COMBAT
WW II

COMBAT
WW II
European Theater
of Operations

Edited by Don Congdon

ARBOR HOUSE

NEW YORK

Acknowledgments

This page constitutes an extension of the copyright page.

"Dunkirk" Copyright 1959 by David Divine. From *The Nine Days of Dunkirk*. Reprinted by permission of W. W. Norton and David Higham Associates.

"The Crisis of Fighter Command" Copyright 1960 by Alexander McKee. From *Strike from the Sky*. Reprinted by permission of Little, Brown & Co. and Souvenir Press of London.

"The Chase of the Bismarck" Copyright 1948 by Russell Grenfell. From *The Bismarck Episode,* published by The Macmillan Company, New York. Reprinted by permission of The Macmillan Company and the author's agent in London, Pearn, Pollinger & Higham, Ltd. A London edition was published by Faber & Faber, Ltd.

"Malta" Copyright 1959, 1960 by Donald Payne. From *Red Duster, White Ensign*. Reprinted by permission of Doubleday & Co. and Harold Ober Associates.

"Tobruk" Copyright 1959 by Anthony Heckstall-Smith. Reprinted by permission of W. W. Norton.

"Behind Rommel's Lines" Copyright 1943 by The Bobbs-Merrill Company, Inc. From *American Guerrilla* by Douglas M. Smith and Cecil Carnes. Reprinted by permission of the publisher.

"Attack at El Alamein" Copyright 1945 by the Executrix of Major H. P. Samwell's Estate. From *An Infantry Officer with the 8th Army,* published by Blackwood & Sons, Ltd., London. Reprinted by permission of Curtis Brown Ltd., London.

"The Raid on St. Nazaire" Copyright 1958 by C. E. Lucas Phillips. From *The Greatest Raid of All*. Reprinted by permission of Little, Brown & Co. and William Heinemann Ltd.

"The Main Assault" Copyright 1956 by R. W. Thompson. From *At Whatever Cost*. Reprinted by permission of Coward McCann Inc. and Hutchinson.

"Montgomery's Mountain Goats" Copyright 1955 by McClelland & Stewart Limited. From *The Regiment*. Reprinted by permission of the publisher.

"Target: Ploesti" Copyright 1957 by Leon Wolff. From *Low Level Mission*. Reprinted by permission of Doubleday & Co. and Longman's Green & Co.

"Salerno" Copyright 1954 by Samuel Eliot Morison. From *History of U.S. Naval Operations in World War II (Sicily-Salerno-Anzio)*. Reprinted by permission of Atlantic–Little, Brown & Co.

Contents

Foreword

Long after the stirring incidents and battles recalled here— from the Allied defeat at Dunkirk in 1940 when the German blitzkrieg overran western Europe to the death of Hitler's Third Reich in Berlin five wounded years later—a young person to whom these names and places must sound like war stories for old movies has a right, indeed an obligation, to demand: What glories are you talking about? With the Cold War's intercontinental missiles and megatons clicking in the chancelleries of power, why stir the ashes of World War II?

Because we cannot escape history, because the past must be distinguished from the present, because we must endure freely. To remember the war is to be antiwar. Shakespeare put it most eloquently: "Of comfort no man speak; let's talk of graves, of worms and epitaphs; make dust our paper and with rainy eyes, write sorrow on the bosom of the earth."

And yet it was a time of great moral response to an epoch of terror and immortality by so-called civilized men and nations such as the world had never seen. All of us, whether serving overseas or in some civilian activity on the home front, saw in the dictator states, and especially in the cruelties of Hitler's Germany, an enemy worthy of our scorn and military retaliation. It took governments and leaders on the Allied side too long to realize that genocide could be practiced a mere two decades after the end of the first Great War of the twentieth century—that the country that nurtured Goethe could worship Goering, that the folks who brought you Beethoven could also stoke the ovens of Buchenwald. Slowly, we came to realize that the concentration camps could be blamed not only on the madness of the Fuehrer and his circle but on the banality of millions of evil German sheep who followed him, who really believed themselves to be a master race.

Yes, in the Furious Forties it was truly defense that caused us to go to war, from bombed Pearl Harbor to occupied Paris. To give in to the dictators would have been indefensible. When the blast of war blew in our ears, it was necessary to stiffen the sinews and summon up the blood, disguise fair nature with hard-favored rage. Yes, it was moral to hate, to sacrifice, to counterattack bravely.

Be aware of the indignities suffered and the shattered dreams of people in all the countries attacked and betrayed by Nazi Germany. Be aware of what it meant to live in London during the Blitz when the Luftwaffe hurled incendiary bombs on your home and families slept in the underground. Be aware of the midnight knock on the door by the storm troopers, the murder of innocent women and children for medical experiments, the war casualties (not to forget the twenty million suffered by the Soviet Union, a statistic that still influences thinking and behavior in the Kremlin down to our own time). Then read these stories of combat with a deeper understanding of what was being fought for. The front lines were everywhere, it wasn't simply democracy that was at stake, it was life itself.

In the great rollcall of place names mentioned in these pages there were terrifying and admirable moments: for the seaman who sailed from cold Atlantic ports zigzagging through U-boat-infested waters on the way to the Near East across the perilous Mediterranean Sea; for the airman who climbed into a thin-skinned, propeller-slow, heavy bomber and flew over a flak alley to a target in enemy-held Europe; for the rifleman who clambered up the beaches of Sicily or Normandy (or name your favorite beachhead; there are still military cemeteries nearby) and learned what it felt like to be nakedly exposed under the efficient machinery of war manufactured by Krupp and other German industrial giants.

In recent years I have revisited some of these places. Driving in a remote mountain region in western Sicily, I had seen some neo-Fascist slogans painted on a few walls and wondered if the wartime liberation had been erased from memories. To me, these island towns had been steppingstones to the Italian mainland, where the Wehrmacht reigned over the Fascist-ruled monarchy. Then something happened that cheered me. A farmer noticed an American's car and his face lit up. He yelled, "Hey, Joe!" As I grinned a return greeting, he raised his fingers in a V-for-Victory sign, and so did I. Not many Americans had come through these mountains over the years. The important ones were those anonymous Joes (some of whose lives ended in these once-numbered hills and are buried above the Anzio-Nettuno beachhead) who, with British Tommies, had brought freedom and kindnesses to Sicily.

I had a similar experience in a little town called Megara, west of Athens, where I had once been privileged to accompany British parachutists who were engaged in the liberation of Greece. In a waterfront restaurant, I met the proprietor, a former partisan. He had only one arm; the other had been lost while blowing up German trains. He and his companions had unarmed the mines that the Germans had planted in the drop zone along the Gulf of Corinth, anticipating where the British sky troopers would land. The partisans had saved Allied lives and I thanked him, belatedly. The proprietor and his wife and son rolled out a feast, called some other ex-partisans, and we dined together. He would not hear of any payment and pressed a couple of bottles of the local wine on me to take home. "You were at Megara," he said, "we are family."

World War II was *not* the Vietnam war. Presidents and high-powered national security advisers in the White House and Defense Department believed otherwise, and that was the fundamental mistake. They have blood on their hands. To this day, neoconservatives are attempting to rewrite the history of Vietnam and America's involvement there, somehow trying to make it noble and a chesspiece in the Cold War; but it won't wash, any more than their effort to justify support for military-industrial dictatorships, without human rights, in Central and South America.

A few days in Saigon and with a First Infantry Division battalion near the Cambodian border in the midst of the Vietnam war made clear the difference. If anything, the war was more complex politically and militarily there, in the cities and the villages, for the Vietcong ruled everywhere after dark. Terror stalked the trails; only the fish in the winding brown rivers were neutral. The young Americans were just as courageous in combat, but it was impossible to uphold unwanted governments in the name of anti-communism or anything else, despite the fact that more bombs were dropped on South Vietnam than on all of Germany and Japan during World War II.

If your experience had been the extended hand, the offered drink, and the cheering V-for-Victory sign in liberated towns in Europe, you could see why Vietnam was a wrong war in the subtle insult of the turned back and the averted eye of the people.

The Second World War multiplied battles and ideals on every continent. Its explosive energy still encircles the globe, and it left a residue of friendship for the United States. Because the next world war, if it comes, will be the last one for a radiated civilization, those who were caught up in the Second World War still have a need to sit upon the ground and write true stories of the death of comrades and conscience; of the blacks and whites of morality peering through the smoke of battle. That is the lesson behind these tales of war. We must unfreeze the mindset of nuclear militarism but still multiply the ideals.

—Herbert Mitgang

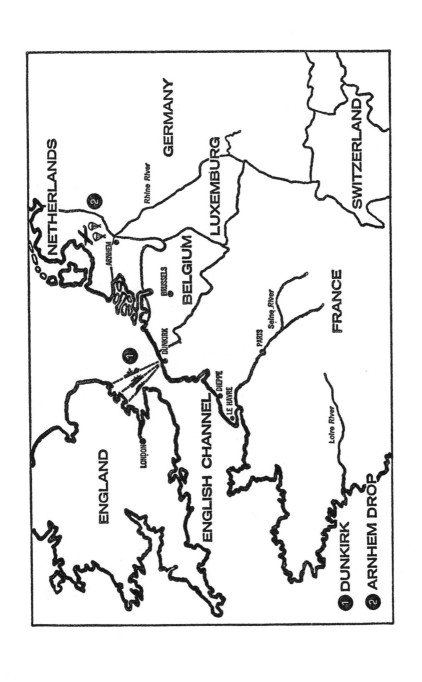

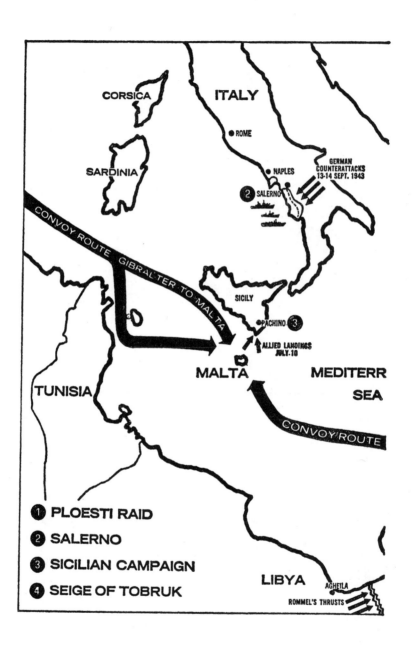

The Beginning

When Hitler invaded Poland on September 1, 1939, he lit the fuse that set off World War II. England and France had guaranteed the borders of Poland by treaty; two days later, they were at war with Germany. Most of the world would be drawn into the conflict in the months to come.

The British and French armed forces were dangerously inferior to Germany's, their peoples were slow to accept the need to fight. The French sat passively behind their Maginot Line, believing the Germans would wear themselves out against its maze of defenses. The British hadn't begun to arm until after Munich, and weren't galvanized into real action until the disaster at Dunkirk. Both of the allies were waiting for the Germans to make the first move—waiting through the fall and winter of 1939, and into the spring of 1940, a time that became known as the "phony war."

The war was no longer "phony" in April; Germany occupied Denmark and Norway, swept through Holland, then overran Belgium.

With Their Backs to the Sea

In May 1940, the German Panzer (armored) divisions plunged into France through the Ardennes Forest, cutting through the weakest sector of the French front near Sedan, just north of the Maginot Line. Before the Allied armies could recover from the blow, the Germans gathered momentum and drove straight for the Channel coast. The British forces were north of this thrust and, as their right flank to the south gave way, they withdrew. Had the French army commanders ordered a general withdrawal earlier, a line might have been established between the French and British armies at the Somme River. But, on May 28, the British left flank was suddenly exposed when the Belgian armies capitulated.

In the event a retreat proved necessary, the British had selected Dunkirk as the debarkation port. Now, as the troops began to retreat toward the coast, a corridor was formed by establishing defense positions along each flank. Troops began to pour down along this corridor to the port area. As the last allied troops were taken in, the end of the corridor was collapsed and defense positions were assumed a few miles closer to the coast.

By May 30, all British troops had arrived within the defense perimeter in front of Dunkirk. In Britain, meanwhile, Operation Dynamo had been set in motion. Masses of small ships gathered in the British Channel ports from all over the coast—lifeboats, pleasure boats, tugs, yachts, fighting craft were all commandeered, anything that could carry men across the channel. On the evening of May 27, this great fleet of small boats set sail for the beaches of Dunkirk.

There, the troops were formed up on the approaches to the harbor and on the beaches. While they waited, they drew heavy fire from German planes strafing and bombing. A British officer describes the scene as he arrived with his men:

"We were now in the region of the dunes, which rose like humps of a deeper darkness. And these in their turn were dotted with the still blacker shapes of abandoned vehicles, half-sunk in the sand, fantastic twisted shapes of burned-out skeletons, and crazy-looking wreckage that had been heaped up in extraordinary piles by the explosions of bombs. All these black shapes were silhouetted against the angry red glare in the sky which reflected down on us the agony of burning Dunkirk.

"Slowly, we picked our way between the wreckage, sinking ankle-deep in the loose sand, until we reached the gaunt skeletons of what had once been the houses on the promenade. The whole front was one long continuous line of blazing buildings, a high wall of fire roaring and darting in tongues of flame, with the smoke pouring upwards and disappearing in the blackness of the sky above the roof-tops. Out seawards, the darkness was as thick and smooth as black velvet, except for now and again when the shape of a sunken destroyer or paddle-steamer made a slight thickening on its impenetrable surface. Facing us, the great black wall of the Mole stretched from the beach far out into sea, the end of it almost invisible to us. The Mole had an astounding, terrifying background of giant flames leaping a hundred feet into the air from blazing oil tanks. At the shore end of the Mole stood an obelisk, and the high explosive shells burst around it with monotonous regularity. Along the promenade, in parties of fifty, the remnants of practically all the last regiments were wearily trudging along. There was no singing, and very little talk. Everyone was far too exhausted to waste breath.

"From the margin of the sea, at fairly wide intervals, three long, thin, black lines protruded into the water, conveying the effect of low wooden breakwaters. These were lines of men, standing in pairs behind one another far out into the water, waiting in queues till boats arrived to transport them, a score or so at a time, to the steamers and warships that were filling up with the last survivors. The queues stood there, fixed and almost as regular as if ruled. No bunching, no pushing. Nothing like the mix-up to be seen at the turnstiles when a crowd is going into a football match. Much more orderly, even, than a waiting theatre queue.

"About this time, afraid that some of our men might be tailing off, I began shouting, '2004th Field Regiment . . . 2004th Field Regiment. . . .'

"A group of dead and dying soldiers on the path in front of us quickened our desire to quit the promenade. Stepping over the bodies

13

we marched down the slope to the dark beach. Dunkirk front was now a lurid study in red and black; flames, smoke, and the night itself all mingling together to compose a frightful panorama of death and destruction. Red and black all the time, except for an occasional flash of white, low in the sky, miles away to the left and right where big shells from coastal defence guns at Calais and Nieuport were being hurled into the town.

"Down on the beach you immediately felt yourself surrounded by a deadly evil atmosphere. A horrible stench of blood and mutilated flesh pervaded the place. There was no escape from it. Not a breath of air was blowing to dissipate the appalling odour that arose from the dead bodies that had been lying on the sand, in some cases for several days. We might have been walking through a slaughterhouse on a hot day. The darkness, which hid some of the sights of horror from our eyes, seemed to thicken this dreadful stench. It created the impression that death was hovering around, very near at hand.

"We set our faces in the direction of the sea, quickening our pace to pass through the belt of this nauseating miasma as soon as possible.

" 'Water . . . Water. . . .' groaned a voice from the ground just in front of us.

"It was a wounded infantryman. He had been hit so badly that there was no hope for him. Our water bottles had long been empty, but by carefully draining them all into one, we managed to collect a mouthful or two. A sergeant knelt down beside the dying man and held the bottle to his lips. Then we proceeded on our way, leaving the bottle with the last few drains in it near the poor fellow's hand so that he could moisten his lips from time to time.

"On either side; scattered over the sand in all sorts of positions, were the dark shapes of dead and dying men, sometimes alone, sometimes in twos and threes. Every now and then we had to pull ourselves up sharply in the darkness to avoid falling over a wooden cross erected by comrades on the spot where some soldier had been buried. No assistance that availed anything could be given to these dying men. The living themselves had nothing to offer them. They just pressed forward to the sea, hoping that the same fate would not be theirs. And still it remained a gamble all the time whether that sea, close though it was, would be reached in safety. Splinters from bursting shells were continually whizzing through the air, and occasionally

14

a man in one of the plodding groups would fall with a groan." *

By June 1, about 200,000 British, French and Belgian troops had been landed safely in England, but the battle was just reaching its climax.

DUNKIRK: JUNE 1ST AND 2ND **

by David Divine

Swiftly, the drama of Dunkirk moved to its climax on the 1st of June. In the morning hours the Royal Navy was to suffer losses as heavy and as significant as those of some of the great sea battles of the past. There is in one of the accounts of the opening of this disaster a phrase that establishes its continuity with history, that links it irrevocably with tradition.

"We were setting our topsail to carry out this operation when a large number of German planes appeared overhead and immediately started bombing and machine-gunning us."

This was the beginning of the heaviest air attack of the operation. Skipper H. Miller of the barge *Royalty* had been ordered to beach his ship opposite the first houses of Malo-les-Bains. "We were setting our topsail" when the whole weight of two air fleets was unleashed for the second time against the crowded anchorage.

Up to this moment, the embarkations of the first hours of the day had achieved new records. The paddle mine sweeper *Whippingham* had started loading, under shellfire, about ten o'clock the previous evening. By 1:30 A.M. she

Return Via Dunkirk, by Gun Buster, published by Hodder & Stoughton.

** This is a condensed version of two chapters from *The Nine Days of Dunkirk.*

estimated that she had loaded 2,700 men and, with her sponsons only about twelve inches above the water, she cast off from the Mole, worked her way out between the wrecks that now, more thickly than ever, studded the narrow channel, and got clear. Her commander, Lieutenant Eric Reed, R.N.R., says that her passage back was slow because she was "very much overloaded." Again this is a classic example of understatement.

Royal Sovereign had been picking up off La Panne. She sailed at 2:30 A.M. with a heavy load, and her master, usually very spare of words, wrote that the beach had come under "terrific bombarding and shelling."

One of the best accounts of the abandonment of La Panne is that of Captain R. P. Pim, R.N.V.R., formerly Assistant Secretary to the Ministry of Home Affairs in the Government of Northern Ireland and, at this time, keeper of Winston Churchill's Map Room. Captain Pim had been on leave at the beginning of the evacuation. He volunteered and crossed with one of the tows. The report of his work says:

"By midnight all the troops which he could find were embarked and placed in ships which sailed for England. Just before midnight he went along some of the beaches to look for stragglers and was told by a staff officer that no more troops would embark from those beaches, but that it was anticipated that the beaches would be shelled and would probably be in German hands the following day. This was a correct forecast.

"He estimates that, from the pontoons and beaches, about 5,000 were embarked. He was impressed by the kindness that was shown to the tired soldiery in the various ships in which they were embarked and also by the fact that the military chaplains were always among the last of their respective parties to leave the beach.

"Anchorage had to be shifted during the night as shells meant for the beaches were ricocheting over H.M.S. *Hilda* [which had towed them over] ....."

Another tow of small craft was operating nearer to Malo-les-Bains.

The Belgian fishing boats were over again in this period.

The *Anna Marguerite* lifted 120 French soldiers and, on her return journey, picked up thirty survivors of a French cargo ship which had been sunk by a magnetic mine. The *Georges Edouard*, which was commanded by a Merchant Marine officer, picked up nearly 500 men this day and, with an earlier trip, carried a total altogether of 1007. The *Guido Gazelle* carried 403 on two trips.

The destroyers *Icarus, Vanquisher* and *Windsor* carried 3000 men between them. Despite the difficulties of the beaches, the loads throughout were tremendously heavy. Mine sweepers, Dutch skoots, trawlers, drifters, paddle-steamers—they all carried enormous numbers of men.

The sun rose and still they loaded. Through this night the Germans had bombed the harbour area intermittently, using brilliant flares. Now, with the sun, the raids redoubled. At five o'clock heavy bombing attacks developed over the whole area from La Panne to Dunkirk, and fighters began to make almost incessant strafing runs along the beaches. The first R.A.F. patrol had been ordered to be over the area soon after 5 A.M. It was heavily engaged on arrival. A second patrol followed at 6 A.M. and again met exceptionally strong opposition. Thereafter there was a gap until nine o'clock, and in this gap the Luftwaffe pounced.

The barge *Royalty*, as has been recorded, set her topsail under fire and ran herself ashore. She was loaded with food, water, and ammunition, and her job was to beach herself as high up the sands as possible so that the troops could unload her as the tide turned. Having carried out his operation immaculately, Skipper Miller rowed out to the tug *Cervia*, which had towed him across. On the way he picked up a launch, with twenty-five soldiers on board, that had broken down. When he joined her, *Cervia* closed the barge *Tollesbury*, which had picked up 180 men.

"At 7:20 A.M.," said W. H. Simmons, *Cervia's* master, "we dropped our anchor and watched the barge. Soldiers began to run down the beach towards her, but guns started to bang away on the outskirts of Dunkirk, and an air-raid siren blew and the soldiers went back to shelter."

The wail of that siren ushered in the attack which, had it been made earlier, might have been decisive in the history

17

of Dunkirk. It is possible that this devastating raid was synchronized with the German's first assault of the day on the perimeter line. At 7:20 A.M. a very heavy force of enemy bombers—predominantly Junkers 87 dive bombers, but with the support of twin-engined Junkers 88s, elaborately escorted by fighters—made its appearance. There were no Allied aircraft in the air at the time; there was no escort for the ships in that narrow channel of destruction. The destroyers themselves, fighting against attack through almost every hour of the past days, were desperately short of ammunition. Many of them had had no time to re-ammunition in the brief spells at Dover. There was only time to discharge their troops, to take on fresh oil, to slip and put to sea again. *Keith*, after fighting all the previous day, had thirty rounds of A.A. ammunition left.

At once the attacks developed on the nearest ships. There is an appalling grandeur in that scene. From behind the beaches, from the harbour, from those ships whose guns could still answer the challenge of the air, the sky was filled with the pock-marks of bursting shells, with the thin trails of tracer bullets, with the whistle and roar of projectiles. Below the sea was flecked with small plumes as the splinters of the shells sang down into the water, between them lifted the monstrous, swirling fountains of the bombs.

Keith was heavily attacked by the first wave. Twisting, turning, at the utmost speed that she could manage in the narrow waters of the roadstead, she eluded the bombs. The account by the master of *Cervia* of these moments—cool, almost dour in its absence of emotion—conveys a graphic picture.

"A British destroyer outside of us began to fire at the enemy planes and bombs began to fall near her as she steamed about. At full speed with her helm hard to port nine bombs fell in a line in the water, along her starboard side, and they exploded under water, heeling the destroyer over on her beam ends, but she was righted again and a sloop joined in the gunfire, also shore batteries, and as the raiders made off over towards the land they machine-gunned us and we returned the fire with our Lewis gun."

To avoid being rammed, *Cervia* weighed anchor and got

under way. She made toward the damaged *Keith* but, as she was doing so, a further air attack took place and the destroyer was again straddled by a stick of bombs. The tug *St. Abbs* and a sloop were also going to the help of *Keith*, so *Cervia* turned round and picked up a motorboat full of soldiers.

Actually *Keith* was damaged in the first attack, though she did not suffer a direct hit. A near miss jammed her rudder, and she turned in small circles for some time. In the second attack she was hit almost at once down her after-funnel and very near misses damaged her side severely. She was moving at high speed and turning at the moment of impact, and she at once listed heavily to port. Enormous clouds of steam came up through the after-funnel and boiler room casings. Still turning, she lost speed rapidly as the steam went, and in a little her commander was compelled to bring his ship to anchor. Captain E. L. Berthon (he had won his D.S.C. at Zeebrugge during the great attack on St. George's Day, 1918) had taken the place of Captain D. J. R. Simson, Captain (D) of the 19th Flotilla, who had been killed at Boulogne on May 24. By the time the anchor took hold, *Keith* was listing almost 20 degrees to port and had no more than two feet of freeboard on that side. At this point, however, she seemed to steady up and sank no farther for the time being.

Though *Keith* was still afloat, she was clearly out of action. Admiral Wake-Walker, with his staff, disembarked into M.T.B. 102, which had closed the destroyer immediately after she was damaged the second time, and headed down the roadstead to call up tugs. But the tugs had already turned towards the battered ship—the Admiralty tug *St. Abbs*, the tug *Vincia*, and the tug *Cervia*. Captain Pim, in H.M. Skoot *Hilda*, was also making his best speed towards the wreck. Before they could reach her she was hit in a third attack. This time the bombs dropped under the bridge, and she heeled right over and sank almost instantly. *Hilda* picked up fifty survivors from the water, including Lieutenant General W. G. Lindsell, the Quartermaster General, and other staff officers. The tug *Vincia* picked up 108 officers and ratings, including staff officers from both British and French headquarters, and *St. Abbs*, which closed her just before she sank, took off Captain Berthon and more than 100 survivors.

All the while there was no cessation in the fury of the Luftwaffe's attack. Farther down the water the dive bombers were peeling off at 10,000 feet and coming down with a terrifying snarl of their motors to within a few hundred feet of the water. While the work of rescue was in progress the destroyer *Basilisk*, which had been held ready to give supporting fire in the event of enemy attack along the beach, was bombed. *St. Abbs*, under the orders of Captain Berthon, turned towards the spot to rescue survivors. Aircraft were flying overhead continuously and a Junkers 88, at high level, let go a single bomb. By a thousand-to-one chance it hit the hurrying tug amidships. She disintegrated and sank, leaving Captain Berthon and the comparatively small number of men who now survived, a second time in the water.

Shortly after, the destroyer *Whitehall* on her first trip— she made two trips this day—found the still-floating hulk of H.M.S. *Basilisk* and sank it. She was herself dive-bombed and suffered damage from near misses. H.M.S. *Worcester* was also damaged by bombing and was to be in collision as she struggled back to Dover.

The gunboat *Mosquito*, which had done magnificent work now for many days, was hit in the same period, badly damaged, set on fire, and had to be abandoned. The Fleet minesweeper *Salamander* was damaged and tugs were sent in search of her. There were other naval casualties, other ships damaged in this period. Admiral Wake-Walker, hurrying to Dunkirk itself in the M.T.B. which had picked him up, was dive-bombed but not hit. All up and down the long, narrow channel of the roadstead there was havoc and the thunder of the bombs. All up and down the roadstead were the long and lamentable pools of oil which marked the new ship graves; and with them, floating on the tide, was the pitiful wreckage of smashed boats and empty rafts, of battered furnishings and splintered planks.

Within little more than an hour the Royal Navy had lost three destroyers, a Fleet minesweeper and a gunboat, and four destroyers had been damaged.

Nor was this the end of disaster. At 1 P.M. the French destroyer *Foudroyant,* the last surviving ship of the 2nd Destroyer Flotilla, came in through Route X. Four miles from the West Mole she was "submerged in a cloud of Stukas," according to a French account. The channel at that point was narrow and manœuvring was impossible. In less than a minute she was hit by a number of bombs and capsized instantly. Small craft and the minesweeper *Sainte-Bernadette-de-Lourdes,* herself damaged by splinters from near misses and listing heavily, picked up her survivors.

The naval losses were desperately serious but the personnel ships suffered almost equally heavy loss in the same period. *Prague,* coming in by Route X, reached Dunkirk at the very height of the first attacks. Her armament was one Lewis gun and one Bren gun, but she closed the entrance and went inside. She berthed at the western side of the outer harbour, close outside the locks, and loaded about 3000 French troops. On the return voyage towards the Downs, the ship was shelled off Gravelines and dive-bombed off No. 5 buoy. Although not actually hit on either occasion, she suffered severe internal damage and the starboard engine was put out of action. Captain Baxter reported:

"From the time of the explosion (10:25) the ship was kept going ahead as fast as it was possible to do on the port engine which was the only one left in service, craft in the vicinity were warned and several naval auxiliaries agreed to stand by us and the ship slowly progressed homewards. It was evident, however, that the water was gaining, and such measures as getting as many troops as possible forward to ease the weight on the after part of the ship were giving only temporary respite, so I decided to try to transfer the troops while the ship was still under way so as to lose as little time as possible. H.M. Destroyer *Shikari* and a sloop and a paddle-minesweeper whose names I was unable to obtain came alongside in turn and very skilfully managed to transfer all except a handful of troops while the ship was steaming as fast as possible towards the Downs. . . ."

H.M.S. *Shikari* transferred under way 500 men. She then called the *Queen of Thanet* to come alongside in her turn. Commander S. P. Herival, R.N.V.R., asked how many troops were left on board and was told, 2000. He embarked most of these—remember both ships were moving at the best speed *Prague* could make all the time—and took them in to Margate. The corvette *Shearwater* then transferred approximately 200 of the remainder and took them to Sheerness.

It was a rescue that in time of peace would have held the attention of the world. There is a tremendous drama, a tension, in the race to beach the ship before she sank under them. There is a desperate excitement in the transfer of those 3000 exhausted men.

As *Prague* came out from the Dunkirk roadstead through the bombing, another railway steamer, the *Scotia,* went in. She was a coal burner, and in addition to the exhaustion and difficulty of the work that she was doing was the necessity to ship coal. There were no proper facilities. For the oil burning ships there were tankers from which they could take their oil direct by pipe line. *Scotia* and the other coal burners had to be supplied with bags and shovels and work their own coal aboard from colliers or hulks. She herself shipped ninety tons from the coal hulk *Agincourt*, then moved to Margate roads and fiinished bunkering from the coaster *Jolly Days*. Her whole crew took part in the work, filling bags and manhandling them to the bunkers. On the way across a homeward-bound destroyer signaled to her: "Windy off No. 6 buoy." The humour was grim. Off No. 6 buoy she was attacked. In the course of the attack British aircraft came in and the enemy disappeared, to re-appear again as soon as the R.A.F. patrol had gone.

Scotia returned to Dunkirk under air attack, being near missed off the entrance. She berthed at the West Mole. "We found Dunkirk quiet except for a few rounds fired from shore batteries," wrote Captain Hughes, and she embarked about 2,000 French troops. As she reached No. 6 buoy on the return voyage she was attacked by three formations of enemy aircraft in groups of four. The ship was hit abaft the engine-room on the starboard side and on the poop deck, and in the final attack one bomb went down the after-funnel. *Scotia* was heavily damaged and began to sink by the stern, heeling steadily over to starboard.

"We carried ten boats, but three of them had been smashed by the bombs. The troops, being French, could not understand orders and they were rushing the boats, which made it very difficult to man the falls—the port boats being most difficult as the vessel was heeling over to starboard. The chief officer had been given a revolver to use by a French officer, threatening to use this helped matters a little. However, they obeyed my mouth whistle and hand signs and so stood aside while the boats were being lowered.

"Commander Couch of H.M.S. *Esk* had received our S.O.S. He was lying at Dunkirk at the time; he came at full speed to the rescue. By now the boat deck starboard side was in the water and the vessel was still going over. He very skilfully put the bow of his ship close to the forecastle head, taking off a large number of troops and picking up hundreds out of the sea. Backing his ship out again, he came amidships on the starboard side, his stem being now against the boat deck, and continued to pick up survivors.

"The *Scotia* had by now gone over until her forward funnel and mast were in the water. Two enemy bombers again approached us dropping four bombs and machine gunning those swimming and clinging to wreckage. The *Esk* kept firing and drove the enemy away. Commander Couch again skilfully manœuvered his ship around to the port side, the *Scotia* having gone over until the port bilge keel was out of the water. Hundreds of the soldiers were huddled on the bilge and some of them swam to the *Esk*, while others were pulled up by ropes and rafts."

While the work of rescue was in progress a fresh bombing attack developed, but the aircraft were driven off by gunfire and the rescue continued uninterrupted until finally only three men were left lying against the bilge keel of the *Scotia*. Captain Hughes fastened ropes round each of these men in turn, they were hauled up to the deck of the *Esk*, and eventually he himself reached the rescue ship. Thirty of *Scotia's* crew were killed or died subsequently, and Captain Hughes estimated that between two and three hundred

Frenchmen were lost. The sinking of the *Scotia* was a tragedy: but for the coolness of Captain Hughes and the brilliant work of the rescue ship it might have been a very great disaster.

H.M.M. *Brighton Queen,* one of the paddle-minesweepers of the 7th Flotilla, which had come down from the Firth of Forth in reinforcement the previous day, made her second trip in the early afternoon. She picked up 700 French and Moroccan troops, and stood out on the homeward passage. At the end of the narrows she was made the target of a concentrated attack by dive bombers. For some while she dodged the rain of bombs, but eventually she was hit in the stern and badly holed. The minesweeper *Saltash* was the first ship to reach her. She reported that "the French troops behaved steadily and intelligently though nearly half of them were killed by the explosion."

Four destroyers had been sunk in a matter of a few hours, four had been seriously damaged. Two of the largest of the cross-Channel steamers and a paddle-minesweeper had been lost. Up and down the roads small ships were on fire and sinking. New wrecks studded the narrow waters of the Channel from No. 6 buoy across the banks. The time had come for a change of plan.

At noon the Commander-in-Chief, Nore, signaled the Admiralty to suggest the "discontinuation of the use of destroyers by day off the French coast." At 6 P.M. a signal from Dunkirk to Admiral Ramsay said:

"Things are getting very hot for ships; over 100 bombers on ships here since 0530, many casualties. Have directed that no ships sail during daylight. Evacuation by transports therefore ceases at 0300. If perimeter holds will complete evacuation tomorrow, Sunday night, including most French. General concurs."

The Admiralty made up its mind. Independently Admiral Ramsay came to similar conclusions. Signals from London and from Dover crossed. The Admiralty directed the suspension of evacuation from Dunkirk at seven o'clock the following morning. Admiral Ramsay's message stated that he had ordered all ships to withdraw from Dunkirk

24

before daylight—the ships could no longer accept the danger of the day. As Admiral Ramsay, considering the problem, wrote:

"In these circumstances, it was apparent that continuation of the operation by day must cause losses of ships and personnel out of all proportion to the number of troops evacuated, and if persisted in, the momentum of evacuation would automatically and rapidly decrease."

But at dusk the ships would go in again—this was not yet the end.

This day criticism of the R.A.F. reached its height. It is not easy to balance the scales in this matter. On June 1 the R.A.F. was asked to provide patrols from 5 A.M. onward. Eight fighter sweeps were made in the course of the day, varying in strength from three to four squadrons. Smaller sweeps had been found impracticable early in the operation. On May 27 twenty-three sweeps had been flown, but the weakness of small patrols invited strong enemy reaction. On this Saturday a second sweep followed at 6 A.M. There was then a three-hour gap until nine. There was another gap through the middle of the day. It was in these two gaps that the heaviest loss took place.

In addition to these fighter operations, Coastal Command and the Fleet Air Arm flew patrols over the approach channels and the open sea, and an astonishing variety of planes was used—Hurricanes, Spitfires, Defiants, Ansons, Hudsons and Swordfish. Three Ansons, reconnaissance aircraft of Coastal Command, engaged nine Messerschmitt fighters at one period of the day, flying almost at water level. They shot down two of them, possibly two more, and drove the rest away. Three Hudsons found "a patch of sky black with Jerrys"—Junkers 87s and 88s ready to dive on transports, with a dense screen of Messerschmitts above them. In thirteen minutes three dive bombers had been shot down, two had dived out of control, and the formation had been driven off. Spitfires claimed twelve German bombers and fighters during a morning patrol, and in the afternoon went up again and claimed another six.

At the end of the day the R.A.F. claimed seventy-eight

25

enemy aircraft destroyed. It was believed that a new record for the war had been established. A more sober analysis of claims brought the figure down to forty-three. In actual fact, German returns examined since the war show that ten fighters and nineteen bombers in all were lost in the course of the day's operations. Of this total, a number must be credited to ships. Naval vessels claimed thirteen 'kills' during daylight hours. On the other side of the ledger, thirty-one British aircraft were lost this Saturday. The legend of qualitative superiority that was built up over Dunkirk rested on perilously slender foundations.

At sea and in the air the battle had reached points of crisis. What was the position on the land?

At 8 A.M., while the Luftwaffe attack against the ships was at its height, General Alexander met Admiral Abrial and General Fagalde again. It was obvious by now that there was no question of a successful completion of the evacuation by the dawn of Sunday. General Alexander agreed to a modification of the original plan. The line was to be held as before until midnight. Thereafter it was proposed that he should withdraw to what is described as "a bridgehead round Dunkirk with all available anti-aircraft and anti-tank guns and with such troops as had not yet embarked."

Already heavy German attacks were developing against the "Canal Line." At Bergues, the 1st Loyals were forced out of the town and took up new defensive positions on the canal bank on its outskirts. At Hoymille, a little to the east, the enemy penetrated a position held by the Warwickshires and secured a foothold across the canal. The position was restored late in the afternoon by the Loyals in a vigorous counterattack. The Border Regiment was also pushed back, and, at dark, the last of the British troops were withdrawn through the French on the intermediate line, which ran through Uxem and Ghyvelde. The Canal des Chats at Uxem was less than four miles from the beaches. The end was very close.

Thirty-one ships in all were lost and eleven were seriously

damaged between midnight and midnight. It was a major disaster, and yet such is the strange quality of Dunkirk that through it all the loading went on, hardly losing its rhythm. Though it was interrupted as the Stukas raided the open beaches, though ships withdrew under attack or were turned back from the approach channels, though the Mole was almost incessantly under fire now, it never ceased. Through it all the small craft worked, pausing sometimes to rescue drowning men from the water, helping to tow a damaged ship, standing by a sinking one.

At dawn from Ramsgate a convoy of eight boats, including *Westerly, Naiad Errant* and *White Heather,* moved off for Dunkirk. The description of Able Seaman Palmer is perhaps the best individual account by any member of the lower deck who took part in the beach work through this time. Palmer was a "Westoe". He came to Ramsgate with a draft from the Royal Naval Barracks, Devonport, where he had been serving for some time past as a member of the Plymouth City Patrol. He was a "stripey," a three-badge man, and held the Long Service and Good Conduct medals, but he was still an Able Seaman. His narrative is simple and graphic with the simplicity of the "Old Navy."

"The adventure began with a sudden draft from Devonport to Ramsgate. For one night at Ramsgate I was billeted with other seamen in the Fun Fair Ballroom, and the next day action began. I was told off with another seaman, two ordinary seamen, and two stokers, to take over two motor yachts, the *Naiad Errant* and the *Westerly*. Being the senior hand, I detailed one seaman, an ordinary seaman, and one stoker to take charge of the *Westerly* and took the remainder on board the *Naiad Errant* with me. I thought she looked the better of the two boats. . . .

"About three miles outside Dunkirk I saw a French destroyer doing about twenty-four to thirty knots, [this was the *Foudroyant*] making her way into Dunkirk. I took my eyes off her for a minute or two and then glanced back, but there was nothing there. She must have had a direct hit from a bomb and sunk within a few minutes. I made my course over to where she had gone and picked up her survivors, which altogether numbered only about twenty.

Those I picked up I put on board a French tug which happened to be in the vicinity, and once more carried on into Dunkirk.

"Eventually I arrived off the beach where the swarms of soldiers were gathered, and at the same time one of our big ships came and anchored close inshore. Three of our little convoy of eight had arrived. The first immediately filled with soldiers and carried on back to England. The second went aground. My first job was to ferry soldiers from the beach to the big ship, and I made a number of trips. Then I tried to tow the boat that had run aground off the beach but the young seaman with me got the tow rope around my propellers, the result being that I had to give the job up and that my own ship ran aground. All around there was ceaseless activity and, jumping over the side, I gave a hand carrying the wounded soldiers to the big ship's skiff which had been launched. . . ."

Naiad Errant's crew was ordered aboard the "big ship," but in turn she ran aground. In the interval soldiers got *Naiad Errant* clear again, and Palmer, after securing enough petrol for the return journey, started back. Shortly after *Naiad Errant's* engines failed.

"With no engineer on board, and me without the slightest knowledge of engines, I had to hope that the soldiers could get her going again. The engineers among them got to work. The others I ordered to break up both the cabin doors and use the pieces as paddles in order to keep a little way on the boat and prevent her from running on to the pier. Although they were dead tired they put all they knew into it and so we managed to keep a little way on the boat and keep her in a safe position. About this time I began to shiver and got very cold as it got dark, for I had on the same togs that I had been swimming in. I was still wet through. Then one of the soldiers tapped me on the shoulder. He handed over a flask, asking me to drink. I did. It was rum, and it certainly put warmth and fresh life into me.

"The soldiers tinkered with the engine in the darkness and it must have been between ten and eleven o'clock at night when there was a clamour of excitement. They had got the starboard engine going! I told them to 'drop everything' and leave the port engine and I would get them over to England all right on the one engine, which gave me about five to six knots. I counteracted the pull of the one engine with the wheel. . . .

"Just after dawn I struck Dover dead centre and then followed the coast up to Ramsgate, arriving there at eleven and I put the soldiers ashore on the pier."

White Heather was abandoned. *Westerly* was damaged and her people were rescued later.

Another convoy left Ramsgate about 9:30 A.M. Between the two there were a number of individual sailings. In the convoy were the tugs *Prince*, *Princess* and *Duke* with the Isle of Wight ferry *Fishbourne* in tow. The *Sun III* had four barges astern of her—*Ada Mary*, *Haste Away*, *Burton* and *Shannon*. She had great trouble with barges breaking adrift, and *Duke* was detached from *Fishbourne* to pick up *Haste Away* and *Ada Mary*. By 2:30 P.M. they were close in to Dunkirk. Air attacks were heavy again at this time, and it was eventually decided that *Fishbourne* should return to Ramsgate. The barge tows, meanwhile, had got well ahead of her and in the middle of the afternoon reached position a little north of Dunkirk during the inevitable air attack. The master of *Duke*, B. P. Mansfield, records, however, that this attack was split up by our own fighter aircraft.

Half an hour after they had left Ramsgate the yacht *Sundowner* began her crossing. *Sundowner* belonged to Commander C. H. Lightoller, R.N.R. (Retd.), who, as senior surviving officer of the *Titanic*, had been the principal witness at the inquiry into the disaster. She was a biggish craft, approximately sixty feet with a speed of ten knots and, with the assistance of his son and a Sea Scout, Commander Lightoller had taken her out of Cubitt's Yacht Basin at Chiswick on May 31 and had dropped down the river to Southend as part of a big convoy of forty boats which had mustered at Westminster. At dawn on June 1 he left Southend with five others and, reaching Ramsgate, was instructed in the casual manner of those days to "proceed to Dunkirk for further orders." His charts were somewhat antiquated, and he was fortunate enough to be able to obtain a new set. At ten o'clock he left by the route laid down.

On the way across Commander Lightoller picked up the crew of *Westerly*, originally one of Able Seaman Palmer's flotilla. She was broken down and on fire. Finding no more men on the beaches, and successfully dodging several air attacks, he headed up for Dunkirk harbour, where he berthed alongside a destroyer and started to load troops. With great foresight every bit of unnecessary gear had been removed from *Sundowner* before leaving Cubitt's Yacht Basin. Commander Lightoller wrote:

"My son, as previously arranged, was to pack the men in and use every available inch of space—which I'll say he carried out to some purpose. On deck I detailed a naval rating to tally the troops aboard. At fifty I called below, 'How are you getting on?' getting the cheery reply, 'Oh, plenty of room yet.' At seventy-five my son admitted they were getting pretty tight—all equipment and arms being left on deck.

"I now started to pack them on deck, having passed word below for every man to lie down and keep down; the same applied on deck. By the time we had fifty on deck, I could feel her getting distinctly tender, so took no more. Actually we had exactly 130 on board, including three *Sundowners* and five *Westerlys*.

"During the whole embarkation we had quite a lot of attention from enemy planes, but derived an amazing degree of comfort from the fact that the *Worcester's* A.A. guns kept up an everlasting bark overhead. . . .

"Arriving off the harbour I was at first told to 'lie off'. But when I informed them that I had 130 on board, permission was at once given to 'come in' (I don't think the authorities believed for a minute that I had 130), and I put her alongside a trawler lying at the quay. Whilst entering, the men started to get to their feet and she promptly went over to a terrific angle. I got them down again in time and told those below to remain below and lying down till I gave the word. The impression ashore was that the fifty-odd lying on deck plus the mass of equipment was my full load.

30

"After I had got rid of those on deck I gave the order 'Come up from below,' and the look on the official face was amusing to behold as troops vomited up through the forward companionway, the after companionway, and the doors either side of the wheelhouse. As a stoker P.O., helping them over the bulwarks, said, 'God's truth, mate! Where did you put them?' He might well ask. . . ."

The old stagers were still carrying on. H.M.M. *Medway Queen* was over again, having left for Dunkirk at 9:30 A.M. With the ships' boats which she towed again was Mr. R. B. Brett. Writing subsequently, he said that he saw one of the crew of the *Medway Queen*, a Royal Naval pensioner, calmly fishing over the stern while the *Medway Queen* was lying off the Mole waiting for her turn to go in.

"When told that there were no fish about and that, if there were, they were dead, he sang out, 'You never can tell, sir. I might catch a bloody Boche helmet.' "

Brett took his boat in until she had almost grounded and then, being the tallest man on board, he waded ashore, calling out, "I want sixty men!" For some time he received no reply. Then, he wrote:

"I sighted a causeway about eight feet wide heading out into the water. To my surprise I found it to be a perfectly ordered straight column of men about six abreast, standing as if on parade. When I reached them a sergeant stepped up to me and said, 'Yes, sir. Sixty men, sir?' He then walked along the column, which remained in perfect formation, and detailed the required number to follow me."

A footnote to the stoicism of Mr. Brett's "human pier" is his account of a blinded man. His hand was placed in Mr. Brett's and he was led to the boat and told that he was being taken to safety. He said simply, "Thanks, mate," and followed patiently and wordlessly into the deep water.

Admiral Wake-Walker, after the bombing of *Keith*, ordered M.T.B. 102, which had picked him up, to proceed into Dunkirk. Landing near the naval dug-out headquarters at the base of the Mole, he was informed of General Alexander's intention to continue the evacuation during the night from the western beaches and Dunkirk, the rear guard retiring at dawn on Dunkirk itself. Fearing the results of a second attack such as the one that had just been experienced, Admiral Wake-Walker returned to Dover for direct contact with Admiral Ramsay. He crossed in the M.T. B., bombed and machine-gunned on the way. At 7:45 P.M. he was off Dunkirk again to take charge of the embarkation operations for the night, and at a conference at Bastion 32 with General Alexander and Captain Tennant the last details of the night's operations were agreed. At that conference he was informed that the French were holding a line in rear of the British positions through which the British rear guard would withdraw.

The whole emphasis had been changed to night loading. Admiral Ramsay's plan provided for all minesweepers, paddle-steamers, skoots, and small craft to work the Malo beach for a mile and a half from Dunkirk. The harbour itself was to be served by eight destroyers and seven personnel ships. Drifters and smaller craft from Ramsgate were to go up into the inner harbour. French ships were to use the guiding jetty and the West Mole, and very small ships the Quai Félix Faure. French fishing craft and drifters were to work with the British on the Malo beach.

The night was very dark. At times as many as six or seven ships were attempting to use the wreck-studded entrance to the harbour at once. Collisions and obstruction were incessant. The confusion of other days seemed to be redoubled, yet again the confusion was apparent rather than real. The sense of individual masters, the seamanship of their crews, the determination of everyone concerned in the operation was such that this vast concentration of ships moved in and out with astonishingly small loss.

Yet loss there was. *Maid of Orleans* was one of the earliest of the personnel ships of the night flight to leave. In six trips she had lifted 5319 men. The utter disregard that this unarmed vessel showed for the almost intolerable dangers of the work and the limitless endurance of her people give her a high place in the record of famous ships.

At 8:30 P.M. she moved out from the Admiralty Pier and within ten minutes was in collision with the destroyer *Worcester*. *Worcester* had been damaged by bombs earlier

32

in the day. She had been towed most of the way across the Channel and then engineers, working in the crippled engine room, had managed to get her under her own steam again. She was slipping thankfully into port now when the two ships met with a tremendous crash. There were many tugs and small craft available; men thrown into the water were picked up, and both ships were towed into harbour. *Maid of Orleans,* however, was so damaged as to be unable to continue her voyage. She had done most gallant work. *Worcester* also was finished as far as Dunkirk was concerned, and she too had matched the very highest traditions of her Service. In the six trips which she had made, two of them under very heavy attack from the enemy, she had brought back 4350 men.

Even endurance has its inevitable limits. The personnel ships had been working now, some of them, for a full week. They were civilian ships—before everything this must be remembered. They were not trained to the necessities of war, they were not moulded to its disciplines. Now, as their weariness grew, there were failures. *Tynwald* should have sailed from Folkestone at this time. She had completed three hard voyages, bringing away 4500 men, but on this evening she failed to sail. Her master stated that his men had been continually on their feet for a week, that his officers were completely exhausted, and that he himself had had only four hours' rest in the whole course of the week and was unfit for further duty. *Malines* and *Ben-My-Chree* were in the same condition.

Exhaustion was beginning to show amongst the naval vessels as well. It was found possible in certain instances to put fresh captains on board. With the personnel ships Admiral Ramsay now took the necessary step of putting a naval commander or lieutenant commander on board with a party of ten seamen. Relief crews were ordered up for *Ben-My-Chree* and *Tynwald*.

As this night went on what was left of the 46th Division, the 1st Division and the 126th Infantry Brigade were taken aboard the ships.

The destroyers still were lifting the greater share of the

total. H.M.S. *Whitshed* had made good the damage that she had received at Boulogne. This night she came back to service. She berthed at one o'clock against the concrete of the outer nose of the Mole.

As she made fast her ropes the Mole was empty. Commander Conder left his ship and walked along the Mole. A little way down it he found a bicycle lying up against a post and on this he rode down to the town. There was damage at various points. At one place the decking of the Mole had gone completely and the gap was bridged by a ship's gangway. At other points there were shell holes patched with any material available. At the far end there was another area of damage, and he had to dismount to circumvent it. Just beyond this he met a naval pier party and was told that troops would be coming at any moment. He went on past the pier party and in a warehouse a few hundred yards farther down found a number of exhausted French and Belgian troops. These he stirred into wakefulness and sent down the pier. There was an air attack on at the time but he was busy hunting. A little farther he found a party of British troops in command of a sergeant—their officers had brought them down as far as the pier and gone back to round up more men. These he took back with him.

The destroyers were taking incredible risks in stowing the vast quantities of men they lifted. It is recorded that *Whitshed* had first unshipped her mess tables and cleared all possible movable gear on the lower deck; now she opened compartments that normally were shut in danger areas, leaving the watertight doors open throughout the ship in order to make "living spaces." Having taken approximately 1000 men on board by these heroic measures, *Whitshed* sent a berthing party to take the ropes of the succeeding destroyers as they came in and, as soon as these were berthed, pulled out stern first between the breakwaters, listing heavily with the weight of men, and got clear.

Her commanding officer's search is typical of many of the efforts made by naval officers at this time. Whenever there was a break in the flow a party from the ships would search. *Malcolm's* navigator marched through the streets of Dunkirk playing a set of bagpipes as a summons to the weary men—there is no evidence on record as to the skill with which he played them.

At 2 A.M. a signal from Dunkirk read:

"C.-in-C. says it is essential that rear guard B.E.F. embarks from the beaches east of Mole on account of French congestion on Mole. Considerable number British troops still on Mole. Military are expecting further arrivals there. Rear guard expects to arrive at beach at 0230."

This was an hour and a half after *Whitshed* had restarted the flow. It seemed obvious that large numbers would not arrive until after the time set for the close of operations. The reaction of Dover was immediate and forthright. It is embodied in a signal which said: "Endeavour to embark rear guard from beach remaining after 3 A.M. if necessary." The wording is simple. It was, however, the acceptance of a challenge. The events of the previous morning were still very vivid in the minds of Admiral Ramsay and the Dover Command. Yet, if the men could not be got down to the beach before dawn, the Navy was still prepared to wait until after dawn to take them.

Through this period the small boats worked steadily. They worked in circumstances of rapidly increasing difficulty. The language problem, now that the French predominated along the beaches, was almost impossible. Amongst certain units discipline had broken down, and it was equally hard without an absolute command of the language to stop men from rushing the boats and settling them firmly into the sand. Latecomers could not be prevented from jumping into overloaded boats. There were not a few cases of small craft that left the beach and sank as soon as they reached deep water and the tumultuous wash of the destroyers.

The great bulk of those of the small boats that still floated and were still capable of progressing under their own steam left in accordance with orders at zero hour. The French continued loading a little later than the British ships. A battalion of the B.E.F., which had marched from Bergues through the night, reached the end of the Mole as the last of the British personnel ships, already fully loaded, cast off for home. The battalion turned and marched off the

35

Mole against the line of the French who still marched down to their own ships. In a little that line ceased also. Those who were left dug themselves into the canal banks and the dunes on the outskirts of the town and lay there till night.

The last ships had held on until sun-up. In full daylight they pulled out to join the end of the long stream that was headed back to the English coast. Over the waters of Dunkirk channel a silence fell. At midnight, when the list for June 1 closed, 64,429 men had been brought safe to the English shore. With all the destruction, with all the loss, this was another Glorious First of June.

A little after sunrise on June 2 a chaplain of the British Expeditionary Force celebrated Holy Communion in the Dunkirk dunes. John Masefield, who tells the story, says that five times before the service ended the congregation of men of the weary rear guard was scattered by low-flying aircraft.

Between 3000 and 4000 of the B.E.F. remained ashore this day. Detachments of these men, with seven anti-aircraft and twelve anti-tank guns, worked with the French throughout the day on the "intermediate line." The French figures were still uncertain. At Dover Admiral Ramsay recorded that the estimate as to "the number of French troops remaining was increasing from the 25,000 quoted the previous evening to figures in the region of 50,000 to 60,000." This uncertainty made planning almost unbelievably difficult. One factor harshly simplified it—the capacity of the embarkation facilities that remained. There was left now only the harbour—almost continuously under shell fire— and a bare mile and a half of beach—equally within range of the German guns.

It was estimated that 25,000 men could be moved during the hours of darkness provided a rapid flow of troops to the embarkation points could be maintained. The night's operation was, therefore, planned on the basis of a lifting of 25,000. Thirteen personnel vessels, two large store carriers, eleven destroyers, five paddle-minesweepers, nine Fleet sweepers, one special service vessel, nine drifters, six skoots, two armed yachts, one gunboat, and a number of tugs towing small craft and free-lance motor-boats were ordered to sail from five o'clock onwards. The French sent altogether forty-three ships, including the Breton fishermen who had worked well the previous day. It was possible for most of the ships' companies this day to get some rest.

There was, however, one aspect of the evacuation for which at this time no provision could be made. The outward flow of wounded virtually ceased this morning. One Casualty Clearing Station remained—12 C.C.S. at Rosendaël. The difficulties which had faced the hospital ships and the accumulating disaster of the morning of June 1 had stopped the movement of stretcher cases. The staff of 12 C.C.S. had abandoned all hope of returning to England.

Late in the morning, however, orders came from I Corps H.Q. to say that one officer and ten men were to be left for every hundred casualties and that the remainder of the medical personnel of 12 C.C.S. was to proceed to the Mole for evacuation. The order led to one of the most remarkable ballots in army history. At two o'clock in the afternoon the names of all medical personnel remaining were placed in a hat. There were by now 230 stretcher cases at Rosendaël, and three officers and thirty men had to be chosen to stay with them. It was decided that "first out of the hat" was first to go, and there were left at the end an officer who had been separated from his field ambulance, another who had been sent over from England for beach duties at Dunkirk, and the surgical specialist of the unit. At ten o'clock at night the remainder of the personnel of 12 C.C.S. moved to the Mole and after an interminable journey reached three destroyers at the end of it.

The wounded, however, were not yet abandoned. The authorities in England decided, shortly after the arrival at Dover of the first of the returning members of the unit, to make a direct appeal to the Germans. At 10:30 A.M. a signal was made by wireless *en clair* to the German Command. It read:

"Wounded situation acute and hospital ships should enter during day. Geneva Convention will be honourably observed and it is felt that the enemy will refrain from attacking."

The Southern Railway steamer *Worthing*, which had been taken over at the beginning of the war for service as a hospital carrier, was lying in the Downs. Two hours after the broadcast she received her orders and at 12:55 P.M. she left for Dunkirk at twenty knots. At 2:32 P.M. she was attacked by twelve enemy aircraft. Nine bombs were dropped, two of which fell within three or four feet of her despite drastic avoiding action. This attack was carried out in good visibility and regardless of the fact that the ship was carrying all the marks and signs of a hospital ship as required by the Geneva Convention. The Convention had been repeatedly flouted throughout the evacuation as it had been flouted on countless occasions before. On this day, however, the attack was more despicable even than upon these earlier occasions. It was made in flagrant, open contempt of the appeal that had been sent out.

While these attacks were taking place the Navy also suffered loss. Though all movements in the area of Dunkirk itself had ceased, the patrols on the approaches had to be maintained. Destroyers, anti-submarine trawlers, drifters, and minesweepers worked throughout the day to safeguard the channels for the night flow.

The diminished perimeter about Dunkirk held. To the west of the town no serious attack had been made on the sector of the line which ran down to the sea in the vicinity of Mardyck, though a number of batteries had been positioned in the vicinity to harass shipping. From Mardyck it held firm along the course of the old Mardyck Canal to Spycker, then along the main canal to Bergues, and from Bergues diagonally across through Uxem and Ghyvelde to the old fortifications on the Franco-Belgian frontier and so back to the sea.

The normal approach to Dunkirk from the south, as has been said, is by the main road which passes through Bergues and, running parallel with the broad Bergues-Dunkirk Canal, moves almost due north into the suburbs of the town. The successful defence of the junction of this canal with the Bergues-Nieuport Canal had so far held the Germans from any attempt at a direct assault, but attacks to the eastward of this road over the level ground which led towards the village of Teteghem had placed the new line there in jeopardy.

At six o'clock in the morning, therefore, the French launched a counterattack in this area. Though it began vigorously, it was brought to a halt by two successive air attacks, each by more than fifty aircraft, and it was finally stopped at the hamlet of Notre Dame des Neiges. At 9 A.M. it was decided to fall back on the Canal des Moëres opposite Teteghem. Throughout the day this position was maintained.

On the other side of the main approach road pressure now increased steadily in the area of Spycker and, as evening fell, the line was penetrated there and a general withdrawal took place. The strength of the holding position in the complicated junction between the canals and roads which led to Dunkirk from the outskirts of Bergues had evidently dissuaded the Germans from a direct frontal assault, and they were plainly endeavouring to find an indirect approach. At nightfall, however, they suspended operations.

Throughout the defence of the perimeter night attacks were rare and hardly ever strongly maintained. The explanation of this lies almost certainly in the nature of the terrain, cut up, as it was, by a complex of navigable canals with, between them, an endless succession of large and small drainage dykes.

As the ships of the night flow approached Dunkirk the position was, therefore, that the perimeter had fallen in but that the line, threatened on either side of the main approach road, still held.

At 3:30 in the afternoon Commander Clouston, who had returned to Dover for a brief rest, left with an augmented pier party in two R.A.F. motor-boats, Nos. 243 and 270, to make the necessary arrangements at the Mole to receive the first ships of the night. Off Gravelines the

39

boats were attacked by eight Junkers 87. No. 243, in which Commander Clouston had sailed, was near-missed early in the attack and became waterlogged. As the attacks continued, both with small bombs and with machine-guns, the crew of 243, with Commander Clouston, took to the water. No. 270 was also damaged but managed, by zigzagging and high speed, to avoid the worst of the attack. Ten minutes after 243 had been hit she returned to the waterlogged wreck. Commander Clouston, who was in the water, waved to her to get clear. Some of his crew had been killed, but with one officer and some of the survivors he set out to swim to a boat that could be seen about two miles away, while the R.A.F. men endeavoured to swim to shore. The water was cold. Commander Clouston, who had for the past week worked almost without sleep and without rest, rapidly became exhausted. He decided finally that he could not make the distance and turned to swim back to the waterlogged wreck of 243. He was not seen again.

The officer with him, after swimming for nearly three hours, reached the boat and found her deserted. With great difficulty he boarded her and was eventually picked up by a French trawler, which had lost her way and which he navigated back to Ramsgate. One of the aircraftmen also turned back to the wreck, reached it and was picked up eight hours later by H.M.S. *Whitshed.*

This is one of the great tragedies of Dunkirk. Commander Clouston was responsible for the traffic of the Mole from the beginning of the operation. Under his guidance 200,000 men had passed down its narrow plankway to safety. It is impossible to exaggerate the importance of his achievement. It was carried out under conditions that could have been surmounted only by a strong spirit. Darkness, wind, sea, enemy shellfire, and incessant bombing conspired always against those who tried to control the traffic of the Mole. The plankway itself was wrecked by direct hits. The loading berths were blocked by sunken ships. The flow of troops was irregular, and the difficulties of dealing with men unaccustomed to the sea and heavy with the exhaustion of defeat were indescribable. Throughout it all Commander Clouston maintained the very highest traditions of the Royal Navy. His service to the B.E.F. and to his country is not to be measured in words.

No. 270 followed her orders and went on to Dunkirk. It had been intended that she should police the fairways and direct traffic. She was, however, so damaged that this was now impossible. Sub-Lieutenant Wake, who commanded her, landed at the Mole and, in the tradition of the Navy, took over the task which Commander Clouston had set out to perform. The inherent difficulty of persuading the inland *poilu* to embark upon an unfamiliar element now reached its height. Coupled with the ordinary language difficulty and the macabre setting of the Mole at night under shellfire and air attack the problem of maintaining the flow was enough to daunt much older men. Sub-Lieutenant Wake kept it going by methods that were at times empirical.

The motor-boat *Blue Bird* crossed under the command of Lieutenant-Colonel H. T. B. Barnard, who had made two previous attempts to get across. This day, however, he left Sheerness with a mixed crew of yachtsmen and ratings. *Blue Bird* closed the eastern end of the beaches but found no troops and, moving down the beach towards the base of the Mole, discovered that water had been put in the petrol tank. This last mishap was a common one through the greater part of the evacuation. Water, as has been described, was being taken over for the use of the Army. The available water cans of the Southern Command—and indeed of the south of England—were used up early, and as a substitute petrol cans were filled and taken over. The petrol for the small craft was also stored in ordinary two-gallon cans. These were appropriately marked, but dumps got mixed on occasion—especially when refuelling was done at night—and the mixture proved disastrous to many ships. *Blue Bird* was towed home by H.M. Skoot *Hilda*.

Sea Roamer, a 40-foot motor cruiser owned and commanded by Mr. J. E. W. Wheatley, also crossed this Sunday evening, with a naval party on board. They towed over a boat to work the beaches and made an independent course across the shallows of the off-lying banks. Outside the harbour they were told to investigate the beaches but, though they closed to within fifty yards of the shore, they could see no signs of life in any part of the area which they examined. While they were doing this the Casino and the Kursaal were hit by incendiary bombs and went up in flames. They searched to two and a half miles north-east of Dunkirk and then, abandoning hopes of picking up anybody from the sands, decided to inspect the wrecks offshore. Circling the first one and shouting, they were rewarded by a head popping up over the side and demanding, *"Etes-vous Allemands ou Français?"* They replied that they were English, and picked up a number of French soldiers who had reached the wreck the day before. These men said that they had seen nobody on the beach for the past twenty-four hours. As she was nearing the next wreck, *Sea Roamer's* people sighted a low, fast-looking vessel carrying, apparently, a heavy gun. There was for some little while considerable exchange of anxiety between the two ships until the new-comer turned out to be the *Massey Shaw* with her powerful fire-fighting monitor on the foredeck. Continuing the search, they worked finally down to the Dunkirk entrance, where they were in collision with a destroyer. *Sea Roamer* herself was slightly damaged, but the boat she was towing was reduced to splinters and the towrope, suddenly freed, fouled her propeller. She was able to move slowly with the auxiliary engine, but she was eventually picked up and towed home by a paddle-steamer.

Sea Roamer, incidentally, recorded one of the better stories of the operation. Discussing the difficulty of persuading French troops to entrust themselves to small boats, her owner said:

"The French, it seems, were not always prepared to wade out and clamber into the dinghies in the surf. A story was told me of a French officer who steadfastly refused to do this. Finally he sent a note to the anxious yacht skipper. It read, 'I have just eaten and am therefore unable to enter the water.' "

The *Massey Shaw* had left Ramsgate at 6:40 P.M. under the command of Lieutenant G. Walker, R.N.V.R., but with eight of her own crew still on board. She found no troops on the beach and Walker took her up the harbour, leaving finally at 3:15 A.M.

Admiral Taylor, having dispatched from Sheerness everything that would float and move, went to Ramsgate in the middle of Sunday afternoon. Discussing the conditions with military officers who had just arrived, he was informed that a pocket of men who had not been able to get into Dunkirk was holding out near Malo-les-Bains, and a special party was organised to get these men away. Three skoots and a dozen fast motor-boats were selected, and sailed late in the afternoon. Commandant Anduse-Faru of the French Navy undertook to arrange for a paddle-steamer and a French ship to be off the beach, and for a number of French fishing vessels to co-operate with Admiral Taylor's boats and ferry off troops to them and to the skoots. He was taken out to the fishing vessels to make arrangements. They had lovely names: *Ciel de France, Ave Maria Gratia Plena, Jeanne Antoine, Arc en Ciel.* They had done good work already and they were very tired but, after argument in the French fashion, they went over again.

Admiral Taylor, who had completed his work ashore, decided to proceed to Dunkirk to supervise the lifting of the pocket from Malo-les-Bains in person. I had at that time stolen a small twin-screw Thames motor cruiser and was ordered to stand by to take the Admiral over. Her name was *White Wing,* she was about thirty foot in length and she had a speed of approximately twelve knots but, owing to trouble with the starboard engine, did not make this speed all the way across. We reached Dunkirk with only minor difficulties and our work for the night is covered in an account that I wrote at the time.

"Having the Admiral on board, we were not actually working the beaches but were in control of small boat operations. We moved about as necessary and, after we had spent some time putting boats in touch with their towing ships, the 5.9 battery off Nieuport way began to drop shells on us. It seemed pure spite. The nearest salvo was about twenty yards astern, which was close enough.

"We stayed there until everybody else had been sent back

43

and then went pottering about looking for stragglers. While we were doing that, a salvo of shells got one of the ships alongside the Mole. She was hit clean in the boilers and exploded in one terrific crash. There were then, I suppose, about 1000 Frenchmen on the Mole. We had seen them crowding along its narrow crest, outlined against the flames. They had gone out under shellfire to board the boat, and now they had to go back again, still being shelled. It was quite the most tragic thing I ever have seen in my life. We could do nothing with our little dinghy."

The rate of flow through this early part of the night was admirable. Steadily the last of the British element of the rear-guard was marched to the Mole and embarked. French troops came down in a continuous stream, and the prospects for the night looked excellent.

One important mishap marred the proceedings. The French cross-Channel steamer *Rouen*, with a number of men on board, stranded on the mud inside the harbour as she was turning. The tug *Foremost* 22 went to her assistance, but ran aground herself and only just got clear. The tide was ebbing fast, and she left the area so that a tug of lesser draught could make the attempt. The *Sun X* then closed the *Rouen*, but 200 feet away she found only ten feet of water and it was obvious that it would be impossible to move her until the next high tide. Both tugs loaded with men, some of them from the *Rouen*.

General Alexander, with his staff, was picked up by Admiral Wake-Walker in M.A./S.B. 10. He was subsequently transferred to a destroyer which was attacked and machine-gunned when close to Dover.

By eleven o'clock the last of the British Expeditionary Force was moving on to the ships. *St. Helier* claims the honour of the final lifting, and appropriate finish to a great record. At about 11:30 P.M., fully loaded, she slipped her ropes for the last time and felt her way out of the harbour, down by the head and leaking badly in her forepeak.

So ended a chapter in the story of the British Army, a story that had begun a bare three weeks before, as the British Expeditionary Force moved through the barriers of the

Belgian frontier and raced into Belgium with lilac on their hats. So ended the story of a great retreat, one of the greatest in military history. So ended, though no man knew it on that day, Hitler's opportunity to break the power of Britain.

At 11:30 P.M. Captain Tennant, Senior Naval Officer, Dunkirk, made the simple signal: "B.E.F. evacuated."

England Alone

Hitler could have tried to drive these troops into the sea before they escaped, and then quickly leapfrogged across the Channel to Britain; instead, he aimed straight for Paris. Outflanking the Maginot Line, he massed more than 100 divisions along the French border against half as many French divisions, and a pitifully small French air force. The "blitzkrieg" tactics of the Wehrmacht had stunned the French, and their government was indecisive; already some members of the French cabinet were discussing an armistice. The French armies steadily withdrew toward Paris, fighting a delaying action. Then Paris was given up without a fight. On June 23rd, the war in France was suddenly over—the aged Marshal Pétain had signed an armistice.

(On June 10th, Italy had declared war on France and England. Mussolini, not willing to risk anything but oratory before, now announced to his generals, "In September everything will be over, and I need some thousands of dead to be able to sit at the peace table as a belligerent.")

The coast of Hitler's Europe now stretched from the borders of Spain to the Arctic. Only England, across the Channel, was unconquered, and she seemed in a state of shock; the island was defenseless, having lost great quantities of arms and supplies at Dunkirk. (At that moment, the British could muster less than 290 tanks and 500 field guns in the home islands; ammunition of all kinds was scarce as hens' teeth.)

If Hitler had been ready to bridge the Channel, if he had been willing to risk big casualties on the beachheads of Britain, the British might have been overwhelmed then and there. The only substantial fire power between Hitler and the coast of Britain was the British Navy. Fortunately, Hitler hadn't enough amphibious craft (by September he would have assembled 3,000 self-propelled barges in European harbors, but by then it would be too late); his navy was crippled and in no shape to give adequate support to landings, and Goering was clamoring that the Luftwaffe could, given a chance, bring Britain to her knees by bombing attacks alone.

46

Hitler himself was busy with plans to invade Russia. If the invasion of Britain couldn't be brought off quickly, he would be caught fighting on two fronts. So Goering was given the signal to throw the Luftwaffe at the British; the U-boats were to tighten the noose around the supply lines to the British Isles and, if all went well, the German command could plan for an invasion of Britain in the fall.

The Battle of Britain

Hitler, who was inclined to believe the British would now surrender, had not reckoned with the new spirit exemplified by Winston Churchill, whose speeches to the British Parliament and to the public had infused everyone with new hope. When evidence of this change was brought to Hitler, he ordered the German Luftwaffe to bomb England to her knees and to destroy the Royal Air Force, preparatory to launching the German Armies across the Channel. Until now, the very threat of bombing from the German air fleets had struck terror in the hearts of Europeans.

Hitler gave the Luftwaffe two primary tasks in the beginning of the Battle of Britain: to drive British shipping out of the Channel, and to crush the R.A.F. if it were thrown over the Channel as a protective umbrella. Churchill said, "Our fate now depended upon victory in the air," and in speaking to Parliament on June 4, he added, "The great French Army was very largely, for the time being, cast back and disturbed by the onrush of a few thousand armored vehicles. May it also be that the cause of civilization itself will be defended by the skill and devotion of a few thousand airmen?" * Throughout July, the Germans flew sortie after sortie over the Channel and the Channel ports. They achieved a partial victory. "After July 4, all big ship convoys on world routes in and out of the port of London had been driven from the Channel; after July 25, all coastal convoys had been stopped; on July 28, the withdrawal of the Dover destroyers had been forced; after July 29, the use of destroyers in the Channel by day had been prohibited."**

The air battle over Britain aroused the whole world; there was horror at the first extensive bombing of civilians, and admiration for the gallant defense put up by the British Spitfire squadrons. But the British also had a "secret weapon," which mystified the Germans for weeks; how did the British get their Spitfires into the air and in position before the German raiders arrived at target? The British had discovered and de-

*Their Finest Hour, by W. S. Churchill, p. 274.

** Strike from the Sky, by Alexander McKee, p. 54.

veloped radar (their experiments before the war had been a closely guarded secret). Later, radar would help the British defeat the German U-boat campaign against Allied shipping.

While the British fighters had suffered some losses, not all the squadrons had been committed and there were still 708 fighters and some 1400 pilots available to throw against the Luftwaffe.

Now the battle moved inland. The new objective was the destruction of the R.A.F. in direct combat to achieve the supremacy necessary for the invasion which Hitler and his generals had agreed could take place no later in 1940 than September 20.

"British fighter pilots had no fear whatsoever of the German bombers which were easy prey for the Hurricanes and Spitfires. The He-111s, Do-17s and 215s and the Ju-88s were not fast enough, particularly when operating in formation. Moreover, they were indifferently armed. They could rarely bring more than one gun to bear on an attacking fighter.

"The attitude towards the Me-109 was different. This type was very effective and accounted for most of the losses suffered by Fighter Command during the battle. It was as fast as the Spitfire, considerably faster than the Hurricane, and it would out-dive and out-climb either. Its armament was formidable. Half a dozen explosive shells from its cannon could do far more damage than the equivalent length of burst of Browning rounds. On the other hand, the firing rate of the Brownings was much higher, which gave the British pilots a better chance of scoring with a short burst.

"In one vital respect the Me-109 was at a disadvantage. It could be out-turned by the Spitfire and the Hurricane. This was a serious handicap to the Luftwaffe pilots assigned to escorting bombers. Their freedom of action was curtailed. They were, therefore, unable to pursue the tactics best suited to their aircraft. They never found a way around this problem and their difficulties were aggravated when Goering, infuriated by the losses inflicted on his bombers, ordered the fighters to stay closer still to their charges.

"At the beginning of the battle the German fighters used their speed to advantage which, coupled with their more recently evolved tactics, played havoc with the antiquated practices of Fighter Command.

"British tactics were completely wrong when the Battle began, but steadily improved. Fighter Command squadrons at the outset flew in tidy tight formations so close that only the leader could see where he was going and what was going on. The other members of the formation concentrated on keeping station.

"This was a handover from peacetime. It looked good at an air display but in combat a close formation of aircraft is easier to see. The result was that many unsuspecting pilots were 'bounced.'

"Since the Battle, the importance of the Hurricane to victory has been slowly undermined. The Spitfire tends to hold pride of place to the extent that a fallacy runs the risk of becoming accepted as historical fact.

"There were more Hurricanes in the Battle of Britain than Spitfires. The Hurricane Mk. 1, with a constant-speed propeller, was a fine fighting aircraft, an excellent gun platform and magnificently maneuverable up to 20,000 feet. It was extremely strong and could take an extraordinary amount of punishment." *

Alexander McKee, author of *Strike from the Sky*, says:

"The limiting factor on the British side was pilots and not aircraft; had another 100 pilots been available, there were sufficient machines for them. The production problem had already been solved; partly because of the planned expansion programme controlled by Air Marshal Sir Wilfrid Freeman, partly by the impact of Lord Beaverbrook's personality, and partly because of the crisis atmosphere after Dunkirk. There was a shortage of A.A. guns, particularly of the lighter type most useful for airfield defence; and here the limiting factor was production—but a number of substitutes were found. This, then, was the force which the Germans had to destroy if they were to win the battle. It was to be found largely in the air, but it was dependent on airfields and aircraft factories for its existence, and for its efficiency on the radar stations located along the coast, and the Sector Operations Rooms located at the main base airfield in each Sector. The controlling headquarters for the whole force was deep underground and beyond the reach of bombers.

"It was a problem quite unlike any other which the Germans had previously faced—fast, well-armed fighters which could not be evaded, a long-range radar warning of the bombers' approach, a radio control system to direct the fighters onto the bombers before they even reached the target, and no possibility of going forward effectively by leaps and bounds, with the tanks driving on to take advantage of the confusion created by the raids before the effect evaporated. Nevertheless, the advance, 'by leaps and bounds,' was the solution adopted, because the Luftwaffe was limited by a technical factor—the

*The Narrow Margin, by Wood and Dempster, pp. 414-415.

short range of their only effective fighter, the Messerschmitt 109. There was not the slightest possibility of unleashing an air attack which could surge at once over the whole of the United Kingdom, striking at the most vital parts of the British war machine, and at the same time confusing the defence by coming in simultaneously from all points of the compass." *

Throughout August the German Luftwaffe bombed targets selected by Goering. British radar installations, airfields, and some factories were hit. Until the end of the month, the Spitfire and Hurricane pilots gave better than they got. Then, for a few days, the Germans intensified their attack on the British airfields. The rate of loss of planes was so severe that the British Fighter Command could not have survived had the attacks continued. But, luckily, on September 7, Goering ordered the major part of the Luftwaffe to begin bombing London. Fighter Command was saved; it could now bind its wounds and be ready to fight another day.

THE CRISIS OF FIGHTER COMMAND**
31 AUGUST-6 SEPTEMBER

by Alexander McKee

In the first week of September the German plan came near to fulfilment. The concentration of German fighters in Pas de Calais swept repeatedly across Kent, shooting to pieces the handful of squadrons sent up against them and carrying the bombers again and again to Sector Stations, laying them in ruins and putting out of action vital parts of the control system. In the air, the British lost

* *Strike from the Sky*, p. 75.

** A slightly condensed version of the above chapter from *Strike from the Sky*.

more fighters than did the Germans, indeed their losses were higher than the total German losses of both fighters and bombers; and on the ground, they lost more fighters, so that the reserve of machines became seriously depleted. If the process was continued, there could be only one end for Fighter Command.

The strain on the outnumbered British pilots was intense. "It was no picnic," said Colin Gray, "despite what anyone might say later. I've seen Al Deere and others push away their breakfast when told to go up. Most of us were pretty scared all the bloody time; you only felt happy when the battle was over and you were on your way home. Then you were safe for a bit, anyway."

The strain on the Germans was equally terrible. Unlike the British, they were not being taken out of the line for rest. Every fighter pilot in the Luftwaffe, apart from those in a small unit held back to guard Wilhelmshaven against possible attacks by Bomber Command, was on the Channel coast and flying two or three sorties a day over England.

The atmosphere on the German fighter airfields can best be gauged by the photographs taken at the time. The pilots are demonstrating with their hands how they shot down that Spitfire or Hurricane, but the faces are tense with strain and at the same time drained of emotion and nervous strength. For the leaders, especially, there was the burden of responsibility. As soon as a *gruppe* commander landed, he had to worry about his losses. How many shot down—or missing? And who? How many aircraft serviceable? How long to repair the damaged aircraft? And then the order for the next take-off. And the crossing, once more, of what the German pilots, with fury, called the, "Shite Kanal," that "sewer," that "bit of dirty water." "I emphasise," said Galland,* "that this fear of coming down in the water did as much damage to our morale as the British fighters." This sentiment, surprising as it is to an Englishman accustomed to regard salt water, and espe-

*German air ace and group leader.

cially the Channel, as basically friendly, was echoed by all the German airmen who fought in the battle, whether in fighters or bombers, but more especially in the single-engined fighters. When the battle was on, they were too excited to feel fear of the enemy, but the nagging thought of that merciless sea waiting for the man whose engine failed either from enemy bullets or a mechanical fault, was continually with them.

On 31 August the Germans struck at three Sector Stations in 11 Group—Biggin Hill, Hornchurch, and Debden —and one Sector Station in 12 Group—Duxford. The 12 Group squadrons, held back to guard the Midlands and to act as flank guard and reserve to 11 Group, were, through no fault of their own, seeing very little action; consequently, they were fit and rested. The Duxford attack, the first of the day, failed.

At 7:30 a.m. the Spitfires of 19 Squadron scrambled from Fowlmere, a satellite field in the Duxford Sector. There were nine of them, led by Flight Lieutenant W. G. Clouston; the second section was led by J. B. Coward, the third section by Flight Lieutenant F. N. Brinsden. Coward had seen action over Dunkirk, but he had been away having his tonsils removed, and had rejoined only two days before, so this was his first action in the Battle of Britain. All nine Spitfires were fitted with two cannon instead of the normal armament of eight machine guns.

With adequate warning of the raid, they climbed away to the east and ten miles from Duxford sighted the enemy —about fifteen Dorniers escorted by perhaps sixty fighters. 25,000 feet below them, at Little Shelford, was Coward's home. The nine fighters pressed on in loose line astern, then Brinsden led his section of three up toward the escort while Clouston took the other six Spitfires into the bombers in a "copybook" pre-war formation attack.

Coward chose the number two Dornier in the second kette, the other two pilots of his section aiming at its companions. Diving in from the beam, Coward aimed at the nose of the bomber and opened fire. "The whole experience was an exhilarating one," said Coward, "for we were fighting over our own homes." His cannons thundered briefly, "boom-boom"—and then stopped. Almost instantly, there was a thud as something hit the Spitfire. Coward felt no pain, but saw his bare foot lying on the floor of the cockpit, almost severed from the leg. The Spitfire went out of control, the nose falling violently in the beginning of an outside loop, which forces the pilot forward against his straps, out of the cockpit.

With the "g" behind him, Coward got out quite easily, but his parachute became caught on the fuselage, his gloves were ripped off by the screaming slipstream and his nearly severed foot was banged repeatedly against the falling Spitfire. He had intended to do a delayed drop, but the pain in his foot caused him to pull the ripcord.

The opening parachute pulled him clear at 20,000 feet and, looking down, he saw the blood pumping out of his leg and dropping away far below. His bare hands, numbed by the cold, were unable to force aside the straps of the parachute harness so that he could get at the first aid kit and handkerchief in his pockets, but if he was to survive, he had to improvise a tourniquet quickly. Frantically, feeling his strength ebbing away and aware that his life depended on it, he struggled with half-frozen fingers to undo the strap and buckle of his helmet, to which was attached a wireless lead.

Once the helmet was off, Coward wound the lead round his thigh, just above the knee, pulling it as tightly as he could to choke off the supply of blood, and at the same time holding his leg almost up to his chin. By these means, he managed to reduce the flow of blood to a trickle. In this position he drifted slowly across Duxford airfield, where the rest of the squadron were now landing. Then the wind changed and he sailed back over Duxford again and came down in a field near the roundabout on the Royston/Newmarket road. The impact was hard and painful and, worried about infection of the wound, Coward tried to keep his leg off the ground.

"A youth came running up with a pitchfork at the charge, obviously thinking I was a German (I was wearing

54

a black flying overall). He stood looking at me, speechless with horror at the sight of the blood. This maddened me because I was hoping for some help. My language was a bit coarse and he departed without saying anything at all."

Years later, when Coward was instructing at a Fighter Operational Training Unit, he met the boy again—now a Pilot Officer. He remembered their previous meeting in the field by the Newmarket road, and told Coward that he had actually run to find a doctor and that the first car he had stopped had contained one. Within half an hour an ambulance had driven him away to hospital in charge of Squadron Leader Brown, an R.A.F. doctor.

Brown had then driven on to Little Shelford to break the news gently to Coward's wife. As he was knocking at the front door, the baker was round at the back, telling the kitchen staff that he had just passed the wreck of Coward's Spitfire; he thought the pilot had been killed. So, when this story reached Mrs. Coward, she already knew that her husband had been operated on and that he had lost one leg below the knee. When he recovered, Coward was posted to Chequers to take charge of the Prime Minister's roof spotters.

The bombers had jettisoned their load before reaching the airfield and 19 Squadron claimed three victories. But they were certain that they would have got more if their cannons had not packed up after firing only a few rounds. Cannon armed Spitfires had been successful in combat against reconnaissance machines off the northeast coast, but in dogfights there occurred these exasperating and inexplicable jams. They caused such fury among the baulked pilots that it was suggested to Lord Beaverbrook that the armament should revert to machine guns. Instead, he ordered an immediate enquiry. Consequently, a few days later, when the attack had begun to switch to aircraft factories, Mr. E. L. Cooper, of the Supermarine factory at Southampton, was to find himself solving the practical aspects of this problem under fire.

Shortly after the Duxford fight had ended, Teddy Morris, leading six Hurricanes of 79 Squadron, was vectored down the Thames Estuary to intercept what was probably the raid on Hornchurch coming in—half a hundred Dorniers with a large escort. The Hurricanes were still climbing, too low to put in a fast attack, but Morris engaged. He passed under the bombers, firing as he went, and then turned to attack the rearmost bombers. He was knocking pieces off a Dornier when he saw a 109 nose up alongside him about twenty yards away. Just time enough to finish off the Dornier, he thought, wrongly. Cannon shells and machine-gun bullets ripped into the Hurricane; Morris, struck by several bullets, his legs sprayed with shell fragments, took violent evasive action and limped back to Biggin Hill where he crash-landed on the airfield. Lying doped in Station Sick Quarters, he was vaguely conscious of bomb explosions and of other casualties being brought in.

Before Morris had even reached Biggin Hill, the raiders were over Hornchurch. Below them, the Spitfires of 54 Squadron were racing across the airfield in a belated attempt to get airborne. Colin Gray, who was flying with them, noted in his diary, "Red Section blown to blazes but no one hurt. Miraculous."

This is probably the most famous single incident of the Battle of Britain. The official *Fight at Odds* prints the Station diary; Richard Hillary, a Hornchurch pilot who saw the affair from the ground, described it in *The Last Enemy* (Macmillan); and Al Deere, the leader of the section "blown to blazes," has given his own account in *Nine Lives*, as it was an occasion on which he lost one of them.

After several false alarms, the engines of the squadron's Spitfires had been started and stopped so many times that they were overheated and difficult to start again when the agitated Controller screamed, "Take off! Take off!" Colin Gray, one of the first eventually to get away, climbing up under the raid, saw Hornchurch disappear in smoke and dust. Al Deere had swung into the wind, to find his take-off blocked by a Spitfire from his own section. "Get to hell out of the way, Red Two!" he bellowed. Deere had got his tail up and was bumping over the grass when he saw the first bomb exploding, ahead and to the left; then the bumping stopped and he was airborne, his section close behind him. The bombs were still falling.

56

"Out of the corner of my eye," wrote Richard Hillary, "I saw the three Spitfires. One moment they were about twenty feet up in close formation; the next, catapulted apart as though on elastic. The leader went over on his back and ploughed along the runway with a rending crash of tearing fabric; number two put a wing in and spun round on his airscrew, while the plane on the left was blasted wingless into the next field. I remember thinking, stupidly, 'That's the shortest flight he's ever taken,' and then my feet were nearly knocked from under me, my mouth was full of dirt, and Bubble, gesticulating like a madman from the shelter entrance, was yelling, 'Run, you bloody fool, run!' I ran."

When Gray landed after the action, he saw Deere's KL-B over on its back, a sorry mess; he thought, "Poor old Al's had it." But no, he found Deere had lost only his helmet and a streak of skin and hair torn off the top of his head. His Spitfire had skated along the ground, upside down, at over 100 m.p.h., dirt and stones battering at his face, and the top of his head virtually in contact with the earth over which the fighter was careering, close enough, anyway, nearly to scalp him. When the wreck wrenched to a halt, he was trapped upside down in the tiny cockpit, with a sea of petrol soaking into the grass around the crash, and no possibility of getting out.

His number three, Pilot Officer Edsell, who had crashed right way up but had hurt his legs so badly that he could not walk, then began to crawl over the aerodrome, which was still being bombed, towards KL-B. While he wrenched from outside and Deere pushed from inside, they got the cockpit door open. Deere wriggled out and, as Edsell could not stand, helped his rescuer to Station Sick Quarters.

Of Sergeant Davies, Deere's number two, there was no sign, although his aircraft could be seen, minus its tail, lying just beyond the boundary fence. His fate was a mystery for some time. He turned up hours later, carrying his parachute—there was no gap in the boundary fence, and he had had to walk several miles around it to get onto the aerodrome again.

The airfield was a mass of craters, in which lay the three

wrecked Spitfires of Red Section, and in the dispersal area four of their reserve aircraft had been destroyed, but not a great deal of damage had been done to hangars and workshops. Hornchurch was bombed again that day and the next morning Deere, Edsell and Davies were in action again; Deere, in particular, had bailed out or crash landed many times before, a split-second escape being involved in each case. Later in the war, the qualifications for the V.C. were amended, in the case of Group Captain Cheshire, to recognise the fact that unremitting performance and endurance may rank as highly as the single exceptional act of courage. Had this been so in 1940, there might have been more than merely a single V.C. awarded to Fighter Command.

In the evening, Biggin Hill, bombed already three times in two days, was the target. Worrall, Frankland and Igoe were in the Operations Room as the raid came in. Frankland was controlling, with Worrall helping him. The W.A.A.F.s continued to plot the steadily approaching bombers as Frankland and Worrall passed the orders to the fighters. "The W.A.A.F.s may have been scared to death," said Frankland, "but if so, they certainly didn't show it and their work wasn't affected." With the bombers right on top, the W.A.A.F.s were ordered under the table. Corporal Henderson, however, remained at her post. The telephone connection with 11 Group, and Sergeant Turner had to be forcibly dragged from the switchboard. Frankland felt as a crunch, rather than heard, the bomb which came through the roof and struck the top of a safe fifteen feet away in the Signal Officer's office. The Operations Room was plunged into darkness as the lights failed, a substantial part of the roof fell in, and choking clouds of dust filled the air.

Desmond Sheen had moved in that morning, from Acklington, with 72 Squadron, which was relieving 612 Squadron at Biggin Hill; he had hardly settled in before he was airborne again on the interception being controlled by Frankland at the time of the bombing. When he landed, most of the remaining hangars and workshops had either been destroyed or were so full of holes that they could not be blacked out for use at night. A W.A.A.F Armament

Sergeant was having the time of her life going round the bomb craters and marking with red flags the small significant holes which indicated delayed action bombs. The W.A.A.F. who drove Sheen across the wrecked airfield with a nonchalant disregard of the D.A. bombs had lost her husband and many of her friends in a previous raid; it was the attitude of this girl and some of the others which impressed Sheen most of all.

Meanwhile, the severe fighting had caused significant attrition among many squadrons. 56 Squadron, for instance, had virtually ceased to exist as an effective fighting unit; in the space of only a few days it had lost most of its leaders and a number of other pilots—dead, burned, wounded, or just badly shaken. The gallant "Jumbo" Gracie —"a fat chap, full of fun, full of life, a most positive cavalier character," Sutton called him—had been shot down and crash-landed on the 30th. He flew again on the 31st, joking about the stiff neck he had got in the crash, then bounced into Epping Hospital for a quick X-ray, cheerfully exaggerating (he thought) with, "I've got a broken neck!" He returned after X-ray, rather white— "It really is broken." Three pilots were in the hospital with severe burns, one of them Barry Sutton.

He was shot down, he always thought, by a Spitfire. At any rate, when returning alone from an attack on a bomber formation, he was "bounced" and the aircraft that circled his parachute was a Spitfire, presumably exulting over the demise of a 109. Just previously, he had been with the squadron, had sighted the German formation, which looked like a "great swarming mass of flies," had reported them, but presumably not been heard, for when he streaked off in their direction he found himself alone, with no sign of the rest of the squadron. His first instinct was to run, but suspecting that the Germans had not seen him and that a quick dive into the middle of them could hardly fail to get one, he went straight through them, spraying bullets. "Looking back on it afterwards with the experience of years, I am quite certain I shot well up out of range and I doubt whether I did much damage."

Grateful still to be alive, Sutton flew back over the Thames Estuary towards Hornchurch, gradually losing height. It was a beautiful evening, so he slid back the hood, raised the seat for a better view—and began to sing.

"Absolutely reprehensible," he commented afterwards. "One should never do this . . . but I thought I was well away from the battle area. Then the instrument panel suddenly began to break up and there was a great explosion, rather like a bang from an oven door." The hood was already open and Sutton got out so fast that all he remembered of it was the tail plane going past his face, very close. He pulled the ripcord, but could not hold on to the shroud lines because the flames which had blown back into the cockpit had raised large blisters on his hands.

"So I just swung about helplessly and listened to the birds, and saw the Spitfire coming round, and finally I began to see the trees and telegraph wires coming up very closely, and a road, and then people running. The people running turned out to be women and I actually landed in the middle of the street in a village near Canterbury, and these old dames came running out, I am not absolutely certain, but I think with rolling pins in their hands—they were very hostile-looking and quite certain I was a German. Then, there arrived an ambulance and a Wolseley 14 car with a soldier in it, and I was not going to get into the ambulance and insisted on the car. I was very rude to the ambulance driver, but he must have won; he put me back in the ambulance—this shows the power of one's will in conditions of shock, which is what I had. Next morning, the Sister produced a 'T' piece from my badly burned tunic, as she thought it might be of value. She didn't know what it was, and I couldn't identify it for a moment, until I realised it was the door-piece of the ambulance, which I had pocketed out of spite because they had insisted that I went in this bumpy old thing instead of the nice Wolseley."

After these losses, 56 Squadron were taken out of the line and sent to Boscombe Down where the few surviving experienced pilots would train the reinforcements. A few days later, 54 Squadron were also to be taken out of the line; but on the 31st Colin Gray got a 109 near Maidstone, which gradually slowed down, spewing glycol, and landed in a field. Circling the crash, Gray saw the pilot get out of the wreckage and three men advancing on him. Each time the Spitfire whistled over the three men, they went down flat on their faces, so that it took some minutes to reach the German; he, meanwhile, took off his parachute and jumped on it. Gray assumed he was an "ace" whose vanity was hurt.

Sunday, 1 September, was the last day of Biggin Hill's "Bad Weekend." Colin Gray attacked a Heinkel formation while they were actually bombing it, and was hit by just one bullet from some German gunner—which severed both elevator control wires. He could turn and bank but not dive or climb, so he turned onto the bearing for Hornchurch, intending to use his trimming tabs to get the nose down. This he did, and brought off a successful landing in the middle of a new rash of bomb craters.

During the day, Desmond Sheen took off from Biggin with 72 Squadron and engaged an escorted Dornier formation coming in south of the Thames; he was brushed off a bomber by the 109s, had to mix it with six of them, collected a cannon shell in his engine—and finally got away. Then he climbed up after the bombers once more. And his engine promptly burst into flames. He slid back the hood, turned the Spitfire onto its back, pulled the harness-release pin—and shoved the stick hard forward, so that the fighter tried to do an outside loop. Out he went, "clean as a whistle," and fell free, somersaulting, until he had counted ten and pulled the ripcord.

"The parachute opened smoothly and there was a reassuring jolt as it took effect," he recalled. "I found myself swaying gently some twelve to fifteen thousand feet above the ground. The descent took some time and was very pleasant; moreover, it gave me a, perhaps, unusual opportunity to survey the battle. It was a clear cloudless day, in fact, a beautiful Sunday morning.

"But, on my right, I could see bombs bursting in the Dover area with the answering fire of the A.A. defences. The A.A. were also very active in the London area on my left, and in between, a series of running fights was taking place. Above all could be heard the crump of bombs and A.A. shells, the roar of bomber engines and the distinctive whine of climbing, diving fighters. There was a smell of cordite in the air. Quite close to me a 109 went down vertically in flames. I think it was the pilot of this one who bailed out but had a faulty harness—he parted company with his parachute. Another 109 turned towards me, but a Spitfire turned onto his tail and both quickly disappeared.

"I landed in the middle of a field with nothing but a slight jar. I got out of my harness and began to roll up the parachute. A young girl came up and eyed me shyly and a few minutes later a young Army Lieutenant appeared, doubtfully waving his revolver in my general direction. I was wearing my old Australian Air Force uniform, which was then a generally unfamiliar sight, and there was no doubt that he wondered whether I was a German. However, I ignored the revolver, continued to pick up my parachute, and started as normal a conversation as possible under the circumstances."

Since Friday morning some seventy people had been killed or wounded at Biggin Hill and every hangar had been destroyed, although the shell of one was still standing. To keep a fighter fit to fly under normal conditions required a team of about five men, who had to carry out daily more than 150 inspections on the aircraft, its airframe, engine, instruments, electrics, radio, and armament. Many of the aircraft were now coming back shot to pieces and if the squadrons were to keep flying at full strength most of the repairs would have to be done on the spot. The sheer pressure of work on the ground crews was tremendous; they slaved to keep the fighters airworthy and suffered casualties while they did it. "Pilots who were on the ground when there was a raid couldn't get into the air quick enough," said Jackson, the Engineer Officer. "When you can hit back it's a build to morale. But to sit on the ground, without a gun, unable to hit back, and just get blasted, is a terrifying experience."

Biggin Hill was the worst hit of the Sector Stations, but what happened there during this climax of the battle against Fighter Command was different only in degree from what happened to most of the other Sector Stations. All except Northolt suffered a similar experience, and the cumulative effect of the attacks was becoming serious.

The attack on the Sector Stations continued without intermission; Hornchurch was raided on 2 September, North Weald on 3 September. The Germans were getting their thrusts home with distressing frequency, partly because of the enormous concentration of fighters in Pas de Calais, partly because they were becoming more expert in protecting their bombers. But the 109s, flying to the limit of their fuel, were vulnerable on the return; they could not fight, but only dive for home. On the 2nd, J. Feric of 303 Squadron pursued a 109 with such enthusiasm that he was still firing at it over France. Park mildly rebuked the Poles, saying that although he appreciated their fine offensive spirit, "this practice is not economical or sound now that there is such good shooting within sight of London." On the 3rd, Colin Gray met a 109 returning from the big raid on North Weald and chased it all the way to the French coast; it was streaming glycol but very determined to get home. As it was steadily slowing down and he was low on ammunition, he waited to fire until he had crept up to 150 yards. It promptly turned over, pretending to be dead, flipped right way up again, and carried gamely on, the propeller slowly ticking over. There, Gray had to leave it, "because its chums were coming out." The Germans were forced to include yet one more refinement in their escort technique—"Fighter Reception"—groups of 109s waiting over the Channel to greet the bomber formations, possibly broken up and certainly with "lame ducks" lagging behind, and possibly separated now from their escort, which would be low on fuel and unable to fight.

4 September marked the introduction of a new type of target for the German bombers on the western flank, those largely under command of *Luftflotte* 3. Whereas in the last week of August they had been employed against targets which had direct connection with the invasion—the bombing of naval bases, particularly Portsmouth—they now began a systematic series of raids on aircraft factories, but without discriminating between those making bombers and those engaged in fighter production. What might have happened if they had concentrated on the fighter factories and done so earlier, in mid-August, is an interesting speculation; possibly, it might have been fatal.

At midday on the 4th, Mr. C. F. Andrews, who is now Public Relations Officer of Vickers-Armstrong at Weybridge, was arguing with a colleague in a bank at Woking, where he was then employed, as to the possibilities of recognising enemy aircraft by the sound of their engines. He maintained that it was not only possible, but easy; his colleague scoffed. "Well now, it's a most extraordinary thing," replied Andrews, "but there's a formation of aircraft coming straight up over the railway line now. And I'll take a small bet that that is a hostile formation, probably Ju-88's." Before they could even reach the door, the guns were firing. When they looked out, the bombers were scattering and they counted at least six parachutes. The man in command of the battery, which had brought down two bombers with its first salvo, was a Sergeant—the officers were away at lunch. He had seen about fourteen aircraft flying low and fast up the main railway line from Portsmouth to London, taken one look at them, roared, "Bloody Ju-88s! Take post! Fire!" (or words to that effect), and the first shell had burst between two of them, bringing both down.

This was most extraordinary. Everything in this case had depended on quick and accurate recognition of the aircraft as German, and most A.A. gunners (the Navy were particularly notorious) had no grasp whatever of this subject. The Army gunners relied on the warnings passed to them by Fighter Command, with which they were integrated. This situation, and the poor quality of the recognition material had caused a group of aviation enthusiasts, mainly whole-time or part-time members of the Observer Corps in nearby Guildford, to form the Hearkers Club. A purely private organisation—it met in a café—it received help from the Technical Editor of *The Aeroplane,* Peter Masefield, and Leonard Taylor, of the Air League, and set such a standard, that it was eventually taken over officially. Andrews was a member and so was the Sergeant who had put his knowledge to such good use.

But he had not stopped the bombers; the remainder, rather scattered, pressed on to their target. This was the Vickers-Armstrong factory, producing Wellington bombers, at Brooklands aerodrome near Weybridge. It was 1:25 p.m., so that large crowds of men and women were leaving the canteen and washrooms or were clocking in; there were not many actually on the factory floor among the machinery, which afforded good protection from blast. Mr. C. Pipe, who had been delayed, had not even reached the building. He had got as far as number three gate, where an old man was standing, leaning on the gate and looking up at a segment of sky across which came four bombers, roaring in low and fast. "Now I don't think I've seen any of those before," observed the old man. There were women and girls passing through, but the sight of the black crosses on the wings of the bombers temporarily distracted Mr. Pipe. "Don't stand there—get down, for flip's sake!" he bellowed, and set the example. One of the four planes banked steeply and a bomb fell away from it, plunging through the roof of the factory.

Watching from the door of the machine shop at that moment was an assistant foreman, Mr. J. Hilyard. His segment of sky contained two planes, from which bombs fell at the exact moment someone exclaimed, "Look at those Spitfires!"

Mr. F. W. Hackney, a storekeeper, had had lunch in the canteen and was just leaving the adjoining washroom; both were on the upper floor with a "well" in the centre. On the floor below was the clocking-in area. Canteen, washrooms, the stairs leading down, and the clocking-in area were crowded with men and girls. The roof above was of glass. One heavy bomb detonated here with maximum effect. It went down through the "well"—passing Mr. Hackney on the way—and exploded, actually underneath him, on the top of a large rubber die-forming press. He heard no explosion. The place just started crumbling away, falling to pieces around him, dissolving, and filling the air with dust. He ran down the stairs, saw the body of a girl, and after a moment's hesitation, took her to the First Aid Post. Because of the dust, smoke, and ruin, every man's view was, for the moment, localised.

Mr. A. G. Bugden, an assistant foreman, had stopped for perhaps one minute later than he usually did, to buy a bar of chocolate in the canteen; so he was coming down the stairs when he heard aeroplanes and was abruptly blown some distance by the bomb. He recovered consciousness, saw a man who was blood-stained, wiped the blood off him —and discovered that he himself was similarly streaming blood. He went into the machine shop, through dense clouds of dust, and saw that the glass from the roof was hanging down in slices, held up by the wire underneath. Two men were lying under the wreckage of the stores, but part of the roof girders had come down on top of it all, and there was nothing that could be done for them. He went to his own desk and found it crushed by a roof support—buying the bar of chocolate had saved his life. Many of the men went home to tell their wives that they were all right, then came back to help.

It was fairly quiet, except for a low, persistent moaning which seemed to come from everywhere. One girl was sitting on her stool, quite lifelike, and quite dead. Of another girl, only the legs were left—with not a crease or crinkle in the stockings. Many other bodies had been wholly or partially stripped of their clothing by the blast, but there was little blood, often none at all, except among the people cut down by the flying slivers of glass. The blast had killed, apparently, without a wound. A.R.P. precautions had familiarised everyone with gas, but not with the effects of large amounts of high explosive inside a thin covering of steel. They were freakish, streams of blast streaking out as unpredictably as water from a running tap when a thumb is placed under it, and striking anything in its path with a force equal to collision with a fast motor car. The delicate internal organs—lungs, liver, spleen—were crushed or ruptured by the blow; the wounded were shocked and bleeding internally. Ordinary First Aid was useless; morphia, not bandages, was required.

Mr. Hackney, anxious to see if his brother was all right, searched for him without result, and then began to help in the work of carrying out the dead. When the supply of stretchers ran out, they piled the bodies on the completed wings of Wellington bombers, and carried them out that way. He saw a man's foot sticking out from under wreckage, but decided to leave him. The general feeling about this was, "They're gone. Leave it." Over one body, he had an argument with another man as to how to move it; they decided to turn the corpse over, and Mr. Hackney got hold of an arm—but it came right out of the body, which had been broken by the blast.

Mr. Pipe saw a removal van drive up to where he, also, was engaged on this task. The driver asked casually, "Can I help?" So they unloaded its cargo of shiny new bicycles, and put in the wounded and the dead as they were brought out from the factory. After three or four trips to the hospital, there seemed to be an end to the job, so the driver calmly took a broom, swept out the thickly caked blood from the floor of the van, reloaded his shiny bicycles, and drove off without even giving his name.

First casualty lists were put up in Sub-Post Offices throughout the district at 6 p.m. One list alone contained 132 names, but the total was not known for several days—88 killed and more than 600 wounded.

"It was eerie walking round the works that night," said a Fire Officer. "Bits of glass kept tinkling as they fell from the roof. Then there was the rubble covering the big press, and you knew, as you went past, that there were people under there. Next day, I remember, there was a chap with a concrete breaker working to uncover the bodies; hat pushed back on his head, he was singing away quite cheerfully."

On 5 September, as 72 Squadron were climbing up over Kent to get height over a raid reported coming in from the east, Desmond Sheen was "bounced" from the rear. He heard a warning shout from one of the "weavers," and almost instantaneously, the Spitfire shuddered from what must have been an accurate and heavy burst from astern. He felt sudden pain in the leg and hand, and then passed out. Possibly, his oxygen bottle had been hit and exploded.

The Spitfire went whining down, vertically, with large pieces missing from the port wing; when Sheen recovered consciousness, he had no control over the aircraft, he could not even level out or roll over so that he could drop clear. And the fighter was going straight down at the deck, speed rapidly building up towards the 500 m.p.h. mark. The hood was already open, and when Sheen pulled the harness pin to release himself from his straps, he was sucked out of the cockpit; but his feet were trapped by the top of the windscreen. He lay straddled along the top of the fuselage, struggling to get free, with no idea how much height or time he still had. Not very much, he suspected.

Then, for no apparent reason, his feet were free and, without waiting to slow down or even get clear of the aircraft, he pulled the ripcord. With a snap that jarred every bone in his body, the parachute opened; Sheen had a split-second glimpse of trees under his feet—and then he was down in Maidstone Wood.

He fell between the trees, his parachute caught on the top branches to act as a brake, and he landed as lightly as a feather, barely touching the ground. He crawled to a path and saw a policeman riding a bicycle, followed by spectators. The policeman's first action was to produce a flask, the second to express surprise that Sheen had waited so long before getting out of his aircraft. His wounds were not serious, but they kept him out of the air for about a month.

When they were jumped, the squadron had been flying in the old tight formation of vics of three, instead of the loose pairs used by the Germans; to offset the difficulties of lookout which made this formation vulnerable, the two rear machines of the last section had been "weaving" but this method was not satisfactory and the "weavers" had seen

68

the Germans too late to avoid the "bounce." Superior numbers and the holding of the initiative, combined with the rigid and inflexible thinking of their opponents, enabled the Germans to inflict heavier losses than they themselves suffered; the Hurricanes particularly, with their comparatively low ceiling and poor performance above 18,000 feet, suffered from the "bounce." Malinowski was three times with formations which were jumped on from the top: the first time, he was shot down; the second time, the attackers consisted only of six 109s, but they got two Hurricanes as they dived through; the third time, there was only one 109, but he also shot down two Hurricanes. These were ambush tactics pure and simple, which, rather than dogfighting, were the essence of fighter v. fighter combat.

On the morning of the 5th, the staff of Vickers-Armstrong had reported for work as usual, but most were not allowed inside the factory because the structure was unsafe. What work there was consisted largely of moving out the machine tools and stacking them for dispersal; this took four days. Lord Beaverbrook's Ministry of Aircraft Production ruled that buildings in the neighbourhood should be requisitioned to house the machine tools as, in effect, small aircraft factories, and that the main factory should do only assembly work, so that never again should such a concentrated, vulnerable target be presented to the enemy. A bookbinding works, a cable works, a timber stores, many garages, and one film studio—which proved ideal for building main wings—were taken over.

The Company had been producing 134 Wellingtons a month, nearly two-thirds at Brooklands, the rest at Chester, out of range of day bombing. Production never actually stopped—the lowest weekly figure following the raid was four Wellingtons—but it was not until eight months later that production again reached peak. Coming three weeks after the raid on Shorts, Bomber Command had been struck a substantial blow. Two important factories in the area were intact, both producing fighters—Hawkers, on the opposite side of Brooklands aerodrome to Vickers-Armstrong, and Supermarine at Southampton. No sooner had Park been relieved of the responsibility for escorting convoys, than he was directed by Dowding, as a result of the Weybridge raid, to give "maximum fighter cover" to the remaining factories, thus imposing maximum strain on his already inadequate forces, whose bases were largely in ruins. Nevertheless, those factories were vital and had to be protected—and they were on the Luftwaffe target list.

On 6 September the debris was being cleared at Weybridge and unsafe parts of the structure brought down. Canadian troops, brought in to do this job, were walking the girders, high above the ground, or sitting on them and knocking out broken glass, singing to their hearts' content. When the whistles blew to signal another raid, and they were told to shelter, they shouted back, "Aw, hell! We came here to work and no goddam Jerry's going to stop us." At midday the raid came in, directed at Hawkers on the far side of the aerodrome. A bomb hit the banked racing car track which encircled the landing ground, bounced along the concrete like a football and ended up at the bottom, unexploded. The Engineering Division was hit and, also, the Home Guard armory, from which rifles showered out: and cannon shells and bullets punched holes in the parked cars of the Directors. But the effect was much less devastating than that caused at the Vickers factory.

The Home Guards—most factories provided their own battalions from members of the staff—worked the unexploded bomb by the banking onto a sheet of corrugated iron and then lifted it onto a truck driven by a Canadian. With one man sitting on the bomb to keep it steady, they drove across the airfield to the nearest bomb crater, lowered the bomb into it—and exploded it there.

While Weybridge was being bombed, the main effort was being made over the eastern outskirts of London; the vapor trails of the dogfight could be clearly seen from the centre of the capital. The target, the oil storage tanks at Thameshaven, was set on fire and burned furiously. Below the battle, busy betting on the dogs at a greyhound racing stadium, were a dozen tired pilots from 66 Squadron who had been flying four and five sorties a day, and had been given the day off. "There was a terrific dogfight going on overhead," recalled Oxspring, who was betting with Rupert Leigh. "He appeared to take no notice, borrowed ten bob off me to put on a dog, then looked up and said, 'You know, I can't help feeling this is a case of Nero fiddling while Rome is burning.'"

Oberst Carl Viek, Chief of Staff to the JAFU 2, had in the beginning been able to do the same thing for his pilots, giving them the day off, by squadrons, to go down to the beach and have a swim, and also, on his own responsibility, grounding the leaders who appeared to be on the point of cracking under the strain. This now was no longer possible; he had been accused of "softness" and nearly lost his job because of it. Nevertheless, in his opinion, greater than the physical strain was the psychological effect of their being told by the high command that, according to arithmetical calculations, there were no British fighters left. "But when they went up they found lots of them—and that caused doubts about the Government."

However, on this day the British defences were torn apart by the improved escort methods of the Germans. The radar system helped the British to offset their disparity in numbers—but only up to a point. Park was trying to engage with as many squadrons as possible—but usually there was insufficient time to assemble more than two squadrons together. The Poles of 303 Squadron, successful the previous day, failed on this day with heavy losses. Squadron Leader R. G. Kellett, who was leading them, saw that the rearguard of 109s was already being engaged by a Spitfire squadron and took his Hurricanes down on the bombers. He alone reached them, setting the engine of a Dornier on fire, before being hit and slightly wounded by cannon fire from a 109. Two of the Polish pilots were wounded and the Polish C.O., Major Z. Krasnodebski, was so badly burned that he was in hospital for a year. Four Hurricanes were lost and two damaged. The new Polish C.O. was Flying Officer W. Urbanowicz, who was to take over the squadron when Kellett left. Later, he became a Wing Commander and Polish Air Attache in the U.S.A., during which appointment he managed, somehow, to visit the Japanese battlefront and to shoot down two "Zero" fighters. His combat report of 6 September contained much pertinent comment.

"Only two of our squadrons in the area—and a hundred Germans," he wrote. "The Germans had now developed a new principle of covering the whole length of the approach to London—a sort of blanket of fighters—under which the bombers had free passage. That made it very difficult to get at them because, invariably, we had to engage the fighters first, and in view of their superiority in numbers, there was no chance to deal with them in time to catch the bombers. So—heavy fighting, considerable losses, where pilots had to engage one Messerschmitt after another and only Kellett was lucky enough to get to the bombers. The English are a bit too cautious in restricting interception to one or two squadrons, which cannot be effective, instead of, on such occasions, putting everything in the air and sweeping it clean." He added, as an afterthought, "I was lucky enough to shoot down a 109. Gave it a very short burst; to my surprise it went straight down in flames; the pilot did not jump."

In the week beginning on 31 August and ending on 6 September, Fighter Command lost 161 fighters in air battles alone, against a German loss of 154 bombers and fighters. The battle in the air—of fighter versus fighter—was being decisively won by the Luftwaffe. If this continued, there really would be no British fighters left, or at any rate, not enough to put up an effective defence. Then the whole of the German bomber force could sweep over southern England, destroy the aircraft factories to make their victory complete, and turn, finally, to the essential bombing of targets connected with the invasion. And that afternoon, from the cliffs of Dover, part of the German invasion fleet was sighted, steaming west past Cap Gris Nez to its embarkation ports in the Channel.

The Polish comment, "the English are too cautious," found its echo later on the German side. The R.A.F. had almost as many fighters as the Germans, certainly enough to sweep that carpet of German fighters and roll it up by squadrons passing across from east to west. In the German

72

view, the British could have brought the German onslaught to a dead stop within three days, instead of being on the verge of defeat, if only they had matched the German concentration of fighters in Pas de Calais with an equivalent concentration of their own. Furthermore, why did the British doggedly carry on from the aerodromes on the southern and eastern sides of London, which were just within the range of German operations, instead of withdrawing to aerodromes north and west of London, which were out of range? They had already withdrawn from their exposed forward aerodromes, why not withdraw the target altogether and leave the Germans to beat at the air? They concluded that the British could not fully have understood the weakness of the German position caused by the limited range of the 109.

Unknown to them were the weaknesses of the British position. Firstly, the limited number of squadrons which the control system could handle, and secondly, the fact that the aerodromes were not merely base aerodromes, as the Germans understood them to be, but Sector Stations of the control system which was too complicated to be moved in a hurry and for which in any case emergency alternatives had been provided. The British therefore felt themselves forced to stand and fight where they were, instead of withdrawing. But certainly they could have engaged with greater numbers, if Dowding had taken the risk of stripping other parts of the country of fighter protection in favour of concentration on the main battle. It was not even necessary to control them, merely to get them airborne in time, so that they could indulge in a British "free hunt" across the German fighter "carpet." In the last analysis, it was not even necessary to retain fighters at the Sector Stations, for the control aspect consisted of an Operations Room and its annexes, together with landlines to a transmitter and telephone lines to Group; it was convenient and efficient for the control staff and the fighter pilots to be in personal contact with each other, but it was not strictly necessary. On the other hand, a withdrawal could produce a momentarily critical situation if the Germans landed suddenly on the southeast coast; the British fighters were

73

just as short-ranged as the 109s, and from bases behind London they could not intervene effectively against bombers supporting the troops on the beaches.

The British reaction to the new German tactics was not altogether satisfactory. Instead of bringing the fresh 12 Group squadrons into the battle area, under Park's control, he was merely given to understand that they would relieve him of responsibility—at some time while attacks were in progress—for guarding his bases northeast of London. In practice, they either did not take part in the battle at all, or came in too late. As these squadrons were fully efficient and, indeed, exceedingly impatient for action, the failure to use them fully partly justifies the criticism of undue caution. But it should be remembered that Dowding held the major responsibility in a battle to which he could see no certain end, at a time when the facts could not be fully known, and when a false move could lose the war. What might have happened if the German attacks on the Sector Stations had continued further to disrupt the effectiveness of his command is guesswork.

Action in the Atlantic

By the end of September, Goering was forced to admit he wasn't accomplishing any of his objectives—he hadn't even knocked out the R.A.F. And bombing the British cities had done nothing but make the British spit on their hands and fight back harder. Hitler was astounded; he had been sure the "decadent" British would ask for an early armistice. Had he realized that the effect was just the opposite, he might have invaded England before turning on Russia. Instead, he ordered the U-boat campaign intensified, and the Battle of the Atlantic began in all its fury.

The U-boats were not the only menace to shipping; the Germans had built a force of surface raiders, including pocket battleships and battle cruisers, which could now operate from bases along the coast of Europe; from air bases in France, their aircraft could bomb and strafe the approaches to the British ports. In 1940 and 1941, eight million tons of shipping were destroyed.

The U-boats were responsible for the major losses, while the surface raiders cost the British little more than three-quarters of a million tons; but the pocket battleships and cruisers in European coastal harbors were major threats to the convoys converging on the British Isles. A pocket battleship in an unprotected convoy could produce a slaughter like a wolf among sheep. The British Admiralty was forced to keep battleships in the Home Fleet, though they were badly needed for convoy duty, against the day when a raider sallied out into the Atlantic.

The British caught the pocket battleship *Graf Spee* off South America in December, 1939, and crippled her so badly the Germans had to scuttle her to avoid capture. Both battle cruisers, *Scharnhorst* and *Gneisenau*, were kept bottled up and inactive by intermittent bombings. But, early in 1941, the Germans finished work on the *Bismarck*, their fastest battleship, with a displacement of 45,000 tons and an armament including eight 15-inch guns. On the 21st of May, the British Admiralty was signaled that the *Bismarck*, plus the light cruiser *Prinz Eugen*, had been sighted escorting a convoy to Bergen. Because of bad weather, both ships got out of the Norwegian harbor undetected by British air patrols.

The British were certain they were out to raid Atlantic shipping routes—but where? *

Admiral Tovey, Commander of the British Home Fleet, had the battleships *King George V* and the *Prince of Wales* (newest and fastest ship in the British fleet), the battle cruisers *Hood* and *Repulse*, and the carrier *Victorious*, all at Scapa Flow. Two cruisers, *Norfolk* and *Suffolk*, were on patrol in Denmark Strait between Greenland and Iceland, and were alerted. Tovey then sent the *Prince of Wales*, the *Hood*, and six destroyers to intercept the *Bismarck* if and when it emerged from Denmark Strait; some hours later another force consisting of *King George V*, aircraft carrier *Victorious*, four cruisers and seven destroyers was sent to cover other approaches south of Iceland. Another force at Gibraltar, which included the aircraft carrier *Ark Royal*, was speeded northward.

The two German ships *had* sailed into Denmark Strait; they were sighted there on May 23rd, and carefully trailed by the two British cruisers (the heavier guns of the *Bismarck* had to be kept at a safe distance). At 5:35 a.m., May 24th, the battleships *Hood* and *Prince of Wales* sighted the *Bismarck* and *Prinz Eugen*, and closed for action at 25,000 yards.

The *Bismarck* straddled the *Hood* with her first salvo.* Within minutes, the *Bismarck's* very accurate shooting broke the *Hood* in two; she sank so fast only three survivors were picked up. The *Prince of Wales*, crippled soon after, was forced to pull out of action.

The news of the *Hood's* loss was a shock to the Admiralty, but they

* At this time, shipping losses had become so serious the British War Cabinet was on the point of not publishing monthly tonnage figures of sinkings.

* Capt. Russell Grenfell, *The Bismarck Episode*—"The principal guideposts in modern navel gun battles are the splashes made by shells hitting the water. These splashes leap up to a great height (in the case of large shells about 200 feet) and are the means whereby gun control officers know where their shots are going. Splashes off the target indicate how corrections are to be made. What the control officer wants is a straddle. That is to say, one or more splashes over and one or more splashes short. He then knows he is 'on the target' and there may be one or more hits. As a rule he will not see those hits. With delayed action fuses, they may crash through the ship side or deck and penetrate deep into a hull before exploding."

76

quickly called for other ships in the Atlantic area to join the hunt. They knew the *Bismarck* had been hit, because the *Norfolk* and *Suffolk*, still trailing, reported a broad oil slick behind her. As the hours went by, the *Bismarck* was lost sight of, then picked up again on the 25th; from her course, the British were certain she was steaming for Brest, a naval port on the French coast.

The *Bismarck* might have made it, with her great speed, but she was losing fuel, and her steering mechanism was damaged, too. Without these mishaps the British battleships would never have been able to get into range.

The chase was to cover nearly 3,000 miles, from the fringe of the Arctic Circle almost to the Bay of Biscay, before the *Bismarck* was cornered. The British themselves were faced with a fuel problem. But Churchill gave orders to keep hard on the scent, even if the battleships had to be towed home.

On the night of the 24th, the *Prinz Eugen* was sent off to rendezvous with an oiler, leaving the *Bismarck* to meet her fate alone. The British ships now moving in for the kill were the *King George V*, with Admiral Tovey aboard, joined by the battleship *Rodney*, plus the *Norfolk*, all pursuing the *Bismarck* out of the northwest; the carrier *Ark Royal*, the cruisers *Sheffield* and *Dorsetshire*, from the south; and a small force of destroyers approaching from the east. Other ships were in the pack, but would not be prominent in the action to follow.

The *Ark Royal* was the first to get within striking distance. Unluckily, the first attack by her Swordfish torpedo-bombers mistook the British cruiser, *Sheffield*, for the target—but no damage resulted. Capt. Russell Grenfell supplies the full account of the battle as it developed from there.

THE CHASE OF THE BISMARCK

by Capt. Russell Grenfell

After emerging safely from the disconcerting episode of the Swordfish attack, the *Sheffield* had gone on to find the *Bismarck*. On her bridge, everyone was scanning

This selection is made up of three chapters slightly condensed from the author's *The Bismarck Episode*.

the horizon ahead for a sign of a ship, and the lookouts had been promised two pounds to the first man to sight her. At 5:40 p.m., on May 26th, the officer of the watch said: "I think I can see something on the port bow." All binoculars were raised to look in that direction and, sure enough, a dim grey shape could just be made out on the misty horizon. Was it the *Bismarck?* At first it was difficult to say, but as the *Sheffield* came closer the silhouette of the *Bismarck* became unmistakable. Once again, a shadowing warship was in contact after an interval of more than a day and a half.

Captain Larcom, of the *Sheffield,* did not want to be seen if it could be avoided, and he altered course away and began to work round to get astern of the enemy at a distance of seven to ten miles. He began also to send in the usual shadower's reports of the enemy's position, course and speed. These reports were supplementing those going out from the *Ark Royal*'s shadowing aircraft who, in successive pairs, had been keeping a continuous watch on the *Bismarck* since 11:15 a.m.

Whether or not the *Bismarck* could see the *Sheffield,* she made no hostile move. Possibly she felt that, as she was obviously being reported by aircraft, it would serve no useful purpose and be only a waste of ammunition to try to drive away the cruiser, anyway during daylight.

Meanwhile, feverish activity was going on in the *Ark Royal* to get the next striking force ready to go. There was no time to be lost and everyone was working at top speed. With the ship rolling heavily, aircraft were refuelled and more torpedoes got ready. This time, too, there would be no mistake about the *Sheffield.* To make assurance extra sure, the aircraft were told to contact that ship on their way to the *Bismarck,* and the *Sheffield* herself was told that they would do so.

By 7 p.m. the striking force was up on deck and ranged. There were fifteen Swordfish, every single torpedo-bomber that remained in the ship. It was still blowing hard. Visibility was exceedingly variable, cloud was at about 600 feet or less, and rainstorms covering very large areas were sweeping across the sea. Once more the ship was turned into the wind and once more the aircraft careered unsteadily along the heaving deck before they rose clear into storm-swept sky. As they formed up in the air and disappeared in the direction of the enemy, everyone in the *Ark Royal* knew that they meant to succeed this time.

About forty minutes later, just before 8 p.m., the *Sheffield* sighted them coming. She made to them "the enemy is twelve miles dead ahead," and they were seen climbing into the clouds. Half an hour later they were back to ask for another bearing, having apparently failed to find the *Bismarck*. Redirected, they departed once more in the enemy's direction. There was too much rain and low cloud about for the *Sheffield*'s people to keep them long in sight. But after an interval there came an outburst of gunfire off the starboard bow and the bright winking of numerous shell bursts in the air which showed plainly that the attack was starting.

The distant display of anti-aircraft fire flashed and sparkled away for some minutes and then died away. There was a pause, and then those on the bridge of the *Sheffield* saw first one and then two more Swordfish flying towards them. They came past very low on a level with the bridge. It could be seen that their torpedoes had gone, and as one Swordfish flew by very close the crew were smiling broadly and had their thumbs held upwards. All those on the *Sheffield*'s bridge and upper deck took off their caps and gave them a cheer as they passed.

The attacks went on, and owing to the bad weather conditions were somewhat protracted. Mostly, the *Sheffield* could see little of what was happening, but at times, in a clear patch, her people saw the *Bismarck* spurting flame from every anti-aircraft gun, while through binoculars it was occasionally possible to spot some of the aircraft as they dived down and flattened out low over the water to drop their torpedoes.

Had the day been fine and clear, a simultaneous assault by the whole force would doubtless have been delivered. As it was, on nearing the enemy's position the aircraft encountered a thick bank of cloud, rising 6,000 to 10,000 feet above its base a few hundred feet from the sea. Inside this cloud bank the striking force got split up. Some aircraft went straight on at the same level till they reached what they estimated to be the correct attacking point. Others spent time in climbing several thousand feet before diving down. Those that did this experienced varying degrees of icing. On breaking cloud cover, some aircraft did not find the enemy where expected and had either to work round in the open or go back into cloud for another approach. One pair and one single aircraft lost the enemy completely and separately went back to the *Sheffield* for redirection. One aircraft found the flak so heavy that it gave up the attack and jettisoned its torpedoes before returning to the carrier. Altogether, the attacks were spread out over about half an hour, from 8:55 p.m. to 9:25 p.m.

While the attacks were still proceeding, those on the *Sheffield*'s bridge noticed that the *Bismarck* was altering course. She would naturally swerve about a good deal to dodge the torpedoes being dropped at her. Now she was getting almost broadside on to the *Sheffield*. Then suddenly from the distant enemy ship there came four rippling yellow flashes from her turret guns. As if stung to fury by the air attacks against her, she had opened fire on the only British ship she could see.

The shells fell a long way, perhaps more than a mile, from the *Sheffield;* and someone on her bridge made a derisory remark about the shooting. He spoke too soon. Again the enemy's turrets spurted their bright tongues of flame, and about fifty seconds later there were some piercing cracks as four 15-in. shells fell very close on either side of the British cruiser, exploding on hitting the water. Huge splashes shot up alongside, and the air was filled with whizzing shell splinters. Captain Larcom went on to full speed, put the wheel over to get clear, and gave the order to make smoke. But before that last order had produced any result four more enemy salvoes had fallen unpleasantly close.

The splinters from the second one had caused casualties among the anti-aircraft gun crews, twelve men being wounded, three of whom died. They had also destroyed the ship's radar apparatus, an awkward piece of damage, as it meant the *Sheffield* could now only shadow by eyesight, and

80

would therefore be ineffective for that purpose after dark.

It was a hectic few minutes, with the sudden outburst of shellfire, the hurried giving of orders, the frantic rolling of the ship as she came beam-on to the sea, the swish and smack of the incoming spray and the rising howl of the gale as she turned at high speed into the wind; and at last, none too soon, the dense volumes of jet-black smoke pouring out of the funnels, blotting out the *Sheffield* from the vicious enemy's sight. The moments had been too crowded for a calm and leisurely observation of the *Bismarck*'s behavior. But she had been seen to continue her turn into the wind. As he swung round away from her gunfire, Captain Larcom ordered a signal to go out that she was steering 340° (NNW). What had been the *Bismarck*'s game? Had she thought this was a good moment to drive away her one surface shadower before dark, when the air attacks were in any case compelling her to twist and turn? Or was there some other explanation? Captain Larcom could not tell.

Many miles below the horizon, Sir John Tovey had even less means of knowing. All he had to go on was Captain Larcom's report that the *Bismarck* had almost reversed her course. What did it mean? In view of the shattering signal just previously received from the leader of the attacking aircraft it probably meant nothing. This signal had been short and very much to the point. It said: "Estimate no hits." It was assumed by the Admiral and indeed by all ships that took it in, that the signal referred to the attack as a whole and indicated that, like its predecessor, it had been a complete failure. The gloom thereby engendered was naturally abysmal. Captain Dalrymple-Hamilton told the *Rodney*'s company over the loudspeakers that no hits had been obtained and added that he very much feared there was now no hope of bringing the *Bismarck* to action. Commodore Blackman of the *Edinburgh* reached the same conclusion. He had been in sight of the *King George V* and *Rodney*, off and on, since early in the day. At about 5 p.m. he had crossed astern of them to make straight for the *Bismarck*'s reported position. But though he ran across both *Sheffield* and *Ark Royal* at different times and therefore must have got very close to the *Bismarck* herself, he did not succeed in sighting her. By this time, his fuel position was verging on the desperate, and the report that the second air attack had gained no hits decided him to give up the pursuit. He turned his ship for home.

To Sir John Tovey the "no hits" signal was the culminating rebuff. All was now clearly over. The *Bismarck* was practically certain to get away and there would be little left for him, Sir John, to do but to make his mournful way back to his base. Then another signal was brought to him. It was from one of the shadowing aircraft and it said that the *Bismarck* was steering due north. The *Bismarck* had undoubtedly turned right round. But this did not necessarily mean a great deal. Such a turn, drastic though it was, was not incompatible with the frustrating of an aircraft attack. The next report would surely show the *Bismarck* as back to east-south-east. But the next report, nine minutes later, did not. It made her still steering north-north-west. Another nine minutes passed, and again an aircraft report was handed to the Commander-in-Chief. Again it said that the *Bismarck* was heading about north-north-west. Sir John and his staff looked at each other with bewildered hopefulness. Could it really be true that the *Bismarck,* for no apparent reason, was steaming back on her tracks? Then, five minutes later, there came a second report from the *Sheffield,* in which the enemy's course was given as north.

There was now no room for doubt. The *Bismarck* was clearly moving in a general northward direction. But if she had not been hit, why was she behaving in this strange, and indeed suicidal, manner? It was to her vital interest to make every mile of progress she could towards the south-east. Yet here she was steering almost in the opposite direction for nearly half an hour. Was it possible that she had been hit after all? The thought was forming among Sir John Tovey and his staff that the *Bismarck*'s otherwise inexplicable movements might be due to her rudders being damaged and she herself being no longer under control.

Whatever the explanation, the situation had turned dramatically in the British favour. Two minutes after the *Sheffield*'s second report reached him Sir John led round to a course of south, directly towards the *Bismarck*'s position.

The *Sheffield* was still steering northward to open the range from the *Bismarck*, and just before ten o'clock she sighted some destroyers coming down from the north-westward. These were Captain Vian's five ships who had been steaming hard to overtake the *Bismarck* for the previous nine hours. They had already seen the *Renown* in the distance and had in turn been sighted by the *Ark Royal*'s aircraft on their way back from the attack. The sun was getting low towards the horizon. Yet even in the evening light, the destroyers made an inspiring spectacle as they came racing up, yawing about and heeling far over as they tore along down wind, the white of their foaming bow waves prominent even among the breaking seas. As they neared the *Sheffield*, Captain Vian asked her for the bearing of the *Bismarck*, and, receiving it, swept past and onwards towards the enemy.

The air striking force had begun to return to the *Ark Royal* at about 9 p.m., but they had a long way to go, and the last of them was not on board till an hour and a half later. Five had been damaged by gunfire. In one 127 holes were counted, the pilot and air gunner having both been wounded. But despite all this and the failing light, only one aircraft crashed.

It was a more cheerful lot of airmen who climbed out of their aircraft and went up to tell their stories. The crews were interrogated separately as they returned, and it was not until well after 10 p.m. that Captain Maund of the *Ark Royal* felt satisfied that one hit had been obtained amidships on the *Bismarck*. He signalled this over by lamp to Vice-Admiral Somerville, who passed it out by wireless at approximately 10:30 p.m. This report did not clarify the situation very much. If the hit had actually been amidships, it would be most unlikely to have been responsible for the *Bismarck*'s northerly course. Nevertheless, the report sufficed to bring the *Edinburgh* back towards the enemy.

Meanwhile, darkness had been coming on, and Sir John Tovey knew that the air shadowers would soon have to return to the *Ark Royal*. But he also knew that, thanks to Captain Vian's initiative earlier in the day, the latter's destroyers were now in the *Bismarck*'s vicinity and would presumably soon be taking over the watch.[1] To assist them in gaining contact, Sir John asked Vice-Admiral Somerville if the air shadowers could guide the destroyers to the enemy, and this instruction was passed to them via the *Ark Royal*. They seem to have left the *Bismarck* at about 10 p.m. and made a sweep in search of the destroyers. These they eventually found, but had by that time become too "lost" themselves to act as guides. Just before 10:30 p.m. they were recalled to the *Ark Royal*.

But Captain Vian was taking his destroyers in the right direction, and at ten minutes to eleven, after a silence of about three-quarters of an hour, the other British forces were cheered by a contact signal from the *Zulu*, showing that the destroyers were in touch. By now, Sir John Tovey was convinced that the *Bismarck* had been injured in such a way as to prevent her maintaining a continuous south-easterly course and to compel her frequently to come round head to wind, which by good fortune was blowing from the north-west. He was satisfied that she could not now escape him; and he therefore decided that, as night was falling, he would not seek an action at once but would wait for daylight. The positions of the enemy and of other British forces were none too certain and there was always the chance of an unfortunate incident if one of the latter was met unexpectedly in the darkness. At 11:36 p.m. Sir John altered course to about north-north-east to work round to the northward and westward of the *Bismarck*, with the object of having her silhouetted against the early morning light when he made his attack. He had hardly got round to his course when he received another signal from Vice-Admiral Somerville to say there had probably been a second hit on the *Bismarck*, on her starboard quarter. Apparently the signal was written out at 2240 (10:40 p.m.) since it bore that time of origin. But it was an hour later when it was received in the *King George V*.

[1] Sir John Tovey had intercepted a signal from the *Renown* saying that the destroyers had been seen passing her at 7 p.m.

84

The word "quarter" was highly significant,[2] and indeed was the sort of evidence for which they had all been waiting for two hours and a half. A hit on the quarter might well mean that the *Bismarck*'s propellers or rudder or both had been damaged, rendering her unmanageable. Sir John Tovey felt more confident than ever that he now had her at his mercy, and he made a signal that she appeared severely damaged and that he would be engaging from the westward at dawn. He also wrote a message to Captain Patterson, wishing the flagship good luck and victory in the coming fight.[3]

Meanwhile, the last aircraft shadowers had just got back to the *Ark Royal* with practically no petrol left, and in spite of the darkness and the lively pitching of the ship had somehow managed to make a successful landing. The crews had some important information to impart. It was that immediately after the aircraft attack the *Bismarck* had made two complete circles and had apparently come to a stop heading north, on which point of the compass she lay wallowing in the seas. This was the final link in the evidence needed to complete the whole chain. Captain Maund flashed it over at once to the *Renown,* and Admiral Somerville sent it on to Sir John Tovey by wireless at a minute before one o'clock, with a time of origin of 0046 (12:46 a.m.).

It was direct and invaluable confirmation of what Sir John had been suspecting for some time. The picture was now indeed reasonably clear to everyone on the British side. After the strain and anxieties of the past few days, culminating in the two wretched disappointments of the previous six hours, when hope of catching the *Bismarck* had declined practically to zero, the enemy's evident disablement seemed almost too good to be true. To the senior officers,

[2] The quarter is that part of a ship about halfway between the middle of her length and the stern.

[3] To *K.G.V.* The sinking of the Bismarck may have an effect on the war, as a whole out of all proportion to the loss to the enemy of one battleship. May God be with you and grant you victory.   JT 26/5/41

particularly, the relief was immense. They, who had known the general strategical situation as their juniors had not, had previously almost despaired of getting the *Bismarck*. They had realized that the air attack which had done the vital damage was virtually the last hope of slowing the *Bismarck* up and thus preventing her escape; and that such a last-minute attempt should be an overwhelming success was beyond reasonable expectation.

All that Sir John Tovey now wanted to bring off his dawn attack were reports of the *Bismarck*'s position during the night, and these he was confident he would get from Captain Vian's destroyers. A few minutes after receiving the "circling" signal, he altered course right round to southwest. Sir John had also requested Sir James Somerville to take his Force H not less than twenty miles to the southward of the enemy. That would be quite close enough for the operation of the *Ark Royal*'s aircraft, and Sir John Tovey thought it best to keep the *Renown* well clear. An hour or two before, Sir James had suggested bringing her over to join the battleships. But Sir John was anxious to avoid any possibility of mistaking her for the enemy in the darkness, while he believed the *King George V* and *Rodney* quite strong enough for the job in hand.

To the north of the *King George V*, the *Norfolk* was still striving to catch up. She had shortened the distance the battleships were ahead of her during the day, but she was still behind them. Being seriously short of fuel, Captain Phillips had been hesitating to go too fast. But when the last air attack was due to be in progress, he could contain himself no longer. He put the telegraphs to full speed.

Another British warship was now speeding towards the *Bismarck*. Captain B. C. S. Martin of the cruiser *Dorsetshire* had been acting as the escort of Convoy SL 74 coming north. At 11 a.m. on the 26th, he and the convoy were about 600 miles west of Cape Finisterre, when the Admiralty's signal was taken in that the *Bismarck* had been sighted just before. The plot of the enemy's position made her 300 miles due north of the *Dorsetshire*, and Captain Martin realized that if the *Bismarck* were making for Brest, he could probably intercept her.

He made up his mind to leave the convoy and steer to meet the enemy. The intercepting course was about east and nearly down wind, which meant that the *Dorsetshire* could maintain a good speed. Captain Martin turned to east-north-east and went on to 26 knots. At 5 p.m., he altered course to east and increased to 28 knots.

When Captain Vian sighted the *Sheffield* ahead of him just before 10 p.m., his destroyers were spread in line abreast, two and a half miles apart, and the *Sheffield* on the opposite course passed through the line a quarter of an hour later. Learning from her that the *Bismarck* was not far off and when last seen was heading north to north-west, Captain Vian reduced speed. In the growing dusk and with heavy seas running, it might be dangerous to make the final approach too fast. It was expected to sight the *Bismarck* ahead of the centre destroyer. But at 10:38 p.m., she was seen a little on the starboard bow of the port wing ship, the *Piorun;* and shortly after the latter's next-in-line, the *Zulu*, also spotted her and was the first to get off a sighting report.

Within a very few minutes, the *Bismarck* sighted the *Piorun* and opened fire on her with both main and secondary armaments. Undismayed, the tiny *Piorun* returned the fire with her 4.7-in. guns. It is very unlikely that she did any good, and she herself, being frequently straddled, was in grave danger. But it was a most spirited display, and the *Piorun* actually kept up the hopelessly unequal contest for over half an hour before she ceased spitting fire at her armoured antagonist and hauled out of range.

Captain Vian had discovered the enemy he was seeking, and he now had to decide what policy to adopt towards him. As his destroyers drew closer and could make a better estimate of the *Bismarck*'s movements, it became apparent that she was proceeding at low speed and was steering erratically. Captain Vian concluded that interception by the British heavy ships was fairly certain in the morning, if not earlier, provided the enemy were successfully held during the night. He therefore made up his mind that his first duty was to shadow the *Bismarck* with a view to guiding the

King George V and *Rodney* to her position. He would, however, as a secondary duty, deliver torpedo attacks as opportunities offered, and provided this did not involve heavy
losses among his ships.

Immediately after sighting the enemy, he had ordered his
destroyers to take up their shadowing positions, and they
were moving over to do that now. The *Maori, Sikh, Zulu,*
and *Piorun* were to form a square round the *Bismarck,* one
on each bow and one on each quarter; while the *Cossack,*
Captain Vian's ship, would shadow from astern. It would
take some time for all the destroyers to get into position,
especially as the two detailed for the farther positions had
to keep out of gun range while reaching them, involving
something of a detour.

At about 11:15 p.m., however, the *Bismarck* made things
easier by altering course in the destroyers' direction. Since
they had first sighted her, she had seemed to be oscillating
about a mean course of roughly north-east. She now swung
round to about north-north-west. But it was nearly dark;
and the outer destroyers did not immediately become aware
of the *Bismarck*'s alteration, and so went on for a short time
in the wrong direction.

At 11:24 p.m., Captain Vian made the signal for taking
up preparatory stations for a synchronized torpedo attack.
His plan, previously communicated to the other ships, was
for three destroyers on one side of the *Bismarck* and for
two on the other all to attack together, coming in on both
the enemy's bows to fire their torpedoes at the same time.
The weather was, however, unfavourable for an organized
attack of this kind. It was blowing very hard and there was
a big sea running. The destroyers could manage a fair speed
down wind, but could make only moderate progress against
it.

It very soon became clear, however, that the darkness was
no handicap to the *Bismarck.* Time after time, she opened
very accurate fire on the destroyers, evidently firing by radar
and independent of visual sighting; moreover, she obviously
intended to show the destroyers they would approach her at
their peril.

The first destroyer to receive her attentions in this way

was Captain Vian's own *Cossack*. At 11:42 p.m., while she was still four miles away from the *Bismarck*, flashes of gunfire were seen from the latter's direction, and salvoes of large and small shells fell close alongside the *Cossack,* the splinters from which shot away some of her wireless aerials. The shooting was too good to be trifled with, and the *Cossack* was forced to sheer away.

Eight minutes later, the *Zulu* received the same treatment. She could just make out the *Bismarck* to the northward and had seen her shooting at the *Cossack*. Now the enemy's guns flashed out again; and a few seconds later a 15-in. salvo straddled the *Zulu* herself. Two more similar salvoes straddled her in quick succession, the splinters wounding one officer and two men. It was providential she was not hit and she made haste to turn away and get farther off. In this progress, she lost touch and did not regain it for more than an hour.

It was the first time in history that radar-controlled gunfire had been used against ships at night; and it was a weird and rather awe-inspiring experience for the destroyers to undergo. Had the *Bismarck* been using searchlights, it would have seemed less unnatural. But there was no such warning. Out of the darkness in the *Bismarck*'s direction would come a ripple of brilliant flashes, momentarily lighting up the sky. A ten- or fifteen-seconds' pause, and then the shriek of approaching shells and a quick succession of terrific, splitting cracks, as they hit the water. Simultaneously, a vast upheaval in the sea near the ship and a number of indistinct masses would tower up ghost-like and immense in the darkness alongside. Then another sudden glare of gunfire, momentarily revealing huge columns of cascading water close at hand.

From half-past twelve till one o'clock in the morning, the *Bismarck* seems to have been unshadowed, all destroyers having lost touch. There was a good deal of excuse. It was an inky-black night and, in addition to the gale and the heavy seas, frequent rain squalls were being encountered, in which the visibility was probably less than half a mile. To lose touch with a darkened ship under these conditions was only too easy. By this time, Captain Vian had come to the

89

conclusion that no set-piece attack was possible. The *Bismarck*'s ability to keep his ships at a distance by radar-controlled gunfire had made the darkness a handicap rather than an advantage. In escaping from the enemy's broadsides, his destroyers had become scattered. If attacks were to be made at all, each destroyer would have to make her own, as best she could. He made a signal at twenty minutes to one that destroyers should attack when opportunities presented themselves.

On receiving this signal, Commander Graham of the *Zulu* at once went off to the westward by himself. As he did so, a star shell winked out into light on his port bow and began its slow descent to the sea. It was from the *Maori*, who was taking a look in the direction where she had last seen the enemy. But it revealed nothing. At about one o'clock, however, the *Zulu* sighted the black shape of the *Bismarck* on the starboard bow, steering apparently a little west of north. The *Zulu* was right astern of the enemy ship and had to get much farther up on or before her beam in order to fire torpedoes. Commander Graham therefore decided to run up on the *Bismarck*'s port side and went on to as high a speed as he could manage. The enemy must have been going very slowly, for it only took the *Zulu* about twenty minutes to get abreast of her, at an estimated range of 5,000 yards. At this point, the *Bismarck* opened a hot fire, and a minute or two later Commander Graham fired all his four torpedoes and then sheered away to open the range. So far as could be judged, none of the torpedoes hit.

The gunfire directed at the *Zulu* showed the *Maori* where the *Bismarck* was, and she steered in that direction. Judging by the gunflashes, the *Maori* was also astern of the *Bismarck;* and Commander Armstrong, like Commander Graham, determined to work forward on the enemy's port side. He got up to a position about 4,000 yards on the *Bismarck*'s port beam apparently without being seen. As it was very dark and he wanted to make sure of his aim, Commander Armstrong then fired a star shell to light the enemy up while he attacked; and as soon as it was burning, he fired two torpedoes. This was at 1:37 a.m.

The moment the star shell broke into light, the *Bismarck*

opened fire, and as usual made excellent shooting. Immediately after firing his torpedoes, Commander Armstrong had begun to turn towards the enemy. He fancied she was altering course towards him and he thought he would cross her bows and fire his other two torpedoes from her other side. The *Bismarck*'s fire was, however, much too fierce, and the *Maori* altered away to get clear, but the *Bismarck*'s salvoes followed her out to a range of 10,000 yards. As the *Maori* retreated those on board her were sure they saw a torpedo hit. A bright glow seemed to illuminate the enemy's waterline and shortly afterwards another vivid glare appeared to betoken a second explosion. A cheer went up from the men on deck.

While the *Bismarck* was firing westward against the *Maori*, Captain Vian in the *Cossack* was engaged in attacking from another direction. He had been stealthily making his way up on her starboard side, and was now in a position whence he could take full advantage of her preoccupation with her other assailant. From the *Cossack*, the *Bismarck* was clearly silhouetted against the glare of her own gunfire, and at 1:40 a.m., only three minutes after the *Maori* had fired two torpedoes, Captain Vian fired three at an approximate range of 6,000 yards. After an interval, the *Cossack* saw what they believed to be an unmistakable hit. Flames blazed up the *Bismarck*'s forecastle,[4] visible not only to the *Cossack* but to all adjacent ships.

The *Sikh* had been driven off by the *Bismarck*'s fire earlier in the night. Losing contact, she had taken in a report by the *Maori* that the *Bismarck* was steering southwest. It was probably a mistaken report for north-east, but it threw the *Sikh* out, and she went on for some time searching for the *Bismarck* in a south-westerly direction. Attracted, however, by the *Bismarck*'s firing in opposition to the other destroyers' attacks, the *Sikh* was now on the way back. The *Zulu* had just reported the *Bismarck* as being stopped, and the *Sikh* believed that this provided an opportunity for a long-range attack. At eighteen minutes past

[4] A possible but unusual indication of a torpedo hit, which, by letting water into a ship, is seldom accompanied by fire.

two, she fired her four torpedoes at a range of about 7,000 yards. After an interval for the passage of the torpedoes, it was thought that there was the sound of an explosion.

Sikh and *Zulu* had now fired all their torpedoes, *Maori* had two left, *Cossack* one, while *Piorun* had not yet attacked. All the first four destroyers had withdrawn out of range after making their attacks.

The *Bismarck* seemed to remain stopped or was only steaming very slowly for an hour from 1:45 a.m. Some of the destroyers were not always in contact, but they knew roughly where the wounded battleship lay.

At about half-past two, there came a signal from the Commander-in-Chief, whose battleships were presumably not far off, for the destroyers to fire star shells to indicate the *Bismarck*'s position. The Admiral was steering to get to the westward of the *Bismarck* for a dawn contact and was anxious for accurate knowledge of her position. His battleships and Captain Vian's destroyers had not yet been in sight of each other, and it was quite possible that, owing to natural variations of reckoning, the destroyers' positions relative to the flagship were appreciably different from what they purported to be. Moreover, the earlier succession of enemy reports had apparently come to an end an hour before. The firing of star shells by the destroyers might therefore give the Admiral a visual indication of the enemy's whereabouts. The destroyers began to comply with this order, but the unseen *Bismarck* quickly showed her resentment by opening an accurate fire on the star-shell firers; and Captain Vian did not think the Admiral would wish him to persist long with this explosive arrangement.

About 3 a.m., Captain Vian decided to take the *Cossack* in to fire her one remaining torpedo. The *Bismarck* was by now apparently under way again and proceeding slowly north-westward. Captain Vian worked round to the northward of her and, closing in, fired from about 4,000 yards. No hit was apparent.

After this attack, all certain contact with the *Bismarck* seems to have been lost till shortly before 6 a.m. But Captain Vian was confident he would find her as soon as it began to get light. It was obvious that she was in an unhappy state. She had been steering a course which varied between north-west and north-east since 11 p.m., at a very low speed. She would not have been doing that on purpose. Therefore daylight was bound to reveal her whereabouts, and it was questionable whether it was sound to court too deliberately any more of her extremely accurate gunfire. At 5 a.m., Captain Vian ordered the *Piorun*, whom he knew to be short of fuel, to return to Plymouth. Commander Plawski, who had been much hampered by rain squalls, was then searching north-west for the *Bismarck*. He went on for another hour before regretfully shaping course away.

Direct touch was first regained by the *Maori*, who sighted the black shape of the enemy battleship at 5:50 a.m., Commander Armstrong making her out to be zigzagging slowly in a direction north-north-west at about 7 knots. Having found her, he shadowed her till daylight. Half an hour later, the *Sikh* sighted her emerging from a rain squall about three and a half miles away. Darkness was gradually giving way to twilight. Just before sunrise when the visibility was getting fairly good, the *Maori* determined to get rid of her last two torpedoes. She closed in somewhat and fired them from a range of 9,000 yards, just before 7 a.m. There was no hit, but once more the *Bismarck* opened fire and straddled several times. It was her last smack at the destroyers that had been snapping at her all night.

With the coming of full daylight, Captain Vian stationed his destroyers in four sectors all round the *Bismarck*, and they continued to keep her in sight. They had had a sleepless and tiring night, keyed up at high tension from dusk to dawn. Each destroyer had been under accurate shellfire from the *Bismarck*'s heavy and lighter guns. All but the *Piorun* had indeed undergone that fiery ordeal at least twice and the *Cossack* had been through it thrice. They were frail craft and their officers and men were well aware that even one hit from the *Bismarck*'s 15-in. guns would probably make an end of them. Considering how often they had been straddled, it was astounding that not one of them had received a direct hit.

There can be little doubt that the periodical losses of contact during the night were mainly due to the accuracy of the *Bismarck*'s radar-controlled gunfire. But for her ability to drive the destroyers outside sighting distance by this means, it should have been a fairly easy matter for them to keep her continuously in sight, had they concentrated on doing so. At the same time, an unexpectedly difficult shadowing problem was still further complicated by the fact that the destroyers did not give it their whole attention. The decision to carry out torpedo attacks could not fail to have a prejudicial effect on the business of keeping the enemy under observation. Successful shadowing calls for the avoidance of damage and the careful maintenance of a suitable shadowing position. The attack, on the other hand, postulates a deliberate exposure to damage and a period of high-speed manoeuvring conducted with the single object of reaching a position for firing torpedoes, regardless of any other consideration. A shadowing destroyer which goes into the attack may emerge, if it emerges at all, five or ten miles from its shadowing station; and where, as in this case, the attacks are made piecemeal, the shadowing arrangements must soon be in disorder if not confusion. Shadowing and attacking by destroyers at night are, in fact, severely conflicting activities.

Nor does it seem that the hazarding of the primary object of shadowing was here compensated by the results achieved in pursuing the secondary object of attacking. It is true that several torpedo hits were claimed at the time. But according to the German records published by the British Admiralty, none were in fact scored. The German statement to this effect may not, of course, be true. On the other hand, the receipt of torpedo hits would probably be known throughout the target ship, and the Germans would appear to have had no incentive to suppress the record of such hits, had they occurred. If anything, rather the reverse; and in the absence of such incentive, the German evidence that there were no hits could well be more reliable than the British belief that there were two. It is very difficult for destroyers attacking at night to be sure that their torpedoes have got home. The tell-tale pillar of water going up alongside the torpedoed ship cannot be seen in the darkness, and the boom of the target ship's own guns firing at the attack-

94

ing craft can very easily be construed into the roar of an exploding torpedo. The force of suggestion is very strong on such occasions. The officers and men of the attacking ships want to see or hear a torpedo hit, and can quite genuinely convince themselves that they have done so when they have not. Especially is this so when they have been through danger and strain to achieve their attacks.

Moreover, the circumstances in which these attacks were carried out were unquestionably most unfavourable to success. A single battleship is a poor target for destroyers at night. It is still poorer when the destroyers are attacking separately and not as a group. Admittedly, a favourable factor in this case was the *Bismarck*'s low speed, making quick avoiding action by her impossible. But against that were the long ranges at which many of the torpedoes were fired. To obtain good torpedo results against a single ship it is generally necessary to get in to about 2,000 yards before firing. Yet on this night, not one torpedo was fired at this range. Three were fired at 4,000 yards, four at 5,000 yards, three at 6,000, four at 7,000, and two at 9,000.

The torpedoing of the enemy was not the only consideration for the destroyers to keep in mind. The screening of the British battleships against submarine attack would be a matter of importance next day, when the danger of U-boat attack would obviously have to be taken very seriously. It was, indeed, for this main purpose that the destroyers had been detached from their convoy and ordered to join the Commander-in-Chief. Yet the performance of this duty would clearly have been impeded, if not prevented, by damage incurred during the night attacks.

It is, however, pertinent to note that Captain Vian's decision to attack was regarded with evident favour in the highest quarter at the time. Though he did not know it, the question of night destroyer attacks had already formed the subject of a communication from the Admiralty to the Commander-in-Chief. About 7 p.m., Sir John Tovey had received a signal, in a code the destroyers did not hold, asking whether he had considered ordering night destroyer attacks to be made. This signal, which the Commander-in-Chief can hardly have been over-pleased to get, was sent out before the *Ark Royal*'s attack and therefore before the *Bismarck*'s rudders had been hit. But it was not cancelled after the Admiralty must have become aware from intercepted signals that the *Bismarck* had probably been rendered unmanageable, nor after the reports of the destroyer attacks had begun to come through. It is therefore a fair assumption that Captain Vian's action in attacking had the full approval of the Naval Staff.

To those on board the two British battleships, the *King George V* and the *Rodney*, keyed up for approaching battle, the dawn seemed to be long in coming. Ships' companies were at action stations but were allowed, half at a time, to sleep at their posts. Neither of the two Captains left their compass platforms during the night, though each of them took an occasional doze, sitting in a chair and resting his head against some control instrument.

At last there came that faint awareness that the darkness was not quite as black as before, which meant that morning twilight was just beginning. Commander Robertson, the Admiral's Staff Officer (Operations), suddenly remembered that his steel helmet was down below in his cabin and he decided it was time he went to get it. As he went down the ladder into the cabin flat, an astonishing sight caught his eye. Round and round the flat were running in obvious terror four large rats. They took no notice of him but continued their frenzied roundabout, slipping and bumping into each other as the ship rolled. In the circumstances, it was not a very exhilarating spectacle, and Commander Robertson was glad to seize his helmet and get quickly back on deck.

Over in the *Ark Royal*, twenty to thirty miles away, the first aircraft shadowers had already been flown off. When they came up on the lift it was still pitch dark, and so strong was the wind down the flying-deck that the aircraft were seen to rise almost vertically past the bridge as they took off. As the daylight strengthened it revealed as stormy a scene as on the day before, while overhead there was the same mantle of ragged, leaden rainclouds driving across the

96

sky. It was raining heavily and visibility was none too good.

Sir John Tovey was watching the weather conditions as they were gradually revealed. He had been up most of the night, examining the movements of the *Bismarck* reported by the destroyers. His main anxiety was how the destroyers' calculated positions corresponded with his. Neither his flagship nor the destroyers had seen the sun for several days and there was therefore plenty of room for errors of dead reckoning on both sides. It had been for this reason that the Admiral had told the destroyers to fire star shells in order to provide a visual bearing. But there was so much rain about that nothing was seen from the flagship and the firing ships reported they were being heavily shot at. The Admiral then ordered wireless transmission on medium frequency in the hope of obtaining wireless directional bearings. But for various reasons, this was no greater success than the star shells. As day began to dawn, the Commander-in-Chief was still full of uncertainty where his enemy was. This and the poor visibility of a stormy horizon convinced the Admiral that conditions were unfavourable for an immediate action, and that it would be better to wait an hour or two for full daylight.

Sir James Somerville had just come to much the same decision regarding the intended dawn air attack. In this vile weather, there was serious risk of the aircraft mistaking friend for foe, which made it prudent for this attack also to be postponed. Sir James was none too sure of the position of either the *King George V* and *Rodney* or of the *Bismarck;* and after the narrow squeak of torpedoing the *Sheffield* the day before, he wanted no more mishaps of that kind.

Shortly before sunrise, Sir John Tovey signalled across to the *Rodney* astern of him to tell Captain Dalrymple-Hamilton that in the forthcoming action he was free to manoeuvre independently, provided he conformed generally to the Admiral's movements. The *Rodney*'s two remaining destroyers had just been obliged to leave her for the return to their base for fuel. They had waited with her as long as they were able, but could wait no longer. Indeed, they had waited, as was to be shown later, rather too long.

The Commander-in-Chief's intentions, made known at this time to his Flag-Captain and Staff, were to close the enemy as quickly as possible to about 15,000 yards and then turn for a broadside battle. But first of all the *Bismarck* had to be located, and there was doubt as to her exact direction. The solution to this urgent problem was provided by the *Norfolk*. She had been rushing south in desperate haste all night, fearful of being too late for the final drama. At a quarter-past eight, she sighted a battleship about eight miles ahead and nearly end-on. Thinking it was the *Rodney*, Captain Phillips ordered the challenge to be made. Getting no reply, he had a more careful look and then realized that the vessel he was approaching at 20 knots was none other than the *Bismarck* herself. Once more the *Norfolk*'s wheel was put hurriedly over, as it had been on the evening of the 23rd, three and a half days before, when she had run out of the mist in the Denmark Strait to find the German battleship also dangerously close.

As the *Norfolk* again sheered away to open the range, she sighted the two British battleships in the distance and was able to give them a visual link with the enemy. It showed Admiral Tovey that he was steering too much to the northward and he adjusted the course of his battleships accordingly. They were roughly in line abreast, a little short of a mile apart and were rolling considerably with the sea on the quarter. For Captain Dalrymple-Hamilton in the *Rodney* it was a family as well as a professional occasion, for his only son was a Midshipman on board the *King George V*.

At 8:43 a.m., the battleships sighted the narrow grey shape of a ship nearly end-on and about twelve miles almost ahead. It was the *Bismarck*. At last she was in sight. It was nearly a week since Sir John Tovey had first heard of her being in the fiord near Bergen; and during the long and anxious days that had followed she had seemed almost too slippery and elusive ever to be caught. But there she was now in front of him, cornered in the end. However, though she had been lamed and overtaken, none of her exceedingly sharp teeth had yet been drawn. There was the prospect of a sharp fight.

At 8:47 a.m., the *Rodney*'s 16-in. guns opened the battle. Just as the salvo was due to fall, the *King George V*'s guns flashed out and both the British battleships were in action. The *Bismarck* had not yet replied and she remained silent for another two minutes. Then she, too, joined in. "Time of flight fifty-five seconds," announced the Fleet Gunnery Officer on the Admiral's bridge in the *King George V*, as the *Bismarck*'s guns went off, and he began to count out the seconds. But he was laughingly silenced by the Admiral, who said he preferred not to be given the exact moment when a 15-in. shell would hit him in the stomach. When the splashes went up, however, it was seen that it was the *Rodney* that was being fired at.

The *Bismarck*'s first salvo was a long way short. But it did not take her long to correct her aim, and her third salvo straddled the *Rodney* and nearly hit her. Having been given latitude to manoeuvre independently, Captain Dalrymple-Hamilton altered course to port and brought his A-arcs to bear. Since he was under fire and the enemy might start getting hits at any moment, it seemed time to develop his full gunpower in retaliation.

Across the way, the *King George V* was steaming straight for the enemy in conformity with Sir John Tovey's belief in an end-on approach. The value of this manoeuvre was not, however, about to be tested. The target ship was the *Rodney*, who had her broadside open, and the *King George V* remained unfired-at during the whole time she was pointing directly for the enemy. Since the *Rodney* was not part of the Home Fleet proper, Captain Dalrymple-Hamilton was unaware of Sir John's views about the end-on method of closing the range, or no doubt the *Rodney* would at this time have been steering a parallel course to the flagship. As it was, the *Rodney*'s early turn to port to open her A-arcs was subjecting the *Bismarck* to heavier gunfire than she herself could develop, and was also taking the two British battleships steadily farther apart.

The *Bismarck*'s salvoes were continuing to fall near the *Rodney*. But the latter, as well as returning the fire with all guns, was zigzagging to dodge the fall of shot, and no hits had yet come to her. At 8:54 a.m., the *Norfolk*, who was six or seven miles to the north-east of the British battleships, opened fire with her 8-in. guns at 20,000 yards. The battleships' range was already closer than that and was shortening rapidly; and at about this time the *Rodney* brought her secondary armament into action. The *Bismarck* was now under the concentrated fire of three ships, and her own gunnery efficiency was noticeably falling off. From being regular and well-placed, her fire was becoming more and more erratic, and the *Rodney* was no longer seriously worried by it. It became known later that the *Bismarck's* main fire control position, the ship's gunnery brain, was hit and destroyed fairly early in the action, and it is possible that the marked deterioration in the volume and accuracy of her fire can be attributed to this cause. But the mass of shells now pouring in on her would have lowered her offensive power in any case.

Twelve minutes after the commencement of the battle, the *King George V* was in to 16,000 yards and Sir John Tovey thought it time to bring the flagship's full fire to bear. After a word up the voice-pipe to Captain Patterson to tell him what was coming, the Admiral made the signal for a course of south, nearly opposite to the very wobbly path the *Bismarck* was following. A minute before nine o'clock, the *King George V* began her swing to starboard towards the new course and her after turrets were soon in action. The *Rodney*, whose independent manoeuvrings had by now taken her out to nearly three miles from the flagship, turned south two or three minutes later. She may or may not have taken in the Admiral's signal, but was under the instruction to conform generally to his movements. The *Bismarck* continued her slow course towards the north-west, yawing considerably each side of the wind. Just before the *Rodney* turned, Captain Coppinger saw a heavy shell burst on the *Bismarck's* forecastle, and gained the impression that one of her two foremost turrets had been put out of action. He was on the bridge with Captain Dalrymple-Hamilton, taking notes of the battle, and he made an entry to this effect.

Just after the turn, the *Bismarck* transferred her fire to the *King George V*, now the leading ship. But some of her guns were no longer firing and only an occasional shot or two fell close. On the British side, fire control had been difficult from the start. Against the dull, rainy horizon, the shell splashes did not show up at all clearly and it was hard to be sure of a straddle, more particularly with three ships mingling their salvoes round the one target. As the range decreased, the spotting of the fall of shot naturally became easier: but the turn to the southward introduced a new handicap. On that course, the resultant of the gale and the ship's speed gave a relative wind straight towards the *Bismarck*. Consequently, the clouds of brown cordite smoke that belched from the British gun muzzles at each salvo were hanging irritatingly in front of the firing ships, forming a semi-opaque screen between them and the enemy, to which the funnel gases added their quota. Fortunately, radar came to the rescue to some extent, but the fire control conditions were far from ideal.

A few minutes after the turn to the south, another British ship joined in the action from the eastward. This was the cruiser *Dorsetshire*. All night she had been coming up at her highest attainable speed, guided by the reports from the destroyers. She had, however, been obliged to turn into the wind about 2 a.m. and heavy seas had been steadily knocking her speed down, first to 25 knots, then to 20. Dawn came without her having sighted anything; but at 8:23 a.m., to Captain Martin's intense relief, the *Cossack* was sighted to the westward and course was altered in her direction. Twenty-five minutes later, gunflashes were sighted almost ahead, and very shortly afterwards the *Bismarck* was seen twelve miles away, firing at something to the westward. At four minutes past nine, with the range at 20,000 yards, the *Dorsetshire* opened fire. But owing to the many shots already falling near the enemy, observation of fire was very difficult, and fire was checked after nine minutes.[5]

[5] A survivor picked up by the *Dorsetshire* is said to have told Captain Martin that it was one of the *Dorsetshire*'s shells which wrecked the *Bismarck*'s fire control position. In view of the heavy concentration of fire against the *Bismarck* and of the fact that

The run to the south by the *King George V* and *Rodney* went on for about a quarter of an hour, with the range nearly steady at 12,000 yards. Interference by cordite smoke, as already mentioned, was bad. The *King George V*'s 5.25-in. secondary armament guns came into action a few minutes after the turn, but as they made the cordite smokescreen worse still, they were ordered to cease fire two or three minutes later. During this period, ten torpedoes were fired at the enemy, six by the *Rodney* at 11,000 yards and four by the *Norfolk* at 16,000 yards. None was seen to hit, and indeed it would have been a great fluke if any had done so when fired from such ranges.

This action on opposite courses naturally made the enemy's bearing draw fairly rapidly aft, and Captain Dalrymple-Hamilton decided to turn the *Rodney* round to preserve the broadside bearing and head the enemy off. The fact that the enemy's fire was now on the *King George V* would enable the *Rodney* to make her turn without danger, and at 9:12 a.m. the wheel was put over for the new course. Once round, the *Rodney*'s full fire was again brought to bear at 8,500 yards, and she was thus able to cover the turn of the *King George V*, who came round some minutes after her.

Captain Dalrymple-Hamilton's decision to turn north on his own responsibility may seem to have been within the discretionary power allowed him to manoeuvre independently. But, in fact, it was something more than that. A stipulated condition of that power was that he must conform generally to the Admiral's movements. By no reasonable standard could he be said to be so conforming if he turned north while his Admiral was continuing to the southward. In fact, though he doubtless did not realize it at the time, Captain Dalrymple-Hamilton was reviving the famous example set 144 years before by one Commodore Nelson at

the survivors are most unlikely to have studied the battle observers' records, this statement can probably be explained by a prisoner's natural desire to ingratiate himself with his captors.

the battle of St. Vincent. Not since 1797 had a British battleship Captain turned out of the line of battle by his own decision until Captain Dalrymple-Hamilton did it on this occasion.

The *Rodney* was now the leading ship and, perhaps for that reason, the *Bismarck* made her again the target. Several of the enemy's shots fell very close, one being only a few yards from the starboard bow. In the *Rodney*'s torpedo flat, twenty feet below the waterline, the torpedo tubes' crew had been listening to the sounds of battle over their heads. They could feel the ship shiver each time the heavy guns roared out a salvo, and the sounds of the enemy's shells falling in the water near the ship were unmistakable. It was a bit lonely sitting down there inactive amid the death-dealing turmoil, and the torpedomen were envious of the guns' crews busy with their job of raising and ramming home the huge shells and pushing over the levers that sent the great breech blocks slamming to behind the cordite charges. It had therefore been very welcome when the torpedo flat got the order "action port" during the run south and for some time the torpedomen were hard at work loading and reloading the three-ton torpedoes into the tubes. Now after the turn, there were more thuds of enemy shells in the water, and one very loud metallic clang. The starboard tube had just been loaded, but the sluice valve door (between the tube and the sea) was found to be jammed and could not be opened. That one had been close.

The turn to the north by *Rodney* and *King George V* removed the nuisance of funnel and cordite smoke interference and enabled a good clear view at last to be obtained of the enemy ship. Both British ships were getting close, being in to 8,500 and 11,000 yards respectively, at which ranges details of the *Bismarck* were easily discernible through binoculars. Obvious signs of punishment were visible on board her. A fairly large fire was blazing amidships. Some of her guns seemed to have been silenced, and the others were firing only spasmodically. Her foremost turrets fired a salvo at 9:27, but shortly after that the *Norfolk*, who had placed herself almost ahead of the *Bismarck* for

103

flank marking purposes, saw two of the forward 15-in. guns run down to maximum depression, as if a British hit had caused a failure of hydraulic power in the turret.

At lessening ranges, the two British battleships steamed north past the slowly moving enemy ship, pouring in a heavy fire from both main and secondary armament guns. At this relatively close distance hits on the upper works were easily seen. A large explosion occurred just abaft B turret (the upper of the two foremost turrets), which blew the back of the turret up over the bridge. Another and very spectacular hit blew away the 15-in. aloft Director, which toppled over the side. The *Rodney* fired another two torpedoes at 7,500 yards, but neither of them hit.

The unsteady crawl through the water to which the *Bismarck* had by now been reduced meant that the British battleships quickly overhauled and passed her, and soon the bearing had grown so far aft that the foremost guns were almost ceasing to bear. It would have been simpler to have shot the battle out on a more or less constant broadside bearing; but this could only be done by using approximately the same speed as the enemy. This was, however, much too low for safety in view of the probable presence of enemy submarines. The *Rodney*, therefore, began to zigzag close across the enemy's bows, firing sometimes at her starboard side, sometimes at her port and sometimes down the length of her hull. At the end of each of the *Rodney*'s zigzags, her foremost turrets would be on their extreme after bearing and firing close past the ship's bridge, where the blast was severely felt. On one occasion, it removed Captain Coppinger's steel helmet from his head with such force that it hit and knocked out a signalman standing some feet away. The former's notebook also flew out of his hand and disappeared, to be picked up later on the quarterdeck.

In order to keep well clear of the *Rodney*, the *King George V* had taken a broad sweep out and back on the enemy's beam. Moreover, she was by now (about 9:30 a.m.) suffering badly from the same complaint that had afflicted her sister ship the *Prince of Wales* in the earlier battle. Gunnery breakdowns were occurring with unpleas-

104

ant frequency. Her three turrets were severally out of action from this cause for varying periods, one for as long as half an hour, while there were in addition several breakdowns at individual guns. There were times when her available firepower was down to 20 per cent of the maximum; a reduction which might, in other circumstances, have had disastrous consequences. Fortunately, the *Bismarck* had by now been pounded almost into silence. Her after turret was still firing occasionally, but the others were dumb. Her A turret guns were drooping dejectedly downwards towards the sea; those of B turret were pointing starkly into the air on a fixed bearing. At the very close ranges to which her enemies had approached, hits were smashing into her one after the other. The *Norfolk* had been firing away all the time, and just before 9:40 the *Dorsetshire* joined in again from the north-eastward, the *Rodney* becoming aware of her presence by some of her 8-in. shells falling close ahead.

By 10 a.m. the *Bismarck* was a silent, battered wreck. Her mast was down, her funnel had disappeared, her guns were pointing in all directions, and a cloud of black smoke was rising from the middle of the ship and blowing away with the wind. Inside, she was clearly a blazing inferno, for the bright glow of internal fires could be seen shining through numerous shell and splinter holes in her sides. Her men were deserting their guns, and parties of them could be seen running to and fro on the upper deck as the shells continued to rain in, and occasionally jumping over the side, to escape by watery death from the terror on board. Captain Patterson of *King George V* would have ceased fire earlier had he known of this, but the *Bismarck*'s port side was so often screened by a wall of shell splashes along her whole length that it was none too easy to notice what was happening on board her.

And her flag still flew. Ostensibly at least, she remained defiant. Though powerless and, like Sir Richard Grenville's *Revenge*, surrounded by enemies, she did not surrender: though under modern conditions the intention to surrender a ship is not too easy to indicate. Surrender or not, however, the British ships meant to sink her and as quickly as they could. At any moment, long-distance German aircraft might appear or torpedoes come streaking in from U-boats that were already quite amazingly late in arriving on the scene; while to add to the urgency there was the nagging anxiety of the acute fuel shortage. Both the *King George V* and *Rodney* should from this point of view alone have been on the way home hours ago, especially the former. There was absolutely not a moment to be lost in putting the *Bismarck* underwater. Sir John Tovey's impatience showed itself by a desire for point-blank range: "Get closer, get closer," he began to tell Captain Patterson, "I can't see enough hits."

It was indeed astonishing that the *Bismarck* was still afloat after the battering she had received. She had been pierced and rent time after time by heavy and light shells from two battleships and two cruisers. She had been torpedoed by the *Victorious*'s, and by the *Ark Royal*'s aircraft. The *Rodney* was now (10 a.m.) firing nine-gun broadsides at her from the 16-in. guns, the huge shells hitting her in threes and fours at a time. At 3,000 yards, the *Rodney* also fired her last two torpedoes, and one of them was seen to hit the *Bismarck* amidships.[8] The *Norfolk* had also fired her remaining four torpedoes from a range of 4,000 yards and believed she obtained at least one hit. But still the *Bismarck* floated.

The *Ark Royal*'s aircraft had one more attack they could make, after which all their torpedoes would have gone. Vice-Admiral Somerville had intended sending them off at dawn. But, as already mentioned, there was so much rain and low cloud about that he was afraid of their mistaking the target. Sir James had been steering north towards the supposed position of the enemy, of whose exact whereabouts he was none too sure. However, at 8:10 a.m., the *Maori* was sighted ahead and gave the *Bismarck*'s position as eleven miles nearly due north. At 0855, the distant boom of heavy gunfire was heard to the northward above the

[8] Said to be the only instance in history of one battleship torpedoing another.

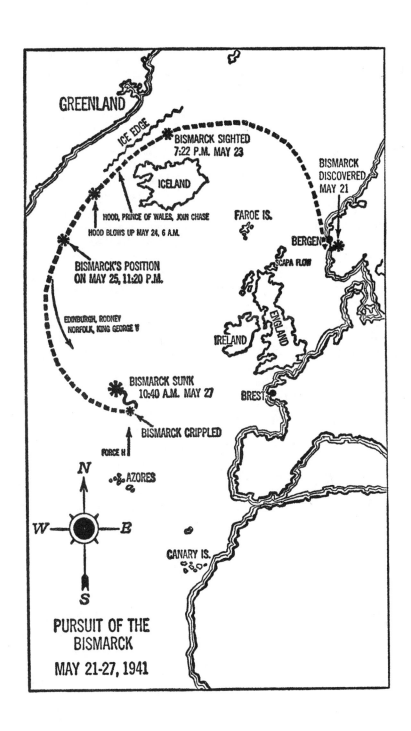

PURSUIT OF THE
BISMARCK
MAY 21-27, 1941

noise of the wind, and Sir James thereupon decided to send off the striking force at once.

It was just as ticklish a job as on the day before, but the twelve Swordfish got safely away at 9:26 a.m. They formed up and went off to the northward; and just as they disappeared ahead, the clouds began to break and from the *Ark Royal* they spotted first one and then another Focke-Wulf.

The striking force soon found the *Bismarck*, but also realised that an attack on her would be very hazardous. She was being fired at from both sides by four ships, and many of their shots were going very wide. At the very close ranges too which the British ships had now got, the trajectories of their shells were almost flat. A very slight error in aim, which the rolling of the ships would facilitate, would therefore take the projectiles that just skimmed the upper works of the *Bismarck* to a distance of two or three thousand yards beyond her before they struck the water. The result was that shell splashes were going up hundreds of feet into the air a long way from the enemy, which would have been death to any aircraft that had flown into them. The aircraft therefore flew on towards the *King George V* to ask for gunfire to be ceased while they went down to the attack. But beyond having some anti-aircraft shells fired at them, they received no attention.[7]

Meanwhile, Sir John Tovey was feeling acute concern at the refusal of the *Bismarck* to sink. He had given her a hammering by gunfire that he had no conception any ship could stand. But there she was, still above water. If she could bear all that without going down, who could tell how much more she might not endure? And Sir John was already quite certain that he could not afford to spend any more time on firing at this ship. It was imperative that his force should start back. He had waited dangerously long, as it was; and every extra half-hour would make his return

[7] It is interesting to record that when Captain Patterson, who knew the mistake was being made, asked the officer responsible if he couldn't see the airmen waving at him, the officer replied he thought they were "Huns shaking their fists."

more hazardous. He looked at the burning hulk, lying deep and sluggish in the water, that had once been a fighting battleship. It was obvious to him that whether she sank now or sank later, she would never get back to harbour. At 10:15 a.m., he signalled to *Rodney* to form astern on a course of 027 degrees (about north-north-east). He was going home.

As Sir John steered away, he signalled that any ship with torpedoes was to close the *Bismarck* and torpedo her. As it happened, the *Dorsetshire* was the only ship in the immediate vicinity with any torpedoes left. Captain Martin, however, had not waited to be told, but was already using them. At 10:20, from about 3,500 yards, he fired two torpedoes at the *Bismarck*'s starboard side, one of which exploded right under the bridge. He then steered round to her port side and fired another torpedo from about 2,500 yards at 10:36. This torpedo also hit. The shattered leviathan, her colours still flying, silently heeled over to port, turned bottom up and disappeared beneath the waves. The time was 10:40. As she was turning over, Captain Martin received the Admiral's order to do what, in fact, he had already done. He at once made a signal to say that the *Bismarck* had sunk.

The great chase was over. The mighty *Bismarck* had been disposed of after a most gallant fight against superior force. All that was left of her were several hundred heads of swimming men, visible on the surface of the breaking seas. The *Dorsetshire* summoned the nearby *Maori* to help her pick up survivors. It was too rough to lower any boats, even had this been permissible. But lines were thrown out and jumping ladders let down the sides. Many of the men in the water were too exhausted to climb up them; but the *Dorsetshire* managed to haul eighty on board and the *Maori* thirty. Then came a lookout's report of a submarine periscope, and Captain Martin considered it high time to withdraw.

The Valorous Island

Halfway between Gibraltar and Alexandria, in the middle of the Mediterranean Sea, lies the island of Malta. Before World War II, the British wrote off Malta as too vulnerable to bombing raids from the Italian mainland. When Churchill became Prime Minister, he was quick to recognize Malta's strategic value athwart the North-South supply routes from Italy to North Africa. The Royal Navy was immediately asked to stockpile foodstuffs. The island's defenses would be strengthened with fighters and antiaircraft guns. Before this action could be taken, war broke out.

The garrison, consisting of five battalions of infantry, was pitifully weak to defend an island of 112 square miles and 300,000 people.

To properly supply the island, the British Royal Navy and Merchant Navy would need to sail 40,000 ton convoys to Malta twice a month. Each convoy would need heavy escort protection and would be subjected to fierce attacks from the Axis air forces; the closer a convoy got to Malta the more perilous its position due to the hazards of the Narrows—a narrow passage between North Africa and Malta, replete with shallows, sandbars, enemy submarines and patrol boats. In fact, Malta's defense outlook was so dim that Mussolini announced to the world that within a month after Italy's entry into the war his main fleet would be in Malta's Grand Harbor.

The British Royal Navy would have something to say about this. If Malta fell, "Allied warships and planes would have been unable to operate in the Central Mediterranean; the German and Italian armies in North Africa would have been reinforced quickly and easily; Cairo and Alexandria would certainly have fallen, and the whole of the Middle East (with its vital supplies of oil) might well have been brought under Axis control." *

The early actions in defense of Malta produced the usual sagas of

*Red Duster, White Ensign, by Ian Cameron, published by Doubleday & Co., Inc., p. 16.

110

courageous sacrifice on the part of a few; "usual" only in that both Britain and the United States earned precious time due to gallant last-ditch stands by those troops caught out on the defense perimeters. The following selection tells of one of the most gallant battles of the early war against fantastically uneven odds.

MALTA

by Ian Cameron

Sixty miles from Malta lay the island of Sicily, its shore line dotted with a series of large modern airdromes—Catania, Augusta, Siracusa, and Pandrino to the east; Comiso, Biscari, Bo Rizzo, Marsala, and Trapani to the south; and, inland, the airstrips of Gela and Gerbini and the great civil airport of Castelvetrano. Based on three dozen airdromes, all of them within fifteen minutes' flying time of Malta, were the cream of the Italian Air Force: some three hundred and fifty bombers (Cants, Savoias, and B.R. 20s) and some two hundred fighters (C.R.42s, Reggiane 2001s, and Macchis); fast modern planes, based on first-class airfields and manned by skilled pilots, many of whom had gained operational experience in the campaigns in Abyssinia and Spain. Only one target was within range of this great armada of aircraft—Malta. Seldom, if ever, had so much strength been ranged against so small and defenseless a target.

Nor was there any doubt about the manner in which, in the event of war, this strength would be used. Giulio Douhet, the high priest of strategic pattern bombing, the man whose theories had been proved in the holocaust of Barcelona, was quite specific on this point. "The guiding principle of bombing," he wrote, "is that the target should be obliterated in one raid. If, however, this is not possible, the target should be 'saturated' by unremitting waves of attackers. A people who are bombed today as they were bombed yesterday, and who know they will be bombed again tomorrow and can see no end to their martyrdom, are bound to call for peace in the end."

Sixty miles away Malta watched and waited. And every day, during the last uneasy weeks of peace, an Italian civil airliner flew openly over the island taking photographs, noting the absence of defending aircraft, pinpointing the dozen or so AA batteries which alone stood between the Maltese people and the acolytes of Giulio Douhet.

Early on the morning of June 11 the expected happened: the sirens started their high-pitched wail; Mussolini had declared war and within a few minutes—to be precise, at 6:57 A.M.—the first wave of Italian bombers were approaching the island.

There were only ten of them in this first wave: ten Savoia 79s, which approached the island at 14,000 feet in two V-shaped formations. The AA that greeted them was spasmodic and ragged, and the Italians, in perfect formation, came steadily on. They dropped their bombs with undisturbed precision; half on Hal Far, half on the dockyard. Then they turned for home.

It had, for the men of the Regia Aeronautica, been as easy as they had expected. They knew Malta hadn't a single defending aircraft; they knew her defenses were pitiably thin. They knew Mussolini had boasted he would be in Grand Harbour within a matter of weeks—and it seemed there was nothing to stop him. In the hindmost Savoia, the rear gunner sang to himself contentedly. *"Vido mare quante bello . . ."* He smiled; for the sea, as they set course for Sicily, really did look beautiful: hushed and very still in the pale half light of dawn.

> *Vido mare quante bello,*
> *Spira tantu sentimente . . .*

And that was as far as he got. For his serenade was cut short by the clatter of machine guns. A neat little row of bullet holes perforated the fuselage not a foot from his head.

He looked back. And—unbelievably—there on his tail was a fighter.

The Air Officer Commanding Malta—Air Commodore Maynard—had been told that the island's official quota of aircraft, in the event of war, was four squadrons of fighters (Hurricane Mk. IIs) and two squadrons of bombers and reconnaissance planes (Wellingtons and Blenheims). But he knew that this was a pipe dream; that there wasn't a chance of the aircraft arriving, for they were needed too desperately elsewhere. In time, the authorities admitted this. "There is no immediate prospect," reads an Air Ministry signal of May 14, "of any aircraft being available for Malta."

Many British commanders, on the eve of war, were faced with the job of making a little go a long way. Maynard's task was more difficult than that. He was faced with the job of making something out of nothing. His efforts to beg, borrow, or steal aircraft from neighboring commands were thwarted. His attempts to convert the island's few civil or nonoperational aircraft were unsuccessful. And it began to look as if the outbreak of war would find Malta without even a single makeshift fighter. Then, at last, Maynard had a stroke of luck.

One day he got to hear that a series of mysterious packing crates were standing on the slipway at Kalafrana. On opening these, he found they contained the component parts of eight naval Sea Gladiators, aircraft which should be embarked on H.M.S. *Glorious* when the carrier sailed for Norway, but which had, in the rush to get her to sea, been overlooked. The aircraft were old, dismantled, and the property of another service. There were no pilots qualified to fly them and no maintenance crews trained to service them. But—of a sort—they were fighters. Maynard went to his opposite number, Rear Admiral Willis, and asked if he could have them.

This request put Willis in a difficult position, for the Admiralty knew all about the Sea Gladiators and had earmarked them for another carrier, H.M.S. *Eagle*. But, fortunately for Malta and the Maltese, Willis was a man who could recognize an emergency. Like Nelson, he turned a blind eye to Admiralty orders, and gave half the Sea Gladiators to Maynard.

Such was the birth of a fighter defense force whose deeds will be honored for as long as the spirit of man is stirred by tales of high endeavor and unflinching sacrifice.

The Gladiators were sturdy little machines, but they were sadly outdated by the planes of the Regia Aeronautica. They were single-bay biplanes, descendants of the Pups, Camels, and S.E.5s that had fought in the First World War. With their fixed undercarriage and one-pitch propellers, their maximum speed was no more than 250 m.p.h. But, on the other hand, they were tough—their compressed-steel lattice ribs making for great internal strength—and they were highly maneuverable—they, if any plane could, could turn on the proverbial sixpence, and, in the Air Display of 1938, three of them had looped the loop, *chained together*. The Gladiators, in fact, though some thing of transition machines between ancient and modern, were not mongrels, but no thoroughbreds either. What they lacked in speed and firepower they made up for in airworthiness. They were the final flower of the sturdy old dogfighting biplanes.

Having got his fighters, Maynard set about finding pilots to fly them and ground crews to maintain them.

There were, on the eve of war, about a dozen pilots in Malta, most of them either in administrative jobs or flying the nonoperational aircraft of Station Flight, Hal Far. Not one of them had been trained as a fighter pilot, but they all volunteered, without exception, to fly the newly acquired Sea Gladiators. In the end, seven were chosen and formed into a Fighter Flight. The names of the seven deserve to be remembered: they were Squadron Leader Martin, Flight Lieutenant Burges, Flight Lieutenant Keeble, Flying Officers Hartley, Waters, and Woods, and Pilot Officer Alexander.

As for the men to service the Gladiators, the Aircraft Repair Section at Kalafrana could boast an experienced and highly efficient team: Maltese ex-dockyard apprentices, Maltese Auxiliary Air Force mechanics, and a nucleus of R.A.F. riggers and fitters. Under the leadership of Flying

Officer Collins, an ex-warrant officer, who had been on the island since 1936, these men had been welded together into a competent, hard-working unit. The fact that they had no experience in handling Gladiators and no spares didn't unduly perturb them. They had faith in their ability to improvise.

So, the Sea Gladiators were taken to Hal Far, assembled, stripped of arrestor hooks and other evidence of their naval ancestry, tested, and flown—though not when the Italian civil airliner was over the island.

The pilots were unanimous about their new machines. They may have been archaic-looking and long in the tooth (officially all operational squadrons had been re-equipped with Hurricanes in 1938), but they were first-class aircraft. As John Waters said, "They could turn on a sixpence and climb like a bat out of hell. Other aircraft all had their nasty little ways, but the Gladiator had no vices at all."

And so, day after day, the seven pilots practiced formation flying, emergency take-offs, interception tactics, and air-to-air firing. They couldn't, of course, help wondering what chance of survival they would have if Italy did enter the war: four planes matched against five hundred and fifty: four obsolescent biplanes facing the cream of a modern air force. But—perhaps luckily—there wasn't much time for thinking. For, a few weeks after their aircraft had been uncrated, the sirens were wailing, Hal Far tannoy was blaring "Scramble the fighters," and the Gladiators were roaring down the take-off strip—and into history.

That first day the Italians, true to the principles of Giulio Douhet, mounted eight raids against Malta. They used well over a hundred and fifty bombers, and in the later raids— as a tribute to the Gladiators—they brought over a fighter screen of Macchis and C.R.42s. When the Italians had a clear run their bombing was unpleasantly accurate. But they didn't like the Gladiators. And the ancient biplanes, whose top speed was actually less than that of the bombers they were trying to intercept, managed again and again to break them up or turn them aside. And they gave the Italian fighters something to think about, too. Here is Timber Woods' report of one of the evening engagements.

"We sighted a formation of Savoia 79s approaching Valletta at approximately 15,000 feet. We climbed until we were slightly above them, then delivered an attack from astern. The enemy turned out to sea. I closed from astern and got in a good burst at a range of about 200 yards. My fire was returned. I broke away and returned to the island.

"While climbing to gain more height, I heard machine-gun fire behind me. I immediately went into a steep left-hand turn and saw a single-engine fighter (a Macchi) diving and firing at me. For quite three minutes we circled each other tightly, then I got him in my sights. I got in a good burst, full deflection, and he went down in a steep dive with black smoke pouring from his tail. He fell into the sea a little to the south of Grand Harbour."

Beneath the bare facts of this report can be seen a story of coolness, resolution, and superior skill. Woods had proved that, contrary to all expectations, the antiquated Gladiators could outfly and outfight their more modern opponents. That, in itself, was heartening.

But more heartening still was the effect on the Maltese of the destruction of an enemy aircraft within full view of hundreds—if not thousands—of onlookers. The sight of the Italian falling like Icarus out of the sky, over which he had so insolently claimed dominion, gave civilian morale a boost at just the right psychological moment. Malta, it seemed, wasn't defenseless, after all. She could hit back.

And from that moment the Gladiators took on, in the eyes of hundreds of thousands of Maltese, a special sort of significance. They became a symbol of the island's spirit of defiance. As long as they stayed in the air, Malta, it was felt, would stay unconquered.

But how long *could* they stay in the air?

That first day all four planes miraculously escaped damage. But such luck was clearly too good to last; and it was decided on the evening of June 11 that from then on one plane (No. N.5524) must be kept permanently in the Aircraft Repair Section at Kalafrana as a source of spare parts: a skeleton which could be stripped to keep the other planes serviceable.

It was decided, too, that new interception tactics were

called for. George Burges put the case very clearly here. In a talk with the A.O.C. after the first day's fighting he said, "The Italian bombers are faster than we are. So our only chance is to scramble and climb as quickly as we can, and hope to get four or five thousand feet above on them by the time they reach the island. Then we must dive on them; but not from astern: from the beam."

And that, in the engagements to come,was just what they did. Day after day. Week after week. Month after month.

The Regia Aeronautica, of course, tried everything they knew to destroy the three little planes which, alone, stood between them and a complete control of the air. They came over in massed formations: fifty to sixty bombers escorted by stepped-up tiers of Macchis and C.R.42s. They sent over decoy planes, with packs of fighters shadowing them, up in the sun. And they deliberately straggled out of formation to try and tempt the Gladiators into dogfights. But somehow the little biplanes, slippery and elusive as eels, always managed to outtwist or outmaneuver them.

But they didn't, of course, escape undamaged. Time and again, in those early days of June and July, a Gladiator landed back on Hal Far so appallingly damaged that it seemed as if nothing short of a miracle would get it back into the air. Three times a plane touched down with its entire tail unit dangling by a single strut and a strand of cable; twice, a wing tip was shredded entirely away; often, the cockpits were ringed with bullet holes, the mainplanes colandered, the landing wheels shot off, the instrument panels shattered. Yet somehow, thanks to the planes' basic toughness and the skill and hard work of the Aircraft Repair Section, the damage was always patched up. Somehow, no matter how often the sirens wailed (and there were, that first month, a total of over a hundred raids), either two or three of the Gladiators always managed to struggle into the air.

And they gave the Italians plenty to think about. Although they scored comparatively few kills, they broke up countless formations, forcing the bombers off their targets, making them bomb quickly, inaccurately, or (in quite a lot of cases) jettison their bombs harmlessly into the sea.

Gradually, in their efforts to avoid the Gladiators, the Savoias and Cants were forced higher and higher: to twenty, twenty-five, and finally to thirty-thousand feet; and from these heights their bombing, of course, was far less accurate. The bombing formations shrank in size, too; to start with, the Italians had sent over, say, thirty Savoias and a dozen Macchis; but soon the ratio was reversed. But the end of June, in an effort to scotch the Gladiators, the Italians were sending over a handful of bombers, escorted by stepped-up tiers of Macchis and C.R.42s. But somehow the little biplanes, against all the odds, still managed to stay in the air.

And so, week after week, the fantastic struggle went on. Three obsolete planes against the might of a modern air force. With the unbelievable happening. The three planes seeming to bear a charmed life, and the air force being reduced to angry impotence.

By the end of June the Gladiators and their pilots had won a niche in history. They had won, too, a unique place in the affections of the Maltese. People showered the pilots with St. Christophers, pasted photographs of them beside their beds, and prayed for them nightly at the shrines in their rock shelters. When the pilots went into the streets, they were followed by admiring crowds; when they took to the air, thousands of people disdained the safety of their shelters and, forgetful of the danger of bomb and shrapnel, stood watching the fantastic dogfights that took place daily over the island. It was history in the making.

One quiet evening in early July, when there hadn't been a raid for several hours, the pilots were sitting on the grass at Hal Far, watching the three Gladiators being refueled.

"You know," Jock Martin said reflectively, "we ought to give them a name."

Someone suggested Pip, Squeak, and Wilfred; but this wasn't received with much enthusiasm. It was John Waters —quiet, good-looking, and technically the most brilliant pilot of the seven—who made the inspired suggestion.

"How about Faith, Hope, and Charity?" he said.

The names caught on. They spread beyond Hal Far, beyond Valletta and the Three Cities, beyond the shore of

Malta itself. Soon, every time the Gladiators took to the air, people would stop, point skyward, and cry:

"Look! There they go. *Faith, Hope,* and *Charity!*"

To most Britishers on the island the names brought no more than a wry, appreciative smile; but to the Maltese they brought something more. For the people of Malta are intensely religious, and it meant a great deal to them that the men and machines which were defending them so valiantly had been christened with the words of St. Paul. Now, more than ever before, the three Gladiators came to epitomize the island's spirit of defiance; they became symbols of a cause which began to take on something of the sanctity of a crusade. As, four centuries earlier, the people of Malta had helped the Knights of St. John to defend their island against the hordes of the Ottoman Empire, so the twentieth-century Maltese now rallied around the British garrison in defense of their island against the forces of another and even greater menace to Christendom. If the British, in spite of the fantastic odds, were willing to make a fight for it, so were the Maltese.

Exactly how many aircraft *Faith, Hope,* and *Charity* shot down will never be known. By the end of a month, each of the pilots could claim at least one kill, and Burges (*"Il Ferocio,"* the Maltese called him) could claim as many as six. And it is now known that many aircraft claimed only as possible did, in fact, fail to make the return journey to their Sicilian bases. In all, in June and July, the Italians probably lost upward of sixty or seventy aircraft in their assault on Malta—about half to the AA and half to the Gladiators. And the island still stood firm. Mussolini wasn't in Grand Harbour yet. Or anywhere near it.

All through June and the first half of July, *Faith, Hope,* and *Charity* kept up their fantastic battle. Then the inevitable happened.

July 16 was a day of heavy raids, and late in the afternoon Burges and Keeble got involved in a dogfight with a mixed formation of Macchis and C.R. 42s. One of the AA gunnery officers has described the combat that followed:

"I watched them twisting and diving and trying to get on

each other's tail. Keeble dived onto a Macchi, but two C.R. 42s followed him down. He managed to shake one of them off, but the other was good—one of the rare ones—and he clung to Keeble's tail. In a desperate effort to elude him, Keeble came down to ground level and flew under the wireless aerials to Pinella, hoping his pursuer would hit one of the cables. But the trap failed. As Keeble dipped under the aerials the Italian followed and shot him down; but he, himself, was so close to the ground that he hadn't time to pull out of his firing dive. The two aircraft crashed in the same field and exploded within a few yards of each other. Both men were brave pilots, and very young."

Peter Keeble's death was felt as a personal loss throughout the island. Normally the death of a pilot in action, though mourned by his friends at the time, is regarded as part of the inevitable price of war. But the outstanding immunity of the little squadron through six weeks of bitter fighting, and in the face of outrageous odds, had lulled everyone into a sense of false security. The Gladiator pilots had seemed to bear a charmed life: to be near immortal. Now it was suddenly brought home how pitiably mortal they were.

But the struggle, of course, still went on. The strain on the pilots was terrific; but the strain on the ground crews (many of whom worked twenty hours out of twenty-four) was even greater. For soon the Gladiators began to crack up.

It was only to be expected, really. They had been flown flat out for a couple of months, and there hadn't been either time or spares for the routine overhauls without which no aircraft can stay airworthy for long. Now, quite suddenly, the engines lost power and began to seep oil; one afternoon when the fitters stripped down *Faith's* engine they found holes, big as florins, in the cylinder heads. They patched the engine up as best they could, working in the open with bombs falling all around them and low-flying Macchis machine-gunning the airstrip, and by the evening *Faith* was airborne again. But everyone knew that the repair was only temporary: that unless something drastic was done the aircraft would soon be grounded for good.

Then Flying Officer Collins had an idea. In the Aircraft Repair Section at Kalafrana were a number of crated Mercury 8 and Mercury 15 engines. These had been intended as spares for the Blenheims; but perhaps, with adaptations, they could be fitted into the Gladiators? At any rate, it was worth a try.

The miracle that followed can be fully appreciated only by those with a knowledge of air engineering. For to fit the engine of one aircraft into the fuselage of another is a stupendous undertaking. In this particular case the Blenheim engines were designed to operate a host of ancillary controls which didn't exist in the Gladiators, and each of these devices had to be laboriously sealed off. Then a number of major components had to be radically adapted—oil sumps, petrol pumps, carburetors, and oil throwers, to mention only a few—and all this the mechanics had to do with improvised tools, *and* in double-quick time and in the midst of near-continuous air raids. Somehow they achieved the impossible: and after forty-eight hours' nonstop ·work the change-over was made, and the surviving Gladiators took on a new lease of life.

A few days later Collins was responsible for another masterpiece of improvisation. It had been decided to use one Gladiator as a high-level interceptor to break up the Italian bombers and the other as a low-level patrol plane to deal with fighter strafing attacks on the airdromes. In the latter plane, maneuverability was less important than firepower, and it was decided to increase the Gladiator's armament. This was easier said than done. But in the end, Collins hit on the scheme of mounting a pair of .303s, Great War fashion, on top of the upper mainplane. The result was that the silhouette of the low-level Gladiator took on an even more archaic outline than ever. With its biplane wings, outsized engine, makeshift propeller, and upper-mainplane guns, it looked, in the uncertain twilight, like the silhouette of a ghost plane flown straight from the Western Front. Somebody, catching sight of it for the first time, aptly christened it the "Bloodiator." It was certainly a bizarre-looking machine. But at least it could fly. And one afternoon it shot down a Macchi *and* a C.R. 42.

So the days passed: days of raid after raid, with the pair of patchwork biplanes continually taking on odds of anything up to fifty to one. It was the sort of hopelessly heroic struggle that caught at the imagination of the Maltese; and the debt that is owed to *Faith, Hope,* and *Charity* lies, not only in the thirty to forty planes they shot down, not only in the thousands of tons of bombs they caused to miss their target, but also in the inspiration they afforded the people of Malta. For the Maltese never forgot the Gladiator pilots' example of fortitude and self-sacrifice. It was an example they, themselves, were to follow, with equal heroism, in the months to come.

By late August, the end seemed very near. The Gladiators and their pilots had flown themselves to exhaustion. They were reeling about the sky like a pair of punch-drunk boxers, fighting instinctively in a haze of tiredness, sleeplessness, and pain. Then the miracle happened. One morning there was a louder-than-usual roar over the airstrip at Hal Far. The AA guns were silent as four sleek monoplanes came hurtling over the airfield. Burges and Waters, who were standing by, dived instinctively for shelter. Then they looked up.

"By God!" Both spoke as one. "Hurricanes!"

The problem of flying fighter reinforcements to Malta was two-fold. In the first place, every available plane was needed, in the summer of 1940, in the Battle of Britain. In the second, there was no Allied airfield within flying range of the island—even with extra fuel tanks and a following wind neither Spitfires nor Hurricanes had the slightest hope of reaching the island without refueling.

Eventually, a system of embarking fighters on an aircraft carrier, convoying them to within range of the island, and then flying them off was perfected; with the result that, in two years, some three hundred and fifty fighter aircraft were flown to Malta with no more than a dozen casualties. These air-ferry operations, being primarily a Navy commitment, were planned and controlled by Admiral Somerville from his headquarters at Gibraltar; and generally speaking, their history is one of effective co-operation between Navy and Air Force.

The smooth running of the later trips, however, was achieved only at a price—the price of men's lives: lives that were lost in the early star-crossed Operation "White," one of the most poignant tragedies of the war.

The first air-ferry operation had taken place in August, when twelve Hurricanes had flown in to relieve *Faith, Hope,* and *Charity*. This operation had been an unqualified success. But from the moment the planes touched down, the Italians stepped up the tempo of their attacks in an effort to prevent the R.A.F. from gaining a permanent foothold: and by October only four Hurricanes and one Gladiator were left. It was, therefore, decided to repeat the operation, and toward the end of the month twelve tropicalized Hurricanes and twelve specially chosen pilots were embarked on the ancient aircraft carrier *Argus* and taken at short notice to Gibraltar. Here they waited, until the warships of Force H were ready to guard them on their way to a flying-off position somewhere south of Sardinia.

The basic plan of Operation "White" was simple. Admiral Somerville would escort the *Argus* and her Hurricanes to within flying range of Malta; the aircraft would then take off in two subflights of six, each subflight being led by a Fleet Air Arm Skua (in which an observer would plot their best course for the island). It was found that the route followed would take the planes very close to Galita Island (off the Tunisian coast); and as an additional safeguard, Air Officer Commanding Malta agreed to have two of his long-range bombers waiting over the island to meet the Hurricanes and guide them back along the last stage of their journey. As soon as the planes had left *Argus,* Admiral Somerville was to retire to Gibraltar. Nothing, it seemed, could be simpler.

There were, however, two outside factors which had to

be taken into account: the weather and the Italian fleet. Bad weather could, of course, jeopardize the whole operation; while if the Italian fleet put to sea it could, all too easily, interefere decisively, annihiliating both the *Argus* and her comparatively light escort. It was, in the end, an unhappy combination of these two factors which was to prove disastrous.

At 4 A.M. on November 15, 1940, Force H pulled out of Gibraltar. The night was fine, with bright moonlight silhouetting the ships as they moved past the Rock.

Admiral Somerville had managed to muster quite an impressive-looking escort. The *Renown* was there, flying the admiral's flag; so was the *Ark Royal*, together with three cruisers and seven destroyers. The Hurricane pilots, as they watched the massive warships positioning themselves around their carrier, must have reckoned that they were in good hands. Yet, in many respects, Force H was more impressive in appearance than in fact. The *Renown*, for example, was something of a white elephant, being slow, lightly armored, and no match for a modern Italian battleship; the *Ark Royal*, with her unarmored flight deck, was peculiarly vulnerable; while the *Argus* (she was *pre*-First World War!) was unbelievably snail-like. Small wonder that Admiral Somerville, as he surveyed his ships, hoped the Italian fleet would remain in harbor.

And within a few hours of sailing, something happened that added to his already considerable anxiety. At 11:30 that morning a Spanish civil airliner, bound from Tetuán to Melilla, passed almost directly over the fleet; and it was well known that Spanish radio operators were prone to forget international law and broadcast on Italian frequencies.

That evening Somerville's suspicions were confirmed, and his anxiety deepened. For at sunset came news of Italian naval forces concentrating in the Gulf of Sorrento.

A couple of hours later the barometer began to fall.

November 16 dawned dull and overcast, with a blustering westerly wind, low cloud, and poor visibility. By noon the weather was too bad for flying, and *Ark Royal's* anti-

124

submarine patrols had to be withdrawn. Withdrawn, too, were Malta's reconnaissance planes from the Gulf of Sorrento; though not before one of them had reported a battleship, seven cruisers, and an unspecified number of destroyers standing south out of Naples.

Admiral Somerville was now in a difficult position. If he kept on, he might well, in the bad weather, run slap into the Italian fleet. If he turned back, Malta would fail to get her badly needed planes. His own words (in the official report written after the operation) explain his dilemma exactly—and his solution to it.

"It seemed to me" [he wrote]
"1. The Italians were probably aware of our departure from Gibraltar.
  2. They might well consider engaging Force H with their superior forces in the hope of balancing their recent losses at Taranto.
"In view of this, I deemed it advisable to fly off the Hurricanes from a position as far to the west as weather would permit. In reply to an enquiry, *Argus* informed me that with the wind as at present the Hurricanes could be flown off from Latitude 37° 40′ N, Longtitude 6° 40′ E. Since all available meteorological information indicated a continuation of the westerly winds ... I decided to accept this as the flying-off position."

Position 37° 40′ N, 6° 40′ E was some forty miles to the west of the flying-off area originally agreed on. But it seemed to Admiral Somerville, and to Captain Rushbrooke of the *Argus,* that this new position still gave the Hurricanes a reasonable margin of safety. For the amended position was rather less than 420 miles from Malta, and the range of the Hurricanes, in still air, was—according to the Air Ministry Handling Notes—521 miles. Bearing in mind the following wind, there seemed not the slightest doubt that the Hurricanes could reach the island without difficulty.

So the new position was unanimously agreed upon.

During the night of November 16-17 the weather started

to clear, but the latest "met." report from Malta (timed 11:30 A.M. on the sixteenth) indicated that the wind in the Malta Channel was still west-southwesterly. And there seemed no reason to believe it would change. On board the *Argus* the first subflight was ranged on deck, ready to take off at dawn.

Force H arrived in position 37° 40′ N, 6° 40′ E at 5:45 A.M. It was still dark. Loath to proceed farther east, Admiral Somerville waited impatiently for dawn. At six o'clock the eastern sky paled imperceptibly; the Hurricanes and the Skua started their engines, and at 6:15 A.M. the first planes roared safely off *Argus'* narrow deck. They circled the carrier several times, climbing to 2000 feet. In the gray uncertain light it took them the better part of fifteen minutes to get into formation and take departure over the center of the fleet. As they left the deck, *Argus'* meteorological officer checked the wind. It was 220° /20 knots. An hour later the second subflight followed the first; and again the meteorological officer checked the wind. It was 250°/16 knots. Veering and falling.

Before the planes were out of sight, Admiral Somerville had reversed course and was heading at top speed for Gibraltar. He thought at first that Operation "White" had been an unqualified success; but toward midday a spate of disturbing signals came streaming in. By sunset he knew the worst. Of the fourteen planes to take off from *Argus,* only five had arrived. Somewhere, in the sea lanes leading to Malta, nine of the aircraft had run out of petrol and crashed.

The leader of the first subflight of Hurricanes was Flying Officer J. A. F. Maclachlan, D.F.C. Though only twenty-one, Maclachlan was an experienced pilot; he had served with 88 Bomber Squadron in France (earning his D.F.C. by blowing up the last bridge over the Marne) and had later transferred to a Hurricane squadron and taken part in the Battle of Britain. Now, he formed up beside the Skua and soon saw the rest of his subflight strung out beside him in loose echelon starboard.

And so, at 150 m.p.h., they headed for Malta. Their height was 2000 feet.

After a while the observer of the Skua noticed something strange. On the surface of the sea, cloud shadows were moving increasingly slowly; and the sea itself was changing its pattern. He dropped smoke floats and found a wind. To his amazement it was east-southeasterly, eleven knots: almost an exact reciprocal of when they had left the carrier. He realized that with the wind now almost dead ahead, they would be hard pressed to reach Malta before they ran out of fuel. Making a slight alteration of course to allow for the new direction of the wind, he kept steadily on. There was nothing more he could do. (All pilots had been briefed to fly at a certain height and speed: the most economic, he assumed, for the Hurricanes.) Soon, to add to their difficulties, visibility worsened; patches of thickening sea mist drifting over the Tunisian shore. By seven o'clock they were flying blind through a baffling patchwork of mist and cloud. But the Skua observer kept his head; he concentrated on his dead-reckoning plot and made an exact landfall—albeit twenty-five minutes late—over the northern tip of Galita Island. Here, much to the pilots' relief, a Malta-based Sunderland was waiting for them, to lead them back on the second stage of their journey.

But this second stage proved even more nerve-racking than the first. For the Hurricane pilots realized now what was happening: realized that with every revolution of their propellers, with the combustion of every drop of their petrol, their expectation of life was draining inexorably away.

Maclachlan—who had recently taken a course on Hurricanes—adjusted his mixture control and his constant-speed airscrew to squeeze the last fraction of a mile out of his dwindling supply of fuel; but several of the other pilots, accustomed to flying older Hurricanes with variable-pitch propellers, were uncertain how to adjust their pitch, mixture, and throttle controls to the most economic setting. They were forty-five miles short of Malta when the engine of the Huricane next to Maclachlan started to run roughly. For several minutes it spluttered and coughed uneasily. Then it cut. Stone-dead. The Hurricane broke formation. Like a slowly falling leaf she spiraled down: down into the sea. Maclachlan watched her. For a moment he hesitated; then he, too, broke formation. Losing height, he began to circle the spot where the Hurricane had ditched. He could see the pilot struggling in the sea. He called up the Sunderland, and soon the big unwieldly flying boat came down to join him. Maclachlan flew low over the pilot, rocking his wings; and the Sunderland landed on the sea, taxied across to the pilot, and hauled him aboard. Then Sunderland and Hurricane again headed for Malta.

Soon they saw the other planes, away ahead of them: five Hurricanes trailing the single Skua. They disappeared into a veil of cloud. When they emerged there were only four Hurricanes. Another of the fighters had run out of fuel: had fallen helplessly into the sea. The pilot was never found.

Visibility in the Malta Channel was very bad, with a light southeasterly wind drifting a mixture of fog, mist, and cloud over the sea. But both Sunderland and Skua were in radio contact with Luqa, and D.F. bearings enabled the planes to home directly on to the island. Without the radio they would hardly have stood a chance; for Malta lay wreathed in cloud: invisible until they were actually over the land. Then, sudden and unexpected, out of the mist rose the plateau of Mdina Rabat, and two minutes later, the dusty runways of Luqa. The Hurricanes hadn't sufficient fuel for a circuit; they plummeted down, higgledy-piggledy, as quickly as they could. The engine of one cut dead before the plane had taxied clear of the runway; the second plane to touch down had three gallons left in her tank; the third had less than four; and in Maclachlan's tank there wasn't sufficient petrol to cover an upended sixpence! Another five minutes and all four of them would have crashed.

The first subflight had been lucky; it was otherwise with the second.

Exactly what happened to them will never be known,

and it is perhaps kinder not to probe too searchingly. But the basic facts are these.

The second subflight missed Galita Island; they never kept their rendezvous with the bomber from Malta. As soon as he realized they were lost, the Skua observer called up Malta for help. But his radio receiver was faulty, and he couldn't pick up the island's reply. Desperately he cast around the Sicilian Channel, hoping every minute to see the longed-for shore. But no shore came. One by one, the Hurricanes that were with him ran out of fuel and fell helplessly into the sea. At last only the Skua was left. Soon she, too, was very close to the limit of her endurance. Then suddenly, through the curtain of mist, the pilot sighted land: a low, green shore line sweeping the width of the northern horizon. He turned toward it. Crossing the coast, he was still trying to identify his landfall when ack-ack guns barked angrily; and the Skua—seventy-five miles off course—fell blazing off the Sicilian shore.

Of the fourteen aircraft that had that morning taken off from *Argus,* only five were left. It was a tragic loss of vitally needed planes and brave men's lives.

Like every other wartime disaster, Operation "White" was followed by boards of inquiry, top-secret reports, and a spate of official findings. After twenty years the ashes are too cold to be raked over again. Yet it is perhaps easier to assess responsibility now than it was at the time, and certainly today the official findings strike an unbiased observer as being more than a little unjust.

For the board of inquiry ascribed the catastrophe as being "mainly due to a lack of knowledge on the part of the Hurricane pilots as to how to fly their aircraft when fitted with constant-speed airscrews"; while a contributory cause was stated to be "bad navigation on the part of the observor of the second Skua." It is easy to blame air crew; especially when they are dead. A more balanced judgment, made today, would seem to indicate that the tragedy was brought about by four contributory factors.

(1) Inadequate weather forecasting. The significant point here is that when the Hurricanes took off at dawn on

November 17 the latest meteorological report they had received from the area they were flying into was timed 11:30 A.M. on the day before: was, in other words, nineteen hours out of date. In subsequent operations far greater attention was paid to obtaining accurate, last-minute weather reports.

(2) Lack of liaison between Navy and Air Force. The Naval Air Operations officers aboard *Argus* and *Ark Royal* were unaccustomed to dealing with Hurricanes; all their information about them had to be gleaned from the Air Ministry Handling Notes. These Handling Notes state specifically that "the range of a Hurricane Mk. II (tropicalized) in still air, at 130 knots, at 10,000 feet is 521 miles." Yet the pilots were briefed to fly at 2000 feet. Naturally their range in the "heavier" lower air was considerably less than if they had flown at the correct height. An R.A.F. liaison officer, to assist in briefing the pilots, would have prevented such a mistake. In every subsequent air-ferry operation, one was carried.

(3) Excessive caution on the part of Admiral Somerville. Bearing in mind that the safe arrival of the Hurricanes was the sole objective of Operation "White," it is reasonable to argue that greater risk to the fleet ought to have been accepted in order to penetrate far enough east to make the success of the operation beyond doubt. Certainly in subsequent trips the carriers concerned nearly always stood well to the east of 6° 40′ E, and as Sir Winston Churchill put it, "Never again were the margins cut so fine, and though many similar operations took place in the future never did such a catastrophe recur."

(4) Pilots' and observers' errors. That some of the pilots and one of the observers made errors of judgment is undeniable. But, looking back, it would seem that these errors were among the lesser rather than the greater of the factors which contributed to the disaster. For even if no air-crew errors had been made, the fate of the Hurricanes would still have hung precariously in the balance. What happened to Maclachlan proves that. It is interesting to note that when planning subsequent air ferries an attempt

130

was generally made to give the pilots concerned a certain amount of practice in long-distance sea flying.

And this underlines the heartening factor which goes far toward relieving the tragedy of Operation "White." Its lessons were well learned, were never forgotten; and subsequent air ferries were conducted with a degree of concentrated efficiency which enabled consignment after consignment of fighters to be flown without loss to the island which had such desperate need of them.

Editor's Footnote: By the fall season of 1941 Malta was garrisoned with 30,000 troops, had some eighty Hurricanes and an antiaircraft defense of 1400 guns—"fiercer than London's," said a Luftwaffe pilot who'd been at the shooting end of both—and foodstuffs for five months.

"It was Malta's growing strength that proved her undoing; that, and the winter stalemate on the Eastern front. For in November 1941, Hitler, balked of quick victory in Russia, again turned his attention to the Middle East. And it soon became clear to the German General Staff that no worthwhile scheme could be embarked on in the Mediterranean while Malta remained unconquered. For the island, which only a year ago had seemed so defenseless, was now proving a poisoned thorn in the Axis' side: a stumbling block to their every plan. They couldn't mount an offensive in Africa because Malta's aircraft and ships disrupted their supply line. (In October, for example, over a quarter of Rommel's reinforcements had been sunk en route.) They couldn't prepare an offensive elsewhere, because Malta's reconnaissance planes reported every concentration of troops and shipping. And soon harbors, airfields, and railways on the Italian mainland were feeling the weight of a not inconsiderable air offensive launched from Luqa and Hal Far. There was, Hitler and Mussolini decided, only one thing to do. Malta must have her teeth drawn; she must be first battered to impotence, then captured by assault from the air. Toward the end of November, Ciano made a note of this decision in his diary. "It has been decided,"

131

he wrote, "that Malta must be obliterated." *

From January, 1942, to early May, Malta was blasted by Axis bombers. To save the island, squadrons of Spitfires were shipped into the Mediterranean aboard the American aircraft carrier *Wasp* to within flying range of Malta.**

The April delivery ran afoul of quick retaliatory raids on the airfields, while the Spitfires were being refueled. Another group landed in May; these were refueled and were airborne within four minutes of arrival to meet the Axis attackers in headlong battle. Thirty-seven Axis planes were destroyed as against a loss of only three Spitfires. It took only several days' battle at these odds before the Germans and Italians abandoned their efforts to knock out the island.

Red Duster, White Ensign, pp. 123-124.
** Heretofore, no British carriers were available for the task.

The Dagger's Point

The siege of Tobruk was one of the longest in contemporary military history. The seaport's position between Alexandria and Sfax* on the Mediterranean coast of North Africa, with its sizable harbor, made Tobruk immensely important in the strategy of the Desert campaign. When the Axis front lines pushed close to the border of Egypt, the British were able to hold and maintain Tobruk as a dagger pointed in the left flank of the Axis troops; when the British pushed westward beyond Tobruk, the port served them as an advance base.

Before the war, the Italians "had constructed a series of wide defenses enclosing an area around Tobruk of roughly 135 square miles. These consisted of a double ring of concrete emplacements eight or nine miles from the town and harbor covering a frontage of some 35 miles. The eastern and western extremities of this perimeter were well protected by steep wadis, impassable to tanks and mechanized vehicles. But for the greater part of its length, the perimeter ran across a flat featureless plain protected by rusting barbed-wire and an anti-tank ditch." **

By the beginning of 1941, the British had pushed the Italians back along the Libyan coast to El Agheila, capturing Tobruk as well as Benghazi. Instead of strengthening the forward units, the British decided instead to send their reinforcements to Greece, while some of the forward units were withdrawn to rest and be refitted in Egypt.

Meanwhile, German General Erwin Rommel had arrived in Tripoli on February 12; in the succeeding weeks German troops reinforced the Italians, and Rommel sent his troops probing into the British lines. On

*Alexandria, Egypt and Sfax, Tunisia.
**From *Tobruk,* by A. Heckstall-Smith, p. 23.

March 21, he launched a solid left jab; the British defenses, now manned by green troops of the Australian 9th Division, suddenly crumbled and Rommel drove their scattered units ahead of him along the Libyan coast toward Egypt.

By April 7, Australian troops began to straggle into the Tobruk fortress. Later that day, General Morshead, the Tobruk commander, announced to his men: "Tobruk will be no Dunkirk; there will be no surrender and no retreat." With these tough words, he hoped to turn the minds of the newly arrived troops away from defeat. Tobruk was to be more than a fortress, the troops should consider it as a "sally-port" as well from which the enemy would be attacked.

On April 9, general reconnaissance was made by General Morshead and his commanders.

"The decision was taken that, until the whole defence system could be put in order and greatly increased in depth, an all-out effort must be made to improve and repair the old Italian perimeter. There, at least, were the series of concrete posts, the barbed-wire, the anti-tank ditch—such as it was—and what remained of the Italian minefields after many of the mines had been lifted or 'deloused' during the January assault.

"For the immediate emergency the perimeter was manned by seven of the garrison's thirteen infantry battalions, each with a reserve company in support dug in about half a mile in the rear. With each company holding a front of more than a mile, Morshead had every reason to warn their commanders to expect penetrations. Nevertheless, every post was to be held to the last man and each foot of ground fought for.

"Later, this defence system was greatly strengthened, and became known as the 'Red Line.' Two miles behind it the garrison constructed a second defence system—the 'Blue Line.' This was composed of a continuous minefield covered by barbed-wire and the fire from anti-tank and machine-guns dug in to well-wired and mined strongpoints. And as the siege went on, so were these positions made stronger, and the area between the Red and the Blue so thickly sown with mines that the sappers themselves could no longer keep track of them.

"But it was many months before this formidable defence system was finally completed; and at the beginning of April the fate of the fortress depended upon the cold courage of its troops rather than the strength of its defences. The garrison's armour at the outset consisted of a regiment of armoured cars, four 'I' tanks, twenty-six cruisers, and

134

fifteen light tanks; these last being useless in an armoured battle. It possessed no medium artillery except a few captured Italian guns. Its field artillery was made up of three 25-pounder regiments from Cyrenaica, and one fresh from Egypt. In addition to these there were two anti-tank regiments, one Australian and the other British, both of which were a battery short. The harbour area was defended by an anti-aircraft brigade with sixteen heavy and fifty-nine light guns.

"For two days while the stifling khamsin lashed the surface of the desert into a raging sandstorm, wearing anti-gas goggles and with handkerchiefs over their mouths, the men of the garrison laboured ceaselessly, preparing the perimeter defences. Day and night the sappers laid minefields, infantry wrestled with rusting barbed-wire and hurled the sand from the concrete posts and the crumbling anti-tank ditch; gunners dug in their 25-pounders; and signallers unwound their miles of wire as they linked the posts one to another. And through the fog of driving sand, thicker than a London 'pea-souper,' struggled the trucks carrying the ammunition and rations up the rocky escarpment to the gun-sites and forward positions.

"Blinded, choking, their sweating half-naked bodies coated with sand, these men had no time to reflect that the very wind they cursed was their staunchest ally. For out in the desert its fury had brought Rommel's armour to a grinding halt and had pinned down his dive-bombers on their airstrips. Under cover of the storm the survivors of the 3rd Australian Anti-Tank Regiment, the 3rd Indian Motor Brigade, and the 3rd Royal Horse Artillery, who had escaped from the hell of Mechili, where they had suffered a hundred casualties, straggled in to the perimeter bringing with them some forty guns to strengthen the lean defences.

"For two days the sandstorm blotted out the sun, filling the water-cans and the dixies, driving into the shallow dugouts and through blankets and ground-sheets. Then, at about noon on April 10, the storm abated. And as the dust cleared, the men in the advanced posts on the western end of the perimeter saw the enemy's tanks and trucks coming down the road from Derna. This was the signal for the sappers to blow the bridge over the road and for a battery of captured Italian 75s and 105s, manned by Australian infantrymen, to fire the first rounds in the garrison's defence.

"By the morning of April 10, Rommel had informed his Staff that the British force in the desert was but a rabble on the run, and had blandly announced that his next objective was the Suez Canal. At the same time he said that on no account must the British be allowed to break out of Tobruk." *

TOBRUK**

by Anthony Heckstall-Smith

The wind that had whipped up the dust-clouds throughout the day had died with the sun. The night was still and the deep blue dome of the sky above the escarpment was bright with stars. The air was cold, and the men in their forward posts sat huddled with their greatcoats over their shoulders watching the young moon rise.

Except for the occasional stutter of a machine-gun, the line was quiet. Too quiet, for all day behind a veil of dust the Australians had watched the enemy's transports, staff cars, and motor-cycles darting about the desert. In the late afternoon German tanks followed by bunches of infantry had moved up towards the perimeter again, but were driven off by our artillery.

Now, the quiet was charged with tension; a tension that caused the men in the forward posts to talk in whispers, nervously fingering the triggers of their rifles and machine-guns. They had been warned to expect an attack that night. But when and where? Sitting waiting for it in the flea-ridden posts behind the rusting wire played hell with a man's nerves. . . .

The mortar barrage which opened up at ten o'clock came almost as a relief to the waiting men, for they knew it was the overture to the night attack. For an hour they crouched in their posts while the mortar shells burst amongst the tangle of barbed-wire in front of them and

*From *Tobruk,* pp. 48, 49, 50.
** This is a condensed version of several chapters of *Tobruk.*

136

the machine-gun bullets ripped into the sandbags along the parapet. Then, as suddenly as it had started, the barrage stopped.

In Post 33, just west of the El Adem road, Lieutenant Mackell, the platoon commander, looked at his watch. The time was eleven o'clock. Beside him, Corporal Jack Edmonston, a sheep-farmer's son from New South Wales, peered into the darkness and the thinning dust-cloud. He gave a low whistle.

"Jerries! A whole heap of the ———s!"

Mackell's eyes followed the corporal's pointing finger. Vaguely he could see the Germans moving through a gap in the wire to the east of his post; twenty or thirty of them.

"Let 'em have it!"

As the machine-guns opened up, to Mackell's astonishment the Germans replied with mortars and light field-guns, plastering the post with shells.

Dug in about a hundred yards away, it was obvious that the Germans were determined to cover a bridgehead through which their tanks could pass. It was equally obvious that they could not be driven out by small-arms fire.

By midnight the situation was fraught with danger, and it began to look as if the line had been breached and that soon the enemy armour would come rolling through the gap.

Mackell decided to drive them out with bayonets and grenades.

With Edmonston and five others, covered by the fire from the post, he sprinted into the darkness, running in a wide semi-circle so as to approach the Germans from their flank. But almost immediately the enemy spotted them and turned all their guns on them, forcing them to go to ground.

A second dash brought the little party to within fifty yards of their objective. Once again they threw themselves down, and as they lay there panting they pulled the pins from their grenades. Then, with a wild yell, which was taken up by their comrades in the post, they charged.

For a few terrible minutes the seven men came under a deluge of fire. Edmonston took the full blast of a machine-

137

gun in his belly just as he hurled his grenade into the midst of its crew. Another bullet hit him in the throat. But he kept on running and, having thrown his second grenade, he went in amongst the Germans with his bayonet.

In a panic of terror they bolted out of their ditch, running blindly into the wire, to hang there screaming as their attackers bayoneted them.

Soon young Mackell was in difficulties, for as he fought with one German on the ground another came for him with a pistol. He yelled to Edmonston for help. With blood pouring from his throat, the Corporal dashed to his rescue, killing both Germans with his bayonet. In the hand-to-hand fighting which followed, Mackell, having broken his bayonet in a German's chest, clubbed another to death with his rifle-butt, while Edmonston and the five others killed a dozen more. The Corporal went on fighting until the last of the enemy had fled, abandoning their weapons. Then he collapsed, and the others carried him back to the post, where he died soon after dawn. He was awarded the Victoria Cross.

All through the night the battle went on. Although young Mackell's charge had routed the enemy's advance guard, by two in the morning the Germans had established a bridgehead several hundred yards inside the wire. In spite of being heavily shelled by two regiments of the Royal Horse Artillery, they held their ground.

Just after dawn, the first German tanks moved through the gap. By a prearranged plan the forward troops made no attempt to stop them, but lay in wait for the infantry. By 5:45 a.m. some thirty-eight tanks of the 5th Tank Regiment's 2nd Battalion, which had made a name for itself in Poland and France, formed up for attack nearly a mile inside the perimeter wire. At the same time the 1st Battalion's tanks were moving up in the wake of the anti-tank and field-guns and infantry. Indeed, the attack was taking on the familiar pattern of all those other German attacks which had proved so invincible in Europe.

But this time the Panzer troops were in for a rude shock, for without suspecting it they had rolled into a trap. Ahead of them were the 25-pounders of the 1st R.H.A. and the anti-tank guns of the 3rd Australian Regiment. To their left were the mobile anti-tank guns of the 3rd R.H.A., and to the right more mobile guns of the same regiment, as well as tanks of the 1st Royal Tank Regiment dug in, in hull-down positions.

The Germans first came under fire from the 25-pounders, sited just inside what were later to become the Blue Line defences. Our gunners engaged them over open sights at a range of less than 600 yards with devastating effect, one heavy tank having its armoured turret blown sky-high.

Altogether seven tanks were knocked out before the remainder disengaged and turned eastward in an attempt to outflank the batteries. Immediately they came under fire from the guns of the 3rd Australian Anti-Tank Regiment and suffered further casualties.

Baffled and battered, the Germans retired. But as they did so they were heavily shelled from both sides by the mobile guns of the R.H.A., mounted on 30-cwt. trucks, as well as the cruiser tanks.

At 7 a.m. the Germans rallied for a further attack against the thin defences of the Blue Line, but were again driven off, for without their anti-tank and field-guns and the 8th Machine-Gun Battalion they had no support. In fact, these units were still struggling to get beyond the gap. To their confusion, they were being savagely mauled by the Australian infantry, whom they had expected to surrender as soon as the tanks had broken through. Indeed, they had even called on the Australians to throw down their arms. But the Diggers answered them with everything they had got and bayoneted those who took refuge in the anti-tank ditch from the hail of small-arms fire.

A typical example of the fighting happened near Post 32, where before dawn some of the 8th Machine-Gun Battalion had established themselves in a ruined building. Early in the morning, Colonel Crawford, commanding the 2/17th Battalion of the 20th Australian Brigade, sent two platoons forward to clear the house. One section went in with bayonets and grenades, while the others gave them covering fire. The Germans returned their fire until the grenades started bursting amongst them and they saw the glint of the Australians' bayonets. Then half of them surrendered. The rest were already dead.

It was because of this and similar infantry operations that after daylight on the 14th no guns or infantry were able to break through to support the tanks. By seven-thirty that morning what was left of the German armour was fighting desperately to escape through the gap in the wire. Soon this retreat became a rout, as the tanks, gunners, and infantry, in a swirling cloud of dust and smoke from burning tanks, fled for their lives. Into this rabble the defenders fired every weapon they possessed: 25-pounders, mortars, anti-tank guns, Brens, and rifles.

A captured Panzer officer described this ghastly shambles as "a witches' cauldron."

For many hours after the main battle had ended the mopping-up operations went on, and it was not until noon that the last of the enemy were rounded up. Some 250 dazed and bewildered Germans, many of them weeping with shame at their defeat, were marched back to the prisoner-of-war cage.

They referred to that Easter battle as "the Hell of Tobruk," admitting that nothing like it had happened to them before.

"In Poland, Belgium, and France when our tanks broke through the soldiers gave in. They knew they were beaten. But at Tobruk you went on fighting," they said, "and fighting like devils out of hell!"

So certain had they been of success that some units—amongst them the 8th Machine-Gun Regiment—had advanced with their administration trucks ready to set up the headquarters in Tobruk. Undoubtedly, their repulse came as a great shock to those proud Panzer troops, and their morale was severely shaken. They had been assured that the garrison would surrender. Instead, the defenders had steadfastly held their ground, and to them must go the honour of winning the first battle against the Germans in the war.

After this setback, Rommel gave up any further attempts

140

against the southern sector. Two days later, he personally directed an attack from the west, employing troops from the Ariete Division and the 62nd Infantry Regiment of the Trento Division. But, although urged on by German tanks, the Italians had little heart for their task, and when the Australians counter-attacked they surrendered in the hundreds, advancing towards our lines waving white handkerchiefs.

Thus ended the opening rounds of Rommel's battle for Tobruk. But, while the enemy still staggered under these first severe blows, General Morshead sent out small patrols and sorties against them.

These sorties so disturbed Rommel that he sent urgent signals to hasten the arrival of the 15th Panzer Division. He was, however, not the only one who viewed the situation outside Tobruk with concern. For the Italian *Comando Supremo* had sent a despatch to the O.K.W. asking for the latter's agreement to call a halt to the advance into Egypt. Time was needed for the attacking force to be reorganized and for its badly strained supply line to be given a chance to recover.

General Halder, Chief of the General Staff, O.K.H., wrote in his diary that he was disturbed by the news from North Africa.

"Rommel," he recorded angrily, "has not sent in a single clear report, and I have a feeling that things are in a mess. . . . All day long he rushes about between his widely scattered units and stages reconnaissance raids in which he fritters away his strength . . . piecemeal thrusts of weak armoured forces have been costly. . . . His motor vehicles are in poor condition and many of his tank engines need replacing. . . . Air transport cannot meet his senseless demands, primarily because of lack of fuel. . . . It is essential to have this situation cleared up without delay. . . ."

To this end the O.K.W. decided to send General Paulus, a Deputy Chief of the General Staff, to North Africa,

141

whom Halder believed to be "perhaps the only man with enough influence to head off this soldier gone stark mad."

General Paulus arrived at Rommel's headquarters to find the stage set for a further assault against Tobruk. It was planned for April 30. He withheld his permission for two days until he had discussed the situation with General Gariboldi. In the meantime he made it clear to Rommel that there was to be no more "high-falutin'" talk about Suez being the next objective. Thanks to "Barbarossa," * the O.K.H. had no resources from which to supply any more troops or weapons to the Afrika Korps. That force's task was now to take Tobruk, and if, and when, the fortress fell, to secure Cyrenaica by holding a line from Siwa to Sollum. Having given his impetuous junior time to reflect upon all this, Paulus then sanctioned the plans for the attack on Tobruk.

The new attack was to be launched in the south-west in the environs of Ras el Medauar. Rommel's plan was that at 8 p.m. on the night of April 30, two German divisions, the 15th on the left and the 5th on the right, should make the break-through. Assault groups of the Ariete and Brescia Divisions would then advance through the breach to roll back the enemy's defences on both flanks. While this was being done, German troops pushing forward east would make reconnaissances to discover whether a main thrust could be made to the harbour. If this could be done, the flanks would then be held by the Italians, and the Panzer troops would attack again on the following morning.

At the section of the perimeter chosen, the line bulged in a salient. The twenty-two concrete posts to the north and south of Hill 209 were held by three companies of the 2nd Battalion of the 24th Australian Infantry Brigade, with a further company in reserve, approximately a mile east of the hill. During the lull between the attacks, the garrison

*Hitler's attack on Russia.

142

had worked night and day strengthening the defences, and fortuitously had laid minefields between the Blue and the Red Lines in the southwestern sector.

For the past two weeks the troops in the southwestern salient had watched the dust-clouds rising between Acroma and Hill 209 as the enemy's lorry-loads of infantry, tanks, and guns assembled some two miles beyond the perimeter. But on the morning of April 30 the dust-clouds thickened, and then in the afternoon the posts were heavily shelled, and out of the red sunset a score of Stukas came screaming down to bomb and machine-gun the forward positions. Their ammunition expended, they turned away, to be followed by yet another formation which hurled its bombs on the barbed wire and the infantry positions around Hill 209. Then, as the last Stuka headed for home, its magazines empty, the Germans laid down a deadly barrage of artillery fire on the same positions and, under cover of the dust and growing darkness, the 2nd Machine-Gun Battalion and sappers of the 33rd Panzer Pioneers raced forward to render safe the mines and blast gaps in the wire to left and right of the hill.

The men in the forward posts had been so heavily bombed and shelled that they were unable to prevent the German penetrations between their widely dispersed posts or to stop them setting up machine-gun nests in their rear. Moreover, as a result of the bombing, the signal lines linking the company holding the hill with their H.Q. had been cut, so that their Commanding Officer, Lt.-Colonel Spowers, was without news of them.

Again and again he sent out runners and signalmen to try to make contact with the company through a curtain of machine-gun fire. Some failed to get through; others to get back. So concentrated was the enemy's fire that one signalman took four and a half hours crawling on his belly to cover the mile and a quarter between his company's post and the Battalion H.Q., mending the wire as he went. In the confusion, patrols got lost in their own minefields, and just before dawn the reserve company, a mile to the rear, reported enemy tanks and infantry to the east of the hill.

When daylight came a thick ground mist shrouded the

desert, and since no one seemed to know where the Germans were, Colonel Spowers did not dare order the artillery to shell the hill. At eight o'clock, when the mist cleared, the situation was even worse than had been feared. The Germans had not only established themselves a bridgehead a mile and a half wide, but had overrun seven of the advanced posts around Hill 209, killing or taking prisoner the men holding them.

Soon after seven-thirty the German tanks which were to thrust eastwards to the harbour began forming up on the hill. But because they were still without information our gunners left them alone. Heading east, forty tanks came straight for the 2/24th's reserve company's positions, blazing at them with cannons and machine-guns. But near the Acroma road the first flight met the fire of the 24th Australian Anti-Tank Company, commanded by Captain Norman. One gun managed to knock out and set on fire a Mark III before it was itself set upon by eleven tanks and its crew all wounded. Two other guns were also silenced, and the tanks swept forward to within a few yards of the reserve company's positions where they ran into a minefield.

In a matter of minutes, seventeen tanks were brought to a standstill, most of them with shattered tracks. But although they were sitting targets, all our anti-tank guns within range had been put out of action. Nor did the field-gunners dare to shell them heavily for fear of detonating our own mines and thus clearing a passage for the enemy.

However, after their initial setback the Germans made no further effort to penetrate the minefield, but turned away to the south.

By early that morning both Rommel's tank thrusts had failed. But he still had large reserves, and our reconnaissance aircraft reported a force of some 200 tanks in and around Acroma and Hill 209. Against this force all General Morshead could muster was twelve "I" tanks and nineteen cruisers. So heavily outnumbered, his only chance was to hold his armour in reserve and rely upon his artillery and the minefields to reduce the enemy's strength. In fact, at this stage Morshead was in a dilemma so far as his tanks

144

were concerned. He had been criticized for using his armour in "penny packets" rather than in strength. But this is an injustice. His air reconnaissance was, to say the best of it, scrappy, and so he had no means of foreseeing from which direction Rommel's next thrust would come. Thus, in order to cope with the unexpected, he was obliged to keep some of his pitifully small force in reserve.

Even as it was, he took risks. On the afternoon of May 1, for instance, he sent out a small force, consisting of five "I" tanks and three cruisers, for the purpose of regaining control of the forward posts. This force was repeatedly attacked by superior numbers of German tanks. First, it came up against fifteen of them. Immediately an "I" tank received a direct hit which killed all its crew except the driver, although the tank itself was not destroyed. As the seven others struggled to withdraw, they were set upon by another batch of fourteen Germans, and a further "I" tank was knocked out and one of the cruisers badly damaged. In these two encounters the Germans lost four tanks. Nevertheless, Morshead can hardly be blamed for holding his little force in reserve and depending upon his artillery, as indeed he had done with such marked success in the Easter battle. But Rommel was aware of these tactics and time and again he sent waves of Stukas to dive-bomb and machine-gun our gun sites. But since they were well dug in, he failed to silence them, and before the battle was over they played havoc with his armour.

Although the defenders could not know it, by the end of the first day's fighting General Paulus had advised Rommel to abandon any further attempts to capture Tobruk and to be content with holding Hill 209 and the positions around it. And so, by the night of May 1, the battle had resolved itself into a struggle for this hill. It was, from then on, a battle of attack and counter-attack, in which both sides fought doggedly, neither gaining nor giving ground.

Throughout May 2, in a thick sandstorm, the Germans fought desperately to hold the posts they had captured, suffering severe casualties in both men and tanks. On the night of May 3, General Morshead threw in his reserve brigade—May 18—in an attempt to retake Hill 209. The

145

attack was planned as a converging one by two battalions. But as they assembled the Australians were so heavily shelled from the hill that zero hour had to be put forward until just before nine o'clock at night. In the darkness, the attack quickly became a series of hand-to-hand skirmishes and individual bayonet raids on the enemy's strongpoints.

Typical of the night's fighting was an incident on the Acroma road when some Australians of the 2/9th, led by Lieutenant W. H. Noyes, saw three Italian tanks approaching. With Sergeant Hobson and three men, he crept on to the tanks and, lifting their turrets, dropped hand grenades inside, blowing them up.

In the early hours of the morning General Morshead called off the attack, since he did not wish his troops to be caught in the open after daylight.

Thus ended the second major battle for Tobruk. As a result of it, Rommel's troops had penetrated the perimeter defences to the depth of less than two miles on a front of nearly three miles. They had captured Hill 209, which gave them an excellent observation point. In achieving this the Axis had suffered more than eleven hundred casualties and had lost a large percentage of its armour. Paulus claimed the battle as an important success. Nevertheless, he gave definite orders that the attack on Tobruk was not to be renewed unless the garrison showed signs of evacuating the port.

There can be no doubt that at the time the defenders' courageous resistance to these attacks by vastly superior forces, employing the same blitzkrieg tactics by which they had conquered half Europe, prevented the Axis Armies marching triumphantly on to Suez.

"Omnis Gallia in tres partes divisa est."

The fortress of Tobruk, like Caesar's Gaul, may be said to have been divided into two parts; the perimeter defences and the harbour area. The whole covered an acreage of roughly the size of the Isle of Wight and was inhabited by an exclusively male population of approximately 30,000.

While it is difficult to generalize about the living conditions within the fortress, since they varied from one area to another, it is true to say that every man's comfort depended largely upon his own ingenuity and resourcefulness. The men quartered in the town lived in reasonable comfort by comparison with those in the forward areas. Generally speaking, the nearer a man lived to the perimeter, the worse was his lot and the more he suffered from the violence of the North African climate, the lack of water, the torment of flies and fleas, and the misery of the dust churned up by the wheels of the trucks and tanks. But dust-storms, flies, and fleas were plagues common to all men in Tobruk.

At the end of the siege a sergeant of an anti-aircraft battery, who had spent seven months in the fortress, wrote:

> "Almost worse than the bombs as a tribulation to the flesh and the spirit were the fleas. The desert fleas are famous, and ours were obviously in the pay of the enemy. How we cursed them on the nights when the moon was late up and we hoped to catch a couple of hours' sleep before the inevitable procession of night-bombers started. The fleas marched and counter-marched up and down our twitching bodies until we thought we would go crazy. . . . And we needed those hours of sleep, for when the moon was up we would get mighty little rest. Twenty-one alarms in one night was our record; and it was nothing to have half a dozen night after night. . . .
>
> No wonder we looked forward to our periodic 'day off' by the sea. Even then we had to keep an eye open for the bombers and dive into the caves for shelter from swooping Stukas, but it was heaven to wash ourselves and our sweaty clothes in the clear blue water, and lie naked on the sand and dream of home, beauty, and beer. . . .
>
> And we had our 'quiet days' when the wind howled and the dust devils swept over the desert so that one could not venture out without goggles or eyeshields;

and as we lay in our shallow dug-outs dozing and reading some tattered paperback, the dust would settle in a floury yellow veil over face, hands, and blankets. We ate it and breathed the stuff so that in the end we scarcely noticed it. . . . Mostly our grouse was plain boredom—week after week, month after month, the same eternal desert, the same discomforts, the same raids. Danger itself becomes tedious after a while. . . ."

None knew better than General Morshead that boredom could demoralize the spirit of his garrison more rapidly than even Rommel's Stukas. So, living up to the nickname of "Ming the Merciless" which the Diggers had given him, he kept his troops constantly working and in continual contact with their besiegers. His infantry battalions were moved every few weeks from the concrete posts in the Red Line back to the Blue Line where they worked on the fortifications, and then into reserve. After a few days' rest, swimming, sun-bathing, and washing clothes, they were usually sent up to the Salient sector, where a night seldom passed without patrols being sent out across no-man's-land to the enemy strongpoints.

Overlooked by the Germans on Hill 209, conditions in the Salient during the early days of the siege were the hardest of all to endure. The positions, due to the rock beneath a shallow layer of sand, were part weapon-pit and part sangar, and, since they were provided with no sort of cover overhead, their occupants were exposed all day to the heat of the desert sun. The majority of these section posts were not even connected by crawl trenches, so that the men were forced to crouch or lie face downwards in what were little better than open graves.

Throughout the long hours of daylight bully beef and biscuits formed their staple diet, while the bitter, chlorinated water in their bottles became so warm that it no longer eased their burning throats. Only by night was any movement possible, and then under cover of darkness the ration-truck came forward and a hot meal was issued, and a further supply of hard rations left for the following day.

Thus, the men had their breakfast at 9:30 p.m., a hot lunch at about midnight, and dinner before dawn. After a week of such living the troops left their sangars thin and weak and often racked with dysentery.

Rommel clung tenaciously to Hill 209 and the ground he had captured immediately to the east of it, since he looked upon it as a weak spot in the garrison's defence through which a way could be forced when the moment came to renew his offensive. But to hold the Salient he was obliged to use a third of his total infantry strength.

For Morshead, too, this sector of the perimeter was a constant source of anxiety. Before the enemy's attack on May 3–4 the garrison had held three and a half miles of the old perimeter, well mined and wired and covered by fire from the old Italian strongpoints. Now it had to hold a front of nearly five and a half miles without wire or minefields, the whole length of which was overlooked by the enemy. Ten companies of infantry were required to defend a sector which had previously been held by only two.

In spite of the fact that he had been reinforced by the arrival of the 2/23rd Battalion by sea, Morshead was hard put to it to hold the Salient. But since his chief role was to keep the greatest number of German troops pinned down outside Tobruk, he never lost an opportunity of taking aggressive action. Now, he took it to shorten the front in the Salient so that he could hold it with two infantry battalions. But, owing to the enemy's complete air superiority at this time, reinforcements were so slow in arriving that Morshead was obliged to draft men, like the Pioneers and the R.A.S.C. from the docks, into the infantry battalions. He also resorted to cunning. By a series of patrols into no-man's-land by night which came to grips with the enemy, by sending out wireless messages that hinted at a forthcoming attack, and by driving trucks and light tanks backwards and forwards from the docks to the western sector of the perimeter in a cloud of dust, Morshead was able to convince the Germans that he was about to launch an attack in force against Hill 209. This ruse succeeded with the result that Rommel withdrew troops from the Sollum area to meet the threat to the Salient, while his sappers and

149

pioneers hurriedly set about strengthening the positions around the Hill itself. But, although he did manage to shorten his front line by the end of June, Morshead was never able to drive the enemy from the high ground overlooking his fortress.

Life all along the perimeter was tuned to harrying the enemy. Except in the Salient where our positions were within easy range of the Afrika Korps' mortars and machine-guns, our troops in the forward area were free to move about in daylight in comparative safety and our trucks could drive up almost as far as the Red Line without risk of surprise attack. This freedom of movement was largely due to the patrols which kept Rommel's troops so far back that no-man's-land along the greater length of the perimeter was never less than a mile wide and at some points as much as four miles of open desert lay between the opposing forces.

After the May battles, this no-man's-land virtually belonged to the garrison, or, at least, our troops had the free run of it. For a while, the Austrailians and the Indians shared it between them. Amongst the Indians were a number of Rajputs, warrior-caste Hindus from Jodhpur, of whom the enemy went in terror. They could move through the darkness without a sound, and never returned from a raid without claiming a high score of Germans and Italians. Indeed, so successful were they that their senior officer became suspicious and lectured them sternly against over-estimating the number of enemy dead. A few nights later, when the patrol returned through the wire just before dawn, its leader, saluting smartly, laid two small sacks at the senior officer's feet. They contained irrefutable, if macabre, evidence of the night's operation, for in one were sixteen right ears, and in the other sixteen left ears, all still oozing with the blood of their former owners.

Apropos of the stealth with which these Indians moved by night, I remember the alarming experience of a South African sapper major while lifting German mines under cover of darkness near Sollum.

"It was one of those nights," he told me, "when the desert was as quiet as the grave. I was on my knees dealing with a detonator when suddenly a hand was clapped over my mouth and a thin arm wrapped itself round my neck. I was so numb with fear that I couldn't move. But my hair stood on end! I felt someone running their fingers over me; feeling the buttons on my tunic, my revolver, my pockets. When they reached the crowns on my shoulders, they seemed to hesitate. Then, just when I'd made up my mind that I was as good as dead, I was released. I heard a voice whispering, but I couldn't hear what was said because the blood singing in my ears deafened me. But I did catch the single word 'Sahib.' I don't know, but I may even have passed out in sheer terror. But when I pulled myself together, I was still kneeling on the ground staring up at two bearded Sikhs. They were out on patrol, and since I was in the Jerry minefield, I'd had a pretty close shave. I still get the trembles every time I think of it!" the Major told me with a shiver.

Every night our patrols went out from Tobruk across no-man's-land, and as the siege lengthened, the men became better and better equipped for their task. In the early days, the Diggers set out with socks over their boots and even in their stockinged feet, while the Indians made themselves special sandals from the rubber of old motor-tyres. Later, the patrols were provided with thick desert boots with soft rubber soles, and special one-piece patrol suits reinforced at the elbows and knees as protection against the thorn bushes and stony ground.

The patrols usually consisted of between ten and twenty men, each with a rifle with fixed bayonet, and carrying two or three hand grenades. In every patrol there was at least one man with a Bren, which he fired from the hip, and often as many as six armed with Tommy-guns. Usually, they were supported by a Bren- or mortar-carrier to give covering fire as they withdrew, and, when necessary, to pick up the wounded. Fortified with a hot meal and a tot of rum, they set out in the darkness, moving on a compass bearing across the featureless desert to the enemy's lines. To achieve surprise, it was their practice to attack a strong-point from the flank or rear; a manoeuvre which called for very accurate navigation by the patrol leader.

One of the main objects of these night raids was to capture a prisoner for interrogation.

One moonlight night when two officers and fourteen men of the 2/23rd Battalion were out on patrol on the Bardia road sector, they had a strange experience.

"As we went forward," their leader, Captain Rattray, told afterwards, "we saw the shadowy figure of a soldier moving out from the forward enemy position to the patrol. . . . Every few yards he would stop and give a low whistle. When he whistled the third time, McMaster whistled back. The figure turned towards us and as he got nearer we could hear him calling: *'Herr Leutnant! Herr Leutnant!'* Mc-Master called back *'Si, si, Comradio!'* and the Eytie walked right into our arms. We had been sent out to get a prisoner and so now we could go back. . . . Next day we all had badly lacerated knees and elbows, but we had the unusual distinction of having whistled a prisoner in."

Such patrols played havoc with the enemy's nerves, particularly the Italians, and to protect themselves against the night raiders the Germans sowed the ground round their strongpoints with mines and booby-traps linked together with trip-wires. They also covered their whole front with an ever-increasing number of mortars and machine-guns. But throughout the siege they were never able to prevent the nightly sorties made against them. They were constantly on the alert and for ever in fear that one of these night patrols might be an overture to a full-scale breakout from the fortress.

It was the spirit of the men in Tobruk which defeated Rommel. Yet that spirit which inspired the garrison is hard to define.

"Throughout all those months," an officer wrote of it afterwards, "it so permeated the whole atmosphere of the place as to be almost tangible. Everywhere one was as conscious of it as the very sand that filled the air we breathed, the food we ate, and the vile brackish water we drank. It manifested itself in the manner of the men. Although most of them looked like scarecrows, and many of them, owing to the lack of fresh vegetables and in spite of the vitamin C tablets, were covered in suppurating 'desert sores,' they bore themselves with pride. Instinctively, one recognized them for what they were; dedicated men, resolutely, grimly determined to endure fear, discomfort, hardship, and, if needs be, death, rather than surrender. Rommel couldn't hope to defeat such a spirit any more than he could understand it. When he came up against it, he was confounded by it. Those ridiculous pamphlets he showered on us from the sky calling on us to surrender proved that."

Yet Tobruk cast something very like a spell over the men who lived there, so that years afterwards they remember it with nostalgia. It would be easy to say that time had lent enchantment to the scene, were it not for the fact that at the height of the siege there were men who wrote home with genuine affection for their beleaguered fortress.

Returning from a twenty-four-hour stint in his battery observation post, a young gunner wrote home of his "day off" by the sea.

"It's my turn down to the beach tomorrow, so I'll have a good scrub and do some washing," he told his mother. "I'm black, or at least grey. This sand gets everywhere, and my clothes stand up by themselves when I get undressed. Sweat and sand make good concrete. I won't have much washing to do, only pants and socks. I don't wear anything else. Furthermore, I'll have to walk around in my boots until my clothes dry. It's nothing here for the boys to walk around stark naked for half the day as most of them have nothing else to wear while their clothes are drying, so at meal-times they line up with nothing on but their boots and hats. . . .

"The sea was like a mill-pond when we got there, the day glorious, so things couldn't have been better.

At night, another chap and I lit a fire and cooked some tinned food, and then lay in bed and had a good feed. . . . You know, when lying there in bed I remarked to my mate that I wouldn't swop beds with anyone in the world, and he agreed. It was beautiful lying there on the sand about five yards from the Med., a lovely still night with every star visible. We were wonderfully warm and comfortable and hadn't a care in the world. . . .

"You women back home sit and worry about us. You don't realize the good times we have, days that we have at the beach or days when Jerry is quiet and we have a euchre party at threepence a game. . . .

"I awoke the next morning feeling great, just crawled out of bed, stripped off, and had a swim before breakfast. . . .

"I'm extremely happy here; I don't know why! There ain't no bird to sing, no flowers or lawns or trees or rivers to look at, but I'm just happy. . . .

"I suppose I enjoy company and I enjoy the wonderful feeling of comradeship in Tobruk. We are more or less cut off from the world, and we have one job and one job only, that is, to hold this place. This is an experience I shall always relish. It will be a privilege later to say 'I was there. . . .' "

Those simple words written home during the summer of 1941, sum up the spirit of the garrison of Tobruk.

But as the months dragged by there crept into those letters an insidious note of resignation—an undertone of philosophic contentment—towards their utterly unnatural existence. They wrote almost with affection about the fly-blown Libyan port in which they were virtually prisoners. In spite of the Stukas, the shelling, the eternal bully beef, the brackish water, and the absence of women, they said they were happy. They didn't know why, but there was something about Tobruk, the blue of the Mediterranean by day and the dark indigo of the desert sky by night, even its detachment from the rest of the world, that tugged at their heartstrings.

Then, one morning towards the end of July, three strange officers presented themselves at the 9th Divisional Headquarters. They wore grey shirts and shorts, comical little pith helmets, and glittering silver insignia. They were very smart, clean, and freshly laundered, and they smelt slightly scented. Clicking their polished heels, they saluted and shook hands with everyone in sight, and then saluted again. They were Poles! And one of them was a general called Kapanski.

Even when the advance party of the 1st Battalion of the Polish Carpathian Brigade arrived, the Diggers had their doubts whether they had come as reliefs or reinforcements. But by mid-August it was confirmed that the Poles were there to release the 18th Brigade. But still there were sceptics who were prepared to wager a month's pay that the old 9th was destined to stay in the fortress until the siege was raised. They were not pessimists, but wishful thinkers.

The Polish Carpathian Brigade had been formed in Syria by General Kapanski. It consisted of regular soldiers who had fiercely resisted the German invasion in 1939, and a large number of volunteers. The majority of the former had been officers who, having escaped from Hungarian, Rumanian, and German prison camps, had made their way to Syria to join the Brigade as N.C.O.s and private soldiers. The rest were patriots who, rather than live under the Nazis, had left their homes and families and suffered ghastly hardships tramping across Europe in order to fight for the Allied cause.

When France capitulated, Kapanski, ignoring orders from Vichy, marched his force into Palestine, taking with him all the arms, equipment, and vehicles supplied by the French. For more than a year the Brigade had remained in Palestine and Egypt, and it had been camped outside Alexandria for several months before the decision was made to send it to Tobruk to relieve the 18th Australian Infantry Brigade.

155

There were Staff Officers in Cairo who predicted that this move was doomed to failure from the start. Everyone knew, they said, that the Poles were raring to kill Germans. But they also had quite a reputation as lady-killers, and so were what was technically known as a "bad security risk." Even if their leave were stopped prior to departure, there were bound to be those truants who would sneak out of their camp at Agomi to take passionate leave of their "lights o' love" in Alexandria. There would be wild farewell parties in the Monseigneur Bar and Pastroudi's, these Staff Officers warned the Navy, and every Axis agent would know exactly what was afoot.

The Navy shrugged its shoulders and remarked that conveying the Poles to Tobruk looked like being a sticky business. So they gave the operation the code name "Treacle."

But no one, least of all Cunningham, really treated this undertaking lightly. The evacuations of Greece and Crete were still fresh in his memory, and although "Treacle" was not an evacuation, it nevertheless entailed the withdrawal of large numbers of soldiers from under the very nose of the enemy. The risks were enormous and the odds even more heavily weighed against his ships than they had been during those desperate days in the Aegean, for now the Luftwaffe were in possession of the Cretan airfields as well as those around Tobruk.

To succeed, "Treacle" would have to be a combined operation in the fullest sense of that term. Its success would depend upon split-second timing and perfect planning by the Staff Officers of the three Services in co-operation with Morshead, the Fortress Commander, Poland, the Senior Naval Officer Inshore Squadron, and Smith, the Naval Officer in Charge, Tobruk.

It was fortunate indeed to have these three able, level-headed officers in Tobruk at such a time; officers who not only inspired confidence in those under them, but who were masters of improvisation. And in Tobruk, where there were no facilities for the quick unloading of ships and handling large numbers of troops, a positive genius for improvisation would be needed.

Morshead had twice left the fortress to confer with the planning staffs in Cairo,* and was confident that his Transport and Movements Control Officers, together with Smith and his staff at Navy House, could cope with their end of the operation. He had given orders that extra mobile 3.7s were to be moved in from the perimeter to strengthen the harbour defences, and had arranged with the Poles that the 'A' lighters and other small craft arriving in Tobruk should be retained there to ferry troops between the ships and the shore. His pioneers, sappers, and the Docks Group had further improved the berthing facilities alongside those wrecks used as wharves by the destroyers. The men leaving would take with them only what they could carry on their backs; the rest of their equipment, including vehicles, would be left behind for the Poles.

No amount of planning, however thorough, could insure against all the hazards of an operation involving so many lives. It was for this reason, therefore, that Operation "Treacle" was an experiment. If it succeeded—and that was a very big "if"—Cunningham, Auchinleck, and Tedder were prepared to repeat it until the 15,000 Australians in Tobruk had been replaced by a like number of British and Polish troops. But in no event could this relief be allowed to delay the start of the new offensive in November, before which all the available destroyers, "A" lighters, and other ships of the Inshore Squadron would be engaged in carrying tanks, guns, ammunition, and supplies to the fortress. Auchinleck made this point clear in his telegrams to Whitehall, and Churchill, who loyally supported his decisions, forwarded them on to Canberra.

A great deal, therefore, depended upon "Treacle." Everyone concerned knew that if the operation was to work it must do so with clockwork precision. Yet, in their hearts, few believed that Rommel would allow it to work. He had vowed that he would either overwhelm the garrison or starve it out. Now that his reputation was at stake, it was

*In June 1941, General Wavell had been removed and General Auchinleck was given the command of the Western Desert Campaign.

inconceivable he would permit the Diggers to escape without making a supreme effort to destroy them.

"Treacle" began on the first day of the moonless period in August when three destroyers and the minelayer *Latona*, loaded with nearly a thousand troops and some two hundred tons of stores, sailed from Alexandria, escorted by other destroyers. All during the day relays of fighter squadrons flew over the ships. Then, as darkness fell and the Hurricanes turned for home, the first of the bombers and long-range fighters set out from their bases in Egypt, heading west for the Axis airfields. Their task was a dual one; to bomb the runways and then circle the airfields so that the Germans would not dare to light the flarepaths for their pilots to take off into the inky darkness.

As the convoy approached Tobruk other bombers roared out of the east to Bardia to drop bombs and flares over the German long-range guns. As they did so, a destroyer was detached from the convoy to fire salvoes into the gun positions. Then, as the three destroyers and the minelayer neared Tobruk bay and swung to port, the batteries of 60- and 25-pounders opened up on "Bardia Bill" and his mates. The timing was superb. Blinded by the smoke-shells and under a deluge of high explosive, the German gunners could see nothing, while the star-shells bursting in the sky guided the ships up the narrow swept channel into the harbour.

In Tobruk the Diggers waited. They stood shoulder to shoulder on the only jetty, on the rusting decks of two half-sunken hulks, packed like cattle in the cavernous holds of the "A" lighters, and on the decks of launches and tugs. On the quay below Navy House, and at the edge of beaches, the lorries waited. All round the harbour, the crews of the 3.7s and the Bofors and the "UPs" waited.

But now, at last, the sun was setting and it would soon be dark—pitch dark, for tonight there would be no moon. Tobruk was strangely quiet. Usually, at the end of these stifling summer days, the port came to life with a sigh of relief. The crews of the landing craft came ashore, the Aussies working on the quay ambled off to wash their sweating bodies in Anzac Cove, the Indian troops, who had

158

been unloading stores, began to chatter like starlings, and a few of the staff of Navy House brought their "Plonk" into the evening air. But this evening Tobruk appeared like a ghost town. Then, as the sky grew dark and the stars came out, the still air was filled by the rumble of approaching trucks. Operation "Treacle" had begun.

Below me, although I could not see them, I knew the Aussies were clambering down from their lorries, rifles slung over their shoulders, and were humping their kit on to the jetty, into the launches and tugs, and over the ramps of the landing craft. I marvelled that so many men, keyed up with excitement, could make so little noise, and listened for the sound of their tramping feet against metal decks. Then I remembered that they were wearing their rubber soled desert boots.

Suddenly, I heard the distant drone of aircraft. All day long I had waited for that sound, and now that I heard it I felt sick. Getting up from the bench, I gazed into the starry sky, expecting at any second the rhythmical hum of the distant planes to be drowned by the ear-splitting crash of the ack-ack batteries. Instead, I heard the far-off thud of exploding bombs and saw their flashes like summer lightning in the southern sky beyond the escarpment, so that I knew the R.A.F. must be bombing El Adem airfield.

The reverberating drum beats of those bombs were the opening notes of an Olympian symphony that I felt was composed by Thor himself. They were joined by the pulsing beat of diesel engines and the throb of giant petrol motors, and, as the tempo quickened, this wild orchestra was swelled by the crash of heavy artillery, the shrill whistle of speeding salvoes, and the staccato crack of bursting shells. The very earth trembled as the symphony soared to a mighty crescendo.

Awed and dazed by this cataclysm of sound, I watched the great pall of smoke rising like a curtain over Bardia change from black to deep crimson, and saw silhouetted against it the shapes of the approaching ships. I saw, too, the jagged wrecks rearing out of the water like dinosaurs.

Slowly, *Latona* glided up the harbour and lost way, and the onyx water sparkled with phosphorus as her anchor

159

cracked its surface. Through my night-glasses I watched two of the destroyers until they vanished into the shadows of the wrecks crowded with waiting troops. The third nosed her way towards the quay, to come to rest alongside yet another wreck. I could see the soldiers lining her deck four deep, and heard above the thunder of the bombardment the clatter of gangways.

Almost before the shore parties had secured her lines, the Indians were aboard off-loading boxes of ammunition, while down the narrow gangplanks the Poles came ashore. As the last of them landed, the Aussies swarmed aboard. There was no noise, no shouting, no flashing of torches, not even a lighted cigarette to be seen; and no confusion.

In less than ten minutes some 350 men had left her deck and another 350, including wounded on stretchers, had taken their places, and the destroyer was going astern on her engines.

Within thirty minutes the four ships were heading for the harbour entrance. High over their masts screamed the salvoes from the 60- and 25-pounders as one by one they merged with the darkness.

The story of "Crusader," which began at dawn on November 18 in a downpour of rain, has been told often enough. Its pattern followed those of all battles waged in that tactician's paradise, the Western Desert, where the protagonists are the armoured units rather than the infantry battalions, and victory is won by the flow of petrol and water rather than blood of soldiers. With their swift outflanking movements by light tanks and armoured cars, their clashes of heavy armour, when, mounting an escarpment, the opposing tanks meet face to face, breathing fire at each other like legendary dragons, and their moments of savage in-fighting between infantrymen with bayonets, rifles, and hand grenades, such conflicts should be an inspiration to any writer. Yet, because they range over the vast, featureless desert, their ebb and flow hidden in swirl-

160

ing dust-clouds, as the opposing armies fight for some un-charted hillock, these battles defy description and accounts of them are deadly dull.

For the first three days of "Crusader" everything went well for the 8th Army, although the reports coming in from the front, in the Commander-in-Chief's own words, "grossly exaggerated enemy tank losses." Nevertheless, Rommel was taken by surprise and forced to give ground.

Briefly, the plan was for the two divisions of the 8th Army, under General Alan Cunningham, to advance north and east towards Tobruk. The 30th Corps, under General Norrie, which comprised the 7th Armoured Division, the 4th Armoured Brigade Group, the 22nd Guards Brigade Group, and two brigades of the 1st South African Division, was to deliver the main attack. Its orders were to make a wide sweep on the desert flank, engage Rommel's main armour, and, having defeated it, to strike north to Tobruk. It was for Norrie to order the garrison to make its sortie from the fortress at the crucial moment. Meanwhile, the 13th Corps, commanded by General Godwin-Austin, and composed of the 4th Indian Division, the New Zealand Division, and the 1st Army Tank Brigade, was to attack and pin down the Axis frontier defences from Halfaya in the north to Sidi Omar in the south, outflank them, and press on to Tobruk. In this overall plan, the relief of Tobruk was merely incidental, for the purpose of the operation was to drive the Axis Army out of Cyrenaica and, finally, North Africa.

The 7th Armoured and the 1st South African Divisions, together with the 4th Armoured Brigade Group, had started off at a gallop in spite of the heavy going. By night-fall on November 18th, they had advanced across the El Abd track running from Sidi Omar to El Gubi, where they split into four columns, which would the next day search out the enemy's armour.

In the morning, the 22nd Armoured Brigade attacked the Trieste Division near El Gubi and knocked out forty-five of its tanks, but lost twenty-five of its own. As the Italians withdrew, the South Africans advanced into El Gubi. Meanwhile, the two center columns were heading north and west. The right-hand column, the 4th Armoured Brigade Group, advanced towards the Capuzzo track leading from Bardia to Gambut, while the 7th Armoured Brigade, finding the going ahead too soft, swung northwest towards Sidi Rezegh. This hundred-foot-high ridge overlooking the Capuzzo track about fifteen miles south-east from Tobruk became the hub of the battle for it virtually was the key to the fortress.

But, at first, Rommel chose to ignore the threat to this important position, and despatched a force of some sixty tanks to attack the 4th Armoured Brigade, whose main armour consisted of some 166 light American Stuart tanks. Although the attackers were outnumbered and forced to withdraw, they had tested the strength of these light tanks and discovered the weakness of their armour and firepower. Thus, the next morning when the 4th Armoured Brigade renewed the attack, it found itself up against a vastly superior German force. It was outgunned as well as outnumbered, but it put up a brave fight. Throughout the whole of November 20, the battle raged, and the reports reaching Cunningham's headquarters led him to believe that not only were Rommel's Panzer divisions committed in battle but had lost a considerable number of tanks.

In fairness to all concerned, these reports were not so inaccurate as they may have seemed. For the Germans did have a number of tanks knocked out. Our troops saw them hit and brought to a standstill. But they underestimated the brilliance of the enemy's recovery organization which enabled many of these tanks to return to action. Even as the battle was on, the Germans sent up their huge wheeled and tracked tank-transporters to recover their damaged tanks and drag them back out of range to the repair bases.

While this battle was being fought, the 7th Armoured Support Group had captured Sidi Rezegh, and the 7th Armoured Brigade had established itself on the aerodrome there. Thus, these two brigades had reached a position of great strategic importance only about fifteen miles from the Tobruk perimeter. Cunningham, therefore, allowed orders to be given for the 13th Corps to start operations and for the sorties from the fortress to begin.

For two days the garrison had been poised ready to spring. Its Commander was no longer Morshead, but General Scobie, G.O.C. British 70th Division, for "Ming the Merciless" had handed over the fortress on October 19 and sailed for Palestine to join the rest of the Australian Corps. Now the only Diggers in Tobruk were the 2/13th Battalion. The new garrison was composed of the British 70th Division, the Polish Carpathian Brigade, and the 32nd Army Tank Brigade.

Its task in Operation "Crusader" was to sally forth from the fortress on the morning of November 20 and drive its way through to El Duda, a point on the ridge about three miles northwest of Sidi Rezegh and approximately the same distance from Bel Hamed. Having done this, it was to hold open this corridor and cut the enemy's lines of communication along the Axis by-pass road.

All through the 19th the men of the garrison sat waiting and listening to the gunfire. But that evening when no signal came from Norrie, they resigned themselves to another bitterly cold night in their posts behind the perimeter wire. The next day, Scobie received the order to break out at dawn on November 21. But this order was tragically premature, for by the time it reached the fortress headquarters everything had started to go wrong for the 8th Army.

Suddenly, Rommel reacted violently to the capture of Sidi Rezegh and hurled the full weight of his armour against the 7th Armoured Brigade and the 4th Armoured Brigade Group. This savage assault changed the whole situation. Now it became a question whether our armour could hold out on the high ground at Sidi Rezegh until the Tobruk garrison could reach El Duda.

The Germans and Italians crouched in strongpoint "Tiger" facing the eastern perimeter, stiff and heavy-eyed after the long winter night's vigil, heard above the intermittent crash of gunfire, the eerie wail of pipes. Borne to them on the chilled dawn wind, the alien sound made their flesh creep, and with numbed fingers they gripped the triggers of their machine-guns and rifles.

Then, like phantom figures in the grey light, they saw

163

their attackers, fanning out to left and right of the tanks. Company upon company, with bayonets fixed, they came charging across the desert, yelling and screaming wild, high-pitched war-cries.

But these were not the mad Australians, whom the besiegers had grown to dread, or the Indians, who attacked at night with the stealth of panthers. They were wild men from north of the Border—the Black Watch—led into battle to the skirl of their pipes. What would the Englishers think of next? The men in "Tiger" had seen Yeomanry officers who led their men with walking-sticks and hunting horns. And, now, these savage Scots with their bagpipes! No wonder Rommel called them amateurs in war.

Even when their piper fell mortally wounded and the music of his pipes died with him in a last fearful screech, the men following him never faltered. On they came, howling like dervishes, their short bayonets glinting in the first light of the rising sun. As they met the first hail of fire from "Tiger," they leapt into the air to fall, kicking like shot rabbits, and then lie still. But there was no stopping them.

By the time they had overwhelmed "Tiger," half the 2nd Battalion of the Black Watch were casualties. But they went on to capture a second strongpoint, known to the garrison patrols as "Butch," and by the afternoon they had taken more than a thousand prisoners, of whom the majority were German. By nightfall, the garrison troops had shortened the distance between themselves and their objective to seven miles. But the enemy's defences were deeper and stronger than had been expected. Furthermore, they were held by Rommel's crack troops brought up for his assault on the fortress. The minefields, too, were thick on the ground, and these, together with the heavy guns, inflicted fearful damage on our tanks, so that it was soon apparent that there was no chance of reaching El Duda by the following day.

Although in Tobruk Scobie had only the haziest idea what was happening at Sidi Rezegh and to the east of Capuzzo, he was left in little doubt that things were not going according to plan with the relieving force. But, by the morning of November 22, the Garrison Commander was in a predicament. His small force of tanks had taken a terrible hammering in the sortie and were sadly in need of maintenance. Without their support, his infantry could make little impression on the enemy's strongpoints. Casualties had been high, the ground gained was thinly held, and there was no telling that if Rommel discovered this, he might not launch an attack against Tobruk at any moment.

But, although Scobie could not know it, Rommel had even more ambitious plans. Flushed with his success against the British armour at Sidi Rezegh, he sent for General von Ravenstein, in command of the 21st Panzer Division, telling him somewhat melodramatically that he was to be given the chance of ending the campaign that very night.

Ravenstein's orders were to take tanks, motorized infantry, and mobile artillery and anti-tank guns, and make a dash for the frontier. He was to look neither to right nor left, but push through and beyond the frontier wire and then swing northward to Sollum. While Ravenstein was doing this, Rommel explained, another force from the 15th Panzer Division commanded by General Neumann-Silkow would follow up and attack General Cunningham's headquarters at Fort Maddalena, while a third force would move east to capture the railhead at Bir Habata with its supply dumps.

Von Ravenstein's force dashed headlong eastwards, shooting up everything in sight. It outflanked the 7th Armoured Division, and threw the 30th Corps headquarters into a state of confusion, so that its administrative and supply trucks turned and fled for the frontier like a flock of panic-stricken sheep before a pack of wolves. By the afternoon of November 24 the rot had set in, and hundreds upon hundreds of British vehicles were streaming eastwards, and they did not stop until they reached the boundary fence. So rapid was both the advance and the retreat that there were times when the fleeing British troops and the pursuing Germans passed and repassed one another in their trucks without recognition, and von Ravenstein's tanks and armoured cars actually swept by our two huge supply dumps at Bir El Gubi and Gabr Saleh and never spotted them. When von Ravenstein was told about them, after he was taken prisoner, he was amazed and said that if he had known of their existence the Axis would have won the battle.

By this dramatic thrust to the frontier Rommel hoped to cut our lines of communication, and so force Cunningham to withdraw right back to his starting point. Once he had achieved this, Tobruk would be at his mercy. And, first and foremost, Rommel's heart was set on capturing Tobruk.

In fact, Cunningham proposed calling off the offensive. To continue it might mean the destruction of his entire tank force and the loss of Egypt. Thus, Rommel's gamble so nearly came off. But he had reckoned without Auchinleck.

Rommel's raid deep behind the 8th Army's lines had left havoc in its wake. The 5th South African Brigade had been cut to ribbons, its headquarters overrun, vehicles blown to pieces and left burning, and some 4000 of its men were either prisoners or missing. Scattered all over the desert were units, which a few hours before had been holding part of a continuous line, now completely cut off. Little groups of guns and tanks, by-passed by the enemy, were stranded in the desert. Hospitals and field-dressing stations found themselves surrounded, their staffs taken prisoners and as quickly abandoned and left to treat British and Axis wounded alike. Their signals trucks destroyed, brigade and battalion commanders, at a loss for orders, manned the machine-guns along with their men, shooting up enemy tanks and armoured cars as they dashed by in a fog of dust. At Army Headquarters, intelligence officers buried their aching heads in their hands and gave up trying to plot the course of the battle.

Into the midst of all this utter confusion Auchinleck arrived by plane, accompanied by his Deputy Chief of Staff, Ritchie, and Tedder.

Faced with such chaos, a lesser man might have conceded to his Army Commander's proposal to withdraw from the battle while the going was good and while there yet remained some armoured units to be regrouped and re-fitted. But Auchinleck gave his categorical refusal to such a plan and issued orders to "attack and pursue the enemy with all available forces, regain Sidi Rezegh, and join hands with the Tobruk garrison," which was to co-operate by attacking the enemy on its front.

This was undoubtedly the Commander-in-Chief's finest hour, for by his refusal to accept even the possibility of defeat, he saved the day. Then he returned to Cairo where he immediately decided to relieve Cunningham of his command, since in his own words he had "reluctantly come to the conclusion that he was unduly influenced by the threat of an enemy counterstroke against his communications."

So at this crucial moment Cunningham went and Ritchie took his place. But from then on it was Auchinleck who fought the battle.

On November 25, Scobie received a signal at the Fortress Headquarters telling him that the 2nd New Zealand Division would make a concerted effort to reach Sidi Rezegh the next day, and that by then the garrison was expected to have captured El Duda. With his tanks hurriedly serviced, Scobie launched an attack early on the morning of the 26th, and after fierce fighting his infantry captured the last enemy strongpoint, "Wolf," between them and their objective. But there was still neither sight nor sound of Freyberg's New Zealanders.

At one o'clock the garrison troops saw some tanks on the horizon, and from the turret of one of them three red flares rose into the clear blue sky. There was a pause and then three more red flares burst above the tanks. As they did so, the men from Tobruk broke into wild cheers, for those six red flares were the 8th Army's recognition signal, and for the first time for seven months the troops from the beleaguered fortress were within sight of the relieving force.

From that moment the men of the Northumberland Fusiliers and Essex Regiment, supported by the tanks of the 32nd Army Tank Brigade, raced for El Duda. By four

167

o'clock that afternoon, after violent hand-to-hand fighting, they had driven the last of the Axis troops from the ridge and the corridor to Tobruk was open at last.

But all through that night the weary garrison troops clung grimly to their positions on the high ground. And it was not until the early hours of the morning of November 27 that the 19th New Zealand Battalion with a squadron of British "I" tanks battered their way through Sidi Rezegh and Bel Hamed to meet men from the fortress at El Duda crest. Then it was that General Godwin-Austin made his famous signal: "Corridor to Tobruk clear and secure. Tobruk is as relieved as I am."

But, once again, this jubilant signal was dangerously premature. For even while it was being despatched, Rommel was regrouping his tanks for another blow at the 8th Army.

On November 29, having gathered his strength together, he launched a major assault into the Sidi Rezegh-Bel Hamed-El Duda area with the 15th and 21st Panzer Divisions, supported by some Italian troops. His scheme was to cut right through the corridor from east and west simultaneously.

Fortunately, through an intercepted radio signal, the 8th Army was warned of Rommel's plan, and was able to muster some tanks to send into the attack. But it was touch and go whether the corridor could be held open. On the ridge at Bel Hamed and Sidi Rezegh, Freyberg's troops, probably the finest fighters in the Western Desert, resisted all the enemy attacks. But at El Duda, the 1st Battalion of the Essex Regiment, finding themselves up against a strong force of German heavy tanks, were forced to give ground.

When night fell it looked as if the western wall of the corridor might cave in altogether and the garrison be forced to rétire within the perimeter again. For eight of Scobie's fourteen infantry battalions were already trying to hold the corridor, thinly supported by the remainder. He then received a signal from 8th Army Headquarters, saying: "At all cost corridor must be held."

Scobie had only one fresh battalion in reserve—the 2/13th Australian. But it had been mutually agreed between

Blamey and Auchinleck that only in an emergency were the Diggers to be committed to battle. Now, however, there was an emergency and a desperate one, and so Scobie sent for the Battalion Commander, Lt.-Colonel "Bull" Burrows.

On paper, he said, the 2/13th no longer existed on the garrison's strength, but, in fact, it was still there, and now, no matter what promises had been made in high places, he was calling upon the Diggers to fight once more for Tobruk.

By six o'clock that evening Colonel Burrows had given his orders for the battalion to move out to El Duda immediately. Two and a half hours later the troops were on their way to the gap in the perimeter to rendezvous with their Commanding Officer, who had gone ahead to contact the Commander of the 16th Infantry Brigade, under whose command they would be.

As they passed through the perimeter wire the oldest inhabitants of the fortress felt a strange thrill—a strange sense of unreality—at driving through the wire in their vehicles, instead of crawling through it on their bellies as they had done so often before.

At "Tiger" strongpoint the convoy halted to await the arrival of another convoy and their escort of armoured cars. Then, at midnight, in the bitter cold, they set off across the eight miles of desert to their positions on the eastern slopes of El Duda, where they were to spend the night.

Their orders were to attack at 11 o'clock the following morning, through the positions held by the Essex Regiment, over some 4000 yards of open country, and to drive the enemy from the lower slopes of Sidi Rezegh.

At first light, the Australians found they were bivouacked on a long low hill, and soon discovered that this position was within range of an enemy heavy battery. Moreover, this proved to be a German battery whose gunners plastered their positions with high and low angle salvoes, forcing the Diggers to scratch shallow holes in the rocky ground with their bare hands to escape the shrapnel raining down on them.

That day the Australians' orders were repeatedly countermanded as the battle for the corridor ebbed and flowed, and all the time they were under heavy shell-fire from the German artillery and tanks.

By dark, when they were due to attack again, Burrows spotted two dozen German tanks ahead of him. While his men took cover, he went back to call up the garrison's tanks. Six of the latter attacked, but the Germans could not be shifted, so Burrows called for artillery support. The heavy barrage knocked out two of the enemy tanks, setting them ablaze, and as the others retired the Australians prepared to attack. As they did so, they were joined by odd troops from the Essex Regiment determined for revenge.

As the moon waned, Burrows gave his men their last orders, telling them to yell "The Australians are coming!" as they charged. And yell they did, as they raced up the slope in the darkness, leaving the lumbering "I" tanks behind them. Ahead they could hear the enemy chattering excitedly and recognized the words: *"Englander kommen!"*

Then, by the livid green light from a Very pistol and to a shout of "Come on, Aussies!" they went in with hand grenades and fixed bayonets.

The odds were more than four-to-one against them, but the sheer weight of their charge overwhelmed the Germans before they had a chance to resist. Indeed, the attack was over so quickly that, except for those in the immediate vicinity, the Germans did not realize El Duda had been recaptured. Throughout the rest of the night the Australians and the Royal Horse gunners were shooting up Staff cars and trucks as they drove unsuspectingly up to their positions.

During the mopping-up after the attack, Private Clarrie Jones took a German captain prisoner. The latter demanded to know the name of Jones's regiment, and, when told, refused to believe it. All the Australians had left Tobruk, he declared knowingly. In the fading moonlight Jones thrust his metal shoulder-titles under his prisoner's nose, and told him to look for himself.

But the German laughed. *"Ach!* You are the English dressed as Australians to frighten us!" he insisted.

For two days the 2/13th held their position at El Duda

before they were withdrawn and their place taken by the 4th Battalion of the Border Regiment. Later, they left in convoy for Tobruk.

> "Never did we dream, during those weary months of siege," Lt.-Colonel Colvin wrote afterwards, "that we would ever welcome a return to the perimeter, but it was with a feeling of relief that we finally passed through the perimeter wire to take over a position from the Durham Light Infantry, astride the El Adem Road."

Day after day the two armies fought for those ridges around Tobruk. When El Duda resisted, Rommel switched his armour against Bel Hamed and Sidi Rezegh, and under the weight of his attacks we were driven from both these positions. Now, although the garrison troops still clung resolutely to El Duda, Tobruk was once more surrounded.

Next, Rommel made a desperate bid to relieve his troops bottled up in Capuzzo and Bardia. But now Auchinleck was at Desert Headquarters, and never for one moment did he allow his armour to rest. His orders were: "Attack everything you see, and keep on attacking." And the "Jock" columns, small roving tank formations that took their name from Brigadier "Jock" Campbell, V.C., one of the finest of all desert fighters, constantly harried Rommel's flank, racing into the attack and off again before the Germans realized what was happening. In this battle of thrust and counterthrust the initiative slowly but relentlessly passed to the 8th Army.

In daylight, Rommel's armour was ceaselessly set upon by the R.A.F., while night after night our bombers went forth to raid his supply bases.

In the first days of December the New Zealanders retook Bel Hamed, while the 4th Border Regiment repulsed no fewer than three heavy attacks on El Duda. On December 5, our fighters reported shooting up huge concentrations of enemy transports all heading west past Tobruk. Two days later, the 11th Hussars from Sidi Rezegh and the South Africans moving up from Bardia joined hands again

171

with the garrison, and it was the turn of the Axis reconnaissance planes to report huge concentrations of enemy transports moving west towards Tobruk.

On the night of December 9–10, the Polish Brigade captured Ras El Meduuar in the Salient, and by the next morning stood triumphantly on Hill 209.

After 242 days of siege the fortress of Tobruk had been relieved.

Duel in the Desert

The Germans had been winning on the European mainland. By the end of May, 1941, they had occupied Yugoslavia, and ousted the British from Greece and Crete. Remnants of the British forces were brought to Egypt. Churchill urgently wanted an offensive to destroy Rommel's forces before the Germans could reinforce him. When he didn't get decisive action, Churchill transferred the desert command to Gen. Auchinleck who, during the autumn of 1941, gained back most of the area along the coast that Wavell had lost. Rommel, unlike the Italians before him, was retreating in good order. He built up his supplies, was reinforced by stronger air elements, and immediately struck back. By January, 1942, he had launched a drive that pushed the British back across Libya again, this time taking Tobruk along the way. On June 24th, Rommel crossed the Egyptian frontier and pushed onward; by the time he reached a position before El Alamein, his lines of communication were over-extended, and he couldn't mount the new attack he needed to break through to Cairo.

The desert war, about to enter its climactic phase, had become a conflict between fast-moving armored and motorized forces. As Churchill says, * "Tanks had replaced the cavalry of former wars . . . the fighting quality of the armored column, like that of a (naval) cruiser squadron, rather than the position where they met . . . was the decisive feature. Tank divisions or brigades . . . could form fronts in any direction so swiftly that the perils of being outflanked or taken in the rear or cut off had a greatly lessened significance. On the other hand, all depended from moment to moment upon fuel and ammunition and the supply of both was far more complicated for armored forces than for self-contained ships and squadrons at sea."

The desert fighting gave both sides a chance to perfect the art of

* *The Grand Alliance* by W. S. Churchill, pp. 557-558, published by Houghton Mifflin Co.

the hit and run raid, slicing clean through the porous defenses. During the autumn of 1942, counterattacks and raids flourished at El Alamein. A typical daredevil raid is reported in the following exploit behind Rommel's lines.

BEHIND ROMMEL'S LINES

by Capt. Douglas M. Smith
(as told to Cecil Carnes)

A British undercover man in Nazi-held Tobruk had reported to headquarters that the enemy had established an airfield outpost somewhere east of the town. He didn't know exactly where it was located, but he knew that every Saturday at dusk a fleet of supply trucks left Tobruk and headed for the outpost. So a party of our men, consisting of a captain, a sergeant and ten privates, volunteered to locate it and blow it to smithereens. They had about 500 miles to negotiate by truck, from our headquarters at Kabrit, Egypt, to the desert objective, and a patrol of Messerschmitts almost spoiled the party as it was stopped in a wadi for tea on the second day out. When the noise of their engines was heard, a camouflage net was hastily thrown over the truck and the men scattered. The enemy patrol, flying at only 1,000 feet, roared across the wadi and continued on. The truck must have looked like a pile of sand to the pilots.

It was a nerve-racking day. The fierce July sun drew out a man's juice, then boiled him in it. The heavily laden truck was stuck twice in patches of soft sand. The second time the churning wheels dug themselves in hub deep, requiring an hour of frantic shoveling to set them rolling again. A lone Nazi patrol plane, hunting for just such ground activity as this, caught them cold in an open, carpet-flat expanse. They spent a hideous hour beneath burlap

174

camouflage mats, tormented by heat and thirst and flies, till the enemy pilot, wearied of describing aimless circles above a seemingly deserted area and droned away to the northwest.

Yet they made fair progress between delays, and did particularly well that night, by blundering onto a camel road from which the boulders had been removed. The succeeding day, too, was kind, so that the captain grunted with satisfaction as he checked their position that evening on his large-scale map.

"Barring an out-and-out catastrophe," he announced, sipping a steaming cup of tea, "we'll be near enough to our immediate goal by Saturday morning so we can cover up and sleep all day. That way we'll be fresh as daisies for the night's task."

The immediate goal was a curve some thirty miles east of Tobruk, along the coast road which was Rommel's main line of communication. It was known that at some point along the coast road, to the east of the town, the truck convoy customarily turned off into the desert. It was the raiding party's job to get into that convoy in the dark somehow —and this particular curve seemed the best place—and travel with it to the airfield outpost.

It worked out as the officer had hoped. At dusk on Saturday evening the truck was parked discreetly in a small deep ravine, out of sight of the coastal road, but not twenty yards from it. A sharp-eyed sentinel with the field glasses established himself on a bluff overlooking the road. An hour later, he came slithering down to announce he had spotted twelve sets of dimmed driving lights approaching in the distance.

"Every man to his place in the truck," said the officer, and waited till the order had been obeyed. "Now I'll let you in on the rest of our program. These trucks will be traveling, as usual, about a hundred yards apart. We will let eleven go by. Before Number Twelve comes in sight around the bend, we will cut into the road and fall in line."

"Mightn't it be better, sir, if we let all twelve go by and then fell in at the rear?" the sergeant asked.

"No," said the captain. "The men on the twelfth truck

will know they're the last in line. They'd probably be sus·· picious if another car turned up suddenly behind them. As it is, Number Eleven will think we're Number Twelve, and Number Twelve will think we're Number Eleven. Right? . . . When we reach the jerry camp, there are bound to be sentries at the entrance. We can't risk one of them noticing thirteen trucks, instead of the expected dozen. So, when we find ourselves getting close to the camp— and we're bound to see or hear some sign of it ahead—we break down in the middle of the road, blocking it. Jerry Number Twelve comes up, stops and asks what the trouble is. Well, we tell him—with knives. Then we park our truck beside the road, where it will be our rallying point for after the show. Privates Brewster and Guffey will stay with the car, ready to use the machine gun, if necessary, to cover our escape. Private Jones will take that gadget Captain Crumper prepared for us and proceed according to orders already given him." Captain Crumper was the explosives instructor at Kabrit. He had a fine, devilish sense of mischief.

"I think they're coming, sir," said Sam Barrett, the driver. His head was sticking out sidewise in the direction of the road. "I can hear somethin' that sounds like 'em."

"Right. Get your engine going, quietly. The noise they're making themselves will drown out ours. Be ready to start when I give the word. . . . You eight men in the back there, get down in the truck and pull the camouflage net over you. Every man check his equipment—canteen, iron ration, knife, revolver, bombs and two grenades. . . . That's Étienne Latour beside you at the rear, sergeant? Good. Better start chinning in German, you two—be in practice if you need it later. And if anything goes wrong, use your knives! One shot would give the show away."

"Here they are, sir!" whispered Barrett.

The dimmed driving lights of a truck swept into view around the curve, followed by another and another. Leaning forward to peer through the dark, the driver was studying the intervals between the units of the convoy as they flashed past the mouth of the wadi at an easy thirty-mile

176

gait. He reported his findings with satisfaction. "Keeping a bit better than a hundred yards between 'em, sir."

"That's a break," muttered the captain. "Get ready, Sam!" He began counting aloud in a tense whisper: "Eight ... nine ... ten. ... Here comes eleven. ... Now!"

The truck shot out from the ravine as if the word had cut some invisible leash. A lurch or two, a few stiff jolts, and it took the highway smoothly, pointing east, some forty yards behind the jerry ahead and comfortably in advance of the one yet to round the curve.

"They're using no taillights!" exclaimed the captain. "Douse ours, quick!"

"Doused already, sir," was the reply from Sam Barrett. "I'd noticed it myself, sir."

"Good man! Now keep your fingers crossed for the next two or three minutes."

He crossed his own, blushing inwardly for his childish superstition. He kept his head turned, staring back at jerry No. 12, which had come out of the curve and was trailing by a scant fifty yards. The captain held his breath. What was the driver of No. 12 thinking? What had he thought when he straightened out from the curve and discovered himself so close to the truck ahead? Would he think No. 11 had fallen off the pace? Would he think he had been driving too fast himself? These Nazis were such methodical devils—would he speed up to investigate?

No. 12 was dropping back! His speed checked perceptibly till he was the required hundred meters to the rear. The captain's pent-up breath escaped in a long sigh of relief. He uncrossed his fingers and rubbed the palms of his hands on his trousers. He swallowed hard and was himself again.

"We'll be meeting Tobruk-bound trucks, I expect," the captain said. "Keep your eyes peeled."

They did presently meet a string of six empty lorries, coming head-on and presumably returning to their base from the German front for further supplies of men or matériel. They rattled past with a genial blinking of lights that Sam Barrett politely acknowledged with blinks of his own, and then the sergeant threw his voice over his shoulder

177

cautiously, "Got a look at Number Twelve in their head-light glare, sir. Small open truck—not much of a load, I'd say—bit of canvas pulled over it. Two men on the front seat, sir."

Twenty minutes later there was an alarm that turned the captain colder than the night itself. It was three short blasts from the horn of No. 12.

The sergeant's voice was anxious as he reported, "Number Twelve put on speed a moment ago, sir. He's overhauling us fast. I think he meant that horn as a signal for us to stop!"

Another short, querulous blast from the German truck.

The captain forced himself to speak coolly, "We'd best pull up. Sergeant, this is your baby, I think. Let Latour do the talking. If a situation arises, meet it according to your best judgment. No more noise than necessary."

"We'll manage, sir," said the sergeant.

Their truck drew over to the side of the road and stopped. Twenty yards to the rear, the German did the same, and the man seated beside the driver jumped to the ground and came forward afoot. Outlined in the faint gleam of the truck lights behind him, his figure showed bulky and powerful.

The Nazi came within a yard of the truck. The sergeant and Étienne Latour sat motionless, their legs over the tail-board, their hands gripping their knives.

The German halted. He spoke, "Please, has anybody here got a match?"

"There isn't a bleedin' match in th' bunch except English," whispered Sam Barrett to the man next to him.

Étienne Latour, who had been born and raised in Alsace, replied in German. "I am sorry, my friend, but neither my comrade nor I has a match. However, here is a lighter which I will gladly lend you."

The captain moaned to himself. Latour's lighter was of French make.

Latour's voice went on serenely, "Please, you must be careful of it and give it back to me later, *hein?* I treasure it highly. It is a French lighter that I took from the body of a French major at Bir Hacheim." He hesitated, then

178

added a detail with the delicate care of an artist. "I bayoneted him myself," he said.

The Nazi grunted his appreciation. *"So!* You were at Bir Hacheim? It must have been fun to stick those dirty French! I have heard they leave slime on one's bayonet instead of blood! Thank you, comrade; I will return your war trophy without fail." An impatient toot from truck No. 12 sped his departure. He called back gruffly. *"Auf wiedersehen!"*

"Auf wiedersehen!" said Étienne Latour.

"Get going, Sam," said the captain rather weakly. "Bear down on it, lad!" He was silent a minute or two while Barrett stepped on the gas, anxious to regain their ordained position before somebody came back to see where they were.

Twenty minutes more and the convoy swung sharply off the coast road to the south. The going was rougher, yet not too bad. It was obvious to the captain that the Germans had done a spot of roadwork. When they came to a steep wadi, the way down was cleared of rocks and the way up on the other side was surfaced with cord matting to afford traction.

He slid back the shield on his luminous wrist watch. It was eleven o'clock. He raised his glasses, and every time the truck mounted a rise he peered hopefully into the black distance. He didn't believe the jerries would go too deep into the desert just to establish a casual camp and airport, and he was right. At the end of an hour, the invisible track they were following topped a height and showed a cluster of pinpoint lights making a pale yellow circle in the blackness.

He announced the news quietly, without lowering his glasses, "That's it, Barrett. Half mile ahead."

"Yes, sir." Mindful of his officer, whose attention was distracted from the road, Barrett added, "Watch out, sir; we're just dipping into a wadi."

"Stop when you get to the bottom and park us across the road," the captain ordered, "as if we'd lost control and skidded, eh?"

The truck stopped with a jolt. A twist of Barrett's wrists

set the truck diagonally across the route, with one of two great rocks at each end.

Bumping and clattering, No. 12 came charging on. Barrett, standing alongside his truck and pretending it was disabled, swung the powerful beam of his flashlight straight into the faces of the two men on No. 12, thereby accomplishing three desirable results. It deepened the darkness in which the sergeant and Latour were lurking behind a rock; it blinded the two Germans, so that they halted their truck with a squealing of brakes; it startled and infuriated them, and angry men lose caution. Grumbling in gutturals, they jumped to the ground, one from each side of the cab. For luck, Sam Barrett gave them both another blinding flash from his torch.

They died quietly. The sergeant and Étienne Latour wiped and sheathed their knives, then hurriedly lugged their victims out of the roadway.

The captain began giving orders, "Tumble out, everybody! Into the jerries' truck! Make it nippy, men! . . . Barrett, get our truck parked fifty yards up the wadi; that will be our rallying point after the raid."

Latour, who was familiar with German truck controls, took the wheel and No. 12 took out after the convoy again.

"You know your mission," the captain went on. "Scatter, keep in the darkest areas as much as possible, set your fuses for thirty minutes, plant your bombs where you think they'll do the most damage. Bateson, Connolly and I will locate the airfield and fix the planes. . . . Jones, you're ready back there with Captain Crumper's gadget? We'll drop you off just before we reach the camp. Couple of minutes now."

No. 12 kept going at a rate which brought it up presently to its proper distance from No. 11. The trucks in the van of the convoy had already disappeared through a gap in what seemed a fence. Private Jones was the first to leave No. 12.

"Right-o, Jones! On your way, and good luck."

"Yes, sir. Good hunting, sir!" A thump and a metallic clunk from the tin container he was carrying announced Private Jones' contact with the desert. Since Brewster and

Guffey were back in the British truck with the machine gun, acting as rearguard and reserve, the party was now reduced to nine.

No. 12 lumbered through a broad gap in a triple fence of barbed wire. The sentries at each side were leaning idly on their rifles, looking at the vehicle incuriously. By the time No. 12 came into the parking space, the men of No. 11 were walking away from the dark bulk of their charge, heading for tobacco and coffee and beer.

A moment later, the driver shut off the engine and put out his headlights. Over his shoulder, the officer gave the order to jump out.

"I think I've spotted the airfield, sir," Bateson whispered. "Got a glimpse against the sky of a pole with what looks like a wind sleeve on it."

They slid through the night. Cautiously, they made a wide detour around the one building that showed signs of human life. A hum of voices came from it, and a paper-thin strip of light from an otherwise closely shuttered window. It was a cookhouse. They reached the airfield without incident and halted for a brief survey.

"Planes dispersed around the edges, of course," murmured the captain. "Connolly, you circle the field to the left. I will go this way. . . . Bateson, there's a group of buildings down at that end; pilots' quarters or repair shops, probably. Take care of them. When you've used up all your bombs, you two, don't hang around waiting for me. Leg it for our truck and hop aboard."

Left to himself, the captain swung to the right for his tour of the field. Presently he found what he was looking for—a wall of rubble and logs and rocks. Tucked behind it were nine planes—bombers and fighters. With typical attention to symmetry and neatness, the Germans had lined them up in threes, their wing tips almost touching. The captain placed one bomb in the center plane of each trio and went on his way rejoicing. He found two more revetments, but to his disappointment there were only three planes in the first and just one in the second. Still, that brought his total up to thirteen. If Connolly did as well, the night's bag would be something to shout about.

He tucked one of his two remaining bombs into the vitals of a small tractor which was probably used for odd jobs around the field. The other he placed under a tool shed. Then he turned and went back over the path by which he had come, moving in the same swift and stealthy fashion.

The officer was abreast of the cookhouse when it happened.

Out of the darkness near the building came a loud, harsh challenge in German, "Halt there! Who are you? Hands up! Quick, somebody! A light here! I've got—"

The shout ended on a gasp. But the alarm had been given. The cookhouse door was flung open and a dozen men boiled out. An arc light flashed on, illumining the whole area. It showed a thickset man on the ground, and another just yanking a dagger from the huddled body. The man with the knife headed for the nearest darkness, running like a frantic deer. Six or seven of the cookhouse contingent chased after him.

When beyond the circle of light, the captain whipped out his revolver and fired at the leading pursuer. The Nazi fell, rolling over and over. The men at his heels dropped in their tracks, flattening their bodies on the ground.

Lights were springing on everywhere. The post was a bedlam of shouting. Then, as the captain sprinted for the exit, from a point in the desert just beyond the southern boundary of the camp came an ear-splitting racket. The staccato explosions rose and fell convincingly, settled to a steady roar, then died away. No more than thirty seconds, just long enough for Private Jones to race away, elapsed between the revolver shot and the moment when Captain Crumper's special gadget went into action.

While the Germans were giving tongue to the south, the raiders made haste to escape to the east. The captain was about thirty yards from the gap in the barbed wire by which they had driven in. He remembered the two guards, and the lamp at one side which lighted the vicinity. He hugged the shadows and went slowly forward, revolver in hand. He stood still when the gap was in clear view. The light was still burning. That meant a nasty twenty-yard sprint in full view of anyone who happened to be around; the unattractive alternative was a try at breaking through or climbing the fences. Hardly practicable, with every passing second cutting into his margin of safety. The truck would not wait long, even for the party leader, nor would he want his men to risk their lives for a laggard. He must make a dash for it. Where the devil were those guards?

Abruptly, he saw them. One was stretched full length on the ground in the straight shadow of a fence post. Across the gap the other was doubled over the top strand of barbed wire, a monstrous human clothespin, his arms and legs dangling grotesquely. Guerrillas had passed that way. The captain put his head down and sprinted into the desert.

The wadi at last. The truck should be fifty yards to his right and a bit farther on. Rashly, he left the road and tried for a short cut. In half a minute he was lost. He stood, panting, a little more nervous than he cared to admit, even to himself. He looked about him and saw only darkness; he listened, and heard nothing. He drew in his breath sharply. Could the truck have gone?

Ears as keen as his own were listening too. Perhaps they had heard his stumbling step. Through the darkness, not at all from the direction he expected, came the softly whistled refrain of a barrack-room ditty then popular in the camp at Kabrit. He whistled it back, and his spirits revived. In a minute he was with his men, asking for reports.

"Three missing, sir," said the sergeant. "No use going back to look for them, sir. They copped it fair. I saw it. Four of us, including Sam Barrett, got twisted and came up against the wire. I found a hole and turned to call them. Then a light went on somewhere. There was a burst of machine-gun fire." The sergeant cleared his throat. "That's all, sir."

With Connolly at the wheel, the truck moved out of the wadi. The officer jumped out when the big car was safely over the sky line. He called his men and led the way back to the crest. "May as well see some of the show," he said, adding, "after all, we paid our admission."

They crouched, looking back in the direction of the Nazi camp. They were barely settled before the night split open in a crimson burst of flame that streamed to the heavens.

A crashing report almost deafened them, a concussion shivered the air, and even at that distance shook the ground beneath them.

"That's Number Twelve, the bus we rode in," said the sergeant. "The first half-hour bomb was planted in her."

With No. 12 still hurling destruction in every direction as lot after lot of ammunition exploded, a minor sheet of flame shot up to the left. Then the show really hit its stride and pyrotechnical effects came too fast and close together to be identified. There were two more major upheavals. One appeared to be a second truck of explosives possibly fired by burning debris from No. 12. The other was a thunderous fiery catclysm. The sergeant said he believed it was an ammunition dump he had mined.

A big stack of gasoline tins sent a great curtain of flame to the sky. By its light, the officer was able to get a clear view of the scene through his glasses. He ran over the score in his mind: twenty planes, an ammunition dump, two truckloads of ammunition and explosives, storehouses of food and miscellaneous supplies, a tractor, the gasoline dump, officers' quarters, a big barracks; he didn't try to estimate the number of smaller buildings and tents demolished. Against it he set the loss of three men killed in action, and the balance did not please him.

"They'll rebuild this camp," he said. "Now that we know the way here, I'd like to come back in a week or ten days and do a really good job."

They did just that, and blew it to pieces again without losing a man.

The Tide Turns

The El Alamein stalemate dragged on. In July, 1942, Churchill himself went to Cairo to relieve Gen. Auchinleck; he appointed Gen. Alexander as Commander of the Middle East Forces, and Gen. Montgomery as Commander of the 8th Army. October 23rd was picked as the jumping-off date against Rommel. The British 8th Army got major reinforcements. Two new divisions arrived from Britain, the armor grew to over 1,000 tanks—half of them Grants and Shermans furnished by the U.S.—and a powerful artillery concentration was put together.

The air force of fighters and bombers now totaled 1,200 planes, and the R.A.F. flew air strikes against troops, communications, convoys and airfields. The Royal Navy harassed Axis shipping, sinking more than 200,000 tons trying to reach Rommel.

The way the troops lived in the desert, waiting for the attack to develop, is described by Maj. H. P. Samwell, author of *An Infantry Officer with the Eighth Army*. He was then a lieutenant with the Argyll and Sutherland Highlanders, slated to lead his platoon in the attack on Rommel October 23rd. (Maj. Samwell was later killed in the Ardennes salient on January 12, 1945.) He wrote:

"Early in October we had taken over a sector in the front just above Alamein Station, a single railroad line which ran parallel to a road which was little more than a track. North of this line there was a further expanse of desert and then the main road to Mersa Matrûh, a modern tarred highway. On the far side of this were cliffs leading down to the long stretch of white sand bordering the sea.

"We had lived in boxes, i.e., large areas capable of holding a complete brigade boxed in on all sides by minefields with several recognizable exits. We were beginning to get used to the sun, but the flies were appalling. One couldn't raise a piece of bread and jam from plate to mouth without being covered with flies. They buzzed around one's head, eyes, mouth and ears. Every precaution was taken with food, latrines, etc., but it was difficult to stop men from throwing rubbish away or even not using latrines during the night, when they had to go anything up to fifteen times (from dysentery) and at night it was quite possible to get lost by moving just fifty yards from one's 'bivy,' so completely featureless was the desert. The training was dreadfully hard and monotonous and nearly all of us were feeling ill in varying degrees."

The task facing the 8th Army was to rip a hole in the German line. It was decided that a night engagement was preferable for the break-through, when a full moon would be up. A path through the mines had to be cleared before the infantry and armor could proceed.

On October 23rd, one thousand guns commenced firing on the German frontal positions. Sgt. J. K. Brown, a mortarman with the 8th Army, in an article that appeared in *The Saturday Evening Post* in 1943, describes the opening barrage:

"At 2140 hours a wide half moon of flashes rent the night sky to the zenith. An instant later the first ear-splitting crash of that perfectly co-ordinated fire order tumbled from the sky. Backward and forward the guns flickered and flashed as battery after battery opened fire. For twenty minutes the mighty artillery concentration roared and hammered a deafening chorus. The sound of thousands of shells falling on the enemy was like the sound of a hailstorm in a city of corrugated iron with the rumble of 10,000 drums. It was appalling."

Then the mortars joined in: "with a hiss and a cloud of sparks, the first salvo leaped from the mortar batteries in what was to be heaviest mortar barrage ever directed against any one position. At the same instant a regiment of heavy machine guns began to add their shrill clamor now to the almost indescribable uproar. Half a million rounds were to pour from the muzzles before cease fire. At 25 minutes to 2 the barrage lifted. The gun crews were exhausted and the barrels were so hot they burned through the thick gloves of the men who handled them.

"For minutes after the barrage ceased there was silence—complete silence. Then of a sudden a weird thin cry rose out of the ground ahead of us. It was the shout of the charging infantrymen. Slowly the sound grew in volume until it was something no longer human. I felt my hair bristle as I listened.

"Scores of bright illuminating flares began to dance along the enemy lines and machine guns raked the minefields and forward slopes of the long ridge. The action was taking place ahead of me and I could see nothing; but presently wounded men, some walking, some on stretchers, began to drift past us. Prisoners came in, and the first accounts of the action with them."

186

ATTACK AT EL ALAMEIN

by Maj. H. P. Samwell

It was part of the battle plan that Rommel should
be made to expect that the main attack would come in the
south across the ground recently fought over in his own
attack. In order to strengthen that belief the whole division
and many others were first moved south, where we camped
in an area which had been made to look as obviously as
possible like a concentration area. Dummy trucks and tanks
were scattered about, and large numbers of real trucks and
armoured cars were concentrated here. The German reconnoitring planes duly came over and reported these concentrations; then on the night of the 22nd-23rd October we
quietly moved back north and took up positions already
dug for us just behind the front. Strict orders were given
that there was to be no movement after dawn, and for a
whole day we had to lie cramped in temporary slit trenches
waiting for night. We could not even move out to relieve
nature, and one can imagine the discomfort we suffered.

The tension was almost unbearable and the day dragged
terribly. I spent the time going over and over again the plan
of attack, memorising codes and studying the over-printed
map which showed all the enemy positions from the air.
Oddly enough, though keyed up, I did not feel any fear
at this time, rather a feeling of being completely impersonal, as if I were waiting as a spectator for a great event in
which I was not going to take any active part.

After dark there was tremendous activity: last-minute
visits by commanders and minor adjustments in plans. And

This selection is condensed from two chapters of the author's
An Infantry Officer with the Eighth Army.

then a hot meal was brought up. Most of us were too excited to eat much, but I felt better after I had had some hot soup. About 9 p.m. we moved forward and took up our positions on the start line—a taped line stretching across the open desert just in front of the forward positions. It was deathly still and a full moon lighted the bleak sand as if it were day. Suddenly the silence was broken by the crash of a single gun, and the next moment a mighty roar rent the air and the ground shook under us as salvo after salvo crashed out from hundreds of guns. Shells whined over our heads in a continuous stream, and soon we saw the enemy line lit up by bright flashes. One or two fires broke out and the ground became clearer than ever. It seemed a long time before the enemy started to reply, but finally they did so, weakly at first, then gradually growing in strength. I could imagine the German gunners having just settled in for another quiet night's sleep, tumbling out of their bivies bewildered and still half asleep. Some of them would never reach their guns, and others would arrive to find their guns blown sky high.

Still I felt the same impersonal air of a spectator. Both sides were concentrating on each other's gun-sites, and no shells landed anywhere near us. Time passed and the firing continued, sometimes dying down only to start again with increased intensity; then suddenly I noticed a difference—our shells were now passing very close over our heads and bursting, it seemed to me, only a couple of hundred yards ahead. It was the signal to prepare to advance; our guns were now shelling the enemy's forward positions. I looked at my watch and saw there was still three minutes to go. I felt ice cool, and remember feeling very grateful that I was. Oddly enough I don't remember the actual start—one moment I was lying on my stomach on the open rocky desert, the next I was walking steadily as if out for an evening stroll, on the right of a long line of men in extended order. To the right I could dimly see the tall thin figure of the major commanding the other forward company. He had a megaphone, and was shouting down the line, "Keep up there on the left—straighten up the line." I turned to my batman, who was walking beside me, and told him to run along the line and tell the sergeant in charge of the left-hand platoon to keep his direction from the right.

I suddenly discovered that I was still carrying my ash stick. I had meant to leave it at the rear Company H.Q. with the C.Q.M.S. and exchange it for a rifle. I smiled to myself to think I was walking straight towards the enemy armed only with a .38 pistol and nine rounds of ammunition. Well, it was too late to do anything about it now, but I expected that someone would soon be hit and I could take his. I began to wonder, still quite impersonally, who it would be; perhaps myself! in which case I wouldn't need a rifle. Then I heard a new sound above the roar of the guns and the explosion of shells. The sharp rat-tat-tat of Breda and Spandau machine-guns—streams of tracer bullets whined diagonally across our front, not more than twenty yards ahead. We must be getting near the first enemy positions. I asked the pace-checker on my right how many paces we had done. He grinned and said he had lost count; then crump-crump-crump! a new sharper note. This was something that affected us—mortar shells were landing right among us. I heard a man on my left say, "Oh, God!" and I saw him stagger and fall. The major was shouting again. I couldn't hear what he said, but his company seemed to be already at grips with the enemy. At that moment I saw a single strand of wire ahead about breast high. I took a running jump at it and just cleared it. My sergeant, coming behind, started to climb over it, and immediately there was a blinding flash and a blast of air struck me on the back of the neck. I never saw that sergeant again. I remember wondering what instinct had made me jump that wire. Strange? I hadn't been thinking of booby-traps. We had broken into a run now—why, I don't know. Nobody had given any order. A corporal on my left was firing his Bren gun from the hip. I wondered if he was really firing at anything. Then suddenly I saw a head and shoulders protruding from a hole in the ground. I had already passed it and had to turn half round. I fired my pistol three times, and then ran on to catch up the line.

The line had broken up into blobs of men all struggling together; my faithful batman was still trotting along beside me. I wondered if he had been with me while I was shooting. My runner had disappeared, though; and then I saw some men in a trench ahead of me. They were standing up with their hands above their heads screaming something that sounded like "Mardray." I remember thinking how dirty and ill-fitting their uniforms were, and smiled at myself for bothering about that at this time. To my left and behind me some of the N.C.O.s were rounding up prisoners and kicking them into some sort of formation. I waved my pistol at the men in front with their hands up to sign them to join the others. In front of me a terrified Italian was running round and round with his hands above his head screaming at the top of his voice. The men I had signalled started to come out. Suddenly I heard a shout of "Watch out!" and the next moment something hard hit the toe of my boot and bounced off. There was a blinding explosion, and I staggered back holding my arm over my eyes instinctively. Was I wounded? I looked down rather expecting to see blood pouring out, but there was nothing— a tremendous feeling of relief. I was unhurt. I looked for the sergeant who had been beside me; he had come up to take the place of the one who had fallen. At first I couldn't see him, and then I saw him lying sprawled out on his back groaning. His leg was just a tangled mess. I realised all at once what had happened: one of the enemy in the trench had thrown a grenade at me as he came out with his hands up. It had bounced off my boot as the sergeant shouted his warning, and had exploded beside him. I suddenly felt furious; an absolute uncontrollable temper surged up inside me. I swore and cursed at the enemy now crouching in the corner of the trench; then I fired at them at point-blank range—one, two, three, and then click! I had forgotten to reload. I flung my pistol away in disgust and grabbed a rifle—the sergeant's, I think—and rushed in. I believe two of the enemy were sprawled on the ground at the bottom of the square trench. I bayoneted two more and then came out again. I was quite cool now, and I started looking for my pistol, and thinking to myself there will be hell to pay with the quartermaster if I can't account for it. The firing had died down and groups of men were

190

collecting round me rather vaguely; just then a man shouted and fired a single round. I afterwards learnt that one of the enemy in the trench had heaved himself up and was just going to fire into my back when my man saw him and shot him first.

Our orders were to consolidate for fifteen minutes before moving on. I suddenly wondered what had happened to Company Headquarters and my company commander. He and I were the only two officers, commander and second-in-command. We had agreed that he should bring up Company H.Q. and the reserve platoon behind, while I led the forward platoons. I started to walk back, and at that moment the strange lull was abruptly ended by four shells exploding all round me. One covered me in sand, but I wasn't hurt; I found the company commander sitting on the ground trying to get through to Battalion H.Q. on the wireless. I gave him a quick report, but he was only half listening, still trying to get through. The commanding officer appeared from nowhere and asked him how things were going; the company commander replied and then turned to me. I told them we had taken the position and the men were lying resting and watching a few yards in front of the position. The commanding officer said, "Good work," and disappeared. The company commander said, "My God, you have left some pretty sights behind you; what was it like? I haven't fired a shot yet." I was quite surprised that he had seen the result of our fight, for I hadn't realised that we had been still advancing while fighting and had thought that the only positions had been those I had just left in front. I asked him to give me the reserve platoon and I would detail the right forward platoon to drop into reserve. There were very few of them left. He agreed, and I went forward again.

The stretcher-bearers were at work carrying the wounded to the battalion line of advance between the two forward companies. I remember reorganising the forward platoons, but again don't remember actually starting forward; I just found myself on the move. I heard the other company's piper starting to play just before we had bumped the enemy, and I wondered what had happened to our piper. I sent my new runner back to ask for him, but he never arrived, and the runner didn't return either. Afterwards I learnt he was wounded on the way.

All this time shells were landing among us, but suddenly there was a new danger: we were walking into our own barrage; shells were screaming above our heads and landing just in front of us. The platoon commander of the left platoon of the other company came across to me just at that moment and remarked, "We're going too fast; those are our shells, aren't they?" I agreed, and he went over to the major, his company commander, and warned him. At first the latter wouldn't agree to stop, but at that moment more shells of our own guns landed just in front and we felt the blast. I went across and persuaded him that we were ahead of time. We agreed to stop.

I pulled my men back a few yards to get completely out of the danger zone, and sent word back to my company commander asking him to come up closer. There was only supposed to be fifty yards between forward platoons and Company H.Q. and I couldn't see him. The runner reported that he couldn't find either the company commander or Company H.Q. or the reserve platoon. While my attention was on this, the other company had decided to advance again as the barrage had lifted. I didn't see them go and they failed to warn me. I found myself out in the "blue" alone with about forty men. I went over to the left flank to find out what had happened to the regiment that was supposed to be there. They weren't there, and I learnt afterwards that they never got past the first minefield.

My first feelings on realising that the company on my right had carried on without me was one of intense irritation, but when I discovered there was no one on my left either, my anger turned to fear. For the first time that night I was afraid; a nauseating wave of terror went right through me as I realised I was quite alone with the remains of two platoons; my company commander and Company H.Q. had disappeared together with the wireless; the "pilot" officer must have gone with the other company (we were sharing him). Instinct told me that I had gone too far to the left. All this time we had been steadily advancing

192

again, and I started to swing to the right. I was still scared stiff, not at the shells that were exploding round us, but at the thought of being all alone, cut off from the battalion and even my Company H.Q. I was to find—and so was the battalion later—that the failure of the unit on my left to keep up was to cost us dearly. We came to another enemy position; they surrendered without fighting, and we didn't waste time mopping up. I was so anxious to make contact with someone again. It appeared that many of the enemy at this position scuttled down the trenches to the left and remained in the gap where the unit on my left should have been, until we had passed, and then filtered back and shot up the reserve companies and Battalion H.Q. who were coming up behind. I was to be blamed for not finishing them off, but if I had attempted to chase them right across a battalion front I should have been hopelessly lost, while at the same time failing to secure my own objective.

I was still feeling terribly afraid and lonely when I heard a shout behind, and up came a platoon of the reserve company under the second-in-command, and with them was the remains of my own Company H.Q. What a wave of relief swept over me! Immediately the fear vanished. I had someone to discuss the position with. It appeared that a shell landed right among my Company H.Q. just after I had left it, badly wounding the company commander and laying out the signals; however, the reserve company's platoon had a wireless with them, so we were all right. The platoon commander told me I was still too far to the left, and we wheeled half-right. Soon we came to another enemy position, which we recognised as our final objective. The enemy put up a half-hearted fight here, but soon gave in; but most of them escaped to the left again, and again I didn't consider it advisable to chase them with the few men I had left. We advanced a further 300 yards and then started to dig in. There was still no sign of the other company, but I was convinced I was in the right place. I got through to Battalion H.Q. by wireless and reported myself in position. The officer who had joined me went off to reconnoitre, and returned shortly to say that the other forward company was already dug in 200 yards on our right.

I felt elated by this news. It was almost dawn before we were finally dug in. We were left completely unmolested by the enemy, and our own and their artillery had stopped firing. Apart from the occasional sounds of small-arms fire well to our right, everything was peaceful. After stand-to I posted sentries, and leaving my company sergeant-major in charge settled into a trench with the two signallers of the reserve company's platoon and went to sleep. The officer commanding the reserve platoon dug in near me.

I was wakened at 8:30 a.m. by my batman with some "breakfast"—half a tin of bully, two biscuits, and a mug of water. I made out reports of casualties, and then, crouching down gingerly, made my way towards the position which had been pointed out to me as Battalion H.Q. Gradually, as there was no sign of firing, I became more daring, and ended by walking normally up to the trench which the commanding officer and adjutant were sharing. It was very small, and their legs were all mixed up together. Just at that moment a tank away on the right started firing, and the shells whistled unpleasantly close by over my head. I hastily jumped into the trench, squatting precariously on the combined legs of the two occupants. I told the commanding officer the main events of the previous night and gave him the casualties, which were high. The adjutant offered me a swig of rum, and after he had pointed out where the ammunition dump was, I started back to the company, passing through the other forward company on the way and stopping a moment to compare notes. There was no sign of the enemy, though I was to learn later that they were less than 300 yards away.

About mid-day on Sunday, 25th October, the commanding officer called a conference; it was obvious to all that our position was precarious so long as the left flank remained exposed. It was decided that one reserve company should stride across the mouth of this gap and capture the original objective of the unit which had still failed to put in an appearance, thus bottling up an enemy element still left in the gap, and at the same time making contact with the unit which had gained its objective on the far side.

194

The attack was to be made early in the afternoon, but was cancelled at the last moment in favour of a three-company night attack timed for 10 p.m. that night. We returned to our company areas, and at this time the major who had led the company on my right was wounded by shrapnel. The loss of officers was already serious; the two original forward companies had two officers between them—myself and one captain transferred from the right reserve company. This company had a company commander and one subaltern left; the fourth company had been split up. One platoon, the one that had joined me the previous night under the second-in-command, was still with me; the rest of the company which had been detailed to come up on the tanks had disappeared together with the tanks. I learnt later that they had been held up by an unexpectedly large and uncharted minefield. The total strength of the rifle companies available was not more than 150 all ranks. Our senior N.C.O. casualties had been heavy also.

We lay in our holes during the afternoon; there was desultory shelling and mortar fire; some tanks came up, and, moving forward to a rise in the ground ahead of us, lined up as if for a review, and we were further depressed by the sight of one after the other being potted off like the sitting ducks they were. In the late afternoon, while we were dozing in our holes, the enemy mortar fire suddenly grew in intensity and shells exploded all round us. At first I thought it was a prelude to the expected counter-attack, but soon we were amazed to see a company of another battalion advancing in extended line diagonally across our front, parallel to the main enemy positions. As they came level with us the enemy opened up with machine-guns to support their mortars, and bullets hissed angrily over our heads as we crouched in our holes, occasionally peeping gingerly over the top to watch this extraordinary and unexpected performance. I was to learn later that our own H.Q. were as mystified as we were. Two or three men of this advancing force fell close to our positions, and we crawled out to pull them into our holes. When they had advanced about two hundred yards beyond us, they went to earth and burrowed themselves in. We never saw them again, and I never discovered how they came to be there.

The rest of the day passed uneventfully. At 9:30 p.m. we prepared to move to the start-line. Some rum had come up, but there was not enough for each man to get the regulation tablespoon swig. Most of the N.C.O.s and myself had to stand down. Just after we arrived at the start-line the two platoons of the missing company came up, and the platoon which had been with me left to rejoin its company. I had now only thirty-two men, a company sergeant-major, two corporals, and myself. I was in the centre with the two original reserve companies on each flank. It was brilliant moonlight and we must have been seen by the enemy before we started; also the last-minute arrival of the last company, and the other reserve company being on the start-line, caused a certain amount of noise and confusion, and before we started the enemy were firing at us.

We started to advance; this time we had no artillery support, for the object had been to surprise the enemy. An officer in a reconnoitring car had reported earlier that the position was only lightly held by frightened Italians who had tried to surrender to him, but as he was alone and under heavy shell-fire, he had been unable to stay to round them up. This was cheering news and we advanced confidently. We had only gone a few yards when streams of machine-gun tracer bullets whistled across our front, intersecting at a point about 100 yards directly ahead of us. The enemy were firing across our front on fixed lines; some mortars added to our discomfort, but we pressed on. It was a strange feeling approaching the first almost continuous stream of machine-gun tracer, knowing that the next step would take us into it; we crossed it with a few casualties, but looking to my flanks I discovered I was again alone, and the fear of the night before returned with the same sickening intensity. We could hear sounds of heavy firing and shouting on our left, and I guessed that the left-hand company had run into some enemy positions. There was no sign at all from the right-hand company.

We continued to advance, and then ahead I saw barbed wire: breaking into a trot we jumped over and started to

196

rush the positions we now saw clearly ahead. We saw German helmets, and I cursed that reconnoitring officer for his misleading information. A machine-gun opened up not more than fifteen yards half left from me; I saw the tracer bullets coming straight for me and I could clearly see the heads and shoulders of the three men manning the gun. The next second I felt a violent blow on my right thigh. I spun completely round and, recovering my balance, carried on; after going a dozen paces my leg suddenly collapsed under me and I fell forward. The men following, mistaking my involuntary action for intention, followed suit, and we lay there, about a dozen of us, not more than twenty yards from the enemy with bullets whistling over our heads. Although I found I couldn't get up, I felt no pain, and raising myself on one arm I shouted for them to rush in at the bayonet point. They did not respond at once; I think they were waiting for me to get up, and there were no N.C.O.s left. Then a corporal from the reserve section doubled up to me and asked what was happening. Almost incoherent with anger at the delay which was making our chances of taking the position less likely every moment, for the enemy were bound to realise soon how few there were of us, I shouted "Get in," and for the first time I remember I swore at my men. The company sergeant-major came up at that moment, and at the same time something little short of a miracle happened. The enemy shouted to us, and we saw that they had their hands up. The men jumped up and rushed in, and I dragged myself after them.

As I drew level with the machine-gun post three Germans jumped out and ran off as hard as they could. I had my pistol in my hand (I must have dropped my rifle when I fell). I fired four times, and saw one pitch forward on his face. The men then returned for me and carried me into a deep dugout and laid me on a bunk beside other wounded. The blankets were still warm from the bodies of the Germans who had been sleeping there. There was a tin of cold coffee on the floor, and a stretcher-bearer gave me a drink.

The company sergeant-major came in and reported that they had rounded up prisoners, including one officer. I asked him to help me out so that I could supervise the defence and interview the officer prisoner. I knew I must get some information at once, for we were in a dangerous position. At first the German wouldn't talk and I had to use a little persuasion. Finally I learnt that they were an Austrian unit with German officers and that they had been rushed up to relieve the Italians that evening after dusk; so the reconnoitring officer's report was true after all.

Just then I saw some of our own men and recognised the company sergeant-major of the right-hand company. He was going off at an angle beyond the position. I shouted to him to come over, but he shouted something I couldn't hear and carried on; then I heard shouting on my left, and the left-hand company came rushing in. I shouted for an officer, for I wanted to hand over quickly as I was feeling very faint. A subaltern came over and rather indignantly asked me what I wanted, saying I was keeping him back from the fighting. I answered rather irritably that the fighting was all over and I wanted him to take over the defence for the inevitable counter-attack which I was expecting any moment. He still answered aggressively, "Why the hell can't you do it? I have my own platoon to look after." The German officer was still standing by, and I felt furious that he should hear this stupid squabbling and prayed he couldn't understand English. I answered angrily, "I order you to take over at once. I am wounded." He said, "Oh! Sorry, I didn't realise." He went off and I lay down again, but I wasn't happy in this dug-out. I felt too closed in and wanted to know what was happening, and if we were to be overrun in the expected counter-attack I wanted a chance to defend myself. I called to my batman, and he helped me out and dug me a shallow hole on the perimeter of a slight rise. He brought me a Bren gun and told me that the company commander of the left company was organising all-round defence and there was no need to worry. I felt much happier with the gun and fired a few rounds to make sure it was O.K. There was a good deal of movement going on on my right, but I couldn't see anything. I heard what I thought was a carrier, and shortly after an N.C.O., who had gone out to reconnoitre on his own initiative, came back to report that there were two enemy anti-tank guns about 300 yards out, and he thought

198

they were preparing to fire on us. I told him to pass on this information to the left-hand company commander who was now in charge: he did so and returned shortly to say with disgust, "He isn't taking any action." I was puzzled, but I knew this company commander was an excellent officer and so presumed there was some reason.

The counter-attack didn't materialise, and later on I got two men to carry me farther into the perimeter, where they prepared a deep trench for me. Shortly after a wounded German was brought in. I got the men to bring him up to my trench and started to question him. He answered very listlessly; told me he was an Austrian, he was too old for active fighting, and that the officers were all Germans and they didn't get on with them. He kept asking when the doctor would be coming. The original plan was for Battalion H.Q. to move forward after us and come up when we had taken the position, so I told him quite cheerfully that we would both be safely in hospital before dawn. This cheered him up a lot, and he said he was glad he was out of it all. He told me he was a machine-gunner and pointed to the post where I had seen the three men running out, and I remembered I had shot one. I asked him where he was wounded, and he said, "In the back." This struck me as a coincidence; perhaps he was the very man that shot me and perhaps I had shot him, and now we were talking together like polite strangers in a railway carriage.

At this moment the enemy, who had obviously heard that we had captured the position, started mortaring us. It was deadly accurate and most uncomfortable. A trench nearby, with some light casualties in it, got a direct hit. The Austrian dragged himself into the other half of my trench; I didn't stop him. We lay in silence together for a long time, and I think I dozed off; at any rate I suddenly realised he was speaking to me again. *"Wann kommt der Arzt?"* he almost whined. I answered rather impatiently, "Oh, he'll be here soon." Then he said something I couldn't understand, but he pointed at my drill shorts, and I realised that they were soaked in blood. He stretched across, obviously in considerable pain, and I tried to stop him, but he insisted. Apparently the bullet had gone through the fleshy part of the

199

thigh, coming out at the other side, and when the stretcher-bearer had hastily bandaged me he had placed the field dressing on the place where the bullet had entered, whereas of course it was bleeding from the place of exit. With great difficulty the Austrian bandaged it again, using his own field dressing. I felt guilty for having spoken so abruptly to him, and when he had finished I did my best to dress his wound. It was a bullet wound right between the shoulder-blades, and the bullet was still in. It was hardly bleeding at all and there was little I could do. I gave him my haversack as a pillow and he was pathetically grateful. I asked him if he was married, and he immediately started to fumble in his tunic pocket and brought out the inevitable family photo. He had been detailed to a machine-gun crew that afternoon and had only been in position two hours before we arrived. He had never fired a machine gun before that night. I talked feverishly, struggling to remember my German. I don't think he understood half I said, but I had to talk to keep my mind off realities; then I saw he was asleep. I relaxed, and suddenly I felt very tired.

The dawn was just breaking, and I thought to myself, "Well, I am excused stand-to this morning." I must have slept for three hours. I had dreadful dreams. When I woke up, the sun was glaring down on me in its full intensity. It was very silent. I was perspiring all over. My mouth was horribly dry and had a dreadful taste. I felt for my water-bottle; I remembered I had unstrapped it to give the Austrian a drink. It was only half full, but I knew I had my reserve bottle in my haversack under the Austrian's head. Then in horror I remembered that I had taken it out the night before while in the dug-out to give a wounded man a drink. Had I put it back? I couldn't remember. It was a pity to disturb the Austrian when he was sleeping so peacefully; but was he sleeping? I looked at him again; his skin was all drawn in and he was deathly white. Had he died in the night? I stretched over and felt his pulse; it was beating weakly. He stirred and murmured, *"Wann kommt der Arzt?"* I replied, *"Bald,"* and he sighed and went to sleep again. I carefully pulled the haversack from under his head and substituted my army pullover which I had taken off.
200

He stirred, but didn't wake up. I feverishly opened the haversack—my worst fears were realised! I had left my reserve bottle in the dug-out. I shook my issue bottle; it was less than half full. I drank very slowly, and then, filling my mouth, washed it out, spitting the water back into my bottle. I didn't feel like eating; I had a packet of hard biscuits and my emergency ration.

It was quiet, and I raised myself to the level of the trench and looked over. I could see two helmets protruding from a trench about thirty yards away. I called out, realising for the first time how painful my wound was now. Someone came doubling over to me after the second shout; it was my batman. I asked him what was happening. Why hadn't the doctor and Battalion H.Q. come? Had he any water? He left me his bottle, and said he would collect my reserve one after he had gone over to the company commander to find out what was happening.

Mortar shells started landing all around me. The Germans were watching our every movement, and had jumped to the conclusion that my trench was the H.Q. Twice I was covered in sand, and once a red-hot piece of metal landed on my chest. The Austrian stirred uneasily and woke up. He started to raise himself by placing his hands over the edge of the trench. There was an ear-splitting explosion. At first I thought our trench had been blown in. I looked carefully over the side; there was a huge crater less than five yards from the Austrian's end of the trench. Then I looked at the Austrian; he was lying half propped up against the trench looking curiously at the remains of his left hand; it had been partially blown away. I was nearly sick, but hastily tore my shirt and bound it tightly round the stump. He thanked me weakly and closed his eyes. His breathing was heavy and laboured; the poor devil was dying. I thought of his wife and children, of how damned stupid the whole thing was. First, he shoots me, then I shoot him, then we talk together as friends and share a trench where he is further wounded by his own side. Why were we fighting each other? Did it make sense? Then I thought of the massacres in Poland, France, Belgium. Yes, I suppose it was necessary. *"Wann kommt der Arzt?"* he interrupted my thoughts. Mechanically I replied, *"Bald!"* Almost petulantly he murmured, *"Bald! Bald! immer bald."* It was no use explaining to him that we were cut off and the doctor wouldn't be coming; he would certainly be dead in a few hours, and I, too, probably, if this shelling went on. As I moved back to my own end of the trench a bullet whistled past my head. That damned sniper was still watching. Our guns opened up now; the shells landed right among us. I hoped the wireless was still working, and the company commander would get through in time. Another salvo—just beyond us this time. I wondered how it would all end. I didn't really care much now.

The day dragged on; the shooting had died down, but it suddenly broke out again, but this time it was the sharp crack of tank guns. I appeared to be almost under their muzzles. A tank rumbled into view: one of ours—I shouted, but it was hopeless. The next moment it went partially over a trench in which some wounded, our own and Germans, were lying. I sank back into the trench. A little later an armoured car came up. I shouted, and this time the officer inside heard me. He got out and doubled over to me. I shouted a warning to him about the sniper; he reached me and lay down beside my trench. He was amazed to find us there; they had no idea we were there. Apparently we were in the middle of a tank battle. I told him we had a lot of wounded; could he do anything to get us out. He said he would report it at once on his return to his H.Q.

It was now early evening. The Austrian was lying peaceful, still breathing, but blood was oozing out of his mouth. I think I slept again; I was getting light-headed. I finished the second water-bottle; my thirst was more painful than the wound. I still had my batman's half-full bottle, but I couldn't use that; he would want it. Another two hours passed, and then suddenly I realised there were people round the trench. I can't remember how many, but the company commander was there and a doctor, not our own. He was wearing a forage-cap, and I thought what a risk he was taking. He was very cool and cheery. "Hold out your arm," he said, and he injected me with morphia. I asked him to give some to the Austrian. He stabbed him, but he

202

scarcely stirred, and murmured, *"Der Arzt ist gekommen."*

The doctor asked where the others were, and I pointed out the trenches I knew and called for my batman to guide him. Never have I seen such cool disregard for personal safety as that man showed. I don't know who he was; he strolled from trench to trench, completely ignoring the bullets and mortar shells which were hotting up again, his forage-cap stuck at a cheeky angle. Finally he returned to my trench unscathed. They held a hasty conference; I couldn't follow much, but I gathered that they were going to try and get the wounded out after dark. The Germans concentrated their mortars with increasing fury on my trench and the little party, which broke up hastily. I had an uncomfortable ten minutes, but I wasn't really caring at this stage. I had such a wonderful peaceful feeling. I must have fallen asleep again; for the next thing I remember, it was quite dark and men were carrying away the Austrian, who was apparently still alive. They came back for me, and pushed me on to the front of a 15-cwt. truck.

Soon we started off, bumping across the rough ground; one or two of the men inside groaned. I felt quite peaceful and had no pain. From time to time I had a feeling of anxiety in case I was going to be cheated out of my hospital bed at the last moment by a mine or a shell, but on the whole I was quite content to leave it to the driver.

We soon arrived at an advanced dressing station. I had another injection here, but after a quick glance at my bandage they left the wound alone. The last I saw of my Austrian he was lying on a raised stretcher having a blood transfusion. I wonder if he lived. I still have his papers.

I was placed in an ambulance, which was sheer luxury after the bumping of the truck, and soon we arrived at a big New Zealand casualty clearing station. They were frantically busy here, and when I assured them that I wasn't bleeding they just put another label round my neck and packed me back into another ambulance. From this I was transferred to a hospital train, and eventually landed at a South African base hospital in Egypt.

Stand By to Ram

The German battleship, Tirpitz, anchored at Trondheim, Norway in early 1942, was a dangerous threat to all North Atlantic convoys. But once the Tirpitz broke out on a raid, the British were sure they could block her return to Norway. The only other Atlantic Coast harbor big enough to handle her was at Saint-Nazaire. "Destroy the Normandie Dock at Saint-Nazaire, and the Tirpitz would not dare to venture out into the Atlantic," so ran the argument in high British naval circles.

The task of blowing up the huge lock (a drydock capable of handling the largest ships in the world) and adjacent installations was entrusted to Lord Mountbatten's Combined Operations. The original objective of this group was to conduct quick hit-and-run raids all along the Atlantic coast—"one operation a fortnight" was Mountbatten's announced goal.

To reach the lock at Saint-Nazaire, it was necessary to sail up the Loire River about six miles. Unless surprise could be attained the mission could hardly succeed, because the river banks were studded with gun installations. Furthermore, the channel was narrow, and on both sides mud flats discouraged ships of more than light draft. Only during extraordinary spring tides could heavier ships get up the river out of channel. Ironically, this "flaw in the defense" appealed to Mountbatten's command as an excellent risk for a spring raid.

The plan of attack finally decided on was as follows:

"A gutted and 'expendable' destroyer of light draft, carrying a commando force, was to cut through the anti-torpedo net and ram the outer caisson (of the lock). A large weight of explosives would be packed at the point of impact and the ship blown up by delayed-action fuses. . . . The troops in the expendable destroyer would meanwhile have landed and would proceed to destroy with explosives all lock gates leading into the Submarine Basin, with the intent of making it tidal.* Bomber Command would be asked to engage the attention of

*German submarine pens had been constructed to service the U-boats in the South Atlantic.

the enemy's guns, searchlights and radar by a bombing operation to be begun before the expedition entered the estuary and to be maintained throughout the assault. Finally the commandos and the skeleton crew of the expended destroyer would withdraw in a second destroyer, which would have followed up and proceeded alongside." *

This plan, if fully supported by the other services, seems almost foolproof in light of what happened. Unfortunately, the inevitable conflict between services during wartime prevented its full acceptance. The Navy was unwilling to risk a second destroyer. CO had to settle for a fleet of lightly armed motor launches. The destroyer chosen to ram the lock was the *Campbeltown*, originally the *Buchanan* and one of the fifty old U.S. destroyers the British received as Lend-Lease in exchange for U.S. use of certain Caribbean ports.

A further blow to the CO battle plan was felt when the R.A.F. Bomber Command reduced the size of their requested contribution, both in numbers of planes and the time span devoted to the operation— Bomber Command hated to give away anything from their own operations.

Because so much depended upon surprise, the overall risks in the operation were now even higher. How high, Lord Mountbatten made clear to Colonel Newman, who would lead the Commando units ashore.

"I want you to be quite clear," he said, "that this is not just an ordinary raid; it is an important operation of war. . . . It is also a very hazardous operation. I am quite confident that you will get in and do the job all right; but, frankly, I don't expect any of you to get out again.

"If we lose you all, you will be about equivalent to the loss of one merchant ship, but your success will save many merchant ships. We have got to look at the thing in those terms.

"For that reason, I don't want you to take anyone on the operation who has any serious home ties or worries. No married men. Tell all your men that quite openly, and give very man the opportunity of standing down if he feels he should. Nobody will think any the worse of him and we must have that quite clear, too." **

The Greatest Raid of All, by C. E. Lucas Phillips, published by Little, Brown & Co., pp. 22-23.

**Ibid., p. 37.

At two o'clock on a sunny afternoon on March 26, the little fleet set sail. "They numbered, apart from the escorts (two destroyers) 611 souls —345 naval officers and ratings, 166 all ranks in the fighting parties from 2 Commando, 91 all ranks in the demolition teams of the combined Commando, together with the medical party, three liaison officers and two press representatives." *

As a feint, their course was set well out into the Atlantic to a point 160 miles west of Saint-Nazaire. There they turned toward France but headed toward a point a good bit south of the Loire River destination. At eight o'clock on the evening of March 27, they turned and sailed toward the open jaws of the Loire estuary.

Mile after mile went by, the little fleet still undiscovered. At 11:30 p.m. British bombers were heard going over but their fleet's position was still a few miles off the coast.**

At 12:30 a.m. the ships entered the river mouth. Their luck held until 1:22 a.m. when the column of ships was suddenly caught and held in the beam of an enemy searchlight. For a few minutes the raiders were able to confuse the Germans with false signals but not for long. Then the firing began from both sides and sounded as though all hell had broken loose.

"Campbeltown was going fast now, making a good twenty knots, her bow wave splaying wide. Every German gun that could bear was now converged upon her; not now those lower down the river but those at point-blank range in the dockyard area itself—from the Old Mole, from either side of the Normandie Dock, from the top of the submarine pens, from the roofs of buildings—and from the east bank of the river. Repeatedly hit, she was now suffering very heavy casualties, among her sailors and soldiers alike, her decks spattered with fallen bodies. But miraculously Campbeltown escaped damage to any vital part as she raced forward. The gunboat and the motor launches of Boyd and

* *The Greatest Raid of All,* p. 68.

** Editor's note: The air raid did little damage, but it did make the Germans suspicious and they went on the alert for that night. To make matters worse, because of an overcast, several bombers continued to cruise over Saint-Nazaire for unexplained minutes before leaving.

Irwin were backing her up at close quarters. Boyd's gunner, Able Seaman MacIver, observed a Bofors immediately to starboard of the caisson engaging the destroyer. With a steady hand, he caught it in the sights of his Hotchkiss and silenced it with a direct hit.

"Not till he was within 200 yards did Beattie see the great steel gate of the lock, discernible as an indistinct black line beyond the 'spill' of the searchlights, dead ahead. At the last moment an incendiary bomb, of the nature of thermite projected by no known agency, but conceivably dropped from one of our own aircraft, landed on the forecastle and burst into flames. *Campbeltown* held steadily on her course. In the wheelhouse there was complete silence. Beattie and Montgomery propped themselves against the front of the wheelhouse, ready for the shock of impact. Throughout the ship every man braced himself.

"Denser and denser grew the black line ahead. A momentary check told them that they had ripped through the anti-torpedo net. All hands could feel the wire dragging along the ship's bottom. The caisson was scarcely fifty yards away and only now could Beattie clearly see it. With extraordinary presence of mind, in order to hit the caisson in the center and in order to swing the ship's stern to starboard, so that the Old Entrance should not be blocked, he crisply ordered at this last moment:

" 'Port 20!'

"Instantly Tibbits obeyed and at 1:34 a.m. with all her Oerlikons blazing at the enemy guns only a few yards away, with her fo'c'sle in flames she crashed into the caisson.

"She struck with such accuracy and force that her bow, up to the level of the caisson, crumpled back for a distance of thirty-six feet, leaving her fo'c'sle deck, which was higher than the caisson actually projecting a foot beyond the inner face.

"Beattie turned to Montgomery with a smile and said, 'Well there we are.' Looking at his watch, he added, 'Four minutes late.' " *

*The Greatest Raid of All, pp. 98-99.

THE RAID ON SAINT-NAZAIRE*

by C. E. Lucas Phillips

Beattie's achievement, executed with such cool precision, marks the attainment of the chief purpose of the expedition. There now began a medley of events difficult to describe in ordered sequence. The battle spread like a flame, to the whole scene by land and water. The motor launches, coming up astern of *Campbeltown*, pressed towards their designated landing places with the greatest daring, adding to the lurid scene the glow of their own conflagrations and the smoke and stench of burning petrol as, one by one, half their number burst into flames or blew up. The battle splintered into innumerable little actions. From the moment of committal command and control of the action was lost, partly through the very nature of the operation and partly through the failure of the gunboat's wireless, so that each boat and each group of soldiers pursued, or attempted to pursue, its predetermined part alone.

At the moment that *Campbeltown* crashes into the caisson, we may imagine Curtis's gunboat and the motor launches of Boyd and Irwin standing off to support her and the two columns of troop-carrying craft coming up close astern, with Platt leading the port column and Stephens the starboard. These beheld the bows of the destroyer erupting in flying timbers, smoke and flames. They saw the commandos leap to their feet on deck and, under a covering fire from the destroyer's Oerlikons overhead, begin to move

*A condensed version of several chapters from *The Greatest Raid of All*.

forward. The guns of both sides began to concentrate their fire on this small area.

Campbeltown herself began to prepare for her last moments. Beattie, excited enough beneath his icy exterior, forgot to give the order to ring off the engines, and for a few minutes there was a little confusion in the engine and boiler rooms, accentuated by the darkness which now enveloped the whole ship below deck. The engines might have been required to hold the ship on to the caisson, but Chief Engine Room Artificer Howard went up on deck, found Gough in the storm of fire that crackled and flashed up there and got sanction to shut off steam. The ship was still being repeatedly hit and down below, where the engine-room staff were bearing themselves with exemplary courage, shells and explosive bullets were still penetrating. Stoker Petty Officer Pyke was going about quietly, maintaining machinery by torchlight. Engine-Room Artificer Nelson was killed while evacuating hands from the forward boiler room.

The first, the most imperative duty, however, was to disembark the commandos as rapidly as possible. Not till this had been done did Beattie give the order to abandon ship. Winthorpe's medical party, their hands more than full to the last minute, were routed out. Howard and Engine-Room Artificer Reay proceeded to scuttle ship by torchlight, opening the valves that would let in the sea and removing the condenser doors. To make assurance doubly sure, scuttling charges were fired under the direction of Hargreaves, the torpedo gunner. Finally Beattie and Gough then went round the ship to make sure that no one was left behind. Then they themselves went onto the upper deck while the ship, held fast by the bows on the caisson, was beginning to settle at the stern.

From this moment we must imagine the seven parties of the commandos, steel-helmeted, with whitened webbing, scattering to their several targets, moving at the double under heavy weights of arms or explosives, past tall cranes, buildings, railway trucks and piles of timber; now brilliantly illuminated by the searchlights, now in a moonlight gloom; sometimes unopposed, sometimes having to fight bitterly for their objectives. In the midst we see the handfuls of the commandos moving to their stations—Roderick scattering his enemies, Roy holding his bridge the teams of destroyers fixing their charges.

Thus the two assault parties carried out their tasks. The demolition teams were hard on their heels. Let us remind ourselves what the targets were they had been ordered to destroy.

These numbered five. At the southern end of the dry-dock area was a group of three tasks entrusted to teams under officers of 5 Commandos. Stuart Chant had the formidable task of destroying the big pump house; Christopher Smalley was to go for the winding-house where the machinery for moving the big southern caisson in and out of position was situated; Robert Burtenshaw was to destroy the caisson itself with magnetic "wreaths" and 18-pound charges if *Campbeltown* should fail to ram satisfactorily. The protection party for all these teams was provided by Hopwood, of the Essex Regiment.

At the northern end of the big dock, Etches, with Gerard Brett and young Corran Purdon, was charged with destroying the caisson at that end, and the winding-house associated with it. For these demolition teams the protection was provided by "Bung" Denison, of Roderick's Troop. All these five demolition tasks in the drydock area were under the control of Pritchard's friend, Bob Montgomery.

During *Campbeltown's* approach Chant's party were lying behind their steel screens, face up and feet forward against the shock of impact. A moment before the destroyer rammed, a small shell burst beside Chant and Chamberlain,

210

wounding them both. A sticky feeling running down his leg told Chant that he had been hit in the knee; splinters wounded his arm and fingers also. The bittersweet fumes of high explosive blew over him. He lay momentarily dazed, but an inner compulsion told him to rise and slip into his rucksack with its load of explosives. Three of the sergeants rose with him, but Chamberlain said, "Very sorry, sir, but I can't move."

Between them, however, they lifted up his hundred and eighty-nine pounds and half-carried him as they moved forward to disembark, together with Smalley's and Hopwood's teams. Then, heavily laden with their explosives, sledge hammers, axes and incendiaries, they scrambled, slid or fell down the scaling ladders on the port side. Somehow Chamberlain was got down and the team made for the pump house by the route printed on their minds through a scene vividly lit, but checkered by the dense angular shadows of the buildings, swaying from time to time as the searchlights swung their beams.

Chant was limping but could move fairly freely. They were right on Roy's heels, seeing the kilts flying just ahead. Without waiting for him to attack the German gunners on the roof of the pump house, they went straight for the entrance, but met an unexpected obstacle when they found it barred by a heavy steel door. Chant was momentarily at a loss, but at that moment Montgomery appeared and from the spare explosives that he carried he took out a small magnetic charge, clamped it on the door and stood back. Chant made to light the short length of safety fuse, but found it difficult to strike the fuse with his bleeding fingers. He was disconcerted to find his hands trembling and he said to Montgomery, "Bob, for God's sake help me light this bloody thing; the chaps will think I'm scared."

Montgomery complied, the door was blown in and Chant and his sergeants entered the pump house.

Chant's team had rehearsed over and over again, including provision for casualties. The task required two demolitions—the first, that of the great impeller pumps forty feet below ground, and the second, the electrical gear on the ground floor where they now stood, particularly the electric motors that drove the impeller pumps below, and the transformers. They flashed their torches around and, with the help of the glow coming in from the searchlights and the fires outside, they noted that everything was exactly as they had seen it in the King George V Dock at Southampton—the straight line of the motors, the transformers, the switch gear, the indicators, all laid out in orderly precision.

Chamberlain was by now weak and moving slowly. Chant was reluctant to take so heavy a man down the steep, zig-zag staircase that led to the pumping chamber far below, but to ease the sergeant's chagrin, he said,

"Stay up here and do guard for us. Don't let anyone in."

The big sergeant lay down at the top of the stairs and Chant started on the long descent below ground, Butler and Dockerill helping him down, with King following, and carrying between them Chamberlain's sixty pounds of explosive besides their own.

Utter darkness lay beneath them, a darkness that the torches at their belts penetrated only as a cold, unfocused beam. Below ground level a cold dampness at once struck their faces. Their blindfold exercises at Southampton came back vividly to them as they counted the steps, but these were not quite the same. The impulse to make haste was upon them, held in check by the risk of losing balance and by thought of the results of taking a false step or of straying off the stairs on to the galleries that ran round the walls of the pit. Chant, limping down by jerks, fought the threat of giddiness.

At the foot of the long stairs, in the pumping chamber at last, their torches showed them that the impeller pumps were exactly as they knew they would be—four main pumps of the turbine impeller type and two subsidiary drainage pumps. They looked rather like giant lifebelts, or huge inverted mushrooms. Inside these big steel ring castings were the fast-revolving vanes which impelled the water in or out of the dock. Standing up in the middle of each ring was the long, shining, steel shaft connecting with the motor that drove it far above at ground level. Each of the four sergeants was to blow up one of the main pumps and Chant himself the two subsidiaries, but Chant now took over Chamberlain's target, leaving the subsidiary pumps to be attacked collectively.

Not much need for torches now. They knew every step and every movement by heart. They wriggled out of their harnesses, laying them on the concrete floor, and took out the specially prepared plastic charges in their waterproof covers. These, reaching up and over the big circular tubes, they slapped and molded firmly onto the casting joints of the impeller pumps, which they knew from the Southampton dock engineers could not be replaced in less than a year. Disturbed by two deep muffled thuds overhead which shook them deep below, they were told by Chamberlain far above that it was "only Captain Donald blowing up the guns." They worked quickly and confidently. Dockerill was quietly singing "Blue Birds over the White Cliffs of Dover" and the other two sergeants chatted casually in broad Norfolk. Their homely, easy voices gave Chant a glow of affection, overcoming the pain of his wound and the handicap of his lacerated fingers. He heard one of them say:

"Nearly finished, sir. Can I help you?"

"No, thanks, I'm all right."

The charges laid, out came the ring main. Together they unrolled and laid it out, hands feeling forward to other hands dimly seen in the checkered light. Out next came the cord-tex leads to connect each charge to the ring main by a clove hitch. Chant, on No. 3 pump, heard successively reports of his companions:

"No. 2 done, sir."

"No. 4 done, sir."

And finally, with a note of triumphant finality:

"No. 1 done, SIR!"

The subsidiary pumps were quickly connected likewise. Finally, out came the two lengths of safety fuse, with igniters and detonators already connected, to be crimped on to the ring main.

A hundred fifty pounds of high explosive were now ready to be detonated at the touch of the duplicated percussion igniters. Three feet of safety fuse gave a delay of ninety seconds, which would give a fit man ample time to run up the stairs and out of the building. It was Chant's duty to fire the charges himself, sending his sergeants up first and being himself last man out. But he was wondering how on earth he was going to get up those forty feet of steep stairs. His knee was now slowing down all his movements. He decided to keep Dockerill with him, sending King and Butler upstairs with instructions to remove Chamberlain to safety and to shout down when the way was clear.

He took one of the igniters and gave the other to Dockerill. Two long minutes passed in the underground darkness. Dockerill continued humming his song. No other sounds were audible and the battle above seemed far away. At last came the expected shout from above and Chant, by prearrangement, gave a simple "one-two-three" to Dockerill. Simultaneously they pulled their igniter pins and the slow fuse began to burn along its three feet passage to the detonator and the cordtex. Subaltern and sergeant turned and made for the stairs. With Dockerill leading and Chant clinging tight to his arm, they went up in the dark as fast as possible, Chant hopping two or three steps at a time.

They arrived out into the bright light and the din and Chant ordered his team to take cover behind the concrete anti-blast wall opposite the door of the pump house, but Montgomery was at hand and ordered them at once to cover further off. They had no sooner reached it than the charges went up, bursting in the confined space below with great violence—"a great roar of sound that cracked our eardrums," as recorded by Copland, who was passing through not far away—shaking the ground and throwing down a great concrete block upon the very spot where they had lain just before. Clouds of debris billowed out and bright showers of broken glass burst outwards from the windows. The "great roar" impressed itself on the whole battlefield, heard with satisfaction by both Ryder and Newman, both now ashore, and heard even by the motor launches in the agony of their river battle.

It was not quite two o'clock.

Christopher Smalley, fresh at the nearby winding-house, came up at a trot to make his report to Montgomery before

214

withdrawing to his last rendezvous. They exchanged quick congratulations and Stuart Chant led his team back to the pump house. They had now to go in again to destroy the motors and electrical gear on the ground floor. Quickly in, they found the building filled with clouds of smoke and dust, the concrete floor caved in, two of the electric motors fallen through it to the pumping chamber far below and the other two lying at crazy angles. It was obvious to them all that the place had already been sufficiently wrecked and that another destructive explosion was unnecessary. Chant contented himself, therefore, with ordering King to smash the transformer pipes and the gauges with his sledge hammer, which that broad-shouldered sergeant did with relish and precision, and as the oil poured out of the transformer pipes it was set on fire with tar babies.

Thus, leaving the pump house completely destroyed and burning fiercely, Chant and his sergeants set out to withdraw according to plan, supporting between them their wounded companion.

When all was done, Montgomery, having observed a large shed at the side of the pump house, opened the door and threw in an incendiary. There shot up, in the words of Copland, "a colossal burst of continuous yellow fire," adding yet another to the series of fires that were now raging in the white beams of the searchlights.

Meanwhile Christopher Smalley and his small demolition team had had equal success in their attack upon the southern winding-house close by. Smalley, of the Manchester Regiment, was somewhat aloof, squarely built, had good looks and a heavy mustache. His little team consisted of Sergeant Bright, the miner, Corporal Howard, Bombardier W. Johnson and Corporal E. Johnson.

His was the nearest of the objectives to *Campbeltown*. Within the building he saw the two big wheels by which the caisson was moved and the motors that drove them. On these motors and on the spokes of the wheels he placed his charges, connected all up with cordtex, and, having had permission from Montgomery, pulled his igniters. There was no result. He reported to Montgomery and fresh igniters and safety fuse were fitted. These fired successfully and the whole building and all its machinery went up with a shattering concussion, the bricks and debris showering down upon the motor craft now in the Old Entrance and narrowly missing Ryder as he stood by the caisson watching *Campbeltown* sink.

Leaving it in ruins and blazing fiercely, Smalley went quickly to report to Montgomery, as we have seen, saying to him, "Bob, I have finished and I'm going to withdraw now." Returning to his team, he saw at that moment Burt's motor launch in the Old Entrance, disembarking his troops, and he decided to take this opportunity of effecting his withdrawal, instead of going to the Old Mole. He and his team ran to the quayside and embarked, but the boat was heavily engaged by the minesweepers and harbor defense boats in the Submarine Basin. The forward Oerlikon was jammed and Smalley took charge of it in an attempt to free it, but was almost immediately shot dead.

All the commandos' demolition objectives on the machinery of the great Normandie Dock had now been fulfilled with almost complete success in less than half an hour from the moment *Campbeltown* had rammed. Even if the destroyer herself should fail to blow up, it was now impossible to operate either of the caissons and impossible to pump out or refill the dock. The great Forme Ecluse was useless for certainly a year at least, useless to the *Tirpitz*, useless to every kind of ship. It was, indeed, to remain useless until long after the war was over. This feat is unique in military and naval annals. No other example exists of damage so vital and so far-reaching in its results being carried out so swiftly and with such economy of force. No guesswork, no "hundred per cent zone," no "permissible error," no "near misses" obscured the exactitude of the commandos' attack, for they placed their charges on those small, vital pinpoints which might never have been hit at all by projectiles launched from bomb rack or gun.

The achievement was not only the visible record of the daring of the men who performed it; it was also a triumph for the man, now at this moment about to die on the doorstep of fulfillment, who had planned it. It was Pritchard whose imagination, invention and fanatical persistence had

216

built the way to this technical achievement, it was his midnight assiduity that had calculated every charge and written out every item of each man's task and load to the last fusee, and it was his patient and meticulous training that had taught each man precisely what to do. In the honors and memorials of the Charioteers his name, denied by death the award of any decoration, stands among the highest.*

Having thus completed all their tasks, the commandos of Group Three began their withdrawal according to plan. Their work was finished and they were now to re-embark for home again.

Except in one instance which will shortly be related, the commandos had not the least difficulty in dealing with any of the troops that they met; what was much more serious to them than the superiority of numbers was the superior weight of fire from the fixed gun positions and from the minesweepers and harbor defense craft, some of them firing from extremely close quarters, to which were quickly added several machine guns. These weapons, particularly those of the ships in harbor and the hastily mounted machine guns, very soon began to turn their attention from the motor launches to the little parties of men that they now saw darting about in the searchlight beams or among the shadows of buildings and dumps and railway tracks. Later the quadruple 20 mm. beyond the Submarine Basin began to sweep this area with their more venomous fire and occasionally, from some unidentified battery, there came the sharp crump of an airburst shell overhead.

With Moss and his important-party missing, Newman was therefore very relieved when his tiny headquarters was augmented by the "special task party" of Troop Sergeant-Major Haines, which joined him soon after he had taken up his impromptu headquarters. The rugged little sergeant-major, in fact, had arrived before Newman and then moved off for his special task of silencing the guns reported to be on the sea wall between the mole and the Old Entrance. Finding none there, he reported to Newman in accordance

*The award of the DSC to Tibbits was made before it was known that he had been killed.

with his orders. Standing to attention as on the parade ground, he listened as Newman told him:

"Stay near me in case I want you; because you are the only reserve I have now got."

He very soon did need him, for fire from one of the 20-mm. guns beyond the Submarine Basin and from machine guns mounted on the roof of the pens began to harass them. Newman called up Haines and said:

"We have simply got to stop those guns. What have you got you can take them on with?"

"I've got a 2-inch mortar, sir. No sights, but it's the only thing we've got."

With extraordinary unconcern, Haines took forward in his great hands a little 2-inch mortar, siting it slap in the open near the quayside of the Submarine Basin just beyond the end of one of the warehouses. Here he knelt down and, taking the small bombs that were passed to him by a chain of hands, including Newman's, from behind the cover of the building, dropped them down the barrel of the mortar, to go soaring high into the air and onto the enemy positions only two hundred yards away. With the enemy fire plunging down on the very spot where he knelt, he successfully silenced one position after another, if only temporarily.

There then came against him one of the armed vessels in the basin, the flash of his mortar and the crump of its bombs being only too apparent. Coming close in, the ship made his position "a veritable death trap." Quite unperturbed, however, Haines leaped over to a Bren gun that some fallen comrade had left, and although the fire from the ship's machine guns was "cascading" in the very place where he was now lying, he sent a series of bursts so well directed that the ship ceased fire and sheered away.

All this time Newman was quite in ignorance of the progress of the battle elsewhere, for he never succeeded in establishing wireless communication with Ryder, though the 38 set on the gunboat had its own independent rod aerial. Sergeant Steele opened up his own set immediately in the shelter of Newman's headquarter building, and almost at once heard Lance-Corporal Fyfe, Copland's signaler in the Normandie Dock area. But Newman was not interested in Copland. He kept anxiously asking, "Have you got the boat yet?" But Steele, swinging his dial from time to time, chanted "Newman calling Ryder—Newman calling Ryder" for over an hour without any effect, till at length there was disclosed a situation in which wireless could only too clearly have no value.

The silence of the radio, however, was not matched by the din and clamor all around, and very soon sounds of fresh Tommy-gun fire on his left told Newman that something was afoot there also.

This was the party successfully landed at the Old Mole by Collier's ML 11, containing Philip Walton's team for destroying Bridge D, Watson's protection squad and Pritchard's demolition control team. Pritchard's tasks were to control the timings of the demolitions, to help where necessary and to attack targets of opportunity.

With Watson's squad leading, followed by Walton's, followed by Pritchard, this little band ran quickly up the steps to the landward end of the mole. Watson had orders that if his was the only squad to gain the mole he was to attack and hold it himself. He could probably have done so, had he not been led to believe that Birney had already arrived. As it was, he stopped to examine and empty his Tommy gun into what appeared to be a new gun position at the top of the steps, until the cry came up from Pritchard in the rear:

"What are you up to, Tiger? Get on!"

Without more ado, the three parties made straight for Bridge D, but very soon came under fire. In commando fashion they did not wait for each other's support, but made straight for their objectives independently. Pritchard, passing two bodies dead or wounded on the ground, reached Bridge D the first, having probably taken a different route from Watson and Walton and perhaps having seen the trouble into which they both ran.

Pritchard's party consisted of four corporals—I. L. Maclagan, a Royal Engineer Territorial, J. Deans and H. Shipton, all of 9 Commando, and S. Chetwynd, of 12 Commando. Approaching the lock of the Southern Entrance, they beheld before them the steel latticework swing bridge which was Walton's objective, looming in the half-darkness

ahead of them like the ribs of some giant skeleton. There
was no cover at all on the bare and open quay, except for
a small concrete hut, about ten feet square, a few yards
from the bridge. To this Pritchard and his corporals
sprinted, dumping their rucksacks on its sheltered side—
four men alone in the half-light with the enemy just across
the bridge and all behind them also. Pritchard, looking
round at once for prey, saw two ships berthed alongside
each other against the quay of the Submarine Basin, forty
yards to his right, and he whispered to Maclagan:

"Mac, I'm going to sink those two ships. Get out two
five-lb. charges."

Under full observation from an enemy scarcely sixty
yards away, the two men ran to the quayside, jumped onto
the nearer ship, crossed to the second and lowered the
charges between the two ships, three feet below water. They
tied them to the rail of the ship, pulled the igniter pins and
hurried back to the shelter of the hut.

There Pritchard gave instructions to the other three corporals, in the absence of Walton's party, to "do what you
can" to the swing bridge, while he and Maclagan went
round to visit, as he hoped, the other demolition parties in
that area. He lingered a moment, however, listening for
what he hoped for, and before they separated, smiled
happily as the charges between the two ships blew up with
a muffled roar, followed by a violent and prolonged hissing
which told convincingly that the charges had been accurately laid against the ships' boiler rooms. When Newman passed there nearly two hours later he found the two
ships sunk. They were the tugs *Champion* and *Pornic*.

Having accomplished this impromptu act, Pritchard and
Maclagan, the tall Welshman and the smaller Scot, set out
at a trot towards the South Entrance, going boldly and
silently along the open lock side, in the half-light from the
"spill" of the searchlight beams and from the moon that
shone through the high cloud. But they passed in turn one
lock gate after another, and the farther bridge likewise,
disappointed to find no demolition parties yet arrived. At
the most southerly gate they turned left to visit the power
station that operated all these southern lock gates, close by

220

on the edge of the Old Town. They could hear the tread of leather-soled boots but they saw no one.

At the power station Pritchard therefore decided that he must go back to find out what was happening. Together with his corporal, he turned about lefthanded and began trotting across the Old Town, making for Bridge D again, Maclagan on Pritchard's left. They passed through a labyrinth of small buildings, making their way through back yards and narrow streets.

They were nearly halfway across the Old Town when, at a sudden corner in the half-light, Pritchard ran straight into a German. The end came swiftly. At one second they met and in the next Pritchard had fallen backwards, possibly bayoneted, for no shot was fired by either. Maclagan took a quick pace forward and riddled the German with his Tommy gun.

He then dropped down on his knee beside his leader. Pritchard was breathing "terribly heavily" and for a few moments could not speak. Then he said:

"That you, Mac? Don't stop for me. Go straight back and report to HQ. That's an order." So far as we know, he never spoke again.

This order the corporal was desperately unwilling to obey, but the tall, strapping Welshman was far too great a weight for his smaller frame. He resolved therefore to return to the concrete hut, send one of his comrades to headquarters, and bring the others to Pritchard's assistance.

He made his way back alone through the eerie, hostile streets and reached the concrete hut safely, but all that there was to be seen was a dead body. It was that of Philip Walton.

Still quite alone, therefore, in the heart of enemy territory, Maclagan continued on his way, across the dangerous and exposed Old Town Place, through the rows of warehouses and so to Newman's battle headquarters. There he asked for help to bring Pritchard in, but was told it was out of the question. At some time or other Corporal Deans and Corporal Chetwynd were also killed, Maclagan and Shipton being the only survivors of Pritchard's party.

Watson's tiny squad comprised young Sergeant Wickson, Lance-Corporal Grief, an irrepressible, ribald Cockney, Private Davidson and Private Lawson.

Coming up immediately behind them was Philip Walton the schoolmaster, with his demolition team for the critical Bridge D, consisting of Sergeant Dick Bradley, Sergeant Alf Searson, Corporal George Wheeler and Lance-Corporal Homer. Watson set off at a smart pace, too smart indeed for Walton's heavily laden demolition team, from whom they soon became separated. At the first group of buildings after passing the landward end of the mole, Watson saw in the half-light what appeared to be a group of French civilians. He shouted to them, as he had been instructed, *"Dedans vite"* (Inside quickly), and fired a burst from his Tommy gun over their heads as he ran. They disappeared, and he saw also a group of German soldiers running away into the Old Town—the second group that he had already seen to run away.

Full of confidence, therefore, he doubled along the broad open space of Old Town Place, but had gone only about one hundred and fifty yards before he met some Germans who did not run away. He called to them, *"Hände hoch!"* (Hands up!) But they answered him with a grenade and a similar summons. Himself a little way in front of his squad, he therefore dropped to the ground to engage them, his orders having been to keep the enemy occupied while the demolition team went on, then to disengage and join up again.

Disengagement became difficult, however, when a machine gun opened up on him from a rooftop to his left. He was almost stunned by a grenade that fell and burst beside him. With a metallic clang a litter tin attached to a lamppost just above his head was riddled with bullets. Another bullet or other projectile burst open his haversack of grenades and the movement of scrabbling about to pick them up drew fresh fire. From an emplacement beyond

222

Bridge D- another machine gun began spraying the area at random. Watson therefore lay low for a minute till the shooting stopped, then rose quickly and darted back several yards to rejoin his squad, who had taken cover behind a railway truck and who would have shot him but for his blue pinpoint torch.

Watson was upset to find the demolition party here also, but without Walton; they had seen him fall while running across Old Town Place, but in fact, unknown to all, Walton was making his way to the bridge alone, there to die in an attempt to lay his charges singlehanded at point-blank range. The subsequent study of the battle by the German naval staff reveals that German troops found charges actually laid on his bridge, though whether by Walton or by one of Pritchard's corporals who was killed we know not.

To Watson's urgent inquiries, Corporal Wheeler replied that they had been unable to cross the road and that he thought Walton must have been killed. Watson shouted for his friend, without result and turned to question Sergeant Bradley, when the sergeant was shot through the lung by the rooftop machine gun. While bending down to administer morphia, Watson himself was wounded in the buttock. Bradley was dragged under better cover, but before long he was shot again.

Some reinforcement was clearly necessary for Watson's tiny squad, but when he raised his Very-light pistol to fire the required signal it was shot out of his hand. He therefore sent Wheeler to run to Newman's HQ with the request for help. He then attempted a new approach, moving half-right through the sheds and warehouses north of him towards the Submarine Basin, closely accompanied by Private Lawson. He had nearly reached the quayside when he heard German voices at the end of an alley between the warehouses, and, instead of ignoring them, he hurled a grenade.

He was answered by a violent burst of machine-gun fire, which enveloped him in clouds of dust from shattered bricks at head level from the wall alongside him and from cement stored in the warehouse. This brusque stoppage came from one of the ships of 16 Minesweeper Flotilla still berthed at the quayside only a few yards from him; he saw her outline clearly, heard her engine-room telegraph and heard the orders from her bridge. He saw also some cement bags lying in the road and thought in the half-light that they were his comrades. His calls to them brought no answer and the way ahead was blocked by wire. Frustrated a second time, he made his way back through the shadows to Newman's HQ, accompanied by the bewildered but obedient Lawson and pursued by the ship's machine gun.

Among all the clamor and the darting tracer Watson found Newman—who was not yet aware of the failure of the Old Mole landings—jovial, kind and reassuring.

"Hard luck, Tiger," he said. "You've done jolly well. I can let you have a couple more Tommy-gunners. Go back and have another shot."

Not much relishing this order, but determined to do his damnedest, the little officer, still accompanied by the faithful Lawson, retraced his steps. "I was convinced," he said, "that it meant certain death, but orders were orders." He made contact again with Sergeant Wickson and the remainder of the party and they turned about. His blood was up. Observing one man straggling, he shouted at him angrily:

"Do you want to live forever?"

The effect of this startling challenge was magical, and by the time that they had all reassembled on the dangerous edge of Old Town Place, they had all become charged with the same ardor. They were at a point close to where they had left Sergeant Bradley, of whom they could see no sign. What they did see on that spot was a party of Germans standing easy, and these they wiped out at a few yards' range.

While they were bracing themselves for the new effort, a runner arrived from headquarters canceling the order and instructing them to assemble with the other parties, for it must have been about now that Newman had seen Maclagan, had learned from him that none of the demolition teams for the Southern Entrance had yet arrived and had begun to realize accordingly that these targets might be beyond accomplishment. Watson complied with mixed feelings, for from now till the end he was in an angry mood, burning to have it out with the enemy in atonement for the

224

failure of his mission; but he had done better than he knew, for his little fight had created a valuable diversion, distracting enemy attention from what was now a more vital area and keeping at bay superior forces that would otherwise have been a danger to the remainder of Newman's troops, who were now beginning stealthily to muster together.

The sounds of Watson's fight had told Newman that some at least of his troops had landed at the Old Mole and were about their business. He had no reason yet to suppose that the mole was not in our hands or that anything on the left wing of the battle had gone seriously wrong. On the contrary, one by one the explosions on his right flank and rear began to tell their tale. He heard Purdon's and Smalley's winding-houses go up, Chant's deep underground explosion in the pump house, and the dull thud and boom of the northern caisson's underwater burst. He felt tremendously exhilarated and began to crack jokes with his staff. On the left, however, no such detonations interrupted the unceasing crash and clatter of guns and machine guns.

Apart from those who were already in his designated headquarters, parties of the enemy in this confused situation were extremely close to Newman's small team. One party was no more than twenty yards away, occasionally lobbing grenades, and small-arms fire seemed to be coming from every direction, besides the vicious air crumps from some unidentified battery from time to time. Mindful of the need of being personally out in the open with his men, Newman abandoned the idea of occupying his proposed headquarter house, and after some grenades had been thrown into it, took up a fresh position behind a shed near the quay (where Haines had fired his mortar), from which he could check the demolition parties as they came in and direct them, as he hoped, to the point of re-embarkation on the Old Mole.

One by one these parties began to come in, the young officers in charge of each—all of them wounded, though

225

Montgomery only slightly—reporting personally. All those who could do so stood up and saluted as though on parade. Tremendously pleased with them all, Newman said, "Well done, old boy. Better move along now towards the mole and wait for Major Bill."

Copland came in very soon after, giving Newman the good news from the Normandie Dock area, and the less promising news of Burn's lone arrival far away at Bridge M. The time had therefore come to fire the rain rockets that were the signal for the withdrawal, but there were no rockets, for they had all been lost when Regimental Sergeant-Major Moss had gone down in the river. Newman therefore called upon Lance-Corporal Harrington to go out and take verbal withdrawal orders to Roderick, a quarter of a mile away, and to Roy. Harrington set out alone at the double. He crossed Roy's fireswept bridge after due challenge and reply, and swung to the right to traverse the dangerous no man's land beyond which lay the *Campbeltown*. On the way he was fortunate enough to meet Roderick, who, as we have seen, had already begun his withdrawal. The lance-corporal returned, passed the order to Roy also and reported back to his CO.

"When the situation is uncertain or confused, collect your forces." By the time that Roderick and Roy had completed their withdrawals, this maxim was being complied with. Newman and his commandos, now reduced by fatal casualties and by the re-embarkation of Smalley's party to something just under a hundred, of whom many were wounded, had collected loosely together in the warehouse area. Newman now knew that the main purpose of the expedition, as Haydon had set it out, had been achieved. The situation on the left was dubious, but, so far, no more than that. The general impression on his buoyant mind, therefore, was that the operation was developing favorably. Of the fate of the motor launches he had little or no knowledge, for where he stood the warehouses and railway trucks acted as a baffle to any view of the river.

Thus when Copland said that he would "push along" to organize the re-embarkation, for which the parties from the

226

north were now ready, Newman said, "I'll come with you, Bill."

Together they made their way southeastward through the ranked warehouses, keeping to the selvage of black shadow that bordered the buildings under the harsh, white beams. Emerging from the buildings and coming to a line of railway cars, they had their first glimpse of the river north of the mole and were all brought up standing.

Struck with consternation, Newman exclaimed:

"Good heavens, Bill! Surely those aren't ours!"

Nothing, in the recorded words of Copland, more exactly resembled a scene from the *Inferno*. The river itself was on fire. Close in to the mole the hulks of burned-out motor launches still glowed red on the water, while in the night beyond, seemingly suspended in the air, there blazed a sea of burning petrol which had spread outwards from each burning ship or had been splayed far and wide like so many fountains of fire as other craft blew up. From this floating furnace a pall of black smoke, frustrating the glare of the searchlights, rolled indolently towards the northwest in the almost still air, mingled with the white withdrawal smoke of the escaping launches. From out this curtain of smoke shot the burning trails of cannon fire from the batteries at Mindin Point beyond. In all this forbidding scene there was no sign of life, or of movement, except the leaping flames and the slowly drifting smoke. And on the Old Mole itself the still-glaring searchlight at its tip and the emplaced gun halfway along its length, firing far downstream on some target that they could not see, betrayed to the watching officers in whose hands the pier still remained.

For a moment they both gazed in silence, the import of the scene only too apparent. Then, with a little, wry laugh, Newman said:

"Well, Bill, there goes our transport!"

The first requirement was to rally, consolidate and organize for the new situation. Copland set briskly to work to re-form the little force, choosing as the rallying ground the loop in the railway 150 yards north of the Old Mole, where there was some field of fire and where a few railway cars gave a little protection. Using the well-armed assault troops to form protective screens, he put out Roy on the southern flank, whence increasing fire was being directed from the Old Town, and Haines to the west, where stood the ranks of warehouses.

Here at this rallying point an extraordinary situation existed. Until the commandos were re-formed, both sides were in considerable confusion. Often only a few yards from each other, friend was not instinctively distinguishable from foe. The winking blue torches, the white webbing and the occasional kilt proved their value but were not infallible. The tread of boots and the shouted orders likewise gave clear indication of German presence, but no one knew who was on the other side of a building nor who had thrown a grenade. In Newman's words, the enemy "were shooting at us round corners." The gaunt dockyard reverberated to the bursts of Tommy and Bren gun, the explosions of hand grenades, the crack of rifle and pistol and the answering fire of the enemy, echoing among the warehouses and accented by the cries of the wounded of both sides.

Steadily augmented in numbers, the Germans were now on all sides of them, except to the north, probing forward with caution, but were kept at bay by fire from troops far more highly trained in the use of infantry close-quarters weapons at night.

Virtually surrounded and their means of withdrawal gone, the commandos nonetheless intended to retain the initiative as long as possible. Newman himself, with the responsibility for men's lives on his shoulders, alone had a moment's doubt. They had, he reflected, accomplished the major part of their mission. To satisfy his mind, he sought a second opinion, calling Bill Copland into a short conference. Did Copland think, he asked, that they ought "to call it a day"?

"Certainly not, Colonel. We'll fight our way out."

Nothing pleased Newman more. He made a quick plan to divide his force up into groups of about twenty, fight their way out of the dockyard, through the town, into the open country beyond and try to make their way in pairs to Spain and thence to Gibraltar.

228

He told Copland and Day his plan, a grenade exploding at their feet as they talked. Copland then moved off to divide the force into detachments of twenty and brought the group leaders to Newman for their orders. Newman's own words vividly illustrate this moment. "The scene at the Old Mole," he said, "is hard to describe. There were flames and smoke everywhere. Some wounded Germans were screaming down an alley and small-arms fire was coming from all the buildings around us. Our own chaps were forming a perimeter round the Old Mole; some railway trucks gave them cover and from behind these they were coolly returning the fire with ever-decreasing ammunition. When the group leaders came up to me for my orders, they saluted and grinned. I told them that, as usual, there was no transport to take us home, and that we should fight our way into the town and from there to open country. No one seemed at all surprised."

Their shortest route into the town was by Old Town Place and Bridge D, 200 yards away, but this broad, open approach was so covered by enemy fire that it would be rash to attempt it. The route decided upon, therefore, was through the area of sheds and warehouses to the north of them, and thence back along the quayside of the Submarine Basin, which Watson had already attempted, this route being chosen because by any other they would have to pass between warehouses with the enemy on both sides of them, for the whole of the warehouse area was now alive with Germans. It was a run of some 650 yards, which would have to be undertaken by the wounded also.

Copland marshaled the force into their groups. Making a final round of the positions, accompanied by Private Fahy, he found a party of Germans trying to break through a weak point, and saw them scatter with casualties as Fahy opened up on them with his Tommy gun.

Then, when all was ready, Copland reported to his colonel.

Some time after 3 A.M. this extraordinary column, encumbered with wounded, short of ammunition, began its dash straight through the serried rows of buildings thronged with enemies. They were fewer than a hundred now, a third of them armed with pistols only and nearly one man in three wounded.

They moved by bounds, keeping to the shadowed ways at the edges of the long warehouses and halting from time to time to squat in some dark patch and collect together—sometimes to rush some open stretch by parties under covering fire, or to overcome some point of enemy resistance or to give time for the straggling wounded to catch up. These, obedient to the precept that the lame must not impede operations, fell out to await the inevitable when they could no longer keep up. Gerard Brett, with manifold wounds, could move no further than the first twenty or thirty yards and, giving his Colt to a man who had lost his own, he sank down in a warehouse.

Throughout the whole route, from concealed positions a few yards away in the dark, a ragged fire, now feeble, now bursting into an angry challenge, was sprayed upon the silent-footed column.

Stumbling through a bomb crater made that night by the RAF, they ran the gauntlet through the warehouse roads, turning left, right and left again, and reaching the approach to the old headquarters building. Contact with Burn had somehow been lost at the first or second turn and Donald Roy was now in the van, a splendid figure in his kilt, a grenade in either hand, now striding along in the middle of the road. As he led, Day and Haines served as whips to the field under Copland's mastership, running up and down the column to bid Roy slow down or quicken up, to urge forward any stragglers and to keep the column closed up. Somewhere always in the van was to be seen the figure of Newman, still cracking jokes, never taking cover, always on his feet and directing fire or calling out, "Keep going, lads!"

Reaching the Submarine Basin, the commandos swung boldly left along the quay. An hour earlier this route would have been impossible, but the minesweepers had now moved from their berths at the quayside and, appreciating that the attack might be directed against the submarines, had taken up positions in front of the pens. In their place, however, the commandos met the fire of the guns across the water on their right, while on their left small-arms fire assaulted them at a few yards range from the sheds. Halted by one troublesome party, Copland took a squad right into the shed to silence them.

Watson trying to rush a rifleman who was firing at close range from round a corner, was hit in the left arm, the bullet shattering the humerus. He sank to the ground and prepared to shoot it out with his Colt, but Roderick appeared, killed the German, administered morphia to Watson and began to carry him, but Tiger called in pain to put him down. Hopwood was there, too, and together they put him down at the side of the road. Very quietly, ignoring the boy's cry of "Hoppy, what the hell are you doing with my gun?" Hopwood slipped his Colt off its lanyard.

Roy, meanwhile, was sweeping along to the southern extremity of the Submarine Basin. At the end of the quay came the most dangerous place of all—the wide, open stretch of Old Town Place, which, turning right, they must cross before reaching Bridge D. At Newman's order they halted accordingly in the pale moon shadows aslant the buildings on their left hand, while Newman himself, accompanied by Roy and Haines, darted across the open space for a quick reconnaissance from the buildings opposite. Immediately they came under fire from a machine gun in a pillbox beyond the Southern Entrance, commanding the open way by which they must all go.

There lay the girdered Bridge D, gaunt and ghostly in the curious light. It was barely seventy yards away. Beyond it the German machine guns looked down from roof and window. Astride it on the far side, and stretching along the quayside, lay a line of enemy riflemen, last remaining elements of the German naval troops.

No means of indirect approach to the bridge was at hand, no cover, no opportunity for finesse. Haines, at his own suggestion, sited a Bren gun to give a little covering fire. Then Newman called to his waiting soldiers:

"Away you go, lads!"

The commandos went for it, moving at a steady double as a hurricane of fire burst upon them from beyond the bridge. The astonished Germans, quite in the dark about the purposes of all these confounding occurrences, shot high and wide, as they had done all that night. A violent storm of bullets swept over the commandos' heads.

Donald Roy made on right in the middle of the road, Newman now beside him. Close behind him were Sergeant Rennie, Denison, Montgomery and Haines. They saw the German riflemen athwart the bridge scramble to their feet and retire. They passed the ships that Pritchard had sunk, passed Philip Walton's dead body and swept over the Bridge of Memories, their rubber boots thudding on the hollow road while the bullets rang and sparked on the steelwork or whistled overhead into the night. To all those who took part it was the most inspiring moment of the night. In the pages of British history there have been many glorious charges, but, on its smaller scale and in its more modest intent, the break-out of the commandos at Saint-Nazaire ranks high among them as a manifestation of soldierly purpose and of the will and determination to defy odds.

As they reached the end of the bridge Sergeant Rennie fell, shot in the knee. A German grenade hit Corran Purdon in leg and shoulder, bowling him over on top of Day. At that moment Copland went straight for the pillbox, emptying his magazine into the slit and others followed his example. Roy, seeing a German run out from behind it, attacked him with a grenade. He ran to a roadside pit with Denison, Haines and a sergeant to attack with fire another machine gun in action from a window a little way up the street. A motorcycle combination, carrying machine-gunners, came suddenly from round a corner at a crossroads. Every commando in sight opened fire and the Germans, riddled with bullets, crashed into a café wall. Further up the road what appeared to be an armored car drove up very fast, spitting out fire at random in every direction and taking station at a crossroads 150 yards ahead, thus barring further progress by that route.

So, about a hundred yards beyond the bridge, ended the commandos' dockyard battle. For the motorcycle combination and the armored vehicle gave notice of the arrival of the first troops of the German Army. They were units of 679 Infantry Brigade, a partially motorized formation, consisting of one or more infantry companies, half a company

232

of machine-gunners, two companies of 559 Construction Battalion and probably a unit of the 333 Division's artillery regiment. The brigade commander himself arrived in the town about this time and took over command of the operations at 4:30 A.M. These troops had arrived too late to mar the splendor of the commandos' break-out from the dockyard, but just in the nick of time to stop them from getting any further. Had they been fifteen minutes later, all the commandos who were fit enough would have made their way through the town and into the marsh country beyond, for once over the bridge, there were no more naval troops to oppose them.

Immediately after having crossed the bridge, the little force, deflected by the armored car, turned left and soon broke up into separate parties. Copland, finding a lorry parked at the roadside, seized the opportunity for escape but inside the cab the only switch he found to work was the one for the headlights, which illuminated Denison, who gave vent to the familiar wartime cry: "Put out those bloody lights!"

From this point all becomes confused as the small parties of commandos, with no maps and not knowing which direction to take, made their way through the streets, sticking close to the shadows of walls. All over the town the Germans were now rushing in reinforcements, uncertain what was afoot, believing that the raid was the spearhead of an invasion. Armored cars or machine guns were being posted at every road intersection. Newman squeezed into a doorway to avoid an armored car that shot past. Everywhere the Germans were shooting at any object that moved, frequently firing at each other, as the watching commandos observed.

To avoid all these patrols and pickets, now being augmented each minute, the British began to forsake the streets, and to engage in what they were afterwards to term the "Saint-Nazaire Obstacle Race," clambering over walls,

233

passing through one back yard after another, even going through houses from front to back. Private Hannon dropped over a wall into a chicken-run, awakening the startled fowls to a premature reveille. Newman also dropped into a chicken-run and, going head-first through a window, entered a parlor with the breakfast things already laid out on a blue-checked cloth, and so passed through the house to the front door.

By now, however, time was running out. It was somewhere about 4 A.M. and only two hours of darkness remained in which to find lying-up places for the day. Ammunition was very short and, with every street corner now picketed by the enemy and every street swept by fire, effective progress became difficult. Worst of all was the condition of the wounded. By now about three men out of every four had been hit. All but a few had kept up but were now weak from loss of blood and fatigue. Here and there small parties, becoming broken off from their main groups, began to seek shelter in cellars and outhouses.

Michael Burn and Rifleman Bushe were surprisingly caught in the boiler room of a ship in the docks. Very few of them had any luck.

Donald Roy, at the head of a party, seeking water for the wounded who were with him, called at a building which unfortunately turned out to be a police station, and the police, after stalling him, had a squad of German bayonets round in a few minutes, for the French police, under orders to collaborate with the invaders, were nearly as dangerous to escapers as the Germans themselves.

Newman himself, with about fifteen others, found refuge in a large cellar equipped as an air-raid shelter, with eighteen palliasses. Of them all, only himself, Copland, Day and Steele were unwounded. Steele was posted as lookout near the head of the stairs and wounds were dressed as far as possible. Here Newman intended to stay until night, when they would set out in pairs for the open country. "But I also decided," he said, "that if we were found in the cellar I should surrender, as the wounded were in a pretty bad way and a single grenade flung down the stairs would see the lot off."

234

They were indeed discovered, the commander of 679 Brigade having ordered a systematic search. Newman himself at once dashed upstairs and offered surrender. Roughly handled, the party was frog-marched across the road and taken into the house immediately across the road, which turned out, to the amusement of Newman, to be the German headquarters. Under heavy guard, they were stripped of their weapons and interrogated by a German officer without much success.

While this was going on one of the commandos had some occasion to take out his fighting knife, which they all wore strapped to their legs inside their trousers and which, as we have noted earlier, they scarcely thought of as weapons, the British instinct (and, one thinks, the German too) being averse to the use of the knife as a soldier's weapon. The interrogating officer, who was what Newman called an "office type," observed this action and flew into a rage. Why had they not surrendered all their weapons? They were then all stripped naked under the muzzles of Tommy guns and lined up against a wall. "I really thought," said Newman, "that that was going to be the end of things." At that moment, however, another German officer appeared who was not an "office type," and he quietly gave orders for the prisoners to resume their clothes.

Back in the dockyard Chant lay by the quay, unable to rise. Wounded a second time in the legs, he had been bowled over in the dockyard battle. Sergeant Butler and Private Brown, of the Argylls, had come to his aid and carried him onward as far as the Submarine Basin, but there he had bidden them leave him. He lay in "the weird half-light" looking straight across to the submarine pens and watching the Germans moving about and manning their weapons on the housetops. A dazed young soldier whom he did not know came and sat down beside him.

There they were found in the morning by a German patrol, who came up to them, Tommy guns leveled, and, shouted, *"Herauf! Herauf!"* (Get up! Get up!). The young soldier, prompted by Chant, obeyed and was immediately shot dead. They turned to Chant and again ordered *"Herauf! Herauf!"* Chant, mad with anger but helpless, pointed to his injured leg. One of the Germans then noticed the stars on his shoulder, and said *"Offizier."* They searched him, taking all his personal possessions, and carried him to a café at a corner of Old Town Place, where Gerard Brett and several other wounded or dying prisoners already lay.

Not far from here Roderick, Hopwood, Sergeant Searson and one or two others, all wounded before or during the break-out (Roderick had been hit a second time), were lying up in a warehouse stored with bags of cement. They all managed to climb to the top of a pile of bags high off the ground and for some hours they avoided capture, watching the German search parties at work.

It was not until 10:30 in the morning that a German, on a higher level than they, looking out from a shed across the dock road, saw, through a bomb-splinter hole in the wall of their warehouse, the bandaged and bloody head of one of the commandos. In next to no time the place was alive with Germans. The wounded men were roughly manhandled to the ground, searched, lined up against a wall, and, like Newman's party, thought that "they had had it." Again, however, some responsible German intervened and instead of being shot they were hustled off to a ship in the Submarine Basin before rejoining their comrades in captivity.

Thus, little by little, what was left of the commandos began to come together again. "It was just like a reunion," Newman recorded. "In spite of personal misfortunes our spirits were high. We never gave in to the Jerries. We all felt that a good job of work had been done, and as each newcomer arrived we pieced the story together. What we were all waiting for, and straining our ears to hear, was the big bang of *Campbeltown* going up in the air."

Not all, however, could maintain this high note. Many were wounded very badly. Wherever the wounded lay, the camera-mad Germans gathered round, clicking from all angles and stepping over bodies to take close-ups. Private McCormack, grievously wounded in the head, lay in an open space in Saint-Nazaire town, with his head between his kilted legs, dying. The Germans gathered round him in crowds, jeering and laughing, while their cameras clicked. One of these pictures was published throughout Europe in

236

the German armed forces magazine as a whole-page picture with the derisory title "Picture of a British Commando."

While the commandos were fighting their dockyard battle and trying to effect their "withdrawal by land," the little motor craft of Ryder's force, or what was left of them, had begun their withdrawal by sea. For some of them the fighting had by no means been ended.

Seven of the seventeen craft we have already seen lost in flames in the immediate neighborhood of the docks—those of Stephens, Platt, Burt, Beart, Tillie, Collier, and Nock. The remaining ten which include Curtis's gunboat and "Wynn's Weapons," have begun their homeward journeys, setting course at full speed for the open sea. There they are to make rendezvous at Point Y, twenty-five sea miles from Saint-Nazaire, with their escorting destroyers *Tynedale* and *Atherstone,* with whom they parted company at 8 P.M. It was intended that, having assembled at Point Y, the force should be well on its way home before first light, which was at 5:48 A.M.

Tweedie and Jenks, commanding *Tynedale* and *Atherstone* respectively, had passed an anxious night, having had no news at all of what was happening in the river. All that they had heard on the air, picked up between 2:18 A.M. and 3:25 A.M. were the "leaving" signals wirelessed by only five of the MLs. Their anxiety had been added to by the knowledge that the five small German destroyers of the 5th Torpedo Boat Flotilla, which had left Saint-Nazaire early that night as a result of the signal from U593, were somewhere in the vicinity and might be encountered at any minute.

While the destroyers waited, the ten remaining motor craft, passing beyond range of the small, rapid-firing flak guns in the harbor area, came under fire from the heavier and more dangerous guns of the coastwise batteries. With the exception of the 75-mm. battery at Pointe de l'Eve, which was not manned, all these batteries engaged them hotly, even the big 9.5-inch guns on railway mountings at La Baule. The 6.6-inch battery at Pointe de l'Eve fired no fewer than 400 rounds that night, mostly in this withdrawal phase, their shells of about a hundred and ten pounds splashing up great fountains of water as they detonated on the surface. Yet all but two of the withdrawing craft successfully ran the gauntlet.

As one may suppose, the Germans lost no time in boarding *Campbeltown*. A group of very senior officers and many technical specialists, to the number of about thirty, climbed on board by the ladders that the commandos had left and carried out an examination. It is said that the Admiral-Superintendent of the dockyard himself arrived and, immediately suspecting the existence of an explosive charge, ordered a search to be made; but none was found, so shrewdly had it been concealed in its steel and concrete jacket. On being so informed, he said, we are told, "Well, the British must be very stupid if they think we can't deal with this." For the problem of disengaging the destroyer from the caisson was not one of serious engineering difficulty. It was apparent that she would sink in the lock entrance if simply towed out, and the methods to be adopted for getting her clear without immobilizing the dock for longer than necessary were being discussed. The acting Harbor Commander also visited the ship, but neither he nor the Admiral-Superintendent stayed very long. Mecke also came, driving up from his headquarters at St. Marc, and he took some photographs.

But these were by no means the only visitors. Orders had been given for a cordon to be placed round the dock, but either the order was never carried out or the cordon was ignored. For the word very quickly flew that here were plenty of cigarettes and chocolates to be had for the taking and a throng of curious sightseers of all sorts began to arrive by car and on foot—the submarine commanders, the gun position officers, officers of the naval shore staff and so on.

And their lady friends. Looking for souvenirs, they roamed the littered upper deck from the shattered bows, where the displaced twelve-pounder stood precariously by the big hole in the fo'c'sle, on past the tangles of twisted metal, underneath the bandstands where the Oerlikons had been so bravely served, and so down the steep incline towards the sunken stern, where the falling tide lapped quietly on the quarter-deck. They penetrated to the darker chaos below, where the officers' sherry lay spilled and wasted in the wardroom, where the butter was plastered on the mirrors, where broken glass, cigarettes, clothing and little personal things littered the cabins and the mess decks and where the inert corpses indifferently lay.

While this tour of his ship was being made Beattie, blanketed and barefoot, was brought ashore in Saint-Nazaire with the other survivors of Rodier's boat. It was probably some time after ten o'clock and he was disappointed to see *Campbeltown* still intact on the caisson. The latest possible computed time for Tibbits's fuses to act was 9:30. What had gone wrong? He supposed that the Germans had discovered the arrangements and found some way of disarming the fuses, though he thought that Tibbits had provided against that contingency also. He had no opportunity, however, to stand and stare and was hurried on, very cold, to some German office, where he was taken for interrogation by a pleasant-mannered German Intelligence officer, who spoke English well. The Intelligence officer got nothing out of Beattie, but he was persuasively talkative, and he remarked:

"Your people obviously did not know what a hefty thing that lock gate is. It was really useless trying to smash it with a flimsy destroyer."

At that precise moment the glass from the window crashed to the floor, as the room, and indeed, the whole town, was shaken by a thunderous explosion sustained for several seconds.

"That, I hope, is the proof," observed Beattie dryly as the vibrations began to abate, "that we did not underestimate the strength of the gate."

The interrogation was brought to an abrupt close.

239

This heartening evidence of their success was heard, or even seen, by nearly all the Charioteers who had now been swept up. The time, as nearly as can be judged, was 10:35 A.M., not earlier. Between them, Beattie and Tibbits had done better than either could know. *Campbeltown* erupted with an enormous flash and a column of black smoke. Under the impact of this blast, reinforced by the hammer-blow of the inrushing sea, the great 160-ton caisson burst open inwards. The sea poured like a tidal wave into the empty dock. The northern caisson, the inner face of which had not been destroyed by Brett and Burtenshaw, held, but the two tankers that lay inside the dock—*Schledstadt* and *Passat*—were flung against the dock walls and damaged and the sunken stern-half of HMS *Campbeltown,* cut off as by a giant saw, was swept inside by the force of the flood. Of the rest of her nothing remained but the fragments that were flung far and wide. All the Germans on board the destroyer—men and women—went with her. So, too, did large numbers of those who clustered about her on hand, dismembered by the violence of that blast.

How shall one explain the fact that this explosion took place so long after the extreme limit of time expected of its fuses? Not one fuse, but at least three. Under normal functioning, they should have burned through at 7 A.M. Even under the extreme expected tolerance, they should have acted by 9 A.M. When they did act, they were nearly four hours overdue.

There persists a belief in Saint-Nazaire that a British officer, either voluntarily or involuntarily, went back on board and, in a deed of self-immolation, refired the quiescent charge. Workmen are said to have seen one or more go on board. The finger of surmise points at once to Pritchard. He understood the charging and the fusing of the explosive ship. He had the professional competence.

Did Pritchard die in the Old Town where Maclagan saw him fall? No shot was fired and the corporal did not know by what weapon he had been struck. Had he only been very badly winded? Or had the wound been not a fatal one?

If there is any truth in the legend, it would, of course, explain the delayed explosion; but it is a legend not easy to sustain. For Bill Pritchard lies buried in the cemetery at Escoublac. Had anyone else gone back on board the destroyer, it is difficult to explain how, without the requisite gear, which he is unlikely to have carried, and in the presence of the Germans, he could have fired the great charge. It was recognized that these fuses were of an experimental and uncertain nature in regard to their timing and we can do no more than suppose that some unknown factor of temperature, moisture or material led to an excessive delay in the action of the acid on the copper. Yet it remains very odd that all the fuses should have been so long delayed without failing altogether, and even a man so little given to fanciful speculation as Hughes-Hallett thinks that "some hero" may have gone back on board and immolated himself.

An alternative interpretation of this persistent French legend is that some one or two British officers, on being ordered or invited by the Germans to go on board, did so in order to encourage the belief that the destroyer was not armed with a deadly charge. That is entirely possible, but there is no positive evidence.

Whatever may be the truth in this matter, nothing detracts from the brilliance of the demolition plans conceived and carried out by Nigel Tibbits, which so conclusively prevented the enemy, for all the remaining years of the war, from using against our most vital convoy route the most dangerous ship that they possessed. And to the memory of Pritchard we owe a like acknowledgment for those acts of demolition against the operating machinery which would have put the big dock out of action for at least a year even if *Campbeltown* had never blown up.

Dieppe at Dawn

The Dieppe Raid was launched at dawn on August 19, 1942. Churchill has called the raid a "successful reconnaissance," a rehearsal for the main landings at Normandy two years later—for it was deemed vital by the Allied commanders to gain experience disembarking major forces of men and tanks from landing craft in face of heavy fire. But in terms of numbers of troops lost, the landings were a disastrous failure. Out of approximately 5000 troops, the casualties numbered 3614, plus 215 officers. And by the end of D-Day, the German commander, Field Marshall von Runstedt, could announce to the world, "no armed Englishman remains on the continent."

The decision for the assault was taken by the Planning Committee of Combined Operations Headquarters presided over by Vice-Admiral Lord Mountbatten. The attack force was made up of 252 ships, of which eight were destroyers assigned to escort duty; air cover was provided by the R.A.F. which had agreed to commit sixty squadrons of fighters and seven squadrons of bombers.

The first landings were made on the outer flanks of the Dieppe sector, British Commando units being landed on Orange and Yellow beaches. They were to destroy big gun emplacements that overlooked the Channel and which threatened the ships in the attack force. The landings on Orange and Yellow were successful.

On the inner flanks of Dieppe, landings were made at Blue and Green beaches. The Royal Regiment of Canada landed at Blue, on the left flank. Here the troops were immediately stalled by anti-troop barriers and then devastated by overpowering fire from the cliffs. Out of 27 officers and 516 men only three officers and 57 men got off the beaches. It is not surprising when one reads the description of Blue Beach.

"The beach of Puits enclosed within the gentle-looking cliffs is a little more than 200 yards from end to end. A sea wall of very solid

242

masonry fills most of this expanse above high-water mark, and at normal tides there is about fifty yards of shingle bank between the wall and the water's edge. This shingle is of large rounded flints of from four to six inches in diameter. It is not an easy or a pleasant beach to walk on.

"At low tide the beach extends to a depth of up to about 300 yards. The shingle soon gives way to sand and flat rocks, and these rocks build up into rocky ledges which narrow the sea entrance to this small haven to less than 120 yards. Even under good conditions the approach is not an easy exercise in navigation, and it is not difficult to miss Puits altogether in the ramifications of that coast.

"The sea wall at Puits is a solid piece of masonry rising vertically about ten or twelve feet above the shingle. The whole crest of the wall was crowned with wire, and the two flights of steps which break the front were filled with tangles of heavy barbed dannert wire . . . From concrete pill-boxes embedded in the sea wall heavy machine-guns were firing point blank, themselves impregnable to small-arms fire, to mortar bombs, and even to the sustained covering fire from the guns of the motor gunboat standing in as near as she dared." *

The South Saskatchewan Regiment landed on Green Beach and moved off the beaches inland with comparative immunity. Its men were up the cliffs by ladder and blowing up gun positions along the tops with a momentum that carried them inland several miles. The Regiment of Queen's Own Cameron Highlanders of Canada followed on their heels and they, too, fared better than the troops on Blue. By nine a.m. the Camerons were more than two miles beyond the beaches.

So far, there was limited success at Green beach, but only a shambles at Blue. Greater success might have been achieved at Green and Blue if the men landing on the main beaches in front of Dieppe had been able to sustain a solid coordinated attack on the objectives handed them, thus mounting pressure on the German defenders at Green and Blue. Failure at the center meant trouble for all.

Let us now turn to the story of the main assault at Red and White beaches in front of Dieppe.

*At Whatever Cost, by R. W. Thompson, pp. 70, 72-73.

THE MAIN ASSAULT

by R. W. Thompson

1

The growing thunder of war closing in upon them from the flanks before the dawn had aroused the people of Dieppe from sleep with a sense of excitement, compounded of hope as well as of fear. They were accustomed, in these years of the Nazi occupation of their land, to the alarms and dangers of air raids. They had listened often, and without comfort, to the harsh roar of anti-aircraft fire and the crump of bombs, but this rousing din of war was of a different texture and pattern.

On all that broad sea front of Dieppe the Germans, too, had awakened to a new alertness. In the grey light of dawn they could see little beyond the fringe of the sea, but the sense of some crisis impending was unescapable, as battles raged on the flanking beaches.

Along the whole length of the foreshore from the end of the west jetty breakwater to the steep white cliffs of the western headland, the heavy barbed coils of triple dannert wire grew out of the half light, seeming a fragile barrier, little more than a snare for the unwary in its almost delicate filigree of outline. Fifteen feet behind the rolls of dannert, a seven-foot wire apron fence built on the knife-rest principle gave a more solid impression to the watchers at their posts behind the sea wall, on the house tops, in the pill-boxes and casemates, behind the anti-tank blocks and barricades, and in the caves of the headlands. Even then, as they stared outwards to the quiet sea, they also looked over their shoulders, for the threat—if threat there was—might come equally well round the flanks of the headlands from Pourville and Puits.

The beach of Dieppe is a steep shingle bank rising from about 1 in 40 gradient to 1 in 10 under the solid masonry and concrete of the sea wall. In places, the high tides had piled up the shingle almost to the top of the wall, which normally rose vertically ten feet above the beach. But this might prove more of a hindrance than a help to an enemy seeking a foothold. The sea wall, protecting the wide promenade, filled all the front for 1500 yards from the harbour to the West headland. It was well fortified. At regular intervals along its whole length men peered out from under cowlings such as shield "prompters" on a stage. These men were Forward Observation Officers. Their stage was the wide beach, and those they must prompt were far behind them, manning the batteries of mortars and field-guns that could bring down concentrations of fire anywhere upon all that steep and stony foreshore at a word. This was in addition to the predicted fire of mortars that would fall upon the angles of the wooden groynes which run up out of the sea to space the beach into tracts 150 yards wide. There were, in fact, a wealth of weapons in great variety concentrated upon this shore.

The Germans, when their own invasion hopes had dwindled, had worked with an energy and skill born of a growing fear throughout all the summer in their preparations to meet an invader. There had been much talk and clamour for an invasion, and the Germans had constructed skilfully an "iron coast" to meet it when it should come. They had burrowed tunnels and dug crawl trenches to their "prompters" boxes and grenade pits from the hotels and boarding houses that stood in gaunt and sombre outline in the half dark beyond the wide boulevards Marechal Foch and Verdun. These boulevards were wide enough to take three lines of traffic, and between them lay lawns and gardens, a seemingly peaceful expanse, 1200 yards long by more than 150 feet wide, and lending a spaciousness to the front of the huddled seaport town. The line of those tall buildings seemed like a wedge, imprisoning the rambling town and holding open the mouth of the narrow valley of the D'Arques that encloses Dieppe within the limits of its white chalk hills.

To the casual eye there were few signs of life at five o'clock on the morning of the 19th August. In all that sober row of hotels and boarding houses looking bleakly out over the grey sea, no guest lay waking or sleeping, and no light burned. The white mass of the casino building with its forecourt and steps breaking the line of the sea wall at the western end of the promenade had a blank deserted look, as though long abandoned. It had long since ceased to be a place of gambling and amusement, and had become instead a minor fortress. In the white cliffs of the headlands there was no sign of weapons or of movement in the blank sockets of the caves. In the docks of the inner harbour armed trawlers and invasion barges lay dark and silent at their berths, while the incessant bursts of gunfire flickered staccato patterns in the sky above the headlands, and beyond to the east and west.

At that hour of five o'clock in the morning the sea in front of Dieppe appeared as deserted as Dieppe itself, revealing nothing to the eyes of the watchers. Even from the snipers high up on the roofs of many buildings the last of the dawn twilight hid its secret.

Three miles offshore at that hour a great concourse of little ships, deployed in a wide arc and carrying the men of the main assault, bore steadily in at 10 knots to close the beaches at the appointed hour. They hoped simply to come in tight on the heels of a brief bombardment from the air and sea. Greater surprise than this they could not hope to gain.

The motor gun boat of Lt. Commander Mullen was in the lead. Gun boats and motor launches, flak and support landing craft guarded the heart and flanks and rear of the convoy, ready to give close support with their machine guns and Oerlikons.

On the left sailed the assault landing craft with the Essex Scottish Regiment under Lt.-Colonel F. K. Jasperson, bound east for the Red Beach. On the right were the assault landing craft of the Royal Hamilton Light Infantry under Lt.-Colonel R. R. Labatt, bound west for the White Beach.

And in their midst with the flak and support craft, and

in the van of those who must be first to land, were the Beach Assault Group of nearly 400 sappers of the Royal Canadian Engineers with their special roles of blasting the sea wall, and all else that might stand in the way of men and tanks.

Keeping station close in along the line in the second rank loomed the larger shapes of the tank landing craft of the first wave. Behind them again came the landing craft with the mortar detachments of the Black Watch of Canada and the Calgary Highlanders, and the machine-gunners of the Toronto Scottish.

Bravely, they came on with all the expanse of Dieppe and its beaches in their minds' eyes, knowing well the slope of the shingle, widening in an arc from left to right from a depth of 180 yards in the east, the Red Beach of the Essex Scottish, to 360 yards in the west, the White Beach where the Royal Hamilton Light Infantry must land. Much they knew; much more they imagined. Above all, they knew that they must seize the beaches at one bound, and press on to their tasks. So they waited like runners poised for the starter's pistol, ready to dash for the sea wall.

In the rear and on the eastern flank of the convoy six assault craft altered course eastward as they made the landfall of the Dieppe Gap. These were the assault craft of the Infantry Landing Ship *Duke of Wellington,* carrying the mortar detachment of the Black Watch for their appointment with death on the Blue Beach of Puits. The main body of ships held on its course, dead ahead. The moment of revelation was at hand.

Out of the northern sky the low hum of aircraft grew to a roar as Bostons and Blenheims swooped in upon the East headland pouring out a dense curtain of smoke, while Hurricane cannon fighters, fighter-bombers and Spitfires dived in a fierce blaze of guns and hurtling bombs to bring all that grey and quiet-seeming front to an instant uproar of smoke and flame, spurting red veins into the sky from the arcs of the answering tracer.

The time was exactly ten minutes past five o'clock.

The leading craft were then less than 1000 yards offshore, and as the aircraft swerved up and away from their brief

247

assault, the guns of the destroyers opened fire to set the whole promenade ablaze and fill the sky above the landing craft with the curious quiet shuffle of shells.

For five minutes that harsh and sibilant music filled the ears of 2000 men crouched ready and waiting for the ramps to go down, and for the rasp of stones that would send them rushing over that shingle bank to storm the wall.

The last half mile narrowed swiftly to 200 yards. Three red Very lights from the leading craft signalled the destroyers, and the barrage switched at once to the flanks, leaving more than a score of tall buildings burning behind the Boulevard de Verdun.

With 200 yards to go, the support landing craft began to lob their smoke bombs to veil all the fringe of the sea. The dawn was shattered now. The silence was ended. Through the smoke and into the guns, the assault craft reached that 1700 yard long curving arc of beach, and deployed upon it from end to end, from the wooden breakwater of the West Jetty in the East to the West headland.

Then the enemy guns roared out, suddenly, to drench all the sea approaches and the foreshore with a deluge of fire that tore the water to frayed shreds of wild spray.

Behind them and in front of them as they landed, the wild uproar of the guns enclosed the Canadians in a terrible cage of din and death from which somehow they had to break out.

The time was twenty-three minutes past five o'clock. They were three minutes late.

2

A terrific battle raged at once on the sea fringe as the Royal Hamiltons charged out of their landing craft to struggle for a foothold on that bleak desolation of stones fenced with its deep barriers of wire. In those first moments the flak and support landing craft joined with the gun boats, motor launches and destroyers, to pour fire into the enemy positions in an attempt to cover the infantry while

248

the smoke held over the East headland. In that opening outburst of fire, the crews of the little ships threw caution to the winds to rise to heights of courage and audacity that were to sustain throughout the long-drawn-out hours of the morning. They were hopelessly outgunned, sitting ducks in the drifting veils of the smoke-screens from which they emerged like Davids to confront the monstrous Goliath of the defence with their puny weapons. From one point alone, near to the Casino, four 3.7 cm. and one 4.7 cm. anti-tank gun with a range of 9,000 yards fired point blank over open sights. A 10.5 cm. gun-howitzer added the weight of its fire from the same area, while from the West headland, Hindenburg, and from a hundred unidentifiable points a deluge of heavy, medium and light machine-gun fire weaving in with the light A/A batteries,* wrought dreadful havoc and confusion.

The tank landing craft, attempting to close the beaches with their ramps down and their doors open, and meeting the full force of the heavier weapons, were stricken, like wounded animals, to wallow in the shallow water, their ramp chains cut, their hulls riddled with the penetrating fire of armour-piercing and high-explosive shells. Yet with a terrible persistence they crawled in while men remained alive upon them.

Worse was yet to come as the smoke cleared, meanwhile the mortars and the machine-guns combined with the brilliant deadly sniping to make a death-trap of the beach as the Royal Hamiltons were caught in the open. Yet in face of that bombardment, spurred on by the courage they knew at their backs, the Royal Hamiltons began to cut and blast their ways through the heavy wire barriers. Many men in that assault were bewildered and confused by the sheer force of the reception, but swiftly those who lived began to fight, to answer with rifles and Brens the deluge that poured upon them.

Within ten minutes of the touchdown, the Beach Assault Groups, many of them trying to land from the crippled tank landing craft, died in scores. Of seventy-one men of one

* Many light A/A guns had dual-purpose roles.

group of sappers only nine survived, and of those, four were wounded. Out of a total strength of eleven officers and three hundred and fourteen other ranks of the Royal Canadian Engineers, nine officers and 180 men were killed or wounded at the moment of landing. Thus at the outset the power of the assault force to demolish their targets was gravely curtailed.

Very few coherent voices speak out of that landing. Private Prince of C Company of the Royal Hamiltons is one of them:

> "When we landed, we were confused for some time but finally got down and began to return some of the fire. We encountered barbed wire and began cutting it. We found it could be crossed without cutting. I tried to go under the last two strands but got hung up. Corporal J. Hartnett was also hung up and was wounded. I think the German sniper is a real specialist. They are wonderful shots and go for the officers and N.C.O.s. We found that they are mostly planted on roofs or in very high buildings.
>
> "The Germans seemed to be able to lay down mortar bombs where they damned well pleased. The beach was well covered by L.M.G.s from the buildings and by Heavy and Medium M.G.s from our flanks.
>
> "After we got over the wire we got down behind the beach wall and were forced to stay there. Going up that wall four of our N.C.O.s were put out of action. Our Platoon Officer was also wounded then. Major C. G. Pirie crawled up and told us to stay put. He got the Colonel on the '18 set' and gave our position and the Colonel told him to stay there. Colonel Labatt was asking the Air Force to bomb the hotels further on. A tank appeared at this moment and after changing direction finally got on the beach. It got a couple of men who were too slow in moving. The tank was hit at this point, three times in the tracks and twice just below the turret, by some sort of A/Tk gun. The tank, after a few attempts, turned round

250

and returned the fire. We stayed in this position until time for withdrawal when we organized parties to help wounded. I would like to mention an act of bravery I saw—the man concerned being Private G. McRichie. He is now missing. McRichie was himself quite safe from fire behind the wall we got to. He looked back and saw Corporal Hartnett who was hung on the wire. George (Private McRichie) got a pair of wire cutters and walked out into that heavy M.G. fire and cut the Corporal loose. He then began to roll him through the remainder of the wire and brought him back into the shelter of the wall."

Even in the first half hour before the smoke cleared from the formidable bulk of the eastern headland, Bismarck, it was plain that the attempt to seize the beaches in one bold stroke must fail. Without the Sappers, the sea wall could not be breached. Without the covering fire of the tanks in close support, the infantry were almost as helpless as men with bows and arrows. Yet after the first moments of confusion they rallied to fight back. With Bangalores and wire cutters they breached the wire while many men struggled over and under the barriers, firing into the yawning cavity of Dieppe as they crawled over the stones. There were very few gaps in that carefully laid pattern of direct and enfilade fire, but in the face of it the Royal Hamiltons reached the wall, and behind them came six tanks that had got ashore in the first wave, climbing, skidding and swerving over the steep shingle. Of these six, five clawed their ways over the wall, and the six climbed the broad steps of the Casino to reach the esplanade. Flying the yellow pennant of C Squadron, three moved off at full speed along the Boulevard Marechal Foch. Two more got into positions on the esplanade east of the Casino, and began at once to shell machine-gun posts and anti-tank guns on the West headland. The sixth tank was caught in a tank trap on the esplanade and its crew died fighting. Seven more tanks were stuck on the edge of the sea, four of them disabled, and three of them with cold engines trying to warm up while fighting their guns with great determination,

251

but unable to withstand the battering that engulfed them.

Nevertheless the partial success of the six tanks in reaching the esplanade had given some cover to the right flank of the Royal Hamiltons, and small groups of determined men were quick to take advantage of the chance to move.

All this time the fighters and fighter-bombers of the R.A.F. dived incessantly upon the enemy. It was in vain. At six o'clock, as the smoke cleared from the East headland, the enemy played his trump card. At that same moment, the gunboat *Locust* was trying to probe the outer defences of the harbour to lead in the Chasseurs, and the second wave of tank landing craft were struggling to close the beach. These met the full force of the terrific armament hidden in the East headland caves. All available destroyers, and *Locust*, turned their guns upon the headland in an endeavour to quell this new fury. It was hopeless. Guns of heavy calibre, probably 88s and 75s, came forward to fire, and immediately withdrew out of sight, invulnerable to guns or the bombs of the R.A.F.*

The official record reads as follows:

> "This appalling enfilade fire made the capture of the beach impossible and all the rest of the plan fell to the ground."

By six o'clock two companies of the R.H.L.I. should have been joining with the South Saskatchewan Regiment in attacks against the light A/A batteries, the Goering battery, and in the assault against Quatre Vents Farm; while a third company should have joined with one company of the Essex Scottish to hold the Dieppe perimeter. But the R.H.L.I. were no longer a battalion measured in companies, platoons, and sections. Units were shattered out of recognition; most of the leaders were killed or wounded, cohesion was lost. The battalion had become

---

*Constant air reconnaissance and daring low-level photographic sorties had failed to reveal the secrets of the caves in the East headland. And they had not been imagined.

252

simply small groups of men ready to take and to accept leadership wherever they could find it. Some of these groups were prepared to do more than sell their lives dearly. A few there were hemmed in under the cover of the wall who could do little, but many more were resolved to harry the enemy wherever they could find him. If the battle could not be won, at least there were many ways in which it might be lost.

The Casino was the first objective. Two groups of men following Capt. Hill and Sgt. Hickson, D.C.M., went in to the attack. Lt. Bell led a third group into the town, while yet a fourth group under an unknown officer attempted to storm the West headland. This officer was seen to fall when halfway up the cliff, and there on the cliff all that group perished.

3

The mile-long beach of Dieppe sweeps away from the East headland and the harbour in a south-westerly direction, broadening like the blade of a scimitar. The Essex Scottish Regiment landed up near the "hilt" where the beach has a depth of approximately 180 yards at high tide. This did not confer any benefit upon them. Instead, they met a weight of fire no whit less than that which greeted the Royal Hamilton Light Infantry on the broad expanse of White Beach, and it was concentrated in a narrower and more devastating field. High velocity artillery fired from concealed positions in the fortified hotels and houses behind the Boulevard de Verdun. Mortars used as howitzers responded instantly to the directions of the Forward Observation Officers using field telephones from their covered positions behind the sea wall. The cross-fire of machine-guns firing from innumerable fortified positions was fully co-ordinated with the mortars, the A/A guns with dual-purpose roles, and the 4.7 cm. anti-tank guns in pill-boxes three to four feet thick, and embedded deeply in the ground.

Yet in the brief interval while the smoke-screen still

blinded the gunners in the East headland to their targets, the Essex Scottish landed and, supported most bravely from the sea, many reached the wall.

In attempting to give a true picture of this succession of events, I find myself imprisoned by their terrible similarity in a narrow framework of words. Men land from landing craft; the beaches are of stones varying from three to six inches in diameter; sea walls, cliffs and headlands enclose them. And within these confines, almost devoid of cover, men are enfiladed by merciless fire and slaughtered in droves. These things beat upon my mind like the strokes of a hammer, day after day. But there is no way out. I must pursue this repetition, seeking constantly to curb the use of words such as "heroism," "courage," "devastating," and "fury" that spring constantly to the end of my pen. Yet even the official record of these events is at times unable to avoid the purple phrase. These things happened. In their emphasis the tragedy may emerge the more starkly.

When they landed on Red Beach the Essex Scottish rushed the first of the wire barriers, flinging themselves down upon it, making bridges of their bodies that their fellows might cross. In that first deluge of fire, men knew instinctively that there was no time for wire cutting, and that only by sheer speed might the battalion hope to reach the wall. There was no shelter, save only the shallow folds of the shingle. While many charged the wire, others burrowed in the loose stones and began to return the enemy fire with rifles and Brens, thus to give some cover to those advancing. In their wake the mortar detachments and some of the machine-gunners of the Toronto Scottish with their guns on A/A mountings, strove to land and set up their weapons. One mortar detachment lived long enough to direct a score or more of bombs against enemy positions before the Forward Observation Officers under their cowlings directed shells upon them. The "average life" of static elements upon that beach was measured in a handful of seconds.

Meanwhile officers and N.C.O.s, the individual prey of snipers, led on towards the wall, many of them maintaining their impetus while suffering mortal wounds, ready only

254

to die when the first objective might be gained. Among these, Lt. D. Green, with one foot blown off by mortar fire within a few seconds of landing, led his men a further hundred yards hobbling on the bleeding stump until a second mortar bomb killed him.

The courage with which Lt.-Colonel F. K. Jasperson led his men is amply testified, but he could not lead them beyond the wall. The role of his battalion had dwindled to this. And there, under that shallow and dangerous barrier, the Essex Scottish fought like animals snarling in a trap. Some of them did more. C.S.M. Stapleton, with twelve men hurling grenades into the grenade pits of the enemy, crossed the wall, the esplanade and gardens, to gain the houses. These few, moving fast in the rear of the hotels lining the Boulevard de Verdun, entered two houses in the town. Firing from the windows for more than an hour, they engaged enemy patrols, killing many, before, by a miracle of retreat, they rejoined their harassed comrades.

The East headland had long since emerged from the veils of smoke to withstand easily the repeated attacks of cannon Hurricanes and fighters and the bombardment of the destroyers. There was no help and little hope for the Essex Scottish. Under the wall, suffering constant casualties, they settled down to fight to the end.

From first to last a wireless operator of C Company maintained contact with Brigadier Southam, at first on White Beach, and later on in the Casino. The incessant crackle of fire in the headphones told as clearly as words of the conditions under which the Essex Scottish were holding out.

4

It had been planned to land four troops of tanks in the first wave; two troops to assist in subduing the armed trawlers in the harbour; two troops to help clear White Beach and silence light anti-aircraft guns, and then to help in the capture of the Goering battery and Quatre Vents

Farm. Three scout cars were to go with Tank Battalion Headquarters, and remain with 6th Infantry Brigade Headquarters. These headquarters with signallers and the beach signalling party were to be established at St. Remy Church in Dieppe and share with the 4th Infantry Brigade landing at Red Beach. With the tank landing craft were also the sappers to demolish the sea wall and let the tanks through.

The first flight of six tank landing craft of Group 8 were less than five minutes behind time when they began to close the beach. The East headland was still masked in smoke, while Dieppe itself was barely visible beyond the swirling chaos of smoke, a cauldron brewing with the appalling din of war, and festooned with the red ribbons of tracer in monstrous profusion.

Two hundred yards out, the tank landing craft met the full force of the anti-tank and light anti-aircraft guns sited and ranged especially to meet them as they emerged to close the beach. Even as the infantry on the beaches met the full force of mortars and machine-guns in the first moment of assault, so also these tank landing craft met the full force of the heavier weapons.

In the face of this great weight of fire, the lightly armed supporting vessels, disdaining the protection of smoke, closed in to point-blank range in their attempts to cover the tanks. On the tank landing craft the machine-gunners of the Toronto Scottish, in exposed positions, offered themselves as sacrifices, manning and fighting their guns until they died.

Shuddering to the frightful impact of fire, the landing craft crept on over that brief stretch of sea. It seemed that not one of them could hope to reach the shore, still less to loose their burdens upon the enemy. The ramp chains of two were cut, the ramps swinging and folding back under the hulls.

The Tank Landing Craft 145, hit in a dozen places, yet with her ramp intact, touched down successfully and landed three tanks. It was her last desperate effort. Hit again as she tried to draw away, she drifted broadside on to the beach and sank fifty yards out.

256

Next to her, the Tank Landing Craft 127 forced her way in with her ramp smashed, and with her engine-room, her ammunition and magazine all on fire, her crew almost all dead or wounded. But a rating still lived at her helm, and two gunners of the Toronto Scottish manned their guns as the tanks crawled out of the burning oven the vessel had become.

The third craft, with her ramp chains cut and her doors jammed, stuck helpless on the beach. A fourth got in on fire, unloaded her tanks, and sank in shallow water. A fifth landed her tanks and struggled out from the beach for sixty or seventy yards before she lost way, and wallowed helpless and sinking.

At the last came Tank Landing Craft 163 fighting a dogged battle with disaster. Early on she had been hit in the engine room and had caught fire. A moment after vards the vessel veered sharply to port as the helmsman collapsed, overcome by fumes. At once a naval rating took the helm, and brought the vessel round, head on, before a direct hit killed him. A third rating took his place, and the distance narrowed in a kind of slow motion to seventy yards before this helmsman also died. A fourth rating then brought Tank Landing Craft 163 to the beach to land her tanks, and with the same rating at the helm of the burning vessel she pulled away from the beach, making a bold attempt to take the sinking craft in tow. In this she failed, but it seemed that the enemy had done his worst to her, and, miraculously, Tank Landing Craft 163 made her own way out to sea.

There were seventeen tanks on shore as a result of this brave endeavour, and six of them reached the esplanade. Of these, the three that had gone off at speed in a westerly direction along the Boulevard Marechal Foch flying the yellow pennant of C Squadron, little is known. A tank commanded by Lt. W. C. Patterson knocked down a house. Another was seen in the Rue Grande. At least two tanks finally made their way back to the beach with all their ammunition gone. No man lived to tell of their exploits.

There were many unlooked-for tank obstacles, especially on the Boulevard de Verdun, that had not been revealed by

257

air photography. By day the enemy had removed all trace, and had hidden his anti-tank guns. These reappeared each night at dusk, and were removed at dawn. Road blocks protected all the entrances to the town and promenade. These were eight feet high and four feet thick, with sloping backs on which fire-steps had been built.

Of the tanks on the beach, two lost their tracks, one lost its turret, and a fourth had the turret badly damaged. An officer climbed out of this tank with one of his eyes shot out, and ran at once to a second tank following up behind. He climbed in, and a moment later this tank knocked out the gun that had wounded him.

But none of these, lurching and floundering, burrowing grooves in the loose shingle, and in the face of deadly fire, reached the wall. Nevertheless, they fought to the last, and gave some cover to the Royal Hamiltons in their fight for the Casino.

Meanwhile, throughout the landing, the large flak landing craft, commanded by Lt. E. L. Graham, R.N.V.R., was conspicuous, closing the beach to attack the enemy at point-blank range. One by one the guns were fought until they were put out of action and the gunners killed. When the Captain was killed, Surgeon-Lt. M. P. Martin, M.R.C.S., the only surviving officer, took command and fought the ship until she sank under him. By so doing, he afforded some protection to the four tank landing craft of the second flight. This medical officer was finally rescued, wounded, from the sea and put aboard *Calpe*. There, throughout the day, despite his own condition, he tended the wounded.

5

The smoke had cleared from the East headland as the four tank landing craft of the second flight came in, exactly on time, at five minutes past six o'clock. They carried with them not only tanks, but also Brigadier Lett and Staff Officers of the 4th Infantry Brigade, together with

Lt.-Colonel Parks-Smith, R.M., of Combined Operations Headquarters, in command of the Beach Provost Party, and Lt.-Colonel J. G. Andrews, commanding the 14th Canadian Army Tank Battalion of the Calgary Highlanders.

These officers were on board Tank Landing Craft 125, to which Lt.-Colonel Andrews had transferred offshore, coming in slightly astern and to starboard of Tank Landing Craft 214. These two craft met the full weight of the barrage unleashed at that moment out of the caves of the East headland. Nevertheless, No. 214, brought almost to a standstill by direct hits, closed the beach in a sinking condition to land her tanks under a tremendous concentration of fire.

This was the target the enemy had longed for and waited for, and a great number of guns were designed and ranged for this purpose. As soon as her cargo was landed, No. 214 crawled away almost along the sea bed, holed like a sieve, and to sink as soon as she was out of her depth.

The Tank Landing Craft 125 with her cargo of commanders and tanks had gained some slight cover in the lee of the stricken vessel. She managed to close the beach and get one tank away before she met the full force of the enemy fire, and then in one burst, with her crew killed or wounded, it seemed that she must be overwhelmed. The vessel was no longer head on to the beach, and those among the wounded who could still move got some way on her astern, trying then to square her up for a second attempt.

The stricken craft had become a vortex of fire, her crew out of action as she drifted again towards the beach. Brigadier Lett had suffered severe wounds, and Lt.-Colonel Parks-Smith lay mortally wounded and dying by his side. At this stage, Lt.-Colonel Andrews, seeing his hopes of getting ashore to take command of the tanks rapidly fading, decided to get away. The vessel was only a few yards offshore, her ramp down and damaged by shell fire that threatened to cut it loose at any moment. It must have seemed to Andrews that he was unlikely to gain another yard. His tank was already out on the damaged ramp, and with a sudden lurch, it left the ship and was drowned in

259

eight feet of water. The tanks had been water-proofed to a depth of six feet.

Like men escaping from the hatch of a submarine just above water, the crew climbed out and swam for the beach. At the last, Lt.-Colonel Andrews climbed from the hatch, paused for a moment to look round, and was heard to shout: "I'm bailing out," before jumping into the sea.

A motor launch, swooping in with her guns blazing in an attempt to cover and rescue the survivors, picked up the Colonel and was immediately engulfed in flames from a seeming deluge of direct hits. It is probable that all on board were killed in that instant before the motor launch sank in the shallows.

Meanwhile, Tank Landing Craft 125 was still afloat, and those alive on board were fighting to save her and the wounded. A Sergeant of Royal Marines had at once cut the ramp cables after the loss of the second tank and the last of the crew. The Sergeant then took the helm. In the engine-room Major M. E. P. Garneaux, a Staff Officer of 4th Infantry Brigade, had reversed the engines, and immediately afterwards manned a pompom.

Slowly, crawling astern, the Royal Marine Sergeant at the helm spotted the engineer struggling to regain the vessel from the water. He had been blown overboard by blast, but was unhurt. Major Garneaux got him back on board, and he at once took charge of the engines. In such fashion the vessel gained the cover of the outer smoke-screens protecting the heart of the convoy, and was taken in tow by a motor launch to safety.

The remaining two landing craft had fought their way in to land their tanks, but with little success. The third vessel, covered to some extent from the full weight of fire from the East headland by the two vessels almost abeam on her port side, landed her tanks without a hitch. Within two minutes all three gained the wall, only to founder there, unable to grip the shingle and to climb to the esplanade.

On that desolation of shifting stones, swept by a fiendish pattern of gunfire no armoured vehicle could withstand, the tanks had the aspect of unwieldy wounded beasts, seeming to flounder almost blindly as they strove to bring their guns to bear upon the targets on the headlands.

Tank Landing Craft 165, the fourth in line, also reached the beach, but the fortune of her tanks was worse. The first tank stalled on the beach, and was an easy prey for enemy guns. The second tank fouled an airduct, and caught fire from a direct hit within a minute of landing. The third tank fouled the port side of the door, and was hit while still on the ramp.

This was a position of the utmost danger for the tank and the vessel, and then with a roar the engine started, and the tank lurched off violently into the sea, pushing the landing craft astern, and dragging a scout car after her through four feet of water. The driver of the scout car hung on, swaying wildly in his small vehicle in the wake of the tank as it roared over the shingle, and on up over the sea wall to the esplanade in one great bound. There, the scout car got free and moved off at full speed along the Boulevard Marechal Foch, while the tank fought like a beast at bay, pouring fire into the hotels and boarding houses that were now wreathed in smoke and flames.

This was the last tank to cross the wall. Of the twenty-four tank landing craft which had sailed, ten landed a total of twenty-eight tanks. Seven of these crossed the wall. One was drowned. Twenty were swiftly casualties. All were lost.

The remaining fourteen tank landing craft of the third and fourth waves, due to go in to land at intervals up to a final landing at ten o'clock, awaited offshore the order to land. It was never given.

All these craft were equipped with barrage balloons to defend them from air attack, in the event no balloons were flown. The R.A.F. controlled the air above all that battleground on land and sea, as yet unchallenged by enemy bombers. Had it been otherwise, the shambles of the beaches might well have been matched by the shambles of the sea.

Through all that day the pennant of Lt.-Colonel Andrews flew from the turret of his drowned tank, a forlorn symbol in an aching void of desolation as the tide receded to leave the tank high and dry on the smooth sands beyond the stones.

Soon after six o'clock the Military Force Commander had decided to commit his Floating Reserve to the support of Red Beach. The messages received at that hour from Brigadier Lett and Lt.-Colonel Andrews, stating that they were about to land, had seemed reassuring. The Military Force Commander could not know that these messages had preceded, by a few minutes the severe wounds of Brigadier Lett and the death of Lt.-Colonel Andrews.

Accordingly, the Fusiliers Mont-Royal, embarked in twenty-six large personnel landing craft, led by Lt.-Commander J. H. Dathan, R.N., set course for Red Beach under cover of smoke. Two of the landing craft were lost by gunfire on the way in, but the smoke-screens in the main masked the approach effectively up to the last moments. Unfortunately, they had also inevitably masked Dieppe itself from view.

At any time up to six o'clock that would not have mattered, but, meanwhile, the tide had taken a strong westerly set, and this was an unexpected and unobserved factor unknown to Lt.-Commander Dathan at the head of the column. Forced to navigate blind through the smoke, and without a chance of a landfall until it was too late, the landing craft missed Red Beach by more than one thousand yards with the left flank, and was off the beach entirely on the extreme right.

Out of the chaos and confusion of the landing, three men had towered above their fellows, and had rallied many to follow them. These three men were Capt. Vandeloe, Sergeant-Major Dumais and Sergeant Dubuc. They were men of rare quality, seeming larger than life even in the bald official record of their deeds. There were no orders now. No battalion. These three, assuming leadership of all who would follow, went in to fight in their various ways, determined to come to grips with the enemy, and to tear him out from behind his guns.

Capt. Vandeloe leading a score of men, and covered by Lt. Loranger's party from the folds of the shingle, stormed up and over the sea wall. Some little way to his right Sergeant-Major Dumais led a smaller group into the attack against the Casino to join with the Royal Hamiltons and Sappers resolved on the same purpose.

Meanwhile, Sergeant Dubuc had landed with his men at a point opposite the western end of the Casino. He had taken in something of the plight of half the battalion under the West headland, yet with no means of knowing that they were trapped. Dubuc's first aim was to liquidate as many enemy guns as possible covering what might be the exit from under the headland. It was the kind of situation for which such men seem to have been born, and which others recognize instinctively in a crisis. With an utter disregard of danger, careless even of whether or not others were with him, Dubuc rushed upon two pill-boxes threatening his immediate front, and overwhelmed them almost, it seemed, with his bare hands.

Sergeant Dubuc now looked for new fields to conquer. At that moment the pennant of Lt.-Colonel Andrews, flying from the drowned tank, caught his attention.

The tank had been left high and dry on the sand by the fast ebbing tide, and Dubuc realized from its position that it must have fallen off the ramp of its landing craft, and that its guns and ammunition might be intact. Without hesitation, beckoning one man to his side, Dubuc bounded off over the stones and the widening fringe of hard sand beyond, running like a stag with his mate at his heels. Together they gained the tank, and from that small isolated fortress on the edge of the sea, Dubuc turned his guns upon the West headland, fighting under the pennant of the Calgary Highlanders until his ammunition was exhausted, and at least six machine-gun posts and anti-tank guns had ceased to fire.

Meanwhile, in the shallows a tragedy was played out to avert a tragedy. In that dreadful moment of revelation, as the assault craft came out of the cover of smoke, it had been as if a curtain had lifted suddenly upon inferno. Upon the instant Lt.-Colonel J. P. Phillipps, the Commanding Officer, recognized the utter hopelessness of the situation. For himself, and all those with him in the first few vessels,

263

there could be but the merest chance of survival. But for those behind, there might be hope. Without a moment's hesitation, and before any man realized his purpose, the Colonel pulled on his white gloves and leapt to the small forward deck to stand upright in face of the enemy. Easily recognizable by his white gloves, he was too prominent to be missed either by the enemy or by his men. He had resolved to halt the landing, if it were possible, and save all those who followed. He had but a few seconds to live, and in those seconds with his white-gloved hands above his head, a proud and most noble figure, he signalled, and clearly made his purpose known, to the landing craft to put about and head back into the shelter of the smoke.

For perhaps ten seconds his body remained upright before he fell mortally wounded to the deck, yet knowing with his last breath, as his men lifted his body, that he had probably saved two hundred men from the murderous fire that must have added their numbers to the final count.

Six landing craft managed at once to turn about on the fringe of the smoke at the Colonel's signal, but the seventh, under Capt. R. R. Devereaux, R.M., remained behind in an attempt to save a few who still lived from one of the sinking vessels. Only then did he turn about to gain the smoke cover with his own assault craft in a sinking condition. The effort would have been in vain had not the Chasseur 43, standing by in close support, gone at once to the rescue to take all on board.

The task of rescue was, indeed, all that now remained to be done. On the Red and White Beaches, in Dieppe itself, in Pourville, and in the woods behind Green Beach, perhaps three thousand men still lived and fought. Even behind Blue Beach some might still survive.

Everywhere, the enemy reinforcements were closing in, and large forces were on the move. The battle could not be won, but all was not yet lost. In the air the R.A.F. remained supreme, still challenging the enemy to fight, and the Navy still ruled the narrow sea.

It was nine o'clock; six hours since the infantry landing ships had put the assault craft into the water.

It is known that at least six small groups of men made

effective raids through the town. There may have been more. At least two tanks fought on in the heart of Dieppe until their ammunition was exhausted, and of their fate nothing is known. But outstanding in the roll of these few are the exploits of Sergeant Dubuc of the Fusiliers Mont-Royal.

For an hour Dubuc and his one companion had fought the stranded tank of Lt.-Colonel Andrews from its exposed position on the sand. As soon as the last shell had been fired, Dubuc decided to make a dash for the sea wall. Two men might easily live where fifty would almost surely die. With his companion, he reached a point under the sea wall close to the invisible boundary between Red and White Beaches. In that area the wounded Lt.-Colonel Ménard strove to hold together a nucleus of his regiment and to organize as much aggressive defensive fire as possible. He was still unaware of the fate of nearly half of his men. They had seemed to disappear, and no contact had been made. In Dubuc's mind was a very strong awareness of his Colonel's plight, and a burning desire to do something to redeem, in however small a fashion, the débâcle of the landing. He was fully aware, too, that his regiment had been sent to the relief of Red Beach.

It is impossible to measure such men as Dubuc by normal standards. It does not seem to have entered his head to sit down under the wall in a defensive role, and at once eleven men of the Fusiliers Mont-Royal rallied to his side. Well armed with tommy-guns, Brens and grenades, they followed their leader in swift bounds to cross the esplanade.

By this time, a murky acrid pall of battle overlay the whole scene, the incessant gunfire, the smoke and flames of burning buildings, the smoke-screens laid continuously at sea and wafted inshore by the freshening wind from the West, all combined to make a twilit world of the broad boulevards and the gardens of the sea front.

The crossing of these wide open spaces presented no problem to Dubuc. Gaining the backyards of the hotels and boarding houses, he pressed on with his men into the town, clearing the streets with bursts of Bren-gun fire, and reaching the Rue de Sygogne almost without incident. There, Dubuc's party came up with Captain Vandeloe of their own regiment, marauding with a body of twenty men in high fettle, having found themselves more than a match for all the enemy they had encountered.

Captain Vandeloe had attacked in the rear the hotels and boarding houses with their fronts on the Boulevard de Verdun. Most of these buildings had been fortified as strong-points, and had added greatly to the direct fire-power of the enemy in the early stages. This much, at least, the withdrawal would be spared, for Vandeloe's party had winkled out the enemy with great effect. They had also brought down most of the snipers from these roof-tops, and those few who remained were no longer able to concentrate with any sense of detachment upon their deadly work.

These successes had inspired Vandeloe, and he proposed to carry on clearing enemy out of houses and key points until it was time to go.

The meeting of these two, the Captain and the Sergeant, seems to have been brief and buoyant, and mutually inspiring.

Dubuc turned East. There lay the tasks he would find for himself, for it was not only in his mind to inflict as much damage upon the enemy as possible, but also to do this in the area to which his regiment had been committed. As for his men, they were eager to follow wherever he might lead. His personal magnetism was astounding, in keeping with the kind of character beloved of a Dumas or a Sabatini, and but seldom encountered outside the pages of romantic fiction. Dubuc led on swiftly towards the docks.

Approaching the dock area, the small party were at once held up by machine-gun posts covering intersections and entrances, but not for long. Moving with great speed and determination round the flanks, and skilfully using covering fire, Dubuc succeeded in destroying the machine-gun posts with grenades used with great daring, and forced a way through to the edge of the *Bassin Duquesne*. Here they were still under intermittent machine-gun fire and sniping, and confronted by a seeming emptiness, bleak and desolate.

266

It was as though they had burst through an outer wall from a world of din and known danger, to an unnatural silence, and a sense of being watched. There were few shots, but those few held a note of peculiar personal menace in the thin whine of their coming.

It would have been simple to have turned back, as men do confronted with a cul-de-sac, and for a moment Dubuc halted on this eerie edge of the dockland, waving his men to crouch in the shelter and shadow while he got his bearings. The *Bassin Duquesne* was empty. Skirting the *Bassin,* moving swiftly in sharp bounds, setting the tempo to those who followed, Dubuc pressed on. There was something indomitable about him, and even at this time an aura of seeming safety.

So they came quickly through to reach the *Bassin du Canada,* and to find there two of the invasion barges that had been earmarked as the prey of the Navy. These were the prizes Dubuc sought. His party was still under intermittent fire, and it was vital to act swiftly before this fire gave warning to the barge crews. A sense of exhilaration seems to have uplifted these few men at this moment: it may have been that their French blood gave them a sense of "belonging," of being native against the alien Nazi. They followed Dubuc as stealthily as cats, to swoop silently and suddenly upon the barges, and to overwhelm the crews in brief and fierce hand to hand fighting. In five minutes Dubuc had won the barges, and it would not have been beyond his imagination to have attempted to sail them out to sea. That task would have been impossible.

Leaving the barges with their dead, Dubuc then turned South on the railway tracks with the idea that his party might in some way hold up enemy reinforcements. This was unwise. Well armed, keeping the initiative, it was credible and even probable that Dubuc and his men might have overwhelmed three times their numbers, but they were now out of grenades, and their ammunition was almost used up.

For about 1000 yards, divided into two groups, one on either side of the tracks, taking what cover they could find, Dubuc and his men moved forward apparently unseen. It was, by that time, nearing half past ten o'clock.

Little time remained, and strong enemy patrols were already moving in Dieppe in the vanguard of reinforcements.

It was in Dubuc's mind to give up this barren course, and move off into the town, when he came suddenly under heavy fire from an enemy patrol. It was impossible to get away. The small party with one mind stood their ground, and fought to the last round. In five minutes it was all over, and Dubuc surrendered. That in itself was a delicate operation, for it is sometimes easier to be killed than to be captured in such circumstances.

At that moment Dubuc appeared to be overcome with exhaustion, and utterly disconsolate. The stuffing seemed to have been knocked right out of him, but the Germans were not disposed to take any chances. Not content with disarming their captives they took the unusual precaution of forcing them to strip down to their underclothes, but they left them their boots. In that sorry state the prisoners were lined up with their faces to a wall near a siding, and left under guard. At a command from the guard they kept their arms above their heads. They were helpless, and to most men, however brave, it must have seemed that the game was up. But Dubuc was acutely alert, his ears tuned to the diminishing beat of boots as the patrol moved on, and sensitive to new sounds.

There could be but a few minutes in which to act— if it were possible to act at all. Dubuc's head had slumped down to his shoulder. He stood in an attitude of dejection, and from that position he was able to watch the guard. The man stood with his rifle at the ready, alert, half turned to keep his prisoners in view while also watching the lines of approach. In postures of weariness and despair, his prisoners appeared to need the support of the wall. Dubuc himself was breathing heavily.

Two or three minutes went by in a silence broken only by the harsh small sounds of men in distress, and the pattern of gunfire that seemed almost to come from another world.

Dubuc had carefully revolved in his mind the chances of a break. He braced himself for action, determined somehow to lure the sentry within reach of his hands. Dubuc, of course, was completely unarmed, standing there, rather ridiculous at first glance, in his Summer singlet and shorts, and with his heavy ammunition boots. He made a sound like a dry groan to gain the attention of the sentry. His hands above his head lay against the wall, as though but for that he must have fallen.

"Water!" he croaked. "Water!"

The guard took two steps towards him, and for an instant was off guard. In that instant Dubuc turned with the speed of a panther and smashed the man down with his bare hands, and killed him.

"Go!" he ordered. His voice was very quiet and gentle. "Back to the beach. Each man for himself."

Within a minute the twelve men had gone without trace, each man taking his way, alone, through the back streets of Dieppe, heading for the beach. If they were seen by the enemy, it may be that the strange sight of men running at full speed through the streets in singlets and shorts was strange enough to make reaction slow. In their various ways they reached the beach.

It was almost exactly eleven o'clock when Dubuc found his wounded Colonel, and reported, excusing himself for his unmilitary appearance. It was a moment of decision. The squadrons of the R.A.F. were swooping down exactly on time over the East headland laying the curtain of smoke that must be a shield to all these men in their hopes of escape. And out of that massive pall, the enemy guns had begun to blaze fiercely at the invisible targets, too numerous and too confined to be missed. In an instant the whole foreshore became an inferno of smoke and sound and fury, and of men moving down over the stones.

Out of the sea smoke Dubuc could see the assault craft coming in through the shallows. It was no short passage now over a steep shingle bank, but a long and perilous journey. Without a word Sergeant Dubuc stooped to lift his wounded Colonel in his arms, and strode out towards the sea.

The End in Africa

El Alamein was a real breakthrough; now the 8th Army was to push Rommel all the way back to Tunisia. And, on November 8th, 1942, the Americans landed with elements of the 1st Army at Casablanca, Oran and Algiers. The common goal of the American and British forces, homing in from east and west, was to push the Germans out of Tunisia, move across the Mediterranean to Sicily, and, once a base of operations had been established, invade Mussolini's Italy.

Long argument and discussion had gone into this plan. The Americans wanted a bridgehead in 1942 in France, somewhere on the Cherbourg peninsula. The British argued for the invasion in Africa and the development of a thrust up from the south against Hitler's flank. The British maintained that, because of the terrible losses of shipping in the Atlantic (losses were again high because of the enormous increase in shipments to Britain from the U.S.), any bridgehead in France could not now be properly supplied and protected against German counterattacks. The Russians had also pressed the Allies to develop a second front, to take some of the German divisions off their backs, and the Americans believed the Russians might not hold out beyond 1942 unless a second front in Europe were established.

Agreement was finally reached only after intervention by Churchill and Roosevelt; Gen. Eisenhower was given command of the North African invasion.

By the end of December, 1942, the British 8th Army had thrust 1,200 miles across North Africa toward Tripoli. But Hitler had in the meantime reinforced Rommel in Tunisia, and this was to delay the Allies' victory by several months. In mid-February, 1943, the Germans had fourteen divisions on the spot, many of them flown in by air, the British and American ships having pretty well buttoned up the Mediterranean by this time. Rommel counterattacked the Americans in the vicinity of the Kasserine Pass, and stalled the American drive for a few days. However, it was only a matter of time before the Germans were pinned down in Tunis and Cape Bon. The remaining German troops were slowly chewed up. The U.S. 2nd Corps broke through and captured Bizerte on May 7th, and on the same day the British 1st Army took Tunis.

270

On May 13th, 1943, the North African Campaign was declared over.

The Germans had suffered a loss of 250,000 prisoners, more than a thousand guns, many tanks and thousands of motor vehicles. Later that month, Churchill visited Roosevelt in Washington, and addressed the Congress. He announced that the Axis had lost almost a million men in North Africa, about two and a half million tons of shipping had been sunk, and nearly eight thousand aircraft destroyed. It was now time for the Allies to turn their combined efforts against Italy.

The Invasion of Sicily

The decision to invade Sicily was made by the Allied Combined Chiefs of Staff at the Casablanca Conference in January 1943. S. L. Morison, the U.S. naval historian, says there was a "serious divergence of views" between the U.S. and Britain as to the next strategic objective after the successful Allied landings in North Africa. There was, however, agreement on the following points:

1. "The basic strategic principle of March 1941 that the European Axis, as the most dangerous enemy in military might and potentiality, must be defeated first.

2. "Anti-submarine warfare was the most pressing and urgent problem.

3. "Some sort of 'second front' must be opened against Germany in 1943.

"The divergences, however, were very wide. The British wished almost complete concentration on the European war and merely to "hold" or "contain" Japan until Germany was defeated. The Americans, especially General Marshall and Admiral King, felt that it was absolutely essential to maintain momentum in the war against Japan, lest she consolidate her conquests and become impregnable. Regarding China as having the same geopolitical relation to Japan as Russia had to Germany, they believed that something must be done in 1943 to relieve Chiang Kai-shek. Admiral Leahy at JCS. meetings kept saying to General Marshall: "Remember this: who controls China at the end of the war, controls Asia. Don't overlook China." The British, on the contrary, regarded China as of slight account as an ally, Chiang as undependable, and the obstacles to rendering him aid through the Japanese blockade as insuperable.

271

"The English-speaking allies also disagreed as to their next move after TORCH. The Americans wished to leave only token forces in North Africa, to concentrate on the United Kingdom build-up and the bomber offensive, and prepare to launch a cross-channel invasion during the summer of 1943. The British, on the contrary, believed that no cross-channel operation had any chance of success before 1944. They proposed to exploit the capture of North Africa by using the ships and troops already there to take Sardinia or Sicily around mid-summer 1943, in the hope of knocking Italy out of the war, and perhaps bringing Turkey in on the Allied side." *

The CCS decided to postpone the cross-channel invasion until 1944, and the U.S. would continue all-out war against Japan in the Pacific. But the Chiefs agreed that "something" must be done in the European Theater in 1943.

"The British Chiefs proposed occupying Sardinia; the Americans, Sicily. Sardinia as the less strongly held of the two could probably be taken about two months earlier and with fewer forces. It would be a good base for bomber raids on the industrial cities of northern Italy, and for commando raids on the coast. But, although Nelson once called Maddalena Bay 'the finest harbor in the world,' it was not ample enough to mount a large modern amphibious operation. Admiral King scoffed at the Sardinia proposition as 'merely doing something just for the sake of doing something.' He predicted that Sicily would have to be taken eventually, and that it could best be taken immediately. Admiral Pound and General Somervell pointed out that the Straits of Sicily were still too risky for troop and tanker convoys, that Allied possession of Sicily would render unnecessary the roundabout Cape route to India, affording a saving in time equivalent to the employment of 225 freighters. On 19 January 1943, the CCS decided on the occupation of Sicily, with four objects in view: (1) securing the Mediterranean line of communications, (2) diverting German forces from the Russian front, (3) increasing the pressure on Italy, and (4) creating 'a situation in which Turkey can be enlisted as an active ally.' " **

Sicily was heavily fortified; 405,000 Axis troops were stationed there to defend against an invasion. The terrain was most difficult for tanks and trucks, because of narrow roads and mountainous country.

*S. L. Morison, *Sicily-Salerno-Anzio,* published by Little Brown & Co., p. 5.

** *Sicily-Salerno-Anzio,* pp. 9-10.

The plan of assault called for a week's bombardment in advance of the landing to knock out the enemy's air and naval defenses. Then on July 10, the invasion forces, consisting of 160,000 men, 14,000 vehicles, 600 tanks, 1800 guns and 3000 ships and landing craft, would land on the Sicilian beaches.

The U.S. Seventh Army was to land between Cape Scaramia and Licata on the southwest coast. Its six divisions, including the 82nd Airborne, were under the command of General Patton. The British Eighth Army, commanded by General Montgomery, would land seven divisions, including the British 1st Airborne, on the southeast coast.

On July 9, bad weather made the prospect of coordinated landings extremely hazardous. But by the morning of D-Day, July 10, the seas had calmed and only moderate surf was on the beaches.

Earlier, airborne troops had been dropped to knock out installations, set up roadblocks, and delay reinforcements. They had only limited success with their tactical objectives. However, the assaults on the beaches by the landing forces were successful and the troops were soon organized into attack groups to move inland.

The Hastings and Prince Edward Regiment of the Canadian 1st Division took part in the Eighth Army assault. Facing only Italian defenders, they had a comparatively easy time of it in the landing operation. But soon the orders came through to form up for the march inland to make contact with German troops who had withdrawn to defense positions in the hills.

Farley Mowat, the Regiment's historian, describes the march.

"The Regiment moved off from its olive grove at noon, turning its back on the sea. The heat was brutal and the dust rose so thickly that it became an almost palpable barrier through which men thrust their whitened bodies with an actual physical effort. It gathered thickly on their sweating faces and hardened into a heavy crust. Their feet sank ankle deep in dust as if in a tenuous slime. There was no water; the occasional foul well along the route dried up when the first few platoons fell upon it. The sun was an implacable enemy, and there was no escape from its brutality. Steel helmets became brain furnaces. The weight of the battle equipment, weapons and extra ammunition was one more agony. The marching troops straggled along the verges where there was no grass, but only dust, eternal dust. Occasional tanks rumbled past, obliterating whole companies in the hanging shroud. They marched.

"Not least of the qualities of good fighting men is their ability to endure. Bravery, military knowledge and expert marksmanship—

273

these things have their place in the making of a soldier, but they are as nothing if the man cannot endure the unendurable. The men of the Regiment were soldiers. They endured.

"The attenuated column, strung out in single file over many miles, worked its way steadily inland, and upward into the hills. There were brief halts each hour, and in those intervals a few men looked back at the broad blue bay with its minute ship models. Most of them looked down at their feet. They dragged at the incomparably bad issue cigarettes that came with the 'compo ration' packs on which the fighting units subsisted; and the smoke was bitter and acrid in their parched mouths. They got to their feet and their boots slithered, clumped, and the dust clouds rose into the shimmering air.

"Before dusk fell the column had passed the limit set for the third day of the invasion. There was no halt. Darkness brought some surcease from the heat, but none from the dust and thirst. The roads became steeper and exhaustion began to take its toll. Men slept on the move; an old habit learned in the English schemes, and they were guided by their companions. Here and there an N.C.O. shouldered extra rifles for those who had reached the apparent limit of their endurance. The troops marched on. Perhaps a dozen men could not go farther and were loaded on the backs of donkeys, to sit swaying with eyes shut.

"At midnight the unit passed through its first Italian town, Rosolini, but the place left little impression on men's minds, and few have any memories of it except that in the central square there was a well.

"A few miles beyond the town, and nearly thirty miles from the start point of the march, the Regiment was halted. Sections and platoons staggered into the open field and fell where they stopped. They were beyond caring even about food. They died on the hard ground, and three hours later they were dragged from their graves, and set upon the road once more." *

"In launching the Sicilian invasion, the Allied Commanders had as their prime objective the capture of the crossings to the mainland of Italy at the Straits of Messina. Accordingly, Eighth Army had been instructed to go directly for this objective up the eastern coastal route while on the far left the American Seventh Army was intended to contain and destroy the major German forces which were then concentrated in the western and central interior.

"But as so often happened, the inital plan had to be drastically

*The Regiment, published by McClelland and Stewart, Limited, pp. 63-64.

modified as a result of the enemy's failure to conform to it. Quickly disengaging the bulk of their forces from the battles with the Americans in the west, the Germans abandoned most of Sicily and concentrated their armour and their best divisions in the path of Eighth Army's coastal thrust. Thirteen Corps on the Catania plains at once became involved in a series of savage and exhausting battles of attrition that gained little ground, and that took much precious time. Its role became that of a holding force engaging the bulk of the German armour. And it was left to someone else to force the path northward towards Messina.

"Thirtieth Corps of Eighth Army, including First Canadian Division and Fifty-first Highland Division, had during the first few days been operating in a secondary role through the interior mountains on an axis parallel to that of Thirteenth Corps. Now Montgomery gave it the formidable task of making the major thrust northward and of opening up the front." *

MONTGOMERY'S MOUNTAIN GOATS

by Farley Mowat

First Canadian Division's thrust through the mountainous heart of Sicily, in its attempt to force the withdrawal of the strong German forces in the Catania plains, was approaching its climax. Catania itself already lay south of the line of the advanced Canadian units and it was nearly time for the Division to swing eastward and drive towards the coast. But before the turn could be made there was a most formidable gate to be opened.

The enemy had established himself on the Leonforte-Assoro base where the mountains swelled abruptly out of the bed of the Dittaino River and lifted steeply towards the peak of Etna to the east. Of the many almost impregnable

*The Regiment, p. 68.

positions available to the Germans, this was by far the strongest. Astride the two roads leading out of the valley the Assoro feature rose nearly 3000 feet from the dead river and thrust itself forward from the main mountain massifs like a titanic bastion. On the slope of the highest peak the village of Assoro clung precariously while a few miles westward the town of Leonforte guarded the back door to the citadel. As long as this position was held by the enemy there could be no further advance of Thirtieth Corps towards Messina; and the Germans had chosen the formidable Fifteenth Panzer-Grenadier Division to garrison this natural fortress.

By July 20 the forward Canadian unit (the Edmontons) had reached the Dittaino and had established a bridgehead across it. From the valley floor men could now look up to the sheer cliffs of Assoro and to the narrow, tortuous road that climbed the crags.

The German defenders were unperturbed by the appearance of the Canadians. They had no reason to be worried, for it was obvious that any frontal attack must be suicidal. And they believed Assoro to be one bastion that could not be outflanked for its only open side, upon the east, was a cliff face rising 900 feet to terminate in the ruins of an ancient Norman castle on the very peak of the mountain.

Brig. Howard Graham, entrusted with the assault of the fortress, believed differently. He knew as well as did the Germans that a frontal assault would be disastrous. But remembering Valguarnera, he found some faint hope in the prospects of an attack from the right flank and rear. The hope was very faint; nevertheless, he called Lt.-Col. Sutcliffe and asked him if the Regiment could do the job. Sutcliffe agreed to try.

With his Regiment committed, the C.O. immediately went forward across the Dittaino to the most advanced positions in order to estimate the chances of success. With him was the Intelligence Officer, "Battle" Cockin. The two men crawled through an olive grove and far down the exposed northern slope, in their anxiety to get a clear view of the enemy position. Crouched beside a single tiny foxhole, too small to hold them both, they were soon engrossed in their study of the great mountain thrusting high out of the dun-coloured earth.

On the Assoro scarp the crew of an 88-mm. gun laid their weapon over open sights. And when the cloud of yellow dust rose clear of the foxhole, Sutcliffe was dead, and the I.O. lay dying.

Prior to this moment all of the soldiers of the Regiment who had been killed had died in the confusion and tumult of action. Their loss had not been deeply perceived as yet, and hatred had not grown from their graves. This new stroke of death was something else again.

The tragedy had a remarkable effect. It irrevocably and utterly destroyed the pale remainder of the illusion that war was only an exciting extension of the battle games of 1941 and 1942. The killing of the C.O. *before* the battle seemed to be an almost obscene act, and when the news came to the men it roused in them an ugly resentment. The emotions stirred by the first skirmishes with war were only awaiting crystallization, and now they hardened and took form. Hatred of the enemy was born.

One more element had been added to the moods of battle and with its acquisition the Regiment reached a new level of efficiency as an instrument of war.

With Sutcliffe's death the command passed to the Regiment's adopted Canadian, Major Lord John Tweedsmuir. Tweedsmuir took over at a moment when the Regiment was faced with the toughest battle problem that it had so far encountered. He reacted to the challenge by accepting and putting into effect a plan so daring that failure would have meant not only the end of his career, but probably the end of the Regiment as well.

It was his appreciation that only by a wide right-flanking sweep through the mountains, culminating in the scaling of the Assoro cliff, could the enemy's position be reduced. Therefore the Regiment would scale the cliff.

It was already late afternoon and preparations had to be hurried. Alex Campbell was ordered to form a special assault force, a volunteer unit, consisting of one platoon from each of the regular rifle companies. The men in this special group were stripped of all their gear except for essential arms and ammunition, for it was to be their task to lead the Regiment; to scale the cliffs, and before dawn broke clearly, to occupy the mountain crest.

The approach march began at dusk and it was the most difficult forced march the Regiment ever attempted, in training or in war. The going was foul; through a maze of sheer-sided gullies, knife-edged ridges and boulder-strewn water courses. There was the constant expectation of discovery, for it seemed certain that the enemy would at least have listening posts on his open flank. Absolute silence was each man's hope of survival—but silence on that nightmare march was almost impossible to maintain.

There were terrifying moments; once, when the scouts saw the loom of a parapet that could only be a masked machine-gun post. Incredibly it was deserted, but so recently that fragments of German bread upon the ground were still quite fresh. Hours later there was a faint sound of stones, disturbed by many feet, ahead of the assault company. Men sank into the shadows tensed for the explosion that never came. Instead a young Sicilian boy came sleepily out of the darkness driving his herd of goats. The youth stared unbelievingly at the motionless shapes of armed men that surrounded him on every side and then passed on, as in a dream.

There was a desperate urgency in that march for there were long miles to go, and at the end, the cliff to scale before the dawn light could reveal the Regiment to the enemy above. A donkey, laden with a wireless set, was literally dragged forward by its escort until it collapsed and died. The men went on.

By 0400 hours the assault company had scaled the last preliminary ridge and was appalled to find that the base of the mountain, looming through the pre-dawn greyness, was still separated from it by a gully a hundred feet deep, and nearly as sheer as an ancient moat. It was too late to turn back. Men scrambled down into the great natural ditch, crossed the bottom, and paused to draw breath. First light was just an hour away. Under the soldiers' hands were the cliff rocks towering a thousand feet into the dark skies.

Each man who made that climb performed his own private miracle. From ledge to ledge the dark figures made their way, hauling each other up, passing along their weapons and ammunition from hand to hand. A signaller made that climb with a heavy wireless set strapped to his back—a thing that in daylight was seen to be impossible. Yet no man slipped, no man dropped so much as a clip of ammunition. It was just as well, for any sound by one would have been fatal to all.

Dawn was breaking and the whole cliff face was encrusted with a moving growth that like some vast slime-mould oozed upward almost imperceptibly. This was the moment. If the alarm was given, nothing could save the unit from annihilation.

The alarm was never given. The two men at the head of the leading assault platoon reached the crest, dragged themselves up over a stone wall and for one stark moment stared into the eyes of three sleepy Germans manning an observation post. Pte. A. K. Long cut down one of the Germans who tried to flee. The remaining enemy soldiers stood motionless, staring as children might at an inexplicable apparition.

Ten minutes later, as the sun cleared the eastern hills, the Regiment had overrun the crest and the companies were in position on the western slopes overlooking the whole German front. Close below them the village of Assoro showed a few thin spirals of grey smoke as peasant women prepared the morning meal. Half a mile below, in the steep valley leading to the front, a peaceful convoy of a dozen German trucks carried the day's rations forward to the waiting grenadiers.

Twenty Bren gunners on Assoro's crest vied with one another to press the trigger first.

The appearance of the Canadians must have come as a shattering surprise to the enemy and had his troops been of a lesser calibre, a debacle must have resulted. But the Germans here were of a fighting breed. Although they were now at a serious disadvantage, they had no thought of giving up.

From the ditches beside the burning trucks German

drivers returned the Regiment's machine-gun fire with rifle shots. The crews of four light anti-aircraft pieces, sited beside the road, cranked down their guns to fire point-blank at the Canadians upon the crest. Machine-gun detachments, hurriedly withdrawn from the front, scrambled up the road, flung themselves down behind stone fences and engaged the Brens in a staccato duel. With commendable, but frightening efficiency, the enemy's batteries, which had been concentrating their fire on Second Brigade in front of Leonforte, slewed their guns around to bear upon Assoro. Within an hour after dawn the crest of the hill was almost hidden in the dust of volleying explosions.

The Regiment dug in. Able company and the assault company on the south and southwestern slopes; the balance of the unit on the north and northwestern side. A series of narrow terraces gave scant shelter but the men scraped shallow slit trenches in the stony soil, using their steel helmets as shovels. The enemy's fire grew steadily heavier, while that of the Regiment died away as realization dawned that this would be a long battle, and there would probably be no new supplies of ammunition until it ended.

But the surprises of that morning were not all one-sided. Before the infantry companies moved off it had been agreed that two green Verey flares, fired by the assault group, would indicate that the enemy position had been overrun and that it was safe for the unit's transport to move forward. Sometime after midnight, while the infantry was still struggling through the maze of hills and valleys far from the objective, a German in the positions overlooking the Dittaino sent a routine signal to his own artillery. The signal that he fired was two green flares.

Although there had been no sounds of battle as yet, the transport group accepted the evidence of its eyes and began moving north. Before dawn it had crossed the valley and the leading carriers had been halted by a crater blown in the road by German engineers some time earlier. Things were still quiet and some of the men of "F" echelon got out of their vehicles and lay down on the gentle slopes to catch a little sleep.

The Panzer-grenadiers defending the road must have

found it hard to credit their eyes as the grey light revealed thirty Canadian trucks and carriers drawn up in a neat line almost under the muzzles of the German guns.

The men of "F" echelon were rudely awakened. Some of them, leaping up out of a pleasant sleep, yelled horrid threats at their comrades who, they believed, had gone mad and were firing upon them. Others, more alert, realized that they were in a most unhappy situation and did what they could to remedy things. While one of the three-inch mortars was hastily put into action, the drivers tried to turn their vehicles on the narrow road. Someone, thinking with great rapidity, began throwing smoke grenades around the leading vehicles and under this thin protection the carriers managed to turn and clatter wildly down the slopes. One of them was driven by a motor-cyclist who had lost his own mount. He missed a turn and his carrier skidded off the road and somersaulted all the way down to the valley floor. The driver was miraculously uninjured and when he had dragged himself to his feet he stood for several minutes, in full view of the enemy, cursing his steed as if it had been a horse that had thrown him, and angrily banging its steel flanks with his boot.

It was fortunate for the transport and carrier men that at this juncture the balance of the Regiment on Assoro's crest carried the battle to the enemy's rear. In the ensuing confusion, and not without casualties—four trucks destroyed and four men badly wounded—"F" echelon managed to make good its retreat to the Dittaino and beyond. But it was in a chastened mood, and for some weeks afterwards it was notably suspicious of all orders to move forward to a "captured" area.

Meanwhile the position of the men on Assoro was becoming critical. The 500 infantrymen were almost completely surrounded on the three-acre crest of the mountain, and they could neither withdraw nor advance. Patrols were sent scuttling through the curtain of small-arms and shell-fire into the village. The place was cleared, but its capture brought little relief. The Regiment's threat against the enemy supply route could not be fully implemented, for already the scanty ammunition supplies carried on men's backs up the cliff, were growing perilously low. Confined to the congested area on the crest, the Regiment was exposed to an increasing fury of artillery shelling which was suddenly, and terrifyingly, supplemented by the fire of a number of German rocket batteries. This was the unit's first experience with the weapon nicknamed "The Moaning Minnie" and there was not a man who was not shaken by the initiation. The shells were nine inches in diameter and they were fired in salvos of five or six. The screaming of their rocket motors was an intolerable sound, as if the heavy shells were being forced through interminable rusty cylinders, slightly too small for their diameter. In addition there were single twelve-inch rockets, each containing 150 pounds of high explosive, that screeched their way slowly overhead and burst with a tremendous blast. More than 400 rocket and artillery shells crashed into the crest of Assoro in the first two hours of that bombardment.

But if the Regiment could not attack, it was not content to remain simply passive under this punishment. The Germans had decided that the crest of Assoro must be held by a very small number of Canadians and that, under cover of the shelling, it would be safe to withdraw the many vehicles which had been at the front. It was not safe. As the armoured half-trucks and open trucks came scuttling up the road the Regiment caught them in a withering small-arms fire and destroyed or forced the abandonment of almost a score of them. The Germans promptly reassessed the danger and prepared to counterattack the hill in force.

The Regiment's situation now became desperate. Unless it could somehow silence the enemy artillery it could not hope to hold on. Desperation sharpens men's wits, and in this extremity someone remembered the captured German observation post. It had been equipped with a fine pair of 20-power scissor telescopes and these were now hurriedly moved to the north end of the hill where Tweedsmuir and his second-in-command, Major Kennedy (who had originally trained as an artilleryman), could sweep almost the entire area from which the enemy guns were firing. There was only one radio—the short-range No. 56 set that had been miraculously carried up the cliff on a man's back. It sufficed to save the unit.

In the next hour the Regiment gave the distant Canadian artillery a series of dream targets. As each German gun fired up at Assoro, its position was radioed to the rear and within minutes salvos of Canadian shells fell upon it. There was no escape, for every movement of the German gunners could be seen. Methodically, carefully, the officers at the telescope directed the counter-battery fire until by noon well over half the enemy's artillery was out of action, and the rest was hurriedly withdrawing to safer sites.

But the vicious bombardment of the hill had added a new emotion to the battle mood. Men had discovered fear.

It was met by the beginning growth of a special type of fatalism, relieved by wit. The sort of thing that led one man to say: "When you dig a good slit-trench nothing can get you except a direct hit, and if it *is* a direct hit, it's because you teased your grandmother—or pulled the wings off flies." And another. "There's no use trying to hide out from a shell. If it's got your name on it, it'll chase you into the house, follow you upstairs, push the pot aside and get you under the bed." The humour was not uproarious—but it was adequate.

On the forward crest of the hill, pinned down behind a rock by a salvo of mortar bombs, Paddy Gahagen replied to the shout of his platoon commander who demanded to know what in the name of all the furies he was doing. "Looking for goddam four-leaf clovers with my nose" was the muffled reply.

Never had there been a greater need for the solace of humour than on Assoro. As the first day drew on, the heat grew worse and though the continuous heavy shelling had ceased, there were spasmodic outbursts from hour to hour. Water was a problem for there was only one well on the crest and those attempting to reach it were exposed to sniping fire. There was little food, for the emergency rations had long-since been consumed. In Charlie company, Pte. Greatrix became the hero of the moment when he produced a can of sardines that had been secreted in his haversack, and gravely offered each man in his platoon one fish.

A small cave near the well had been converted into a medical station and here the wounded lay in silent rows. The padre, Capt. Reg. Lane, a man of more than forty-five years of age, who was not equipped either by nature or by training for the hardships he had undergone, performed his own private miracle of endurance as he helped the stretcher bearers care for the living, or helped the living bury the dead.

In the late afternoon the C.O. gave up hope of a relief column breaking through to the Regiment that day, and called for two volunteers to return to the Canadian lines and attempt to guide a carrying party forward with rations and ammunition during the night. The R.S.M. and an officer accepted the task and set out down the great cliff, and across four miles of enemy dominated country, finally reaching safety in a state of complete exhaustion. But when darkness fell they were still able to guide a hundred men of the Royal Canadian Regiment laden with food and ammunition, back through the gorges to the foot of the mountain. The next morning the garrison received its first rations in thirty-six hours.

While the supply party was toiling over the hills and gullies, the battle situation had reached its climax. The Germans were being fiercely attacked at Leonforte by Second Brigade and they could not stand firm there while the threat of Assoro lay on their supply routes. They understood that Assoro would have to be retaken or the whole position would have to be abandoned; so at 2200 hours the enemy counterattacked. They came through the north end of the town, two companies of grenadiers, under cover of an intense mortar and artillery barrage, and they met Dog company on the lower slopes. Dog had very little ammunition left, but when the attack broke and fell away, Dog company had not given any ground and had taken a heavy toll of the attackers. It was the Germans' last effort. As darkness fell, they began to withdraw both from Assoro and from Leonforte to the west. The gates were opening.

The ordeal of the men on the mountain was not yet at an end for the road up to Assoro had been so badly cratered that it was not until late on July 23rd that the Regiment could be relieved.

At the precious well a group of a dozen soldiers relaxed contentedly, drinking to their hearts' content, and splashing cold water over their faces and arms. Below the town, supply trucks at last rumbled forward. Now the Regiment could rest.

And then, somewhere far to the north, the crew of a German rocket-launcher prepared to abandon their position. One 21-cm. rocket was set up for firing with its electric igniters wired and ready. And someone, in a last defiant gesture, paused for a moment to close the circuit and send the rocket screaming into the quiet sky.

The indecent shriek of the projectile drifted over the brown hills. The men by the well heard, but they had only time to stiffen warily before the rocket struck. It hit the curbing of the well, and when the black and acrid smoke had cleared, four dead men lay in the new crater, while five others moaned in mortal agony.

It was a brutal way to learn the grim lesson that in battle there can be no escape—until the war is done.

The Treetops Raid

About one-third of the oil—especially the high octane fuel necessary for aircraft—used by the German war machine came from refineries in Ploesti, Rumania. In the early years of the war, an oil refinery did not receive top priority in the bombing lists of the Allied air forces; rather, electrical plants, transportation centers, and industrial centers manufacturing tanks, planes, etc., took precedence. But in May 1943, during a meeting in Algiers, the Allied leaders decided a strike should be made against the Ploesti refineries.

In June, the 44th and 93rd groups of the VIII Bomber Command, 2nd Bombardment Wing, then undergoing combat over Europe, were withdrawn and given special new flying assignments. At the end of the month they were sent to Benghazi where they joined two other groups of the Ninth Air Force, the 98th and 376th. Altogether a force of approximately 200 B-24 Liberators was now assembled for the 2700 mile strike.*

In July, during the invasion of Sicily, these bomber crews were sent on daily missions against carefully selected targets. It was not until several planes were shot down that air force brass realized that some of the crew officers had already been briefed on the Ploesti strike. As a precaution against information leaks from any captured officers, all future combat missions were canceled until August 1.

According to Leon Wolff, the Ploesti "complex as a whole was fairly

*This would not be the first Allied raid on Ploesti. On June 11, 1942 a small force of 13 B-24s took off from the Egyptian air base at Fazid and dropped two tons of bombs. Little damage was done but the Germans and Rumanians immediately took pains to improve antiaircraft installations and warning systems against further raids.

286

concentrated around the major refineries and their most vital installations—mainly the six cracking plants. Distilling units, too, were particularly fragile, as well as the boilerhouses, power plants, and a few gas-liquefying plants. A vast scattering of over 2000 storage tanks dotted the area. Snake-like rail lines threaded everywhere, requiring in turn several key marshaling yards. A network of pipe lines connected the distant oil wells with the refineries. It all added up to a dream of an aerial target . . ." *

A most important condition for the success of the raid was surprise; a new and daring tactic was to be tried—planes were to hit Ploesti in successive waves but at "zero altitude." ** The planners believed such a maneuver would cause the greatest possible damage to the refineries.

The B-24s were fitted out with additional armor plate to protect against small-arms ground fire; an extra .50 caliber machine gun was placed in the nose, and the top turret guns in lead planes were made operable to fire forward to increase the overall strafing power of the leaders.

There were many doubts about the tactics of the low-level raid. For instance,

"The enlisted gunners were not told of the detailed bombing plan until the night before the mission. But unofficially the word had seeped down, or the men had made a remarkably good guess, and they too expressed many doubts. Some top officers began to wonder whether an unusual number of personnel might not find a reason—such as illness—to evade the mission. It cannot be doubted that fear had begun to permeate the five groups as the date for the ominous venture neared. Daily it seemed more and more suicidal. The consensus was that surprise was improbable, low-level or high. Flak would slaughter the low-flying, cumbersome monsters. Fighters would knock down dozens, at least on the way back, if not sooner. The balloon cables would be murderous. And 2700 total miles of unescorted flying, in itself, was no joke over enemy territory or water. It all seemed to add up to a desperate and needless gamble.

"In the desert, in July, everything was that much more exasperating. It was hot. Countless little sand flies made the fliers fretful. Scorpions

*Low Level Mission, by Leon Wolff, published by Doubleday & Co., Inc., p. 84.
** Minimum possible altitude.

prowled through the tents and took up lodging in the men's clothes and bedding; their sting was nasty, flashlights were prized, and walking barefoot was unheard of.

"But first, last, and foremost was the sand. Reddish and talclike, it seeped into everything and became an invariable part of life. Every afternoon the wind came up and the desert began to swirl. To evade the dry, gritty, blinding sandstorms, men even welcomed combat flying. The wind tore out tent stakes, it ballooned out the canvas tents in an afternoon, it covered everything inside with sand piled inches deep. The battle was without end." *

Then on July 31, the day before the mission, official briefings were held and the success of the assignment could be seen to depend on unusually delicate timing. "Plans called for the five groups to proceed northward in column after the original forming up over Benghazi. Then, regardless of what happened in the interim, there would be a time check over the Danube. Each group had its own assigned time of arrival at that point. From there the five groups would proceed in column to their first Initial Point. And finally, still in line, one after the other according to their time of arrival at the I.P., they would bomb their targets in the order that had been designated in the field order and by the briefing officers day in and day out for weeks on end. While the less experienced 389 had been assigned the easier separate target of Campina, the other four groups would be bunched together from Pitesti onward. This was the first I.P.; the second was Floresti, from which the run would be made to the target in bunched waves as swiftly as possible." **

*Low Level Mission, pp. 100-101.
** Low Level Mission, pp. 121, 122.

288

"TARGET: PLOESTI"*

by Leon Wolff

SEVEN-TEN A.M.

It began badly. One of the planes from the 98th never got off the ground, ran to the end of the runway, crashed, and exploded, killing all crew members aboard instantly.

Take-offs continued amid billows of orange-red dust, with the 44th and 98th using the adjacent Benina field and the other groups taking off from the strips near Benghazi proper. The weather was good except for a slight haze which reduced visibility to about ten miles. Each plane was flown to 2000 feet. There it wheeled overhead awaiting the remainder of its group. The men plugged their radios into the jack marked "interphone," and the pilots interrogated each man in turn ("pilot to navigator . . . pilot to radioman . . . pilot to tail gunner . . ." and so on). Each crew member stated that his guns and station were in order, that he had checked his oxygen (it would probably not be needed on this trip), that his Mae West was on (they would be over water half the way), that his parachute was in proper condition (it would be useless during the low-level phase). Everybody checked his machine gun by firing short bursts into the Mediterranean.

7:40 A.M.

Now all five groups were aloft and formed up. One aircraft had been scratched before dawn, one had already

*A somewhat condensed version of several chapters from *Low Level Mission*.

crashed, and the remaining 176 assembled in follow-the-leader order behind Compton's 376th. Next came Baker's 93rd, then Kane's 98th, then Johnson's 44th, with Wood's 389th bringing up the rear. The first group flew low over the water. Each successive group was a little higher than the one in front of it, and the last group, Jack Wood's 389th, held an altitude of 4000 feet. In this alignment the great task force swung north and headed across the Mediterranean Sea, cobalt-blue, brilliant, and glistening in the slanting morning sun that glanced off the whitecaps.

7:50 A.M.

One of the planes (the Kickapoo) flown by a squadron leader of the 376th began a long curving sweep out of formation to the right. Major Ramsey Potts had stood up to stretch, turning his controls over to his co-pilot, when he noticed this. "He seemed to slide off on his right wing and burst into flames. The radio operator on my airplane, who was standing beside me looking out across the sea—toward the lead formation which was off to our right and below us —said, 'Gee whiz, look at the flame!' And that was quite an incongruous sort of reaction, I thought, so I half-pushed him back into his seat and told him to shut up . . . We were all keyed up, and to have this happen to a lead plane in the lead formation was kind of shocking."

The Liberator on fire was still partially under control, and the pilot thought he could make it back to the Benina strip. This he did, but as the ship neared the ground it was flying fast and not quite level. The field was still a swirling fog of red dust stirred up by the prop-wash of the last planes to take off several minutes previously. With a sickening jolt the Kickapoo hit the runway, bounced twenty feet into the air, hit again, skidded down the extreme edge of the field, smashed into a concrete telephone pole, and exploded. Eight of the ten men were killed. Sergeant Eugene Garner came out almost unharmed, but the navigator, Lieutenant Russell Polivka, survived with fearful burns from head to waist.

Radio silence had been put to the test during this incident, but not a word was spoken by the horrified on-lookers aloft. The plane behind the ill-fated one moved into the vacant slot, and the group flew wordlessly on.

All across the Mediterranean the planes flew on in a flat V, wing tip to wing tip, none more than twenty-five feet away from another. It was a pleasure, at least, to be flying so low that annoying, efficiency-robbing oxygen masks were not needed. As time passed planes began to turn back because of mechanical failures. Captain William Banks of Kane's 98th observed: "Every once in a while I would look off to my left and see one or two Liberators feather a prop, wheel out of formation, and start for home. A little later one of the crew would call over the interphone, 'Another plane's turned back!' Most of them went under us. We could see them about halfway down between us and the sea, trying to make it to safe, Allied land before they piled into the Mediterranean. Others would turn back close enough for us to see the men in the plane. We waved goodbye . . ."

Eleven planes in all aborted. Major Shingler thought that the number was "a little high," but pointed out that "it was up to the pilots to use their own discretion," and that a mission as long and hazardous as this called for air-craft in top condition "especially as we were anticipating the interception of fighters from the time we entered the coast off the Adriatic Sea, all the way in and all the way back." (It is true that seven of the eleven aborts came from Kane's group. This percentage seems out of line and may have been caused by the fact that Kane often strongly ad-vised his people to fly beyond their operational limit. It is known that in this mission, especially, he had exerted great pressure, even to the point of delaying certain men stateside leave until their return from Ploesti.) As each plane turned back the hole in the formation was plugged up. Each group remained intact, but the haze had caused the five groups to become partially separated from each other. The 98th, for one, had become completely isolated after three hours. No enemy shipping or planes were sighted; thus far the element of surprise was still on the side of the invaders.

11:30 A.M.

While the 376th Group was proceeding over the coast line of the island of Corfu, Brian Flavell's lead plane spun into the sea with the loss of all crewmen, including the lead navigator, Captain Anderson. When this crucial plane and officer went down, a chill of foreboding passed through all members of the group. Momentarily the 376th began to scatter in confusion, trying to select a new leader. Then the plane carrying Compton and Ent moved out of their section and up into the lead position of the group. In theory lead navigating was now in the hands of a young, inexperienced second lieutenant. In actuality Compton and Ent took over, since they doubted the ability of the youngster to handle the assignment of penetration to the target accurately.

The attacking formation, which had originally been conceived by General Brereton to include 178 aircraft, was now reduced to 163 effective sorties, and the five groups were considerably scattered as they began crossing the coast line in the vicinity of the Greek-Albanian border. Now they turned gently northeastward. Over the land, swelling white cumulus clouds were beginning to form well under 10,000 feet. As the planes crossed Albania and approached Yugoslavia they began to climb, for ahead of them lay the North Albanian Alps.

12:20 P.M.

Here the cloud build-ups had become fairly dense and towering, rising to about 15,000 feet, a mile and a half above the average height of the mountains. Four of the leaders elected to fly above the clouds, while Kane led his group under them at about 12,000 feet. The winds at the higher altitude favored those groups. Imperceptibly their ground-speed increased.

1:30 P.M.

As the four high groups crossed the final mountains above the clouds and neared the Bulgarian border, a cer-

292

tain amount of confusion had taken place. Even some individual squadrons were now quite separated. In going through clouds twice (up and down) most aircraft had temporarily lost sight of each other. Obviously many adjustments would have to be made if each group individually were to pull itself together before reaching the target.

Killer Kane and his outfit were, for the moment, nowhere. Unfavorable winds had left them far behind, struggling somewhere over the Alps. Keith Compton's aircraft were first to break through into the open country. In fair order they headed for the Danube without pause. By now Jack Wood had overrun both Addison Baker and Leon Johnson (unavoidably so, because of his higher altitude and speed). Since he was supposed to be last in line, this would require a correction. Under ordinary circumstances the use of inter-plane radio communication would have straightened the jumble out, but this was not possible today. So the four groups proceeded toward the little town of Lom on the Danube, losing altitude and trying to sort themselves out in the process. By the time they reached the great river most squadrons were down to about 2500 feet. The clouds had thinned out. A beautiful, nearly clear, sunny day welcomed them in Rumania.

1:50 P.M.

At this point the laggard 98th broke through the Alps and the cumulus and headed for the Danube in the vicinity of Lom, Bulgaria. There much skillful but nerve-racking maneuvering was already taking place. Compton and Baker had reorganized in good fashion and were precisely on time as briefed. Congratulating themselves on their accuracy, they set out for their first I.P.—the town of Pitesti.

This was an understandable but regrettable move, for it brought the 376th and 93rd toward the target far ahead of the other formations. For during this interval the succeeding groups continued to circle over the Danube, arranging themselves into their proper elements; and while so engaged they were surprised to see Killer Kane's straggly collection of aircraft approach from the south. Since these belonged in front, the others were forced to wait for them.

The feelings of the men during this seemingly interminable delay can well be imagined. At 2500 feet they were in plain view of anybody on the ground. The entire mission had been planned on the basis of at least partial surprise, and this had been one reason for the decision to execute it at low level. Now the concept was being apparently nullified by faulty timing, which in turn had been caused by a mere cloud obstacle.

More than likely the defenders had already been alerted, especially since Compton and Baker had already gone on to the I.P. Yet minutes passed without a sign of enemy fighters or anti-aircraft fire. The Rumanian Cabinet, including Marshal Antonescu, weekending at the little town of Snagov, heard the sound of airplanes above but thought nothing of it.

2:10 P.M.

After these agonies of readjustment and realignment the three late groups set off toward Pitesti, losing altitude and picking up speed in a shallow dive. They knew they were twenty minutes behind schedule.

It was about now that the crew of Hadley's Harem, piloted by Lieutenant Gilbert Hadley, claims they were spotted and shadowed by two enemy fighters who made no attempt to close. (If true, this meant that the attacking bombers had lost the element of surprise long before reaching even the first I.P., a likelihood more or less verified by subsequent information and events.)

2:30 P.M.

The two early groups, under Compton and Baker, reached the first I.P.—Pitesti—at an altitude of 200 feet. Here they came down even farther, perhaps to twenty or thirty feet above the ground.

The reaction of the people below to this fantastic sight and sound was one of wild excitement. Details could be seen vividly from aloft. An elderly man and woman fell to

294

their knees and prayed. People in the villages stood still and gaped upward. Most of them had their Sunday finery on. "You could see people going to church . . . man, wife, and child walking along the country roads." Bombardier Herbert Light, through his binoculars, saw an open-air festival in progress, with the women dressed in colorful skirts and blouses. One of them threw her apron over her head in panic.

As they roared over the wheat fields, the first unfriendly acts occurred: farmers threw stones and pitchforks at them. One farmer leading two horses was startled by the advancing planes and leaped into a nearby stream. A girl swimming in another river was reported by ten separate crews.

And still there was not a plane, not a gun to challenge the Americans. At about 200 mph and rock-bottom height (one plane had to pull up to avoid hitting a man on a horse) everything went by swiftly and dreamlike. In fascination the men watched the kaleidoscopic sights hurtle below them, and looked above for the enemy interceptors that they had been awaiting for two hours. They cleared their guns in short bursts, stared, and waited, but nothing happened and nobody came.

2:50 P.M.

The remaining three groups arrived at Pitesti and began to drop to treetop level, the 98th and 44th for the run to Floresti, the 389th for its private target: Campina. The 98th had been specifically "directed to get down to fifty feet, and we knew fifty feet would put us below some of the stacks in the refinery. But we figured we could pull up over those and get back down . . ."

Meanwhile the new lead plane of the lead group, piloted by Colonel Compton, in which General Ent was a passenger, was on its way to Floresti, the second and final I.P., from which the turn to the target would be made. A railroad line led from Floresti straight into Ploesti. The same was true of Targoviste; and here a blunder of major magnitude was made. As their aircraft approached the latter, Compton and Ent decided to turn with that railroad, having mistaken the town for Floresti—an error not too difficult to make in a plane moving so fast and so low. Their young navigator protested, but General Ent hastily overrode him. Scarcely before anyone could realize what was happening, they had turned sharply down the railroad and were roaring downhill to the southeast at nearly 300 mph, followed by the rest of their group and Baker's 93rd. But this route led to Bucharest, not Ploesti. What ensued is described by Major Potts of the following 93rd:

"We had gone through this maneuver of turning from the run-up to the Initial Point and make the run-down on the target many times. And as we drew near that point I had a map of my own in the cockpit, and my navigator was checking with me constantly. I was trying to jockey myself into position so I would be trailing a little bit, so when the turn to the right took place I could wheel into line and we could present a frontal string of airplanes to the target as we came into it.

"However, just about nine minutes before we were due, according to my calculations and those of my navigator . . . the lead formation started to turn to the right. And the second formation, taken by surprise, turned in a kind of following position. We were boxed in, and I had no choice but to turn. At that point I broke radio silence and started calling the leader . . ."

It will be noted that radio silence had been enforced thus far. However, all surprise was lost now—the formation led by Compton, followed by Baker's puzzled group, was already on the outskirts of Bucharest. The spires of the buildings in the center of the city, white and delicate in the distance, could be seen clearly. German and Rumanian staffs were already in an uproar, and no doubt wondering why the Americans would want to attack Rumania's innocent capital city. Dozens of air-raid sirens began to yowl. All flak batteries had been called into action. Radio and telephone had alerted every fighter field in the Balkans.

"At that point the leader of the formation called back and said he realized he had made the wrong turn and was turning back to the left. We made a left turn but this maneuver had taken us south of the target, and we were now coming in on an axis of attack for which we had not been briefed, and with which our navigators and bombardiers were unfamiliar.

"I thought that I might turn left again and go back to the Initial Point. But by the time I had run the thought through my mind I found that we were practically on top of some of the refineries, and we were getting shot at in all directions. It just would have been useless to try to turn around and come back on the right axis."

3:00 P.M.

Unaware of all this, Jack Wood and his aircraft had reached Campina; Killer Kane and Leon Johnson had made their turn at Floresti and were running toward Ploesti. It did not strike them as unusual that the defenders seemed unusually alert, although this was largely caused by the premature turn made by the 376th some twenty minutes earlier. One of Lieutenant Robert Sternfels' gunners called him on the phone to ask, "When can I start firing, boss?" He replied, "Any damn time you see something worth shooting at." A few miles from the main target the raid paid its first dividend. Gunners of Kane's own plane blew up several dozen oil cars sided at a rail junction along the Floresti-Ploesti spur.

At this point Kane was shocked to see several pink B-24s pass under him heading southwest. Since pink identified Compton's outfit, Kane realized for the first time that the 376th had already entered and left the target area.

As yet not a single one of the five groups had reached their assigned target, but already they had run into a small-caliber hornet's nest. Most of this was ordinary machine-gun fire. One or two planes had already been brought down by it, and others had been seriously damaged by the puncturing of hydraulic lines and injury to electrical systems. Dozens of these smaller flak batteries and machine-gun nests sprouted from nowhere. Roofs of cottages unfolded and guns swung out; haystacks parted to reveal gun emplacements. Lightninglike duels were fought between many air crews and these gunners, in which some of the latter were killed. But as yet there was little or no interference from heavy flak batteries, partially because the planes were too low to be hit by them. This factor and the approach to the target are described by Colonel Johnson:

"We got down on the deck . . . most of us had studied those maps so much that we needed no maps from the time we left the Danube. I remember them saying, 'North of this town on a hill there will be a monastery four miles out of town.' I remember seeing it distinctly. 'You will cross a big sandy river and there will be two bridges across it.' So from the time we crossed the Danube to the time we turned in to the target I personally never needed a map. We had moving pictures of the target area, and we had sand table models made up—it was so similar to what we'd seen that we had no difficulty . . .

"We turned—98th, 44th, in that order—until we came to a point where we all turned in abreast . . . And the 389th had pulled out to go to their target, which was in a little valley up ahead.

"As we approached Ploesti we could see heavy smoke and fires over the town, and at the same time we could see guns firing at us in the vicinity of the target and to the north of the target, as we were running from north to south. As these guns fired we would dive to get as low as we could. I remember distinctly being lower than some high-tension wires and pulling up over them in formation.

"We had over a hundred airplanes there down below treetop level . . . because our salvation seemed to be there. They couldn't get their artillery trained on us if we were that low . . ."

All the ingredients necessary to bring about a calamity of the first water were now present:

The cloud structure which had caused a mix-up of the formations also brought about a long delay over the Danube which, doubtlessly, had led to their tentative detection.

The premature attack of the two leading groups would

bring in its wake two penalties for the following two groups attacking Ploesti itself: First, the immediate defenses would be even more alert to subsequent aircraft. Second, these would have to fly into the fires left by their predecessors.

The false turn toward Bucharest finally and definitely alerted all defenders elsewhere, as well as in the immediate vicinity, twenty minutes too soon. This particularly meant fighter aircraft and insured that the bombers would receive their maximum attention on the way back.

The 376th and 93rd would now be forced to approach the target from its most heavily defended sector and, as pointed out by Major Potts, from an angle with which they were not acquainted. Therefore there was likely to be a good deal of waste motion in their bombing of the assigned objectives, assuming that they would be able to recognize them at all.

The element of surprise having been dissipated, lack of friendly fighter escort would tell even more heavily than had been expected.

Thus, long before the various elements had begun their final run into the targets assigned them, nearly 400 German, Rumanian, and Italian fighter pilots were already racing toward their waiting ME-109s, HE-111s, and Macchis, which were being hurriedly warmed up on a dozen flight lines by startled mechanics in Italy and Hungary as well as Rumania itself. As for flak and machine-gun emplacements, every one had been at least partially manned a half hour ago, and by now the full complement of each crew was ready and waiting. And, to complicate matters, the defenders had been given enough time to set off several dozen smoke pots at the southeast section of Ploesti which were beginning to obscure, to some degree, the various aiming points assigned to the bombardiers.

So the worst of all possible nightmares was now a definite reality: surprise was lost, the defenders were 100 per cent alert, the bombers were stranded twenty feet above the ground, 1350 miles from home without escort, and were about to be hit by fighters . . . "flak, small arms, everything but slingshots." Already some of the younger, more panicky American gunners had begun to fire at anything that moved, including cows that grazed quietly in the fields below.

After the run-up through the valley (referred to as "difficult" by General Brereton in his memoirs) and the wrong turn toward Bucharest instead of Ploesti, Compton found his formation in an uncomfortable predicament. To go back toward the I.P. and start all over again seemed impossible. Pandemonium had already broken loose. On the other hand, to run through the strongest sector of antiaircraft guns in a dubious effort to locate the target from an unfamiliar direction would, in effect, base the entire 376th operation on pure guesswork. After discovering the mistake he had, at most, one minute in which to make up his mind. All thirty planes were now flying over the suburbs of Bucharest itself.

Following a hurried conversation with General Ent, Compton decided to head straight for Ploesti from the southwest. Thereupon, the 376th, still followed by Addison Baker's group, executed the tightest possible turn toward the target twenty-five miles away. The closer Compton's men approached Ploesti, the more intense became the flak, fired by German gunners at remarkably oblique angles directly into the path of the oncoming planes; 88-mm. cannon fired point-blank over open sights, like so many shotguns. Machine-gun bullets came up in sheets. Three bombers apparently crashed during this phase.

In desperation Compton then led his remaining aircraft in a great twenty-mile semicircle around Ploesti, hoping to get at it from a northerly direction. While this would be a roundabout route, at least the final approach would be more or less as planned, and the planes would be coming in from the direction where Intelligence had forecast the least number of defending guns.

So the 376th drove in from the new angle, northeast of

300

Ploesti. Though obscured by smoke, their target, Romana Americana, could be dimly seen in the distance. However, the volume of AA fire seemed as great as it had been previously to the south. At this point General Ent himself got on the inter-plane radio and directed the 376th Group to attack "targets of opportunity." This was, in effect, an admission that the individual attack of this group had misfired. The five squadron commanders, each leading six planes, were now on their own.

Most of these planes ranged over the general Ploesti target area and unloaded on anything that looked good. It was in this action that the volunteer, Major Jerstad, and most of his crew were killed. When a burst of flak caught his plane it began to burn. He continued to fly toward the refinery that he had selected, and stayed on course for three miles while the flames sheathed both wings and began to envelop the body of the plane as far back as the top turret. After bombing the plant, his plane plummeted into the target area.

Major Norman C. Appold, a tall, thin youth with a large Adam's apple, decided to make a try for the Concordia Vega installation. He led his squadron straight in, and all aircraft unloaded practically at once. An inferno of fire and smoke burst skyward. The six planes plunged through it and emerged on the other side, miraculously unharmed but covered with soot. While the target was in this fashion well plastered, it had been intended for Addison Baker's target force.

And, finally, a few planes from the now thoroughly dispersed lead group set out for Campina, where they bombed the Steaua Romana refinery, which had already been smashed by Jack Wood's outfit.

Bitter and frustrated over the turn of events, Colonel Baker and his 93rd had been dragged willy-nilly into this imbroglio from the south, behind Compton's formation. Compton, as noted, had turned right (east) at the outskirts of Ploesti. It was the second time his group had turned unaccountably right, and perhaps Baker was becoming annoyed, for he ignored the leading group and the

AA fire and plunged directly into the target from the south, followed by his intact group of thirty-five aircraft. Prior to the mission Baker had emphasized the stringent necessity of keeping a tight formation so as to hit their small targets with the greatest number of bombs. He had warned: "If anything happens to the lead ship pay no attention. Don't swerve. No matter what happens, keep straight . . ."

Baker's Target Force No. 2 Liberators had been assigned Concordia Vega, but they could not locate it from their reverse approach. However, as noted, Major Appold's squadron had been kind enough to bomb it by mistake, and with excellent results.

Meanwhile, Target Force No. 3, also under Colonel Baker and commanded by Major Potts, was doing its best to find something resembling its assigned targets. As related by the Major, "Several of the planes in my formation had dropped by this time . . . we went ahead and bombed what we thought was the right target, but probably not more than five planes in my formation bombed the right target. The others were dropping their bombs on what they thought was the target, but they were confused. As we went over . . . coming in, as I say, from the south, the wrong direction, the planes on my right and left went down . . ."

Meanwhile a shell had struck the right side of the cockpit of Colonel Baker's Liberator, killing the co-pilot and injuring the colonel. The forward section of the ship began to burn. Almost immediately it was hit again, by a heavier-caliber shell. A wavering mass of flames, the bomber stayed on course long enough for Baker's bombardier to dump his entire bomb load into a single refinery a few dozen yards below. Baker tried to pull up so that his crew could bail out, but the plane would not respond. It began to somersault end over end lightning-fast, like a boy's toy, and then crashed heavily on the edge of the refinery it had just bombed, with all men still aboard.

Enemy fighters, portents of things to come, had already begun to appear in small units. In spite of them and the flak the 93rd accurately bombed its improvised targets from heights as low as 100 feet. These later turned out to

302

be Astra Romana, Phoenix Orion, and Columbia Aquila, refineries which had been intended for the attentions of Kane and Johnson and their respective men. Eleven B-24s from the 93rd Group were lost over these targets alone. One plane crashed into a women's prison, allegedly killing about a hundred inmates.

The easiest objective had been given to Jack Wood and his somewhat less experienced collection of thirty crews, the 389th Bombardment Group. They were to fly to the suburb of Campina and bomb only the Steaua Romana refinery, giving Ploesti and the other squadrons a wide berth coming and going. But here again things did not work out quite as planned.

"We had been warned," said Colonel Wood, "to avoid drifting left after we crossed the Danube because of a G.C.I. station in that direction, and to stay strictly on our northeast course. But what do the two groups in front of us do but veer left at exactly that point.

"I was checking my navigator to the fraction of an inch —I wasn't at the controls—I had a pilot and co-pilot flying the plane and I was squeezed in almost between them with a map on my knees. As soon as I saw Kane and Johnson swing left I turned to my pilot and said, 'I don't know where the hell those fellows are going, but from now on we're on our own.' We kept straight on for Pitesti."

Wood could afford to be more independent than the other commanders, for his group was the only one with a single, separate target not in Ploesti proper. After reaching their I.P. they banked slightly northward and at 4000 feet headed laterally across the mountain ranges which temporarily prevented them from coming down to zero altitude. Their task was to pick out a particular valley about three miles wide, and then to follow it straight into Campina. They then proceeded to descend into the wrong valley. When this mistake was discovered, Wood calmly led his outfit up to 4000 feet again, and over into the next valley, which turned out to be the right one. The bombers coasted down to minimum altitude once more, and raced toward their target. At this stage machine-gun nests on the sides of the hills were firing down on them—a novelty, certainly, in anti-aircraft annals. Some of the planes ripped their wings through the treetop branches. As they approached the target many gun duels ("like a wild-west movie") took place between the bombers and the flak and machine-gun batteries concealed below in haystacks, in railway flatcars, and in farmhouses. Over four hundred .50-caliber American machine guns, including the new nose armament, which was used to good advantage, poured a flood of millions of bullets from all directions at anything that moved. This sweeping mass of fire killed, wounded, and scattered great numbers of the defenders during the earsplitting sweep toward the town.

Youthful Second Lieutenant Lloyd Hughes was among those killed at Steaua Romana. His plane was hit by machine-gun bullets during the run-in through the valley, and sheets of gasoline poured out of the left wing and bomb bay. But since the plane was not yet afire, Hughes decided to make his run to the target. In doing so he passed through a tongue of flame which touched off the left wing. After releasing his load of explosives and incendiaries he tried to land in a dry creek bed, found a bridge in the way, pulled up and tried again; but it was too late, and his B-24 spun into the ground. (From another plane moving pictures were taken of the entire sequence of this tragedy, from the moment when gasoline started pouring out of the tanks until the flaming machine crashed—a remarkable film still on secret Air Force file.)

Lieutenant John Fino, bombardier of the 389th lead plane, dropped a thousand-pound bomb directly through the large double doors of one power plant which apparently had not had time to reduce its steam pressure. As a result this single bomb created innumerable explosions within the plant by tearing out high-pressure steam conduits.

Another plane from a later wave was destroyed like a moth in a flame when a boilerhouse hit by a previous bomber blew up just in time to catch it in the explosion. But the 389th hit Campina accurately and as briefed. In ten narrow waves of three planes each the group passed over the target exactly as planned and practiced over the mock-up in Libya. At this point one stray squadron from Compton's 376th began to show up, for, it will be recalled, some of them had decided to go to Campina after General Ent's order to attack "targets of opportunity."

"We could see these aircraft about three or four miles to our right coming in at right-angles to our line of approach, and we couldn't figure out what they were doing around here, especially since they were bound to arrive after we were all finished." And several minutes after the 389th made its turn back to home base the bombers from Compton's group reached the holocaust that had once been the Campina refineries, and inflicted further damage on the roaring, blackened remnants of this installation.

"We had expected to take losses," Colonel John Kane said, "but I never will forget those big Libs going down like flies." His radio operator, Ray Hubbard, added, "I looked through the open bomb-bay doors and could see flames from exploding gas tanks shooting right up into us. The fire wrapped us up. I looked out of the side windows and saw the others flying through smoke and flames. It was flying through hell . . . I guess we'll go straight to heaven when we die. We've had our purgatory." Official AAF historians admit that the 98th and 44th Bombardment Groups would have been morally justified in turning back from the target under the circumstances.

Kane's 98th was after Phoenix Orion and Astra Romana, but Baker's squadrons had been there first. So for Killer's aircraft to bomb them, which they proceeded to do, they were forced to fly directly into the fires and explosions left behind by their own people. In addition, the delayed-action bombs were now beginning to detonate. This, in fact, was the most insidious hazard of all, not only for Kane's group but later for Johnson's as well. A sheet of flame and a billow of smoke could often be avoided by an oncoming plane, but nothing could be done about sudden explosions from delayed-action fuses dropped previously by planes which had attacked refineries not assigned to them. Possibly a total of six aircraft were cremated in mid-air by these gigantic and unexpected blasts.

Kane's plane itself was hit in one engine just as it came over one of the targets. He feathered the propeller and added power to the other three engines. "From below, ack-ack batteries were firing at us point-blank . . . like a skeet shoot."

Wringing wet with perspiration from the roaring fires on the ground and from the emotional tension of the mission, Kane's men severely damaged Phoenix Orion, left it behind, and drove on doggedly for the great Astra Romana plant. It was unbearably hot in the planes from the wall of flames and explosions rising over 300 feet, the August heat of the day, and the machine guns, which had been firing steadily until the gun barrels were blistering to the touch. The colonel reported, "We could see reservoir tanks exploding, with fire shooting up like ruddy tongues in the middle of the smoke. It was so hot the hair on my arms was singed. I thought I could smell it burn . . ." The smoke was a constant worry, for it obscured chimneys and balloon cables lurking within it.

An unexpected factor over the target area was the violent turbulence caused by flames and explosions. At best a B-24 is not easy (like a B-17) to fly steadily; even in routine formation it tends to wander and slide when not on automatic pilot. Over Ploesti this defect was dangerously magnified. Only with difficulty could the planes be kept under control near the heart of the inferno. They rolled and pitched like sheets of paper in a breeze. Many a bomber could be seen hanging crazily on a wing tip; others sagged and then were wafted upward by a hot billow of uprushing air. Crew members had to strap themselves down. Pilots and co-pilots flew their ships simultaneously; the job was too much for one man. There is little doubt that several planes went into the ground purely through accidental dives and sideslips. Sometimes pilots were forced to change course right in the middle of a bomb run; off they veered to attack another refinery instead, in split-second switches caused by the simple necessity of avoid-

306

ing collisions with other bombers off course or out of formation.

The ships swept on, weaving in and out of the smokestacks, through several miles of storage areas and small farms. "We [had] many airplanes come back with corn stalks hung in their bomb-bays," remarked Major Shingler. "In a B-24 the bomb-bays open up like a clam-shell, and of course we were right down on the deck. When they shut the bomb-bay doors . . . they just gathered up a little corn with it." The remnants of the 98th hit Target White 4 in four waves at a speed over the objective of about 185 mph. The smudge pots, fortunately, turned out to be no great nuisance.

Enemy fighters began to hover over the wild scene, waiting for the bombers to leave the area and come up from the floor. A few of them tried to attack the heavy planes hugging the ground, but the majority of the ME-109s and other interceptors grimly bided their time. The bombers stuck to their assignment, manifold and prop settings as low as possible, and mixtures lean, to save gasoline.

"Our pinpoint was a smokestack," said Captain William Banks. ". . . all we needed was a split-second to sight it. And we had to get it with the first try; there would be no time to turn around for another run this trip. Somebody ahead of us had bombed our target by mistake. We all felt sick when we saw the oil tanks exploding and great swirls of smoke pouring up from the ground. There was nothing to do but try to hit it again . . .

"Oil tanks were still going off right under us, and on both sides German ack-ack batteries were firing in unison. We were so low that they were actually trained down on us.

"We kept straining our eyes for that stack. We couldn't see it yet, and I began to worry. It looked as if we weren't going to get the damned thing after all . . . We just plowed on, sweating blood and not saying a word. The Sad Sack was bristling with guns for this mission and we were firing every one of them as we roared in. The whole plane shuddered with the fire.

". . . Finally I decided to pull away. We had finished our run and hadn't even seen our pinpoint. At that moment

Joe Souza yelled. He had spotted our smokestack and power plant through an opening in the smoke. I held her steady for a split second while Joe sighted and let his bombs go, and then I almost jumped out of my seat. Carl shouted, 'Jesus!' and I pulled back with all the strength I had. Right in front of us, square in the middle of the windshield and looming up almost out of sight was the tallest . . . smokestack I have ever seen.

". . . Shaking all over with the racing of her motors, the *Sad Sack* leaped up and climbed for the top of it. I prayed as she lost speed and the stack rushed at us. We cleared it as if we were pole-vaulting . . ."

Some contact bombs failed to explode, but few of the crewmen noticed this in the confusion around them. Banks continued: "There were B-24s going down all around us now. We saw two fall right in front of us that had apparently climbed up out of formation and had been hit by pursuit planes. The ground was spotted with them, including some that had managed to land safely. The crews of these last were beside them, watching the planes burn and waving to us as we went by . . . We ducked even closer to the ground and scooted for home."

The squadron in which Captain John Palm was flying had been ordered to climb to 100 feet when they arrived thirty seconds from their assigned target. This he did, but when he reached it his plane was the only one of the six left. And as he was nearing the refinery, his own forlorn Liberator was finally hit. An anti-aircraft shell knocked out three engines. The plane went into a shallow dive. Two men in the nose were killed outright. Captain Palm's right leg was blown off. He glanced down and noted, almost absently, that it was hanging by a few strands. At the moment he had other problems. The plane was going in fast, just above the refinery that was to have been bombed. He yanked the emergency release.

As the action increased in intensity, a pall of dense black smoke added to the difficulties and caused several near-collisions. B-24s were crisscrossing the area. Much of the confusion was caused by Compton's earlier aircraft, which were roaming haphazardly over the entire target area seeking targets of opportunity, as instructed by General Ent. This meandering, plus the maneuvers of Baker's aircraft in bombing installations not under their briefed jurisdiction, and from a reverse direction, created a particular hazard that no one had dreamed would take place during this meticulously planned operation. Yet all but eight of Kane's element got over the target, one having cracked up in the take-off, and seven others having turned back with mechanical troubles. This group suffered the worst losses of all; twenty-one of Kane's thirty-eight American heavies that arrived at Ploesti were knocked down.

The last was the most unfortunate group of all, for it perforce arrived at a scene of unparalleled confusion left by the previous three groups assigned to Ploesti proper. This was the 44th, originally from England, led by Colonel Leon Johnson.

"It was more like an artist's conception of an air-battle than anything I had ever experienced," Johnson said. "We flew through sheets of flame, and airplanes were everywhere, some of them on fire and others exploding. It's indescribable to anyone who wasn't there." Engineer James E. Cailliar added, "As we passed over [Brazi] our ship filled up with smoke and it was quite awhile before it all cleared out."

Two of the planes from this group (and possibly others from other groups) ran into balloon cables and crashed. However the British briefing officers were partially vindicated, for other planes had in fact snapped the cables, as predicted, though their wings were slashed back to the main spar in the process.

The 44th experienced the same keen disappointment as Kane's formation before them: their Ploesti target (though not the one in Brazi) was burning before they arrived. So they would have to bomb it all over again, or go home emptyhanded, or find something else to bomb. The decision is described by Colonel Johnson: ". . . we had all agreed ahead of time that we weren't going that far without trying to get our targets, so even though they had been fired on . . . we made our runs . . . and we'll point out for the interest of the people that weren't there that the

309

fires were so close together that some of the planes had the paint on their wings burned and scorched . . . I remember the cracking plant loomed up and we let our bombs go.

". . . we found that we could weave around the fires like we weaved over the trees and over the high-tension wires, because the fires were not a continuous line across. There would be a tank burning on your right, and maybe one staggered back—well, it seemed like only the width of an airplane, but it must have been more than that. You could weave through with a formation, although it looked . . . too narrow to get three airplanes through."

Thus Columbia Aquila was tagged again for good measure, and the first blows were delivered to Creditul Minier at nearby Brazi. Each time one of the incendiaries struck home there would follow a hoarse roar, a sheet of flame, and a billow of black smoke. In the course of these actions eleven of the big planes were shot down by machine guns and heavier AA fire, or burned to a crisp in gigantic explosions beneath them.

Johnson later remarked: "We saw the 93rd and 376th groups swinging below us . . . or even with us, and some of us had to pull up to let the others go by. It was a sight that was hard to forget, because you see planes going in on fire, and I remember seeing one pull straight up, and two chutes come out of the window of this big bomber, and I saw it pull straight up and then fall to the ground.

". . . Then the anti-aircraft opened up on us. We were headed almost parallel to it . . . We decided that the only thing to do was to head over it—we didn't think they would traverse 180 degrees overhead . . . If we went parallel we knew they'd knock us all down. As a result we flew immediately over them. And we shot and fired at all the gunners as we went by . . . I distinctly remember seeing a number of them leaving their guns and running for cover . . ."

If the two early groups (Compton and Baker) had been even earlier, or if the two later groups (Kane and Johnson) had been later, affairs would not have been so bad. As it was, the time spent by the formations that had gone to Bucharest and then belatedly swung around toward Ploesti and Campina brought them there, by an unfortunate coincidence, at almost the same moment that the other formations arrived, and from an opposite axis of attack. Thus, according to Johnson, "We had airplanes going in at just all the directions you could think of . . . We'd have to pull up and find airplanes below us and other airplanes above and around us. I mean, it was just a general confusion around the target area—of squadrons and groups, not individual flyers." But part of Compton's lead outfit had arrived several minutes earlier—for example, Appold's squadron. When later aircraft came in, they saw what had happened. The timing was all wrong. The delayed-action bombs of the first wave were going off ahead of them and under them. They barreled through nonetheless and unloaded. Twelve of one outfit went into the smoke and only nine broke through on the other side.

There is a saying among bomber crews that while en route and over the target they were employed by Uncle Sam, but after "Bombs away!" they were out of work. The Ploesti raid of August 1, 1943, was over to the extent that the explosives had been laid on the target to the best of the ability of the participants. Their problem now was to save their skins. From this standpoint the raid was less than half finished.

All the ground fire that had been traversed on the way in would now have to be met on the way back. Also, there had been no fighters worth mentioning on the way to the target and over the target, but now they were wheeling overhead in swarms, and they would hang on all the way out into the sea "like snails on a log." Many bombers had already been lost. Therefore the concentrated fire power of the rest was reduced. And all planes were damaged now to some degree. Some were limping on three and even two engines. These could not possibly keep up and had to be more or less discounted from defensive calculations. Many crewmen were dead or wounded, reducing the gun strength of their aircraft that much more. The odyssey of the Ploesti warriors was many hundreds of miles, many hours, many deaths from done.

By a stroke of unpremeditated luck, the scurrying bombers were for the moment relatively safe from the enemy fighters above them: They were actually too low. To dive on them at roughly 300 mph would not allow enough time to pull out. Some enemy planes tried it, and either pulled up before coming within effective range or dove in too close, sprayed their opponents briefly, and then piled into the ground an inevitable split second later. After several Germans had killed themselves in this manner, the others gave it up and turned to different methods of disposing of the disorganized Liberator formations clinging to the protection of the ground and streaking for home. They could not stay down there indefinitely; in fact they would have to start climbing very soon in order to clear the Alps.

A renewed hail of flak met the bombers as they emerged into open country, knocking down a few more and damaging almost all the rest in varying degrees. There the interceptors got to work in earnest. The experience of Captain Young of the 98th is typical of many return trips:

"After the bombs were away, we dropped back to twenty feet and about fifty ME-109s and 110s jumped us from the right. We were flying so low they couldn't dive on us, but they did lazy-8s all over our formation and caused us plenty of trouble.

"The housing around the propeller and three cylinders of our No. 4 engine were shot out. Two feet of the prop on the No. 1 engine was smashed, tearing a foot-and-a-half hole in the left aileron. The motor was vibrating like a bucking bronco. And we had a wing-cell leak in No. 3 . . . The fighters kept coming in, and we acounted for three. They attacked for about twenty minutes, and we just put the ship on the ground and ran like hell.

"We muddled through the fighter attack, and staggered away from the target on two-and-a-half engines. About 200 miles south of the refineries, we realized that we

312

couldn't return over the Mediterranean with our battered ship. We decided to hug a land route going back. The chief topic of conversation was picking a good place to set her down. Everybody was pestering our navigator, Lt. Norman Whalen . . . He finally had to tell the Colonel, 'Look, if you guys will just leave me alone for a while, maybe I'll find a field.' We left him alone. Whalen was navigating for two other damaged planes which were following, and the three of us were being covered by Lt. Royden LeBrecht. Nothing had happened to his ship.

"We crossed an enemy airfield at 1500 feet, and the flak batteries opened up. I don't know who was more surprised. But we got away without trouble.

"In order to gain altitude to cross a mountain range, we threw out everything that was movable. We released the extra gasoline tank and tossed out oxygen bottles, gas masks, ammunition, radio equipment, and anything that a screw driver could dismantle. LeBrecht called and inquired: 'What the hell are you doing, redecorating?'

"We finally got up to 6600 feet, but we needed 7000 to cross the mountains. By picking our way through canyons and ravines, and with some lucky updrafts, we managed to get over.

"The plane was hobbling along now at 130 mph, and we knew that it might stall around 125. We kept plugging along. We had a choice of putting her down on land or flying across open water to the nearest Allied landing field. The Colonel and I realized that there was a good chance the ship would flop into the water, but we had come too far to worry about that. As we crossed the coast, Whalen gave us an ETA (Estimated Time of Arrival) of 2110 for the selected airfield.

"Whalen was on the nose to within a minute. Exactly fourteen hours and forty minutes after we left Africa, we let her down.

"We had to crash-land the plane, but nobody was hurt, and the first thing I did after we got away from the ship was to kiss the navigator. Yes, I really kissed him."

The Axis threw every available fighter at the Americans, scraped the bottom of the barrel, and even came up with

313

a few obsolescent biplanes—Gloster Gladiators built by
Britain in 1935 (top speed 250 mph), a few of which had
been sold to other countries later in the decade. They,
said Major Shingler, "had a chance of making just about
one pass at us. And then of course they had their other
fighters . . . and they would hover over you and drop
fragmentation bombs . . . I saw a few B-24s lose their tails
that way. Nobody dove into us, but I did see B-24s with
their tails knocked off, and the minute you knock off one
of the verticle fins it goes into a chandelle, stalls in, and
then comes right straight in on its nose.

". . . They were right down on the deck . . . strafing the
whole bomber formation at fifty or a hundred feet. And
they seemed to have an intercept system, whereby they
would relay us from one control point to another . . . and
then when we'd go fifty or sixty miles another control point
would pick us up, and we'd have fresh fighters coming in."

Theoretically the plan was for all surviving aircraft to
assemble at a rendezvous point some fifty miles from Ploesti, whereupon those in good condition would group together and head for Benghazi, while the cripples were
supposed to make a formation of their own and try to get
to Cyprus or some other escape area. The 376th and 93rd
Bombardment Groups had come and gone about twenty
minutes earlier than the others and headed south at once
in fairly good order. But the three later groups got together
more or less as briefed, after hitting their targets.

The situation, however, was too confused and dangerous to permit any leisurely maneuvering and regrouping.
Lurking in the background, also, was a gasoline problem,
especially in the case of those planes flying on three (or
two and a half, or even two) engines. The cripples knew
that their chances were better in formation; for even a battered, limping B-24 carries a good deal of fire power, and
in combination with other such casualties is hard to knock
down. So most planes, in good condition or otherwise, hurriedly contrived something resembling a combat box and
turned south.

Shingler continued: "We climbed up to about 12,000
feet, as I remember, and we were still being intercepted

314

by fighters. About 45 minutes before we got to the coast the fighters stopped. We came out over the Adriatic in good weather, and my personal opinion is that everyone relaxed. I think they said, 'Well, the show is just about over' . . . The formation got sloppy . . . we started letting down to around 8000 feet. All of a sudden we looked up and here were Italian fighters coming across from Foggia, which was across the sea. They came in under us and they did shoot down five aircraft—*zip, zip, zip,* just like that . . . I still think they wouldn't have shot down any of the boys if we had been in formation and the gunners had been manning their guns. They were taking care of some of the boys who had been shot up on the aircraft and trying to make them comfortable . . . I would say there were in the neighborhood of twenty-five or thirty fighters that hit us just as we came out over the Adriatic, heading back to Benghazi. We lost about eighteen aircraft."

Shingler blames his own people for this crowning misfortune, but Colonel Johnson of the 44th is more lenient: "[The enemy fighters] ran out of fuel and couldn't keep up with us. They took quite a beating, too. We knocked down quite a few of those fighters that came up against us. There were no more fighters until we got over the Adriatic . . . A number of us started chattering back and forth on the radio . . . and fighters did come up from the heel of Italy and knocked down a few of our bombers. Actually, if I remember correctly, they took five out of the 98th Group. Fortunately, although we were talking just as much, they didn't hit my particular group—it was just happenstance more than anything else."

As the laborious exodus continued, Liberators continued to fall, new fighters rose and pressed their shallow attacks, occasional ack-ack continued to annoy the bomber crews hanging on grimly with their precious gallons of fuel, forcing them to make small, wasteful detours to avoid them. The planes that "had lost an engine had to start lightening their load for the climb [across the Alps]. It startled us at first to see equipment fly out . . . and float back under us. We thought the planes were disintegrating in mid-air. The crews threw out everything that was loose or could be

315

yanked loose, and we left behind us a long, wobbling trail of seats, tanks, belts, shoes, boxes, and first-aid kits with gauze bandages unrolling in great circles, figure-eights, and curious, sometimes beautiful designs."

It began to rain. The atmosphere aboard the plane carrying Ent, Compton, and their navigator was particularly depressing.

Flying at 100 feet, Major Potts started down a valley he hoped would afford a little extra protection from AA fire surrounding the main target. "The tension relaxed just a bit. A young gunner that was flying the left waist gun position—named Sherman, not more than nineteen—let go at what looked like a distillation plant—not one of the [assigned] targets . . . it suddenly exploded and burst into flames. Everybody on the plane started cheering . . . it was kind of an anti-climax and a good feeling to see something burst into flames that you figured was sort of a dividend.

"Well, as we started back other planes in my formation, numbering nine, gathered around and we started to climb back over the mountains . . . One of my very close friends, Captain Roper, was . . . leading two other planes . . . He pulled off a little bit so he wouldn't be flying in too close to me. He seemed to go into a cloud. And we suddenly saw dropping out of this cloud various pieces of airplane. Well, that was a shock . . . much more than losing somebody in the target area . . .

"After we landed back on base I realized that only seven planes out of thirty-seven had come back from the mission. That created an additional damper on everybody's feelings. Matter of fact, I was feeling so depressed that I had a hard time sitting through the interrogation by the Intelligence officers . . . It was kind of an ordeal . . ."

The 44th, under Leon Johnson, was so mauled and dispersed in the course of the strike that he was able to gather only three other planes around him for the return trip. Following a skirmish with enemy fighters, one of these feathered a propeller and headed for Turkey. The remaining three plugged on, cleared the mountains, and reached the Adriatic, where one plane was forced to ditch into the sea. Two got back to Benghazi.

The aircraft flown by Captain Banks, of the 98th, was one of eleven which made it to Cyprus. "The next morning we spent hours refueling the plane. The airfield didn't have any fueling apparatus, and we had to fill her up with piddling little five-gallon cans of gasoline. It was one hell of a job. We finally got her refueled and checked over, and took off at noon. It was an easy run down to Tel Aviv." There the captain distributed a wad of "escape money" to his crew and said, "I don't want to see a sober man within the hour."

Killer Kane wound up in typical style, crash-landing spectacularly in Cyprus, where he dined on pork chops and a bottle of wine in a night club. But he got little sleep that night. "I kept thinking about those guys going down, some of them in flames—big Libs like broken flies."

One of the favorite stories of Keith Compton's outfit had to do with the plane known as the Lucky, flown by "Hap" Kendall. It had two insignia—one a Teddy bear holding a bomb, and another (for no special reason) of a girl. Damaged and running out of fuel, this plane had no chance of reaching Africa, and Kendall decided to try a landing at a small British field in southern Sicily. The first complication arose when it was discovered that a break in the hydraulic system required the landing gear to be cranked down by hand. The brakes were also gone. When the great bomber landed on the tiny 800-foot strip it raced to the end of it in a flash, ran over a ridge, smashed through two fighter planes under repair, crashed through five tents, and finally stopped with the camp kitchen directly under the starboard wing. A gunner named Miller jumped out, yelling, "At least we can eat!" and the rest followed.

Hadley's Harem had been hit hard before reaching its target. One large hunk of flak blew off part of the nose of the ship. Another slammed into the chest of the bombardier, Bud Storms, killing him instantly, and at the same time Harold Tabicoff of Brooklyn, the navigator, was also wounded. Engineer Russell Page decided to go aft to see what could be done and, since Storms had not had the chance to get his bombs away, Page salvoed them simultaneously by using the emergency release. He adminis-

317

tered first aid to Tabicoff and then noticed Storms, whose chest had been torn to shreds. Page hurried forward, muttering, "I never want to see a mess like that again."

Lieutenant Hadley had turned south, warily watching the No. 2 engine upon which burning oil was flickering. He feathered the propeller. At this point the Harem staggered and went into a steep dive, but Hadley and his co-pilot pulled back on their wheels to the limit and the plane came out of it. Wind was now pouring like a torrent through the gaping nose. The forgotten bomb-bay doors were still wide open.

When the next burst of flak hit, the floor of the ship buckled like a smashed tin-can, throwing the men about and knocking two of them unconscious. Three birds were flying overhead. In a daze the waist gunner cut loose at them, thinking they were enemy interceptors.

In their doomed bomber the men watched two others settle on the ground of Rumania with their tanks aflame. Then a third was seen flaming from wing tip to wing tip. She climbed agonizedly to nearly 3500 feet; then, in a single, blinding explosion, the Liberator totally disappeared. "I guess they were trying to get up and bail out," said Blacky Holweger, the armorer-gunner. The vision preyed on him for a long time. "For a split-second I saw that. It was the most horrible thing I had ever seen. It is stamped on my mind."

The Harem, too, was climbing tortuously for altitude with which to clear the Alps. When they passed over a Sunday excursion train, the passengers leaned out and waved. Farmers saluted them from the fields below. Chickens scurried for safety in tiny eddies of dust. One girl in a brilliant peasant blouse ran out of her house to look up. The No. 3 engine cut out just as they reached the Aegean Sea when they were at 5000 feet. All hands were told to be ready to bail out and warned not to smoke, for gas fumes were leaking throughout the fuselage.

The day was turning hazy and dim at eight-fifteen, when the No. 1 engine began to lose oil; in a flash the gauge dropped to zero. Hadley turned to the co-pilot: "What do you think we'd better do?" Lindsay suggested that they should try to make land first, but pointed out that engines Nos. 1 and 4 would soon be definitely out. Hadley then queried the crew over the intercom; all the men said they preferred to stay with the ship. The discussion, at any rate, was now academic, for the plane had lost so much altitude so quickly that parachuting was impossible. Everybody took off his shoes and adjusted his Mae West. When they were less than a mile from Turkey, Hadley asked Page to read the air-speed gauge. He replied, "No, the co-pilot will read it," for, to do so, Page would have had to lean over while standing between the two pilots and would have been killed instantly in that posture if the plane hit. He opened the top escape hatch and braced himself against the armor plate behind the pilot.

Just as the last two engines sputtered out the plane went in. There was a paralyzing shock as the right wing tip snagged a wave and twisted the plane into the water at an awkward angle. The Mediterranean rushed through the flak holes and especially the torn-open nose, filling the Harem instantly with water. Outside a slap of water slammed the escape hatch shut. The crew was now trapped.

The nine live men groped and swam in their underwater tomb. As Page held his breath a hundred confused thoughts passed through hs mind. He saw his wife's face and said to himself in wonderment, "My God, am I going to die this way?" He, Hadley and Lindsay, half blind from the salt water, tried without success to burst open the jammed escape hatch. With his lungs near bursting Page worked back to the top of the gun blister and tried to break through the Plexiglass. In despair he turned and saw the pilot and co-pilot splashing frantically in the nose. A half minute had passed since the plane had gone under.

Lindsay and Hadley never did get out. Trapped in a welter of debris, they drowned while the Harem settled slowly to the bottom of the sea. The remaining seven men forced their way through various natural and artificial openings and reached shore. As they staggered up the long beach they found fifteen ragged peasants awaiting them with long rifles, relics of wars long since ended—"Just like those revolutionary movies." They dozed on the beach under guard beside a big fire all night long, and the following morning were spotted by an English Wellington bomber. Later an air-sea rescue boat from Cyprus landed, three British Navy men furnished first aid, and arrangements were made to smuggle the Americans back into Allied hands.

The experiences of the hundreds who crash-landed or parachuted in or around the target area were perhaps the most grueling of all, in addition to which they faced the bleak prospect of untold years in concentration camps awaiting the end of hostilities. A few were shot by Germans in the process of being captured. Most of the others were treated reasonably well, one of whom was Captain Palm. Holding the remnants of his right leg, he had dived through the window of his crashed plane and hopped into a cornfield while hanging to a crew member, Bill Love. There the rest of the crew congregated abjectly, waiting for Rumanians to surrender to, and hiding from the Germans. Finally a group of peasants appeared, and the fliers shouted, "Doctor!" at them—a word they believed was similar to the Rumanian word. For a few moments nothing happened. The Rumanians looked at the Americans. The latter began to wonder how popular they were. At this stage several German soldiers arrived. A discussion followed as to who was entitled to the American prisoners. Eventually the Germans left, but not before one of them had reached over and snatched Palm's wrist watch, while he was clasping the remnants of his leg with both hands.

When the Rumanians tried to carry the captain, he nearly fainted from the pain, and because his dangling leg kept slapping him in the face. A litter was hurriedly whipped together out of saplings and he was lifted into a truck. Next he was driven to a hospital for women and children, where he was turned away, and then moved again to another hospital where a Dr. Petrescu—"a hell of a good old Joe"—snipped off the leg.

Now Rumanians began to come in to see Palm. He understood their curiosity. It was as though Chicago had been bombed by Rumanians, or it was like a visit by a man from Mars. In Palm's ward lay five other Rumanian victims

320

of the American bombing. "I wouldn't have blamed them for being sore," Palm relates; but, in fact, they tried to shake hands with him. Delayed-action bombs continued to explode throughout Ploesti during the entire evening. The six men in the hospital ward tossed and muttered, and tried to sleep.

The sun had set, leaving in its wake a cloud-streaked twilight, when word came at seven-thirty that the first planes were calling in from a hundred miles out at sea. Officers and men jumped into jeeps and staff cars and dashed over to the Benghazi strip. Some ground crews were already there, looking for their own planes, and as the ships arrived they called out their names—Old Baldy, Vulgar Virgin, and so on. On one the bomb doors were still grotesquely swinging open. A few arrived with dead engines. All were riddled by machine-gun bullets or the scars of 40-millimeter shells. Brereton personally greeted Ent and Compton as they crawled unhappily out of their plane. Many bombers had a curiously blackened appearance, as though they had been toasted over an open fire. Some fired flares during their approaches, to indicate wounded on board. The main spar had buckled on the right wing of one bomber. Holes in the tail surfaces could be clearly seen from the ground. Some of the landings were poor, for the planes were now so light that they bounced like rubber balls down the strip, too battered to respond efficiently to the controls. It was a sorry, bedraggled formation that made the initial landings at Bomber Command.

One of the bombers in Jack Wood's section had the manual controls shot away, but by putting the ship on automatic pilot and manipulating the engines the pilot got it back to Benghazi. Remarkably enough, he even managed to make a fairly decent landing despite the absence of tail or aileron controls.

Still another bomber from the 389th had been the cause

321

of much anxiety on the way home. Over the Mediterranean the pilot began to complain by radio that his gas was running low. Every few miles he reported that the end was near, and finally he drifted away. There was nothing to do but hope that he had been able to ditch safely so that the men could be picked up later by rescue boats. But when Wood landed at Benghazi the first people he saw were these supposedly doomed fliers, who had not only reached base but had even beaten him there.

The night dragged on, black as Pharaoh's tomb. There was no moon. At infrequent intervals other forlorn single planes found their way home, guided by the thin, bluish glare of a searchlight that swung slowly back and forth over the field. The service and officers' clubs stayed open all night; there was much drinking and strained, nervous celebrating. Every man had a whole Southern fried chicken for dinner. Voices and incongruous laughter drifted across to the Operations tent, where a little group of men still watched the pitch-black sky, against which the stars shimmered with a hard, gemlike intensity. The Ploesti raid was over.

Into Italy

The prospect of an Italian campaign heated up the arguments between British and American High Commands all over again. The Americans still wanted to invade France across the English Channel, and as early as possible. The British now argued for an immediate attack upon Italy —a momentum had been developed by the victories in North Africa which ought to be sustained by an advance to the Italian mainland.

The British were intent on an Italian campaign partly because they had their eyes on the Balkans; Churchill felt this was the place to establish a common front with the Russians, and also foresaw the need for a foothold there in the post-war power struggle. And then there was the attractive possibility of knocking Italy out of the war, for it was thought that Italy had little stomach left for fighting.

But the Americans were convinced the main task was to defeat Germany—and the quicker the better. Any grand strategy not directly aimed at this goal didn't appeal to them.

What is interesting is that the Germans expected the Allies to invade Europe through the Balkans; not even the successful capture of Sicily changed their minds. They kept twice as many divisions in the Balkans as they had in Italy.

The original Allied strategy provided for the 8th Army to invade the toe of Italy, but in the middle of July, 1943, Mussolini's government was overthrown, and the Italians under Marshal Badoglio began to discuss an armistice with the Allies. The surrender of Italy was to remove more than thirty divisions of Italians which would have opposed the Allies in Italy. As it developed, the Italian people regarded the Allies more as liberators than enemies. This brought about a revision of the invasion plan. The 5th Army was created out of three American and three British divisions, for an assault landing in the Gulf of Salerno. On September 3rd, the British 8th Army invaded Italy at the toe, and six days later, on September 9th, the 5th Army landed on the Salerno beaches.

Avalanche

The British 8th Army under Montgomery moved across the Strait of Messina on to the toe of Italy, almost unopposed; their progress was slow up the boot. There was little opposition but roads were mined and bridges blown and the 8th Army, used to traveling on wheels, took its time. This was unfortunate because the Allied command had hoped that the 8th Army would reach the Salerno beachhead quickly in order to put pressure on the left flank of the German defenders. However, it would take the 8th until September 16 to make contact with the 5th Army, and then only advance patrols of each Army had met.*

Operation Avalanche commenced with some degree of optimism on the part of the Allied Commanders. In retrospect, it does not seem justifiable. Hugh Pond, author of the recently published *Salerno* says:

"The beaches along the thirty-six-mile curve of Salerno Bay were ideal for an assault landing. There were no shoals or river-mouth ridges to impede the boats and the sand shelved gently and evenly. But the coastal plain behind the beaches—largely reclaimed land—was narrow, and in some places almost non-existent, dominated by the mountains from which a beachhead could be observed and pounded by artillery. The only exit from this plain was through two narrow passes, which could easily be held by light, strongly entrenched forces.

"The nearest air bases for our fighters, apart from carrier-based planes, were in Sicily, which meant that Spitfires fitted with ninety-gallon wing tanks would be able to remain over the area for a maximum of twenty minutes, an operation which called for tremendous co-ordination to be effective. For the first three days the ground troops would have the support of a hundred and twenty Seafires of the Fleet Air Arm, operating from five Royal Navy carriers under the command

---

*Twenty-four hours earlier, several war correspondents had driven the length of the gap between the Allied Armies and had met no enemy resistance.

324

of Rear-Admiral Sir Philip Vian.*

Again, optimism plus plain bad strategy seems to have overcome the 5th Army Commander, General Mark Clark. Admiral S. L. Morison says:

"Of all decisions about AVALANCHE, the most unfortunate was the Army command's insistence on no preliminary gunfire support, in order to obtain tactical surprise. Admiral Hewitt argued against this in vain, as he had before HUSKY. He pointed out that the Germans knew something was on, as evidenced by their August air raids on Bizerte; that any officer with a pair of dividers could figure out that the Gulf of Salerno was the northernmost practicable landing place for the Allies; that reconnaissance planes would snoop the convoys; in short, that it was fantastic to assume we could obtain tactical surprise. He was right in every particular. Implicit in the denial was the fear that preliminary bombardment would attract German forces to Salerno. But on 6 September the Germans had already sent the 16th Panzer Division into the Salerno plain. The enemy had several days in which to set up 88-mm and other guns, cut down trees, build strong points, site the Italians' Breda machine guns and fieldpieces on the beaches and their exits, bring up tanks, and cram nearby airfields with their planes. As it turned out, a good selective shoot on strong points on the edge of the Salerno plain, for a day or two before D-Day, would have rendered the landings much less arduous." **

In the meantime negotiations between the Italians and General Eisenhower were carried on, which led to the unconditional surrender of Italy. The announcement of the surrender was made by Eisenhower on September 8 while the assault troops were approaching the Salerno beaches. "In justice to the Italians the armistice had to be announced before we landed on their soil, but it was singularly ill-timed with reference to embarked troops. These, naturally assuming that they were to have a walk-over at Salerno, proceeded to relax, mentally and otherwise. Senior officers tried to undo the mischief by warning the men by loud-speaker that they would still have to fight Germans; but Admiral Cunningham states 'that many took no heed of these warnings and viewed the proceedings with a sense of complacency.' Complacency is hardly the word for it; the general impression seemed to

*Salerno, by Hugh Pond, published by Little, Brown & Co., pp. 40-41.

** Sicily-Salerno-Anzio, pp. 249-250.

be that the war was over. We were landing in Italy, and the Italians had quit, hadn't they?

"So the tenseness that one usually feels just before an amphibious landing dissipated; the approach continued under a sort of spell. It was a beautiful, calm, bright night. To many of the ships Capri was visible, swimming in a silver sea; the jagged outline of the Sorrento peninsula made a dark cut-out against a floor of heaven . . . thickly inlaid with patines of bright gold and beyond lay the Bay of Naples redolent with history, beauty and romance. . . .

"This illusion lasted even after the beacon submarine—HMS *Shakespeare*—flashed her guiding light seaward, and until the transports began easing into their release points at one minute past midnight. Then orders rang out, boatswains' whistles shrilled, and the clang and clatter of lowering landing craft broke the spell." *

Sicily-Salerno-Anzio, pp. 252-253.

SALERNO*

by Samuel E. Morison

Paestum, the American Sector

Daylight revealed to lookouts in the crow's nests a superb panorama, unsurpassed even on the west coast of Italy. The Gulf of Salerno, Longfellow's "blue Salernian bay with its sickle of white sand," loosely embraced by a jagged mountain wall, stretches 30 miles from the Sorrento peninsula to Cape Licosa. Between mountains and sea lies a plain shaped like a second-quarter moon, with the bright little city of Salerno at the upper and the small town of Agrópoli at the nether tip. The Naples–Reggio coastal highway and railway pass through Salerno, skirt the plain, and at the town of Battipaglia are met by another road and railway from southern Italy.

The planners for AVALANCHE decided to put the British X Corps ashore near the northern end of the gulf, for prompt capture of Salerno, Montecorvino airport and Battipaglia; while the American VI Corps landed opposite the temples of Paestum in order to protect the Allies' right flank and make contact with Montgomery's Eighth Army marching up from Calabria. It may seem odd that the two sets of beaches should have been eight miles apart, instead of contiguous; but the beaches near the mouth of the Sele are more obstructed by sand bars than those farther away, and the exits are not good.

At 0001 September 9 the leading transports, three British LSIs, were in position. *Marnix van St. Aldegonde* had her

* A somewhat condensed version of the Salerno chapters in *Sicily-Salerno-Anzio*.

landing craft in the water in 20 minutes. She and four United States transports carried the 142nd RCT, which was to land on the two northernmost beaches (Red and Green) at H-hour, 0330. Simultaneously, five U.S. transports were to land the 141st RCT on the two southern beaches, Yellow and Blue. Five other U.S. transports and one LSI carried the 143rd RCT, which was destined to follow up on Beaches Red and Green at 0630.

The same Scouts and Raiders who had functioned in HUSKY were embarked in four scout boats (LCS), one for each beach. Using a radar fix on Monte Soprano obtained by *PC–624*, reference vessel for the Southern Attack Force, each of the four scout boats took a position a few hundred yards off its assigned beach, and started blinking seaward, to guide the boat waves. The boat commanded by Ensign G. Anderson USNR arrived at a point 400 yards off Beach Red at 0230 and began blinking red. That of Lieutenant (jg) Grady R. Galloway USCG located Beach Green by sighting, against the starlit sky, the Torre di Paestum—a medieval stone watchtower that adjoins the road exit between the two pairs of beaches. Galloway started blinking green at 0310 from 100 yards off shore. Ensign J. G. Donnell's boat found the center of Beach Yellow from a bearing on the tower, and took station 600 yards off shore. (During the hour of waiting, the men in this scout boat heard clanking and clattering ashore and saw the lights of vehicles; German troops were moving down to the water's edge.) Ensign Ross E. Schumann USNR, commanding the guide boat for Beach Blue, found that beach by a bearing on Monte Sottane.

Next after the scout boats came Commander Richards's minesweepers to clear a channel through the mine field reported to lie between the line of departure (6000 yards off shore) and the transports. This was done by the same group of fleet minesweepers (*Seer* flag) that had been used in Sicily, and ten small motor minesweepers (YMSs). According to Admiral Hewitt, the sweep plan was too ambitous, requiring not only the boat channels but fire support areas to be swept by 0330. That was more than the available craft could possibly accomplish. Several boat waves were held up by reports of floating mines, and one LCVP was blown up.

The American beaches were well selected for an orderly night landing. There would have been no trouble if tactical surprise had been obtained, or if the enemy had been lukewarm fighters, as had happened on the coast of Sicily. Unfortunately for us, the Germans were almost as well prepared to contest landings at Salerno as the Japanese would be at Tarawa two months later.

General von Vietinghoff, commanding the German Tenth Army, had been expecting a landing in the Salerno Gulf for several days. On 7 September when he heard that large convoys were heading thither, the 16th Panzer Division and the Italian 222nd Coastal Division were already busy installing mine fields along the beaches, building strong points at the most likely landing places, digging tank traps and preparing bridges for demolition. By D-day there was a series of strong points along the shore between Salerno and Agrópoli, armed with light and heavy machine guns, quads of antiaircraft 20-mm, and either 75-mm or 88-mm cannon. In the hills and along the Salerno-Battipaglia road were several batteries of 88-mm mobile artillery, and the Germans were in process of taking over all Italian coastal and fieldpieces. The commanding general of the coastal division, who objected to taking German orders, was quietly taken out and shot. By D-day all beaches between Salerno and Agrópoli had been mined, and pioneers were preparing the port of Salerno for demolition.

When Vietinghoff got the word of the Italian surrender, during the evening of 8 September, he ordered the 26th Panzer Division, then delaying Montgomery's advance in Calabria, to break contact and hasten north. Still uncertain of the main Allied target, Vietinghoff made no further troop dispositions until daylight revealed that the Allies had made a *Grosslandung*, not a Commando raid.

The higher levels of German command also were well prepared. Hitler's headquarters, as early as 1 August, had drawn up a plan for Operation ACHSE, to start when and if

Italy surrendered. This involved the swift occupation of Genoa, Leghorn, Venice and Trieste by Marshal Rommel, now commander in northern Italy; of central and southern Italian ports by Marshal Kesselring, commander in those parts of Italy; the evacuation of Sardinia and Sicily by German troops, and a brisk transfer of German divisions to Italy. At 1950 September 8, Kesselring ordered Operation ACHSE to be executed. When news of the Salerno landings reached him, the Marshal was apprehensive of an American air drop on Rome; but when nightfall came, with no paratroops, he felt confident enough to issue a grandiloquent proclamation:—

> The invading enemy in the area Naples-Salerno and southwards, must be completely annihilated and in addition thrown into the sea. Only by so doing can we obtain a decisive change of the situation in the Italian area. I require ruthless employment of all the might of the three army units. Every commanding officer must be aware of his historical responsibility. British and Americans must realize that they are hopelessly lost against the concentrated German might.*

As first light broke on D-day, at 0330, the initial waves for the four American beaches were nearing the ends of their eight- to ten-mile runs over a calm sea. All hit their respective beaches within seven minutes of one another (0335 to 0342) and the second and third waves followed at the proper intervals. Both waves were guided to the line of departure by patrol craft; but, unlike the British, they had no close fire support from that point to the beaches. Admiral Hewitt offered to furnish rocket craft or small gunboats, but the U. S. Army would have none of them; the soldiers imagined that they could obtain complete surprise if they landed silently. This decision was unfortunate; for want of close support, many men in landing craft were killed by German gunners ready and waiting behind the beaches. And, what made matters worse, the Luftwaffe at

*War Diary German Naval Command Italy 10 Sept. 1943.

the same time began to bomb and strafe the beaches, on a scale never before or since equaled in a Mediterranean landing. Fortunately this did not long continue.

Colonel John D. Forsythe's 142nd Infantry went ashore on Beaches Green and Red. Heavy fire from mortars, 88-mm cannon, and machine guns, descended on and around his landing craft, and the troops, even when wading ashore, came under machine-gun fire from the Torre di Paestum. Relentlessly they worked around to their prearranged assembly area, and made it by sunrise, 0436. Plenty of Germans were left near the beach for later arrivals to mop up. Dukws carrying fieldpieces arrived from three Killer-class British LSTs at 0530. An hour later, the 143rd Regiment began to land on Beach Red. By 0800 that beach had become very congested, owing to the usual failure of Army shore parties to do their job of stevedoring.

Lieutenant Galloway's scout boat for Beach Green was, by exception, provided with a few rocket launchers which were used to silence gunfire directed at the first wave. The second wave of landing craft for this beach was delayed by mines and became mixed up with subsequent waves, beaching only at 0630. Thirty dukws hit Beach Green as early as 0525, one in every twelve bringing much-wanted 105-mm howitzers, and the others, ammunition. They unloaded in good order behind the dune line and most of them returned to the transports. No fewer than 123 dukw landings were made on the Amercan beaches between 0530 and 0730—a remarkable achievement. The 2nd Battalion of the 142nd Regiment here had a hard time getting through barbed wire and lost men from exploding land mines; but it managed to reach the same assembly area as the battalion from Beach Red. The southern half of Beach Green was interdicted by enemy gunfire throughout D-day.

Much of the trouble here and on the next beach (Yellow) came from machine guns mounted on the 50-foot stone tower and from one or two tanks that lurked behind the farm buildings attached to it. This tower was too near the beach for naval gunfire to take on. It was finally captured, the tanks put out of business, and all German defenders killed or made prisoner by the 531st Shore Engineers, who had already lost a number of officers and men in the early air attacks.*

The two southernmost American beaches, Yellow and Blue, were the most difficult for the invaders to negotiate. Behind them, the Germans had constructed a strong point, and both beaches were within range of coastal batteries near Agrópoli. As the landing craft approached, a loudspeaker blared in English "Come on in and give up. We have you covered!" The first three assault waves of the 3rd Battalion 141st Regiment were indeed covered. Tank fire from behind the stone tower stopped them, but there was no giving up; and a reserve battalion came in at 0500 to help them get off the beach. From 0830 to 1330 Beach Yellow was completely interdicted, and on Beach Blue the 1st Battalion was pinned down for 20 hours. Heavy gunfire prevented six tank-laden LCTs from landing there at about 0640. Four of the six were hit by 88-mm shell; in *LCT–244*, Ensign S. J. Cavallaro USNR, guiding the formation, was killed, and the tank nearest the bow started to burn; the crew promptly lowered the ramp and shoved the tank overboard. The LCTs retired out of range, awaited orders, started in again about noon with gunfire support from a destroyer, and at 1330 discharged their tanks on Beach Red. Tank-laden *LST–389*, which also carried pontoon units, beached at Blue at 1241. Her crew bravely rigged this pontoon under enemy fire and at 1354 her tanks began to roll off. Within twenty minutes enemy gunfire forced another closing of Beach Blue, but it was reopened at 1600 and became the principal beach for discharging tanks.

Thus, the 36th Division had very little armor ashore on D-day, but German Mark IV tanks had been active from 0700, maneuvering both in the open and behind the old Greek city walls, on which machine guns were mounted.

*Company D of this engineer regiment, commanded by 1st Lt. G. L. Shumaker USA, did fine work preparing the beaches with bulldozers and steel mat, under heavy fire from the tower. Disparaging remarks directed at Army shore parties do not apply to the 531st Shore Engineers.

The GIs, with the aid of a dismounted cavalry reconnaissance troop, bazookas, 105-mm howitzers and naval gunfire, prevented these tanks from reaching the beaches, and by noon forced them to retire; but some of their fire still reached Red and Green. At 1020 thirteen more Mark IVs rumbled down the highway from the north, threatening the 142nd Regiment's command post which had just been set up in the Capaccio railway station, a few miles north of Paestum. A dukw hauling a 105-mm howitzer arrived just in time to shatter two of the tanks; a third was destroyed by an Invader (A-36) divebomber; gunfire from a naval vessel, probably H.M.S. *Abercrombie,* accounted for two more, and the rest retreated.

The landings at Paestum and the British sector were among the most fiercely contested in World War II. Few soldiers suffered so severe a baptism of fire on landing as did those of this yet untried division, or came through it so well. Like the Sons of Tola, the 36th "were valiant men of might." Yet even they could not have carried on without naval gunfire.

Rear Admiral Lyal A. Davidson in *Philadelphia,* tempered by his experience in North Africa and Sicily, commanded naval gunfire support in the American sector. He also had *Savannah* at his disposal, and four destroyers, while H.M.S. *Abercrombie,* screened by Dutch gunboat *Flores,* stood by to serve when 15-inch shell was wanted. The monitor was the first to get into action. Between 0825 and 0915 she fired 11 rounds at an enemy battery, with aircraft spotting. At 1025, as we have seen, she fired on a tank concentration, and again at 1112. Next, she bombarded the town of Capaccio. All at ranges of over 25,000 yards. This hard-hitting monitor, whose help had already been appreciated in HUSKY, struck a mine that afternoon, took a 10-degree list, reached an even keel by counterflooding, but was so badly damaged that she had to steam to Palermo.

Delays in passing through mine fields and in establishing communications with harassed shore fire-control parties prevented the other fire support vessels from functioning as early as they wished. In Admiral Hall's opinion, they did not do so well this day as on D-day in Sicily; but there was no complaint from the troops. At 0914 *Savannah* established communication with her shore fire-control party, which wanted a railway battery silenced. That was accomplished with an expenditure of 57 rounds. For more than an hour, beginning at 1132, *Savannah* fired on a concentration of tanks at the good range of 17,450 yards, yet (so it was reported from shore) forced them to retire. Other targets were German infantry, artillery batteries, observation posts, and the town of Capaccio. The cruiser answered eleven calls for fire support on D-day and expended 645 rounds of 6-inch ammunition. For spotting she used her own SOC observation planes, as well as Army Mustangs; for the 111th Fighter Reconnaissance Squadron had been trained to spot naval gunfire. These P–51s, flying in pairs, turned in an excellent performance at Salerno; one would spot while the other covered against enemy air attack.

Flagship *Philadelphia's* work on D-day, the first of ten spent off the Salerno beaches, began at 0943 when, on call from shore fire-control party, she opened on an enemy battery. At 1033 she launched an SOC spotting plane, and two minutes later took a bridge under fire to hold up approaching panzer units. At 1057 she launched a second spotting plane and then followed a minesweeper through a swept channel to close the beach. From 1220 to 1309, with destroyer *Ludlow,* she fired at a German battery which was shelling beached LSTs on Beach Blue, then recovered her planes. Shortly before 1400 she launched another plane which, simultaneously with one of *Savannah's,* discovered a covey of German tanks concealed in a thicket adjacent to Beach Red. *Philadelphia's* 6-inch salvos flushed 35 of these birds and kept them under fire as they scurried to the rear; about seven were destroyed. Continuing almost to midnight, this cruiser expended 305 rounds of 6-inch shell on D-day.

Outstanding performance in gunfire support was given also by the destroyers.

Owing to the interdiction of Beaches Yellow and Blue by enemy gunfire, Beach Red became horribly congested after noon. A veritable mountain ridge of boxed ammunition and baled supplies lined the water's edge and extended several feet into the sea. Landing craft could not even find room to let down ramps. Troops detailed to unload drifted away, as usual, leaving boat crews to do the stevedoring. Admiral Hall at 1036 appealed to General Clark to assign 200 men to each beach to clear up the mess, and the General gave him about that many from his headquarters troops in *Duchess of Bedford;* but they were untrained for such work and were unable to cope with the sea-wall of supplies.

Landing craft crews functioned even better here than in HUSKY; discipline and seamanship alike were excellent. And although the sea was much calmer than it had been off Sicily, enemy fire on the boats was far heavier. The crews stuck by their craft, and worked around the clock to unload transports. When the operation was over, the incredibly small number of eleven boats had to be abandoned, and all but one of these had been knocked out by enemy action.

Despite this fine boat performance, the unloading of transports and assault cargo ships was unduly delayed. Distance of the transport area from shore (10 miles for some ships), beach congestion, lack of LCTs,* and defective combat loading at Oran were responsible. Disregarding the lessons of TORCH and HUSKY, the Army had again taken charge at that port, stowing equipment urgently needed for the assault where it could not be got at, and piling in stuff that would not be needed for days—as if the expedition were bound for some far-off Pacific island. At the end of D-day, the transports of the Southern Attack Force were only partially unloaded, the percentage ranging from 17 to 65. They would not have done even this well but for an extensive use of cargo nets which enabled bulk cargo to be hoisted out of landing craft by portable cranes onto trucks and dukws.

Surmounting all difficulties, the 36th Division reached important objectives by the end of the day. It had taken the

*Only 16 out of 54 LCTs promised from the Northern Attack Force area actually turned up on D-day.

459-foot hill called Templo San Paolo, two miles inland from Capaccio railway station; another hill south of it; and the town of Capaccio, from which the Germans had already retired. One company had fought its way almost to to summit of Monte Sottane. On the right flank, the 141st Regiment was still pinned down on Beach Blue. These fell short of D-day objectives, but General Clark was on the whole satisfied; he "felt that we had achieved as much as could be expected."

If anyone then imagined that the Germans had shot their bolt, he was destined for a great disappointment. They were still able to challenge from the air; they now had full control over the roads and railways of southern Italy, and of communications with the north. Reinforcements were rolling in from the mountains, and the Hermann Goering Panzer Division was coming south from Naples; leading elements of the 29th Panzer Grenadiers had reached the Salerno beachhead at 1900, less than 24 hours after they had been ordered north. During the three following days, the issue was continually in doubt.

That the Army achieved so much was, in some measure at least, due to the quality of naval gunfire support; the boldness of the destroyers driving in through mine fields to deliver accurate shoots was especially praised. It inspired a generous message from the divisional artillery commander of the 36th Division, Brigadier General John W. Lange, which was relayed to every fire support ship and joyfully entered in their logs:

Thank God for the fire of the blue-belly Navy ships. Probably could not [otherwise] have stuck out Blue and Yellow beaches. Brave fellows these; tell them so.

The British Sector

"What's the weather like at Salerno?" wrote Horace to a friend, about the year 20 B.C.; "and what sort of people shall I encounter there?" That's just what the Northern Attack Force wanted to know in A.D. 1943. The weather could not have been better for an amphibious landing; but

336

the people, instead of the friendly Italians whom the troops expected to find on the beach, turned out to be very tough and uncooperative Germans of the 16th Panzer Division.

The general plan for this northern sector was for Commodore Oliver to land Lieutenant General McCreery's X Corps on beaches between three and six miles south of the city of Salerno. On the northernmost pair, designated "Uncle," the 46th (North Midland) Division, Major General Hawkesworth, was to swing left after landing and secure control of the high ground behind Salerno. One column was to capture Salerno and then move through the Cava gap toward Naples; the other to move up the valley of the Picentino and through a pass to Mercato, north of Salerno. The 56th (London) Division, Major General Graham, would land on the "Sugar" and "Roger" pairs of beaches south of Uncle, capture Montecorvino airfield and then drive toward Ponte Sele, apex of the desired beachhead line, ten miles inland. None of these objectives, unfortunately, were attained for many days.

On the Sorrento peninsula, whose astonishing beauty— a unique combination of rugged mountains and sophisticated building and planting—must be seen to be believed, two subsidiary landings took place. At Maiori, two miles east of Amalfi, there is a shingle beach with a gradient so steep that small cruising yachts anchor within a stone's throw of the shore. Maiori is the terminus of a road from Naples through the Chiunzi pass, and it was to seize this pass that three United States Ranger battalions were landed under Lieutenant Colonel Darby, the hero of Gela. A few miles farther east, and very near Salerno, the Marina de Vietri, with a short sand beach, lies at the foot of the Cava gap, through which the main road and railway run to Naples. British Army and Royal Marine Commandos under Brigadier R. F. Laycock RM, augmented by an American mortar battery, landed here to destroy nearby coast defenses and seize the gap.

Darby's Rangers, embarked in two LSIs and five American LCIs, began landing at Maiori at 0320. Unexpectedly, for Rangers, they met no opposition; succeeding waves and supply runs were sent in smoothly; by 0615 all supplies and

337

equipment were ashore and the landing was completed. By this time the troops had reached the height of the Chiunzi pass, and the ridges which overlook the main road and railway running from Salerno to Naples. And their positions also dominated the defile of Nocera, a bottleneck where a network of roads converged.

At Vietri the British Commandos (embarked in *Prince Albert* and three British LCIs) were less fortunate. The first wave landed unopposed at 0330 after H.M.S. *Blackmore* and a gunboat had silenced a shore battery. For the next two and a half hours the landings continued "according to plan." But Vietri was too near Salerno for the Germans to ignore the threat. They infiltrated the town, mounted mortars and machine guns on several houses which overlooked the beach, and drove off landing craft attempting to come in after 0630. After almost two hours' fighting the enemy was driven out. As early as 0600 the Royal Marine section of the Commandos had reached the defile of La Molina about a mile inland, where they were counterattacked by a German force supported by tanks, and were pinned down for some time.

All these landings were subsidiary to the main operation. The main body of the Northern Attack Force sighted the outer ship of a string of reference vessels at 2317 September 8. Six fleet minesweepers of the Royal Navy and seven American YMSs preceded Admiral Conolly in *Biscayne,* commanding "Uncle" group, on its final run-in. By 0150 September 9 they had swept a channel through the mine field. Next after the minesweepers came three Hunt-class destroyers, which took fire support positions only one mile off the beaches—a bold plan, the wisdom of which was soon proved. Conolly received word from Admiral Hewitt at 2341 that shore installations were not to be engaged unless they opened fire—hoping that all would be abandoned, owing to the armistice.

The enemy soon canceled this restriction. At 0121, as the 15 six-davit American LSTs bearing assault troops were deploying in their allotted area, gunfire was observed on the beach ahead. Shortly after 0200, *Biscayne* and the LSTs were subjected to severe shelling by 88-mm guns. One LST

338

had several members of her crew and 25 soldiers put out of action by the first three salvos. Admiral Conolly immediately ordered the supporting destroyers to return fire, while *Biscayne* stood across the inshore boundary of the transport area to lay a smoke screen. At 0225, when shore fire slackened, Conolly ordered the landing to proceed. As the first boat wave for the two Uncle beaches, Red and Green, made its run for the beach, gunboats picked up the ball from fire support destroyers and, just before the boats touched down, an LCR discharged 790 rockets onto Beach Red. The first wave landed precisely at H-hour, 0330, met stiff resistance and quickly overcame it. Artillery and ammunition followed, and at 0645 the Brigadier Commanding was on the beach with his staff.

Unfortunately the rocket barrage intended for Beach Green was almost half a mile off in deflection, and fell on Beach Amber of the Sugar pair. Guide boats were stationed off Beach Green and the commander of the first wave could easily have landed there; but, as rockets were considered necessary to explode beach mines, General Hawkesworth and Admiral Conolly had agreed that, if they went wild in the darkness, the boats must follow the rockets and not the plan. So the first wave destined for Beach Green landed at Amber instead, and three more waves followed at 15-minute intervals.

Landing behind the rockets may have saved some soldiers from being blown up by beach mines, but it crowded the 56th Division off Beach Amber, left intact an enemy strong point near Beach Green, and forced two assault battalions of the 46th Division to the wrong side of the Aso River. These battalions, working north to link up with the rest of their brigade, encountered German troops and, without vehicles or supporting weapons, suffered many casualties. And when their vehicles and artillery finally landed on the correct Beach Green, heavy 88-mm fire pinned them down.

German artillery and the Luftwaffe concentrated on the Uncle beaches and roadstead, and made things very hot afloat as well as ashore.

Throughout D-day, fire support ships were blazing away

in reply to aerial bombing and enemy artillery fire. Rangers and Commandos each had a destroyer and an LCG (converted beaching craft armed with 4.7-inch guns) to cover their landings on the Sorrento peninsula. Three British destroyers and three LCGs were assigned to support the 46th Division in Uncle, and the same number, with one more LCG, were assigned to the 56th Division in Sugar and Roger. Cruiser Squadron 15, commanded by Rear Admiral C.H.J. Harcourt RN in H.M.S. *Mauritius,* with *Uganda, Orion,* monitor *Roberts* and two destroyers, operated directly under Commodore Oliver in support of the entire X Corps, but the cruisers had such difficulty communicating with their F.O.O.s and ascertaining the relative positions of friend and foe that they were unable to do much on D-day.

The destroyers more than made up for the cruisers' silence. Off Uncle beaches, H.M.S. *Mendip* and *Brecon* and three small gunboats were busily engaged from 0215 on. They found it easy to silence enemy batteries temporarily, but the German 88s for the most part were mobile and constantly shifted position. When daylight made direct observation possible, enemy fire increased. The German artillery was so well camouflaged that gun flashes and smoke could seldom be detected by ships lying off shore. Admiral Conolly, from the bridge of flagship *Biscayne,* spotted a battery firing into the transport area from a hill southeast of Salerno. Unable at that moment to raise the destroyers by radio, he ordered his flagship to take care of the battery; she moved in and silenced it with 12 rounds from her two 5-inch guns. Soldiers and sailors had begun to call this flag officer "Close-in-Conolly" after his performance off Licata; this incident confirmed his nickname.

The same destroyers, together with H.M.S. *Blankney,* throughout the morning carefully pounded every German battery that they could detect. Liberal use was made of smoke to cover both transports and ships approaching the beach. Smoke provided good protection, since enemy artillery did not fire on floating targets unless they were clearly visible. When Beach Uncle Green was (falsely to be sure) reported overrun by the enemy, during the mixup over Green and Amber, these destroyers steamed so close to shore that they even came under rifle fire. *Loyal* had a boiler knocked out by an 88-mm shell. After *Laforey* had blown up the ammunition dump of a troublesome battery, a second battery nearby straddled her, but she silenced it at 0600, after receiving five hits. Her crew made temporary repairs in the roadstead, and she returned to action within an hour. The 56th Division reported that her fire had reduced several German guns to scrap and inflicted many casualties on their crews. *Lookout* closed Green Beach and put out of action a battery which had sunk an LCT. She remained off the Roger beaches all day, firing at every target seen, although she had but one contact with her F.O.O.

When a strong enemy tank column attacked the 167th Brigade on the right flank of the 56th Division, gunfire from *Nubian* was decisive in breaking up and driving off the assault.

Air defense of the beachhead, controlled by Brigadier General E. J. House USA from his fighter-director center in Admiral Hewitt's flagship *Ancon,* was adequate on D-day because the Luftwaffe put in but few and feeble appearances after the early morning attacks. The British escort carriers, operating well out to sea, placed Seafires over the transports and beaches from dawn to 0745, when fighter planes from the Sicilian fields took over. They started "home" at 1800, when the Seafires resumed combat air patrol and continued until after dark. There were only four "Red" alerts on D-day; and during the first three days, 10–12 September, only 156 enemy air raids were plotted by fighter-director control. Most of them were intercepted by Allied fighters and broken up before entering the assault area. Allied pilots had begun to feel that their activities were wasted, and top air force officers were beginning to suggest using them for "offensive missions," when the Luftwaffe disclosed a new secret weapon that made necessary an increase rather than a decrease of fighter support.

With the exception of the Uncle area, landings in the British sector were less strongly opposed than at Paestum.

But the X Corps became just as heavily engaged ashore as did the United States VI Corps at the same time. By evening the left flank of the 46th Division was about three miles from Salerno, whence its front ran east to a line about two miles inland, where the 56th Division took over. Its right flank joined the coast four miles northwest of the Sele River mouth, leaving a gap of about seven miles between the British X and the United States VI Corps. The Salerno harbor, Montecorvino airfield and Battipaglia—three important D-day objectives—had not been attained.

The pattern of assault in the British sector was very similar to that in the American. Amphibious technique was almost identical, troops were equally aggressive, landing craft crews as skilled and industrious and gunfire support ships equally bold. Commodore Oliver reported that "there was not enough space to bring into action all the artillery landed; naval gunfire filled the gap." Admiral Hewitt concluded that "without the support of naval gunfire, the assault of the beaches could not have carried and the Army could not have remained ashore without the support of naval guns and bombing aircraft."

Although the German command in Italy found D-day both confusing and critical, it quickly recovered balance. On 10 September the Hermann Goering Division and part of the 15th Panzer Grenadier Division began to move toward Salerno. With Rome secured, the 3rd Panzer Grenadier Division was able to start south from near Orvieto; and in Calabria the whole LXXVI Corps was hastening north, after disengaging Montgomery. At 1000 September 10 Kesselring received a cheerful report from the 16th Panzer Division at Salerno that the beachhead front was stabilized; half an hour later General Herr, commanding LXXVI Corps, arrived from the far south and took over. He promptly ordered the 16th Panzers to counterattack VI Corps from Eboli down the Sele Valley toward Paestum,

342

and, as a diversion, to launch a tank attack from Battipaglia against the British X Corps. Both movements started at 1610, but neither succeeded.

Action ashore during the first four days, 9–12 September, is difficult to follow because almost nothing was "according to plan." Heavy fighting started even before the first landing waves beached, and continued with little let-up. We shall attempt to describe the ground action in a general way in order to lay the foundation for our account of the vital part that naval gunfire support played. The intensity and volume of naval gunfire delivered in direct support of troop operations here set a new high in that aspect of naval warfare; one that would not be exceeded in the Pacific until Iwo Jima and Okinawa. Unfortunately no accurate or complete log was kept of these shoots, or even of the calls. On the basis of incomplete reports it has been estimated that during the Salerno operation the ships delivered more than 11,000 tons of shell in direct support of troops ashore. This was the equivalent of 72,000 field artillery 105-mm high-explosive projectiles, and in total weight greatly exceeded that of the bombs dropped by the Northwest African Air Force on the Salerno beachhead, which amounted to only 3020 tons.

In the American sector of the beachhead, VI Corps met slight opposition, enabling it to reorganize, to get the floating reserve (two regiments of the 45th Division) ashore, and to consolidate positions. The gunfire support ships had a rest—few calls came. On the 11th the beachhead was expanded by nightfall against mounting opposition and VI Corps had reached a line starting at Agrópoli on the coast, running thence inland through hilly country and high ground for about ten miles, through Albanella and Altavilla, and to a point near Persano on the Sele River. The 179th Infantry of the 45th Division very nearly reached Ponte Sele, apex of the desired beachhead line, but was stopped short of it by German tanks and artillery. For the 29th Panzer Grenadier Division arrived that day in the foothills behind the Salerno plain, tipping the balance of forces in favor of the Germans; it attacked down the Sele

River, on the 45th Division front, while the 16th Panzer Division thrust outward from Battipaglia toward Salerno, in order to clear the way for the Hermann Goerings to reach the plain through the passes north of Salerno and Maiori. The 157th Regiment, just committed from Fifth Army reserve, moved up the right bank of the Sele River to help the rest of the 45th Division, but was held up by German troops who had occupied a large stone tobacco factory on the other bank of the river. The best the 45th could do by nightfall was to dig in along a line seaward of Persano.

Heaviest fighting on 10 and 11 September occurred in the British sector. Facing a long, 2000-foot ridge which dominated the beach and accommodated a strong concentration of enemy artillery, X Corps made little progress. From Salerno southeastward, Highway No. 18 skirts the base of this ridge and leads past the Montecorvino airfield to the rail and road center of Battipaglia, nearly five miles inland from the beach. On the right flank of X Corps, patrols of the 56th Division were in Battipaglia early on the 10th. Intense fighting continued there throughout the day. At dusk a counterattack by German tanks drove the British out. During the 11th, the 46th Division beat off several enemy counterattacks, and by nightfall it had captured Montecorvino airfield. But this important airdrome, the only one on the plain, remained under German artillery fire for several days. And X Corps had only a weak contact on its right flank with the American VI Corps to the south.

Toward Salerno itself the 46th Division had to fight on a narrowing strip of plain dominated by German artillery on the long ridge. The city was captured on the 10th. A British naval port party entered soon after to open the harbor, but their efforts were countered by the German gunners, who continued to range so accurately on the harbor that Salerno remained useless to the Allies for another two weeks.

At least 37 calls for naval gunfire were answered on 10 September in the British sector. Destroyers *Tartar, Lookout* and *Loyal*, which had been in the thick of the action on D-day, continued their active support on the 10th. *Loyal* departed for Palermo at 1030 to replenish ammunition, but was back on the job by dawn 10 September. Typical of the support rendered was that of H.M. destroyer *Nubian,* which fired 341 rounds of 4.7-inch shell on that day. In the early morning she broke up a German tank concentration, between 1000 and 1145 she bombarded and destroyed an enemy battery, besides demolishing a building which her F.O.O. thought to be a German strong point; for half an hour from 1250 she engaged an enemy battery that was firing on British troops, and destroyed it. Next targets were an ammunition dump and a concentration of enemy vehicles; at 1648 she shifted again to tanks, and closed a busy day at 1951. Cruiser *Mauritius,* flagship of Rear Admiral Harcourt, answered 17 calls for fire and expended nearly 500 rounds on a variety of targets ranging through enemy troops, artillery and tanks to road intersections. Cruisers *Uganda* and *Orion* and monitor *Roberts* joined in some of these shoots, which were very accurate — "Target destroyed" or "Battery silenced" being the usual closeout comment on a specific target. The cumulative effect of naval gunfire in checking German attacks and helping the hard-pressed British troops to hold their positions cannot be precisely assessed, but there can be no doubt that it was very important.

Commandos and elements of the 46th Division moved north through the pass from Vietri against mounting resistance, and held a good position against a heavy infantry and tank attack in which the Royal Marines suffered 198 casualties out of a total strength of 350. On the heights of Mount Chiunzi the Rangers held firm against determined German attacks. Dug in as they were in positions as high as 4000 feet, supply was their major problem; they fought on with skeleton rations and little water. Even mules collapsed when bringing water and ammunition up from the beach by the steep path. From observation posts high in the hills, the Rangers directed artillery and naval gunfire onto the roads below.

On 11 September, the 4th Battalion seized Monte Pendolo, far to the left of the 3rd Battalion, with a gap of several miles between. In order to strengthen their lines on these important positions overlooking the passes between Salerno and Naples, General Clark on 11 September lifted a battalion of the 143rd Infantry, reinforced with artillery, tanks, tank destroyers and engineers, in beaching craft, from the VI Corps sector to Maiori.

By nightfall 11 September, Fifth Army beachhead at deepest penetration reached about ten miles inland, but on the northern flank it tapered to about a mile. There was a lightly held gap between VI and X Corps north of the Sele River that was in the course of being plugged with the 157th Regiment.

Enemy air attacks on troops ashore on 10 and 11 September were little more than nuisance raids. But the Luftwaffe made serious raids on the roadstead, using the new radio-controlled glide-bomb. Two types of radio-controlled bombs, fitted with fins and with rocket-boosters, had been developed, one with a range of about 8 miles and maximum speed of 570 m.p.h.; the other with a range of 3½ miles and maximum speed of 660 m.p.h. Both were guided visually by radio from a high-flying plane which released them at a safe distance from the target; each carried a warhead explosive charge of 660 pounds. The existence of these bombs was already known to Allied naval commanders, since they had been used to a limited extent earlier in the war. Their employment in this theater was anticipated, but as yet no good defense against them had been devised.

Savannah was put out of action by one of these bombs. She was lying-to in her support area, awaiting calls for gunfire support, at 0930 September 11, when 12 Focke-Wulf 190s were reported approaching from the north. The cruiser rang up 10 knots' speed, which she increased to 15 knots after a heavy bomb had exploded close aboard *Philadelphia*, nearby. Ten minutes later, *Savannah* received a direct hit on No. 3 turret. The bomb, which had been dropped by a Dornier–217 from 18,000 feet, detonated in the lower handling room. The blast wiped out both the crew of the stricken turret and the No. 1 damage-control crew in central station, blew a large hole in the ship's

346

bottom and opened a seam in her side. Fires were extinguished in several boilers, and for a short time the ship had no power. She settled by the bow until the forecastle was nearly awash. Surviving damage-control parties worked smartly to seal off the flooded and burned compartments; salvage tugs *Hopi* and *Moreno* moored alongside to assist. *Savannah* was kept on an even keel by shifting her fuel oil. At 1800 she retired under her own power, screened by four destroyers, and arrived safely at Malta.

Although enemy resistance had been so strong that several D-day objectives had not yet been reached, the beachhead seemed secure by the evening of 11 September. After a visit to X Corps, General Clark reported to General Alexander that he would soon be ready to launch an attack northward through Vietri toward Naples. The Germans, despite their rapid reinforcement and partial success in counterattacks, were none too happy. The commanding general of the 16th Panzer Division reported to General Herr that the situation was critical. His troops were under heavy pressure at Battipaglia and his lines had been breached by American tanks near Persano. But the tables were soon turned.

Ominous reports began to flow in to General Clark's headquarters ashore, shortly after 0930 September 12. Elements of the Hermann Goering Division moving south from Naples had been identified opposite X Corps, and the presence of the 15th Panzer Grenadier Division in the same area was ascertained. Elements of the 26th Panzer and 29th Panzer Grenadier Divisions arrived at the beachhead from Calabria and went right into action against VI Corps. The Eighth Army was supposed to be hot on their trail; Alexander on the 10th ordered Montgomery to hurry, and on the 12th sent his chief of staff "to explain the full urgency of the situation." But Montgomery's advance patrols did not make contact with VI Corps until 1400 September 16, after the crisis had passed.

On the right center of VI Corps, a battalion of the 142nd Infantry occupied Hill 424 behind Altavilla early on 12 September. Before it could organize this position, an important one to deny the enemy since it commanded a complete view of plain and beaches, the Germans counterattacked and forced them to adandon Altavilla. On the left of VI Corps, elements of the 45th Division drove the enemy out of the tobacco factory, with the help of gunfire from *Philadelphia,* captured Persano and advanced inland. General Dawley regrouped his troops during the night of 12–13 September to strengthen and tighten his lines; but there was still a wide gap between VI Corps and the British. General Dawley planned to drive against Hill 424 on the 13th.

On the extreme left flank of Fifth Army, the Rangers captured several more heights overlooking Castellammare on the 12th and sent a night patrol into that town, where they ran into stiff resistance. This thrust was little to the Germans' taste, as it threatened to break a way for the Allied forces to enter Naples. But the élan of the Rangers gave the enemy an exaggerated idea of their strength and he decided to reinforce before launching a major counterattack. The Rangers were strong enough to dominate the Sorrento peninsula and control the road-railway gap at Nocera, but too weak to exploit their positions.

No significant gains were made by X Corps on 12 September, although it was well supported by the gunfire of monitor *Roberts* and several destroyers. The 167th Brigade 56th Division was driven out of Battipaglia, sustaining such heavy losses that it had to be relieved. Despite comparative quiet in the British sector, X Corps had suffered some 3000 casualties—from 5 to 7 per cent of its strength—by the evening of 12 September, and the troops were exhausted.

Thus Fifth Army lost Battipaglia and Altavilla on 12 September, a day of more intense fighting than any that had preceded. It became obvious that the Germans were rapidly and dangerously building up their strength in front of Salerno beachhead. By the 12th, Kesselring had at his disposal 600 tanks and mobile guns, on which he relied to throw Clark into the sea before Montgomery could come up to relieve him. The day closed for the Allies on a very different note from that on which it had opened. General Clark began to think that he would have to evacuate the southern beaches and concentrate his entire army north of the Sele River.

Although the Montecorvino airport had been in British hands since 10 September, it was still dominated by German artillery fire on the 13th, and unusable. Army Engineers met the emergency by constructing a strip on the plain two miles north of the Greek temples at Paestum, and had it ready 12 September. On that day the British escort carriers had to retire to fuel at Palermo, but 26 of their Seafires were flown in to the Paestum airstrip from which they operated until replaced by planes of the Northwest African Air Forces. By 13 September a second strip was ready near the first, work had been begun on a third, and the British sappers had two emergency strips ready in X Corps area.

To strengthen the VI Corps left flank and also to close the dangerous gap between it and the British, General Dawley ordered many front-line units shifted during the night of 12–13 September. When news reached him that night of the German recapture of Battipaglia, he withdrew two more infantry battalions from the right flank of the 36th Division and sent them to the threatened left.

A tactical group, called the Martin Force from the Colonel commanding, composed of three battalions from the 142nd and 143rd Infantry, counterattacked Altavilla and Hill 424 at 0600 September 13. It did very well during the morning, but later in the day a German column isolated the Martin Force and stopped its offensive. It had to withdraw during the night of 14–15 September.

The crux of the German counterattack on 13 September came on the VI Corps left flank, especially in the angle formed between the Sele and the Calore River that empties into it.

At 1542, one column of six German tanks attacked the left flank of the 1st Battalion 157th Infantry, which was dug in on the north slopes of the tobacco factory hill, and at the same time 15 more tanks rolled down the road from Eboli, followed by a battalion of the 79th Panzer Grenadier Regiment and towed fieldpieces. They captured the tobacco factory and drove the 1st Battalion back to the railroad. Another force of infantry-supported tanks hit the 2nd Battalion 143rd posted on the road to Ponte Sele and forced it to retire across the Calore, with a loss of 508 officers and men.

Then, fortunately for us, the German commander made a bad tactical error. At 1715 he sent his main body of tanks right down into the fork between the Sele and the Calore. His intention, obviously, was to cross the Calore where the maps showed a bridge, and drive through the VI Corps to Paestum and the beach. But the bridge had been burned, the dirt road chosen by the tanks was lined by deep drainage ditches, so they could not deploy, and, on the rolling open grassland south of the burned bridge, two battalions of United States field artillery, the 189th and 158th, were posted. Lieutenant Colonels Hal L. Muldrow and Russell D. Funk USA stripped their batteries of all but minimum gun crews, commandeered every stray GI and truck driver they could pick up on the road, put headquarters company and band into line, and posted these improvised infantrymen, armed with rifles and machine guns, on the slope between the batteries and the river. The fire of these men, added to that of the artillery, crossed the tanks' "T" as neatly as Admiral Togo did that of the Russian fleet, and forced all surviving tanks to retreat.

Although *Philadelphia* and several destroyers were available, they were not called upon for gunfire during this critical battle. Probably there was no shore fire-control party among the impromptu defenders at the river fork. *Boise,* arriving off the beachhead that afternoon to replace stricken *Savannah,* divided 36 rounds of 6-inch between a German tank concentration and a battery at the rear, checking fire when her shore fire-control party reported the battery demolished. *Philadelphia* was busy brushing off enemy air attacks. Two of the new radio-controlled bombs were aimed at her, but nimble "Philly" eluded both and they exploded harmlessly in the water, one 100 yards, the other 100 feet from the ship.

Even after the tank attack in the river fork had been defeated the situation ashore was still critical. Several American units had been decimated, and there were few reserves to throw in next day. When the ground commanders assembled at VI Corps headquarters at Paestum

350

that evening, things looked bad. Only the two artillery battalions had prevented a complete break-through, and X Corps was still heavily embroiled. General Clark, as a precaution in case the Germans had worse things in store for the morrow, sent Admiral Hewitt an urgent request to prepare plans to evacuate the VI Corps from the beachhead and re-land it north of the Sele to aid the X Corps, or vice versa. The Admiral did not like the idea—but, as the Navy was there to support the Army by any and every means, he went ahead with the plans.

Although the main strength of the German attack on 13 September was directed at the weak left flank of VI Corps, there was heavy fighting on the British X Corps front as well, especially near Battipaglia. To support the troops, H.M.S. *Roberts*, three cruisers and six destroyers delivered shoots on troops, batteries, tanks and road intersections, as called for by their F.O.O.s. Cruiser *Uganda* was struck by a guided bomb at 1440 when no alert was on; the attacking plane was not seen. The bomb penetrated seven decks and exploded below the ship. Although flooded with some 1300 tons of water, she was saved by prompt shoring of threatened bulkheads, and left the combat area early next morning under tow of U.S.S. *Narragansett,* escorted by three destroyers. Within an hour of *Uganda's* hit, destroyers *Nubian* and *Loyal* were narrowly missed by guided bombs. Now that two light cruisers were out of action, and other ships running low on ammunition, Admiral of the Fleet Cunningham ordered H.M.S. *Aurora* and *Penelope* up from Malta. They arrived off Salerno by sunrise 14 September.

Important reinforcements arrived on the 13th—the 82nd Airborne Division which would have performed the drop on Rome had it not been canceled. Some of the paratroops were landed at Maiori to reinforce Darby's Rangers; the rest, standing by on Sicilian fields, were requested by General Clark, at 1330, to fly in that very night. General Ridgway, equal to every emergency, organized the drops at an hour's notice. Mindful of what had happened in Sicily, he asked that all antiaircraft guns on the beachhead or in the roadstead be forbidden to fire that night; General

Clark and Admiral Hewitt so directed. The first planes took off at 1930. Led by three Pathfinders with paratroops and ground signaling equipment, 82 C–47s and C–53s, starting from Cómiso and Trápani–Milo fields in Sicily, dropped over 600 paratroops exactly where they were wanted behind the VI Corps lines south of the Sele; only one man was injured. The following night 1000 more paratroops were dropped successfully in the same zone.*

Throughout the night of 13–14 September weary Army officers worked to arrange a new defensive line, starting at the crossroads west of the tobacco factory, along the rise whence the artillery had stopped the tanks, and around the east edge of a line of foothills, almost to the hill town of Roccadáspide. At dawn 14 September the Germans renewed their attack with probing tank and infantry thrusts; but, thanks to the night time regrouping, VI Corps held its ground. In the X Corps sector the 46th Division was well dug in on hills near Salerno, but the 56th was still in the open plain southwest of Battipaglia, under enemy observation from the nearby hills. The Coldstream Guards and the 9th Royal Fusiliers repulsed a strong enemy tank attack during the night of 13–14 September, and on the 14th moved over to close the dangerous gap between the X and VI Corps. Although the rest of the 26th Panzer Division from the south, and a regimental combat team of the 3rd Panzer Grenadier Division from the north, arrived in the battle area that day, these were the last reinforcements available to the Geman command, and when darkness descended over the Salerno plain on 14 September the situation of the Fifth Army had greatly improved.

Naval gunfire support was a material contribution to this result. Of the 14th Vietinghoff wrote: "The attack this

*A third drop during the night of 14–15 September at Avellino was less successful, because the mountains forced it to be made from altitudes between 3000 and 5000 feet. Only 15 of the 40 planes carrying 600 paratroops hit the right place; the rest dropped their men from 8 to 25 miles away in small groups. Most were captured; some worked their way south and made contact with the Fifth Army.

morning pushed on into stiffened resistance; but above all the advancing troops had to endure the most severe heavy fire that had hitherto been experienced; the naval gunfire from at least 16 to 18 battleships, cruisers and large destroyers lying in the roadstead. With astonishing precision and freedom of maneuver, these ships shot at every recognized target with very overwhelming effect."

Philadelphia, as usual, was to the fore. She continued to shoot at targets designated by her shore fire-control party throughout the night of 13–14 September, firing 921 rounds of 6-inch on tanks, batteries, road intersections and massed troops, and receiving such messages as: "Very good—we are under attack—stand by," and "Thank you—stand by." Between 0844 and 1345 September 14, *Boise* relieved her, firing almost continuously at tanks and troops—18 different targets—and expending nearly 600 rounds. Shore fire-control party reported "Very well!" after a tank concentration had received 83 rounds. At 1503 *Philadelphia* returned for a two-hour session. There followed another lull in naval gunfire support; then, at 2130, *Boise* was called on for rapid fire on troops. With shore fire-control party reporting "No change" and "Straddle, straddle!" she unloaded 72 rounds in short order. An hour later she was called on again, and after firing 121 rounds got the word, "Cease firing; thank you, stand by." At 2310 she delivered interdiction fire on German troops marching down from Eboli; "You are doing well," said the shore party. All night 14–15 September she continued firing on call. In the British sector the pattern of gunfire support was much the same. Four light cruisers and four destroyers got into the shooting, with good results.

Although Fifth Army and supporting fleets were successfully beating off German attacks on 14 September, the situation still seemed grave to the higher Allied commanders. Admiral Hewitt, it will be remembered, had been making plans for a possible shifting of VI Corps to X Corps sectors, or vice versa, at General Clark's insistence. That afternoon he sent an urgent message to Admiral of the Fleet Cunningham: "The Germans have created a salient dangerously near the beach. Military situation continuing unsatisfactory. Am planning to use all available vessels to transfer troops from southern to northern beaches, or the reverse if necessary. Unloading of merchant vessels in the southern section has been stopped. We need heavy aerial and naval bombardment behind enemy positions, using battleships or other heavy naval vessels. Are any such ships available?"

Admiral Cunningham reacted promptly to the request for naval reinforcements. At 1732 September 14 he ordered Admiral Vian to expedite the loading of troops at Philippeville and to sail immediately with H.M.S. *Euryalus, Scylla* and *Charybdis* to Salerno. An hour later he ordered battleships *Valiant* and *Warspite* to depart Malta with six destroyers and report to Admiral Hewitt as soon as possible after daylight next morning. Unfortunately Hewitt's dispatch reached an important addressee, General Eisenhower, in a garbled form which suggested that he and General Clark were contemplating a complete evacuation of the Salerno beachhead. There was consternation at headquarters over what appeared to be going on, and consternation at the beachhead over what Hewitt thought he might have to do, if General Clark insisted. Both Commodore Oliver and General McCreery, in no uncertain terms, opposed the idea of transferring troops from one part of the beachhead to another, insisting that they should fight it out where they were, with all the gunfire support the Navy could provide.

General Alexander, after reviewing the situation on the spot, killed the plan for shifting troops. It was fortunate that the shift never had to be made, since a reverse amphibious operation under hostile fire is exceedingly difficult to carry out. But neither General Clark nor Admiral Hewitt at any time contemplated a complete withdrawal from the beachhead.

Northwest African Air Forces were not idle through all this. On 13 September General Eisenhower ordered Air Chief Marshal Tedder to send every plane that could fly against sensitive spots in the German formations. This great air attack was delivered on the 14th. Although in part ill-directed, owing to the lack of ground air-control units with the troops, it badly disrupted German mobility and communications, and materially helped the Allies to regain the initiative.

In retrospect, it appears that the German drive to the beaches was defeated not only by the stout resistance of all three Allied arms, but by the German dual command in Italy—Rommel in the north, Kesselring in the south. A single commander could, on 9 September have sent south to Salerno several divisions of the Army group stationed around Mantua, and they could have arrived by the 13th. But Rommel, who never believed in the southern Italy campaign, would not let them go. Even two divisions more would have enabled Kesselring to make good his threat, and wipe out the beachhead.

Before Cassino

Rommel commanded eight divisions in northern Italy, and Kesselring, eight divisions south of Rome. The invasion of Salerno had been no surprise to the Germans; Kesselring had expected a landing there, and ironically a Panzer division was carrying out anti-invasion exercises at the very time the 5th Army hit the beaches. The issue was in doubt for almost a week. As Fred Majdalany puts it in his *The Battle of Cassino*, "With a semi-circle of high ground overlooking the beaches, the battlefield resembled half a saucer with Germans sitting on the rim." The battle turned against the Germans partly because of constant pressure from air strikes and naval bombardment.

The British 8th Army, landing two divisions in the south, now moved up alongside the 5th, and by October 1st, Naples was taken. Both armies now prepared themselves for the drive to Rome. But they were to pay a heavy toll first to the harshness of the terrain, and the Germans' skillful tactics in utilizing it. Italy was beautifully suited to the kind of punishing defensive tactics the Germans adopted. Down the middle of the Italian peninsula is a formation of mountains, their highest points in the center, with riblike slopes moving out to either side to the coasts. Because of these mountains, and the poor roads, the two Allied armies had no common front. Here in Italy the Allies had to fight an entirely different war than they had in North Africa. In the desert plains, the war was one of maneuver; in Italy, it was one of attrition. And the Allies never did commit enough men and supplies to hit the Germans with the solid punches necessary for a real knockout.

Kesselring set his line of defenses along the Garigliano and the Rapido rivers, through Cassino into the central mountains, and then to the River Sangro on the east coast; the Germans worked tirelessly on the Gustav Line, as it was called, while the 5th and 8th Armies worked their way up the peninsula. Seven divisions were moved over from the Balkans now, and reorganized into two armies under Kesselring. (Rommel, incidentally, had been transferred to a command in western Europe.) The Germans had twenty-five divisions to call on in Italy—the Allies, only eleven. Two Allied divisions previously available had been recalled to Great Britain for the forthcoming strike across the Channel.

About January 15th, 1944, the 5th Army arrived in front of Cassino, where they looked forward to rest, reorganization and replacements for the casualties suffered over the previous four months' campaign. But rest wasn't in store for them; a plan had been developed in the previous weeks for a landing at Anzio, some sixty miles back of the Gustav Line. One British and one American division were to land and establish a beachhead to pull some of the Germans off the defense line at Cassino. Because landing craft to be used at Anzio had to be returned to Britain for the forthcoming invasion, and supplies had to be moved up along the coast by sea in these same landing craft, the date for the landing at Anzio had to be fixed as early as possible—late January.

Gen. Alexander had taken over command of the land armies in Italy (Eisenhower and Montgomery had been recalled to London to assist in planning for the invasion); he now ordered the 5th Army, under the American Gen. Mark Clark, to attack. This was to co-ordinate with the two Allied divisions expected to be moving out of the beachhead at Anzio. The Cassino attack ended in a disaster for the 36th American Division, and two days later the American 34th Division was thrown into action. At the end of ten days' fighting, the 34th had won a bridgehead on one of the many hills in the Cassino area, but it was clear to the men doing the fighting that little progress was going to be made until the big hill overlooking the town of Cassino, on which the Benedictine monastery stood, was either taken or successfully bypassed. In the meantime, the French had put two of their divisions into action to the right of Cassino, and gained some ground after gallant fighting. But in the second week of February the whole operation ground to a halt. Both American divisions had lost more than 2,000 casualties apiece, and worse, the Anzio beachhead had now become a liability rather than an investment. While 70,000 men had been landed, the Germans were about to throw several fresh divisions against them in a counterattack. Without time for proper regrouping and a closer study of the Cassino problem, the Allied Command was forced to commit the troops to a second attack almost immediately. Gen. Alexander moved over several divisions from the 8th Army, which had slugged their way up the east coast of Italy. The news from Anzio grew worse. By February 15th, the second battle of Cassino had to be launched. Majdalany, who was at Cassino in the British army and who has written an account of the whole operation, says, "Wilson [the Allied commander] urged Alexander, Alexander urged Clark, Clark urged Freyberg, and Freyberg urged his two divisions to attack immediately."

THE BATTLE FOR CASSINO

by Fred Majdalany

No event of the war caused more heated and lingering controversy than the bombing, on February 15, 1944, of the Abbey of Monte Cassino.

It is possible to understand the bitterness and bewilderment of the Cassinese monks themselves. The cloister is not the place in which a detailed grasp of military practicalities can be expected to flourish.

One can discount the naïve foolishness of the uninformed —like the English newspaper correspondent who spent a few hours at Monte Cassino after the war, and then published the complacent view that the bombing was "vandalism" and the verdict on those who ordered it must be "guilty but insane."

It is more than a little surprising, however, that those who have emotionally wanted to believe that the bombing was a criminal act should have been fortified in their judgments by, of all people, the army commander who ordered it, General Mark Clark.

In his personal memoir *Calculated Risk*, General Clark wrote:

> I say that the bombing of the abbey . . . was a mistake, and I say it with full knowledge of the controversy that has raged round this episode . . . Not only was the bombing of the abbey an unnecessary psychological mistake in the propaganda field but it was a tactical military mistake of the first magnitude. It only made the job more difficult, more costly in terms of men, machines, and time.

358

This might be read as an admission of error, but in the pages that follow, Clark, who gave the order for the bombing, disclaims responsibility for it. If Clark had confined himself to a military reappraisal of the bombing, there could have been no objection to his being as outspoken as he liked. In fact, he ignores the special circumstances, conditions, and pressures prevailing at the time. He ignores the important psychological impact of the Monastery. He ignores the hard fact that two Commonwealth divisions were now being required to tackle a task that had just knocked the heart out of two American divisions. He makes little attempt to re-create the context in which the difficult decision had to be taken. He merely devotes himself to an angry apologia—disclaiming responsibility for an order which he himself gave, and blaming it on his subordinate commander General Freyberg.

It is unusual, to say the least, for an army commander to repudiate his own actions by blaming a subordinate for forcing them on him.

The great red herring that has been drawn across the bombing has been the relating of it to the question whether or not the Monastery was actually occupied by the Germans. It was afterwards reasonably well established that it was not. But this could not be known at the time. And in any case the question is irrelevant.

The simple inescapable fact is that the building was an integral part of a physical feature that was not only occupied but to a high degree fortified. The fortified mountain and the building at its summit were in military terms a single piece of ground.

Ground is the raw material of the soldier, as weapons are his tools. Ground is the factor which more than any other eventually controls the shape of a battle. Like pigment to the artist and clay to the potter, ground is the material which the soldier must study, cherish, understand, and adapt to his purposes. This is the basis of all military tactics.

A mountain is one kind of ground. A mountain crowned by a building is another. If the building happens to be inordinately strong, the ground is something else again. To

359

the soldier the mountain and the building are not separate
things but together comprise a whole. Ground is indivisible.
The mountain and the building are one and must be considered as one. Their relationship may be likened to that
between a coconut shy and a tray of china set in its midst.
It would be foolish to tell someone to aim as hard as he
likes at the coconuts but on no account to hit the china.

The piece of ground called Monte Cassino comprised
a 1,700-foot mountain with rocky sides; a zigzag shelf of
roadway twisting for five miles up one face of it, and providing both shelter and mobility for tanks and guns; and,
at the summit, a building, more than two hundred yards
long, with the thickness, strength, design, and structure of a
powerful fortress.

Occupation of a piece of high ground like Monte Cassino can take two forms. It can be garrisoned with soldiers.
Or it can be occupied by one soldier equipped with binoculars and a wireless set through which he can accurately direct the fire of guns on to any point of the landscape within
his view. There is absolutely no limit to the number of guns
that can be so directed by one man. A trained observer is
therefore an even more potent defensive garrison than a
battalion of soldiers.

It follows from this that any high ground likely to be
used by the enemy as an observatory is an automatic target
for attack by the other side. The attacker must use everything in his power to make this observation point untenable
until such time as he can deprive the enemy of it by seizing
it himself. Thus the pattern of advance of a modern army
is from one line of good observation to the next.

The relationship between the summit of Monte Cassino
and the important main route which it commands is so exceptional that it invariably impresses military men as the
finest observation post they have ever seen.

To observe from the summit of this particular mountain,
a man might set himself up comfortably (and because of
its thick walls, more safely) inside the building. Alterna-
tively he might (to get a wider view) install himself in a
trench outside it, with a telephone link to an orderly stationed securely inside the building. If an observation point

360

is of exceptional quality—as is the case with Monte Cassino —there are likely to be a number of separate observation posts set up by the different artillery formations and headquarters who will want to use it. A prominent peak of this kind may well become a mass of observation posts providing eyes for the many different departments of the army it is serving. Along the razorback of Monte Trocchio, for instance, where the Allied armies had their main view of the Cassino front, there were at one time more than a hundred observation posts.

The key to the German defense of the area for convenience called Cassino—though it comprised a combination of river line, mountain mass, and fortified town—was not the garrison, nor was it the prepared system of fortifications, formidable though both were—but the superlative observation which enabled such good use to be made of them.

> From the vantage point of the Monastery the enemy can watch and bring down fire on every movement on the roads or open country in the plain below [reported Freyberg to the New Zealand government].

> At New Zealand Divisional H.Q. [wrote Kippenberger] we felt certain that the monastery was at least the enemy's main observation post. It was so perfectly situated for the purpose that no army could have refrained from using it.

> This famous building [recorded Alexander in his final report on the campaign] had hitherto been deliberately spared, to our great disadvantage, but it was an integral part of the German defensive system, *mainly from the superb observation it afforded.*

The italics are mine.

Observation was the overriding issue at Cassino, not the relatively unimportant question whether the Abbey was occupied. And allied to the question of observation—in fact a corollary of it—was the psychological impact of this altogether exceptional observatory.

Because of the extraordinary extent to which the summit of Monte Cassino dominated the valleys; because of the painful constancy with which men were picked off by accurately observed gunfire whenever they were forced to move in daylight within its seemingly inescapable view; because of the obsessive theatrical manner in which it towered over the scene, searching every inch of it, the building set upon that summit had become the embodiment of resistance and its tangible symbol.

Everybody has experienced the sensation, when walking alone past a house, that invisible eyes were watching from a darkened interior. Hostile eyes can be sensed without being seen, and the soldier develops an exceptional awareness of this. Monte Cassino projected this feeling over an entire valley, and the feeling was being substantiated all the time by gunfire that could only have been so accurate and so swiftly opportunist through being directed by quite exceptionally positioned observers. Even in peacetime, Monte Cassino overwhelms even the least imaginative visitor gazing up at it from below. In the cold desolation of winter and the fatiguing travail of unresolved battle, the spell of its monstrous eminence was complete and haunting.

This was the psychological crux of the matter. To the soldiers dying at its feet, the Monastery had itself become in a sense the enemy.

Only the generals on the spot could be fully aware of this. It was their responsibility to order men to die attempting a task about which no one could feel optimistic. Theirs in the end are the only opinions which count.

This was the equally balanced, reasoned summary of General Kippenberger.

> Opinion at New Zealand Corps H.Q. and New Zealand Divisional H.Q. as to whether the abbey was occupied was divided. Personally, I thought the point immaterial. If not occupied today it might be tomorrow and it did not appear that it would be difficult for the enemy to bring reserves into it during the progress of an attack, or for troops to take shelter there if driven from positions outside.

It was impossible to ask troops to storm a hill surmounted by an intact building such as this, capable of
sheltering several hundred infantry in perfect security
from shellfire and ready at the critical moment to
emerge and counter-attack.

I was in touch with our own troops and they were
very definitely of the opinion that the Abbey must be
destroyed before anyone was asked to storm the hill.

It is difficult to see how Freyberg could have come to any
other decision than that the Monastery must be destroyed
whether occupied or not.

But since so much has been made of the question of
occupation, it is worth examining the evidence available
at the time to the Allied commanders, and it will be seen
that there was a considerable doubt about this.

During the conference at which the Second U.S. Corps
handed over to the Second New Zealand Corps, General
Butler, deputy commander of the U.S. 34th Division (who
made the first attacks on the Monastery feature) said:

I don't know but I don't believe the enemy is in the
convent. All the fire has been from the slopes of the
hill below the wall.

During the same conference a senior intelligence officer
said:

With reference to the Abbey, we have had statements from our own observers who believe they have
seen observing instruments in the windows. We have
had statements from civilians both for and against.
Some have said that Germans are living there but this
is not supported by others. It is very difficult to say
whether it is being put to any military purpose this
time.

Questioned further, the officer estimated that the Germans had a battalion-plus on top of the hill.

According to the official history of the U.S. Army Air
Forces in World War II, the American Generals Eaker
and Devers "flew over the Abbey in a Piper Cub at a

363

height of less than 200 feet and Eaker states flatly that he saw a radio aerial on the Abbey and enemy soldiers moving in and out of the building."

There is one possibility, though it cannot be supported by evidence, which I think worth noting. Civilian refugees were lodged in the Monastery corridor being temporarily used as a rabbitry for the breeding of rabbits for food. This gave access to the open kitchen garden on the western, that is the German, side of the Abbey walls.

Anyone with experience of the more human side of front-line soldiering knows that no soldiers—lonely, uncomfortable, in danger, and bored—can be entirely restrained from making contact with any civilians within reach, either to exchange pleasantries with a woman or to barter cigarettes for eggs.

We know that three weeks before the bombing the military police guard was removed from the main entrance. For three weeks German soldiers were within a hundred yards or less of the kitchen garden to which the refugees had access. It can never be proved that some of them did not make contact with these civilians for one purpose or another, and that they were not seen doing so—thus giving rise to the reports that reached the Allies that German troops were in the Abbey: and perhaps explaining how it was that Generals Eaker and Devers were convinced during their flight over the Abbey that they had seen German soldiers moving about within its precincts.

Such unofficial excursions to a building which their Higher Command had formally placed out of bounds could easily have been accomplished without the monk's knowledge. The soldiers would merely have to wait until the sound of plainsong indicated that Abbot Diamare's small remnant community were safely inside the depths of the building at their devotions.

Finally, Sir D'Arcy Osborne, British Minister to the Vatican, had formally asked the Cardinal Secretary of State for an assurance that the Germans were not using the Abbey for military purposes. Sir D'Arcy's personal diary kept at the time shows that he received no reply until the evening of February 14 (the eve of the bombing) and then only a vague statement denying, on the authority of the German Embassy and German military authorities, that there were any considerable ("*grössere*") concentrations of German troops in the "immediate vicinity" of the Abbey. This was the only communication from the Vatican and it was hardly one on which action could be taken.

There remains the argument that a building becomes even more defendable after it has been destroyed. General von Senger, writing of the battle after the war, had this to say:

> As anyone who has had experience in street fighting —as at Stalingrad or Cassino—is aware . . . houses must be demolished in order to be converted from mouse-traps into bastions of defence.

This may be true as a general rule, but it is not necessarily so in the case of a building with walls ten feet thick, and the structural characteristics of a fortress. Nor had this consideration been overlooked by the New Zealand Command. They had discussed it thoroughly and had concluded that while the building would continue to be useful to the enemy after destruction, it would be more valuable intact. I again quote Kippenberger:

> Undamaged it was a perfect shelter but with its narrow windows and level profiles an unsatisfactory fighting position. Smashed by bombing it was a jagged heap of broken masonry and debris open to effective fire from guns, mortars and strafing planes as well as being a death trap if bombed again. On the whole I thought it would be more useful to the Germans if we left it unbombed.

It will be seen, therefore, that it was only after long and earnest deliberation, and after every aspect of the matter had been most thoroughly discussed, that General Freyberg reluctantly came to the conclusion that the destruction of the Monastery, by the only means powerful enough to have any effect on it, was tactically and psychologically necessary.

It may be added that General Clark was not in the clos-

365

est touch with the Cassino front at this time. He was necessarily preoccupied with the bigger problem of Anzio—the crisis center where a German counteroffensive was known to be due very shortly. His opposition to the bombing—of which he has since made so much—was mostly expressed at second hand through his Chief of Staff. He was not, like Freyberg, continuously on the spot. So that it became necessary for General Alexander, as Army Group Commander, to influence the situation by stating unequivocally that he had complete faith in Freyberg's judgment.

And so, after days of doubt—the situation not being helped by the public airing of the pros and cons by the British and American press for the benefit of Goebbels and other interested parties—the decision was made. And General Clark gave the order for the bombing which he afterwards so bitterly repudiated.

If all the factors are considered dispassionately there can be little doubt that it was the only possible decision. The tragedy was that once the decision had been made, the matter became an Air Force responsibility. The Air Force, working alone without reference to the Army, projected it as a separate operation without co-ordinating it with the ground attack which was the only reason for its happening at all. The Air Force went ahead and carried out the bombing before the Indian division could possibly be ready to make the attack it was intended to support.

So the bombing, when it happened, expended its fury in a vacuum, tragically and wastefully. It achieved nothing, it helped nobody.

From the Air Force point of view the timing of the bombing depended mainly on the weather and on operational requirements elsewhere. A forecast of twenty-four hours of good weather was the first stipulation.

This operation was something new. For the first time the heaviest bombers of the Strategic Air Force were to operate with the Mediums in close support of infantry. Hitherto this had been the function of the Mediums only. These aircraft, based on forward airfields and bombing from a relatively low level, were the ones whose job it was to at-

366

tack at short notice targets designated by the forward troops. The Mediums of the tactical air force were in effect another form of artillery under army control. The forward troops could indicate a target and the bombers would be over it within a short time.

The introduction of heavy bombers into an infantry battle created new problems. The operation had to be mounted from many airfields scattered through southern Italy, Sicily, and North Africa. Many of the aircraft would have to travel a long way to the objective. The Flying Fortresses bombed from very high altitudes, and it was something new for them to be asked to attack a pinpoint target. Sustained good weather was therefore more than usual a factor in timing the operation.

The second factor—requirements elsewhere—meant, of course, Anzio. The combined air forces could not make a maximum effort at Cassino and Anzio simultaneously. It had to be one or the other. Anzio was at this time the major anxiety. The new German counteroffensive was expected to go in there not later than February 16. (In the event, this forecast proved to be correct.) Cassino had to be disposed of before then.

It was inevitable in the circumstances that the timing of the bombing should have been a matter for the Air Commanders to decide. But this does not excuse the lack of liaison between the air and army. At the same time there seems to have been a failure on the part of General Freyberg to appreciate the difficulty the Indian division was experiencing in getting ready to make their attack. Otherwise he must have requested that the bombing be delayed until they were ready to take advantage of it.

"Ask of me anything but time," Napoleon once said. It is common to most operations that the subordinate commanders protest that they have insufficient time. It is the duty of senior commanders to treat such protests with some reserve. In this case Freyberg, himself under extreme pressure from above, appears to have carried skepticism too far.

The difficulties of the Indians were not being exaggerated. There were some extraordinary hazards attending the re-

lief of the Americans by the Indians' assault battalion—
the shortage of mule transport; the loss of their entire
reserve of grenades and mortar ammunition; the laborious process of trickling the division across the Rapido
valley—the false no-man's-land—to the remote and separate battleground in the mountaintops; the insufficiency of
mules; the necessity to manhandle stores and supplies up
the final stretches of the precipitous tracks; the limitation
on daylight movement owing to the positions being overlooked; the impossibility of reconnaissance of the ground
over which attacks were to be made; the constant casualties from shellfire, including the shells of Allied guns that
had not yet mastered the intricacy of this isolated salient
that, in relation to the gun lines, was *behind* the German
positions.

There was the question of the all-important Point 593,
the peak adjacent to the Monastery. The Americans had
claimed that they held it, and it was not until the Indian
division arrived to take it over that they found that the
Germans still held this key piece of ground, and that
it would have to be cleared before the attack on the Monastery could go in. This does not appear to have been understood at New Zealand Corps H.Q. which continued to
show 593 in its Intelligence Summaries as held by the Allies.

An illuminating comment on this situation is that of General Kippenberger who, writing long after the event about
the difficulties of his opposite number Brigadier Dimoline,
had this to say:

> Poor Dimoline was having a dreadful time getting
> his division into position. I never really appreciated
> the difficulties until I went over the ground after the
> war. He got me to make an appointment for us both
> with General Freyberg, as he thought his task was
> impossible and his difficulties not fully realized. The
> General refused to see us together: he told me he was
> not going to have any soviet of divisional commanders.

So Dimoline protested that he needed more time; Freyberg insisted that he could not have any; and the United

States Army Air Force waited with one eye on the meteorologists and the other on Anzio. On February 14, after a great storm which raged throughout the 13th, the experts promised a twenty-four hour period of clear weather. The bombing was accordingly ordered for nine-thirty the following morning, the 15th.

In the early afternoon of February 14, the monks were preparing to take to his last resting place Dom Eusebio who had died the previous day of the unidentified epidemic [1] which had broken out among the refugees in the Abbey. Still in his monk's habit, he lay in one of the underground passages where the others had taken turns to maintain a twenty-four hour vigil over his body. Now they were ready to consign him to one of the improvised coffins which he himself had been constructing in the carpenter's shop for those refugees who had died of the same disease.

As the monks prayed for the last time over the body of Dom Eusebio a group of refugees rushed up to them in high excitement. They brought with them leaflets that had just been dropped by an American aircraft. The leaflets, addressed to "Italian Friends" and signed "The Fifth Army" bore this message:

> We have until now been careful to avoid bombarding Monte Cassino. The Germans have taken advantage of this. The battle is now closing in more and more around the sacred precincts. Against our will we are now obliged to direct our weapons against the Monastery itself. We warn you so that you may save yourselves. Leave the Monastery at once. This warning is urgent. It is given for your good.

At once there was a great commotion. Alarm quickly spread among the refugees scattered in pockets throughout the vast building. They began to stream in to where the Abbot stood, reading and rereading the leaflet. The best thing, the Abbot said, would be to find a German officer and see if it could be arranged for the Abbey to be evacuated.

[1] Subsequently diagnosed as paratyphoid fever.

369

Three young men volunteered to leave the safety of the Abbey walls and make a dash for one of the German posts not many yards away. This meant showing themselves in the open. They set off, but before they had traveled very far they were frightened by the shellfire and turned back. Panic broke out afresh, and while the Abbot deliberated, and the monks and the refugees argued about what should be done, the Sacrist and half a dozen helpers quietly lifted Dom Eusebio into his coffin, and bore him off along the corridors and staircases to the Chapel of St. Anne where he was laid to rest in the central grave of the presbytery.

By the time the burial party had returned, the refugees were barely controllable, still demanding from the Abbot a magical solution. One monk suggested a mass exodus under a white flag, but another opposed this with grim stories of massacres he said had taken place in similar circumstances. Another argued in favor of staying and making the best of it. Before long the uncertainty had prompted one of the men to start a rumor that the monks were in league with the Germans, and that the leaflet was a trick concocted between them to get the Abbey cleared of the refugees—whose relationship with the monks was always inclined to be strained. In desperation the Abbot ruled that it was everyone for himself. They could make a run for it or stay—whichever they preferred. Another effort would be made to get in touch with the Germans after dark.

Shortly after nightfall two men did succeed in making contact with the German armored car troop which patrolled the road up to the monastery entrance during the hours of darkness. They said that the Abbot wished to speak to an officer and were told that this could not be arranged before five o'clock the following morning. Then two representatives of the Abbot—but not more than two—could come along to their headquarters. So they resigned themselves to a night of fear and uncertainty, and from time to time, unable to bear the suspense, the refugees would shout from the rabbitry to the nearby German posts, which were within earshot—but the soldiers did not reply. At five o'clock, just as the Abbot's secretary and the man chosen to accompany him were leaving the building, the officer they were to try to locate turned up. He was introduced to the Abbot and shown the leaflet.

The Abbot suggested that it would be convenient if he and the monks could be allowed to make for the Allied lines, and the refugees were removed to the German rear. There was a wistful irony in the old man's suggestion that his own small group and the refugees should move in opposite directions, and also, perhaps, in the choice of directions he proposed.

The officer, a lieutenant, said that there could be no question of anyone being allowed to walk to the Allied lines. He pointed out that it would be a risky business leaving the Monastery at all, and they would have to take full responsibility for any move decided upon. He added, however, that during the night he had discussed the situation of the Monastery with his commanding officer, and the latter had arranged for one of the paths leading down to Highway Six to be opened to the refugees from midnight until 5 a.m. the following morning, February 16.

The Abbot protested that it might be too late then. The officer said that this was the best he could do and after being taken, at his request, into the cathedral for a few moments, he left. It was still half an hour before daylight. Those civilians who were at hand dispersed to the various passages and corners that had become their temporary homes. The monks repaired to their small subterranean chapel in the *torretta,* the oldest part of the building, the one link with St. Benedict's original abbey, and there they prepared to start the day's devotions which in winter begin at five-thirty.

Tuesday, February 15, 1944, began, like any other day, with the celebration of Matins and Lauds.

The morning of Tuesday February 15 was cold, but the sky was clearer than it had been for many days. In that part of their refuge which they had turned into a temporary chapel, the Abbot and the monks were addressing themselves as usual to the succession of holy offices which make up the Benedictine day: to that rhythm of prayer and

371

psalmody and meditation precisely laid down for them fourteen centuries before by their founder.

It had begun, after the departure of the German officer, with that part of the Divine Office that ended with Lauds. At eight-thirty they recited together the psalms and prayers prescribed for *prime* and the first of the Little Hours, *terce*. And then, as it happened to be the week of the Feast of St. Scholastica—St. Benedict's sister, whose bones lay alongside her brother's in the great tomb below the high altar of the cathedral of Monte Cassino—they celebrated the conventual mass appropriate to this particular saint.

Not long afterwards they went to the Abbot's room for the second and third of the Little Hours, and then they returned to their temporary chapel. They had improvised an altar there, and on it they had set the little Madonna of De Matteis which normally rested on the tomb of St. Benedict in the cathedral. Kneeling before this altar, and chanting antiphonally, they invoked the blessing of the Madonna.

It was a little after nine-thirty and they had just sung the words "Beseech Christ on our behalf" when the first of a succession of great explosions sent a shudder through the thick abbey walls and great gusts of thunder echoed along the vast stone passageways, giving continuity to the crashes so that they were no longer a succession of explosions but a single great cataclysmic roar.

To these men whose lives had been passed in near-silence; whose scant conversation was in a low voice; whose meals were taken in silence; whose habitation was a mountaintop that was the apotheosis of tranquillity; whose most violent acquaintance with sound was the Gregorian chant of the Divine Office, the bombing was, apart from anything else, an overwhelmingly terrifying baptism of sheer noise beyond anything they could conceivably have imagined. They huddled together in a corner on their knees, numb with terror. Automatically the eighty-year-old Abbot gave them absolution. Automatically they composed themselves for death.

The explosions seemed incessant. A great haze of dust and smoke was discernible through the narrow window, and great yellow flashes as the bombs crashed about the building, dispassionately destroying. All the time the thunder of the explosions echoed and re-echoed along the vaulted corridors and stone passageways, adding immeasurably to the noise.

After the first few minutes of petrifying shock there was a diversion, marked by that quality of melodrama which was never long absent from Cassino. A breathless figure, covered in dust, appeared suddenly at the side of the praying monks. He was gesticulating like a man demented, but he uttered no sound. It was the deaf-mute servant. In the sign language of the deaf-and-dumb, heightened by terror into almost maniacal convulsions, he was trying to tell them that the cathedral had gone. It had been one of the first parts of the Abbey to receive a direct hit. A bomb had passed through the frescoed dome.

The bombardment continued throughout the morning, and though only about ten per cent of the heavy bombers succeeded in hitting the Abbey, this was enough to wreck the interior.

Inside the cathedral the pipes of the celebrated Catarinozzi organ, which had cost 10,000 ducats, were shredded like paper foil; the high altar, incorporating parts of an original attributed to Michelangelo, subsided into a mound of rubble about the tomb of St. Benedict; the wooden stalls of the choir, a masterpiece of the Neapolitan carvers who have no equals in this work, were reduced to a tangle of splinters. Fragments of marble inlay were scattered everywhere like outsize confetti.

One by one the five cloistered courtyards were shattered into dumps to contain the rubble of the elegant cloisters and the solid buildings which had formerly surrounded them.

The entrance cloister was a series of broken stumps and a heap of debris that was knee-deep. The Cloister of the Priors, around which the boys' college had formed a square, had been totally submerged by the collapsed college, and nearly one hundred refugees were buried under the ruins. The Bramante Cloister, the one unquestionable architectural masterpiece of Monte Cassino, no longer existed.

This cloister had been built round three sides of the central courtyard. Along the top of its arches ran the celebrated gallery known as the Loggia del Paradiso—and from the fourth side rose a magnificent stone stairway, sixty feet wide, leading up to yet another cloister, the Cloister of the Benefactors, decorated with the marble statues of seventeen popes and kings who had befriended the Monastery. This cloister led to the cathedral. In the center of the courtyard, too, was a cistern, decorated with a handsome pillared fountainhead.

By noon the central courtyard was unrecognizable. The cloisters were like broken teeth. The great flight of steps had vanished. The portico above the cistern had been leveled to the ground leaving only a gaping hole filled with water that was now colored red.

Once during the morning, when there seemed to be a lull in the bombardment, the Abbot left his shelter to inspect the damage. He found that most of the upper stories of the Abbey had gone and that all that remained of the cathedral was its shell, wide open to the sky. He heard the groans of refugees buried under the ruins of the Priors' Cloister, and found that nothing could be done to rescue them. He saw other refugees making a dash for the open, and about a hundred got away during this interlude. And he was accosted by the three peasant families, who from the earliest days of what might be termed the siege had been allowed to stay on in the Abbey. They asked if they might now go down to the monks' refuge, and the Abbot gave them permission to do so. Then the sound of aircraft was heard again, and everyone hastily returned to his shelter.

The monks were safe in their chapel, and the lay brothers, it turned out, had been able to make themselves comfortable and secure in the bakery. Meanwhile the Sacrist had made a hazardous journey through the rubble and the half-collapsed walls to bring the Holy Sacrament from another chapel so that the monks could celebrate Communion.

The bombardment reopened. It was now the turn of the medium bombers. They dropped smaller bombs, but they dropped them more accurately. The Mediums attacked from a low level in tight little formations of twelve, and their

374

bombs fell in a compact carpet. Once again the Abbot, those monks who were still with him, and the three peasant families who had attached themselves to him, prepared for the worst. Soon an explosion more powerful than any they had yet experienced seemed to tear the heart out of the crumbling abbey. A great wave of debris thundered about the refuge, blocking the entrance to it, but the thick walls held.

To Allied observers, watching the bombing with a sense of uncomfortable awe, it did not for a long time seem as effective as they had expected.

Christopher Buckley, the British war correspondent, noted:

> As the sun brightened and climbed up the sky I could detect little modification in the monastery's outline as each successive smoke cloud cleared away. Here and there one noted an ugly fissure in the walls, here and there a window seemed unnaturally enlarged. The roof was beginning to look curiously jagged and uneven . . . but essentially the building was still standing after four hours of pounding from the air.
>
> Just before two o'clock in the afternoon a formation of Mitchells (Mediums) passed over. They dipped slightly. A moment later a bright flame, such as a giant might have produced by striking titanic matches on the mountain-side, spurted swiftly upwards at half-a-dozen points. Then a pillar of smoke five hundred feet high broke upwards into the blue. For nearly five minutes it hung around the building, thinning gradually upwards into strange, evil-looking arabesques such as Aubrey Beardsley at his most decadent might have designed.
>
> Then the column paled and melted. The Abbey became visible again. Its whole outline had changed. The west wall had totally collapsed . . .

The Mediums, operating in tight formation, had administered the *coup de grâce*, and this had been the explosion more powerful than any that had gone before, the one that had blocked the entrance to the monks' refuge.

(The wall, though breached, had not been split from top to bottom, as it had seemed to Buckley watching from a hillside five miles away. The lower part, the battlemented base, ten feet thick, was still intact. The Abbey had been wrecked but there was still no easy way in for any soldiers who succeeded in storming their way up the slopes of the mountain.)

During the afternoon the Abbot and those with him dug their way out of the refuge they had been using, and made for the chapels under the largely intact *torretta*, which now seemed the safest place left. There they did what they could to help the injured. A little food was located and distributed. But there was no water. With the arrival of darkness, and periodical collapses of walls and ceilings— not to mention the artillery fire that was by this time following up the work of the bombers—a new kind of terror set in. Should they attempt to get away at once, risking the shells? Or should they wait for the German officer to whom they had spoken in the morning?

At eight o'clock this same lieutenant arrived at the Abbey. But it was not, as they had hoped, to guide them to the escape route that had been promised early that morning.

The lieutenant had come to say that Hitler, at the request of the Pope, was asking the Allies for a truce so that the monks and the civilian refugees might leave Monte Cassino. They would be taken away in German army transport, but owing to the state of the road, would have to make their way to the transport on foot. Kesselring would ask for a truce that night. If the Allies failed to grant it the responsibility for the fate of the monks and the refugees would be theirs.

The Abbot was then asked to sign a statement to the effect that there had been no German soldiers in the Monastery before or during the attack. The statement was already prepared:

> I certify to be the truth that inside the enclosure of the sacred monastery of Cassino there never were any German soldiers; that there were for a certain period only three military police for the sole purpose of en-

376

forcing respect for the neutral zone which was established around the monastery, but they were withdrawn about twenty days ago.

Monte Cassino   *(Signed)*   GREGORIO DIAMARE
February 15, 1944   Abbot-Bishop of
                                       Monte Cassino.
                             DIEBER
                             Lieutenant.

On the altar of the Chapel of the Pietà, his black habit still white with the clinging dust, the eighty-year-old Abbot signed the document and the officer left. Although his feelings were by no means pro-Allied at this moment, the Abbot and the remaining monks had little doubt that the statement about the request for a truce meant nothing. There is an innocent pathos in the way one of them expressed his doubts: "The truce did not take place. It is indeed doubtful whether the request for it was ever even put forward, and whether it was not a case of deception." But at this extreme time they needed some sort of hope to cling to, and the mention of a truce, however skeptically they felt about it, provided them with it. It was this hope of a truce that helped them to face the long twelve-hour night in darkness that was penetrated only by the flash of bursting shells, the moans of the wounded, and the fearful rumble whenever some further part of the ruins collapsed.

As they composed themselves to await the morrow there was one result of that day that affected the monks more profoundly than any other. In a devastation that had spared no part of the extensive monastery buildings, except those below ground, the cell used by St. Benedict himself, and preserved through the ages, had unaccountably escaped. They would have been filled with even greater wonder had they known (what was discovered many months later after the war had passed on) that during the afternoon a large-caliber artillery shell had landed within a foot of the saint's tomb, but had failed to explode.

So it happened that in all this destruction the cell where Benedict lived in his lifetime and the tomb in which his remains had rested during the fourteen hundred years since his death were the only places to escape injury.

That night the Air Command announced flatly that 142 B-17 Fortress bombers and 112 Mediums had by nightfall dropped 576 tons of bombs on Monte Cassino. The Monastery buildings had been wrecked and breaches made in the outer walls, but because of the great thickness of these walls the bombs had not breached them from top to bottom.

On this same Tuesday morning, February 15, the foremost troops of the 4th Indian Division were facing their third day in the uncomfortable mountain salient. The conditions were unlike anything they had previously experienced. Only a shallow jagged hump separated their forward posts from those of the Germans seventy yards away. The whole of this isolated private front line was overlooked from enemy-held heights on three sides, which made daylight movement out of the question. It had been difficult enough to relieve the Americans in the first place, and since taking over two nights before, it had been even more difficult to bring up the supplies they would need for the major attack they were being pressed to launch almost immediately. Living conditions were not improved by the presence of over a hundred unburied—and unreachable—bodies scattered about the area.

The best way to visualize this salient, cutting into the heart of the German mountain positions, is to imagine a rocky, uneven ridge roughly in the shape of a boomerang and a thousand yards long. From the British side the boomerang curved away to the left, the Royal Sussex being astride the near end, the Germans occupying most of the rest of it, and Monastery Hill being just beyond the far end. At the "elbow" of the boomerang was the dome-shaped mountain known on the map as Point 593. The Germans manned its forward slopes in strength.

The boomerang-shaped ridge, which the Americans had called Snakeshead, provided an approach to the Monastery, but blocking the way was the natural obstacle of Point 593. The sides of the ridge sloped away sharply, at times precipi-

378

tously, and the only alternative to an advance along the ridge (taking 593 en route) was to cut directly across the open "elbow" to Monastery Hill, giving Point 593 in the middle a wide berth. This, however, would entail crossing a chaos of slopes, gullies, ravines, boulders, gorse thickets, and shattered walls where shells had churned up the terracing. On the whole the approach along Snakeshead seemed the lesser of the two evils, but first Point 593 would have to be captured.

Two basic (as well as a score of minor) difficulties influenced the projected operation over this unpromising ground. The first was supply. Everything, including water, had to be brought seven miles across the valley on mules by an oblique route, and then manhandled for the last few hundred yards up the final steep paths to the forward positions. This supply route took five hours to cover, was constantly shelled so that only a proportion of the mules actually got through on most nights. The wounded had to endure the same long and hazardous journey in the opposite direction.

The second basic difficulty was that the ground itself—this tangle of rocky ledges, slopes, ravines, boulders, narrow ridges, and gorse thickets—was such that only a few troops could be deployed on it at a time. To adapt itself to these conditions, the Division's plan had been to establish one of its three brigades (the 7th) in the forward area as a firm base and assault force, and to feed battalions of a second brigade (the 5th) into the 7th as required. The 7th Brigade would therefore act as a funnel not only for its own jug of water, as it were, but also for that of the 5th Brigade. The third brigade of the division, the 11th, would be used as a corps of porters, carriers, and laborers to keep the other two supplied.

By Tuesday morning the 7th Brigade were just beginning to become acclimatized to their spearpoint position. The 1st Royal Sussex were astride Snakeshead Ridge, seventy yards from the Germans, a thousand yards from the Monastery. The 4th/16th Punjabis were echeloned down the slope to their left. The 1st/2nd Gurkhas were in reserve a few hundred yards behind.

To the Royal Sussex, who were the point of the spear, the focal point of the landscape was, of course, the cream-colored Abbey on which they looked slightly downward from this height. But what worried them more was the rocky dome of Point 593 rising up immediately to their front. While everyone else could talk of nothing but the Monastery, the Royal Sussex were doing their best to make it clear that Point 593 would have to be captured first. No 593, no Monte Cassino. At the headquarters of the Second New Zealand Corps across the valley this had not been fully appreciated. Thus it was that the 4th Indian Division, now gloomily aware of all the local difficulties, was thinking in terms of a preliminary clearance of Point 593, to be followed by an attack on the Monastery: while Second New Zealand Corps, constantly being urged to get a move on, was visualizing an immediate direct attack on the Monastery as soon as the bombing had taken place.

While the officers were preoccupied with these problems on that Tuesday morning there was nothing for the soldiers to do but to make themselves as tolerably comfortable as they could in the circumstances. They would try to sleep, or read, or even shave if they had saved the dregs of their tea—for when water had to be brought seven miles by mule it had also to be severely rationed. They would clean their weapons, but not themselves. They would smoke, if they had not run out of cigarettes, for ammunition had to take precedence over comforts while mules were still in short supply. They would write letters. They would stare at the Monastery.

When, shortly after nine-thirty, the formation of Fortresses passed high overhead, no one paid any attention. Except when the weather was bad, Fortresses were always flying over—so high that they were only just visible—to those regular assignments: marshaling yards, railway bridges, communications centers, that to the soldier seemed always so remote and useless. Then the bombs began to drop on the Monastery and some of them quite a distance from it and a few of the soldiers were wounded by flying rock splinters before they had quite grasped what was happening.

As the first salvo crashed down, Colonel Glennie, C.O. of the Royal Sussex, picked up his telephone and called his brigade headquarters, but before he had time to speak the voice at the other end said: "We didn't know either!" No one had remembered to tell the ground troops primarily concerned that the bombing, which they had been warned to expect on the 16th, had been brought forward a day. "They told the monks," remarked Colonel Glennie, "and they told the enemy, but they didn't tell us!" Of this curious lapse perhaps it may be said that army-air co-operation was still in its adolescence, if not its infancy, and that this was yet another occasion when a number of lessons were learned the hard way.

For the soldiers, the bombing was a spectacular diversion in the monotony of the front-line day—albeit a nerve-racking one, for many of the bombs fell close to their positions and caused several more casualties. For the officers it was the background to a day of feverish planning, for it wasn't long before the order came through that, however unexpected the advancing of the date of the bombing, however unready they might think they were, an attack must be made that night. The preliminary clearance of Point 593 must be disposed of immediately. The Royal Sussex must deal with it that night.

The factors were brutally simple. The nearest German posts were 70 yards away: too close for the British battalion to employ direct artillery support. The peak of 593 was only another 100 yards farther on. The ground was rock hard, and littered with loose stones, making silent approach virtually impossible. There had been no time to build up a picture of exact enemy dispositions through patrolling and continuous observation. This was a battle that would be settled by grenade, bayonet, mortar, and light machine gun, and the unfortunate Sussex would now have bitter cause to regret the loss of their mortar and grenade reserves on the journey forward when the two lorries carrying them plunged off the road. (In passing, one may wonder why the Divisional Staff failed to make good this loss.)

This must have been one of the few battlefields of the second world war which reproduced the close conditions of

381

1914-18. The Flanders phrase is entirely applicable. What the Royal Sussex had to do was to go "over the top."

In view of their limited knowledge of both the ground and enemy dispositions the Sussex decided to make their first attack with one company only. That night, about the time that Abbot Diamare, propping himself against the altar of the Chapel of the Pietà, was signing the document declaring that there had been no German soldiers in the Monastery, a company of the Sussex, 3 officers and 63 men strong, moved stealthily forward astride Snakeshead Ridge toward Point 593 at the "elbow" of the boomerang.

They moved in normal formation of two platoons abreast, the third following behind in reserve. They moved very slowly. On this ground there was a danger at every step of a stone being dislodged and rattling against another: and in these high places sounds of this kind were audible a long way away. On this ground, too, it was fatally easy to turn an ankle, or stumble. It was especially easy for a man laden with something heavy, such as a Bren gun. With every single step there was a danger of breaking the silence that was essential to their approach—with an alert enemy a bare seventy yards away.

The leading troops had advanced no more than fifty yards when they came under a withering fire of machine gun and grenade. They went to ground. They wriggled across the sharp, stony ground from one position to another, trying to work round to the flanks. Time after time individuals and groups made a new effort to find a way round, a way closer to an objective that was so near and yet so inaccessible. But the steep ground defeated them. And their grenades began to run short, though the Germans, sending them over in showers from their positions up the slope, had unlimited quantities. To help them out grenades were collected from the other companies of the battalion and passed forward, but long before dawn these too had been used up.

If they had remained in the open after daybreak they would have been wiped out to a man. Before first light they were therefore ordered to withdraw. February 15, a calamitous day for Monte Cassino, had not spared the Royal Sussex either. Of the 3 officers and 63 men who had undertaken this exploratory trial of strength against a preliminary objective, 2 officers and 32 men had been killed or wounded no more than fifty yards from their start-point. It was a foretaste of things to come.

During the morning the Sussex were ordered to try again that night, using the whole battalion. At the same time it was learned that the counteroffensive against the Anzio beachhead had started, as expected, a few hours before.

The Germans had massed four infantry divisions on a 4,000-yard front and were making an all-out effort to cut through the heart of the beachhead to Anzio, eight miles away. This was their biggest offensive operation of the campaign. It was supported by 452 guns. Following up the infantry divisions and their supporting tanks ready to exploit their success were two Panzer divisions, each reinforced by a battalion of the newest and heaviest tanks, the Tiger and Panther.

There was no doubt at all where the Allied Air Forces were going to be needed for the next few days. Everything that could fly would be wanted at Anzio. Cassino could look for no help from the air for a few days. The bombing offensive that had started the day before with the destruction of the Monastery had to end with it.

Poor Abbot Diamare and his reduced party of monks and refugees could not know this, however, and they spent a forlorn day in the Abbey ruins waiting in vain for the Germans who had promised to return and help them get away.

By now the party was reduced to about forty. Most of the able-bodied survivors of the bombing had got away during the night or at dawn. There remained the three dogged peasant families who never left the Abbot's side now; some children—three of them badly injured—who had been deserted by their parents; a number of other injured including an old woman whose feet had been blown off; about half a dozen able-bodied men, and a few of the lay brothers. Only two monks remained. One, as we saw, died in the epidemic. Two others were killed in the bombing.

Apart from one brief visit from fighter bombers during the day, there was no air activity, but there was a great deal of artillery fire. Quite early in the day the Abbot decided that he could expect no further help from the Germans and that he must organize the evacuation himself. He decided that first light the following morning would be the best time, as he had noticed that there was generally a lull in the fighting then. Once again he and the monks had to resign themselves to another long night in the ruins.

There were two small comforts in a day of otherwise unrelieved fear and hopelessness. One of the lay brothers managed to rescue a breviary from the rubble: it enabled the Abbot and the monks to celebrate the divine offices as usual. The other, and more earthly comfort was the discovery that a small water tank was undamaged in the ruins of the kitchen.

The first thing the Sussex C.O. did when he was ordered to attack 593 again that night was to send a strongly worded SOS for grenades. The company battle of the night before had confirmed that grenades more than anything else were what were wanted for this close-quarter fighting among the rocks. Then he planned his attack.

B Company, reinforced by a platoon of A Company, were to be the main effort company: they were to attack 593 from the left and take it. Simultaneously the depleted A Company were to make a diversionary effort on the right, to distract the German defenses. When B Company were on the hill, they were to send up a light signal, whereupon D Company, fresh and carrying as much ammunition as they could, were to rush through, relieve B on the newly captured height and immediately prepare to repel the inevitable counterattack. C Company, the one halved in strength by the battle of the previous night, would remain in reserve.

With the objective beginning only seventy yards away, it was not possible to have it shelled in advance.

The shortage of ammunition for the mortars was solved by salvaging the bombs (of a different caliber from the British) left behind by the Americans. These could be fired through some captured German and Italian mortars which the Sussex had brought back from North Africa as souvenirs.

No one was happy about the operation. The trial of strength the previous night had shown how strongly defended 593 was. The impossibility of prior reconnaissance made night movement over this broken and difficult ground a dangerous gamble. Ammunition was still far from adequate—it would take many nights to build up the necessary stocks. But Anzio was facing its gravest crisis and the Cassino attack had to go in. It would be something if the all-important grenades arrived in time. For the Royal Sussex it was a day of tension.

The attack was ordered for 2300, because that was the earliest time by which the mule train bringing the grenades could arrive. By 2300 the mules had not arrived. The supply route had been heavily shelled that night, and many mules had been lost. The attack was postponed for half an hour. By 2330 the mules had still not arrived, and the attack was postponed for another half hour. A few minutes later the mules did arrive, but owing to losses on the way through the shelling, they brought only half the number of grenades required.

The attack at last started, calamitously, at midnight. As we have seen there could be no direct artillery support on an objective so close to the attackers. Instead the task of the artillery was to neutralize the adjacent peaks, especially Point 575, 800 yards to the right of 593. From the point of view of the guns—firing from the far side of the valley, 1,500 feet below the altitude of these hills—the ridge along which the Sussex had to advance was a crest only slightly below that of Point 575. To hit the latter, it was necessary for the shells to skim the top of Snakeshead by a few feet, and gunnery as precise as this allowed no margin for error. The tiniest fraction of a variation in elevation and the shells would hit the top of Snakeshead instead of Point 575, 800 yards away.

This is precisely what happened. As the two leading companies, closely followed by Battalion Headquarters and the Reserve Company, formed up on the start-line of the attack, the artillery opened fire on Point 575. But several shells failed to clear Snakeshead, and burst among the leading companies and Battalion Headquarters. It is axiomatic that the most demoralizing beginning to any operation is for the attacking force to be shelled on its start-line. It is not less disturbing if the shells happen to be from its own guns. Only one company—the one that was to take over and consolidate the hill if it was captured—escaped.

After a hurried reorganization the attack went in according to plan. As on the previous night fifty yards were covered before the advancing troops ran into a withering fire. The reinforced main effort company worked round by the left, as they had been ordered, while the smaller company set about creating their diversionary display of fireworks on the right. This company at once ran into trouble. Just in time they stopped on the edge of a forty-foot precipice not indicated on the map. There was no way round by the right, so they edged leftward, and then found themselves faced with a crevice fifteen feet deep and twenty feet across. There was nothing they could do except go to ground and give fire support.

Meanwhile the main effort company on the left, thanks to a number of individual feats of valor which destroyed some of the German machine-gun nests, did succeed in forcing their way on to the main part of the feature. But the Germans, defending ruthlessly, could not be dislodged from well-prepared positions in which they were determined to stay. A hand-to-hand battle then raged, and in the confusion a number of the Sussex pushing through to the rear of the objective went beyond it, and fell down another of the small precipices in which the area abounds. They were wounded and taken prisoner. Another party, driving through to the rear of the peak, unluckily ran into a more numerous party of German reinforcements on their way in. As on the previous night it turned into a grenade battle, but while the Germans were sending them over in showers, the British battalion soon began to run out. After about two hours of this, the right-hand company had had all their officers killed or wounded, and the reserve company went to reinforce them. On the left the main effort force was

386

rapidly running out of ammunition, and all of their officers had been wounded.

The one fresh company—the one that had been intended to exploit the captured position—was sent in as a last resort, but they came up against the deep crevice that had halted the right-hand company, and at the same time they were caught in a murderous cross fire.

The attack had failed and there was nothing for it but to withdraw the remnants of the four companies to the point from which they had started.

Out of 12 officers and 250 men that had taken part in the attack, 10 officers and 130 men were killed, wounded or taken prisoner. In the two nights, therefore, the Sussex casualties had been 12 out of 15 officers, 162 out of 313 men. In two nights a fine battalion that had fought since the earliest days of the war, and which had never previously failed to take its objective, had been cut to pieces.

The casualties speak for themselves. The battalion could not have tried harder or more gallantly. It wasn't their fault that they had to attack before they were ready. With the supply line what it was—the night was barely long enough for the mule trains to make the round journey of fourteen miles—they had no chance to build up their ammunition stocks to the level required.

At dawn on Thursday (by which time Tuesday's bombing seemed an age ago), while the commanding officer of the Royal Sussex was reorganizing the remains of four powerful companies into three small ones; while General von Mackensen's Fourteenth Army, after a nonstop attack which had driven a mile and a half into the Anzio beachhead, was approaching the climax of its tremendous onslaught; Abbot Diamare, summoning up the last reserves of his strength, prepared for the final stage of his long ordeal.

He called the surviving monks and refugees together by the entrance arch of the Abbey (above which the inscription PAX was still intact) and gave sacramental absolution to each one of them. Then, taking hold of a large wooden crucifix, he led the way through the rubble on to

387

one of the bridle paths leading westward through the mountains. Before the party of forty left there was a last distressing decision to be taken. Three small children, a sister and two brothers, had been found in the ruins. All three were injured. Their mother had been killed in the bombing and their father had since abandoned them. It was clear that the girl and one of the brothers had a very short time to live. When an attempt was made to lift them they screamed with pain, and it was thought kinder to leave them. To have carried them up and down steep mountain paths would have only made their last moments more painful. The other brother was less badly hurt, he was only paralyzed in both legs. A lay brother hoisted him onto his shoulders. A ladder was found which could be used as a stretcher for the old woman whose feet had been blown off, and two of the very few survivors who were not either sick or wounded carried her at the rear of the column.

Progress was slow and painful, the paths being steep and rough. But the Abbot, supported by the monks and lay brothers, insisted on holding up the heavy crucifix as they stumbled down the mountainside. Whenever they came to a German post the Abbot asked for permission to pass, saying that he was abandoning the Monastery with the consent of the German High Command. For the most part (one of the monks recorded) the soldiers just stared open-mouthed at this strange company and said absolutely nothing. Inevitably the little column straggled and after a time there were shouts from the rear. The men carrying the ladder bearing the woman who had lost her feet shouted that they could not keep up, the track was too steep and too difficult. Those in front shouted back encouragement. There was not much farther to go, they must keep up. After they had been walking for some time they came to a level piece of ground and the Abbot called a halt so that they could rest a little, and to give the stragglers a chance to catch up. It was discovered then that the two men who had been carrying the old woman had given up some way back and abandoned her. They were too exhausted to carry on, they said. The column moved off again and after a time they came to a cottage in which the Germans had established a medical post. There the injured were given some attention, but when the Abbot asked to be put in touch with a headquarters he was told that the telephone line was cut. The Germans said it would be better for the party to keep moving until they were farther to the rear. They would receive help there. They pointed out a suitable path and suggested that it would be safer (there was a certain amount of shelling) if they moved off at intervals in small groups.

This was arranged and one by one the groups moved off. The last to leave were to be the Abbot and the Sacrist. For the time being these two rested inside the cottage as the Abbot was by this time close to collapse. While they were there a messenger arrived to say that an urgent search for the Abbot had been instituted and all forward units had been warned to look out for him. As soon as he had reported back that the Abbot was found, a further message was sent to the medical post ordering them to look after him until he could be picked up. The ambulance arrived during the afternoon.

The German corps commander, General von Senger, has described the end of the story:

> I had the Abbot picked up there by car and brought to my Headquarters . . . I lodged the venerable old priest, who was accompanied by a solitary monk companion, for one night.
>
> While the Abbot was my guest I received orders from the German High Command to induce him to make a radio statement regarding the attitude of the German troops and their respect for the neutrality of the Monastery. I decided to comply, as the destruction of the Monastery was an event of historic importance in which my personal honour as a soldier and as a Christian was involved. After a conversation with his companion the Abbot agreed, and we conducted a dialogue into the microphone which went even further than I had intended, complaining of the deplorable ruin and destruction of many valuable and irreparable works of art. After the broadcast I had him taken by car to Rome, appointing an officer to

deliver him safely to Sant' Anselmo, where he informed me he wished to go. Sant' Anselmo on the Aventino is the centre of the Benedictine Order . . .

My plan to convey the Abbot safely to Sant' Anselmo was thwarted. On the road to Rome the car was waylaid by agents of Goebbels, the Propaganda Minister. Goebbels had no intention of missing this excellent piece of propaganda and according to the methods of the Fuehrer Principle meant to act with complete disregard of what others might do in the same line. The frightened old priest was accordingly brought to a radio station, kept waiting a long time without food, and finally induced to make another statement as prescribed by the radio columnists . . .

But this was not sufficient. Hitler's most stupid and most arrogant henchman, the Foreign Minister, also wanted his share of the cake. The statement which he required was shaped upon distinctly political propaganda lines. The unfortunate old priest at last broke down, refused to make any more statements, and asked to be released, as he now understood that he was no longer a protected guest but a prisoner.

War exacts its wages indiscriminately. In the mosaic of suffering and endurance created by the battle of Cassino, Gregorio Diamare, eighty-year-old Abbot-Bishop of Monte Cassino, has an honorable place. So, it may be thought, has the old peasant woman with the severed feet, whom they carried part of the way to safety on a ladder and then left to die alone on the cold mountainside. For it was her fate to be a battle casualty without even knowing what the battle was about.

That evening, the German propagandists having completed their work, the Tenth Army was able to make some small adjustments in its dispositions on and around the summit of Monastery Hill by establishing posts in the Abbey ruins.

For the 4th Indian Division and the New Zealanders it was a day of urgency. Both divisions were at last ready to make the concerted attack originally designed to follow the bombing. That night the Indians would attack not with one battalion, but with three.

At midnight the 4th/6th Rajputana Rifles would pass through the Royal Sussex and attempt to storm Point 593. If they succeeded where the Sussex had failed, the depleted Sussex would then follow up the success, and sweep along the ridge to Point 444 at the far end of the "boomerang."

At 0215, with the help of the moon which would then be rising, two battalions of Gurkhas, the 1st/2nd and 1st/9th, starting from the left of the Sussex would sweep across the slopes and ravines in a direct assault on the Monastery. It was an appalling route that they had to cover, but the Gurkhas, born and bred in the foothills of the Himalaya, were the most expert mountain fighters in the Commonwealth armies. If anyone could negotiate the impossible mountain terrain, the Gurkhas could. Two entire reserve battalions of the division were organized into carrying parties to provide the necessary replenishments of ammunition and other essentials.

While the Indians projected themselves at these mountain strongholds, the 28th (Maori) Battalion of the New Zealand division was to advance from the direction of Monte Trocchio along the railway causeway and take Cassino Station.

The New Zealanders had not had the same difficulty as the Indians in getting into position, but like the Indians they had found themselves on ground where few troops could be deployed at a time. Owing to the flooded state of the valley, the causeway was the only usable line of approach.

On the heels of the Maoris would follow a company of sappers to remove mines, deal with the demolitions that the Germans had left behind to make the causeway impossible for transport, and to erect Bailey bridges over two waterways—a canal and the Rapido—which lay between the start-point and the station. The success of the operation depended on the sappers making the route fit for transport by dawn, so that tanks and anti-tank guns could join the Maoris on the objective by daylight. Massed behind Trocchio, ready to exploit the Maoris' success, was the rest of the Division supported by 180 tanks of the U.S. 1st Armored Division.

The Maoris had a special place in the New Zealand division. They were cheerful ebullient men, with a keen sense of humor, and a natural fighting spirit: great soldiers in the assault and pursuit. Temperamentally, they were the "wild Irish" of the New Zealand division. The advance started soon after dark to give the engineers as long a period of darkness as possible in which to complete their vital bridging and repairs to the route. In the closing stages of the advance the Maoris came up against minefields and barbed wire, and they were continuously mortared. But they fought their way through, and shortly after midnight they had stormed into the sheds and buildings of the Station, and triumphantly taken possession of them—and also of a number of prisoners.

Meanwhile, two thousand feet above them in the mountains—just faintly discernible from the Station in the dark—the Rajputana Rifles edged along Snakeshead Ridge toward Point 593. But, as on the previous two nights, within an hour or so the battalion was pinned down by impenetrable fire as it crouched at the base, and on the lower slopes, of the rock. They tried everything they knew to work their way round the boulders and ledges, and more than one small party succeeded in reaching the summit, but they were invariably killed or wounded. It developed into the same story as on the two preceding nights: successive small individual efforts that made no progress but always cost a few more lives. By two in the morning one company commander had been killed, two of the other three wounded.

While the Rajputs fought it out on 593, the 1st/9th Gurkhas, only 300 yards to their left, set off on the rough direct route to the Monastery, about 1,000 yards away. Their preliminary objective was Point 444 at the end of the "boomerang." Almost immediately they came under heavy cross fire from 593 and points on their left, and their efforts to deal with these positions brought them up on the left of the Rajputs, but neither battalion could make any headway. The stronghold of 593, supported by the neighboring high points, was well able to take care of both.

392

The second Gurkha battalion, the 1st/2nd, then moved off, but some way further to the left, with a direct approach to the Monastery via Point 450. As they worked their way down to the steep ravine which was the final obstacle—the ravine at the bottom of the northern slope of Monastery Hill—they approached a belt of what looked like scrub. It stood out in a landscape that had been bereft of so much of its vegetation by shellfire. They remembered noting it on their air photographs, on which it showed up as a long, prominent shadow. As the leading platoons approached it, a shower of grenades came down on them from the higher ground behind, and swiftly they dashed forward to take cover in this patch of scrub.

There was a series of staccato explosions. The scrub was not scrub at all, but a thicket of strong thorn, breast-high. It had been laced with barbed wire, and was thickly sown with interconnected anti-personnel mines set to explode when any of the trip wires, cunningly placed across all approaches, was touched.

As the leading platoons dashed into what they took to be cover, half of them were blown up by mines, those that weren't were mowed down by the rows of machine guns a little way to the rear, which had only to pour their fire into the cries and flashes and the silhouettes grotesquely lighted up on the thorn and barbed wire every time a mine went off. The colonel, shot through the stomach, was among those who fell wounded at this place. Despite this setback, the follow-up companies tried to press on with the attack, but a line of machine guns across the full width of Monastery Hill presented a curtain of fire through which they could not break, though they did not stop trying. The Monastery was only four hundred yards away, but they were four hundred of the longest yards in the world.

The full story of these deadly night battles can never be known, because too many of its authors died writing it. Undersupplied, without sufficient time to prepare, these few fought a lonely battle in the mountains and no one in the rest of the army had any idea of what they were facing. They had nothing to sustain them except that potent imponderable, their regimental identity. It mattered to the

393

Rajputana Rifles that they were Rajputana Rifles: it mattered to the Royal Sussex that they were Royal Sussex. In the end it was probably this alone that enabled them to keep on. His mother in a village near Katmandu would never know about her stretcher-bearer son making sixteen

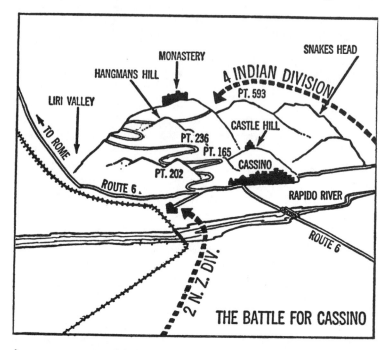

THE BATTLE FOR CASSINO

journeys across this inferno until, as he raised his last load, he fell dead with a burst of tracer in his back. Like the English officer who lay dead at his side, he had done what he had done not only because it was his job as a soldier, but because over and above that he was conscious of being a Gurkha Rifleman.

By first light on Friday the situation on Snakeshead was exactly as it had been the morning before, except that there were three battalions instead of one pinned down among the boulders of this nameless three acres of mountain. Once again there was nothing for it but to withdraw the survivors before daylight.

By first light in the area of Cassino Station, the New Zealand sappers had almost completed the night's work. They had lifted scores of mines, despite the additional time-wasting labor of having to dispose of the blown-up railway line. (It could otherwise not be known whether the mine detectors were picking up the metal of the mines or the line.) They had cleared wire, and booby traps; they had thrown Bailey bridges across two water obstacles, a canal and the River Rapido; they had spanned with rubble or bridging material several smaller gaps the Germans had blown in the causeway. By one means or another—and in spite of being under shell and mortar fire for half the night —they had managed to create behind the advancing Maoris well over a mile of usable roadway along which the tanks and anti-tank guns could race at daybreak. Now they were working desperately to finish by the end of the night, which for sappers can never be long enough.

They very nearly succeeded. But as the sky began to lighten there was just one more gap to be bridged. They had been beaten by a few minutes. The work could not be done in daylight. The Maoris would have to spend the long twelve-hour day without tanks or anti-tank guns.

To infantry who have carried out a successful night attack, the arrival of the tanks and anti-tank guns at dawn is a matter of life and death. Without these aids, they are naked and exposed if the enemy counterattacks with tanks. They would have the support of their artillery, but ordinary artillery can do little from long range against armor. Tanks have to be tackled with the armor-piercing shells of anti-tank guns firing from close range in the infantry area.

Like the Indian division nearly two thousand feet above them, the Maoris had had severe casualties: 128 of them had been killed or wounded. But by dawn they were well established and dug in. The station buildings provided plenty of cover and also room for maneuver. They cheerfully accepted the order to hang on, in splendid isolation, until the next period of darkness, twelve long hours away.

At daybreak of this same day, Friday, the German Four-teenth Army, now two and half miles into the heart of the Anzio beachhead, committed its armored reserves, an indication that this day was to prove the climax of the counteroffensive. Lowering black clouds there warned the hard-pressed American and British beachhead divisions that they could expect no help from the air forces that day. The Germans had also introduced a new weapon, the "Goliath," a small tank filled with explosives which was directed by remote radio control into the Allied positions, and then exploded.

In Rome a citizen recorded in her diary:

> All Rome is thickly placarded today with posters showing photographs of the ruins of Monte Cassino with monks and refugee civilians, and reproductions of handwritten signed statements by the Abbot and his administrator. This is certainly a trump card in the German propaganda game.

It was an uneasy morning all around for the Allied commanders.

In the mountains the Indian division made a melancholy count of the night's losses. The Rajputana Rifles had lost 196 officers and men including all their company commanders. The Gurkha battalion so many of whom had been crucified on the thorn and barbed wire of that mined thicket had lost 7 British officers including their colonel, 4 Gurkha officers, and 138 N.C.O.'s and men. The other Gurkha battalion had lost 96 of all ranks. In three nights four crack regular battalions had been cut to pieces, without a chance to do anything but die well. Nothing whatever had been gained.

Its crest only a hundred yards away, Point 593, the intermediate rocky eminence they had hoped to dispose of with a preliminary clearing operation, had proved to be a major fortification in its own right—thanks partly to the fragment of an old fort which provided its forward slope with a steel heart, but also to the skill and tenacity of first-class soldiers who knew how to make the best use of it; and to the closely co-ordinated fire of the adjacent German-held peaks. If you attacked one, six others could come to its rescue with machine-gun and mortar fire.

Everything now depended on the Maoris. Could they hold on to the Station for a whole day without the means of dealing with tanks, if tanks should be sent against them? If they could, the battle could be saved. As we have seen, the Station area—a thousand yards from the town and half that distance from the corner where Highway Six swung round Monastery Hill into the Liri Valley—not only provided a means of bypassing the core of the Cassino defenses, but made a jumping-off point for an armored break into the valley. It all depended now on the Maoris.

At daybreak General Kippenberger went forward to visit them. He found them cheerful and confident. They are the kind of soldiers who thrive on success. Their leading companies were well dug in, and they had good cover from the buildings, for the Italians construct their stone buildings well, even in railway stations and yards.

The chief difficulty was Monastery Hill, its southeastern corner a mere five hundred yards away, towering over the Station area so overwhelmingly that it made a man feel puny and helpless just to look up at it. There were tanks and artillery pieces at all the key points of that corkscrew road which cut across the face of the mountain, and many eyes to direct their fire. To be in the Station so near to the base of Monte Cassino was like being stared at hugely and malignantly. But the position must be held. If they could only hang on till nightfall, the engineers could hurry along the causeway, deal with the last gap, and the whole weight of the division could then pile up behind the Maoris.

When he had seen the position for himself from a forward viewpoint, General Kippenberger decided to cut off the Station from the view of the Monastery by laying a smokescreen and keeping it going all day. There was no difficulty about making the screen, the gunners said, but to keep it going all day would require many more shells than they had available. The artillery do not normally lay much smoke—it is generally left to the mortars—and the standard proportion of smoke shells at the gun sites is small. Where were the nearest reserves, Kippenberger asked. In Naples, seventy miles away. Then someone must go to Naples and get some. The Service Corps rose to the occasion. A column

397

of lorries was sent off to bring back the necessary quantity of shells (to keep the screen going all day would require about 30,000) and within a few minutes the Maoris were relieved to find themselves screened from Monastery Hill by a thick artificial fog.

There was nothing for it now but to wait. The hours passed slowly. By ten there had been no counterattack. By midday there had been no counterattack. One o'clock, and no counterattack—but reports from the Maoris that they were being mortared. Two o'clock. Only four hours to dusk. The lorries were back from Naples, and the gunners were thickening up the screen confident that they could now keep it going indefinitely.

But soon after three, the ominous grating of tanks was heard in the Station. A few minutes later German infantry and tanks, skillfully using the New Zealand smokescreen to disguise the direction of their approach, burst through it into the Station area from two sides. Unluckily the men manning the bazookas were early casualties. The Maoris had nothing to pit against the tanks. There was a short sharp fight; the New Zealanders lost a number of prisoners: a few more were killed or wounded; the remainder were pulled back. The smokescreen had proved a two-edged weapon. But without it few of the forward troops would have survived the day.

The sweating gunners, who in relays had been pumping smoke shells into their guns without respite for more than eight hours, stood down exhausted. The battle was over. The single net gain on both divisional fronts was a bridge over the Rapido.

Viewed from a distance, the second battle of Cassino may be thought—especially after the world-wide commotion which preceded and followed the bombing—to have been something of an anticlimax. In the mountains a company attack on Tuesday night, a battalion attack on Wednesday, and a three-battalion attack on Thursday—all unsuccessful. In the valley, an attack by a single battalion, also unsuccessful.

Commentators at the time and since have been inclined

to dismiss the failure as a simple case of attacking in driblets instead of strength. The criticism is not valid. Ground and weather were the factors which determined the number of troops that could be used in this battle. We have seen already how these factors controlled the Indian division's operations. In the valley, though the New Zealand division did not have the same difficulty over the supply line, ground and weather imposed the same limitation on deployment. The valley was waterlogged, and the only feasible approach to the Station objective was along the railway and on a two-company front.

It must also be realized that there are two ways in which the might of a division can be used. It can attack with several battalions on a wide front, in which case its action is that of a scythe. Or it may initially use a small force on a narrow front, in the hope of making a penetration which can be followed up by the rest of its battalions piled up behind. In that case the action is that of a chisel, with a large number of hammer blows ready to force it through in a series of sharp thrusts. The ground and the weather made the second method the only possible one in this battle, and the New Zealanders nearly succeeded.

It was subsequently known that the Germans had been extremely alarmed by the capture of the Station. They did not expect their counterattack to succeed, as is shown by the following conversation between Kesselring and Vietinghoff on the night of the 18th:

V: We have succeeded after hard fighting in retaking Cassino Station.
K: Heartiest congratulations.
V: I didn't think we would do it.
K: Neither did I.

Had the New Zealand sappers been able to bridge the final gap on the causeway, and make it possible for tanks to come up on the objective, it seems likely that it would have been held.

The second battle of Cassino was notable, also, for two other things.

399

It showed how, in the most mechanized war in history, conditions of ground and weather could arise in which machines were useless, and the battle had to be fought out between small forces of infantry with rifle, machine-gun and grenade. An army that could call on six hundred tanks, eight hundred artillery pieces, five hundred airplanes, and sixty or seventy thousand vehicles of all shapes and sizes found itself dependent on the humble pack mule. In the mountains above Cassino in February a mule was worth half a dozen tanks.

The other lesson was that when Army and Air Force are working together there must be unity of command and the closest co-ordination of plans. Retrospectively this may seem too obvious to be worth mentioning. The plain fact is that in the last year but one of the war it was a problem that had still to be solved.

Out of Anzio

Four major attacks were necessary before the final breakthrough was made at Cassino. The 8th Army was brought over to work with the 5th, on a twenty-mile front. In the meantime, the 5th Army's Anzio forces were increased to six divisions. On May 11th, 1944, the last offensive opened in front of Cassino, and finally on May 18th, Mt. Cassino fell to the Polish Corps. The Germans were suddenly in full retreat, and Alexander gave the signal for the attack from the Anzio beachhead. The Allies waited for victory for weeks; if the Anzio force could break out of the beachhead and cut off the Germans' retreat, they would be in a position to destroy the German 10th Army utterly.

ANZIO TO ROME

by Eric Sevareid

The Allied armies waited, contesting now with time. Only the airplanes moved in their formations, preparing the earth behind the enemy lines. The belated spring arrived; the peasants were plowing up the soft, black soil; the snowline moved high on the mountains of frustration, and the roads to the front were arrows of beige-colored dust. Shawled Italian women trudged barefoot, carrying great baskets on their heads; their faces were stolid until a truckload of Italian men in remnants of uniform would pass

This selection is condensed from the author's *Not So Wild a Dream.*

on the road, and then the women would show their white teeth as they shouted greetings. The gathering engines caused dust to settle upon new acres of peace and permanence, stippled with white crosses. These acres contained the bodies of the first conquerors from the New World ever to invade this much violated land. They lay as dead as Visigoth or Saracen, and in the afternoon the broken arches of the ancient aqueduct shadowed these acres with unaltered precision.

Behind the Allied fronts the earth trembled in the night under the tread of silent convoys. Whole armies switched positions unnoticed by the enemy; the Americans on the central front moved down to the Tyrrhenian Sea; the French faced impossible peaks to our right; the British and the Poles looked at Cassino and the Liri Valley. Each prong of the steel rake was imbedded in position; very soon the signal would be given, and the rake would move northward up the length of the peninsula, furrowing the earth, heaping the mangled houses and bodies together as it moved. It was May. Everywhere the fields were delicately tinted with flowers.

The Allied commander-in-chief invoked the name of God; the German commander invoked the name of Adolf Hitler. The moon was high and full and impartially illuminated both sides of the front, blessing and betraying both defender and attacker. It lighted the way for the men who crawled on their bellies up the Italian drawbridge toward Fortress Europa; it exposed them to Europe's jailers, touching with iridescence coat buckle, water bottle, gun shaft, and wide young eyes. From Cassino to the sea on the central front the soft spring earth shuddered and heaved in grunting convulsions; the venerable olive trees burst their trunks, bent beneath the blasts of air, and then, half erect, exhibited to the moon their leafless limbs, thin and naked as the arms of an obscene hag.

The first blow for the freeing of Europe had fallen in the night, and in the first hour personal friends lay wounded and dead. Two divisions of young Americans who had never before seen combat moved forward over the rolling hills at which they had stared for weeks until they knew each tree and stone in this small area of fate, which to them had become all the planet, its beginning and its end. Within twenty-four hours they were veteran soldiers. By the next dawn, fear was a secondary impulse, and they moved like automata, their limbs stiff with chill, their nostrils black with grime, their beards one day dirtier. They smelled the clover and the dead in alternation and were aware of neither.

It seemed to me that I had been living with the war since that month of September five years before; while the faces, the instruments, the talk were all familiar now, still the moving picture of the fight was new to me, for always before I had known only stalemate or retreat. This was victorious attack, and the spectacle was not at all as the military writers had pictured it. Troops did not "sweep ahead," "wave after wave," tanks did not "charge" the enemy, divisions did not "plunge" nor "pour" at or into anything. It was far more the slow, deliberate behavior of a surveying party than the agitation of a football team. One never saw masses of men assaulting the enemy. What one observed, in apparently unrelated patches, was small, loose bodies of men moving down narrow defiles or over steep inclines, going methodically from position to position between long halts, and the only continuous factor was the roaring and crackling of the big guns. One felt baffled at first by the unreality of it all. Unseen groups of men were fighting other men that they rarely saw. They located the enemy by the abstractions of mathematics, an imagined science; they reported the enemy through radio waves that no man could visualize; and they destroyed him most frequently with projectiles no eye could follow. When the target became quiet, that particular fight would be over and they moved ahead to something else. Never were there masses of men in olive drab locked in photogenic combat with masses of men in field gray. It was slow, spasmodic movement from one patch of silence to another.

The men were real, and the results one saw all around were shockingly real. There is an atmosphere at the front, a heightened feeling which can never be transmitted nor de-

403

scribed. Until one becomes drugged with exhaustion, every scene is a vivid masterpiece of painting. The tree and the ditch ahead are all the trees and ditches of creation, informed with the distillation of sacred *tree*ness and *ditch*ness. Each common odor goes down to the final nerve endings; each turn of the road is stamped indelibly upon the brain; every unexplored house is bursting with portent; every casual word and gesture bears vibrant meaning; those who live are incredibly alive, and the others are stupefyingly dead. Obscure villages which were meaningless names on the map —Minturno, Castelforte, Santa Maria Infante—soon acquire the significance of one's native town, each street and each corner the custodian of intimate, imperishable acquaintance.

A young German soldier lay sprawled just inside a sagging doorway, his hobnailed boots sticking into the street. Two American soldiers were resting and smoking cigarettes a few feet away, paying the body no attention. "Oh, him?" one of them said in response to a question. "Son of a bitch kept lagging behind the others when we brought them in. We got tired of hurrying him up all the time." Thus casually was deliberate murder announced by boys who a year before had taken no lives but those of squirrel or pheasant. I found that I was not shocked nor indignant; I was merely a little surprised. As weeks went by and this experience was repeated many times, I ceased even to be surprised—only, I could never again bring myself to write or speak with indignation of the Germans' violation of the "rules of warfare."

Not a single tree in the ravine had retained its leaves; it was exactly as though a cyclone had just swept through. We sat down on the gray earth with a young captain from West Point named Aileo. He had had six hours' sleep in the last seventy-two, but he merely relaxed in the sun, closing his eyes and smiling to himself as our great shells chortled over sounding like locomotives at high speed. An indolent cook handed us hot, fresh cherry turnovers with a wink, as if to say: "All the comforts of home." The shells were sending up sudden plumes from an enemy-held castle on the next ridge. No one watched it; everybody was already bored

404

with battle. A young corporal trudged by, lugging his personal equipment and a book. The captain asked: "Corporal, are you happy in the service?" "Yes, sir," said the corporal. "Why?" "Because I found a room to sleep in tonight," the boy replied. Then he looked at the volume he carried, *The Return of the Native.* "Only thing bothering me right now is that character here they call the Reddleman. That guy keeps coming in and out of the story, and he confuses me." Puddles of dust advanced up the road, and a lieutenant with a smug and happy look on his face emerged, leading a dozen German prisoners walking with their fingers locked behind their necks. They were exhausted and without expression. Between victorious youth and defeated youth no manner of human transaction occurred.

Battles were large or small; points at issue were vital or of minor consequence; but always and everywhere procedure and pattern were monotonously the same. German guns betrayed their presence. We called our planes to bomb them, and we concentrated our own artillery, too numerous to be opposed, and they shelled the German guns. Thereupon the infantry flowed slowly ahead. At each strong point or village there were always a few snipers to be blasted out, always mines which exploded a number of vehicles, always booby traps which filled a few rooms with smoke and mortal cries. Bulldozers would clear the rubble, engineers would fill the craters, the medical troops would set up their aid stations, a few half-starved Italian families would be rooted out of evil-smelling cellars, and while silent men hoisted limp bodies into trucks the news would go out to the world that the place was "liberated." This is the way it was, day after day, town after town, as the enemy moved back and the line of corrosion moved northward across the peninsula leaving an ever-growing area of stately Italy in blackened ruins which were final beyond despair.

Columns of infantry emerged from side paths and with a censor—a Minnesota classmate, Arthur Burck, who voluntarily went to the front to see the events he had to judge with the blue pencil—I stepped into line to take part in the occupation of Scauri on the coast. They were bearded and unwashed, and they walked very slowly (the headlines said

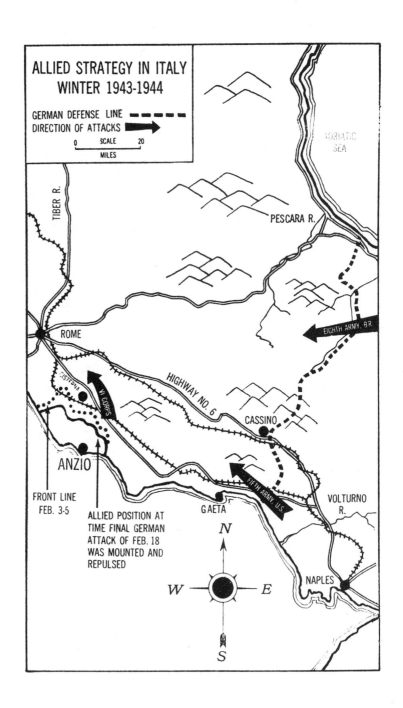

ALLIED STRATEGY IN ITALY
WINTER 1943-1944

GERMAN DEFENSE LINE
DIRECTION OF ATTACKS

0   SCALE   20
MILES

ADRIATIC
SEA

TIBER R.

PESCARA R.

EIGHTH ARMY, BR

ROME

HIGHWAY NO. 6

VI CORPS

PACISTIO

CASSINO

ANZIO

FRONT LINE
FEB. 3-5

ALLIED POSITION AT
TIME FINAL GERMAN
ATTACK OF FEB. 18
WAS MOUNTED AND
REPULSED

GAETA

FIFTH ARMY, U.S.

VOLTURNO
R.

NAPLES

N

W   E

S

they were "racing" along the coast), carrying their packs and clusters of bright yellow hand grenades at their belts. They would fight before they slept again, and only those two things were on their minds. You noticed that their bodies were relaxed, but their faces were not. If you grinned at a man, he grinned back at once. I realized suddenly that in a way these men were happier now than during the long months of waiting. At long last they were doing what they had trained themselves to do, and if death was closer now, so was climax and the end to their bestial routine. A boy walking toward his life's crisis would call: "Hey, Mac, how about puttin' my name in the paper?" Another would ask: "When's the war going to end, correspondent?" Another: "What's going on, fella? They never tell us nuthin'." I realized, too, that I was happy to be with them; that, however officers at the rear regarded a reporter, these men at the fighting front were glad to see me. They knew I did not have to be there, and perhaps that made them one small degree less afraid. Certainly the presence of journalists gave them some slight lifting of the heart in the knowledge that they and their work were not obscure and unnoticed, that if they became victims, somebody somewhere would know why and how it happened. Nothing is quite so awful as anonymity.

A German sniper, no more than a boy, stumbled back down the line under guard, his trousers widely ripped so that his buttocks were exposed. There was muttering as he passed, and I wondered that he was still alive. While we talked with a young lieutenant who was still breathing hard from a reconnaissance by armored car out from the town, a pink-cheeked private approached and hesitantly said: "Lieutenant, sir, pardon me. I can't find my officer. We've got some civilians in a house back there. What shall we do with them, sir?" The excited, puffing lieutenant snapped out: "If you can spare a guard send them back. If you can't, why, shoot 'em in the back. That's what we always did in my outfit. Don't take no nonsense from 'em." The pink-cheeked boy received the order to commit mass murder, saluted, and trotted off.

The sea lay serene and blue before us. In an orange

orchard the birds were singing, and between the thunderous claps from the big guns one could hear their sweet, untroubled notes. Two jeeps halted beside me. One contained General Clark and his aides; the other contained the army photographer who always accompanied the General. Clark said: "Sevareid, aren't you a bit off limits here?" I had the impression he was slightly disgruntled at seeing a reporter at the point of advance before *he* had reached it. He drove slowly on between the two lines of infantry, leaning out now and then to call encouragement and praise to a soldier who would be startled, then draw himself up and walk more stiffly for a few moments. It was good behavior for a general; it was a help. Just outside the town, the General's party halted, and we overtook them on foot. No one could proceed farther on the road without being shot. While Clark looked at a map and pointed toward the hill where the "fire fight" was in furious progress, his photographer scrambled about to snap the pictures. They were always taken of the General's left profile. I noticed that, although an ordinary soldier risked a fine for not wearing his helmet in a combat area, the General was wearing his little overseas cap. When the pictures were finished and he had seen what he wished, he shook hands all around, mounted his jeep, and turned back toward the pacified area. Then he replaced the overseas cap with his steel helmet.

Newly routed civilians, now homeless like the others, with no idea of where they would next sleep or eat, with all their future lives an uncertainty, trudged back from the fighting zone. A dust-covered girl clung desperately to a heavy, squirming burlap sack. The pig inside was squealing faintly. Tears made streaks down the girl's face. No one moved to help her; the thought did not occur to me any more than to the others. There was too much misery, so much that no one could possibly feel sorrow or compassion. We strolled back through the town and came upon a group of filthy, white-faced Italians standing before a ruined house. One merely noted that they had not been shot, after all. The children were the color of paste and looked more dead than alive. The men gestured as we approached, pleaded for food, and showed us how they had eaten grass and roots while they huddled in the cellar. They were in stocking feet, the Germans, they said, having confiscated their shoes.

A few miles up the hills, I knew, the French, who advanced so rapidly that the communiqués could not keep up with them, were taking their towns, running up their flags, talking loudly, and sending up organized cheers. My countrymen around me here were a different kind of conqueror. It was quiet in the town now, and they stood about, a bit awkwardly, wondering what to do. A youngster with fuzz on his chin uttered a low whistle before a tank which was standing foolishly on its nose. One, who looked like a farm boy with great red hands, surveyed a perforated resort hotel. "Ah'll take a room with a southern exposure," he drawled. Conquerors? They had no sense of conquering a country; they were just after the Germans and had to walk over this particular piece of the earth's surface to get at them. Liberators? The Italians were merely harmless creatures who sometimes got in the way. The New World had returned to the Old. America was now in the world. The American Century, perhaps. This was the way it looked.

Allied army authorities nearly always told the journalists everything. It was a wise method. We did our work more intelligently and reduced to a minimum the errors that embarrassed both generals and reporters. But it also entailed certain risks for the generals. If we were told and asked to publicize the fact that General Alexander was making all decisions, this helped to glorify him, but it also left him no easy way out if the decisions brought poor results. If we were told, as we were, that the whole object of the campaign was to "destroy the German armies in Italy," with Rome a secondary objective, that only complete destruction of the enemy here would aid the coming second front in France, and that merely pushing the Germans back would amount to failure of the Italian mission—then the issue was irrevocably stated, and the commanders would be judged by their own statements and standards.

The night before the assault out from the [Anzio] beachhead was to begin, we were ushered into the illuminated

409

caves, and they told us all their plans. It was the custom of assembled correspondents to rise when a general entered in recognition of his rank. It had always been a voluntary gesture on our part, but in this headquarters the ceremony followed a different pattern. As we sat in the rows of benches, a beefy staff colonel would rush in and bellow: " 'Tenshun!" We were always startled and a little resentful, but we would rise. Just as we got to our feet, General Clark would stride in, cut the air laterally with his palm, and call: "Sit down, gentlemen!" in a tone which indicated that this was all a mistake, we were all men of parts together, and that he was embarrassed by his colonel's unjustified command. We frequently wondered if they rehearsed it beforehand—it went off with such dramatic flourish.

The German radio often called Anzio "a prison camp where the inmates feed themselves." If that is what it was, this would be the greatest jail break in history. We had overwhelming superiority in men, vehicles, guns, tanks, and planes, and we needed them, for the Germans held the arc of hills and we must assault them directly. As Clark outlined the plan, the main impetus of our attack would be straight north to take Cisterna, continue on to cut Highway Six at Valmontone, carry on farther in a straight line to cut other roadways, and thus bottle up the main body of the German army from the Cassino front, which the British and others were pushing back up the Liri Valley. Thus the greater mass of the enemy in Italy would be eliminated at once, Rome could be taken almost at leisure, and the Germans would have to pour immense forces into northern Italy to hold that valuable industrial region—thus aiding the second front—or give up Italy altogether. The attack would begin at dawn. We would be allowed by the censors to say very little about its aims, of course, but it would be all right, the press officers told us, to say that General Clark was in personal command.

At dawn, I stood on a slight rise in the flat prairie among the tents of a field aid station attached to the First Armored Division. It was chill and cloudy. There were daisies and flowering thistle at our feet, and as we looked at our watches we could hear the meadow larks singing. A veil of fog partly obscured the German hills. At 5:45 the gun flares spurted in clusters from the left, then far to the right, then all around us they sounded, and the earth began a faint trembling. Shells passed over our heads, and our jackets flipped from concussion. The planes began to arrive. Through a break in the clouds we saw their tight formations, the fighter bombers wheeling and darting and disappearing in the curtain dividing the two armies. Around us now sleepy men crawled from their holes in the ditches and grubbed for cigarettes with stiff and dirty hands. They were waiting for the first violated bodies to be passed back into their care. The tanks came clanking up the highway, moving very slowly and well apart, their radio antennae nodding behind like the drooping pennants of armored horse and knight, jolting slowly to take the field. In and out of their ranks courier jeeps scuttled like agitated beetles. The barrage slackened off; it was 6:30, and we knew that up ahead the infantry was moving into battle. It was now irrevocable; the men had been "committed." Now one could only wait and hope; if any prayed he did it unnoticed. We slid down into a ditch and drank coffee with the medics. One man read and reread an old American newspaper that lay on a sandbag. The black headline said "Joan Sobs on Stand," and the story had a Hollywood dateline. Another man studied and restudied a single page in a book on photography. Nothing portentous was said. One remarked: "They can hear this in Rome, maybe." A shell screamed too close overhead, and we slid deeper into the ditch. A lad grinned at us and said: "Are you noivous in the soivice?"

An ambulance jolted off the highway into our camp. The man with the book, who had not yet turned the page, carefully marked his place and got up. Others, with artfully pretended boredom, followed slowly. The soldier lay unmoving on the grass floor of the tent, staring at the roof. Blood was seeping rapidly through the bandage on his head. His helmet lay on the grass beside his litter, the steel bent back from the hole the shell fragment had caused. I bent down to the boy to say: "You're going to be all right." There was only the faintest flicker in his staring eyes; he said nothing. Two men entered, supporting a German prisoner who

411

hopped on one leg. He sat on a chair and smiled as they bandaged his leg, then nodded briskly and hopped out again into the waiting ambulance. Everyone talked now. The man sterilizing instruments began to whistle. Another ambulance bumped into camp. The familiar routine of war and systematized suffering was well under way.

On the exposed tableland one felt unnaturally large and vulnerable, if not expendable. My jeep driver said: "On this road if you smile Jerry can tell if you have brushed your teeth."

I could never quite reason out the reactions of soldiers to danger. Men seemed to behave in two completely opposed ways. If somebody related a dramatic occurrence in which he had figured, part of his audience would react by saying something like this: "Aw hell, that ain't nothing like what happened to me on the Volturno. Why, lemme tell you, we was . . ." Those were the men to whom nothing was quite real except as it involved themselves. The other part of the audience would have a feeling of wonder and awe at the story, even though they themselves had had experiences equally astonishing, if not more so. They were the men for whom anything that happened to themselves was not quite real or valid, who could never come to think of themselves as actors in this performance, as the very persons everybody was writing and thinking about. If such men were stationed in the rear, no matter what their tasks, they thought of those at the front as the ones who were really in danger. Those like them at the front line thought of those out on patrol, and as likely as not when they were out on patrol they thought of those immobilized farther back as the men really in danger. As someone else has pointed out, it was the same with the air force. Men on the ground thought of those in the air as "the ones." Those in the air thought of the wounded, and the wounded thought of the dead.

The offensive was going well; after thirty-six hours we had taken more than a thousand prisoners, and the key town of Cisterna seemed certain to fall. But our attention was now fixed on the progress of the Americans from the southern front who had passed Terracina and were moving

412

rapidly up the coast for an inevitable juncture with the Anzio forces. When they met, the beachhead would no longer be a beachhead, and all the allied armies in Italy would have overland connection. In the late night of May 24 I wrote a broadcast script saying that in a matter of hours there would be only one front in Italy. I fell asleep on the floor while awaiting the broadcast time. I awakened because someone was shaking my shoulder. General Clark's Press Colonel was standing over me, shining his torch in my face. "Eric, old boy, I'm sorry to wake you up. I just wondered if you wouldn't do me a favor and change that script to read: 'There will be one *Fifth Army* front in Italy.' "

The join-up had caught everyone by surprise, and even General Clark, who got there as fast as anyone else, had to re-enact the greeting for the photographers. The Germans had pulled out of the low marshlands along the coast, and the troops from the southern front had simply driven overland without opposition. At a small bridge that was blown, Captain Ben Souza of Honolulu encountered Lieutenant Francis Buckley of Philadelphia strolling up the road. "Where the hell do you think you're going?" the former demanded. Buckley replied: "I've come to make contact with the Anzio forces." Souza said: "Well, you've made it."

The Fifth Army publicity machine promptly issued a statement saying that Anzio was now justified and broadly implying that the commanders responsible for the landing there had been right all along, always knew they were, and that, in fact, the whole operation proved the wisdom of the high command whose subtle methods were frequently misunderstood by grosser minds. If any correspondents sent off the statement I did not observe them.

Military commentators in London and New York were enthusiastically saying that day that "up to a hundred thousand Germans" were trapped in the coastal lowlands by the juncture. I drove that afternoon down to Naples for an overnight stay and it was clear that the Germans had escaped through the hills. We had captured a few dozen. The net result was that the Allies now had a connected front, shipping could be diverted elsewhere, and the advancing southern troops found great stores waiting for

413

them at Anzio. It was all very dramatic, and it seemed like a great victory; in truth, we had merely extricated ourselves from our own stupid mistake, committed when we landed on those beaches in January.

Something happened now to change the whole strategy of the Fifth Army offensive. We learned that the impetus of the drive had been radically switched. Although we had taken Cisterna and were interdicting Highway Six with a constant rain of shells, we were abandoning the officially stated strategy of continuing north to cut the remaining German escape roads, the move designed to bottle up their main forces. We were now to turn west with our spearheads and try to drive to the left and right of the Alban Hills, straight for Rome. What had happened? Was the Eighth Army coming too slowly up the valley to effect a mass capture of the enemy? Or had orders arrived from some higher authority to get Rome without delay? It seemed to some of us that, in view of Alexander's declaration that the aim of the campaign was the destruction of the enemy in Italy, this was a serious mistake. In a broadcast script I wrote: "There is a question whether the two aims [of getting Rome and of destroying the enemy] are compatible or mutually exclusive." The censors cut this line out. But General Clark, who saw each morning all press and radio copy of significance, reacted strongly to my suggestion. Before all the correspondents he referred to "a broadcast" that suggested that we might be able to capture the bulk of the Germans. "That is sheer nonsense," he asserted with vigor, and with his pointer he indicated various side roads to the north by which, he said, the Germans could easily escape. No amateur could prove otherwise. (Almost nothing can be proved or disproved in the realm of strategy and tactics, for "military science" is not a science at all, but only a rude kind of art.) Yet such a capture had been our unquestioned aim. Now the General spoke in a manner that seemed to deny that the idea had ever entered his head. Some of us remained puzzled and skeptical. What had happened that we must now rush straight for Rome?

On Memorial Day the white crosses in what was probably

414

the largest American cemetery in the war at that time were shimmering in the hot morning sun. Detachments from every division assembled with their banners. Thick smoke from our concealment screen drifted across one edge of the field, and one could hear the sound of our guns and the motors of the ambulance planes which lifted away toward Naples every few minutes, bearing the injured. On this day each white cross bore a small American flag fastened above the name plate and the number. A crowd of shirt-sleeved Italian laborers stood by the great mounds of fresh earth where the unfilled graves were ready. The unfilled graves were so neatly aligned, and there were so many of them, waiting. The General spoke of the glorious achievements of the fighting men and the imminent freeing of the first European capital from tyranny. The corps chaplain (the Baptist who kept a neat file of clippings about himself and always had a new story of his exploits for the reporters) announced over the loud speaker that the men who lay dead before us had died in the cause of "true religion." When orators and formations had marched away, I came upon six new bodies stretched in the sun behind the canvas curtains at the field's edge. The burial sergeant was a West Virginia schoolteacher who begged me not to write a story about what he was doing in the war. One of his assistants said: "You get used to it after a while." The sergeant answered: "That isn't true—I never get used to it." He looked at the bodies and went on: "With a thousand, it would be just a problem of sanitation. With six, it seems like a tragedy."

One saw so many dead each day, so many bleeding bodies. I realized that I was becoming a little obsessed with the tragedy of these youngsters, tending to write about death more and more. Sometimes in the long, lovely evenings when we sat by the sea, the old feelings about the death of youth which I had experienced as a college boy began to steal back, unnerving and frightening me. It would not do; one had to shake off these moods. But it was becoming harder and harder to escape them. I realized now with a start that the sight of a dead German boy did not affect me, while the sight of a dead American did. Did this reaction **come from the deep-seated national feelings which go back**

415

to childhood, or was it due to simple propinquity? I was unsure.

Even to noncombatants in the field like myself the Germans were not quite real any more as human beings, such is the mental derangement of war. Their bodies did not affect me. But when a colleague showed me some letters, written in a girlish scrawl, which he had taken from a dead German boy, I was moved. I saved the letters, which in part went as follows:

Vienna, April 14. Dear Robert: First of all heartiest greetings. Since I don't hear from you I write you a few lines. I hope they will not be unwelcome. I sent an Easter card to your grandmother, and when she answered she enclosed your address with the hint that I should write to you. And now that I have time, I write, as you see. How do you like the army? I would like to see you as a soldier. How are your girls? Do they write to you often? I want to close now with the heartiest regards. Best regards from Mother.—Feli.

The letters became bolder, more intimate:

Vienna, May 1. Dear Robert: I received your dear letter on the 22nd of last month with great joy. . . . I'm enclosing some writing paper to make sure that you write me more. Maybe I'll take a ride to your grandmother this week. Say, dear Robert, what do you mean by telling me that she is not the only one who loves me? I can't imagine who has the courage to love me. I'm sorry that the army doesn't agree with you. . . . I feel sorry for the poor girl you broke off with. Don't you think she feels hurt? Well, what do I care? . . . I close for today with heartiest regards.—Your Feli.

Vienna, May 7. Dearest Robert: . . . Your grandmother worries very much about you. Please write cheerful letters to her. She worries very much about you and more so when you write her that the going is

416

bad.—Your Feli.
P.S. A stolen kiss.

The attack toward Rome slowed to a stop, embarrassing
for the generals and deadly for the fighting men. It was the
bitter situation so familiar in the Italian campaign: the
enemy was holding the high ground—in this case the Alban
Hills, the last breastworks defending Rome. Clark had sent
the First Armored across the flat ground between the hills
and the sea. Every vehicle was easily spotted in the enemy's
gun sights and within ten minutes we lost twenty-five tanks.
The other divisions could get nowhere in the vineyards,
which were dominated by the hill city of Velletri, key to the
German defense. Hitherto the summer campaign had been
a straightaway, bludgeoning business of hammering frontally with our great superior weight of shells and bombs. I,
at least, had never seen anything subtle or unorthodox attempted at any time. Unorthodox ideas are generally
frowned upon in military commands, and, to be sure, they
are usually not worth the risk when one has overwhelming
superiority in everything. But the proposal of Major General
Fred Walker of the Thirty-sixth Division was accepted. He
drew two regiments from in front of Velletri, circled them
around to the right in darkness, and started them climbing
the two-thousand-foot height *behind* Velletri. It was a gamble. If the Germans could close their lines again, these men
would be lost. If not, the final defenses of the Eternal City
were breached.

With that brave and tender-hearted photographer-writer,
Carl Mydans of *Life,* I set out to witness this seemingly impossible feat. By noon we had found the advance C.P. of
the division, which now consisted of several bearded officers
squatting under a railroad trestle studying a map. General
Walker gave me a curt nod and continued pacing back and
forth under the trestle. He was a solemn, self-contained
man, and this was the first time I had ever observed him in
a state of perturbation. A good friend, Lieutenant Colonel
Hal Reese, smiled benignly at me as he drew a map with
his cane in the dirt to indicate the route we would have to

417

follow in order to mount the hill—"if you get past the snipers." I had bunked with Reese in the LST that brought his division to the beach.

A husky young major with a full pack hitchhiked a ride with us. He was John Collings of Detroit, who had just come from the Pacific and was seeking his new battalion, somewhere up the mountain. We left the highway, bumped across the rail tracks, and thumped our tortuous way up a newly cut trail among cornstalks and vineyards. Only a jeep could do this, but there were sharp descents and sudden upthrusts where we thought the jeep would go over on its back. It was very silent. The sun filtered down through the thick trees. A lone sentry stepped out. "Watch for the snipers, sir," he said to Collings. Freddie looked back from the steering wheel, a question on his face. He had orders, as did all the press drivers, to go only as far as he himself considered safe, regardless of what the correspondent passengers requested. With a casual gesture that somehow held the impact of drama, Collings flipped out his pistol, held it cocked in his hand, and, keeping his eyes steadily upon the trees ahead, remarked: "Go ahead, driver. Snipers aren't so bad." A machine gun began to sound near by, like corn popping in a deep kettle. The jeep trudged over ruts and roots, and a party of approaching peasant women carrying great water bottles through which the sun's rays filtered, squeezed against the trees to let us pass. They were one of the invariable signs of fighting just ahead.

We emerged again upon the highway. Three soldiers rested in a ditch. "You're visible to the enemy next couple hundred yards," they told us. Implied was: "We are alive by the grace of God; you may die in the next few minutes." The tone was the tone of men saying that it looked like rain. This is the way it was, nearly always, among men in the regions of death. The jeep darted the next stretch and was halted by a soldier who seemed no more than a boy in his teens, the artless, helpless type which ought never to be taken into any army. His eyes were unnaturally large, and his hands were twisting a towel, rapidly, senselessly. "Do you know where the aid station is, sir?" he asked through trembling lips. We thought it was just ahead. "Are you hit?"

"No, sir, it's my nerves, I guess." We left him. Though he was a casualty, as surely as any man with a bullet in his head, he could be condemned for desertion.

Another quarter-mile and we could go no farther on the highway. Velletri was invisible, but lay only another thousand yards to the west. Machine guns were sounding again, and it was certain death to proceed. Here now was the cut-off, a narrow "jeepable" trail, mounting sharply between high banks. Freddie would have continued with us, but he had nothing to gain by getting the "story," and it was foolish to risk another man. He stayed at this point with the jeep, which was a mistake. We began hiking upward in the hot sun; we rounded a bend and there were *tanks* chugging up, their massive breadth plugging the whole road cut, scraping down dirt and stones from the banks. Scrambling around the tanks, we found the ubiquitous bulldozer, simply carving the trail into a road, roaring and rearing its ponderous way at a forty-degree angle upward. This was all madly impossible, and yet it was being done.

The men themselves, bearded, silent with fatigue, swung their shovels through the loose dirt and pitched it over the banks. A rifle snapped very close at hand, and we heard the sigh of the bullet this time. A trained soldier is generally more afraid of snipers than of artillery; I found I had the reverse reaction. Heavy shell fire was unnerving to me after a while, and I could hardly bear the sense of helplessness and exposure if it were coming in while I was in a vehicle. Rifle fire, though it might be directed right at me, left me completely calm; and it was reassuring to be standing on my own feet, able to take cover by a simple muscular reflex. Perhaps most amateurs are this way; they react to noise and concussion rather than to the missiles themselves.

A couple more bullets whistled overhead and a party of shovelers stood upright. "Oh-oh," one said. Mechanically, as though they had done it a thousand times, two of them let their shovels fall, slipped their carbines from their backs, and crawled over the bank, disappearing in the direction of the sniper. Now a jeep with the Red Cross marking tilted precariously down the trail. Strapped across the hood was a stretcher with a man upon it. His head was almost covered with bandages, only the eyes, nose, and lips exposed. The lips held a cigarette. When Carl pointed his camera, the boy turned his head toward the lens and, in an unforgettable voice tinged with irony, asked: "Do you want me to *smile?*"

We found ourselves with a rifle company, men I had last visited in the fields before Velletri. They had detrucked in the night, then made a ten-mile hike around Velletri and gone straight up the hill, carrying their heavy mortar shells in their bare hands, clutching them to their stomachs. The weighty metal boxes of rifle ammunition they had strapped to their backs, and they had climbed all night, silently, like Indians, forbidden by Walker to have a cartridge in the chamber of their rifles. He would permit no firing, to avoid alerting the Germans. Only a grenade could be used, if absolutely necessary, for the Germans would easily mistake that for a mortar shell and remain ignorant of its origin. (The Germans were ignorant enough—later we learned that they believed that two companies, not two regiments, had made the infiltration.)

In a sun-speckled grove the men lay sprawled on their backs, oblivious to the traffic's dust or the spasmodic machine-gun fire so close at hand, catching any moment that fortune provided for precious sleep. A soldier walked past, going downhill. He held up his hand to show bandages covering what remained of his thumb. "How's that for a cheap Purple Heart?" he said. No one cared for the medal; what he was saying was: "I'll never have to fight, sleep in mud, and be frightened again." One witness muttered: "He's got the war made." "Lucky bastard," said another. Battalion headquarters was a farmhouse. Inside, three young officers sat at ease around the kitchen table while the farm wife served them wine. One of the men had flown from Cairo with me. We drank and discussed Cairo cafés, like two casual acquaintances in a smoking car. Outside the door lay a dead German sniper wearing American army boots. A Texas lieutenant jerked his thumb toward the body. "That guy shot two of our medics. He made us sore." The German had violated the "rules of war"—or rather, he had outraged his youthful opponents. When they captured him, they in-

420

structed him to turn and run for it. He ran and fell with thirteen tommy-gun bullets in his square body.

We debated whether to try to reach the summit. The way seemed clear, but it was growing late, and we must reach Anzio before dark. In any case, the mountain position was safely established; everything was in order. We said good-bye to Collings and started down. (Two months later Mydans met Collings in Rome and learned that the major had pulled away from the farmhouse in a jeep with four other men. They proceeded upwards a quarter-mile and received a burst of German machine-gun fire. Collings alone survived.)

On the highway, we found Freddie crouched in the ditch, clutching his rifle. Machine-gun bullets had just been whispering around his ears. We wrenched the jeep around and departed at full speed, hanging to our helmets.

In the night the Germans tried a counterattack and failed. Our men clung to the heights and fired remorselessly upon the desperate enemy within Velletri. In the morning General Walker, his tanks, and his men rushed the town, entering upon the highway. Lieutenant Colonel Hal Reese insisted upon walking ahead of the tanks; a shell burst killed him at once. When he was informed, Walker averted his face and said: "I asked him not to go ahead like that. I asked him not to." Why did Reese, who was not a professional soldier, who had everything to live for, who understood prudent behavior, act in this rash manner? I do not know. I do not know what lay behind his serene and gentlemanly countenance. But in his notebook they found that he had written: "I got through the last war all right, but I will not survive this one." It is my impression of men who have lost many comrades and who feel no escape for themselves, that they not only take risks in a fatalistic manner—they welcome them. They seek death.

Rome must now fall. Generals Alexander and Clark would soon receive the key to the city, but surely it was General Walker who turned the key. From him they were really receiving it.

Perhaps it is true that we love best those to whom we

give and dislike those who give to us. We were never told the reason, but a few weeks later General Walker, whose love for his division was returned in his men's respect for him, who was at the height of his brilliant combat career, was relieved of his command and sent back to the States.

In the morning again we drove around the eastern slopes of the lovely green hills, past mutilated Valmontone (another old city we had shot up to no purpose in our reckless way, for the bridges and skirting roadway were all that we required), and as we progressed it began to dawn upon us that the German defenses were falling apart so fast that we would be into Rome within hours. The air was charged with excitement, with savage triumph and obscene defeat. German vehicles were smouldering at every bend of the road, and dead Germans lay sprawled beside them, their faces thickening with the dust sprayed over them by the ceaseless wheels that passed within inches of the mortifying flesh. Shells were screaming over in both directions, but in the general frenzy not even the civilians paid them much notice. By wrecked gasoline stations, in the front yards of decapitated homes, flushed Americans were shoving newly taken prisoners into line, jerking out the contents of their pockets and jabbing those who hesitated with the butt ends of their rifles. A child was vigorously kicking a dead German officer, until a young woman shoved the child aside and dragged off the man's boots. Infantry of the Third Division were arriving in trucks, and their general, "Iron Mike" O'Daniel, jumped from his jeep before it had stopped and in stentorian voice shouted the orders for their detrucking and deployment. One of our tank destroyers ahead burst into flames, and shells began falling nearer. American officers, throwing themselves down and clutching their helmets, shouted questions at one another about how the race for Rome was progressing. While Mydans remained with his camera—he spent a frightening night under bombs—I turned back to Anzio, impelled by the realization that things were now moving faster than anyone had expected and that somehow the press installation, the censors, and the radio transmitters must be uprooted at once and taken to the front lines, or the story of the fall, the whole impact of the "psychological and political victory" that Rome was to be, would surely be delayed and half ruined. In the wrecked villages to the immediate rear, medical aides were pulling our wounded from their ambulances, shabby civilians were gathering in the rubble-strewn public squares, all looking toward the capital city, and standing beside their ruined parents the children, in their innocence of tragedy and death, were clapping their small and grimy hands as we passed them by.

I was black with a thick covering of grime and dust when I reached the press villa on the now silent beach. I was exhausted by the hectic journey and by sheer nervous excitement, and my hands were trembling when I tried to eat at the mess. It appeared that no orders whatsoever had been given for uprooting the transmitters—indeed nobody there seemed quite aware of what was happening; and I fear that I transgressed the limits of dignity in urging immediate action. But nothing could move until morning. At midnight I did my last broadcast from Anzio and was up again with the others before dawn. Nearly all the other correspondents had vanished in the night toward the front, and it appeared that I would have to guide the slow caravan with Vaughn Thomas of the BBC, since no others knew the detours. We moved with agonizing slowness, and I was certain that I would miss the entry into the city. Near Valmontone the transmitter van behind us hesitated at a crossroads, and I ran back a couple of hundred yards to direct them. Returning to the jeep was one of the most horrible experiences of my life. Perhaps it was that the breeze shifted or died; I do not know. But I walked into a veritable lake of stench. There was not a body in sight; the bodies must have been dragged into the brush just off the road, but the hot sun was directly on them. I had smelled the sharp, sweet, gaseous odor of death before, but nothing like this. It inflamed the nostrils, and I could even taste it in my mouth. Each breath drew it in deeply. I began to choke, and water streamed from my eyes. I started to run blindly up the road, which made me breathe more heavily. All my insides were convulsed, and I felt vomit in my throat. I was almost in a

423

fainting condition when I reached the jeep, and I stayed sick for hours afterwards. The sight of death is nothing like its smell.

The army had not yet crossed the city limits; German antitank guns were interdicting the highway, delaying us, while the enemy hurriedly pushed the bulk of his troops out of Rome by the northern gates. A few hundred yards from the city limits we turned off into a group of workers' apartment buildings, while an army captain named Wickham, who was something of a technical genius, threw up the antennae in an open field. It was Sunday noon. Rome was just ahead, yet all the city proper was obscured in haze and smoke. Guns and shells sounded loudly near us, and from somewhere in the city came the dull sound of explosions— evidence, we thought, that the Germans were blowing the bridges on the Tiber. We hiked up the road and crouched beside cement ramparts along the trolley line, as far as one could go. There was a curious feeling in the air: a combined spirit of battle and of holiday. Reporters sat typing with their machines balanced on their knees. A dying German lay groaning in the hot sun on a cement driveway by a villa while a group of civilians silently watched him. An old man held a cup of water to his lips with one hand and stroked his hair with the other. People hung out of every window and gathered before every gate. The girls and children tossed flowers at the two lines of slowly walking American soldiers, and bouquets were now displayed on the turrets of our tanks.

Rome was falling, and all the world was waiting and watching. It was a day of climax and portent, a day for history. I sat before the microphone at a portable table while shells passed over and the concussion whipped my papers. I could say nothing of consequence. I could only say that Rome was falling and that we were all tired and happy. In a thousand editorial columns, on a thousand public platforms, men far from the scene would utter the big thoughts about this. Here, none among us seemed to have anything to say.

(Up the highway a short distance, a conversation was
424

going on, which was not then publicly recorded, but which also, perhaps, merits a footnote in the history of the war and of the personalities who directed it. Brigadier General Robert Frederick, the young and capable commander of the special "commando" regiment of Americans and Canadians, was watching the progress of his men who led the assault. A jeep drew up, and Major General Keyes, corps commander, descended. "General Frederick," he asked, "what's holding you up here?" Frederick replied: "The Germans, sir." Keyes then asked: "How long will it take you to get across the city limits?" Frederick answered: "The rest of the day. There are a couple of SP guns up there." "That will not do. General Clark must be across the city limits by four o'clock." Frederick asked: "Why?" The corps commander answered: "Because he has to have a photograph taken." Frederick looked at Keyes steadily for a long moment and said: "Tell the General to give me an hour." The guns were silenced, the General and his faithful photographer arrived, and the pictures were taken of the conqueror within his conquered city.)

Early in the morning the big entry by troops and correspondents was made. Many great cities were liberated after Rome, and the spectacle was nearly always the same. But to me this entry was a new thing, and I found myself having to hold tight to my emotions. Everyone was out on the street, thousands upon thousands from the outlying areas walking toward the center of the city. A vast, murmurous sound of human voices flooded everywhere and rose in joyous crescendo at every large avenue we crossed. There was a gladness in all eyes, and now and then, as when a German sniper in his green-daubed cape was marched out of the Colosseum, remembrance of hate contorted the faces, even the young children uttered savage cries, and the fists that had held bundles of flowers were doubled in anger. The Piazza di Venezia was jammed with a monstrous crowd, and our jeep proceeded at a snail's pace, while flowers rained upon our heads, men grabbed and kissed our hands, old women burst into tears, and girls and boys wanted to climb up beside us. One tried to remember that they had been our recent enemy, that they were happy because the war was over for them as much as because we had driven out the Germans, that noncombatants such as I had no right to this adulation. But one tried in vain. I felt wonderfully good, generous, and important. I was a representative of strength, decency, and success, and it was impossible at this moment to recollect that Germans or Fascists had also once received this same outpouring of gratitude.

In the *Stampa Estera* building the correspondents were typing madly, shouting for censors, and demanding to know how the copy was to be transmitted to London and New York. Everything was in confusion. All the elaborate army plans for joint broadcasts to the world, to give dramatic effect to the great "psychological victory," had apparently broken down. The press reporters were in a frenzied state of fury. Then the chief public relations officer burst into the room to announce that General Clark would hold a press conference at the Campidoglio building immediately.

The General was lounging against the balustrade that overlooked the square when we hurried up the outside stair-way. There was a jam of people around him, and already the news-reel men were grinding away, photographing the lean, smiling victor against the appropriate background of the great city spread out below. General Truscott arrived, then General Keyes. They worked their way to Clark's side and regarded the mob of reporters and photographers with a questioning look in their eyes. General Juin of the French Corps hastened up the steps and also looked at us with an expression of bewilderment. Clark shook hands with them and in a modest drawl said to us: "Well, gentlemen, I didn't really expect to have a press conference here—I just called a little meeting with my corps commanders to discuss the situation. However, I'll be glad to answer your questions. This is a great day for the Fifth Army." That was the immortal remark of Rome's modern-day conqueror. It was not, apparently, a great day for the world, for the Allies, for all the suffering people who had desperately looked toward the time of peace. It was a great day for the Fifth Army. (Men of the Eighth Army, whose sector did not happen to include Rome but without whose efforts this day

could not have occurred, did not soon forget the remark.)
Then Clark spread a map on the balustrade, and with the
whole mob pressing close proceeded to point out something
or other to his commanders. The cameras ground, the corps
commanders, red with embarrassment, looked back and
forth from us to the map. We pushed down the steps.

Casting the Net

Two huge Arctic convoys with supplies for the Russians were scheduled to be sent on the Murmansk run in November and December, 1943; they would be escorted by strong units of the British Navy. Since the previous May, when it was necessary to draw off Allied naval strength for the operations in the Mediterranean, none had been sent by the Northern route. Now the pressure was building up from the Russians to renew the convoys to Murmansk.

The Germans, who had suffered defeats on the Russian front, were determined to prevent the convoys from making their delivery; they knew from past experience that the arms and supplies delivered by the Allies to the Russians immediately stiffened their resistance to German attacks.

The terrible toll of convoys by the German U-boats had been effectively reduced in 1943 but any British convoy traveling north still must be on constant guard against enemy submarines, as well as the danger of a hit-and-run raid from the German 1st Battle Group which lay at anchor in the Alta Fjord of northern Norway. This group was comprised of the battle cruiser *Scharnhorst* and five destroyers. The real killer in the Group was the *Scharnhorst*; if she could once get into a merchant ship convoy, with her nine 11-inch guns, her secondary complement of twelve 5.9 inch guns and fourteen 4.1's, she could do great damage. She was also able to outrun any heavy British naval ship because of her speed.

The first convoy in November got through safely. But the December convoy was spotted by German air reconnaissance. Quickly, the German Naval High Command issued orders for 1st Battle Group to sail on Christmas Day and make contact as soon as possible. The weather conditions could hardly have been worse—for all ships at sea in northern waters. "A southwesterly gale was blowing in the opera-

428

tional area. A heavy sea had come up while dense snow squalls seriously reduced visibility. The term 'heavy sea' as used by seamen meant waves up to thirty feet high. They rolled up in long roaring swells, dark, foam-flecked, white crested. The gale tore sheets of spray from the crests and shot them flat across the water. The eddying snow was thicker and heavier than the men had ever known it before, either in the North Sea or the North Atlantic, and it was cold as the icy breath of the Pole itself.

"The Arctic convoys sailed round the most northerly end of Norway to Murmansk. The farther north they kept, the safer they were from attack, but their voyage took proportionately longer and this was at a time when hours could be decisive. Furthermore, the sea to the north became increasingly rougher. The wind which blew in directly from the Pole churned up mountainous seas, while visibility was obliterated in furious flurries of snow. The dark sky precluded light and it was, literally, impossible to see one's own hand. Only occasionally would the green-yellow or red-violet Northern Lights cast an unsteady, erratic gleam. At noon the day would turn a pale grey for about two hours, although the sun never rose above the horizon. The cold was almost unbearable. Watchkeepers on warships and freighters shivered in spite of sheepskin clothing and many layers of woollens. Depth charges froze fast to the decks, gun-sights and breeches became encrusted with ice, and the lubricants on the munition-hoists froze hard. A warship which failed to take special precautions to safeguard the lives of her crew and keep her armament free of ice, could not hope to survive an action in these waters." *

The British convoy escort was made up of fourteen destroyers and three cruisers. To the southwest of the convoy was the battleship *Duke of York*, the cruiser *Jamaica* and four destroyers; this unit was attached almost solely for the purpose of doing battle with the *Scharnhorst* should she sally out after the convoy.

*From *Holocaust at Sea*, pp. 48-49 and 72-73.

SINKING OF THE SCHARNHORST*

by Fritz-Otto Busch

During the night of December 25–26 the *Scharnhorst* proceeded on her sortie with the five escorting destroyers. Set on a northerly course, blacked-out, with war-watches closed up at action stations, the battleship rolled on before the south-westerly gale. Slowly the Radar beams scanned the darkness, while look-outs on the bridges, control positions, searchlights, and guns scrutinized their allotted sectors.

Sailing before the wind with the gently swaying motion and rhythmical pitching characteristic of the long ship, the *Scharnhorst* was spared the worst effects of the gale blowing from astern. But snow squalls impeded visibility, the sky was as dark as the sea, and the escorting destroyers were hardly discernible. From time to time a breaker reared up before the battleship, stood for seconds in a column of pale foam, then collapsed over the bows, and ebbed away before the breakwater in gurgling eddies. Smaller breakers, churned up to left and right by the great curving bows, disintegrated in white pennants. The night was icy cold. Cold, too, were the lashes of salty spray which flung themselves across the armour of the forward triple turrets and whipped up to the bridge.

Little was to be heard above the roar of the sea and the intermittent howling of the gale. Here, a water-tight door would bang; there, the clatter of heavy boots on wooden gratings could be heard as one of the watches on the bridge stamped to keep his feet warm. The soft regular hum of the electrical generating plant spread its soothing sound

*Condensed from several chapters of *Holocaust at Sea.*

through the stillness of the control positions and turrets. Otherwise there was silence. Every man was tense with expectancy. Any moment the alarm might sound and the ship that was gliding so smoothly ahead would be suddenly transformed, as if ignited, into a volcano belching fire.

During the whole of December 26, Acting Chief Petty Officer Willi Gödde stood at his port forward searchlight-control column on look-out duty. These installations, known to the ratings, not quite correctly, as "director columns," were fitted on either side of the bridge, somewhat abaft the armoured fire-control position, and were used for look-out duty because of their outstanding optical performance. P.O. Gödde, a quiet, serious type of man with religious leanings, could not be relieved all day because the Petty Officer who usually took over from him, a trainer in "B" turret, was away on leave.

Gödde was wearing his telephone apparatus slung round his neck and so was in constant communication with the ship's command. He was able to listen to everything that was discussed at the control position and follow the entire sequence of events.

Suddenly, at 0920 hours, huge columns of water, nine feet in diameter, spurted up out of the darkness about 500 yards abeam of the control column. Phantom-like in their pale unreality, they were clearly visible through the drifting snow.

"Shell splashes," darted through the P.O.'s mind "Eight-inch shells at least." He turned the speaking-switch of his telephone . . .

And then everything happened at once.

The forward Radar reported the enemy. Alarm bells rang. Gödde heard a confusion of voices; directors on all stations picking up the target; orders, commands. Then the barrels of the after "C" turret began to thunder.

An action had started, but not against the convoy and its cargo ships; warships had opened fire on the *Scharnhorst*.

A far-off angry rumbling snarled across the sea and the night was lit with flashes of fire. On the port quarter, on a bearing of 245°, orange-red flames burst out of the darkness. Gödde could see quite clearly the snowflakes dancing in the fiery light, and shortly after the German guns had fired their second salvo, he heard the answering roar of the enemy's guns. Then he was momentarily dazzled by the long sheets of flame which burst from the *Scharnhorst's* own armament, while the ship was wrapped in a cloud of warm acrid fumes. Gödde pressed his eyes hard against the rubber-cushioned lenses of his apparatus, but in vain; he could see no more than the enemy's gunflashes; of the ship that was firing he could see nothing. Perhaps there were two ships, perhaps three—he could not tell. But one thing was certain: the ship that was hidden there, sending over salvo after salvo, must be a heavy cruiser with 8-inch armament.

Starshell was also being fired, obviously from another ship, to allow the heavy cruiser to observe the fall of shot around her target, the *Scharnhorst*.

The action lasted fifteen minutes, that is until 0940 hours. It was impossible to say whether any hits had been scored on the enemy. Shortly after opening fire, the *Scharnhorst* altered course to 150°, almost a complete turn round, and increased her speed to 30 knots. Her task was to annihilate the convoy. To engage in battle with enemy cruisers that were certainly armed with torpedoes, in the pitch darkness—dawn would not begin to break until 11 a.m.—was certainly no part of her duty. The German Commander-in-Chief could now assume that the cruisers were standing to the southward of the convoy, and that he would certainly have come upon the convoy itself had not the cruisers fallen upon the *Scharnhorst* like angry watch-dogs. The convoy could not be far off now; it must be steaming somewhere to the north of the cruiser line, and as the speed of the *Scharnhorst* was thought to be superior to that of her opponents, she could easily disengage, try to work round the cruisers and attack the convoy from a different direction.

The *Scharnhorst* did not, however, emerge from this

encounter unscathed. A report reached the forward fire-control position from the port III 5.9 gun:

"Hit between port III gun and torpedo-tubes. Shell has not exploded."

Ordinary Seaman First Class Sträter serving in the IV 5.9 turret heard later that this shell had penetrated the upper deck, and come to rest in compartment IX, the office of the technical P.O.s in the forward crew space of the 4th Division. The gun crew had only just been apprised of this when the Signals-Transmitter turned the talking-switch of his telephone and raised his hand:

"Attention! The foretop Radar is out of action. A direct hit in the foretop. Casualties among the A.A. crew."

As a result of the same hit, splinters were falling, fortunately, without causing further damage, on to the small open platform where P.O. Gödde stood at his control column. Through his earphones he, too, heard the reports of the two hits. He learned also that fire had broken out on the lower deck when the unexploded shell had come through, but that it was quickly got under control.

While the *Scharnhorst* was disengaging, the Captain ordered a smoke screen, and as the ship sped away at 30 knots great clouds of dense white smoke formed a solid wall behind her. Then the loudspeaker was heard again:

"Lull in action. We are trying, once more, to get at the convoy, the destroyers from the south, we in the *Scharnhorst* from the north."

The sequence of events during the first encounter between the *Scharnhorst* and the cruisers of Force 1 were, from the British point of view, as follows:

At 0840 hours the Radar in the *Belfast*, Admiral Burnett's flagship, picked up the *Scharnhorst* at a range of 35,000 yards. At this time Force 1 (10th Cruiser Squadron) was heading for the convoy which was still 48 miles distant to the north. The *Scharnhorst* was at this time 36 miles away from the convoy. From 0900 to 0930 hours the British Radar recorded a second echo. It was assumed that this was either one of the merchant ships in the convoy or possibly an enemy destroyer seeking to approach the convoy. As the cruisers intended to attack the *Scharnhorst*, the echo was ignored as being of only secondary importance. Vice-Admiral Burnett, therefore, kept course in the direction of the German battleship. At 0924 hours the *Belfast* opened fire with starshell, and five minutes later Force 1 was ordered to engage with main armament. The *Norfolk*, the only cruiser with 8-inch guns, opened fire with her four twin-turrets at a range of 9800 yards. She continued firing until 0940 hours. Upon firing the second and third salvoes, the British observed that the *Scharnhorst* had been hit. The *Belfast* and *Scheffield* did not participate in the direct firing.

When the *Scharnhorst* retreated and the range opened, the *Norfolk* ceased firing and the squadron pursued the German battleship to the southward. When, at 0955, the *Scharnhorst* turned on to a northeasterly course, the Admiral appreciated at once that she was trying to work round to the northward of the convoy and attack again. As the *Scharnhorst's* speed was estimated at 30 knots and Force 1 could steam at a maximum speed of only 24 knots in the prevailing gale and sea, Admiral Burnett decided to take a short cut and interpose his force between the convoy and the *Scharnhorst*. He knew that the cruisers' Radar could sight and report the enemy in good time. He had the cruisers alter course accordingly so that at 1020 hours contact with the *Scharnhorst* was lost. The last Radar echo was obtained from the *Scharnhorst* at 36,000 yards when she was steering to the north-east.

The *Scharnhorst*, concealed by her smoke-screen, had disappeared on a southerly course. As contact with the British cruisers appeared to have been broken, Rear-Admiral Bey gradually altered course to the northward. His plan of action had been well considered. The battleship's superior speed should allow her to turn the enemy's flank and take him completely by surprise. The one thing which the Commander-in-Chief and his Staff had not reckoned with was the great range and—as was later explicitly acknowledged by the British Commander-in-Chief in his despatch—the outstanding performance of the British "Rotterdam apparatus."*

The black Arctic night at last yielded to a faint grey dawn. Gale, sea and snow squalls increased. The *Scharnhorst* men remained closed up to action stations, the Commander-in-Chief was on the bridge. With the collar of his heavy sheepskin coat turned up and the big Zeiss nightglasses hanging on their leather slings round his neck, Rear-Admiral Bey gazed into the dancing snow flurries. Next to him stood the Captain, hands encased in fur-lined gloves and thrust deep into his pockets. Korvettenkapitän Bredenbreuker, the Gunnery Commander, in company with his Chief Signals-Transmitter, stepped from his control position on to the bridge. In such thick weather more could be seen from outside than through the lenses of the directors and gunsights. The Gunnery Signals-Transmitter, an able seaman of long service, leaned nonchalantly against the armoured walls of the control position. He had put on his head-phones and the telephone cable coiled like a thin black snake at his feet. With the sea on her quarter, the ship rolled with a smooth and gentle rhythm. Shortly after 1100 hours, the Navigating Officer appeared on the bridge with a wireless message. It was now sufficiently light for him, immediately, to recognize the Captain's broad-shouldered figure and he made his way straight to him:

"Report from a reconnaissance aircraft, Sir."

Captain Hintze freed his right hand from his pocket and took the wireless message.

"Splendid. It's remarkable how these chaps manage to keep it up in this foul weather!"

He read the text, frowned and turned to the Commander-in-Chief:

"Not too pleasant, Herr Admiral. But it need not worry us for the time being."

The Admiral took the message form. The report was disquieting. Five units had been sighted far to the north-westward of North Cape, approximately 150 miles to the

*Radar.

westward of the *Scharnhorst*. The Commander-in-Chief looked at the Captain with half-closed eyes:

"We'd better make sure exactly where it is. Come along."

They went down to the chart-house together. The Navigating Officer, Korvettenkapitän Lanz, had already plotted the position on the chart. He indicated it with his pencil:

"Here, Herr Admiral."

Rear-Admiral Bey considered for a while:

"In my opinion," he said, "it can only be an enemy Battle Group. One or more heavy units with the usual screen. Or just one heavy unit."

The Admiral took a packet of cigarettes from his coat pocket and offered it to the Captain, while Chief-Quarter-master Jürgens—who had been keeping respectfully in the background—stepped forward to offer them a light. Inhaling deeply, the Admiral thanked him and offered the tall, fair Friesian a cigarette. Then, in company with the Captain, he left the chart-house and returned aloft. Back on the bridge, he said:

"The look-out, Hintze, must be first-class. Everything depends on it. Do impress that again on the Gunnery Commander."

In the *Scharnhorst*, between 1100 and 1130 hours, P.O. Gödde, at the port forward searchlight control column, heard the voice of his Captain. Captain Hintze did not, on this occasion, use the loudspeaker system, but spoke, instead, on the artillery telephone:

"From the Captain to all stations: Situation Report. This morning as expected, we ran into the forces covering the convoy—three cruisers of the 'town class' type. We have altered course and are now trying to get at the convoy from the other side, that is from the north. We have shaken off the cruisers. An important reconnaissance report has just come in from the Luftwaffe. A British heavy battle group has been sighted 150 miles to the westward; I repeat 150 miles to the westward. That is to say, well out of our way. We are forging on towards the convoy. End of announcement!"

Gödde nodded. He was satisfied. It was very satisfactory,

436

he thought, how the Captain always took the men into his confidence, and kept them informed of the situation. He knew from comrades serving in other ships that this was not always the case.

About two hours after the first engagement of that day, Gödde heard contact with the enemy again reported by the after Radar. Soon the alarm bells were sounding their shrill warning through all decks.

Gödde applied himself to his apparatus with redoubled concentration; carefully he scanned the way ahead.

At 1221 hours Gödde thought he saw a patch of darkness against the midday twilight on the port and starboard bows. Soon afterwards, this became definite shadows. Turning the wheel of his director apparatus with his right hand, he felt for the talking-switch with his left and pushed it over:

"Port and starboard ahead three shadows!"

At the same time Gödde was able to hear how similar reports were coming in at the control position from other stations. As the initial orders went out to the heavy guns, and the directors in the control tower picked up the target, flashes of fire came from the distant shadowy forms, the silhouettes of which were gradually sharpening against the twilight. Once, twice, three times gun flashes broke from the dark shadows that were the enemy ships. Dull explosions above his own ship, and the sudden appearance of a yellow glare around him, caused Gödde to take his eyes off the targets and look upwards. Three or four dazzling yellow-white suns hovered phantom-like above the *Scharnhorst*, their falling rays starkly illuminating her superstructure and decks. The outlines of the triple turrets and barrels, the bridges and tower roofs rose sharply delineated out of the whirling snow.

"Starshell!" The thought was mechanical, objective. Gödde again glued his eyes to the sights of his apparatus. Great splashes raised steep plumes from the sea close to the ship, and at the same moment, the two forward 11-inch triple turrets of the *Scharnhorst* opened fire against the enemy ship lying to starboard. The second encounter of December 26 had begun.

437

Standing in the open on the bridge, Rear Admiral Bey observed the enemy's fire, while the Captain and Gunnery Commander rushed to their stations in the control position immediately the sighting of British forces was reported. The Admiral then stepped to the port armoured bulkhead of the control position which was still open and shouted his order to the Captain:

"Turn to port; we must get out of this!"

"*Jawohl*, Herr Admiral! Hard a-port! All engines full speed ahead! New course: 135°. To Gunnery Commander: Ship is turning hard a-port."

Quickly increasing her speed, the *Scharnhorst* hauled round on to her easterly course, heeling over heavily to starboard while the fire-control directors of the main and secondary armament held steadily on to their target. In the turrets, the gunners followed the pointers to offset the ship's turning. Now, the after "C" turret on the quarter-deck could also pick up the target and add the golden-red flames of its triple barrels to the second and third salvoes. Kapitänleutnant Wieting, the Second Gunnery Officer, added the fire of the two forward 5.9-inch twin turrets for as long as they could still reach the target.

P.O. Gödde observed that after the first three or four salvoes from the *Scharnhorst* fire broke out in one of the three British cruisers—the outlines of which were now clearly visible—roughly abreast of her after funnel. Another cruiser was evidently also well ablaze at bows and stern and was giving off a great deal of smoke. Between two salvoes Korvettenkapitän Bredenbreuker announced:

"To all stations: Heavy explosions with the enemy."

Then the heavy guns fired their next salvo. Ahead and astern of the British cruisers the splashes of the 11-inch shells rose mast-high from the sea, stood erect for several seconds, like giant fountains, and then broke. Broad circles of foam formed in their place and swung up and down with the rhythm of the waves. Gödde noted to his satisfaction that the salvoes which the Gunnery Commander was ordering in quick succession were straddling the enemy almost in every instance. The *Scharnhorst* kept turning round on to her easterly course and the British cruisers were dropping more and more astern and to port. Once more Gödde, who was keeping his sights trained on the enemy, observed what he thought was a hit in the bows of one of the cruisers. A giant sheet of flame shot from her fore-deck but soon subsided in a cloud of black smoke. It appeared that the enemy's fire, which at first had been well placed, began to falter under the quick-firing salvoes of the *Scharnhorst's* main armament, though the range was much closer than during the first encounter in the morning. After about twenty minutes the enemy was, in the driving snow and rain, completely out of sight.

At 1241 hours the British checked their fire. A quarter of an hour later, at 1300 hours, the Captain transmitted an order to the Gunnery Commander which was thereupon repeated by all Signals Transmitters:

"Lull in action!"

In this action, the second encounter with Force 1 (10th Cruiser Squadron, Admiral Burnett), the *Scharnhorst* was not hit.

Everywhere, the gun crews set to work. The brass cartridges of the used ammunition were salvaged or thrown overboard where they had not already been washed away by the heavy seas. The heavy turrets, from which the cordite gases could not always be drawn off quickly enough, were briefly turned into the wind for ventilation. Munition hoists rattled; munition racks were replenished, and the ordnance personnel checked consumption in turrets and batteries. Minor damage was quickly repaired by the artificers. Soon the all-clear reports were reaching the Gunnery Commander.

Meanwhile, the Commander-in-Chief was discussing the situation with his staff, the Captain, and the Navigating Officer, in the charthouse.

"Damn it," grunted the Admiral, "we're not getting at the convoy at all. The cruisers are always just where we want to strike. They were the same ones as this morning, weren't they, Hintze?"

The Captain pulled the leather cover over the lenses of his big double glasses and remained thoughtful for a moment before replying:

"I'm inclined to agree, Herr Admiral. The AO (Artillery Officer, i.e. Gunnery Commander) thinks so, too. It was impossible to see the cruisers this morning, but the shell splashes, which I observed myself, were of the same calibre. The AO thinks they were 8-inch and 5.9-inch shells."

"Apparently we're still being shadowed," continued the Rear-Admiral, "according to the after Radar reports at any rate. There's nothing actually to be seen. Let's hope we shake her off in due course. I can see no point in making a third attempt to get at the convoy."

He paused and everyone was silent.

The Admiral went up to the chart table, checked once more the distance to the north Norwegian coast, glanced at the course and speed indicators and looked at the Captain:

"Return to Norway, Hintze. Alta Fjord."

A few minutes later, the *Scharnhorst* slewed round on to her new course. She now had the gale and the sea ahead and to starboard as, her bows washed by the heavy breakers, she pitched southward. The short twilight was already over. Darkness had settled around the ship. She was no longer closed up at action stations, but intensified look-out had been ordered.

It seems probable that Rear-Admiral Bey—possibly concerned by the report that five enemy units had been sighted—chose to make for the Norwegian coast after his second attempt to strike at the convoy had failed, so as not to be cut off by the British Force. From the measures taken by the Commander-in-Chief and from the Captain's words to the crew—as recalled by survivors—one may conclude with reasonable certainty that in the *Scharnhorst* they thought that one of the five units reported was a heavy unit, and the Grand Admiral's explicit instructions were that the *Scharnhorst* was on no account to enter into an engagement with a heavy unit.

At 1345 hours, that is to say, after the conclusion of the second encounter with Force 1, the 4th Destroyer Flotilla received an unsigned wireless signal:

"Fourth Destroyer Flotilla break off!"

Upon inquiry from the destroyer leader in Z 30 it was

440

stated that the signature *Scharnhorst* had been transmitted in a garbled form. To Captain Johannesson, leader of the flotilla, the order—quite naturally—seemed incomprehensible. As it was not clear to him whether it referred to the attack against the convoy as located by U-boat Lübsen, or meant that the entire operation was being called off, he asked the Commander-in-Chief, by wireless signal, for further instructions. The *Scharnhorst's* reply, received at 1420 hours, was:

"Return to base!"

The British dispatch concerning the second engagement of Force 1 with the *Scharnhorst* contains, among other things, the following details:

At 1024 hours the 10th Cruiser Squadron closed the convoy and met up with the 36th Destroyer Division. Then the cruisers—because of the danger of U-boats—zigzagged 10 miles ahead of the convoy, with the 36th Destroyer Division disposed ahead of the cruiser force as a screen.

Towards noon it became clear to Admiral Fraser in the *Duke of York* that, owing to the fuel situation in the destroyers, he would be obliged either to turn back or go on to Kola Inlet for refuelling. If the *Scharnhorst* had already been on her way back to base at this time, there would have been no chance of catching her.

At 1155 hours Admiral Fraser ordered the convoy to alter course to 125°, that is, more to the south, his idea being to keep the cruisers between the convoy and the *Scharnhorst*. At 1137 hours the *Norfolk* made contact with the German battleship by Radar at 27,000 yards, but lost it a few minutes later. Then, at 1205 the *Belfast* picked up the *Scharnhorst*, this time at 30,500 yards. Vice-Admiral Burnett now concentrated the 36th Destroyer Division on his starboard bow and altered course to 100°. At 1221 hours the *Sheffield* reported, "Enemy in sight," and Force 1 was ordered to open fire at a range of 11,000 yards.

At the same time the 36th Destroyer Division was ordered to attack with torpedoes. The destroyers, however, owing to the extraordinarily bad weather conditions which greatly reduced their speed, and to the fact that the *Scharn-*

horst was all the time retreating, did not come within torpedo range at this stage of the battle. The *Musketeer* opened fire at a range of 7000 yards at 1222 hours and continued firing for 14 minutes.

During this second action, at 1233 hours, the *Norfolk* received a serious hit through the barbette of her after turret "X," which put it out of action, and the turret's magazine had to be flooded as a precaution. A second shell hit the *Norfolk* amidships. All the cruiser's Radar apparatus became unserviceable except for one set of the Type 284. One officer and six ratings were killed and five ratings were seriously wounded. At the same time an 11-inch salvo straddled the *Sheffield* and pieces of shell— some the size of footballs—according to the British report —crashed inboard; smaller fragments also penetrated the ship at various places.

With the *Scharnhorst* retreating at 28 knots, the range, which during the action had narrowed to 4½–8 miles, opened more and more. Vice-Admiral Burnett decided to check fire and shadow with the whole of Force 1 until the *Scharnhorst* could be engaged by Admiral Fraser with Force 2. The 10th Cruiser Squadron, therefore, increased speed to 28 knots so that from 1250 hours onwards the enemy range remained steady at 13,400 yards. The 36th Destroyer Division, too, continued the chase. Later the range between the *Scharnhorst* and the pursuing cruisers opened to 20,000 yards and then remained steady.

Admiral Sir Bruce Fraser, sailing in the *Duke of York,* and acting on enemy reports received from Vice-Admiral Burnett, had on this December 26 been proceeding eastward with Force 2. His sole aim was to approach the *Scharnhorst,* cut off her retreat to Norway, and sink her, thus disposing of the most serious threat to the Arctic convoys.

A quarter of an hour after the *Scharnhorst* had been

442

engaged by the cruisers of the 10th Squadron, one of the young officers from the Radar plot of the *Duke of York* reported in the chart-house of the Admiral's bridge:

"Enemy reconnaissance aircraft, Sir."

The Admiral, who with his Chief-of-Staff, had been checking Vice-Admiral Burnett's reports on the first action just concluded, looked up quickly:

"German reconnaissance aircraft? Where?"

"Eight and a half miles on the starboard quarter, Sir. We picked them up by Radar as well as by D/F. Three aircraft. One of the planes must have Radar; it's started sending radio location signals and is transmitting reports."

Sir Bruce exchanged glances with his Chief-of-Staff and placed the report sheet on the chart before him:

"Nothing else? No further signals?"

The Sub-Lieutenant shook his head:

"No, Sir. We're keeping contact with the aircraft."

"Good. Thank you."

For about four hours the *Duke of York's* Radar observed the German reconnaissance aircraft shadowing the Force and sending out signals. Then it was seen no more; either it had lost contact or had returned to base.

At 1400 hours Sir Bruce sought out his Chief-of-Staff in the plotting-room. "I'm beginning to wonder," he said, "if our respective positions have been incorrectly reported. They seem too good to be true."

The Chief-of-Staff pointed with conviction to the large-scale chart on which all data were precisely recorded as they came in:

"Impossible, Sir. The D/F bearings here fully confirm the positions. Our approach is being made on a steady bearing."

Sir Bruce was relieved. "If the *Scharnhorst* maintains roughly her present course, she will run directly across our bows. I shall attack with the *Jamaica* on the same course, open fire at 13,000 yards and at the same time give the escort destroyers the order for torpedo attack. Burnett is keeping excellent contact."

The Chief-of-Staff traced with his pencil the course of the 10th Cruiser Squadron, Vice-Admiral Burnett's Force 1.

"Up to now, Sir, there's no indication that the reports of the German reconnaissance aircraft have influenced the movements of the *Scharnhorst* in the slightest. If she continues as she's going now," he cast a quick glance at his watch, "we shall be in action with her at about 1715 hours."

About two hours later, at 1617 hours, the Admiral was seated on a metal stool by the rapidly rotating disc which permitted a clear view through the large window of the bridge, in spite of the driving snow, when suddenly one of the officers from the plotting-room appeared before him like a spirit conjured from the darkness.

"We've got her, Sir! The first report has just come in: 45,000 yards, bearing 020°. The Chief-of-Staff wishes to report that the bearing agrees with the plotted course. The *Scharnhorst* has turned on to a rather more southerly course. Force 1 has made the same report."

The Admiral jumped to his feet:

"Splendid; well done, Radar. Flag-Lieutenant: Pass on this Radar report with our own position to all ships!"

"Yes, Sir," came the voice of the Flag-Lieutenant out of the darkness.

Exactly twenty minutes later, at 1637 hours, the escorting destroyers received the order to take up the most advantageous positions for torpedo attack in subdivisions. (Sub-divisions stationed on either bow of the *Duke of York* had previously been formed.) At the same time, it was reported that the Radar had also picked up the *Belfast* which was coming up behind the *Scharnhorst* in pursuit.

Five minutes earlier, the *Duke of York's* fire-control Radar had found the *Scharnhorst* at 29,700 yards.

Sir Bruce gave a further order to the Flag-Lieutenant and requested the Captain of the flagship to come to the voice-pipe connecting the Admiral's bridge with the ship's bridge below. When Captain Russell reported, the Admiral himself was already standing at the voice-pipe:

"In two minutes Force 2 will turn to 80°, Russell. You can then bring all heavy guns to bear at once."

At 1647 hours the *Belfast* opened fire with starshell. One minute later, at 1648 hours, the *Duke of York* joined in also with starshell, and at 1650 hours the first heavy salvo

444

thundered from the ten 14-inch barrels of the British flagship. The *Jamaica* followed with her twelve 6-inch guns, while the *Norfolk* and the *Belfast* opened fire somewhat later. The initial range was 12,000 yards.

Stationed at his control column, P.O. Gödde, who was searching slowly and systematically from dead ahead to the port beam, became suddenly aware that the Radar reports were taking a new shape. He took his eyes from the lenses, all attention now on the headphones. What was that? The after Radar, which had been putting through in routine fashion reports on the British ship shadowing astern, had suddenly discovered another target to starboard. And now, at the Captain's request, it was reporting the range and bearing of the new target. The P.O. suddenly recalled what the Captain had announced to all stations at 1130 hours: that an enemy Force was 150 miles away. Gödde pondered on this. Three hours previously the *Scharnhorst* had turned on to her present southeasterly course; before that she had been in the second action with the cruiser squadron. What would be the speed of this new Force? Twenty-eight to 30 knots, Gödde thought. That would mean 90 miles in the last three hours at the most. But this Force would obviously have been receiving continuous reports on the speed, course and position of the *Scharnhorst*—from the shadowing cruiser; hence, Gödde reasoned, if the enemy are out to intercept us on our return journey, they will have been able to take a short cut. This battle group must now be just about ready to strike.

Suddenly the piercing sound of the alarm bells shrieked through the ship.

It was 1600 hours.

Heeling over heavily, the *Scharnhorst* slewed round and increased speed at the same time. The unbearable pitching changed into rolling, then into a soft rhythmical swaying now that the battleship was almost running before the sea again.

445

The Signals-Transmitter passed on a further announcement from the Gunnery Commander:

"Enemy opening fire to starboard. A.A. crews below deck. Skeleton crew only to remain on deck."

Then it came. Blow upon blow. In a matter of seconds ship and crew were swept along in the confused headlong rush of events. Gödde observed gigantic splashes 100 to 150 yards on his port side from what must have been shells of the heaviest calibre. Then, while the battleship was still turning round, her own heavy turrets opened fire. Gödde heard the Second Gunnery Officer, Kapitänleutnant Wieting, order single guns of the starboard secondary armament to fire starshell in between salvoes, evidently with the idea of enabling the visual range-finders to pick up the enemy. The enemy's own starshell firing seemed to slacken during the few starshell salvoes of the German 5.9-inch guns. The P.O. now heard an interchange between the Gunnery Commander and the Second Gunnery Officer on the artillery telephone. The Gunnery Commander thought it inadvisable to take guns from the batteries and thus weaken the defensive fire. The Second Gunnery Officer, accordingly, stopped the firing of starshell, and the guns which were ready for the next salvo were at once unloaded.

The enemy's shells which had been falling to port and starboard of the *Scharnhorst,* now began to fall wide and well behind the ship.

Anxiously Gödde searched for an enemy on the port side. Nothing could be seen but the glistening white columns of water which rose steeple-high as the 14-inch shells hit the sea. They rose from the water like pale phantoms trailing white shrouds, stood poised for a while, and then fell in mighty cascades of water. The German heavy armament kept up continuous fire from all triple turrets.

At 1655 hours a 14-inch shell hit the starboard bows abreast of "A" turret and the blast threw P.O. Gödde to the deck. Overcome with shock and the greenish-black lyddite fumes he gasped for air and lay for several seconds on the wooden grating of his small platform, incapable of moving. Just at this moment the Captain appeared. The lenses of the optical apparatus had become temporarily

446

unusable—from the effects of the hit and the fumes—and had to be cleaned from the outside by ratings sent up from below. Captain Hintze saw the prostrate man and helped him to his feet:

"Are you wounded, Gödde?"

The P.O. pulled himself together:

"No, Herr Kapitän, only stunned."

The Captain pointed to the apparatus:

"Stay at your post. We can't afford to be taken by surprise from this side."

"A" turret was now jammed in its bearings with its barrels elevated and could no longer be trained. Shortly after the first hit, a second was scored amidships.

Later, when Gödde's artillery-telephone had been put out of action, and he had switched over to the ship-control telephone system, he heard a report from one of the stations to the Gunnery Commander:

"A" turret is no longer reporting. Fire and smoke around the turret prevent entry."

This meant that "A" turret was completely out of action and that the *Scharnhorst's* defences were deprived of three 11-inch guns. Her remaining heavy guns, six 11-inch barrels, meanwhile stepped up their fire to a quick succession of salvoes and the range opened to 17,000–20,000 yards. It was observed that the enemy was frequently straddled by salvoes and that many near misses fell close to the British ship. This gunnery duel lasted some twenty minutes and was conducted by both sides with the utmost ferocity. Throughout this period a continuous stream of starshell were exploding over the *Scharnhorst*. The flares hung over the ship for minutes on end like so many huge floodlights exposing everything with stark, pitiless clarity, the cruel brilliance sharpened by the fiery flashes of the German's own salvoes. The whole battleship from bridges to foretop, masts and funnels was bathed in a ghastly pink to blood-red light. Smoke and cordite fumes clung to the ship, driven now by an almost following wind, and at times completely obscured visibility in the direction of the enemy. Through the thunder of the German salvoes, the British shells could be heard screaming over and thudding

447

into the sea, while those that met their target caused the ship, already rocked by the recoil of her own guns, to tremble from stem to stern.

P.O. Gödde concluded from the gunnery orders that the range was opening while German and British fire slackened appreciably. The *Scharnhorst* was steady on her easterly course and seemed to increase speed still more. The intervals between salvoes lengthened and visibility gradually improved.

As the action was being fought to starboard, the crews in the port IV 5.9-inch twin turret could open the turret trap-hatch occasionally and observe the continuous explosion of starshell over the ship stabbing the darkness with their glare. At 1650 hours the turret Signals-Transmitter repeated an announcement from the Captain:

"From the Captain to all stations. The heavy enemy units are turning away, they can't match our speed." Then after a short pause: "The *Scharnhorst* has again proved herself."

The lull following the Captain's last announcement, during which the *Scharnhorst's* heavy artillery temporarily checked fire, lasted only five to ten minutes. Then once more the ship was exposed to the dazzling light of starshell and the heavy shock of an underwater explosion, amidships on the starboard side, shuddered through her hull. Soon after this, her speed slackened.

In the port IV 5.9-inch turret the Signals-Transmitter passed on the report:

"Torpedo hit in boiler-room 1. Speed 8 knots."

By 1840 hours the first sub-division (*Savage* and *Saumarez*) were astern of the *Scharnhorst;* at the same time the second sub-division (*Scorpion* and *Stord*) closed in from the south-east to about 10,000 yards, and were on the *Scharnhorst's* starboard beam ready to fire their torpedoes. The *Scharnhorst* opened heavy fire against the *Savage* and *Saumarez* with her secondary armament and

448

A.A. guns which the two destroyers returned. At the same time they fired starshell. The second sub-division *Scorpion* and *Stord* turned for the torpedo attack, *Scorpion* firing eight torpedoes at 2100 yards and *Stord* another eight at 1800 yards. *Scorpion* observed one hit. The *Scharnhorst,* turning to southward ostensibly to get out of the line of fire, put herself just where the first sub-division wanted her. Thus, while the second sub-division on its retreat came under heavy secondary armament and A.A. fire from the *Scharnhorst,* the first sub-division hastily trained its torpedo tubes from port to starboard and turned in to attack. *Savage* fired her eight torpedoes at a range of 3,500 yards. *Saumarez,* which owing to casualties and damage had only one set of tubes clear for action, and lying as she was under heavy fire, could launch only four torpedoes at 1800 yards.

Savage remained miraculously intact, but *Saumarez* was damaged above the waterline and sustained casualties. Shells hit her director and penetrated below her rangefinder director without, however, exploding. Splinters from other shells caused further damage which reduced her speed to ten knots on one engine only. One officer and ten ratings were killed and eleven ratings wounded. *Savage* claimed to have observed three hits on the *Scharnhorst, Saumarez* one.

The attack of the two sub-divisions was carried out without support from the *Duke of York* or the *Jamaica.* The *Duke of York* observed three heavy underwater explosions on the *Scharnhorst,* the *Belfast* six—an indication of how uncertain and unreliable observations made during a night action are, though they may be made and reported in good faith.

After delivering their attacks the destroyers withdrew to the northward.

While the *Scharnhorst's* heavy guns were still firing at the retreating destroyers, P.O. Gödde heard the after Radar reporting new targets; the Captain asked for their respective bearings and ranges, and these were given.

Shortly afterwards, the 11-inch guns opened fire on these as yet shadowy opponents, one of which was soon identified as a battleship; heavy shells fell into the sea around the *Scharnhorst*. The Second Gunnery Officer, Kapitänleutnant Wieting, ordered the secondary armament to open fire on the battleship and on a second opponent which, judging by its shell calibre, was obviously a cruiser.

Hit upon hit crashed on to the *Scharnhorst*. Heavy explosions followed one upon the other, and as each bout of violent rocking subsided it was replaced by a slow vibration as if the very hull were trembling. Steel crashed upon steel; fire broke out and the smoke which billowed from the quickly spreading flames mingled with the acrid cordite fumes of the German salvoes and the strangely stinging odour from the British explosives. The two remaining triple turrets kept up their relentless fire in company with the 5.9-inch battery and the 4.1-inch A.A. guns. Between the German salvoes one could hear the dull rumbling noise of starshell exploding over the battleship, the detonations of torpedoes and the impact of shells. The rending steel groaned and hissing splinters hammered like hail on superstructures and decks. The enemy's wide shots came screaming over the *Scharnhorst* and fell with heavy thuds into the sea beyond, flooding decks and guns with the swell and marking their trail with a rain of deadly splinters.

This hurricane of fire, this ghastly concentration of assault from heavy guns and torpedoes, took place—according to the British dispatch—between 1901 and 1937 hours.

In the fearful din of battle in which the *Scharnhorst* was now enveloped, none but the well-trained ear, tried in exercise and action, could distinguish voices and interpret the reports and orders which the ship's telephone system was picking up from every side. P.O. Gödde possessed such a practised ear. He had his eyes pressed closely to the lenses of his control column, raising them only occasionally to look round him, when a particularly heavy explosion

450

shook the ship. Through the noise came word from the Captain:

"Scharnhorst immer voran!"

It was the ship's motto. Gödde gritted his teeth and looked up. He realized that the long bows of the *Scharnhorst* had nosed straight into the path of a shell. The noise of the explosion mingled with the sight of wood, iron and steel torn asunder as by giant, flaming ploughshares. Then the blast flung the P.O. from his apparatus, lifted him bodily into the air and threw him violently on to the deck. Gödde lost consciousness and lay inert. When he wearily opened his eyes again he saw the Captain.

Captain Hintze had left the control position through the port door opposite Gödde's control column to take a quick look round. The lenses of the optical instruments in the control position had for the most part been destroyed by flying shrapnel; the rest had been made temporarily unserviceable by clinging snow, water and slime. Just as the Captain was squeezing through the narrow aperture of the slightly open armoured door, the 14-inch shell—the one which tore Gödde from the control column—hit the bows. Splinters grazed the Captain's face but he seemed hardly to notice them. He had only the sensation of something warm trickling down his forehead and on to his cheeks and he dabbed it with his handkerchief. Then he saw Gödde crumpled up on the wooden slats of the control column platform. He bent over him:

"Are you wounded, Gödde?"

The same question as he had asked the P.O. two hours previously. The Captain helped the prostrate man to his feet. Gödde rubbed his eyes and looked at his apparatus.

"No, Sir. It was only a few splinters. The gear's all right."

The Captain nodded:

"Good. See what's wrong with the starboard control column. It's not answering."

With this the Captain withdrew once more to the control position and Gödde hurried round to the other control column. In the harsh light of starshell one glance sufficed. The men on the platform were all dead. The apparatus was

451

totally destroyed. All that remained was an unrecognizable mass of twisted steel, shattered instruments and torn, half-melted cables. As quickly as he could Gödde rushed back to his own control column, slipped on his telephone and reported:

"Starboard forward control column destroyed. Crew dead."

This hit must have occurred a few minutes after 1900 hours. About twenty minutes later, roughly at 1925 hours, Gödde felt the impact of a torpedo which brought the battleship practically to a standstill. Then a shell of medium calibre, fired no doubt by one of the cruisers now stationed to the north and south of the *Scharnhorst*, crashed into her bows. A fragment of this smashed the upper mobile portion of the control column at which Gödde was stationed and flung it from its bearings, while other splinters severed the cables of the head-phone. He himself remained unscathed. While Gödde was still occupied in investigating the damage, a Quartermaster sent out by the Captain appeared:

"The Captain wants to know what's happened here? Why don't you answer?"

"The control column's gone. And the telephone too."

The Quartermaster disappeared into the control position again and then returned once more.

"Order from the Captain: Come into the control position. The old man says there's no point in staying outside any longer."

Casting a last look at the shambles around him, Gödde followed the Quartermaster and squeezed himself through the armoured door into the control position.

It was the British torpedoes which finally brought about the end of the German battleship.

One, two torpedo detonations thundered above the indescribable pandemonium of the battle and the *Scharnhorst* slowly took a list to starboard. Whatever there was that could still fire—"C" turret and the remaining 5.9-inch guns—went on firing. And again two, three torpedo detonations crashed forth. They hit on the starboard side and the list increased. Simultaneously came the order:

"From the Captain to all stations. Destroy all secret papers and installations. To damage control party: prepare for scuttling! All men detailed for scuttling to their stations!"

More violent explosions. Torpedoes again. The port 20-mm. A.A. gun was still firing from the fore-top, the only one which had remained in action after the fore-top had been hit during the morning. It fired down from the main A.A. gun tower and with it the port IV 5.9-inch twin turret. Then, because of the heavy list, the hoist in the twin turret jammed in its shaft. At the same time, the order was passed down from the bridge:

"Abandon ship."

Staff Chief Gunner Wibbelhoff rose from his seat:

"Leave the turret!" he ordered.

The men hesitated. During the whole operation the turret had suffered neither damage nor casualties.

"Leave the turret, boys," Wibbelhoff repeated, raising his voice. "I'm staying where I belong."

Chief Petty Officer Moritz went at once to Wibbelhoff's side:

"I'm staying too."

Not another word was spoken. Slowly, the men turned away and prepared to leave, returning the Battery Commander's last salute.

They clambered out slowly, one after the other, still a little uncertain, turning round for a last glance. Sträter, one of the last to leave, saw Wibbelhoff put his hand in his pocket and quietly produce a packet of cigarettes. He saw him light up and in the calm deliberate manner so familiar to his men, swing back into his seat. Moritz, likewise, lowered himself onto his laying-seat. Sträter felt a lump in his throat as he gazed on the scene for the last time, a scene which was to be indelibly printed on his mind and swim before his eyes whenever he thought of his ship.

453

Both men were still at their stations when the *Scharnhorst* capsized and sank.

Shortly before the first torpedoes of this last phase of the battle hit the *Scharnhorst*, Gödde, now in the control position, heard that enemy destroyers were closing from astern.

The Captain, who received the report, looked at the Commander-in-Chief:

"They want to finish us off like the *Bismarck*, Herr Admiral. Torpedoes into rudder and screws!"

He stepped to the side of the Signals-Transmitter at the emergency line which the Torpedo Officer, now standing by at the torpedo tubes, had had hurriedly laid. Then Captain Hintze gave the order to fire torpedoes. By a supreme effort, the Torpedo Officer, Oberleutnant Bosse, and those of his men who were left, had carried out emergency repairs on the damaged tubes; now with the help of a few ratings, he succeeded in training them and firing torpedoes first to port, then to starboard at the targets indicated by the Captain. After the appropriate interval the stern look-out reported to the control position that he had observed a brilliant blaze astern.

According to British sources, this was yet another of the mistaken claims made in good faith by both sides during the night battle.

The *Scharnhorst* was hit by the first enemy torpedo salvo at about 1927 hours, and six minutes later, at 1933 hours, by the second. Four minutes after that, at about 1937 hours, the last torpedoes detonated with a thunderous roar against the ship's starboard side.

The fate of the *Scharnhorst* was sealed.

Gödde, deeply moved, heard reports coming in from all parts of the dying ship; in accordance with the Captain's orders to prepare for scuttling, the damage control parties had fitted the explosive charges, and, one-by-one, the

454

various installations were being destroyed or rendered useless.

The *Scharnhorst* was listing more and more to starboard as Captain Hintze beckoned the Navigating Officer to him.

"Pass to the Action Information Centre," he ordered, "a last report of our position in clear text. Quickly Lanz. Time is running out!"

Then he gripped the Chief Signals-Transmitter by the arm:

"To all stations. From the Captain: Abandon ship. Every man to the upper deck. Life-jackets on. Prepare to jump overboard!"

Summoned by the Captain, the First Officer, Fregatten-kapitän Dominik, had come up from the Commander's office through the armoured shaft. Rear-Admiral Bey, Captain and First Officer now discussed the measures still to be taken. Then Gödde saw the slim figure of the First Officer leaving the control position to go across the bay of the bridge and down the port companion-way to the upper deck. The list was becoming increasingly marked and Captain Hintze urged the twenty-five men in the control position to leave.

"Off with you, men. Put on your jackets. Just think of yourselves now. And don't forget to inflate them. Don't go overboard to starboard, my friends. Go over from the port side, and slide from the rail into the water."

As Gödde prepared to leave the bridge, the *Scharnhorst* was rolling heavily in the rough sea and was enveloped in dense smoke and fumes, but she was still moving slowly. Her starboard side lay in the water practically to the folded wing of the bridge, while the highest waves washed the main mast. Snow squalls, mingled with hail, had again set in and starshell still hovered over the sinking ship.

In the target area there were present at this time: one battleship, three cruisers and eight destroyers. The *Duke of York* withdrew to the northward to avoid the mêlée of ships. All that could be seen of the *Scharnhorst* was a dark glowing mass within an enormous cloud of smoke lit up by starshell and the searchlights of the surrounding ships. From the British side neither the glare of the starshell nor

455

the beams of the searchlights could penetrate behind that smoke-cloud. Thus no ship actually saw the *Scharnhorst* sink. It seems certain however that she sank after a heavy underwater explosion which was heard and felt by various ships at 1945 hours.

Jamaica, Matchless and *Virago* were the last ships to sight the *Scharnhorst* (at 1938 hours). When the *Belfast* turned in for her second torpedo attack at 1948 hours the German battleship had finally sunk. She went down in approximately 72° 16′ N., 28° 41′ E. The *Jamaica* joined the *Duke of York* on her northerly course while *Belfast, Norfolk* and most of the destroyers continued until 2040 hours to search for survivors. During this time *Scorpion* picked up thirty survivors and *Matchless*, six. *Scorpion* reported that the German Admiral and the *Scharnhorst's* Captain had been seen in the water seriously wounded. The Captain was dead before he could be reached. The Admiral grasped a life-line but died before he could be hauled on board.

The deck was already tilted at a steep angle, so Gödde and the Bos'un's Mate, Deierling joined hands and moved carefully across the icy surface. As the port companion-way was crowded with men, they decided to use, instead, the starboard companion-way leading to the upper deck. The starboard bridge was already on a level with the water and heavy breakers lashed the main mast. Suddenly the two Petty Officers lost their footing and a receding wave swept them from the ship, separating them.

Gödde was drawn down by the suction around the hull. He felt an unbearable pressure in his ear drums, then he was tossed to the surface. He tried desperately to get clear of the whirling waters which eddied round the ship.

It was a gruesome scene that met his eyes as Gödde, lifted on to the long crest of a wave, looked about him, a scene illuminated by starshell and the chalk-white beams of searchlights. Where their light met the blue-black ice-cold water it shone in flashes of dazzling silver. Gödde swam on slowly and steadily, his head turned towards the capsizing *Scharnhorst*. Through the whirling veil of great snowflakes he saw, garishly illuminated, the outline of the

456

battleship now lying practically on her side. The sight seemed unreal, improbable. It flashed through his mind that a fighter plane, banking, would have seen the *Scharnhorst* like that. Everything was oblique, foreshortened, contradicting the laws of gravity. Only a few men were swimming on her starboard side, most of them having followed the advice of the Captain and left the *Scharnhorst* over the rail on the port side.

He saw the light of an emergency raft flickering close to him. Uncannily, like a ship's distress signal, its flame quivered restlessly in the gale. Gödde could see a young officer and several men on the raft. He swam towards it and saw the officer suddenly stand up. Through the raging storm he heard him shout: "Three cheers for the *Scharnhorst!*"

Gödde was two to three hundred yards from the ship which was now lying so much on her starboard side that he could look right down her funnel as into a dark tunnel. He was amazed that she was still afloat. He and many of his shipmates could still plainly hear the turbines revolving inside her. Fuel oil had spread across the sea, covering the surface with a tough, pungent, rainbow-colored film. It was nauseating if it was washed into the mouth or even came into contact with the face. But, as Gödde quickly observed, it cushioned the violence of the breaking seas.

At the same time Sträter saw the *Scharnhorst* capsize and settle deeper into the water, bow first. All three propellers were still revolving at fair speed.

Gödde now tried to reach a raft which was drifting near him. Some twenty men were already sitting on it or clinging to it, so that, pressed below the surface by the combined weight of the men, nothing could be seen of the raft itself. Seeing this, Gödde abandoned his attempt and swam towards some wooden props such as were used by the damage control parties for propping up hatches, etc. They were drifting close together and when at last he reached them, they offered him some support. Of the ship's rafts only a few were in the water. Most of the rafts and life-boats had, on the Captain's orders, been cut free from their lashings in good time, but splinters and fragments of

457

shell had riddled them with holes and rendered them useless. Clinging to the wooden props Gödde let himself drift about in the swell. Now he could relax sufficiently to look back to his ship; the *Scharnhorst* had turned turtle after capsizing and her superstructure, which Gödde had been able to see for so long, had disappeared. The wreck was drifting on the sea, bottom up, and men were moving about on the ship's keel, among them Artificer 1st Class Johnnie Merkel, one of the survivors. He remained perched on the keel until he saw a raft drifting by, then he jumped into the water. Sitting on the raft Merkel then helped several men over from the ship's bottom.

Meanwhile the cold began to take hold of Gödde; paralysis crept from his lower extremities and threatened to numb his whole body. Lumps of ice were drifting by, the snowstorm was still raging, and gusts of hail drove almost horizontally across the dark waters. Gödde was weakening. He had just reached the point when he felt he could keep his grip on the props no longer when he caught sight of the raft bearing Merkel and three other men. Summoning his last reserves Gödde managed to reach the raft. He let go of the props and Merkel helped the half-paralysed man to push the upper part of his body over on to the raft. Utterly exhausted Gödde cast a last glance back to the *Scharnhorst*. Only part of the stern was showing above the water. Then the long rolling swell of the Arctic sea closed over her.

Gradually, the sound of starshell firing ceased and darkness reclaimed the sea. The little groups huddling on the few rafts could hardly see each other, still less the isolated swimmers. A young rating who had left his own raft because of overcrowding joined Gödde's company. He too was helped on by Merkel so that he could keep his hold by lying, like Gödde, with his body across the raft. They were all completely exhausted, incapable of feeling, half-numbed, stricken by a leaden weariness. For one to one and a half hours they drifted, the raft swinging up and down with the sea, floundering in monotonous rhythm between wave-crest and trough. Pressed tightly together, one supporting the other, they would, whenever the raft was lifted to the crest

458

of an unusually high wave, look around them with eyes red-rimmed and swollen, encrusted with hoar-frost and caked with salt and oil.

Then, suddenly, they started: there was a flash quite near them, the thunder of guns broke loose again and the screaming of shells passed over their heads. Were they under fire? There came the sound of dull detonations, then the sky lit up around them. Flares shed their harsh light and a few seconds later the long white arms of searchlights pierced the darkness. For a moment the men thought that their raft was being fired on, then they realized their mistake. A great ship had concentrated her searchlights and was now spot-lighting the raft. In the light of starshell they saw two destroyers approach and stretch the thinner fingers of their searchlights too on to the raft, their raft. Then one of them turned away. The other continued towards them and, maneuvering cautiously, approached the raft. It struck Gödde, now fully conscious again, how skilfully the destroyer was managed in the heavy sea-way; she left the raft on her starboard side and then let herself drift with the wind towards it. Great climbing nets were laid out on the side of the destroyer and as soon as the vessel was close enough the British seamen threw bowlines over the heads and shoulders of the men on the raft. They were pulled on board one after another in this fashion. When Gödde had the sling thrown to him he had not the strength to slip it over his elbows, and as the British seaman went to pull him up he slipped out of the sling and back into the water. Four times they threw him the line: at the fifth attempt the end of the line hit him directly across the mouth. In desperation he sank his teeth firmly into the hemp rope and in this manner was hauled up. As he reached deck level he felt a pair of giant fists grasp the collar of his uniform and pull him over the rail.

Attack by Air

But the Allies were already carrying the attack to the heart of Europe—
by air. The aim was to destroy the German war industries, knock down
the Luftwaffe (which by now had become a defensive unit), and reduce
the land defenses facing the British across the Channel. The R.A.F. conducted their raids at night, preferring area-saturation bombing; the
Americans flew their missions of Flying Fortresses during the day, bombing their targets as accurately as their instruments and daylight observation allowed. Losses were murderous in late 1942 and early 1943.
Heavy damage was being visited on German war industry, but it was
obvious that bombing missions in daylight needed fighter protection.
The trouble was that, at this time, we had no fighters of long enough
range to protect the bombers to the target and back.

Both air forces pounded aircraft factories, a job in which the bomber
crews had a great stake. Successful raids could help cripple aircraft production, meaning fewer replacements for the Luftwaffe's air defense
squadrons in the following months. When the Germans began to dis-
perse their assembly plants, the Allies followed them tenaciously, continuing to do serious damage.

From November, 1943, through the following March, Berlin was heavily bombed. The second raid on the city, November 22nd, saw 2,300
tons of bombs delivered in one of the greatest raids of the war. Another 1,400 tons were delivered on the 23rd, and, on the 26th, another
thousand tons. The Allies were bent on shattering the hub of the German government, and striking at civilian morale.

Through the spring of 1944 even more attention was paid to all elements of German air power; the date of the invasion of France had
been set for the following June, and it was essential that the Luftwaffe
be crushed so the Allies could hold complete air supremacy. The Allies
offered battle at any time to German pursuit planes. A shuttle system
was worked out so that on long raids British and American bombers
could land at Italian bases, and now industrial cities such as Regensburg and Wiener Neustadt were in reach. Winter weather always caused

difficulties for large-scale bombing, but when the weather began to clear in February, heavier raids than ever were launched on German industrial centers. Such fierce attacks meant heavy casualties. But the German air force was crippled—their aircraft production could no longer keep pace with their losses.

The following description of one of the raids on Regensburg is written by Lt. Col. Beirne Lay, Jr., American pilot of a day-bombing B-17 Flying Fortress.

RAID ON REGENSBURG

by Lt. Col. Beirne Lay, Jr.

In the briefing room, the intelligence officer of the bombardment group pulled a cloth screen away from a huge wall map. Each of the 240 sleepy-eyed combat-crew members in the crowded room leaned forward. There were low whistles. I felt a sting of anticipation as I stared at the red string on the map that stretched from our base in England to a pin point deep in Southern Germany, then south across the Alps, through the Brenner Pass to the coast of Italy, then past Corsica and Sardinia and south over the Mediterranean to a desert airdrome in North Africa. You could have heard an oxygen mask drop.

"Your primary," said the intelligence officer, "is Regensburg. Your aiming point is the center of the Messerschmitt One Hundred and Nine G aircraft-and-engine-assembly shops. This is the most vital target we've ever gone after. If you destroy it, you destroy thirty per cent of the Luftwaffe's single-engine-fighter production. You fellows know what that means to you personally."

There were a few hollow laughs.

After the briefing, I climbed aboard a jeep bound for the operations office to check up on my Fortress assignment. The stars were dimly visible through the chilly mist that

461

covered our blacked-out bomber station, but the weather forecast for a deep penetration over the Continent was good. In the office, I looked at the crew sheet, where the line-up of the lead, low and high squadrons of the group is plotted for each mission. I was listed for a copilot's seat. While I stood there, and on the chance suggestion of one of the squadron commanders who was looking over the list, the operations officer erased my name and shifted me to the high squadron as copilot in the crew of a steady Irishman named Lieutenant Murphy, with whom I had flown before. Neither of us knew it, but that operations officer saved my life right there with a piece of rubber on the end of a pencil.

At 5:30 a.m., fifteen minutes before taxi time, a jeep drove around the five-mile perimeter track in the semi-darkness, pausing at each dispersal point long enough to notify the waiting crews that poor local visibility would postpone the take-off for an hour and a half. I was sitting with Murphy and the rest of our crew near the Piccadilly Lily. She looked sinister and complacent, squatting on her fat tires with scarcely a hole in her skin to show for the twelve raids behind her. The postponement tightened, rather than relaxed, the tension. Once more I checked over my life vest, oxygen mask and parachute, not perfunctorily, but the way you check something you're going to have to use. I made sure my escape kit was pinned securely in the knee pocket of my flying suit, where it couldn't fall out in a scramble to abandon ship. I slid a hunting knife between my shoe and my flying boot as I looked again through my extra equipment for this mission: water canteen, mess kit, blankets and English pounds for use in the Algerian desert, where we would sleep on the ground and might be on our own from a forced landing.

Murphy restlessly gave the Piccadilly Lily another once-over, inspecting ammunition belts, bomb bay, tires and oxygen pressure at each crew station. Especially the oxygen. It's human fuel, as important as gasoline, up where we operate. Gunners field-stripped their .50-calibers again and oiled the bolts. Our top-turret gunner lay in the grass with his head on his parachute, feigning sleep, sweating out his thirteenth start.

We shared a common knowledge which grimly enhanced the normal excitement before a mission. Of the approximately 150 Fortresses who were hitting Regensburg, our group was the last and lowest, at a base altitude of 17,000 feet. That's well within the range of accuracy for heavy flak. Our course would take us over plenty of it. It was a cinch also that our group would be the softest touch for the enemy fighters, being last man through the gantlet. Furthermore, the Piccadilly Lily was leading the last three ships of the high squadron—the tip of the tail end of the whole shebang. We didn't relish it much. Who wants a Purple Heart?

The minute hand of my wrist watch dragged. I caught myself thinking about the day, exactly one year ago, on August 17, 1942, when I watched a pitifully small force of twelve B-17's take off on the first raid of the 8th Air Force to make a shallow penetration against Rouen, France. On that day it was our maximum effort. Today, on our first anniversary, we were putting thirty times that number of heavies into the air—half the force on Regensburg and half the force on Schweinfurt, both situated inside the interior of the German Reich. For a year and a half, as a staff officer, I had watched the 8th Air Force grow under Maj. Gen. Ira C. Eaker. That's a long time to watch from behind a desk. Only ten days ago I had asked for and received orders to combat duty. Those ten days had been full of the swift action of participating in four combat missions and checking out for the first time as a four-engine pilot.

Now I knew that it can be easier to be shot at than telephoned at. That staff officers at an Air Force headquarters are the unstrung heroes of this war. And yet I found myself reminiscing just a little affectionately about that desk, wondering if there wasn't a touch of suicide in store for our group. One thing was sure: Headquarters had dreamed up the biggest air operation to date to celebrate its birthday in the biggest league of aerial warfare.

At 7:30 we broke out of the cloud tops into the glare of the rising sun. Beneath our B-17 lay English fields, still blanketed in the thick mist from which we had just emerged. We continued to climb slowly, our broad wings shouldering a heavy load of incendiary bombs in the belly and a burden of fuel in the main and wing-tip Tokyo tanks that would keep the Fortress afloat in the thin upper altitudes eleven hours.

From my copilot's seat on the right-hand side, I watched the white surface of the overcast, where B-17's in clusters of six to the squadron were puncturing the cloud deck all about us, rising clear of the mist with their glass noses slanted upward for the long climb to base altitude. We tacked on to one of these clutches of six. Now the sky over England was heavy with the weight of thousands of tons of bombs, fuel and men being lifted four miles straight up on a giant aerial hoist to the western terminus of a 20,000-foot elevated highway that led east to Regensburg. At intervals I saw the arc of a sputtering red, green or yellow flare being fired from the cabin roof of a group leader's airplane to identify the lead squadron to the high and low squadrons of each group. Assembly takes longer when you come up through an overcast.

For nearly an hour, still over southern England, we climbed, nursing the straining Cyclone engines in a 300-foot-per-minute ascent, forming three squadrons gradually into compact group stagger formations—low squadron down to the left and high squadron up to the right of the lead squadron—groups assembling into looser combat wings of two to three groups each along the combat-wing assembly line, homing over predetermined points with radio compass, and finally cruising along the air-division assembly line to allow the combat wings to fall into place in trail behind Col. Curtis E. Le May in the lead group of the air division.

Formed at last, each flanking group in position 1,000 feet above or below its lead group, our fifteen-mile parade

464

moved east toward Lowestoft, point of departure from the friendly coast, unwieldy, but dangerous to fool with. From my perch in the high squadron in the last element of the whole procession, the air division looked like huge anvil-shaped swarms of locusts—not on dress parade, like the bombers of the Luftwaffe that died like flies over Britain in 1940, but deployed to uncover every gun and permit maneuverability. Our formation was basically that worked out for the Air Corps by Brig. Gen. Hugh Knerr twenty years ago with eighty-five-mile-an-hour bombers, plus refinements devised by Colonel Le May from experience in the European theater.

The English Channel and the North Sea glittered bright in the clear visibility as we left the bulge of East Anglia behind us. Up ahead we knew that we were already registering on the German RDF screen, and that the sector controllers of the Luftwaffe's fighter belt in Western Europe were busy alerting their *Staffeln* of Focke-Wulfs and Messerschmitts. I stole a last look back at cloud-covered England, where I could see a dozen spare B-17's, who had accompanied us to fill in for any abortives from mechanical failure in the hard climb, gliding disappointedly home to base.

I fastened my oxygen mask a little tighter and looked at the little ball in a glass tube on the instrument panel that indicates proper oxygen flow. It was moving up and down, like a visual heartbeat, as I breathed, registering normal.

Already the gunners were searching. Occasionally the ship shivered as guns were tested with short bursts. I could see puffs of blue smoke from the group close ahead and 1,000 feet above us, as each gunner satisfied himself that he had lead poisoning at his trigger tips. The coast of Holland appeared in sharp black outline. I drew in a deep breath of oxygen.

A few miles in front of us were German boys in single-seaters who were probably going to react to us in the same way our boys would react, emotionally, if German bombers were heading for the Pratt & Whitney engine factory at Hartford or the Liberator plant at Willow Run. In the making was a death struggle between the unstoppable object and the immovable defense, every possible defense at the disposal of the Reich, for this was a deadly penetration to a hitherto inaccessible and critically important arsenal of the *Vaterland*.

At 10:08 we crossed the coast of Holland, south of The Hague, with our group of Fortresses tucked in tightly and within handy supporting distance of the group above us, at 18,000 feet. But our long, loose-linked column looked too long, and the gaps between combat wings too wide. As I squinted into the sun, gauging the distance to the barely visible specks of the lead group, I had a recurrence of that sinking feeling before the take-off—the lonesome foreboding that might come to the last man about to run a gantlet lined with spiked clubs. The premonition was well founded.

At 10:17, near Woensdrecht, I saw the first flak blossom out in our vicinity, light and inaccurate. A few minutes later, at approximately 10:25, a gunner called, "Fighters at two o'clock low." I saw them, climbing above the horizon ahead of us to the right—a pair of them. For a moment I hoped they were P-47 Thunderbolts from the fighter escort that was supposed to be in our vicinity, but I didn't hope long. The two FW-190's turned and whizzed through the formation ahead of us in a frontal attack, nicking two B-17's in the wings and breaking away in half rolls right over our group. By craning my neck up and back, I glimpsed one of them through the roof glass in the cabin, flashing past at a 600-mile-an-hour rate of closure, his yellow nose smoking and small pieces flying off near the wing root. The guns of our group were in action. The pungent smell of burnt cordite filled the cockpit and the B-17 trembled to the recoil of nose and ball-turret guns. Smoke immediately trailed from the hit B-17's, but they held their stations.

Here was early fighter reaction. The members of the crew sensed trouble. There was something desperate about the way those two fighters came in fast right out of their climb, without any preliminaries. Apparently, our own fighters were busy somewhere farther up the procession. The interphone was active for a few seconds with brief admonitions: "Lead 'em more." . . . "Short bursts." . . . "Don't throw

466

rounds away." . . . "Bombardier to left waist gunner, don't yell. Talk slow."

Three minutes later the gunners reported fighters climbing up from all around the clock, singly and in pairs, both FW-190's and Me-109-G's. The fighters I could see on my side looked like too many for sound health. No friendly Thunderbolts were visible. From now on we were in mortal danger. My mouth dried up and my buttocks pulled together. A co-ordinated attack began, with the head-on fighters coming in from slightly above, the nine and three o'clock attackers approaching from about level and the rear attackers from slightly below. The guns from every B-17 in our group and the group ahead were firing simultaneously, lashing the sky with ropes of orange tracers to match the chain-puff bursts squirting from the 20-mm. cannon muzzles in the wings of the jerry single-seaters.

I noted with alarm that a lot of our fire was falling astern of the target—particularly from our hand-held nose and waist guns. Nevertheless, both sides got hurt in this clash, with the entire second element of three B-17's from our low squadron and one B-17 from the group ahead falling out of formation on fire, with crews bailing out, and several fighters heading for the deck in flames or with their pilots lingering behind under the dirty yellow canopies that distinguished some of their parachutes from ours. Our twenty-four-year-old group leader, flying only his third combat mission, pulled us up even closer to the preceding group for mutual support.

As we swung slightly outside with our squadron, in mild evasive action, I got a good look at that gap in the low squadron where three B-17's had been. Suddenly I bit my lip hard. The lead ship of that element had pulled out on fire and exploded before anyone bailed out. It was the ship to which I had been originally assigned.

I glanced over at Murphy. It was cold in the cockpit, but sweat was running from his forehead and over his oxygen mask from the exertion of holding his element in tight formation and the strain of the warnings that hummed over the interphone and what he could see out of the corners of his eyes. He caught my glance and turned the controls over to me for a while. It was an enormous relief to concentrate on flying instead of sitting there watching fighters aiming between your eyes. Somehow, the attacks from the rear, although I could see them through my ears via the interphone, didn't bother me. I guess it was because there was a slab of armor plate behind my back and I couldn't watch them, anyway.

I knew that we were in a lively fight. Every alarm bell in my brain and heart was ringing a high-pitched warning. But my nerves were steady and my brain working. The fear was unpleasant, but it was bearable. I knew that I was going to die, and so were a lot of others. What I didn't know was that the real fight, the *Anschluss* of Luftwaffe 20-mm. cannon shells, hadn't really begun. The largest and most savage fighter resistance of any war in history was rising to stop us at any cost, and our group was the most vulnerable target.

A few minutes later we absorbed the first wave of a hailstorm of individual fighter attacks that were to engulf us clear to the target in such a blizzard' of bullets and shells that a chronological account is difficult. It was at 10:41, over Eupen, that I looked out the window after a minute's lull, and saw two whole squadrons, twelve Me-109's and eleven FW-190's climbing parallel to us as though they were on a steep escalator. The first squadron had reached our level and was pulling ahead to turn into us. The second was not far behind. Several thousand feet below us were many more fighters, their noses cocked up in a maximum climb. Over the interphone came reports of an equal number of enemy aircraft deploying on the other side of the formation.

For the first time I noticed an Me-110 sitting out of range on our level out to the right. He was to stay with us all the way to the target, apparently radioing our position and weak spots to fresh *Staffeln* waiting farther down the road.

At the sight of all these fighters, I had the distinct feeling of being trapped—that the Hun had been tipped off or at least had guessed our destination and was set for us. We were already through the German fighter belt. Obviously, they had moved a lot of squadrons back in a fluid defense in depth, and they must have been saving up some outfits

468

for the inner defense that we didn't know about. The life expectancy of our group seemed definitely limited, since it had already appeared that the fighters, instead of wasting fuel trying to overhaul the preceding groups, were glad to take a cut at us.

Swinging their yellow noses around in a wide U-turn, the twelve-ship squadron of Me-109's came in from twelve to two o'clock in pairs. The main event was on. I fought an impulse to close my eyes, and overcame it.

A shining silver rectangle of metal sailed past over our right wing. I recognized it as a main-exit door. Seconds later, a black lump came hurtling through the formation, barely missing several propellers. It was a man, clasping his knees to his head, revolving like a diver in a triple somersault, shooting by us so close that I saw a piece of paper blow out of his leather jacket. He was evidently making a delayed jump, for I didn't see his parachute open.

A B-17 turned gradually out of the formation to the right, maintaining altitude. In a split second it completely vanished in a brilliant explosion, from which the only remains were four balls of fire, the fuel tanks, which were quickly consumed as they fell earthward.

I saw blue, red, yellow and aluminum-colored fighters. Their tactics were running fairly true to form, with frontal attacks hitting the low squadron and rear attackers going for the lead and high squadrons. Some of the jerries shot at us with rockets, and an attempt at air-to-air bombing was made with little black time-fuse sticks, dropped from above, which exploded in small gray puffs off to one side of the formation. Several of the FW's did some nice deflection shooting on side attacks from 500 yards at the high group, then raked the low group on the breakaway at closer range with their noses cocked in a side slip, to keep the formation in their sights longer in the turn. External fuel tanks were visible under the bellies or wings of at least two squadrons, shedding uncomfortable light on the mystery of their ability to tail us so far from their bases.

The manner of the assaults indicated that the pilots knew where we were going and were inspired with a fanatical determination to stop us before we got there. Many pressed

469

attacks home to 250 yards or less, or bolted right through the formation wide out, firing long twenty-second bursts, often presenting point-blank targets on the breakaway. Some committed the fatal error of pulling up instead of going down and out. More experienced pilots came in on frontal attacks with a noticeably slower rate of closure, apparently throttled back, obtaining greater accuracy. But no tactics could halt the close-knit juggernauts of our Fortresses, nor save the single-seaters from paying a terrible price.

Our airplane was endangered by various debris. Emergency hatches, exit doors, prematurely opened parachutes, bodies and assorted fragments of B-17's and Hun fighters breezed past us in the slip stream.

I watched two fighters explode not far beneath, disappear in sheets of orange flame; B-17's dropping out in every stage of distress, from engines on fire to control shot away; friendly and enemy parachutes floating down, and, on the green carpet far below us, funeral pyres of smoke from fallen fighters, marking our trail.

On we flew through the cluttered wake of a desperate air battle, where disintegrating aircraft were commonplace and the white dots of sixty parachutes in the air at one time were hardly worth a second look. The spectacle registering on my eyes became so fantastic that my brain turned numb to the actuality of the death and destruction all around us. Had it not been for the squeezing in my stomach, which was trying to purge, I might easily have been watching an animated cartoon in a movie theater.

The minutes dragged on into an hour. And still the fighters came. Our gunners called coolly and briefly to one another, dividing up their targets, fighting for their lives with every round of ammunition—and our lives, and the formation. The tail gunner called that he was out of ammunition. We sent another belt back to him. Here was a new hazard. We might run out of .50-caliber slugs before we reached the target.

I looked to both sides of us. Our two wing men were gone. So was the element in front of us—all three ships. We moved up into position behind the lead element of the high squadron. I looked out again on my side and saw a cripple, with one prop feathered, struggle up behind our right wing with his bad engine funneling smoke into the slip stream. He dropped back. Now our tail gunner had a clear view. There were no more B-17's behind us. We were the last man.

I took the controls for a while. The first thing I saw when Murphy resumed flying was a B-17 turning slowly out to the right, its cockpit a mass of flames. The copilot crawled out of his window, held on with one hand, reached back for his parachute, buckled it on, let go and was whisked back into the horizontal stabilizer of the tail. I believe the impact killed him. His parachute didn't open.

I looked forward and almost ducked as I watched the tail gunner of a B-17 ahead of us take a bead right on our windshield and cut loose with a stream of tracers that missed us by a few feet as he fired on a fighter attacking us from six o'clock low. I almost ducked again when our own top-turret gunner's twin muzzles pounded away a foot above my head in the full forward position, giving a realistic imitation of cannon shells exploding in the cockpit, while I gave an even better imitation of a man jumping six inches out of his seat.

Still no letup. The fighters queued up like a bread line and let us have it. Each second of time had a cannon shell in it. The strain of being a clay duck in the wrong end of that aerial shooting gallery became almost intolerable. Our Piccadilly Lily shook steadily with the fire of its .50's, and the air inside was wispy with smoke. I checked the engine instruments for the thousandth time. Normal. No injured crew members yet. Maybe we'd get to that target, even with our reduced fire power. Seven Fortresses from our group had already gone down and many of the rest of us were badly shot up and short-handed because of wounded crew members.

Almost disinterestedly I observed a B-17 pull out from the group preceding us and drop back to a position about 200 feet from our right wing tip. His right Tokyo tanks were on fire, and had been for a half hour. Now the smoke was thicker. Flames were licking through the blackened skin of the wing. While the pilot held her steady, I saw four crew members drop out the bomb bay and execute delayed jumps. Another bailed from the nose, opened his parachute prematurely and nearly fouled the tail. Another went out the left-waist-gun opening, delaying his opening for a safe interval. The tail gunner dropped out of his hatch, apparently pulling the ripcord before he was clear of the ship. His parachute opened instantaneously, barely missing the tail, and jerked him so hard that both his shoes came off. He hung limp in the harness, whereas the others had shown immediate signs of life, shifting around in their harness. The Fortress then dropped back in a medium spiral and I did not see the pilots leave. I saw the ship, though, just before it trailed from view, belly to the sky, its wing a solid sheet of yellow flame.

Now that we had been under constant attack for more than an hour, it appeared certain that our group was faced with extinction. The sky was still mottled with rising fighters. Target time was thirty-five minutes away. I doubt if a man in the group visualized the possibility of our getting much farther without 100 per cent loss. Gunners were becoming exhausted and nerve-tortured from the nagging strain—the strain that sends gunners and pilots to the rest home. We had been aiming point for what looked like most of the Luftwaffe. It looked as though we might find the rest of it primed for us at the target.

At this hopeless point, a young squadron commander down in the low squadron was living through his finest hour. His squadron had lost its second element of three ships early in the fight, south of Antwerp, yet he had consistently maintained his vulnerable and exposed position in the formation rigidly in order to keep the guns of his three remaining ships well uncovered to protect the belly of the formation. Now, nearing the target, battle damage was catching up with him fast. A 20-mm. cannon shell penetrated the right side of his airplane and exploded beneath him, damaging the electrical system and cutting the top-turret gunner in the leg. A second 20-mm. entered the radio compartment, killing the radio operator, who bled to death with his legs severed above the knees. A third 20-mm. shell

472

entered the left side of the nose, tearing out a section about two feet square, tore away the right-hand-nose-gun installations and injured the bombardier in the head and shoulder. A fourth 20-mm. shell penetrated the right wing into the fuselage system, releasing fluid all over the cockpit. A fifth 20-mm. shell punctured the cabin roof and severed the rudder cables to one side of the rudder. A sixth 20-mm. shell exploded in the No. 3 engine, destroying all controls to the engine. The engine caught fire and lost its power, but eventually I saw the fire go out.

Confronted with structural damage, partial loss of control, fire in the air and serious injuries to personnel, and faced with fresh waves of fighters still rising to the attack, this commander was justified in abandoning ship. His crew, some of them comparatively inexperienced youngsters, were preparing to bail out. The copilot pleaded repeatedly with him to bail out. His reply at this critical juncture was blunt. His words were heard over the interphone and had a magical effect on the crew. They stuck to their guns. The B-17 kept on.

Near the initial point, at 11:50, one hour and a half after the first of at least 200 individual fighter attacks, the pressure eased off, although hostiles were still in the vicinity. A curious sensation came over me. I was still alive. It was possible to think of the target. Of North Africa. Of returning to England. Almost idly, I watched a crippled B-17 pull over to the curb and drop its wheels and open its bomb bay, jettisoning its bombs. Three Me-109's circled it closely, but held their fire while the crew bailed out. I remembered now that a little while back I had seen other Hun fighters hold their fire, even when being shot at by a B-17 from which the crew were bailing. But I doubt if sportsmanship had anything to do with it. They hoped to get a B-17 down fairly intact.

And then our weary, battered column, short twenty-four bombers, but still holding the close formation that had brought the remainder through by sheer air discipline and gunnery, turned in to the target. I knew that our bombardiers were grim as death while they synchronized their sights on the great Me-109 shops lying below us in a curve

473

of the winding blue Danube, close to the outskirts of Regensburg. Our B-17 gave a slight lift and a red light went out on the instrument panel. Our bombs were away. We turned from the target toward the snow-capped Alps. I looked back and saw a beautiful sight—a rectangular pillar of smoke rising from the Me-109 plant. Only one burst was over and into the town. Even from this great height I could see that we had smeared the objective. The price? Cheap. 200 airmen.

A few more fighters pecked at us on the way to the Alps and a couple of smoking B-17's glided down toward the safety of Switzerland, about forty miles distant. A town in the Brenner Pass tossed up a lone burst of futile flak. Flak? There had been lots of flak in the past two hours, but only now did I recall having seen it, a sort of side issue to the fighters. Colonel Le May, who had taken excellent care of us all the way, circled the air division over a large lake to give the cripples, some flying on three engines and many trailing smoke, a chance to rejoin the family. We approached the Mediterranean in a gradual descent, conserving fuel. Out over the water we flew at low altitude, unmolested by fighters from Sardinia or Corsica, waiting through the long hot afternoon hours for the first sight of the North African coast line. The prospect of ditching, out of gasoline, and the sight of other B-17's falling into the drink seemed trivial matters after the vicious nightmare of the long trial across southern Germany. We had walked through a high valley of the shadow of death, not expecting to see another sunset, and now I could fear no evil.

With red lights showing on all our fuel tanks, we landed at our designated base in the desert, after eleven hours in the air. I slept on the ground near the wing and, waking occasionally, stared up at the stars. My radio headset was back in the ship. And yet I could hear the deep chords of great music.

Up to Overlord

The Americans had entered Rome on June 4th, 1944, by the end of the day the city was fully taken. Alexander now had twenty-eight divisions in Italy, hard on the heels of the retreating Germans. But great disappointment was in the cards for Alexander. At the Teheran Conference the previous year, it had been decided that an invasion of southern France, labeled Anvil, was needed to effect a pincers with the Normandy invasion against the German forces in France. On June 6th, the Allies landed on the Normandy beaches and the eyes of the world turned to the invasion efforts there. The American general staff insisted that Anvil now be carried out. The objections of Alexander and the field commanders in Italy, who fought the decision, were overruled; Alexander was deprived of seven of his divisions, three American and four French, for Anvil.

The battle for Italy was to be a bitter, frustrating engagement to the end, but the campaign had, and would continue to have, important effects upon the main target, Germany. One of the chief strategic goals was to subdue the German Luftwaffe. Airfields were now available in Italy to raid the Rumanian oilfields, and heretofore unreachable targets in Germany and the Axis satellites. Furthermore, the Allies in Italy were holding down twice as many German divisions as they themselves had committed, at the very time the Germans on the Russian front were in need of reinforcement.

Meanwhile the plans for the invasion of France, Operation Overlord, had been shaped, refined and elaborated on from conference to conference among the Allied leaders. In the beginning, the initial assault was to provide for three seaborne divisions and two airborne brigades, with two more divisions to follow right behind. Churchill, however, argued throughout 1943 to enlarge the strength of the assault by twenty-five per cent. To support the increase, additional landing craft would have to be provided. They were available only if withdrawn from U.S. Pacific operations, and the American Naval Commander, Admiral King, fought against this.

475

Depending upon whether one consults the American or the British view, the arguments that hammered out the final invasion strategy range from good logic to national prejudice.

The Americans were deeply involved in the Pacific campaign, and planning for both theaters created an inevitable conflict. And the Americans still kept up the initial drive and optimism of the early days of war mobilization. Result: a policy of immediate attack, without waiting for reinforcement from the Pacific.

The British wanted to be certain that the German army would give way at the Atlantic Wall; they still recalled the stalemate and bloodletting in the trench lines of World War I. They had also been mobilized for war since 1939. And had already seen three land operations thrown off the continent. Result: a policy of caution, of not moving until overwhelming power had been built up.

This conflict was resolved at the top level, by Montgomery and Eisenhower. Gen. Eisenhower had been appointed the Supreme Commander-in-Chief on December 6, 1943, with Field Marshal Montgomery to command all ground operations. When they met in London later that month, both men saw the need to strengthen the invasion forces. The plans for Overlord now moved forward in earnest.

Just where on the long European coast the Allies would invade worried the German High Command. Hitler was already fighting on two fronts, soon to be three. His armies were being chewed up and pushed back in Russia. The Italian front held down twenty-one divisions. The long western coastline that was once the symbol of Hitler's victories was now a liability to German strategy. Behind the Atlantic Wall, the Germans finally decided to keep a central reserve of troops in France, which could be quickly shifted to any point along the coast once the invasion point was known. While this was sound strategy, Hitler sapped it by constantly draining the reserve for the Russian front.

In the spring of 1944, Von Rundstedt, the German Commander-in-Chief in the west, had fifty divisions spread along the coast, to be increased to sixty by June 6th. He expected the Allies to make a successful landing and breach the Atlantic Wall, but he hoped to be able to mount a strong enough counterattack immediately after D-Day, by maneuvering the central reserve force, to drive the Allies back into the sea. Partly because of this strategy, Von Rundstedt hadn't paid much attention to the condition of the Atlantic Wall. Rommel, who, under Von Rundstedt, commanded the German armies in Holland, Belgium

476

and France to the Loire River, inherited the job of strengthening the Wall in 1944. He soon found the defenses in poor shape.

Rommel foresaw the Allied superiority in the air, and realized the Germans therefore wouldn't be able to deploy their mobile reserves in time for the counterattack. And so he set to work strengthening the fortifications all along the coast under his command. The beaches were heavily mined, many kinds of underwater obstacles were planted, and new pillboxes were constructed, with guns set to rake the beaches with enfilading fire.

The Allied plans for Overlord, as now revised, provided for an air drop of three airborne divisions, and five divisions to assault from the sea, with two more divisions to follow up. This meant increasing the beachhead area to approximately fifty miles, increasing the aircraft operational support, and supplying the previously mentioned landing craft, plus adding a U.S. naval task force to help escort the enlarged convoys and bombard the beaches. The lessons learned from other landing operations were put to use in Overlord. The British, from their bitter experiences at Dieppe and Norway, knew that pre-assault air and naval bombardment wouldn't necessarily knock out the Germans long enough to enable the troops to reach the beaches safely.

Small support ships were devised to increase firepower close in to the beaches, providing covering fire as troops spread out and took up positions on shore. Batteries of rocket and mortars were mounted on small boats. The infantry was to be followed immediately by heavier artillery anti-tank guns, and then by tanks themselves to give stronger support to the men moving up the beaches.

There were also special tanks designed—flail tanks to beat through the mine fields, DD tanks which could swim ashore under their own power, and flame-throwing tanks to subdue stubborn pillboxes.

A further innovation was the creation of two artificial harbors, to be constructed in England and floated across to the French coast. Until the port of Cherbourg could be captured, they would receive the supplies that would pour across to the continent.

The Allies hoped to land eight divisions on D-Day, another two on D-plus one; by D-plus four, they hoped to have fifteen divisions ashore. The Russians had agreed to launch an offensive to coincide with the landings, and pressure was to be increased against the Germans on the Italian front.

It was enormously important that the Germans discover neither the

477

exact landing areas for the invasion nor the date it was to be launched. Unusual security measures were taken to restrict travel in the United Kingdom, and two weeks before the invasion the troop assembly camps and embarkation ports were sealed off from all civilians. The Allies outdid themselves to mislead the Germans and to camouflage invasion preparations. The British had conceived of Operation Fortitude, a plan to suggest to the Germans that the invasion would occur at Pas de Calais, a section of the French coast north of the real landing area. The Pas de Calais was the point of shortest distance between France and England. The British hoped that if the Germans swallowed the bait they might also be led to consider the landings in Normandy a diversionary tactic, and *still* expect major landings in the Pas de Calais area.

To make a convincing show of it, divisions to land after D-Day were assembled in England in an area opposite the Pas de Calais; fake landing craft were assembled in ports near by, dummy gliders were staked out on fields—all the signs of a huge staging area were exposed. The British also released dozens of messages, orders and signals all designed to be guided along into the hands of known enemy agents. And finally, right up until D-Day, bombing was twice as heavy as usual in the areas immediately behind the Pas de Calais.

On the eve of the invasion, Operation Fortitude really came into its own. Through use of aircraft and small ships of the Royal Navy, the impression of "big ship echoes" was produced on enemy radar (according to Wilmot in his *The Struggle for Europe*) while bombers created the effect of huge air armadas, again on radar, by dropping quantities of metalized paper in front of Pas de Calais. Every tactic suggesting a realistic invasion was pursued.

In fact, Von Rundstedt had already persuaded himself that the invasion would be at the Pas de Calais; it was closest to England, and he knew the British Spitfire's range was severely limited and, in providing proper air cover, would be most effective here. (Operation Fortitude seems to have accomplished everything and more than the Allies hoped for; on D-plus ten the Germans were still expecting a major attack from the fake divisions in the staging area across from the Pas de Calais.)

Air force strategy raised a new argument in the Allied staff. Through the winter of 1944, with the combined air forces of Britain and the U.S. hammering German industry, the air commanders still believed that bombing raids alone could bring Germany to her knees—if only enough sorties could be flown. But Overlord's planners wanted rail traffic in France paralyzed to keep the Germans from maneuvering for anti-inva-

478

sion counterattacks. The airmen would have to shift their attention to this job. Finally, the air forces came around and, beginning in March, rail lines, depots, and traffic centers were strafed and bombed. By D-Day rail traffic throughout France had been reduced by seventy per cent. The immediate effect of this was to keep reinforcements from reaching the Atlantic Wall.

The invasion plans in their last details were made irrevocable in early May. Gen. Montgomery was to lead and command the land forces. His aim was to secure the beachheads, and send armored columns probing inland as fast and as far as possible, to offset the expected counterattacks from Rommel's Panzer divisions. Montgomery had guessed that Rommel would try to throw the Allies off the beaches at once, to try to produce another Dunkirk, and this Montgomery had to prevent at all costs.

The landings, after long rehearsals, were to be carried out by the following forces:

Three airborne divisions would be dropped on the evening of D-Day, the 6th British Division into the Orne Valley, and the 82nd and 101st American Airborne Divisions on the Cotentin Peninsula. Their objectives were to strike at the beach defenses from the rear, and secure the flanks of the bridgehead: the Americans, the right flank to the south; the British, the left flank to the north.

On D-Day itself, the 1st U.S. Army under Gen. Omar Bradley was to land on two beaches, at two separate invasion points: Utah Beach, and Omaha Beach on the left. The 2nd British Army, under the command of Gen. M. C. Dempsey, was to land between Bayeaux and Caen on three beaches: Gold Beach, Juno Beach (to be assaulted by the Canadians), and Sword Beach.

In early May, June 5th had been set as D-Day, but only after the most comprehensive research into weather, problems of tide, circumstances of German reinforcements, availability of all naval support and landing craft, etc. The month of May provided perfect invasion weather, and the Germans, it is now known, expected the invasion almost daily. The Allies were not yet ready.

On the weekend preceding June 5th, a storm brewed up in the Atlantic off Great Britain that would affect the Channel waters, and this forestalled plans for the 5th. Some naval elements had already been started across the Channel early on the morning of the 5th, and had to be called back—several convoys were more than halfway to France before the signal reached them to return. Soldiers already committed to the invasion ships had to be kept aboard as their ships pitched and tossed at anchor—some men had been aboard for three and four days. They couldn't be taken off the ships; their places in the invasion camps had already been filled by the divisions slated to follow them after the beachhead was established.

At the Allied headquarters, there was to be a brief period of comparative calm on the evening of the 5th, although the weather outlook was still not good. Any postponement beyond June 6th would involve a delay of at least two weeks before another attempt could be made; Eisenhower decided late on Monday morning the 6th to give the signal again, and the invasion ships headed out into the storm-tossed Channel. Even though the weather was to clear later on, there were still high winds and waves. Some of the smaller landing craft had to return to port. By mid-afternoon of June 6th, there were more than 3,500 ships in the Channel, of which more than 500 were warships to escort the convoys and lay on the first bombardment.

The waters off the Normandy coast first had to be swept of mines, and the minesweepers worked in the last few hours of daylight, surprisingly without interference from the Germans. Operation Fortitude was now producing some effect, but the Germans were simply not alert. The Luftwaffe flew only one reconnaissance mission, and that was too far north to spot the invasion fleet while at sea; the Luftwaffe was grounded by the bad weather, and what was left of the German navy kept inside the harbors. Rommel himself was on his way to Berchtesgaden where he hoped to get Hitler to agree to move a Panzer division into the St. Lô area where, ironically, the Americans were to drop their airborne divisions later that night.

The minesweepers and underwater demolition teams had done their work. After dark had closed in, the three airborne divisions filed into their planes and gliders, every paratrooper armed to the teeth. Just before midnight, 1,100 air transports filled with British and American troops headed for their drop points behind the Atlantic Wall.

The following account of the drop is taken from the regimental history of the 501st Parachutists of the 101st Airborne Division, as set down by Capt. Laurence Critchell.

AIR DROP ON NORMANDY

by Capt. Laurence Critchell

The night of June 6th was sullen and rainy. Fitful gusts of wind rocked the planes. Twilight was late in England at that time of year and, though the planes did not take off until 10:21—in military time 2221—a desolate blue light still showed behind the storm clouds. The C-47s climbed to their formations and straightened out, at two thousand feet, to head for France. Within the cabins we sat with darkened faces and stared out at the lampless countryside far below. Those of us who had taken the round, pink seasick pills felt drowsy. The wild excitement characterizing the scenes at the field prior to the takeoff had subsided, and no one talked very much. In the planes ridden by the Catholic and Protestant chaplains, the men said short prayers, bowing their blackened heads where they sat. Forward, by the pilot's compartment, were equipment bundles waiting to be kicked out the open door; on racks under the planes, like bombs, were more.

Over the English Channel a familiar and tranquil moon came out. Looking down to the indigo water, we could realize for the first time the stupendous effort of which we were a part. As far as the eye could see on the rough surface of the Channel, extending from beneath the plane to either wing-tip and dissolving into the far-off murk, were the ships of the Allied invasion. The thought crossed many of our minds that, down in each one of those tiny fragments, were men like ourselves, sitting in darkness and waiting dry-mouthed for the unknown. And suddenly it seemed as though we could see the whole great, sprawling, disconnected plan, which had begun at the induction centers ("Did they ask you about the paratroops?"), coming together into a single arrow of assault. And we were the tip.

The man who is going into combat does not feel much different from the man who is going to make his first parachute jump. What lies ahead of him is too unfamiliar to be frightening. He may realize that his heart is beating a little faster than normal, that the skin of his face is hot and his hands are cold. Otherwise he feels all right. But all his faculties are keyed up to abnormal alertness. And if the inner nervousness has not made him drowsy—which is one effect of tension on the system—he is acutely aware not only of himself, his physical presence in the plane or ship, but also of everything around him. From the moment he leaves the security of the rear to go forward he lives completely in the present.

The weather was clear across the Channel. By the time the planes began to encounter scattered clouds near the French coast, most of us were asleep. We were awakened by an unfamiliar sound, like the close-by popping of an outboard motor. Looking out the celluloid windows, we could see what it was: we were being fired at. The tracer bullets were speckling up into the sky in streams, thousands of them. Curiously enough, they were all colors—red, green, yellow, blue. It seemed unreal; it gave the darkness a nightmarish quality, like a multicolored blast furnace.

For all of us, pilots and soldiers alike, this was our first instant under fire. Nobody stopped to analyze his feelings. But if we felt anything at all it was surprise—surprise that anybody actually hated us enough to want to kill us. It was a feeling that tightened us in around ourselves painfully. And if the reader is interested in knowing what causes the gulf between a civilian and a veteran soldier, it is simply the difference between a man who has lived all his life in a reasonably friendly world, compared to the one who has existed where other people are literally trying to spill his brains on the earth.

The machine-gun bullets turned on Sergeant Rice's plane. They appeared out of the darkness below as little colored specks and whizzed past at the same instant. The popping noise sounded, oddly, as though it were close underneath the plane. It was not a loud noise, but it was distinct above the roar of the motors.

At the shouted order we shuffled to our feet. Hooking up, we checked our equipment. The familiar rote of parachute school was reassuring. But then we had to wait, pressed close against each other in silence. And we were having a hard time keeping on our feet. Almost at the first shots from below, the inexperienced pilots—men who later were to take us through enemy anti-aircraft fire as nervelessly as on a bomb run—had begun evasive action. This was contrary to orders. Their formations loosened up. A cloud bank near the Merderet scattered them still further. Sergeant Rice's plane dipped and turned, sometimes rising a hundred feet in a second or two, buckling the men's legs under the pressure.

All this had taken only a few moments. Now there was a new sound in the sky—the noise of explosions. The distant ones made an odd, enveloping *wop*, like a sound curling in on itself; close by, they had the concussion of dynamite. A noise like the rattling of chains beat against the walls of the plane; it was expended shrapnel. Nothing had prepared us for the surprising discovery that flak made noise. A glare lit up the sky. Rice saw a plane on fire as it dipped down below him, curling off on one wing. One—two—three dark figures hurtled out of it; then flames enveloped the cabin. In his mind's eye he saw the men shriveling up inside— maybe Suarez, maybe Colonel Johnson . . .

He wanted to get out of the plane . . .

A red light glowed over the door. There were more explosions. All semblance of formation had been lost. In the steady popping of the machine-gun bullets, the *wham wham wham* of the 20-mm. tracer shells and the explosions of the 88-mm. flak, the sharp arrow of the invasion seemed hopelessly blunted. One or two pilots slammed the doors of their compartments and circled back for England; they had had enough. But for the most part the planes blundered on. Men got sick and vomited on the floor; shrapnel tore up through the greasy pools or through the seats they had quitted. In the planes carrying loads of high explosives known as Composition C-2, the men held their breaths, waiting to find out what it would feel like to be blown to pieces.

"Take it easy, boys!" yelled Lieutenant Jansen at the door of Rice's plane. "It'll be all over in a minute!"

Fifty-caliber machine-gun bullets tore through the wings like the chattering of gravel. Rice's plane was much too high. Everything was going wrong.

Over the door, like a signal of relief, the green light went on.

How the hell did the pilots know where they were?

A K ration bundle lay in front of Lieutenant Jansen. He kicked it out the door. That was the last they ever saw of it. The second bundle weighed three hundred pounds. Before he and the crew chief could get rid of it, sixty seconds had passed. In that time the plane, going too fast anyway, had traveled almost two miles. What none of the men realized was that those chance sixty seconds were taking them—as in Colonel Johnson's plane, where a similar delay occurred —to La Barquette.

The anxious men dove out. Rice was wearing too much equipment; his left arm caught in the door. For three seconds he hung outside in the hundred-mile-an-hour wind. When he was torn free, the metal edge of the door scraped his skin almost to the flesh, taking with it his hundred-and-fifty-dollar wrist watch. He scarcely felt it. But his body position was so bad that the opening of the parachute almost knocked him unconscious. Dazed, he floated down. The only sounds were the sharp cracking of bullets that struck the edge of his nylon canopy. One arm was almost useless; with the other he slipped to earth as fast as he could. It was dark. He lay still on the ground for a moment. Machine-gun bullets firing to his right were thirty and forty feet in the air. He could hear the explosions of mortars and the sounds of planes going away, going back to England . . .

The pilots were hopelessly confused. The area had looked right that was all. How could anybody be sure of anything in all this confusion? But it would work out. It had to work out . . .

All over the Cotentin Peninsula the parachutists were coming down that way. Out in the English Channel the great armada of ships moved steadily towards set destinations—beaches later called Utah and Red Leg and Omaha, where hundreds of infantrymen died in the bleak daybreak. But that was four hours away. Meanwhile, we had no encouragement, no assurance, even, that the seaborne invasion would actually take place. And we were scattered. Where we had expected to land in selected drop zones, to assemble as complete battalions, each man found himself virtually alone.

A prize military secret—the dim locator lights on the equipment bundles—was quickly rendered useless; the German machine gunners fired on the lights. Later they booby-trapped the abandoned bundles. The biggest secret of them all—the pathfinder radar devices, the operators of which were dropped in Normandy half an hour before the first wave of planes—also turned out poorly: the operators were unable, as a rule, to reach their sets. All over Normandy, that night, the long prepared plans and the careful strategy were going awry.

Small groups of men worked their way across country, collecting more men as they went. Privates or sergeants or colonels led them—whoever kept his wits. Staff Sergeant Clarence J. Tyrrel of Georgia, who had been dropped twenty miles beyond his objective, gathered enough men to act as a tactical unit and on his way back through the darkness destroyed two light tanks. Lieutenant Colonel George Griswold and Captain Eldia Hare collected another group of men and brought them to the division command post at Hiesville, knocking off a horse-drawn German ammunition train enroute. But some of the groups were so small and so thoroughly lost that they fought for days before they learned that the invasion had really taken place.

This scattered fighting in the darkness seemed useless at the time. In effect, however, it worked out all right. The German soldiers had been accustomed to a pattern of formal war, with front lines, outposts and command posts. They found themselves fighting all around the clock. They themselves had developed vertical envelopment at Crete and Holland, but counter-offensive had evidently not occurred to them. There was nothing in their books to prepare them

485

for situations where fire came from one direction one moment and from another the next. War waged by small independent groups of soldiers without leaders or without strategy was inconceivable. It was not war; it was chaos. How were such men controlled?

The Americans were not controlled. They just killed Germans.

Colonel Johnson was near Sergeant Rice when he landed. A dark building suggested one way of finding out where he was. But he left it alone—it was a German command post—and worked his way along the ditches in the general direction of the south, killing his first German when an enemy soldier opened up at him with a machine pistol. He was looking for La Barquette. He crawled for half an hour before he met anyone. Then he encountered a small group from one of the other battalions. None of the men knew where he was.

Tom Rice, meanwhile, had done all right. He and a small number of men moved into the apparently deserted village of Addeville. Finding no Germans there, the platoon leader, Lieutenant Rafferty, set up a temporary command post. Addeville had not been an objective. Everybody knew it. But just then they were not thinking about the plans that had been laid out for them in the sanity of England. They considered themselves lucky to hold what they had.

General Eisenhower, listening to the first word of the seaborne landings early next morning, had no idea of what had really happened to his airborne troops. But neither, as a matter of fact, had his airborne troops.

Across the Channel

The 101st Airborne Division got down out of the air with comparative safety, but then their troubles began. Because of heavy anti-aircraft fire and the bad weather, the troops were dispersed over such a wide area that out of more than 6,000 men, less than half had been brought together by the evening of D-plus one. They captured many of their objectives but they, like the 82nd Airborne, had trouble organizing enough men to achieve all they had been assigned to do.

On the eastern flank, the 6th British Airborne Division was to land near Caen and hold that flank against an expected counterattack from Panzer divisions in the area. Compared to the Americans, the British had a more successful drop, accomplishing most of their objectives by the time of the sea landings later that day.

Even the airborne operations hit the Germans with an element of surprise. Most of their radar warning system had been knocked out by bombing, and what was left was taken in by the deceptions of Operation Fortitude. Reports that did come in to German headquarters only helped to compound confusion. The Germans knew nothing of the invasion fleet's approach until it had gotten close enough to launch landing boats, and even then they were sure this wasn't the "real" invasion. They still held themselves in readiness for the Pas de Calais thrust. By early morning, part of the German Command had asked permission to move some armor in against the Normandy landings, but Hitler advised them to wait until the main direction of the invasion could be determined in the coming daylight hours. The late Chester Wilmot, Australian correspondent, describes what happened on Utah and Omaha beaches.

ASSAULT FROM THE SEA

by Chester Wilmot

A rising, surging sea carried the invasion fleet uneasily into the night. To the men whose destiny lay beyond the black horizon, the voyage seemed lonely and interminable. Cold, stinging spray swept the decks, but it was better there than it was below, where the pitching and throbbing of the ships was magnified and the humid air reeked of sickness. Nausea accentuated the natural anxiety of expectation. They did not imagine that the enemy was ignorant of their approach and his failure to respond seemed to many not only surprising but sinister. The sense of anticlimax added to their qualms, and they were slow to draw reassurance from the German inactivity.

Because the voyage was uneventful, it took on an air of unreality, which still prevailed at 2 a.m. when Naval Force "U" (Rear-Admiral D. P. Moon, U.S.N.) began assembling undisturbed in its transport area off the Cotentin, 12 miles north-east of Utah sector. Aboard its ships, nearly a thousand all told, were 30,000 men and 3,500 vehicles due to be landed that day on this beach alone.

Good fortune smoothed their way. The E-boats, which had been ordered out from Cherbourg to patrol the Bay of the Seine, turned back "on account of the bad weather" without making contact. The twin islands of St. Marcouf, lying athwart the line of approach, were found to be undefended. The coastal batteries were silent, for their radar was being jammed. Moreover, during the night they had been severely hammered by R.A.F. Lancasters and at first light they came under fresh onslaught from air and sea. At 5:20 a.m. 300 medium bombers of the Ninth U.S. Air Force flew in below the clouds to strike at these guns again and at strongpoints on Utah beach, which was already shuddering under shellfire from two battleships, two cruisers and a dozen destroyers. The accuracy of this double bombardment was evident as the assault craft, carrying two battalions of the 4th U.S. Infantry Division, drove in-shore leaving great white wakes on the dark-green sea. Even then there was little response from the coastal artillery and the beach defences were subdued by drenching fire from the "mosquito fleet," which moved in behind and on the flanks of the assault craft to rake the shore with rockets, flak-guns and howitzers.

In the vanguard of the invasion were two squadrons of DD tanks. These were to have been launched four miles off-shore, but because they were delayed by the weather, the LCTs carried them more than two miles closer before setting them to swim. By then they were under the lee of the Peninsula, which gave them considerable protection from the wind that was lashing the beaches farther east, and 28 out of 32 "DDs" got safely ashore. At least a dozen of them touched down with the first wave of infantry at 6:30 a.m. and began firing from the shallows as the men leapt from their landing-craft.[1]

With the tide still well out, most of the craft came to rest short of the belt of obstacles set up for their destruction and the troops had nearly 500 yards to run before they reached the long, low line of dunes. From these there came not the expected torrent of fire, but fitful and erratic spurts, for the defenders were numbed by the bombardment which still rang in their ears. They were slow to realise that it had switched to targets on the flanks and those Germans who did come up to man their weapons found their fire answered at once by tanks on the water's edge.

[1] The authors of *Utah Beach to Cherbourg*, a campaign study prepared by the Historical Division of the U.S. Army, say (at p. 44) that "the 32 DD tanks played little part in the assault" and that they "beached approximately 15 minutes after the first assault wave." This view is supported neither by the commander of the leading American regiment (Col. J. A. Van Fleet), nor by the reports of prisoners.

Although Rommel had given warning that the Allies would employ "water-proofed and submersible tanks," his troops do not seem to have taken his admonition seriously, for the appearance of the "DDs" unquestionably came as a shock to them. They had thought that they would turn their guns against soft human targets advancing unprotected over open beach, but now the Americans were covered by fire from armour which had come up out of the sea. Nothing in war is more unnerving than the unexpected. Surprise gave the DD tanks an influence far beyond their fire-power, striking terror in the hearts of the Germans and adding confidence to the resolution with which the Americans swept ashore. By 9 a.m. the leading regiment and the tanks had broken the crust of the Atlantic Wall on a two-mile front between the sea and the coastal lagoon.

In this they were aided by a mistake which proved no misfortune. Owing to the early swamping of two control vessels, a slight error was made in navigation, with the result that the assault battalions were landed nearly a mile south of the prescribed beach. This brought them to a sector where a single battalion of doubtful quality was manning defences less formidable than those the Americans would have encountered farther north. The Germans had presumed that the double belt of inundations in this extreme corner of the Peninsula would effectively discourage any attempt at landing or at least render nugatory whatever foothold might be gained there.

In the wake of the assault waves came naval demolition units and special squads of army engineers to blow and bulldoze clear lanes through the beach obstacles, thus preparing the way for the rapid and early landing of the rest of the 4th Division. This clearing operation was doubly hazardous, for most of the obstacles were mined and the foreshore came under increasingly heavy shellfire from long-range guns now able to operate without the aid of radar. Nevertheless, adequate gaps were cleared by the time the main body of the follow-up regiment began landing at 10 a.m. The infantry moved quickly through the shellfire and swung north along the dunes to attack the sector where the landing should have been made. There they

490

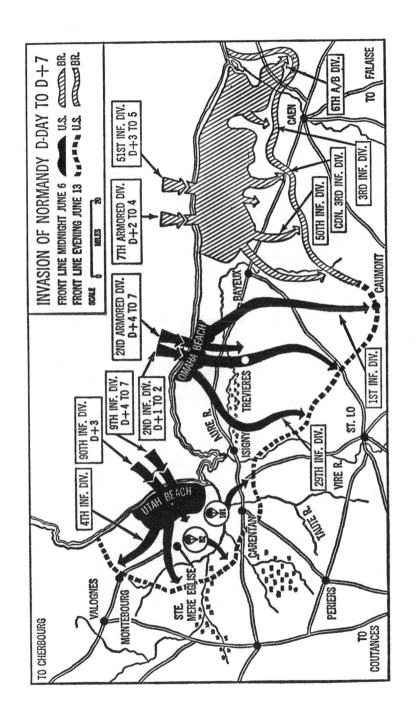

INVASION OF NORMANDY D-DAY TO D+7

FRONT LINE MIDNIGHT JUNE 6
FRONT LINE EVENING JUNE 13

U.S. ▬▬ BR.
U.S. ▪▪▪ BR.

SCALE
0   MILES   20

51ST INF. DIV.
D+3 TO 5

7TH ARMORED DIV.
D+2 TO 4

2ND ARMORED DIV.
D+4 TO 7

9TH INF. DIV.
D+4 TO 7

2ND INF. DIV.
D+1 TO 2

90TH INF. DIV.
D+3

4TH INF. DIV.

29TH INF. DIV.

1ST INF. DIV.

50TH INF. DIV.

CDN. 3RD INF. DIV.

3RD INF. DIV.

6TH A/B DIV.

TO CHERBOURG

VALOGNES

MONTEBOURG

STE. MERE EGLISE

CARENTAN

PERIERS

TO COUTANCES

UTAH BEACH

OMAHA BEACH

AURE R.

TREVIERES

ISIGNY

BAYEUX

CAUMONT

ST. LO

VIRE R.

TAUTE R.

CAEN

TO FALAISE

encountered determined opposition, and they were not able to reach the guns, which continued their harassing fire in spite of counter-battery bombardment by the Navy.

This enemy shelling did not seriously delay the landing and unloading, and a stream of men, tanks, guns and vehicles came in to consolidate the division's hold on the coastal strip and to strengthen its westward advance. In the middle of the morning the infantry set out across the causeways with amphibious tanks moving through the water in close support. A few enemy positions on the far shore of the lagoon were still active, but the tanks subdued them and by 1 p.m. the seaborne and airborne forces had met. Already the parachutists had seized the exits from four causeways, while a fifth was found to be undefended and unmined even though it linked the beach with the main road leading straight through to the Merderet Valley.

No junction had yet been made between the 101st and the 82nd Divisions, but it was clear that a strong grip had been established on the Peninsula. Shortly before midday, Moon signalled to Kirk, commanding the Western Task Force, "Initial waves made landings on exact beaches after accurate air and naval bombardment. Fifteen waves landed by 0945B.[2] Succeeding waves continue to land. Both beaches cleared of obstacles. Roads under construction and vehicles proceeding inland. Little opposition. Coastal batteries under control."

This signal idealised the situation beyond the facts, for no one who was on the beach that morning would have reported in such glowing terms. But the general impression it conveyed—that the battle was developing according to plan—was justified and it brought profound relief to Omar Bradley, the Army Commander, who was in Kirk's flagship, the U.S. cruiser *Augusta*. There throughout the morning Bradley had been receiving reports of a very different character from the other American sector, Omaha, where Gerow's V Corps was still fighting for a foothold against what proved to be the fiercest and most sustained resistance of the day.

[2] That is, 9:45 a.m. British Double Summer Time.

492

Omaha was a concave beach four miles long and dominated at either end by cliffs which rose almost sheer for more than 100 feet. Between these two bluffs the gently curving strand sloped up to a cultivated plateau which reached a height of 150 feet half a mile inland and commanded the whole foreshore. The escarpment of this plateau was indented at four points where small watercourses had cut their way to the sea and these narrow valleys provided the only exits for vehicles. On the beach itself the tidal flat, some 300 yards deep, was firm sand, but it ended in a bank of heavy, smooth shingle which sloped up rather sharply.

On the western third of Omaha this shingle ran up to a sea-wall and a paved road, beyond which the escarpment soon rose at a steep angle. On the rest of the beach the shingle bank was backed by sand dunes which were impassable by vehicles, as was the shingle in many places. On the far side of this line of dunes was a broad stretch of sand which was marshy and tufted with coarse grass at the entrances to the valleys. Here the rough slope was less steep, but it could not be negotiated even by tracked vehicles except in a few places. Apart from the paved road under the lee of the western bluff, the routes running inland were little more than cart tracks and all led through thickly-wooded cuttings into the stout stone villages of Vierville, St. Laurent and Colleville, which thus commanded every exit.

The inherent strength of this sector had been well exploited by the Germans in designing their defences. On the tidal flat there were three belts of obstacles; the beach above the shingle, and parts of the slope, were mined and wired; all the natural exits were blocked by mines and by either concrete obstructions or anti-tank ditches. The main strongpoints, consisting of entrenchments, pillboxes and bunkers equipped with machine-guns, anti-tank guns and light artillery, were concentrated on the bluffs at either end of the beach and at the mouths of the four valleys. There the fire positions were terraced up the slopes on either side and were echeloned inland, so that they were almost impregnable against head-on assault. From these the Ger-

493

mans could cover most of the beach with direct and flanking fire.

Between the exit valleys, however, the defences were less formidable. There were trenches and weapon pits along the crest of the escarpment and some minefields on the plateau, but the Germans relied on their reserves in the string of coastal villages to cut short any penetration between the main strongholds. These villages formed a second defensive chain and three miles inland the flooded valley of the River Aure provided a further barrier which the Americans would have to force in order to avoid being contained in the narrow coastal belt.

This stretch of beach, thus fortified, was hardly inviting, but it was the only part of the entire 20 miles between the mouth of the Vire and Arromanches, north-east of Bayeux, where a landing could be made in strength. Elsewhere in this zone sheer cliffs or outcrops of rock off-shore provided natural protection and allowed the Germans to concentrate on the defense of Omaha.

When the American plan was made it was thought that this four-mile sector was manned by little more than a battalion of the 716th Division, which was then holding 45 miles of coastline from the Orne to the Vire. This was an indifferent formation, containing many foreign conscripts and equipped only for a static role, but a mobile division of good quality, the 352nd, was known to be in close reserve around St. Lô. In May British Intelligence had come to suspect that this division had moved up to strengthen the coastal crust by taking over the western half of the Orne-Vire sector, but the evidence of that move was slender and the Americans were disinclined to accept it. When some confirmation was received early in June, it was too late to pass the warning on to the assault troops who were already embarking. Consequently, they went into action believing that though Omaha was strongly fortified it was not particularly heavily garrisoned.

The plan provided for the 1st U.S. Division (Major-General C. R. Huebner) to assault with two Regimental Combat Teams, each of three battalions, supported by two battalions of DD tanks and two special brigades of engineers. On the

494

right the 116th Regiment (attached from the 29th Division) was to land between Vierville and St. Laurent, and on the left the 16th Regiment, between St. Laurent and Colleville. For the assault both these regiments were to be under Huebner's command, but once a foothold had been gained, the 29th Division (Major-General C. H. Gerhardt) was to take over the western sector and clear the area between the coast and the Aure as far as Isigny. Meantime, the 1st Division would swing east to link up with Second British Army at Port-en-Bessin and drive south to secure a bridgehead over the Aure, east of Trévières. It was hoped—a little ambitiously perhaps—that by nightfall V U.S. Corps might have a beachhead 16 miles wide and five to six miles deep, but it was realised that whether or not this "phase-line" could be reached depended primarily on the whereabouts of the 352nd Division.

Soon after 3 a.m. Naval Force "O" (Rear-Admiral J. L. Hall, Jr., U.S.N.) began lowering the assault-craft from their "mother-ships" into a rough and unfriendly sea twelve miles off-shore. Several craft were swamped within a few minutes of touching the water; others were kept afloat only by strenuous bailing by troops who used their steel helmets as buckets. None but the most hardened stomachs were unmoved by the pitching and tossing and men became weak from sickness long before they began the run-in. Perhaps the most unpleasant experience was that suffered by a boatload of the 116th Infantry. "Major Dallas's command party," says the regimental account, "made their start under inauspicious circumstances. In lowering the boats from the davits of H.M.S. *Empire Javelin,* the command boat became stuck for 30 minutes directly under the outlet of the ship's 'heads' and could go neither up nor down. During this half-hour the ship's company made the most of an opportunity that Englishmen have sought since 1776."

The rough seas had more serious consequences in the case of the DD tanks. One battalion decided not to attempt any launchings; the other put 29 tanks into the water, but some sank like stones as soon as they left the LCTs, others were swamped on the run-in and only two reached the shore. The weather was the primary factor in this disaster, but the casualties might not have been so severe if the tanks had not been launched so far out (they were set to swim nearly four miles) and if the training and maintenance had been more thorough. But whatever the reason, the plan to land the DD tanks ahead of the infantry miscarried, and the men themselves approached the shore under the gravest disadvantages. As one report says, "Men who had been chilled by their wetting, cramped by immobility in the small and fully-loaded craft and weakened by sea-sickness were not in the best condition for strenuous action on landing." [3]

While the assault battalions were heading for the shore, warships and aircraft began the bombardment of the coast defences. Owing to low cloud, visibility was poor when the shelling began and after a few minutes the dust and smoke made it almost impossible to pinpoint targets on shore. The task of the bombers thus became extremely difficult and, fearful of hitting their own troops, they left a good safety margin. This was unquestionably wise, but it meant that most of the bombs fell behind, not upon, the beach defences. In addition, many rocket-firing craft, confused by the smoke and over-anxious about the coastal guns, loosed their salvos well out of range and the in-coming troops had the mortification of seeing most of the projectiles burst in the water short of the beach.

Batteries and strong points were still active when the bombardment lifted, and the assault craft came under heavy shelling and mortaring over the last half-mile before they touched down on a beach almost unscarred by friendly bomb or shell. The severest fire came from the bluff which commanded the western end of the beach and from the Vierville exit, directly in front of which the 1st Battalion of the 116th Regiment was due to land in column of companies.

[3] *Omaha Beachhead,* p. 38. This authoritative account of the landing, prepared by the U.S. War Department's Historical Division, is admirably frank and comprehensive.

496

At 6:30 a.m., as the leading company approached this beach, known by the code-name Dog Green,[4] one of its six craft foundered and another was sunk by a direct hit, but the rest went on till they ran aground on a sandbar several hundred yards short of the sea-wall. The ramps went down and the men leapt into water which was waist to shoulder deep. Then, says the battalion's own story: [5]

> As if this were the signal for which the enemy had waited, all boats came under criss-cross machine-gun fire. . . . As the first men jumped, they crumpled and flopped into the water. Then order was lost. It seemed to the men that the only way to get ashore was to dive head first in and swim clear of the fire that was striking the boats. But, as they hit the water, their heavy equipment dragged them down and soon they were struggling to keep afloat. Some were hit in the water and wounded. Some drowned then and there. . . . But some moved safely through the bullet-fire to the sand and then, finding they could not hold there, went back into the water and used it as cover, only their heads sticking out. Those who survived kept moving forward with the tide, sheltering at times behind under-water obstacles and in this way they finally made their landings.
>
> Within ten minutes of the ramps being lowered, A Company had become inert, leaderless and almost incapable of action. Every officer and sergeant had been killed or wounded. . . . It had become a struggle for survival and rescue. The men in the water pushed

[4] Between the Vire and the Orne the Normandy coast was divided by the planners into beach sectors labelled alphabetically from the West. The three sectors of Omaha—D, E and F—were known from their lettering as Dog, Easy and Fox, and sub-sectors were designated by colours. Thus the 116th Regiment landed on Dog Green, Dog White, Dog Red and Easy Green; 16th Regiment on Easy Red and Fox Green.

[5] This account was prepared by the U.S. War Department's Historical Division after close interrogation of the survivors.

wounded men ashore ahead of them, and those who had reached the sands crawled back into the water pulling others to land to save them from drowning, in many cases only to see the rescued men wounded again or to be hit themselves. Within 20 minutes of striking the beach A Company had ceased to be an assault company and had become a forlorn little rescue party bent upon survival and the saving of lives.

The vanguard of the assault on this flank of Omaha was still at the water's edge when the next company came in 25 minutes after H-Hour. Several boatloads, which landed on Dog Green, the same sector as the first wave, were riddled on the water's edge, but the others, carried farther east and farther inshore by the tide, touched down on a less heavily defended stretch of beach which was enveloped in smoke. This shielded them as they dashed for cover of the sea-wall and from there two groups, each less than twenty strong, struggled through the wire and minefields and up the ridge to Vierville, 700 yards inland, not stopping to deal with the fortifications but infiltrating between them as best they could.

Because of the drag of the wind and tide, all six boats of the following company came in east of the Dog Green death-trap, and moved across the foreshore and up the slope with less than a dozen casualties, for they found an unmined gap between the strongpoints which guarded the natural exits. Before 10 a.m. this company and part of 5th Ranger Battalion, which landed behind it, had joined the two earlier groups in Vierville, just in time to beat off a sharp counter-attack. There some 200 men stopped a thrust which would have carried through to the beach, where the remnants of the 1st Battalion lay almost helpless in their foxholes, lacking the support of armour or heavy weapons.

A mile to the east, the other two battalions of the 116th Regiment, landing in succession on either side of the Les Moulins exit, met less opposition on the beach, because the Germans were blinded by smoke from grass and buildings on the crest set afire by the naval bombardment. This unintentional smoke screen saved many lives, but it caused great confusion. Most companies came in farther east than had been planned and "officers, knowing they were to the left of their landing areas, were uncertain as to their course of action, and this hesitation prevented any chance of immediate assault action." [6] They were slow in rallying, slower still in advancing up the slope, since they tended to move in single file through the minefields, and those who did reach the crest soon lost cohesion and direction, for there the smoke was so thick that the troops had to put on their gas-masks.

There was little progress until someone discovered, east of Les Moulins, a sector where the minefields had been detonated by the bombardment, opening the way for elements of both battalions to infiltrate towards St. Laurent before the enemy closed the gap with shellfire. This accentuated the congestion on the beach, for supporting weapons and transport had begun to land before the engineers had cleared any exits and before the infantry had subdued the strongpoints which raked the foreshore with fire. Wrecked landing-craft, burning vehicles, exploding ammunition and intermittent shelling added to the confusion, making it extremely difficult for commanders to organise the scattered and bewildered groups who had taken shelter under the sea-wall or the shingle bank, and impossible for the follow-up regiment to come in as planned at 9:30 a.m.

Meantime, the counterpart of this battle had developed along the eastern half of Omaha, where two battalions of the 16th Regiment had landed at half-past six. Here, too, the bombardment had missed the beach defences and the assault craft were dragged by the run of the wind and tide half a mile and more to the east of their appointed stations. The whole assault side-slipped with most unfortunate results. On Easy Red, where the enemy fire at first was relatively light, barely 100 men were set down during the first half-hour, but the best part of three companies made their landfall on Fox Green directly beneath the unscathed guns of formidable strong points which covered the exit leading to Colleville. The terrible story of Dog Green was repeated.

[6] *Omaha Beachhead,* p. 47.

On Easy Red, where the 2nd Battalion should have landed, the first meagre assault forces were pinned to the beach until "a lieutenant and a wounded sergeant of divisional engineers stood up under fire and walked over to inspect the wire obstacles just beyond the embankment. The lieutenant came back and, hands on hips, looked down disgustedly at the men lying behind the shingle bank. 'Are you going to lay there and get killed, or get up and do something about it?' Nobody stirred, so the sergeant and the officer got the materials and blew the wire." [7] This courageous gesture rallied the men and the lieutenant led them to the top of the ridge in single file along a narrow pathway which was under fire and sown with anti-personnel mines. By that route, this platoon, followed by another company, got within striking distance of the strongpoints which had turned this sector into a slaughter-ground. One by one these were silenced but the hazard of the minefields remained. One false step and a man lost a foot or a leg, if not his life. The wounded lay where they fell, afraid to move lest they might set off another mine, and the men in the shuffling line stepped over them. Shells dropped close but none dared to go to ground, for every yard was lethal. When the reserve battalion tried to find its own pathway, the minefield claimed 47 victims in the leading company, but some 300 men finally got through and headed for Colleville. The gap thus opened became a funnel for movement off Easy Red during the rest of the morning, but that movement was slow and perilous.

On the extreme left, however, the 16th's other assault battalion was able to make reasonable progress, in spite of early mishaps which might have proved disastrous. Rough sea and bad navigation delayed the landing. Several craft were swamped, or sunk by direct hits, one assault company was an hour and a half late and the other came in half a mile too far to the east. This, in fact, proved an advantage, since the men were able to organise under the lee of the cliffs and, instead of trying, as intended, to force the strongly-guarded exit from Fox Green, they found their

[7] *Omaha Beachhead,* p. 58.

way up a steep but ill-defended gully farther east. The rest of the battalion followed and opened a clear breach in the defences with the aid of fire from destroyers and small craft operating close in on the flank. Here by 9:30 a.m. the Americans were moving slowly but steadily east along the cliff-top towards Port-en-Bessin, where they were due to link up with the British.

Elsewhere on Omaha, however, the situation was still extremely grave. By half-past nine, according to the After-Action Report of V U.S. Corps, the assault units "were disorganised, had suffered heavy casualties and were handicapped by losses of valuable equipment. . . . They were pinned down along the beach by intense enemy fire. . . . Personnel and equipment were being piled ashore on Easy Red, Easy Green and Dog Red sectors where congested groups afforded good targets for the enemy. The engineers had not been able to clear sufficiently large gaps through the minefields with the result that companies attempting to move through them off the beach suffered considerable casualties. . . . Action in this early period was that of small, often isolated groups—a squad, a section or a platoon without much co-ordination. Attempts were made to organise units but . . . the beaches were too confused to permit it."

In this confusion the forces already ashore were powerless to break the deadlock, and the men, tanks and guns which were so urgently required could not be landed because the engineers had not been able to clear the underwater obstacles or the general wreckage on the foreshore. Even those tanks and vehicles which had been landed were still immobilised on the narrow strip of sand between the rising tide and the shingle bank through which as yet no gaps had been cleared. The assault regiments were clinging to barely a hundred yards of beach. A few small parties, which were to reach Vierville, St. Laurent and Colleville, had made minor penetrations, but these had been partially closed behind them by enemy fire. The Atlantic Wall was holding firm, and the Americans now knew that the Omaha sector was held by units of both the 352nd and the 716th Divisions.

In May, during the general strengthening of Normandy following Hitler's intuitive inspiration and Rommel's policy of strengthening the coastal crust, the 352nd Division had moved up to garrison the Bayeux-Isigny sector. There it took under command the regiment of the 716th which was holding this extensive front, and proceeded to nose in three of its own six battalions to defend Omaha and another likely beach at Arromanches on the British front. This left three battalions of the 352nd in close reserve behind Omaha and by chance one of these was carrying out an exercise on that stretch of coast on June 5th-6th.

There were thus eight battalions in the area between Bayeux and Isigny, where the Americans had expected to find four, and the defences had some depth, provided moreover by troops of fair quality, equipped for something more than a static role. This meant that when the bombardment miscarried and the amphibious armour failed to arrive, the Americans entered an unequal struggle with every advantage of weather, position and armament against them. The presence of the 352nd Division in and close behind the beach made it a matter of the most vital consequence to break through the coastal defences before they could be further reinforced.

This was the prospect at 9:50 a.m. when a signal from the troops ashore told Huebner, "There are too many vehicles on the beach; send combat troops. 30 LCTs waiting off-shore; cannot come in because of shelling. Troops dug in on beaches, still under heavy fire."

Huebner acted promptly. He called on the Navy to engage German batteries and strongpoints regardless of the danger of hitting his own troops, and he ordered the 18th Regiment to land at once on Easy Red. Of that regiment, however, only one battalion was loaded in craft which could make what amounted to an assault landing. The others had to be transhipped from their LCIs into small craft, and it was early afternoon before they were ready to go ashore.

By that time, the situation had been improved by the landing of one battalion on Easy Red and another on Easy Green. Both battalions found the beaches still under fire, but they curbed it by capturing several pillboxes. In the attack upon these they were supported by DD tanks, which had been landed dry-shod, and by sustained and accurate shelling from destroyers standing only a thousand yards off-shore.

At noon a report from Easy Green said, "Fire support excellent. Germans leaving positions and surrendering." A few minutes later came another report, from Easy Red, "Troops previously pinned down on Easy and Fox now advancing inland."

Even more important, by this time the last enemy strong-points at the main exit from Easy Red had been reduced and engineers had begun clearing the minefields. Thus after a six-hour battle the defences began to crumble and the foreshore was gradually freed of small arms fire, but the shelling of the beach continued, in spite of counter-battery bombardment by warships and fighter-bombers. There were still no exits for vehicles; most of the passages through the minefields were little more than single-file tracks; and the enemy was opposing most strenuously any attempt to deepen the penetration. The first crisis had passed, but the battle was by no means won.

In the early afternoon movement off the beach was limited and sluggish and the enemy had time to re-form his front roughly along the line of the road that ran through Colleville and St. Laurent. Within an hour and a half of landing part of the 18th Regiment, by a very remarkable effort, reached the northern edge of Colleville, a mile inland, where several weakened companies of the 16th Regiment were waging a house-to-house battle. But the enemy, too, had been reinforced and throughout the afternoon the Americans could do no more than hold on and hope that additional support in men and weapons would get through from the beach.

Unfortunately, movement inland was delayed, primarily because of the psychological supremacy of German mines over the American engineers and infantrymen. Even when the minefields were no longer under direct fire, the engineers were tardy in tackling them and the infantry were so ill-schooled in the art of "de-lousing" mines that they pre-

503

ferred to pick a dangerous passage through them rather than set boldly about the task of clearance. In mid-afternoon, for instance, one battalion was led slowly and painfully in single file up the ridge, stepping over the wounded who lay on the mined path. By resolute action the way could have been cleared in half the time it took to pass the battalion man by man along it. Yet no one would grasp the nettle.

It was 2 p.m. before the engineers succeeded in clearing any exit track. Another two hours elapsed before tanks and vehicles began moving off the beach, and then full use could not be made of the exit because of shelling. Late in the afternoon this became so severe that Huebner's third regiment did not finish landing until after seven o'clock and two battalions of artillery were even further delayed. Thus the infantry who had battled inland were left without adequate supporting fire until some time after 7 p.m., when a few tanks and tank destroyers came to their aid as the fight for the coastal villages hung in the balance.

Even the possibilities of direct air support could not be fully exploited, mainly because so many of the leading companies and battalions had lost their radio sets in struggling ashore. No one in the H.Q. ships knew where the front line was, the troops on the ground were far too busy to put out visual signals, and the smoke and dust which overhung the beachhead made accurate identification of targets impossible. This obscurity also handicapped the warships, but their bombardment was the most effective aid the infantry received.

It was only at the end of the long day that the Americans forced the line of the coastal road, and this success was principally due to the unquenchable spirit and drive of the 1st Division. On the right the units of the 29th Division, fighting their first battle, made little progress after taking Vierville and reaching St. Laurent in the morning. In the face of aggressive German probing, it was all Gerhardt's troops could do to hold a beachhead 1,200 yards deep, for only two of his infantry regiments and one artillery battalion were landed during the day, and that battalion lost all but one of its 12 guns. At dark the situation was still confused and St. Laurent was not completely clear. The American grip on this stretch of Omaha was by no means secure, and there was considerable anxiety about the danger of a counter-attack against the tired and weakened battalions during the night. The opportunity was there and the Germans could exploit it—if they were to commit their reserves in the right place.

For eight hours after the airborne assault began, the H.Q. of the German 84th Corps (Marcks) was handicapped by lack of reliable information. Reports of the main paratroop and glider landings were reasonably prompt and accurate, but the jamming of coastal radar prevented the enemy from gaining any indication of the strength and dispositions of the forces at sea until after daylight, and by that time the coast defences were under fire from aircraft and warships. Although this bombardment did not cause serious damage to the defences on Omaha, it did disrupt communications, especially in the Cotentin area. The start of the naval shelling was duly reported by 84th Corps to Seventh Army at 6 a.m., but Marcks received no word of the seaborne landings until two hours later, and it was nearly 11 o'clock before he learned that troops were landing from the sea on the Cotentin. This news, which came only from the German Navy, could not be confirmed, and at 11:45 a.m. 84th Corps signalled, "Regarding East coast [of Cotentin] no reports available since at the moment communications are severed." [8]

In the meantime, the news from the Omaha sector, though scanty, was encouraging. At 9:25 a.m. Marck's H.Q. reported, "The forward positions in the area of 352nd Division have been penetrated but the situation is not so critical as in the area of 716th Division," i.e. between Bayeux and Caen, and it was for this sector that he requested immediate counter-action by panzer divisions. This policy seemed justified when at 1:35 p.m. it was stated by the Chief of Staff of the 352nd that "the Division has thrown

[8] This, and the other messages that follow, are taken from the Telephone Log of Seventh German Army H.Q.

the invaders back into the sea; only near Colleville is there, in his opinion, a counter-attack still in progress." On the strength of this news Seventh Army informed Rommel's H.Q. that "the situation in the area of 352nd Division is now restored." There was no contrary report from this division until 6 p.m. and in the meantime all armoured reserves had been directed against the British with the object of preventing the fall of Caen. None were sent to the area west of Bayeux.

In any case the reinforcements which Marcks could have thrown into the Omaha battle were not as great as Allied Intelligence had feared they might be. Around St. Lô there was only a mobile brigade, and its mobility was limited to the skill of its members as cyclists, for it had no motorised troop transport. Nevertheless, if it had intervened at Omaha during the afternoon the consequences might have been serious, but at midday it was ordered to counter-attack the British east of Bayeux. Thus the only reserves which could be employed against Omaha that day were three battalions of the 352nd, deployed in close reserve between Bayeux and Isigny. Before dawn in response to the airborne landings on the Cotentin two of these battalions were ordered to move west "to establish and maintain the link through Carentan." One had started moving before Marcks learned of the Omaha assault and the other, which had been stationed around Bayeux, was drawn into battle with the British. This left only a single battalion in position to reinforce the Omaha defences, and it was pitted against the American right flank at Vierville and St. Laurent. It was here that the Germans should have made their counter-stroke during the night with the battalion which had started for Carentan and been recalled, but they made the fatal mistake of looking over their shoulders at a landing which was not and could not have been any real threat.

Soon after seven o'clock that morning three companies of Rangers (the American counterpart of British Commandos) had landed three miles west of Omaha at the base of Pointe du Hoe, an almost sheer cliff 100 feet high. Their primary task was to silence a powerful coastal battery

506

capable of firing upon both Utah and Omaha beaches. The cliffs appeared to be unassailable, but the Rangers shot grappling hooks and rope ladders to the top with rocket charges and scaled the heights under covering fire from two destroyers. This fire drove the Germans into their dug-outs and the Rangers met little opposition as they moved to the battery position. They found it so cratered by bombs and shells that it looked like the face of the moon; the casemates were wrecked, and the guns had gone.

Patrols were sent inland and after going half a mile two men found the missing battery, camouflaged and intact. There were stacks of ammunition on the ground, the guns were ready to fire on Utah, but there was no sign of the crews or of any recent firing. The battery was put out of action with explosive charges, but the mystery of the silent and deserted guns on Pomte du Hoe remains unsolved. Whatever the reason, the most dangerous battery in the American assault area was never used and was exposed to destruction by a two-man patrol!

As the day wore on the small Ranger force, numbering 130 men, drew increasing attention from the enemy. There were two counter-attacks in the afternoon and three more after dark, when the Germans pitted against the Rangers the reserves which should have been used for an attack against the western and most vulnerable sector of the Omaha beachhead.

There was no such diversion to aid the 1st Division in the slogging battle which carried it across the Colleville-St. Laurent road in the last few hours before dark. The recovery Huebner's men had made since the middle of the morning was extraordinary. It had seemed then that the leading regiment was broken and beaten, but at the critical moment its survivors had responded to the intrepid leadership of its commander, Colonel G. A. Taylor, who became famous that morning for the rallying cry, "Two kinds of people are staying on this beach, the dead and those who are going to die—now let's get the hell out of here."

In that spirit the first small parties had made the break and the follow-up regiment had exploited this slender advantage with a thrust to Colleville and beyond, which ended by cracking the second German position. This village was the keystone of the defence once the coastal fortifications had begun to yield. At dark some Germans were still holding out in Colleville, but they were so hard pressed by infantry and tanks that the village had lost its tactical significance. Maintaining the pressure south and east so long as the light lasted, the 1st Division's own regiments extended their beachhead to an average depth of a mile to a mile and a half on a four-mile front by the end of the day. It was a slender enough footing, but it was held by men who had been ashore before in North Africa and in Sicily, and who could not be dismayed even by the most desperate situation. Had this sector of Omaha been assigned to troops less experienced, less resolute or less ably commanded, the assault might never have penetrated beyond the beaches.

The near-disaster which befell the Americans at Omaha was in some degree due to the weather, which led to the miscarriage of the preliminary bombardment and the mislanding of the assault units, but the sea off Omaha was hardly, if at all, more hostile than it was on the more exposed British beaches farther east. In so far as they suffered more severely from the rough sea, this was chiefly due to the fact that the U.S. Navy, concerned about the fire of coastal batteries, insisted upon lowering the assault craft as much as twelve miles off-shore, whereas the British "lowering areas" were less than eight miles out. The longer passage not only added to the strain upon the assault infantry but greatly increased the danger of swamping and of faulty navigation. The leading assault craft had to start their run-in while it was still dark, and were excessively and unwarrantably exposed to the vagaries of wind and tide. On the other beaches very few mislandings were made on D-Day, but on Omaha less than half the companies in the assault battalions were landed within 800 yards of their appointed sectors. The U.S. Navy's unwillingness to take advice from Ramsay was the start of the trouble.[9]

[9] In his public comment on this Ramsay was tactfully restrained, for in his *Dispatch* (paragraph 40) he was content to say: "The

So far as operations on shore are concerned, it is suggested by the War Department's historians that "the principal cause of the difficulties of V Corps on D-Day was the unexpected strength of the enemy on the assault beaches." [10] This is only a partial explanation, for there were grave defects inherent in the American plan. The first of these was the fruit of the American predilection for direct assault. The plan for Omaha was a tactical application of the head-on strategy which Marshall had so consistently advocated in pressing the case for cross-Channel invasion. The Americans knew that the main enemy fortifications covered the natural exits, and yet they deliberately planned to make their heaviest landings directly in front of these strongpoints with the object of taking them by storm. They scorned the lessons of earlier amphibious operations, which had shown the wisdom of landing between the beach strongpoints, not opposite them, infiltrating and assaulting them from the flank and rear. The plan for Dog sector was typical. Dog Green and Dog Red were each known to be covered by powerful "exit" strongpoints. Between those Dog White was comparatively weakly defended. The American intention, however, was to land four companies in succession on each of the former during the first hour and only two companies on the latter where prospects of success were greatest. The results might have been anticipated. Two companies of the 2nd Rangers landed according to plan opposite the Vierville exit on Dog Green; only 62 men out of 132 reached the sea-wall. But 450 men of the 5th Rangers landing at the same time on Dog White between the strongpoints "got across the beach and up the sea-wall with the loss of only 5 or 6 men." [11]

There might have been some justification for the policy of direct assault if the Americans had accepted Montgomery's plan for landing armour *en masse* at the start of the

---

longer passage inshore for the assault craft of the Western Task Force appeared to add appreciably to their difficulties."

[10] *Omaha Beachhead,* pp. 109-10.

[11] *Omaha Beachhead,* p. 53.

attack, and for using the specialised equipment of Hobart's 79th Armoured Division to deal with the fortifications and the underwater obstacles. When Montgomery first saw this equipment he ordered Hobart to make one-third of it available to the Americans, and set himself to interest Eisenhower and Bradley in its revolutionary employment. Hobart's account of the reaction of the three generals is illuminating.[12]

"Montgomery," he says, "was most inquisitive. After thorough tests and searching questions he said in effect: 'I'll have this and this and this; but I don't want that or that.' Eisenhower was equally enthusiastic but not so discriminating. His response was, 'We'll take everything you can give us.' Bradley appeared to be interested but, when asked what he wanted, replied, 'I'll have to consult my staff.' "

Bradley and his staff eventually accepted the "DDs" but did not take up the offer of "Crabs," "Crocodiles," "AVREs" and the rest of Hobart's menagerie.[13] Their official reason was that there was no time to train American crews to handle the Churchill tanks in which most of the special British equipment was installed, but their fundamental scepticism about its value was shown when they rejected even the "Crabs" which offered few training difficulties, since the "flail" device was fitted to the standard American Sherman tank.

The terrible consequences of this short-sightedness were only too apparent on Omaha on D-Day. The failure of the bombardment and the non-appearance of the DD tanks left the infantry at the mercy of the strongpoints which they were required to take by storm. Where tanks were available, landed direct from LCTs, they proved invaluable, but they were too few and too dispersed, and they found great

[12] This account was given to me by General Hobart on November 10th, 1946.

[13] "Crabs" were "flail-tanks" and "Crocodiles" were flame-throwing tanks. "AVRE" stood for "Armoured Vehicle, Royal Engineers," "AVREs" were used in demolishing fortifications and surmounting obstacles.

difficulty in manœuvring because of the congestion of vehicles on the foreshore.

This congestion was chiefly due to the absence of specialised armour capable of dealing with the natural obstacles and fixed defences. The British had learned from the Dieppe Raid that engineers cannot consistently perform under fire the deliberate tasks required of them unless they are given armoured protection. No such protection was available on Omaha. Apart from lightly armoured bulldozers the Americans had no mechanised equipment for dealing with the obstructions and fortifications. They were expected by their commanders to attack pillboxes with pole-charges and man-pack flame-throwers, to clear barbed wire entanglements and concrete walls with explosives manually placed and to lift mines by hand, all under fire. That they often failed is not surprising. Throughout the morning tanks, guns and vehicles were immobilised at the water's edge because the engineers could not clear gaps in the shingle bank, a comparatively minor obstacle. Throughout the afternoon, infantry were compelled to move across the beach in single file because the sappers had no mechanical means of dealing with mines and hand-clearance was too slow. At the Vierville exit the last strongpoints were reduced by 2 p.m., but it was another eight hours before the mines and obstructions had been cleared, for they had to be cleared by hand.

At dark only this road and one other were open for vehicles, and the full sweep of the beach was still under fire from artillery and mortars. The corps beachhead was six miles wide and less than two miles deep at the point of greatest penetration, and there was a grave shortage of tanks, anti-tank guns and of artillery generally. Most of the battalions were seriously weakened, for the day's fighting had cost 3,000 casualties. In short, although the Americans were ashore, they held an area barely large enough to be called a foothold, and were in no condition to withstand any large-scale counter-attack with armour during the next two critical days. But whether or not the Germans would, or could, develop such an attack depended on the course of events on the front of Dempsey's Second British Army.

Off the Beaches

The British assault on their three beaches was a larger operation than the Americans'. Three British divisions were landed, their chief objective being Caen, the Germans' main base for the defense of Normandy. The British met fierce resistance on the beaches, but flailing tanks were employed to knock out mine fields and flame-throwing tanks to reduce pillboxes. The British were also lucky to have longer naval bombardments; their jumping-off time for the beaches was scheduled later than the Americans' because of tide conditions, and the Royal Navy had four times as long to smash at the German coastal batteries. And their landings were only seven to eight miles offshore, which, as we have seen, shortened the tortuous ride to the beaches.

At the end of D-Day the British had captured Bayeux, one of the two principal objectives, but they had not taken Caen. (They would not occupy it for a month.) Montgomery knew the Germans would hurl their heaviest counterattacks against him, because Caen guarded the road to Paris, and the Germans believed Paris was the Allies' prime objective.

The day's best success went to the 3rd Canadian Division, supported by the 2nd Canadian Armored Brigade, which pushed farther inland than any other division in the Normandy landings. They almost reached Caen, but lacked enough support, and their unloading on the beaches had been delayed. The 21st Panzer Division prevented the capture of Caen; it was firmly lodged between the 3rd Canadian Division and the 3rd British Division between Caen and the coast. Here the German coastal defenses were still intact. But Rommel was unable to move enough reserves to reinforce the 21st Panzer—he lacked air superiority, and the German High Command had lost the initiative by wavering in the early hours of the invasion. When the 12th SS Division was finally sent to help on D-plus one, it was badly strafed; by the time it reached Caen there was not enough fuel for an immediate counterattack.

The Luftwaffe was nowhere to be seen on the coast during the daylight hours of D-Day or D-plus one—an astonishing lapse. What was even more amazing, on D-Day only about 120 fighter planes were available to the Luftwaffe on the Channel front. Against this the Allies had more than 5,000 fighters available in Britain. The Allies had air supremacy throughout the day, and the invasion fleet steamed across the Channel without the slightest interference through D-Day and D-plus one.

The Allies hadn't reached all their objectives, but there was reason for cautious optimism. Neither the two American beachheads nor the British beachhead had been able to consolidate with each other, but they were established, and only major counterattacks could dislodge them.

In all, the Allies, had lost fewer than 2,500 men killed; while there were many more casualties, the blood-letting feared by the peoples of the United Nations was not to take place on the beaches.

Then the German counterattacks finally materialized; they were successfully beaten off during the next few days, but there was fighting of the most stubborn kind in all sectors. As the Allies held firm, they knew the decision lay in whether they could beat the Germans in the build-up of supplies and reinforcements.

The Americans' first objective was to seal off the Cotentin Peninsula and then free the port of Cherbourg at its tip, giving the invasion a real port of supply; if the Germans had committed more of their heavy armored units here, the offensive would have been in real trouble. But the Germans still held back divisions to the north of the British beachhead, expecting another landing, and they continued to throw the majority of their armor at Montgomery.

Hitler and the German High Command believed the Allies were only feinting at the Cotentin Peninsula, to make the Germans swing their main forces in that direction; the Allies would then follow up with a second landing of even greater force, driving into France farther to the north. The Germans were still without effective reconnaissance, and they were suffering serious difficulties in all their troop movements.

The over-all SHAEF strategy was this: the 1st U.S. Army, once it had cleaned out the Cotentin Peninsula, was to capture Cherbourg to the west and drive for St. Lô to the east; the British 2nd Army would protect the Americans' flank and keep pressure on the German armored divisions, so they wouldn't be sent south. Bradley's first efforts to move on St. Lô brought the American infantry and tanks into the

Bocage country, where the hedgerows turned out to be Hitler's best allies—dirt banks, with thorn-bushes growing on top, that lined the small lanes and roads in Normandy. This natural defense was so rugged that heavy tanks could operate only on the roads. Bradley decided that his troops would have to have special help. Until his tanks were equipped with new cutting devices, not much progress was to be made, other than cleaning up the Cotentin Peninsula. Here Gen. J. Lawton Collins, commanding the 7th U.S. Corps, fought up the peninsula. Actually the Bocage was at its worst on the peninsula; it is interesting to note that hedgerows held fewer terrors for Collins, who had commanded infantry on Guadalcanal, than they did for some of the other generals. Collins's men moved up the peninsula in quick jabs, with the infantry having little fire support other than rifles, mortars and bazookas.

The fall of Cherbourg was official on June 26th, 1944. The port would not be in working order for some time, but the fate of the German divisions left in the peninsula had been sealed when Eisenhower ordered two American airborne divisions dropped to cut off their escape to the east.

The Americans could now ready the drive on St. Lô, while the British held the main German offensive power around the Caen sector.

Alan Moorehead's description of the St. Lô breakout follows.

BREAKOUT AT ST. LÔ

by Alan Moorehead

Towards the end of July nearly a million American and British troops were either ashore in Normandy, or about to come ashore. The bridgehead was stretched like a drum. Even though a completely new system of roads and ports had been built, the traffic blocks sometimes extended for ten or fifteen miles. We were approaching the crisis of the campaign, the crucial moment for the whole of western Europe. Montgomery remained Allied commander in the

514

field, working from a headquarters near Bayeux, midway between the American and the British armies.

Rommel lay on a hospital bed fighting for his own life. The long personal struggle between him and Montgomery was over. Allied fighters, little knowing what they were doing, had swooped on the German commander's car near Lisieux. Rommel was sitting in the front seat beside the driver, and the smashed corner of the windscreen had splintered against his temple. A chemist from the neighboring French village looked at the unconscious figure on the road, and said he could do nothing. After that Rommel lay for a long time in the field hospital without regaining consciousness. At last, when he had sufficiently recovered to be removed to Paris, it was seen that it would be months at least before he could return to active command, and indeed his death followed soon afterwards in Germany. His place was taken by Von Kluge, a Nazi.[1]

Everywhere the Allies were moving into position for the great battle: the Americans at St. Lô, the British towards Pincon and the southwest of Caen. It is quite true to say that the bulk of the German armor and some of their best divisions were spaced round Caen, opposite the British; it is quite untrue to suggest that because of this the Americans had no serious opposition at St. Lô. Both armies had immense battles to fight; the British a static battle, the Americans a breakout battle. In neither sector were the opening stages particularly brilliant; many mistakes were made. These errors were followed by a most memorable stroke of arms, when the American First and Third Armies fanned out through Brittany and western France; and still another

[1] July 4th until July 17th (the date of Rommel's injury): There were constant upheavals inside the enemy command. On the 4th Rommel told Hauser there was an express order from Hitler he "must not withdraw an inch." Hauser replied the enemy had already broken through. "In that case," Rommel answered, "the enemy will be in St. Germain tomorrow." It is interesting to see the steady disintegration of Rommel's morale right up to the moment of his wounding; it is almost as if he knew that both he and his army were doomed.

extraordinary feat when the British took up the running and headed straight for Belgium. These vast and fast pursuits took the headlines. Being easily explicable operations, and in themselves the proof of victory, they engaged the public's attention, and no doubt will remain longest in everyone's mind. In actual fact, they were no more than the intelligent and courageous exploitation of a *fait-accompli*. The real decisive issues were fought out on the bridgehead perimeter, and later round the Falaise pocket. It was here in Normandy that the German army was defeated, and in military history the battles of St. Lô and Caen will take precedence over the subsequent rush to the Rhine.

It was already late in July when Montgomery decided to try and smash the German hinge at Caen. Caen, though occupied by the Allies, was still under fire. We now wanted to push beyond the town, and run out over the flatter wheatfields of the Falaise plain, which was said to be excellent tank country. All this time Caen had been in the position of the hinge of a door which stretched out westward towards St. Lô. The plan was for the Americans to keep pushing the door open until General Patton and his fresh Third Army could slip round the corner at Avranches, and over-run Brittany. At the same time the British were to try and unseat the door at its hinge. Then, when the whole structure was wobbling, the Americans would run round behind the open door and pin against the British such Germans as were left on the spot.

General Dempsey, the commander of the combined British and Canadian forces, now had three full armored divisions—the Seventh, the Eleventh and the Guards—plus several independent armored brigades. He decided to move these in secret to the extreme eastern part of the bridgehead. Bridges were to be thrown up at night across the Orne Canal north of Caen. The armor, some five or six hundred tanks, would then cross and charge due south through the German lines in the general direction of Falaise. Some three divisions of infantry would follow to consolidate. The bombers would prepare the way for the tanks.

At this moment the whole question of the use of heavy

516

four-engined bombers was in debate. One school believed that they should be used exclusively for the strategical bombing of Germany; the other school argued that every available weapon should be thrown into this Normandy crisis. The latter school won. We were committed to the use of a new and immensely powerful weapon in circumstances for which the personnel had had no proper training. When you fly over a battlefield you can very rarely see where the front-line runs. For the most part, nothing shows on the ground except a few indeterminate puffs of smoke. Since all the Normandy countryside looked alike it was extremely difficult to pin-point targets. And now the four-engined bombers were asked to bomb not clearly defined targets like towns and bridges but the open countryside where, unseen to the crews, the Germans were hiding. Furthermore, they were asked to bomb targets within a thousand yards or less of our own troops. There had already been a series of mistakes. British and Americans alike had been hit by their own bombs.

By the time Dempsey came to make his tank drive there had been some advance in technique. It was now at last accepted that you do not necessarily hit armies in the field by knocking down towns, and you do frequently retard your own advance because of the craters and the piles of debris. And so this time it was resolved that we should bomb in "strips." The four-engined planes would lay a path of bombs along either side of the projected tank run. This was designed to silence the anti-tank guns and infantry on the flanks. Then the lighter machines would scatter non-cratering anti-personnel bombs along the central strip, where the tanks had to travel. In addition, as soon as the tanks started their run the artillery would commence a creeping barrage. The shells would fall just ahead of the oncoming tanks, and the barrage would advance about the same rate—five miles an hour. In other words, the armor would go into action surrounded by a wall of our own explosive. It was a plan that depended on perfect timing. It went wrong. The bombs failed to silence the German gunners. The gunners simply stayed underground until the bombing was over, and then they emerged and opened up at very close range on the hundreds of vehicles deployed across the plain. Two hundred British tanks were lost within a few hours. A number of villages were destroyed by the Lancasters, but the Germans were sheltering outside. And now the enemy rushed his Panthers and Tigers with their superior guns to the front. Only three bridges had been laid across the Orne canal; blockages quickly occurred. The Luftwaffe managed to catch a number of replacement crews while they were sheltering for the night. And so the advance faltered and stopped after a few miles.

We tried again a few days later, using new devices. Pink smoke was put up to blind the enemy to our movements. Searchlights were shone against the clouds at night to give the effect of moonlight. Colored lights were fired into the enemy lines to direct our bombers. All these maneuvers were countered by one means or another. The enemy, for instance, quickly seized on the idea of firing colored guiding lights into *our* lines as soon as aircraft appeared.

It was decided to bomb still more closely to our own infantry, and then we really began to take casualties. It was impossible to strike the targets accurately. I watched one great salvo fall five or six miles inside our own lines. It wiped out a headquarters and caused hundreds of Canadian casualties. Exactly the same thing was happening on the American sector at the opening of the battle of St. Lô. The army was growing distinctly nervous about its own air force, and although much more good than harm was done by the bombing the effect upon morale was becoming serious. A senior American general had been killed, and in the forward platoons the soldiers became just as apprehensive about the bombing as the Germans were. There is always something particularly unnerving about being hit by your own side.

Fortunately the need for heavy, close-support bombing vanished soon after this, and subsequently the technique was greatly improved. One brilliant exception all through had been the British Typhoon rocket planes. They had by now developed such accuracy that they were diving upon single tanks and even if they did not get one-hundred-per-cent results, they often succeeded in scaring the crews into hiding.

All through this period, too, our artillery was increasing

and increasing until it reached fantastic proportions. It was an unsettling thing to drive anywhere near the front. Hundreds of guns would suddenly erupt out of the bushes on either side of the road, and the blast would make your eardrums ache for hours on end. In numbers of tanks also we had immense superiority. Provided the crews had been saved, it was no great tragedy to find a hundred wrecked Shermans lying about the fields; one knew that another couple of hundred had just been put ashore. The whole plan was to keep attacking, never to let the enemy rest; to bomb him all the way to the Seine, to shell him all night, to submit him to infantry rushes day after day. We now had overwhelming fire-power, and at the end of July it was in continuous operation for a hundred miles along the front.[2]

[2] Conditions in the enemy lines were going in just the opposite direction: towards disintegration. At the end of June German coastal commanders were complaining "the fire of enemy naval guns is unimaginable." On July 5th there was much discussion at German headquarters about the possibility of new Allied sea and air landings. On the same day Seventh Army headquarters was reporting that all their counter-attacks were "suffocated" by the Allied air force. The Chief of Staff added: "Our ground forces will be simply slaughtered if it goes on." July 7th: General Jodl, back at supreme headquarters, told Rundstedt that he "could not" put up to Hitler proposals for new withdrawals. But on July 15th the Germans were describing the battle as "one tremendous blood bath." Appeal after appeal went out for more fuel, more tanks, more aircraft, more men; and above all, permission to withdraw.

Hitler followed the battle very closely, village by village, unit by unit. His occasional direct orders were treated with the utmost reverence even by such seasoned professionals as Rundstedt. "The Führer says"—that was enough to make every German soldier spring to obey. All through this period one has a picture of Hitler, tormented, harassed and blindly angry as the appalling news kept coming in. Even his closest advisers like Jodl were balking at the job of acquainting him with the worst disasters. Possibly there were moments when Hitler was not sane. In the midst of his passionate megalomania one can conceive the bitter per-

There was little enough to show on the map. Villages were won and lost by the dozen, and still the front-line did not move. All the way down the Odon river to Pincon and thence to St. Lô the German line bulged under an intolerable weight, and still somehow it was patched up and kept together. When prisoners were taken they came out of the line with gray lined faces, suffering not so much from wounds as from shock. Their pocket diaries told the story of the gradual crumbling of the will under persistent fire. The belt of destruction thickened and lengthened every day, until all the area of the perimeter began to assume that beaten, worn-out appearance of the French battlefields in the last war. Great stretches of forest were uprooted. One after another the villages went down into dust. Hundreds of bulldozers struggled to keep pace with the wreckage of the bombing. It did not matter in what direction you turned; within an hour's run by jeep from the beaches you found yourself involved in a battle, and the incessant aching noise of gunfire never ceased. One began to marvel at the German endurance. Somewhere surely the line had to break.

It broke at last at St. Lô. General Bradley, who controlled the American armies under Montgomery, was rapidly developing into one of the ablest field commanders of the war. At St. Lô he was determined to force the issue one way or another. Old friends like the American Ninth Division were being cut to pieces, but still he persisted. On July 24th St. Lô collapsed, a heap of ruins. Patton raced through the gap. He was round the corner at Avranches, a bloodhound in full cry. Aircraft patrolled ahead of the armored columns. At the slightest opposition the tanks and armored cars raced round, attacked on the flanks and pressed on. Prisoners who were completely bewildered began to come in by the thousand.[8]

---

sonal struggle in trying to force down his mind to the humiliating facts. And the final bitter awakening must have come when the attempt was made upon his life by his own people in the middle of July.

[8] July 31st: The German Seventh Army headquarters informed the High Command, "The left flank has collapsed."

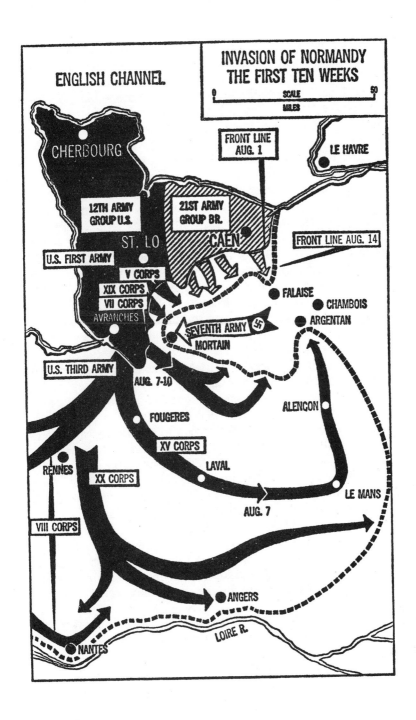

INVASION OF NORMANDY
THE FIRST TEN WEEKS

ENGLISH CHANNEL

SCALE
0   50
MILES

CHERBOURG

FRONT LINE
AUG. 1

LE HAVRE

12TH ARMY
GROUP U.S.

21ST ARMY
GROUP BR.

ST. LO

CAEN

FRONT LINE AUG. 14

U.S. FIRST ARMY

V CORPS

XIX CORPS

VII CORPS

FALAISE

CHAMBOIS

AVRANCHES

SEVENTH ARMY

ARGENTAN

U.S. THIRD ARMY

MORTAIN

AUG. 7-10

ALENCON

FOUGERES

XV CORPS

LAVAL

RENNES

XX CORPS

LE MANS

AUG. 7

VIII CORPS

ANGERS

NANTES

LOIRE R.

And now the whole line began to give way. Bit by bit the door was pushed wide open. On August 7th the British at last surged up to the crest of Mount Pincon, and for the first time since D-Day looked down over the bridgehead and out across the Loire valley, where the Americans were already beginning their great encircling movement. Village after village collapsed on the Falaise plain, and the Canadians battled their way into the burning ruins of Falaise itself. The trap was being laid.

The German Seventh Army and all its reinforcements now found itself in a rough rectangle bounded by Falaise, Vire, Mortain and Argentan. Since the Americans had passed right round the south of their position, one escape route remained: the area between Falaise and Argentan. But they were not yet thinking of retreat. Rommel's successor, Von Kluge, sitting in his underground headquarters at St. Germain, outside Paris, was on the telephone to Hitler every night. And always he received the same order: Resist. Counter-attack. No retreat. It did not matter that corps commanders were reporting that they could not hold, that their lines were already breaking, that the chances of re-grouping on a better line were diminishing every day. They had to hold. They were ordered to a counter-attack at Mortain.

On paper it was an attractive idea. Here were the Americans strung out all over Brittany and the Loire valley on a very thin line. Everything had to pass through Avranches, since we still had no ports in Brittany. The Germans at Mortain were only twenty miles from Avranches. Once break through to the sea there and the bulk of the two American armies were cut off.[4]

Two panzer divisions led the attack. For a while things were locally critical. If there was any deficiency at all in the American equipment it was in anti-tank guns. Then at the height of the battle the rocket-firing Typhoons arrived. They continued throughout the entire day, remaining only

[4] July 31st: Von Kluge's appreciation of the position was: "The whole western front has been ripped open. Avranches is the anchor of Brittany. It must be recaptured." And he himself came down to the battle area to supervise the operation.

522

long enough on the ground between trips to reload. Nearly a hundred German tanks were destroyed. Their entire striking front was broken up, and the attack turned abruptly into defeat. Whatever Hitler ordered now, only one course remained for the Seventh Army: retreat. But could they retreat?

A revolutionary change had overtaken the situation while the Germans were wasting time round Mortain. Rennes had fallen. So had Laval and Le Mans, Angers and Tours on the Loire. Orléans was falling. So was Chartres. Paris itself was in immediate danger. The Americans raced on and on through the unguarded south. Their tanks roared through one city after another, leaving behind great empty stretches of road, great regions of open countryside; and still they kept on. It had the effect of an octopus laying tentacle on tentacle round a victim, and now the grip began to tighten. Everywhere the French Resistance was rising. Little groups of maquis ambushed the German garrisons along the path of the American advance. Snipers were surprised, road blocks cleared, mines torn up. It became unnecessary for us to occupy the country we took; the French were doing that for us.

In Brittany the scattered remnants of the enemy army gathered themselves into the coastal fortresses, chiefly at St. Malo, Dinard, Brest, St. Nazaire and Lorient. Here at least they could stand aside from the general route and take refuge behind concrete and minefields. The German policy of denying us the ports was started in good earnest. A series of sieges began, and this was later to develop into the only coherent line of action the Germans were able to adopt to the west of the Rhine valley. For the moment, however, the battle for the ports was secondary, just as the fall of Paris was secondary. Everything was focused upon that Homeric scene round Falaise where the German armies in the west were about to fall headlong into one of the greatest military defeats in history.

Even those of us who were visiting different sectors of the front every day were unable to grasp the enormity of the thing that was happening. All we knew was that somewhere to the south of Falaise, in an ever-dwindling pocket of rolling countryside, there was a horde of broken and bewildered men, the survivors of some thirty or forty divisions. And now they were being killed and captured and maimed at the rate of several thousand every day.

It had been a dull and indifferent summer. Since D-Day we had never been able to rely on the weather for two days at a time. But now the sun shone out day after day. The trampled corn turned brilliant yellow. The dust rose up with the smoke of the explosions. And through this hot August sun the Allied aircraft streamed down on to the trapped German armies with such a blitz of bombing as western Europe had never seen. No German convoy could take the roads in safety before nightfall. But now in their extremity they were forced out into the open, and the carnage along the roads was horrible. Unable to stay where they were, unable to go into hiding, little groups of enemy began feeling their way blindly towards the east. They used side-roads. They traveled as much as they could by night. It made no difference. Sooner or later they found the forests on fire around them, and Allied troops cutting in from the flanks. The pressure on the western end of the pocket became unbearable. Conde and Tinchebray fell, and with them all the villages of the upper Orne.

The Germans now abandoned all pretense of keeping up a continuous or coherent line. Their regular units lost all identity. Little battle groups were formed, given a sector and told to look after themselves as best they could. In one day alone we captured men belonging to thirty different German formations. As the refugees streamed back they were grabbed at the mouth of the pocket, re-formed, and put into the crumpling line. Cooks and signalers were fighting side by side with gunless gunners and grounded airmen. Tank fitters became infantry, along with butchers and staff officers and road menders. Then presently, towards the concluding stages, the battle groups lost contact with one another. In a blind instinct for self-preservation the Germans were either surrendering or deserting in little companies, in the hope of reaching the Seine on foot. There were no drugs for their wounded; no time to bury their dead. One after another their field hospitals were over-run.

524

The time when half or even a third of the diminishing army could retreat had long since disappeared. Nearly all their vehicles had been lost. The horse-drawn traffic was utterly disorganized. Those who had struggled back to the Seine came under a new and still fiercer blitz from the air on the river itself. Barges and ferries were shot up in scores. The bridges were already down.[5]

A little group of surviving German generals met in the forest of Chambois for a conference. What should they do? General surrender? One last effort to get the best of their men away? They took a vote, and by a narrow margin decided on the latter course. Foreign troops, raw and second-rate troops, wounded men and men who had got themselves isolated—all these were abandoned. The surviving panzers and SS troops climbed on to what was left of their tanks and vehicles and headed northeast for the Seine. Already the British and American armies had locked the gate. But this last desperate column determined to smash it open again for a few hours; for just sufficient time to enable them to get away. They struck through a village called Trun, outside Falaise. A Polish division in the Canadian army took the first blow. Then for the next thirty-six hours all this sector of the battlefield disappeared under continuous smoke and explosion. Broken staccato reports came out of the arena. A few German tanks were getting through. Canadian reinforcements were rushed in. There was a final headlong onslaught round the hamlet of St. Lambert. I do not think I can do better than to describe the scene in the same words I used in a message to my newspaper at the time:

"If I were to be allowed just one more dispatch from this front this would be it; not because the dispatch itself is important, but because we have begun to see the end of Germany here in this village of St. Lambert today.

"The best of Von Kluge's army came here *en masse* forty-eight hours ago. They converged upon the village to fight

[5] August 8th: The Seventh Army reported: "A break-through has occurred at Caen the like of which we have never seen." August 10th: The order at last came down from Hitler: "Disengage." In the opinion of the army staff it was already too late.

525

their way out; long caravans of horses and gun-carts, tanks and half-tracks, hospitals and workshops, artillery and infantry. It was the sort of panzer battle array that the Germans have used to terrorize Europe for four years. We knew no combination to stand against it.

"And now, here in the apple orchards and in the village streets one turns sick to see what has happened to them. They met the British and the Allied troops head on, and they were just obliterated. Until now I had no conception of what trained artillerymen and infantry can do, and certainly this is the most awful sight that has come my way since the war began.

"It begins in the back streets of St. Lambert, where the German columns first came in range of the British fire. The horses stampeded. Not half a dozen, but perhaps three hundred or more. They lashed down the fences and the hedges with their hooves, and dragged their carriages through the farmyards. Many galloped for the banks of the river Dives, and plunged headlong with all their trappings down the twelve-foot banks into the stream below, which at once turned red with blood. Those animals that did not drown under the dragging weight of their harness, or die in falling, kept plunging about among the broken gun-carriages, and trampled to death the Germans hiding under the bank. The drivers of the lorries panicked in the same way. As more and more shells kept ripping through the apple trees, they collided their vehicles one against the other, and with such force that some of the lighter cars were telescoped with their occupants inside.

"At some places for stretches of fifty yards vehicles, horses and men became jammed together in one struggling, shrieking mass. Engines and broken petrol tanks took fire, and the wounded pinned in the wreckage were suffocated, burned and lost. Those who were lucky enough to get out of the first collisions scrambled up the ditches and ran for cover across the open fields. They were picked off as they ran. One belt of shell fire fell on the Dives river bridge at the moment when two closely packed columns were converging upon it. Those vehicles and beasts and men on the center of the bridge were all pitchforked into space at once.

526

But so many fell that soon the wreckage piled up level with the bridge itself, and made a dam across the river.

"At the far entrance to the bridge, where a number of heavy guns were attempting a crossing, a blockage was caused and took fire. Those in front apparently tried to struggle back. Those behind, being utterly bewildered, tried to push on. And so the whole column was wedged immovably until it was reduced to flames.

"I suppose there were about a thousand German vehicles of every sort lying out in the fields behind. All these came under fire. The Germans made no attempt to man their guns. They either huddled beneath them, or ran blindly for the futile cover of the hedges.

"They ran in the direction of the fire, shouting that they had surrendered. They gave up in hundreds upon hundreds. There was no fight left in them any more, and now, here, you can see what is left by the battle in the warm midday sunlight. It is exactly like one of those crowded battle paintings of Waterloo or Borodino—except of course the wreckage is different. Every staff car—and I suppose I have seen a hundred—is packed with French loot and German equipment. There is a profusion of everything: field-glasses and typewriters, pistols and small arms by the hundred, cases of wine, truck-loads of food and medical stores, a vast mass of leather harness. Every car is full of clothing, and every officer seems to have possessed a pair of corsets to take home.

"If you want a car you walk up and take your pick—anything from a baby tourer to a volkswagen or a ten-ton half-track. The Tommies start them up and go off through the orchards. Two Russians in German uniform stand stupidly on the river bank, and they timidly hold out cigarettes to anyone who comes by. They stand in the middle of piled-up riches they never dreamed of before; purses crammed with notes that have fallen from dead men's bodies, radio sets and dumps of rich clothing looted from the French. I have just picked my way across the wreckage to the house on the far side of the orchard. It is full of Germans—Germans beaten and numbed into senselessness. Like animals, they seem to have no will of their own. They are all armed with machine-pistols and rifles, but no one takes the slightest notice of them. It would be absurd to think that they would fire, and nobody has time to take their arms from them and lead them into captivity.

"Over at the hospital it is far worse. The dead and the wounded lie together. Living or dead there is not much difference in the appearance of the men. Many hours ago life ceased to count for anything at all. The wounded keep dying, but quietly, so that one is not aware at any given moment of just how many are surviving. They are all jumbled on top of one another, and the stench makes it difficult for one to refrain from being sick. Outside a Canadian soldier is mercifully going round shooting wounded horses with a Luger pistol. It would be equally merciful if he did the same for some of these enemy patients who are beyond hope and too weak to cry any more. At any rate, I have just directed this mercy-killer down to the river, where there are about thirty horses wounded and unable to get up the steep banks. Long ago they stopped trying, and they stand patiently in the water waiting unconsciously to die.

"I do not know the limits of this battlefield, since I have been here only four hours. It stretches I know for about a mile up the Falaise road, because for a good part of that distance you see the line of many hundreds of German helmets flung away by the enemy at the moment of their surrender. A young Canadian lieutenant explains: 'They kept coming up the road in bursts every three minutes. We shot the leaders of each group and captured the others.'

"I have just selected a volkswagen to get me back to my billet. The back seat is piled with the belongings of the man who now lies dead by the front wheels. He had taken the precaution, I note, of procuring a civilian suit, which is always a good thing to use if you are going to desert.

"Well, there it is; there could be no reason in this ghastly scene. I say again I think I see the end of Germany here. This was their best in weapons and men, their strongest barrier before the Rhine. It has been brushed aside, shattered into bits. The beaten Wehrmacht is a pitiable thing."

In The Hedgerows

The hedgerow country before Saint-Lô was especially rugged for infantry. As tanks moved up the roads between the hedgerows, they were sitting ducks for German 88s emplaced just around curves. Machine guns and mortars were cleverly situated by the Germans to exploit the hedgerows as natural defenses. Instead of traveling up the alley-like roads, the infantry were forced to take to the fields. But soon they were sure to come to a hedgerow at right angles to the road. In consequence, it is not hard to see why progress before Saint-Lô was measured by one hedgerow after another, and there always seemed to be another one beyond the last.

Taking part in the war through this country was the 1st Battalion, 115 Infantry of the 29th Division, under the command of Major Glover S. Johns. These people landed at D-Day on Omaha Beach and were in combat steadily for the next two months. The Major's portrait of this action is remarkably frank for an officer; he unashamedly records his own feeling, his own inexperience in combat, and his times of indecision—all the while accepting the need to press on ahead.

Early on in his story he says, speaking of himself in the third person:

"They walked rapidly for a hundred yards. The firing began to die away. Then it stopped all along the whole front. The Major slowed a bit. These sudden changes in the tempo of the action puzzled him. He wondered if C Company had repulsed the attack, if A Company had driven in from the flank and forced the enemy to retreat, or if Ryan had been stopped and had pulled back into the woods to re-form and try it again.

While these questions passed through his mind a nasty feeling of failure grew inside him. Night was closing in. He had not succeeded in taking his first objective as a battalion commander. His stomach was knotting slowly but tightly with that overpowering fear, not fear of death or injury, but of failure. He kept moving forward." *

And, again:

"He looked at what he had written, but didn't like it. He was damned if he would squall for help so soon in the first fight.

"He was drawing a line through the last sentence when the world suddenly exploded all around him. Sharp ballistic cracks pounded his eardrums so rapidly they seemed like one impossibly prolonged rifle shot. He was instantly paralyzed with overwhelming fright.

"The radio operator, Jimmie, slumped forward at his feet, another man stumbled past to fall into the ditch ahead, and Newcomb cleared the eight-foot hedgerow apparently with one jump. But the Major was too shocked to move. His stomach knotted itself into a tight ball. It jammed against his pounding heart while his breathing stopped completely for an instant, then came in jerky gasps. The hair on his head felt as if it were rising like the hair on a cat's back. His skin prickled all over. But the most awful thing was the cold, empty feeling in his guts." **

Later as his men are hung up outside Saint-Lô he tells the story of attack and counterattack, the ebb and flow of infantry fighting which was the meat and potatoes of combat, and is still today.

BEFORE SAINT-LŎ

by Glover S. Johns

As the sun climbed higher the temperature rose with it. The day was going to be hot. And it was hot in more ways than one. The Germans began warming things

*The Clay Pigeons of St. Lô, by G. S. Johns, p. 11.
** Ibid., p. 13.

up all along the line by throwing over more and more artillery and mortar fire. By mid-morning there had been several casualties in each company and the command post had been shaken up twice. The battalion commander issued orders that no man would leave his position unless absolutely necessary. Obeying his own order, he stayed in the hole.

The battalion's mortars and supporting artillery were returning more than they received, but there was no quieting the Germans that day. Martin was watching the situation with interest. One of his jobs was to receive and forward "shell-reps." A shell report, or "shell rep," was supposed to be sent in by any man who witnessed the fall of enemy artillery fire. The report included the exact location in which each shell hit, its caliber, and, as nearly as possible, the direction from which it had come. At the Fire Direction Center, the artillery S2 placed the location of each hit on the map and projected the estimated direction of flight back into enemy territory. The lines thus plotted always crossed somewhere. If enough of these rays intersected near the same point, it was a good bet a hostile battery was located somewhere in that vicinity. By studying the terrain, as indicated on the map, it was often possible to guess just about where that battery would be. Then, when the S2 was satisfied, from this information, that he had a good chance of drawing blood, he could take the matter to his own commander and ask for a counterbattery mission. If approved, the big 155's would reach out and search the selected area. Sometimes they were lucky. Sometimes they weren't, but every shell that burst in enemy territory was money in the bank to the infantrymen who heard it going over, so it was never a complete waste.

Martin was puzzled. He kept a rough record of the shell reps for his own information and by the middle of the afternoon he had enough data to make him want to talk to his boss. He called Lieutenant Colonel Cooper, the commander of the 110th Field Artillery Battalion.

"Sir," said Martin, "I believe the Germans have moved some more artillery in opposite us. The way these reports are coming in makes me think they are registering on us. What worries me is how they could be getting any observation on some of the targets they shoot at."

"We think the same thing," Cooper replied, "and I'm asking General Sands for some corps artillery to give us a hand with counterbattery today. Call me again if you get any definite ideas."

Some of the enemy fire falling that day was on targets that had never been hit before, and which couldn't possibly be observed from the enemy lines. The Germans had no equivalent of the American light observation plane that provided the artillery with a bird's-eye view of any front. Therefore there seemed to be only one answer to the accuracy of the fire—the Germans must have infiltrated artillery observers into the battalion lines for the express purpose of registering on vital new targets.

Major Johns ordered out several search parties. They beat through every wooded area and combed every hillock or bush-covered hedgerow. They examined every tall tree and even prodded into suspicious-looking ground that might have covered trapdoor-type holes. They found no observers. After two men were hurt by incoming shell fragments, the Major ordered them back to their holes, none the wiser.*

Martin was defeated. He said it was impossible for artillery to fire with such consistent accuracy from a map. If his first "only" answer had been wrong then all that was left to

---

*Many times during the campaign in Europe did American units suspect that the Germans had observers concealed behind our lines. This probably did occur in some instances. However, the answer usually comes from a less mysterious source. The Germans told us after the war that our radio security was consistently poor, that by monitoring our transmissions they were generally able to keep themselves well informed as to our movements, and that by goniometric intersection on our transmitters they were able to locate most of our command posts as well as other installations. Our people never seemed to realize that in many German units were men who had lived in the States and

believe was that the German artillery had registered on all those targets while the area was still in their hands. Nobody could answer that question, but it didn't stop the accurate fire from coming in steadily.

The mortars were the worst, though. They were even more effective than the 88's there in that position at Dufayel, because the rolling terrain produced many dead spaces which the 88's with their flat trajectory could not reach. It was later that the men came to fear the 88's more than the silently falling mortar shells.

The German mortar gunners must have registered, too, because they had the exact range of every foot of hedgerow held by the battalion. On the 10th of July they covered almost every foot of every hedgerow. That sort of gunnery was rough on the men. They never knew when the first round would fall. But once it had splattered with its flat crash, they all knew that six or maybe a dozen more were coming, each one a little farther up or down the hedgerow. When you heard that first one you pulled the bottom of your foxhole right up into your belly and prayed. When you heard the second one you knew whether or not they were coming your way. If they were coming toward you it got right rough. Each round was a little closer, and they were so damned deliberate about it that the waiting was worse than the crash of the shell itself. You lay there and counted the seconds between the shells until you knew that the next one was YOURS.

The twenty seconds or so was the longest in the world

understood American slang perfectly, and that the so-called double talk which we indulged in rarely fooled them. Even more interesting is the fact that our supposed short-range transmissions during the Louisiana and Tennessee maneuvers were picked up in Germany owing to a phenomenon involving reflection from the Heaviside Layer of ionized particles in the stratosphere. A study of these intercepts often told the enemy when our units were preparing for oversea movement. The German artillery was also skilled in sound- and flash-ranging, but this method did not, of course, locate for them anything except active artillery positions.—Editor.

because you'd never know if you were safe until the shell hit. It could hit anywhere outside your hole, even a matter of inches, yet you were okay. If it hit in the hole with you you'd never know it, of course. Actually, only a few shells ever made direct hits on foxholes, but some did and nearly every man had seen a foxhole that had been hit. There was always the little tail-fin section left on the surface, and after the litter bearers had come and gone there was only a pool of dark muck to show that somebody had been in the hole.

It happened twice that day.

A little after 1700 General Gerhardt came striding through the trees behind the command post hole. His manner was neither light nor gay. He came on serious business, that of giving orders for an attack. If he carried them himself they were important.

He wanted to brief all the company commanders but he didn't have time to wait for Able and Baker to worm their way out. Consequently he talked to Kenney; and to Mc-Carthy, who had succeeded Captain Nabb in command of Dog Company; and to Mentzer, together with Major Johns and the staff. All crowded into The Hole.

"Gentlemen," he said, with an edge to his voice that was impressive, "the division attacks tomorrow morning at 0600. All along the line. This is the drive for St.-Lô."

He stopped to consult a notebook. "Your objective will be the town of Belle Fontaine. Of course you will get details from Ordway. But I want to tell you that this is the beginning of a very big and very important operation. I can't tell you more now, but I expect every one of you to do your best tomorrow."

With that he was gone, Weddle and Grimsehl scurrying to get off the steps to make room for his passage, and his aide scrambling to get out of the phone hole and catch up.

Before he got well into the woods, the General stopped suddenly and called, "Oh, Johns."

Major Johns was on his heels. "Yes, sir?"

"Look, boy, you're the sole survivor of the three volunteers who wanted to come with me. Did you know that?"

534

He didn't wait for an answer. "Whitehead caught an 88 the other day while you were back in those woods." He paused and looked sharply at the Major. "I don't know if it's lucky to ask to get into a war or not. But you stay in there and pitch. I'm counting on you."

He waved and was gone again before Johns could reply.

The staff ate their C-ration supper in thoughtful silence, waiting for the CO and Weddle to be called back to Regiment for particulars concerning the attack. They were called soon enough.

There were few details. The battalions would attack, as the General had said, at 0600. The 1st Battalion would advance in the southwesterly direction, with the village of Belle Fontaine as its initial objective. It was hardlly a thousand yards, across country, but every man in the battalion knew it would be a long thousand. It was just as well that they didn't know just *how* tough that thousand yards was to be.

The 2d Battalion would move on La Forge and the 3d would be in reserve.

That was about all there was to it, except for the usual information concerning artillery support, supplies, location of the regimental command post, and that sort of thing.

Johns and Weddle got back just at dark. Though it was very quiet, the company commanders who were waiting in The Hole were uneasy. None of them wanted to attack from that position. It was too screwy a setup. But there was nothing they could do about it now. The Major had no choice in his order of attack. From the direction of the objective he could do only one thing, let Able and Baker take off from right where they were, with Charlie, in reserve, protecting what would become the exposed and dangerous left flank.

Johns expected trouble on that left flank because they would be moving slantwise across the Charlie front, at least at first. Even in that difficult terrain it was too much to expect that they could get clear without trouble. He told Kenney to try to protect the flank with one platoon

535

while holding two platoons free for him to use to shove through a soft spot, if one was found, or to bolster a weak place if they were hit hard with a counterattack.

By the time the order got down to the platoon leaders their part was pretty simple; all they, in turn, had to say was "All right, gang, let's take that next hedgerow."

When the company commanders had gone, the staff discussed the plan of attack. The question bothering Johns most of all was where to put the advance command post group. He wanted to hold casualties to the barest minimum, yet he wanted to be as far forward as possible. There were a number of good reasons for this. In the first place, keeping the command group close to the companies made a lot of difference in communications, particularly in this close, wooded country. A clump of heavy trees or a high hedgerow could spell the margin between having contact and not having it. That was of supreme importance. Second, if he had to move to a bogged-down company or to any trouble spot, he wanted to have the shortest possible distance to go. Third, the group couldn't afford to stay far behind, in any event, because they fully expected the German paratroopers to close in around them as soon as they started to advance. If the command post group were too far from the rifle companies it would have a good chance of getting cut off and destroyed or captured. Then there was always the consideration that the men liked to know that the Old Man was not far behind, and to see him once in a while when the stuff was flying around. Major Johns was acutely aware of this, but he'd already suffered losses in his command post group by getting them up front and he didn't want that to happen again. There wasn't a good route of advance in the center so he decided to move along close behind Able. That would put the command post on the open flank, away from the known threat to the left but exposed to anything that might come from the right. If danger did materialize, the command post group could always help defend the flank then shift toward the center as soon as they could conveniently disengage.

At midnight the whole staff, less only the S4, was still in The Hole talking about the attack. The night was almost

536

eerily still. Only a quiet voice or two and the occasional passage of heavy shells, high overhead, disturbed the silence.

There was no mortar fire, largely because mortar men don't like to fire at night. The flash of their guns, so comparatively close to the lines, looms bright and clear in the darkness and sometimes a little trail of fire follows a shell for several hundred feet up into the air, making it plain as a tracer and spelling out, "Here I am. Why don't you shell me back?"

There was a rare rifle shot or brief burst of machine-gun fire as some gunner on one side or the other fancied he saw a target. But the stillness between was so heavy that these puny outbursts hardly made a ripple on the great pond of silence.

By 0100 the last patrol was in safely. Only two had been sent out, just to make sure the enemy was still in the same positions and to listen for signs of movement behind his lines. Nothing was stirring.

The radiomen turned on their sets and checked with each other as they did every half hour throughout the day and night, so they would never be completely out of touch for more than 30 minutes if the wires should go out.

The staff was uneasy. They didn't want to turn in. They couldn't say why; there had been other nights like this. They all sensed that everyone shared their own nameless fears.

Mentzer broke the spell. They had all come out of The Hole for a breath of air and were standing by the hedgerow, looking at the few stars that showed through a light overcast that had drifted in since dark. Mentzer was a light-hearted individual, not usually concerned with thinking deeply about abstract matters. He had been a cab driver back in Frederick, Maryland, home of his Headquarters Company. "Ah," he said, "them bastards are just tired after throwin' all that heavy stuff in here all day. They've shot their wad. I'm gonna hit the sack."

He turned and disappeared into the extreme darkness of the woods, headed for his nearby hole.

Down in The Hole the phone rang softly. Weddle went

537

down to answer it, staying nearly two full minutes before he came back up, saying, "That was the Doc. He says one of his men saw a German out by the medics' latrine. I asked him how could he know it was a Kraut in this dark and he said because the guy crawled over a hedgerow not ten feet from him and he got a good look at his little paratrooper helmet silhouetted against some stars that happened to be in the clear just then. He said the guy grunted when he slid off the hedgerow and he didn't sound like any of our people. The Doc checked but couldn't find anybody else who had been out there. Nobody uses that latrine but the medics."

Major Johns snapped to full alert. "Doc's man was probably seeing things. Nevertheless get Mentzer to grab some of his people who are off duty right now and beat out the area. Get the whole A and P Platoon if you want to, but have a good look around. We can't take any chances."

He wouldn't have admitted that he was nervous. He just believed in playing it safe.

Weddle went after Mentzer while the Major turned to Grimsehl. "George, wake everybody up and check the CP close-in defense. Get the Commando Platoon on their toes. See that there is an alert, tight ring around here tonight—all night."

Grimsehl lost no time in moving out to look for Sergeant Turner, who had charge of the so-called Commando Platoon, which was a group of 10 or 12 men specially picked and trained for tough patrol work. They were kept around the command post for its defense when they were not out on a mission. In a quiet position a double guard at each entrance was usually enough, as all the others slept nearby in holes dug in a circle around the command post. Tonight the battalion commander wanted every man in every hole to be awake and ready for business. He proposed to take no chances on a quick rush by a few determined paratroopers overrunning the guard and tossing grenades into all the holes, including The Hole.

Suddenly a terrific firing broke out.

Every German cannon, mortar, rifle, and machine gun that had fired a round that day cut loose simultaneously.

538

The sound of mortars coughing on the German side blended with the scream of incoming shells. Grimsehl and Hoffman slid down the steps of The Hole before the first round hit.

It was Ryan's war all over again on a broader front. The sharp roar of artillery shells overrode the flatter crunching of the mortars, while the vicious, snarling, still sharper crack of 88's stood out above both, and the ripping of German machine guns filled in the tiny intervals between explosions. Although the fire was concentrated chiefly on the edges of the gap between the two companies at the orchard, it was hitting all along the front. Some rounds tore into the field and hedgerow near the command post while others rushed overhead to burst in the trees as they searched for the mortar positions.

The phone rang. Major Johns grabbed it. "Red 6."

"Charlie 6, sir. We're catching hell down here with mortars and artillery. I think there is enemy infantry coming in under the fire."

Stoen broke in, the operator having wisely sensed a crisis and cut him into the circuit, "Same here, Major. Only I KNOW there's infantry coming in. They're already in the road with us."

His voice and manner were normally extremely quiet and easy-going. Now his tone was strident with urgency. Had it been anyone but Julian Stoen, the Major might have thought it showed near-panic. "Okay to both of you," he answered as calmly as he could. "Stuff's coming in up here too. Fight 'em and keep me informed."

He spun the crank and said to the operator, "Give me Regiment."

Nothing happened. You can tell when a field wire is dead because it is so very dead. The operator's voice was rising now, too. "Sir," he shouted, "that line is out. I'll get a crew on it right away."

Before Johns could lay the phone down it rang again. It was Stoen. "Sir, for God's sake put all the artillery we got down in front of the lines . . . you know my concentrations . . . call for all of 'em . . . . the bastards are all over us." The phone went dead.

Martin was frantically spinning the artillery phone crank

but there was no answer and the crank spun easily. There was no resistance in the circuit, indicating that the line had been cut. Martin stuck his head out the entrance and called to the radio operator. "Call for concentrations 175 through 183 as fast as they can fire 'em. Tell 'em it's an attack. We need all they can give us."

The operator turned on his set and started calling. He called and called, but he got no answer. They all knew that the set at the Fire Direction Center was not on because they had checked in exactly 8 minutes before, and it would not come on again until 0200. That meant that for 22 minutes the battalion would be cut off from outside support of any kind. A lot could happen in 22 minutes.

The mortar observers, up with the companies, found their lines were out too; but they had radios, and the men at the mortar positions did not need orders to start firing anyway. They could hear what was going on. The mortars started pouring out shells before the first message came back. So, at least, the battalion had its own support working.

"That Kraut back by the aid station!" cried Weddle, suddenly. "He must have been part of a patrol that came through and cut all our wires! Hell, there haven't been enough shells falling to cut 'em ALL. The smart bastards! They even knew when we checked the radios, too."

Major Johns nodded. He was calling Able Company. No answer. That wire was out. They were all out, front and rear. He took the 300 handset from Bein, his new radio operator, and tried to get Charlie Company. Kenney answered, reporting that his whole line was heavily engaged. There was no reply from Baker.

Johns cursed his impotence. His communications, with which he had been so satisfied, were shot to hell. For all the influence he was having on this battle he might as well be back at Division. It was up to the men on the front line now. He had no reserves and no way of getting any. He knew the radiomen were trying to get through to Regiment and the Fire Direction Center. There was absolutely nothing he could do but wait.

The enemy fire was still heavy. The German gunners pounded every company, then searched every position that

540

might hold reserves. The command post was shaken up again and again. Bein's radio lost an aerial, which he replaced in seconds. One of the commando gang took a fragment in his leg. Tracers flew overhead in all directions, ricochets screamed and yowled, and the tearing crackle of German machine gun bullets never stopped.

Only minutes after the barrage hit, the hollow, clumping roar of grenades came from the direction of the Able Company command post. Major Johns rushed into the open to listen more carefully. The sound of the grenades kept coming, punctuated with the short high-pitched burrrrp, burrrrp, burrrrp of the MP 38.* The center of the noise was moving slowly but steadily toward the rear, right through the center of A Company. Johns' stomach crawled up in his chest again, so that nothing but a cold vacuum was left in his belly. His defensive line was broken! The paratroopers were running over Able Company! He took two running steps in that direction, then stopped. It would be pretty silly for him to go tearing off into the dark in the middle of this melee, thus virtually surrendering control.

He turned to Grimsehl. "George! Send a runner to A Company to find out what's happened down there."

Grimsehl went to get the man, who in a few seconds trotted off down the hedgerow, his M1 ready in his hands.

Twenty age-long minutes crept by. The fury of the attack did not diminish. Johns stayed outside to listen, as he could learn more from the nature and location of the firing than he could from his useless radios and telephones. Twice he had to duck back inside, once when a battery volley struck along the other side of the hedgerow, and once when the enemy mortar fire started its orderly march down the near side. The German mortar gunners were, as usual, deadly accurate in their location of the hedgerow, but they were not so effective in the spacing of the rounds.

*Maschinen Pistole Model 38 (Schmeisser), a "Tommy" gun issued to parachute troops. Americans called them burp guns, from the sound of their high cyclic rate.

One shell hit between the old phone hole and The Hole and the next struck harmlessly on the far side.

At last came the sound of still more artillery. But this was the good kind—the going-out kind. It was hard to distinguish it from the rest of the din. Nevertheless there are always lulls in any battle, no matter how fierce, and in these intervals the familiar outgoing whine came through clearly. But the volley went out much too far; the first few rounds would have no effect on the Germans, who were storming through the battalion defensive lines.

The artillery fire kept going out, way out, until both Martin and Johns were almost beside themselves with frustration. Suddenly the monotonous calling of Martin's artillery radio operator changed to sharp attention. He had got an answer!

"Fire mission. Concentrations 175 through 183 at once! Request all available fire. Enemy attacking strongly all along front!"

Thank God! breathed the Major. Then he yelled in Martin's ear, "Tell the FDC to tell Regiment what's going on and that if they have any reserves to rack 'em up behind us, we may need 'em."

The message went out quickly.

"On the wa-a-a-ay" came back as an answer.

This time the artillery hit much nearer. It had that authoritative crack to it which told that it was close in, almost as close as the German stuff. And it kept coming.

Somehow the wires to Charlie and Baker were re-spliced time and again. They always went out, but after that first 30 minutes or so they were in most of the time. When they were not, the 300's did the job. The companies had settled down a bit after the first shock and the operators did whatever was necessary to reestablish their communications. Kenny and Stoen both asked for reinforcements, both getting the same answer, "Sorry. There aren't any. Do the best you can."

There was no contact with Able. No runners came in to report, no fire missions were requested. Nothing! There was no longer any heavy firing in the direction of the line originally held by A Company, but there was plenty from an area to the rear of that line. Oddly enough, there was an occasional flurry of fire from well in front of the center. It looked very much as if the company lines had been completely overrun and were falling back.

Martin called for the A Company defensive concentration anyway.

Around 0300 the runner came back. His eyes were very big. "Sir," he reported, "there are Krauts in the A Company CP."

"Nuts," said the Major."

"Yes, sir, there really are."

"How do you know?"

"Well, I had a little trouble, running into people on the way. Some were Krauts, some our own men, so when I got close I crept up sort of easy-like. 'Fore I saw anybody in the road a Kraut challenged me and when I didn't answer he cut loose at me with a burp gun. Missed me, though."

"Nuts," repeated the Major. He didn't want to believe Able had been overrun. He turned to look for Grimsehl but saw instead the man he really wanted. It was Private First Class Gay, Silver Star hero of a lone patrol back at the Bois de Bretel. Gay was sitting very calmly on a corner of The Hole, chewing gum. Johns snapped at him, "Gay! Get the hell down to Able and see for sure if there are Germans in the CP and what the situation is generally."

Gay looked at the Major. His jaw motion slowed to a halt. Then he remembered that he had a reputation to maintain. He rose, checked his carbine, gently detached a grenade from his belt, and started down the hedgerow fiddling with the pin on the grenade.

The German artillery and mortars began to let up some. They seemed more uncertain, as if they weren't too sure just where their own people were. They kept beating the flanks of the salient they had driven into the battalion line, but the rolling barrage under which the paratroopers had first come in had slackened materially. The savage ferocity of the small-arms battle was either increasing, or the lessening of the artillery and mortar fire let the sounds of the rifles, machine guns, submachine guns, and grenades come through more clearly. The indefinite center of the fire was

543

coming from a point that moved farther and farther to the right rear of the command post. Major Johns could not be sure, but the sounds seemed to indicate that A Company was pulling back from in front of the enemy, fighting as it went.

Stoen had managed to report that his right was holding but he had had trouble on his left at the orchard. His whole line had been in action ever since the first shells fell. Germans had gone through his company, he said, on through the orchard in rear, but they had not driven him out of his position. There had even been two grenades thrown into his command post.

The center of the battle surged in close, no more than a hundred yards to the right of the battalion command post. Bullets cracked through the trees, chunked solidly into wood or earth, or snapped overhead in the clear. One long burst, flashing straight down the hedgerow, bored into the top of The Hole between the Major and radio operator Bein. It was beginning to look as if the command post were going to get into the fight. Johns ordered every man into a fox-hole. There would be no moving around and no shooting unless the enemy attacked in force. There was no use starting a fight with the little handful of people near the command post. If they had to shoot they would, but there was no point in asking for trouble.

Grimsehl loomed up out of nowhere, prodding a prisoner ahead of him with a bayonet. Some instinct led him to the Major who rose from his hole to see what the S2 had got from the prisoner. "Sir!" Grimsehl said excitedly, "I got this bird from a couple of A Company men. He says they are hitting us with four companies, three infantry companies in the assault and one engineer outfit fighting as infantry in reserve—all paratroopers and about 110 men per company."

"Four companies! And on a narrow front! Wait till Regiment hears this. Maybe we'll get some help now!"

The paratrooper, his hands locked behind his head, must have understood a little. He smiled as if confident that he would not be a prisoner for long.

Grimsehl faded into the dark returning a moment later

544

without the prisoner, whom he had given to a commando for safekeeping.

"He says they had committed the reserve just before he was grabbed, which was about 0215 or 0230. They were already through the A Company center and right flank by then and they shoved the reserves on through to keep going. But I don't know where they could have got to, because the fighting still isn't much past our line here."

While he was speaking, the center of the battle surged toward the rear, as if it had just gotten free of snag. There was a beating of feet up the hedgerow a few yards toward A Company and the sounds that men make scrambling over a hedgerow. Johns and Grimsehl sank to the ground. The safety on Hoffman's M1 clicked loudly as he pushed it forward into the "Off" position.

But the rushing sounds went straight to the rear, punctuated by brrrrps from German guns. They did not pause at Mentzer's domain or at the aid station. They were headed for the mortar positions.

Major Johns whispered to Bein, "Call Dog and tell them some Krauts are coming toward them from the direction of Battalion."

Bein called, but the only answer he got was the sound of firing from the direction of the nearest mortar position.

The telephone operator, taking the Major by the arm, whispered in his ear, "Phone, sir. It's Regiment. Colonel Ordway."

"Johns? What's going on up there?" The Colonel was excited too.

"Full-scale counterattack, sir. Prisoner says four companies, 440 men, hitting us. Didn't you get my message through the artillery?"

"Yes, but they just said an attack."

"I asked for help. Able was overrun and maybe part of Baker. I think you better . . . ." Realizing that he was talking into a dead line, Johns rang for the operator. "Send the wire crew out again, and ring Message Center for me."

Sergeant Wilson answered the Message Center phone himself, "Yes sir?"

"Sergeant, haven't you got that radio working yet?"

545

"Yes sir, it's working, but we can't get an answer from Regiment." The sergeant sounded completely unperturbed about the whole business.

"If you ever get through, tell 'em they're going to have Krauts back there very shortly if they don't send me some help to restore these lines."

"Yes, sir. I'll write a message and bring it to you later for signature."

"Oh for Pete's sake! All right." Johns dropped the phone to look for Martin. He found him at a post on the hedge-row, watching the dark field beyond.

"Martin! Get your people to tell Regiment that we have been hit by an enemy force of 440 men, that our line has been broken, and that we are requesting reinforcement."

"Okay, Major, but I'll have to encode that, which will take a while."

"Encode hell. The Jerries know about it. Send it in the clear." The Major was having "security" trouble again.

"If you say so . . . ." The artilleryman repeated the message to his radio operator who reluctantly put it on the air.

The Artillery Fire Direction Center was horrified at the breach of security. They lectured the operator briefly but thoroughly. He replied with a rude sound that was not in the Signal Operating Instructions, adding, "The Major said send it. We need help and the Krauts know it. Now get it for us!"

Kenney called for artillery fire at a new point. Instantly Martin, his operator, and the Fire Direction Center became coldly precise again. They had been firing concentrations on every spot where the paratroopers could possibly form up or through which they would have to move to reinforce the attacking force. Most of the Division artillery and some from Corps must have been supporting, because the whine, scream, crash, roar, crack, and rumble of the shells going overhead and thundering down into enemy territory was almost constant. The sound was extremely comforting, even though the small-arms fight was still raging behind the command post.

A man staggered up to the command post and nearly fell

into Martin's arms. Only some instinct had prevented the CP guards from shooting him, as he had made no attempt to answer their low challenge or to halt. It was an officer, a forward observer who had been with Able Company.

He was pantng, incoherent. Martin and Johns half carried him down the steps into the command post, where they sat him on an ammunition box that served as a chair. In the light of the single candle he made a horrible sight. Blood was smeared over his face, his hands, and his shirt. But Martin could find no wound. The man was dazed, dumb. He sat with his head down, still panting, paying no attention to questions. He stared at the blade of a hunting knife in his right hand. It was still sticky with blood, as he raised and lowered it. He seemed almost to be weighing the knife. He opened and clenched his fingers around the handle, never taking his eyes from the red-stained blade.

Martin heated some coffee over a K-ration box and forced it gently on the forward observer, who was a close friend. The young officer took the coffee and began to settle down. The wild look went out of his eyes. His trembling lessened until it nearly ceased. Finally he began to talk, the words falling out in chunks, sometimes incoherent, "We were out on Able OP 2 . . . . I was asleep . . . . the stuff started falling all around us . . . . Before I knew what was going on . . . . the Krauts were in there with us . . . . They killed two Able boys—right in front of me . . . . I held up my hands and my radioman did too. . . . They took my pistol belt . . . . then the others went on and one Kraut pushed us toward the rear, his rear. . . . We walked a long time . . . . I don't know how far . . . . or where we were . . . . then some of our own mortars came in close. We stopped and the Kraut looked around for cover. There wasn't any so we ran a ways . . . . then the artillery started . . . . it was hitting in front of us. We stopped again . . . . and found some old German fox holes. They had tops on. The guard turned his back on me. He was kicking at a hole to see if he could get in it . . . . and my radioman jumped him. My man jerked off his helmet, hit the Kraut in the back of the neck with it. . . . Then I remembered I still had my knife." He pushed the bloody blade forward and

547

looked at it for a long time, his fingers still closing and opening around the hilt.

"I jerked it out." He stopped talking and put his head down almost to his knees, still holding the knife at an awkward angle in front of him. He didn't move for a full minute—then, with an effort, he sat up again and went on. "I jumped him just as he turned around . . . I hit him with the knife and it went into him . . . then I hit him again and again and again. I couldn't stop hitting him even after . . . after I knew he was dead. My radioman pulled me off him, finally . . . We started back."

Major Johns was bouncing with impatience to ask questions but something held him in restraint until the man stopped. "Where were you? How did you come back? Did you see any more Krauts?"

The lieutenant looked at him dully, as if he didn't understand. But he answered. "I don't know. We didn't see anybody until we got here. I don't know where we were, or how we came back. I didn't know where we were until . . . until I recognized the battalion hedgerow."

It was obvious they were going to get no useful information out of this man. He was another combat exhaustion case, shocked more by the awful experience of killing a man with his own hands than by the fire he had been under and the fact that he had been captured. The Major motioned to Martin, who led the still-dazed man away, and sent him to the aid station.

Gay came back from A Company. He answered the challenge flippantly and slouched into The Hole. There were no grenades hanging from his belt. He reported.

"That runner was right, Major. There WAS some Jerries in the CP."

"What do you mean, 'was'?"

"Just that. There ain't so many now as there was before I got there, least not so many live ones."

"What happened?" The Major was impatient. It was obvious that Gay was enjoying the spotlight again and wanted to draw it out.

"I crawled up to the edge of the sunken road right over

the CP, coming in from around on one side. I couldn't make out who was there, so I made a noise and some bastard challenges me in Dutch. I answers him in Dutch, too, but it don't sound right to him and he asks for the password. I gives it to him with grenades, and hightails it out of there. The stupid bastard never even got a shot at me."

Johns couldn't help smiling. "What about the rest of the line? Could you tell anything about it?"

"Naw, Major, it was too dark to see anything, but there was some shootin' out on the left front and a helluva lot in the right rear. None at all along the road where most of the line used to be."

"All right, Gay, thank you very much. Stick around close, I may need you again."

Gay went out and took his place on the corner of The Hole. He treated himself to a fresh stick of gum.

No battle goes on for hours without lulls. This one, fierce as it was, was no exception. After the flurry of fire back at the mortar positions there was a long pause in the small-arms firing although the artillery was still going over, mostly outward bound now. As Gay went up the steps of The Hole the firing started again, back by the mortars. It grew until it was a first class row, with grenades, burp guns, and rifles all mixed together.

It lacked the size of the earlier fighting, but not ferocity. Nor did it rise and fall in volume quite so much. It gave the impression of determined, plugging fire, kept up by a comparatively few men on both sides, men who weren't going to quit. From the mortar positions it began to move slowly back toward the front again.

As soon as the direction of the sound was definite, the Major began to exult although he could not be sure that the battle had turned. He was puzzled because the sound of German burp guns stood out clearly and dominated the other firing.

The sounds came closer and closer, then died out completely for a few seconds. In the near silence the sound of running feet came not far from the aid station. Then an M1 rifle cracked sharply 8 times from a point no more than a hundred yards back of the command post hedgerow. A burp gun answered. More M1's fired. Two or three other burp guns opened up. Then a light machine gun joined in, its tracers flying toward the enemy lines, a few ricocheting off the hedgerow.

The running feet pounded nearer. In another momentary lull there came again the sound of men scrambling over a hedgerow. Then a burp gun and several rifles fired from the far side of the hedgerow. The machine gun and other burp guns answered them. A rifle grenade burst on the hedgerow itself. More running feet, then grenades and scuffling noises, more grenades. Then came the clear cry, "Goddammit, somebody kill that sonuvabitch before he gets away again."

Every man in the command post group laughed aloud at that. They knew the show was about over. The battalion's lines would be restored before morning.

The firing, with more bloodthirsty yelling, receded toward the A Company line.

Kenney called from C Company to report that the attacks on his line had let up and they were now free from any flanking threat. Stoen, his line out and the radio not working at the moment, sent a messenger to say that they were holding. He had picked up about a squad of A Company men who had been wandering around in the rear. They were using the squad to bolster their own right flank.

There was still no word from Able Company.

It was after 0400. The dawn would soon help clear things up one way or another. If it showed most of four companies of paratroopers in the lines formerly held by Able there might be some trouble. On the other hand if the Krauts were scattered and had not been able to consolidate a position during the darkness, it might be possible to pull some men away from Charlie and Baker, to clean up such enemy as were left.

It occurred to Johns that if the enemy were still around, the command post group might find itself with a fight on its hands as soon as people could see. He again ordered everyone to stay out of sight until he could tell what the score was. There had never been a thought in anyone's mind of withdrawing, even though the attack had carried well to their rear.

The line to Regiment was in again and Colonel Ordway was on the phone. Major Johns gave him a brief report. "Sir, things are getting quiet up here again, but I can't tell yet who owns the area. I don't have the faintest idea where any part of Able is. Baker may have lost some of its left platoon by the orchard, although Stoen tells me they are still in most of their original positions. The Germans got clean through our middle and went as far back as the mortar positions but I think we've got everything in hand now." He waited while a long burst of machine-gun fire snapped overhead, then added, "But you never know."

Colonel Ordway was impatient. "Some sergeant from A Company rushed in here about 3 o'clock with a wild disaster story. Said the whole battalion was destroyed and he was the sole survivor."

"One of MY men said that?"

"Yes, one of YOUR heroes. That was bad enough but he put the wind up for a battalion of 4.2 mortars that are digging in behind you. That whole gang took off." The Colonel paused a moment, then went on. "He picked up about half of my Cannon Company as he went through the woods, too."

Johns was nearly speechless—a man from the Red Battalion—a sergeant too—running away from the enemy! He sputtered into the phone, "Why . . . . why that dirty . . . . ! I'll court-martial him for cowardice if it's the last thing I do!"

The Regimental Commander ignored him. "Can you attack at 0600?"

That stopped Johns cold. It was the first time he had even thought of the attack and, if he had, he would of course have assumed that another outfit would be put in their place. People don't attack too well after fighting for their lives half the night.

"Colonel," he answered, "we couldn't attack a hot break-

551

fast at 0600. I've got most of one company, at least half of another, all of my headquarters, and Lord knows how much of my Weapons outfit. I don't know anything about Able Company yet, nor do I know that we aren't going to be fighting Krauts out of the CP in the next ten minutes. What about the reinforcements I asked for?"

"Nothing doing. Division wouldn't let me send you anything. They still won't believe you had anything but a combat patrol up there. They know about your prisoner's report and I told them about the runaway sergeant. But they still wouldn't let me turn loose anything. They wouldn't even believe what I told them about the 4.2 battalion running off. Had to send their own man down to check, but he'll be until noon getting back with a report."

"Very well, sir, I think we can handle the situation alone now anyway, but I repeat that I can't guarantee ANYthing. You may have a good part of our hostile paratroopers in your lap by the time it gets light, because I believe a lot of them just kept right on going after they got through us. I don't have any idea where they could have got to, but it's quiet now. Stoen and Kenney have even stopped calling for artillery for the first time in more than 3 hours."

That ended the conversation. Johns swung around on Weddle and Hoffman, cursing fervently. "That goddam Division! The ornery SOB's wouldn't believe what we told 'em! I hope that bunch of Krauts gets clean through to where they are, if they can walk that far! Maybe they'll believe us then!"

Stoen called in. The wires had been restored again. He reported that his position was secure and that he was sending a patrol out to the left to see what he could find in the Able Company line. He also said that his 60-mm mortar people, whom he had directed to pull back one hedgerow in order to keep them out of the fight, had found all three of Able's 60's, abandoned. They had picked them up, together with their ammo, and had fired all 6 guns all night long until they were now down to only a few rounds per gun.

Johns looked toward the spot in the darkness that he

552

thought was occupied by Weddle. He did not often call the S3 by his first name, but this was a special occasion. "Leroy," he said, "I want you to take about six of the commando boys and go down to Able to see if you can tell what happened and what the situation is. I figure it's better to do it in the dark, taking it easy, than it is to wait till it gets light and maybe run into something and get into a fight. Don't get involved in anything unless you have to. If you find it advisable, stay down there and get things straightened out, but send me a message so I'll know what you're doing. Watch out for that Baker patrol, although I don't think you're apt to run into it."

Captain Weddle groped for his helmet and M1, said "Okay," and was gone up the steps.

Once more there was nothing for Johns to do but wait.

It wasn't long until the sky began to lighten. There was no word, of course, from either Weddle or Stoen. It was too soon to expect anything. But the Germans started to throw 88's into the area, which was encouraging. They wouldn't be doing that if they had any reason to believe their own troops were occupying the lines. Johns went outside to look around. As he did so an 88 smashed viciously into a tree just behind The Hole. He grinned as he sniffed the acrid smoke. Dallas and his German paratroopers, hunh!

It was a little past 0500, light enough to see clearly, when the first runner came from Weddle. He was grinning broadly as he trotted up, rifle in hand. "Sir," he said, "Captain Weddle says tell you he has found what is left of two whole platoons of A Company and that Sergeant Shaff has the old CP back again."

He saluted and turned to go back to Weddle. The Major returned his salute, calling after him, "Tell the Captain that makes me very happy."

A little later Stoen called in to say that he was occupying every foot of his old line and that his patrol had returned to tell him about the two Able platoons that were still in position. He had lost a lot of people but didn't know how many more were being found all the time. He had also lost the two .50 caliber machine guns that Regiment had ordered them to use in the attack that morning. Neither Stoen nor Major Johns was concerned about the guns as they had thought all along that it was silly to try to use such heavy guns in an attack in that kind of country.

Weddle got back about 0630 with a strange story. He came into The Hole, demanded a breakfast ration, and sat down on the shelf before he would tell it. Finally he got started.

"Here's what happened to A Company, as near as I can tell now: The mortars and artillery hit them sudden and hard. They hit the outposts at the same time they did the main line. Every SOB in the company put his head down. The Krauts come in under that fire like they loved it. Shaff said they weren't thirty yards back of it. They run plumb over the outposts before the sentries knew there's a Kraut within a hundred yards, so the main line got no warning. One sergeant looked up and saw the shine of a shell burst on a box of machine gun ammunition a Kraut is carrying and he hollers, 'Krauts,' but by then it's too late in most places. The Germans poured right over the edge of the road and run up and down it throwing grenades into the holes where the guys were still hiding from the artillery, shooting anything that moved.

"That bird you got running the company says he was stunned by a grenade in the first assault. He wasn't able to get out of his hole, or to give an order. He seems to be okay now, except a little shaky. He's trying to get things together. He's damn lucky he isn't dead.

"Anyway, the Germans ran through the company CP in nothing flat. Everybody that isn't killed takes off for the rear. That's where our sergeant hero that went back to Regiment come from, I think. But the two platoons in the middle are cut off. You know they aren't all in the road. They can't run if they want to, 'cause they know by now that there're Krauts behind 'em, probably more than in front. So they stayed right there, fighting like good little boys all night long. That was the shooting we heard out front from time to time and couldn't figure. Kee-rist! There's dead Krauts and our dead people all over the place.

554

"Those of Able that take off, about a platoon plus, altogether, I reckon, hit for the battalion mortar positions.
They join up with a few guys from Baker and beat the
Krauts back there by quite some time. Then the noncoms
and a couple of officers who are around—I still don't know
who—rally the whole gang, put them in some sort of
position along with the mortar crews. By the time the
Krauts get back there they're ready for 'em and kick hell
out of 'em. I heard about one bird who waited for a Kraut
to come right alongside of him, then raises up, grabs the
Kraut's burp pistol, kicks the guy in the crotch, and shoots
him with his own gun. That was why we heard so many
burp guns. Our guys were taking 'em away from the Krauts
and using them against 'em. Our boys like the Schmeissers
better'n anything we got, for this kind of fighting.

"This took most of the night. It didn't go quick, mostly
because the Heinies were taking it pretty easy after they get
through the line, like they don't want to lose contact with
one another. Then they had that scrap down by the mortars.
Some of the Germans pulled back, just as slow." The S3
stopped, took his helmet off, and scratched his head
seriously.

"You know," he went on, "I just can't figure out what
happened to all those paratroopers. The boys from Able
said there must a been at least two hundred went through
the orchard. But I don't believe there was more'n about 40
or 50, maybe 60 at the outside, ever got as far as the
mortars."

Johns interrupted, "Could be a lot of 'em got separated
in the dark and decided it was no good so they filtered out
around the flanks, or went back the way they came."

"Yeah, could be. Then we got to remember that Kenney
and Stoen and the two Able platoons had a quota apiece.
From the way the Krauts chewed Baker there must'a been
quite a few in that crew.

"And I nearly forgot—the artillery knocked hell out of
a lot of Germans before they ever got going. That was
probably what saved our tails, really. The Able boys said
that first concentration, the one that hit so far out, went
right into the middle of something, because they heard all

kinds of yelling and screaming and carrying on out there. Could of been their reserves, I guess.

"Well, however it happened, it all boils down to the same old story: they hit us, pushed through, took casualties, and got disorganized. We counterattacked and shoved 'em out again—just like the book says."

Grimsehl came in with more details obtained from his prize prisoner. The man, who was from the headquarters company of the German battalion they were facing, seemed to know all about everything. He claimed that the whole attack was a direct result of the visit of the medical officer two days before, when the truce had been requested and granted. The Major stared hard at Grimsehl when he reported that, and the S2 flushed. If this were true the battalion had paid a terrible price to save the life of that one American they had got out of the orchard alive.

Grimsehl went on, "He said that medic came back and told their commander that he had been in our lines and they were lightly held. Of course, he never was in our main line, only in an outpost. If he thought that was the main line I can see how he would believe it to be pretty thin. But I guess they got a surprise when they hit Baker and Charlie, who wouldn't give. Anyway, the German battalion commander decides to have a try at us, because we are sticking out a little and they wanted to straighten their lines and maybe get back the main road behind us, there. He got some more artillery to come in for the show. They were registering and covering it up by firing so much yesterday. Then he got that company of engineers to fight as infantry and act as a reserve.

"This prisoner says what Weddle guessed about our artillery is about right, because the Germans took one hell of a beating in that first concentration. It knocked the engineers cockeyed while they were forming up and delayed their push through the orchard quite a bit.

"I think they had a couple of platoons worrying Charlie and maybe a couple more trying to get around Baker's right, while the rest hit right in the middle. But by the time they got through they were so shot up that the engineers didn't have what it took to roll us up. So they chickened out when they hit the mortars, and decided to quit."

Major Johns accepted the story without comment. It was probably correct. But at that moment he was more concerned with what was going to happen than with what had already happened. He wanted to know how many casualties he had suffered, to get the companies untangled, bring up more ammunition, and see that the men got a little rest. They hadn't had much sleep lately. It still did not occur to him that the attack order would not be cancelled. As far as he was concerned, the 1st Battalion had had enough fighting for the day.

He called the companies for a strength report, and told them to hurry up the reorganizing process. All companies reported some dead, but none had an accurate count as yet. The Doc reported that the aid stations had treated 42 casualties, with more coming in all the time.*

*The facts concerning the German attack were all verified in a German after-action report which the 29th Division captured later at Brest. Major Johns' estimate of the number of troops involved, the casualties suffered, and the progress of the action were all confirmed exactly, showing that the Battalion's information was accurate. Division, which had exhibited such skepticism, was mildly embarrassed, and the Battalion was ultimately awarded the French Croix de Guerre for the action.

To the Rhine

But over a third of the German 7th Army did get out of the Falaise Gap, partly because the Allies couldn't keep the noose tightly closed; the men escaped, but they were unable to save their equipment.

The Germans withdrew to the Seine, in a state of high disorganization, expecting the Americans to turn on Paris itself. But Patton's 3rd Army kept driving east, under orders to seize a bridgehead over the Seine southeast of Paris. Patton was stalled only by the insurrection in Paris. To help out the beleaguered French, the Allied High Command sent an American and a French division into Paris to help liberate the City of Light.

Paris was freed on the 25th of August, 1944, and Patton loaded up with gasoline; now his 3rd Army lashed out once more south of Paris, pounding for the German Saar; the 1st U.S. Army pointed for the Ardennes to the north; farther to the northwest the 1st Canadian Army and the 2nd British Army headed for Belgium, aiming to cut off the German 15th Army which held the V-rocket sites on the coast, and to open up another major port. A port in the north, to shorten the supply route for the thrust into Germany, was an essential. The American armies were being supplied from Cherbourg; by the end of summer the supply lines stretched out 400 miles. The British were supplied from Bayeux, some 250 miles away, and this would be lengthened as they drove on Belgium. The irony was, the supplies were ashore, but they couldn't be moved to the front fast enough to launch an Allied smash to the Rhine while the German armies were still reeling.

The supply problem fed a disagreement between Montgomery and Bradley over the strategy of mounting the knockout punch. Montgomery's idea was for the American and British forces to move out together north of Paris; the 1st and the 3rd Armies would then fan out toward the Ardennes, while the British and Canadian armies would free the Channel ports, move into Holland and then wheel to the east aiming a punch at the German Ruhr. He asked for forty divisions and a majority of the supplies during September to build up the knockout punch,

558

and planned to attack on a short front. To get the forty divisions, the 1st U.S. Army would have to be placed under his command. The 3rd would proceed to the Meuse River and hold there to protect the flank of the northern operations.

Eisenhower showed some interest in this, but Bradley and Patton were thoroughly aroused. Patton, a restless and aggressive commander, had continued his drive, and he couldn't abide the idea of waging a defensive campaign, particularly after the success of the breakthrough at St. Lô. SHAEF had also laid down that American armies were to serve under American commanders only, once they were fully established in France.

To resolve the conflict, Eisenhower took over as commander of all the land armies, giving Montgomery part of what he wanted—the major share of supplies for the strike into Belgium and Holland, and the promise of some of the divisions from the 1st Army. This didn't really calm things between Montgomery and Bradley. Patton continued to press for supplies, particularly gasoline, so that he could keep pushing the Germans in front of the Meuse River.

On August 29th, Montgomery opened his attack toward Belgium. The British 2nd Army's armored columns drove north, pushing the Germans ahead of them, crossed the River Somme, captured the German 7th Army at Eberbach and entered Belgium on September 2nd. To the east, two American armored divisions also crossed the border on the same day. The British met little resistance on their way to Brussels, taking the city on September 3rd; the British 11th Armored Division pushed on to Antwerp, entering the city on September 4th. The German 15th Army was now cut off, isolated along the Channel coast (they could save themselves only by getting across the Scheldt estuary to the west of Antwerp.) Remnants of the 7th Army were being cut up, those not captured were being driven back against the Ardennes and the Meuse River to the south. Now the German Ruhr, the heart of the German steel industry, might be vulnerable to Montgomery. From the Ruhr, Berlin was only a jump away.

Montgomery now urged Eisenhower to put his strategy for the solid punch at the German Ruhr, and the outflanking of the Siegfried Line, into effect while the Germans were still staggering. Eisenhower, under pressure from Bradley and Patton, felt the Allies could still operate on a broader front; not only could Montgomery strike at the Ruhr, but Patton, too, could undertake limited offensives toward the Saar (particularly while Montgomery was held up at Antwerp flushing the Germans

559

out of strong positions on the Scheldt estuary that blocked access to the port). Eisenhower was a leader who assessed all opinions, and tried to arrive at the best common denominator; he never took a strongly defined stand on the long-range strategy, never committed himself to one or the other of the opposing views, and so was buffeted between Bradley and Montgomery for the rest of the war.

Eisenhower decided to give Patton's 3rd Army half the supplies available, with a go-ahead to cross the Moselle River and force the Siegfried Line; Montgomery was to secure the approaches to Antwerp, then launch his attack across the Rhine River at the Ruhr. The U.S. 1st Army, now commanded by Gen. Courtney H. Hodges, was asked to cover Patton's northern flank while he pushed to the south, and to furnish flank support to Gen. Miles Dempsey's 2nd British Army to the north, preparing to strike across the Rhine. This was stretching his resources over an ever-widening front, a condition that would make for trouble later in December.

Meanwhile, Montgomery was given some assurance that his supplies would be built up for the impending British drive into Holland. This drive, labeled Operation Market Garden, was to begin September 17th with an airborne drop north of the jumping-off point of the British 2nd Army. This was to be the largest airborne operation ever undertaken; three divisions, 1st British Airborne, the 101st and 82nd American Airborne, were to form a corridor stretching fifty miles north to Arnhem. Holland would be split in half, and Montgomery would move his armored columns up the corridor. Strong resistance was expected from the Germans from *both* sides, for to the west they were still holding on to their V-2 rocket sites; if Montgomery could consolidate the corridor, the sites could no longer be supplied from Germany.

But the Arnhem operation met with only limited success. The attack was stalled cold by September 25th. Bad weather at the airfields in Britain prevented reinforcements from being dropped to the British 1st Airborne, holding the northern end of the corridor at Arnhem. In any case, the 1st Airborne hadn't been dropped close enough to the Arnhem bridges, which the Germans then used to reinforce their besieged elements down the corridor. Also, the British 43rd Division didn't move as fast up the corridor as planned. Wilmot says this failure was largely due to the conservative tactics of the British commanders. He maintains that if the British hadn't been so cautious about casualties, and if the Americans had committed larger supplies, concentrating on a smaller front, Montgomery could have succeeded at Arnhem; this would have put him in a position to persuade Eisenhower to give him what he needed to punch through to the Ruhr.

Instead, the British succeeded only in driving a narrow wedge into Holland; the approaches to Antwerp could now be taken without any counter-pressure from the Germans to the east. But the British had lost 6,000 casualties. Instead of being in a secure jump-off point for the push to the Ruhr, the British to the east of the corridor faced tough fighting, while the Canadians to the west had hard work to free the port of Antwerp.

The following selection is taken from Capt. Andrew Wilson's *Flame Thrower*, an account of war seen from one of the British Crocodile tanks, which were designed for flaming stubborn pillboxes and heavily entrenched positions in the kind of fighting that now engaged the British infantry.

FLAME THROWER

by Capt. Andrew Wilson

The three Crocodiles which Wilson inherited were called "Supreme," "Sublime" and "Superb."

"Supreme" was the troop leader's. The driver was a quiet, fatherly man, who went into battle as phlegmatically as if he were driving a bus. When he came out, he spent hours trying to straighten damaged headlamps and track guards. The co-driver was a cheeky Welshman called Randall, who, when he wasn't arguing with Wilson, was constantly at war with the gunner and the wireless-operator.

The squadron was sent to Winssen to the west of Nijmegen. At first the farm at Winssen looked forbidding. It stood on the edge of a cheerless marsh, and the rain and wind

This selection is condensed from the author's book *Flame Thrower*.

which blew across the polder beat hard on the flaking paint of the doors.

The front was all around. To the east was Germany; to the west a big enemy pocket which reached to the sea; to the north a desolate stretch of heavily-shelled ground called "the island."

Nijmegen was in the front line. In the streets were big smoke canisters, which were set alight whenever the enemy started shelling. The great steel bridge was guarded by Royal Engineers, who watched for mines which the Germans were floating down the river. Fire engines waited in the streets to put out fires which the shells started, and all the time the remaining civilians were going about their business.

One morning the squadron left on the road to 'sHertogenbosch. It was a fine day with a touch of autumn in the air. For a while they ran through the quiet countryside. Then they heard the sound of guns and turned off the road where a knocked-out Sherman stood facing an abandoned anti-tank gun.

The ground was held very thinly here. The squadron stopped by some cottages and a woman told them that the enemy came round in the night, foraging for bicycles.

The crews not on guard spent the night in a hayloft, and next morning the squadron joined up with a squadron of Cromwells from an armoured brigade, which had been probing the enemy's defences. They made a common harbour in two adjacent fields. Away to the east, across the flat countryside, you could see the broken spire of Rosmalen church, with an even round shell hole in what once was the belfry. The enemy had a look-out there.

Wilson met the Lancers' Sergeant-Major. "What's the form?"

The sergeant-major winked. "Watch haystacks," he said. "They've got a habit of changing position."

They were to attack Rosmalen next morning. In the afternoon Barber came back from an infantry battalion order group and told the troop leaders to go up and do a reconnaissance.

They found a lonely company dug in behind a hedge.

"O.K.," said the Company Commander. "Keep your heads down and follow me."

They crawled along a ditch, which struck out into no man's land. The mortars were crumping gently a little way down the line, and somewhere a Spandau zipped. Now and then, as they worked their way forward, a bird would fly up.

"There you are," said the Company Commander. "The village is in the trees. The red roof by the church is what we call the Rectory. There's some sort of anti-tank gun to the left, and a bit of a stream in the dead ground just before it. O.K.?"

"O.K.," said Wilson.

They crawled back faster than they came. The mortars were ranging on them, hitting the ditch and throwing up clods of earth.

Wilson fell asleep, wondering what kind of gun it was by the Rectory. He was sure that death, when it came, would be from an anti-tank gun. He saw in his mind's eye the muzzle of the gun as it moved behind the leaves of some bush or in a shadowy space between buildings. He had learned the aspect of every gun by heart. It had a certain advantage: it made him almost indifferent to shelling.

Someone pressed his shoulder and said, "Reveille." He looked at the luminous dial of his watch: it was four-fifteen. He put on his belt and beret and picked up his map-case.

The darkness was absolute. A breeze swept the harbour, cold and edged with rain. Around the vehicles the first shadowy figures were moving, opening up and stowing away the blankets. An hour to zero. At any moment now the five-fives would open up. He waited in the shelter of his tank.

At the fixed moment the sky to the rear was lit with a sheet of flame, and the earth shook gently beneath him. He stood listening. From high in the darkness came the long, fluttering thrum of the shells. He strained to look eastwards, away beyond the village where the enemy's support line ran.

Two, three, four seconds passed. He was aware of other figures round him, which had stopped whatever they were doing and were looking eastwards too. But all that came back was a deep, protracted rumbling of the ground.

"All right," he said. "Get mounted."

563

In the turret the operator was answering the netting call. Dunkley came up on the air, and then Sherrif, reporting their troops ready to move. A moment later a dozen long shapes came looming through the darkness and went clanking out of the harbour. It was the Lancers.

The squadron followed. They moved slowly. Sometimes there was the exhaust-glow of the tank in front to follow, and sometimes only a cloud of dust. Down below the gunner was asleep, his head lolling against Wilson's legs. He was a funny little country lad, and the others were always teasing him because he was so scruffy and tongue-tied. Wilson wondered if he dreamed down there, and if so, what. It was always the gunner who got out last when a tank brewed up.

Suddenly the Lancers stopped. It was the forming-up point.

Wilson and the co-driver dismounted and opened up the valves on the trailer. Outside the tank, away from the hum of the headphones, there was a world of noise and death. The enemy was shelling along the start-line, and every now and then something solid and heavy slammed through the air. You couldn't mistake an anti-tank gun. This one was firing blind, perhaps at the sound of the engines.

They re-mounted, and Wilson looked at his watch. He thought of the dials in the trailer, which would still be going up, showing the rising pressure of the nitrogen on the fuel tanks; he wondered about the gun again; and suddenly he remembered that they hadn't had breakfast.

Zero came.

"Driver advance."

Everything was blotted out except the few yards of grass and bushes in front of the tank, the place where he had to pass through the infantry. As the tank moved forward, he saw helmets where men crouched low in a trench, waiting for the order to get up and walk upright. Then there was just the pressure of his brow on the periscope pad, and ahead an open flatness, ending in a line of flickering explosions.

He tried to see which of the explosions was the gun; but it might have been any one of them. The shots went slam-

564

ming through the air. It was still more than three-quarters dark.

"Hello, Oboe three . . ."

A Lancer troop moved up on his left, their Besas spitting tracer. They were going to shoot him in. He felt an intense comradeship with the long Cromwells. They and he were out ahead—the little black arrows on the war maps.

"Co-ax, five hundred, fire!"

His own gunner opened up, and the fumes blew back into the turret, sharp and choking, towards the ventilator fan.

"Just keep spraying, gunner."

They moved with infinite slowness. It seemed to be getting lighter, but really it was just the distance closing. The low black line of the trees emerged; the spire of the church, dim against the dawn.

"Get ready, flame-gunner—fire!"

The flame shot out, fell, broke, rolled along the ground.

"Left, sir. Left!"

Suddenly, from the side of the periscope, Wilson saw something flash against the armour of a Cromwell. The driver jerked the Crocodile towards a small, dark opening in the trees, and for one long moment the flame-gunner pumped in the fire.

They worked down the trees which masked the front of the village, pouring the fire into the darkness. Now and again there was the sound like men screaming, which Wilson had once heard in Normandy. When they reached the end of the trees, Wilson halted the troop and they stood off the target while the infantry went in.

Two minutes later Barber came on the air. "Our friends are held up," he said. "Go in and help them."

He led the Crocodiles into another opening in the trees, and everything went dark again. The front of his tank began to nose up a tall bank; it lifted slowly, reached the top and stood poised for a moment. All at once the bank gave way.

"She's slipping," shouted the driver. "I can't hold her."

One of the tracks started to race. The tank began to turn over, sliding a little, rolling on its side. Wilson thought: We shall be helpless, like an upside-down turtle. Next moment the tank slid off the bank and crashed into a dark space

565

below.

His head must have struck the gun mechanism. When he came to, the tank was on its side. The seventy-five and the Besa were useless. The wireless was dead. All he could see was the red indicator lamp of the flame gun, which still glowed on the turret wall.

"Are you all right in front?"

The flame gunner answered, sounding dazed.

"Can you see anything?"

"Yes, a house."

"All right, flame it."

The flame shot out. Its sudden glow lit up the periscopes. He leant against the seventy-five ejector shields and tried to manipulate them, straining to see the enemy who must be coming in with their Bazookas. But the periscopes would move only a few degrees.

He directed the flame to the only other target he could find—a group of cottages, a little to the right, about a hundred yards away. The fire crashed in and ran through the buildings from end to end. It's always the same, he thought. Flame anything in sight and you're terrifying. Stop, and you're a sitting target for the Bazookas. But, fired continuously, the flame lasted only a few minutes.

All at once, the gun gave the snort which meant that the fuel tanks were empty.

"Take your guns and get out," he said.

They climbed out with their Sten guns, and made a small group round the Crocodile. He saw now that, coming over the bank, it had run onto the roof of a small house. The house had collapsed and the tank had fallen down among the rubble. The battle was going on all around.

"Wait here," he said. "I'll try to find the others."

He took a Sten and went through some bushes to the left, where there was firing. A few moments later he found himself in a sunken garden: it must have been the garden of the place they called the Rectory. There was an ornamental summerhouse in the middle, and a gate in the wall on the far side.

It seemed quite empty. Then he saw the German officer.

He was standing ten yards away, with a pistol in his hand; and he saw Wilson at the same moment.

Wilson pressed the trigger of his Sten. He thought: It's the first time I've killed a man this way. But nothing happened. He tugged at the cocking handle. The Sten was jammed.

Slowly the German raised his pistol and fired. The bullets smacked dully into the bushes at Wilson's back. It seemed so stupid. He was struggling to get out his own pistol, which was caught in the lining of his pocket.

Then the German turned and ran. As he went through the gate, a Bren gun fired on the far side of the wall: he tilted sideways and fell in a little heap.

Wilson found the Bren and a corporal in charge of it.

"Have you seen the Crocodiles?"

"Frig, no," said the corporal. "But the place is lousy with Jerries." He was going in to clear the Rectory. His men were all-out. They'd been doubling in through the Spandau fire, and now he was urging them on again.

At last he got them to their feet. They ran across a lawn and the corporal threw a grenade through the door. As they went in, he shot left and right through every door with the big German Schmeiser he was carrying.

Wilson watched them, and then went off through the trees again, hoping to pick up track-marks or perhaps find Barber. At the foot of a big oak a German lay clutching his stomach. He was half moaning, half shrieking. As Wilson passed, the noise subsided to a sob, and he saw that the man was dying.

Beyond was a kind of garden shed, ripped open by a shell and full of smashed bicycles. There must have been twenty or thirty—tall Dutch bicycles, with pieces of German equipment tied to them. Then there was a trench with a pile of bodies. When Wilson crossed, he found the open ground.

He was facing the knocked-out Cromwell. The crew had tried to bale out. One, a boy of about nineteen, was lying on the ground with his head on his arm; he was smiling, as if asleep, and his brain had spilled out on his battledress.

Further on, Barber's Support tank was trying to pull a Crocodile out of the stream. Wilson ran over.

"What's happened?" said Barber.

Wilson told him. "Whose tank is this?" he asked.

"One of Sherrif's."

"Let me have it."

Just then the Support tank pulled the Crocodile free. The corporal tank commander handed over the headset, and Wilson took the Crocodile into the village.

He found the rest of the troop and told them to follow him. At the end of the village six or seven Cromwells were firing across the fields. He led the troop into position among some broken buildings.

The ground ahead was utterly flat, except for a single hedge, and away in the distance a row of haystacks. For a moment it was difficult to see what the Cromwells were firing at. Then, unexpectedly, the early morning sun broke through a cloud bank, lighting up the ground in clear detail.

Wilson ran his glasses over the pattern of greens and browns, which a moment before had been monochrome. Almost at once his eye caught something moving—a line of grey figures which doubled and paused and doubled again, moving across the front, left to right, towards the 'sHertogenbosch road.

"Co-ax, traverse right. Steady . . . on. Six hundred. Got them, gunner?"

The gunner spun his elevating wheel.

"On, sir."

"Fire!"

The Besa broke into a roar, hosing out tracer in a flat arc. The burst fell short but quickly moved up, cutting into the figures as they ran. Through his glasses Wilson saw some stumble and fall. The rest went to ground.

Then another group was running.

"Co-ax, stop. Up two hundred, left."

The gun began to hose them. Quickly the sergeant and corporal picked up the target. But the group went on, a man or two dropping at a time. Wilson saw now that they were making for one of the haystacks. Suddenly he remembered what the sergeant-major had said.

568

"Co-ax, stop. Seventy-five load A.P."

The operator opened the breech, ejected the high-explosive round which lay there, and threw in the long black armour-piercing shot.

"Seventy-five traverse right."

The turret swung right with a gentle whine from the traverse motor.

"Steady . . . on. Haystack eight hundred. Fire!"

There was the usual convulsion as the gun fired; the breech running back on recoil; a haze of flame and heat above the muzzle; the shot with its single red trace, spinning towards the target.

As it struck, there was a violent flash. The haystack burst into flame and poured out smoke—the thick black smoke which comes from fuel oil.

The operator threw in another round.

Suddenly the Lancers were firing A.P. too. Then, without warning, something big and square emerged from a haystack further along the line. It moved sedately from left to right, gradually gathering speed. Wilson brought over his gun, and twice the gunner fired at it. But it was no good. The thing disappeared in a sunken road.

He wirelessed back to the Lancers squadron commander, who was at the other end of the village.

"Hello Item Two, there's a Tiger just gone across our front, moving your way. Over."

"Hello, Item Two. Thanks for the tip. Out."

For the first time Wilson felt sure of himself in battle. More than that, he was elated. He'd led in the infantry, flamed an anti-tank gun, burned down half a dozen buildings which might or might not have held enemy, switched tanks, knocked out what was generally thought to have been a Mark IV in a haystack, and seen a Tiger long enough to fire at it.

"Well," said Barber. "Did you have a good time?"

"Fine," said Wilson.

The squadron was going back to refuel, and he went off to find his own crew. When he reached them, the fitters had arrived with the A.R.V. and were fixing tow-ropes to pull the Crocodile upright. The place was full of smoke from the burned cottages. Every now and then a mortar bomb fell, and they all dived under the A.R.V. for shelter.

Presently the mortaring slackened, and they made breakfast. There was a tin of bacon and some jam and biscuits. They ate happily and almost silently in a place where they could see no dead, knowing that the Crocodile would be out of action for a good many hours yet.

When they had finished, the gunner disappeared in the direction of the Rectory. A few minutes later he came back with a handful of black cigars.

"Have one, sir. They're out of a Jerry funk hole."

But Wilson shook his head. He pulled a crumpled Player's from his pocket and stood for a moment, listening to the sound of firing, which now came from far on the other side of the village.

"I'm going for a walk. If you want me, I'm up where the anti-tank gun was."

Ever since his first action in Normandy he'd been drawn by a fierce curiosity to see what happened where they'd flamed. Yet he'd never done so, because always they'd be switched from one place to another, and there was never a chance to explore the objective.

He walked down the front of the trees, where here and there the brushwood still smouldered among the blackened trunks. The burning away of the undergrowth had completely uncovered some trenches. He looked in the first and for the moment saw only a mass of charred fluff. He wondered what it was, until he remembered that the Germans were always lining their sleeping-places with looted bedding.

Then, as he was turning to go, he saw the arm. At first he thought it was the charred and shrivelled crook of a tree root; but when he looked closer, he made out the hump of the body it was attached to. A little way away was the shrivelled remains of a boot.

He went on to the next trench, and in that there was no concealing fluff. There were bodies which seemed to have been blown back by the force of the flame and lay in naked, blackened heaps. Others were caught in twisted poses, as if the flame had frozen them. Their clothes had burned away.

570

Only their helmets and boots remained, ridiculous and horrible.

He wanted to vomit. He'd vomited before at some sights. But now he couldn't.

Suddenly he heard someone behind him and he looked round with a start. It was Randall, his flame gunner. He must have come round from the opposite direction.

One didn't make favourites in a crew, but from the moment he'd taken over, Wilson had felt a special affection for Randall. With his constant cheekiness, his eternal arguments with the turret crew, he was utterly free from all false sentiment. He was a soldier because he had to be. He took no pride in killing.

"Come up and see what's by the gun," said Randall.

They went. The gun itself was crushed. One of the Cromwells or one of the other Crocodiles had run over it. A little to the side were the bodies of the crew. One of them had been caught by the flame as he ran away, splashed with the liquid which couldn't be shaken off. His helmet had fallen off and now he lay with black eyeballs, naked and charred and obscene.

There came from it all an enormous disgust, which couldn't be expressed, yet somehow one had to say something.

"We certainly did a proper job of it," said Randall.

About midday they had the Crocodile upright and joined the broken tracks. It was a makeshift job, because they had to break off some steel keepers which held the track pins in place.

On the way back to the refuelling point they met the rest of the squadron coming out.

"Catch us up when you're ready," shouted Barber.

As the column passed, Wilson saw his sergeant—Warner. Barber had put him with Sherrif's troop to replace a corporal who'd been killed in the village. Warner waved as he went by.

A little further on they had to let a scout car pass. As the car came level, it stopped, and the man in the commander's seat dismounted. It was Waddell.

He asked Wilson how the action had gone and where the

squadron was. Wilson told him. The C.O. looked at the Crocodile, scored with bullets and with all its track guards ripped away, and grinned.

"Fine," he said, and then with a curious finality: "Good luck." Next moment the scout car disappeared towards the squadron in a cloud of dust.

The refuelling-field was littered with piles of empty drums. Wilson took the Crocodile round the perimeter until he found his own drums, full and neatly stacked, together with five new nitrogen cylinders.

They started heaving the heavy drums to the top of the trailer and pouring in the four hundred gallons of white, treacly flame-fuel. While they were doing it, the fitter sergeant arrived.

"You're not taking her out again without those keepers fixed?" he said.

"They'll hold a bit longer."

Sergeant Pye shook his head. "I'll go back and get the welding kit."

"Too long," said Wilson. "There's a R.E.M.E. section down the road. Go and borrow theirs."

Pye went off in his half-track.

"What did you do that for?" said Randall. "We could have been here till tomorrow."

Wilson didn't answer. Even if he had wished to answer, he couldn't have explained what the sight of those bodies at Rosmalen meant—that either one threw up everything and made one's protest, or else one did everything more thoroughly and conscientiously than ever before, so that there was no time to think.

On the Border

At SHAEF headquarters the great Montgomery-Patton duel dragged on. During the fall months, Montgomery had pressed Eisenhower to hold back Patton in the south. Eisenhower, seeing that Montgomery couldn't be ready for his strike at the Ruhr until Antwerp could supply him (the port wasn't opened until November 27th), allowed Patton and Bradley to build up for a limited offensive; if Patton could reach the Rhine and threaten the Saar, a breakthrough might occur at a weak spot, or at least the Germans would have to commit reserves to the south rather than hold them in the north against Montgomery.

The 3rd Army struck across the Moselle River on November 8th, in the midst of rainy weather. The Germans gave ground but there was no real breakthrough, partly because the attack was launched on a thirty-mile front. They still had a long way to go before their backs were to the Siegfried Line, in the Saar.

North of the Saar the 1st and 9th U.S. Armies had been trying since September to smash through to Aachen, but they hadn't enough supplies to get very far, since Patton was now getting priority. And the Germans had had time to construct a solid defense line, from the Huertgen Forest all the way north of Geilenkirchen, where the 2nd British and the 9th U.S. Armies joined fronts. (According to Wilmot this was the most strongly defended area in the western front.) In the Huertgen Forest the 1st U.S. Army met some of their toughest fighting; with constantly bad weather, the American troops measured their gains in inches.

The following selection is taken from *Yank*, the famous Army weekly newspaper written by and for the American serviceman.

IN THE HUERTGEN FOREST

by Sgt. Mack Morriss

The firs are thick and there are 50 square miles of them standing dismal and dripping at the approaches to the Cologne plain. The bodies of the firs begin close to the ground so that each fir interlocks its body with another. At the height of a man standing there is a solid mass of dark, impenetrable green. But at the height of a man crawling there is room, and it is like a green cave, low-roofed and forbidding. And through this cave moved the Infantry, to emerge cold and exhausted when the forest of Huertgen came to a sudden end before Grosshau.

The Infantry, free from the claustrophobia of the forest, went on, but behind them they left their dead, and the forest will stink with deadness long after the last body is removed. The forest will bear the scars of our advance long after our scars have healed, and the Infantry has scars that will never heal.

For Huertgen was agony, and there was no glory in it except the glory of courageous men—the MP whose testicles were hit by shrapnel and who said, "Okay, doc, I can take it"; the man who walked forward, firing Tommy guns with both hands until an arm was blown off and then kept on firing the other Tommy gun until he disappeared in a mortar burst.

Foxholes were as miserable but they were covered, because tree bursts are deadly and every barrage was a deluge of fragmentation from the tops of the neat little firs. Carrying parties were burdened with supplies on the narrow trails. Rain was a constant but in Huertgen it was cold, and on the line there was constant attack and a stubborn enemy.

For 21 days the division beat its slow way forward, and there were two mornings out of those 21 when the order was to re-form and consolidate. Every other morning saw a jump-off advance, and the moment it stopped the Infantry dug in and buttoned up because the artillery and mortars searched for men without cover and maimed them.

There was counterattack, too, but in time the Infantry welcomed it because then and only then the German came out of his hole and was a visible target, and the maddened Infantry killed with grim satisfaction. But the Infantry advanced with its battle packs, and it dug in and buttoned up, and then the artillery raked the line so that there were many times when the Infantry's bed rolls could not be brought up to them.

Rolls were brought to a certain point, but the Infantry could not go back for them because to leave the shelter was insane. So the Infantry slept as it fought—if it slept at all—without blankets, and the nights were long and wet and cold.

But the artillery was going two ways. The division support fire thundered into the forest, and it was greater than the enemy fire coming in. A tired battalion commander spoke of our artillery. "It's the biggest consolation we have," he said. "No matter how much we're getting, we know the kraut is getting more." So the Infantry was not alone.

Tanks did the best they could when they could. In the beginning they shot up defended bunkers and dueled with machineguns in the narrow firebreaks, and they waddled into the open spaces so that the Infantry could walk in their tracks and feel the comfort of safety from mines. At the clearing before Grosshau they lunged forward, and some of them still dragged the foliage of the forest on their hulls when they were knocked out.

One crew abandoned their tank, leaving behind all their equipment in the urgency of the escape. But they took with them the mascot rooster they had picked up at St. Lô.

The advance through Huertgen was "like wading through the ocean," said S-3 at the regiment. "You walk in it all right, but water is all around you."

There were thickets in the forest where two battalion CPs had been in operation for three days, and physical contact between them had been routine. Thirteen Germans and two antitank guns were discovered between them. The CPs were 800 yards apart. "Four thousand yards from the German lines," said S-3, who had been one of the battalion commanders, "and we had to shoot krauts in our own front yard. Our IPW team got its own prisoners to interrogate. The engineers bridged the creek, and before they could finish their work they had 12 Germans sitting on a hill 200 yards away, directing artillery fire on them by radio." These things were part of Huertgen, a green monument to the Wehrmacht's defense and the First Army's power.

At that, the monument is a bitter thing, a shattered thing. The Germans had four lines of defense in the forest, and one by one those lines were beaten down and the advance continued. This was for the 4th Division alone. There were other divisions and other lines. And these MLRs were prepared magnificently.

Huertgen had its roads and firebreaks. The firebreaks were only wide enough to allow two jeeps to pass, and they were mined and interdicted by machinegun fire. In one break there was a teller mine every eight paces for three miles. In another there were more than 500 mines in the narrow break. One stretch of road held 300 teller mines, each one with a pull device in addition to the regular detonator. There were 400 antitank mines in a three-mile area.

Huertgen had its roads, and they were blocked. The German did well by his abatis, his roadblocks made from trees. Sometimes he felled 200 trees across the road, cutting them down so they interlocked as they fell. Then he mined and booby-trapped them. Finally he registered his artillery on them, and his mortars, and at the sound of men clearing them he opened fire.

The first two German MLRs were screened by barbed wire in concertina strands. The MLRs themselves were log-and-earth bunkers six feet underground and they were constructed carefully, and inside them were neat bunks built of forest wood, and the walls of the bunkers were paneled with wood. These sheltered the defenders. Outside the bunkers were the fighting positions.

The Infantry went through Huertgen's mud and its splintered forest growth and its mines and its high explosives, mile after mile, slowly and at great cost. But it went through, with an average of perhaps 600 yards gained each day.

The men threw ropes around the logs of the roadblocks and yanked the ropes to explode the mines and booby traps in the roadblock, and then they shoved the trees aside to clear the way. The engineers on their hands and knees probed the earth with No. 8 wire to find and uncover non-metallic shoe mines and box mines which the Germans had planted by the thousands. A wire or bayonet was shoved into the ground at an angle in the hope that it would touch the mines on their sides rather than on the tops, but they detonated at two or three pounds' pressure. Scattered on that ground there were little round mines no larger than an ointment box, but still large enough to blow off a man's foot.

At times, when there was a clearing, the engineers used another method to open a path. They looped primacord onto a rifle grenade and then fired the grenade. As it lobbed forward it carried with it a length of primacord, which was then touched off and exploded along the ground with enough force to set off or uncover any shoe mines or S mines hidden underground along its path. In other cases, when the area was known to be mined, it was subjected to an artillery concentration that blew up the mines by the force of the concussion. There could be no certainty that every mine was blown. The advance was costly; but the enemy suffered.

One regiment of the 4th Division claimed the destruction of five German regiments in meeting 19 days of constant attack. The German had been told the value of Huertgen and had been ordered to fight to the last as perhaps never before. He did, and it was hell on him. How the German met our assault was recorded in the brief diary of a medic who was later taken prisoner, and because it is always good for the Infantry to know what its enemy is thinking, the diary was published by the 4th Division. The medic refers to the Infantry as "Ami," colloquial for American. These are some excerpts:

It's Sunday. My God, today is Sunday. With dawn the edge of our forest received a barrage. The earth trembles. The concussion takes our breath. Two wounded are brought to my hole, one with both hands shot off. I am considering whether to cut off the rest of the arm. I'll leave it on. How brave these two are. I hope to God that all this is not in vain. To our left machineguns begin to clatter—and there comes Ami.

In broad waves you can see him across the field. Tanks all around him are firing wildly. Now the American artillery ceases and the tank guns are firing like mad. I can't stick my head out of the hole—finally here are three German assault guns. With a few shots we can see several tanks burning once again. Long smoke columns are rising toward heaven. The Infantry takes cover, and the attack slows down—it's stopped. It's unbelievable that with this handful of men we hold out against such attacks.

And now we go forward to counterattack. The captain is leading it himself. We can't go far though. Our people are dropping like tired flies. We have got to go back and leave the whole number of our dead and wounded. Slowly the artillery begins its monotonous song again—drumming, drumming, drumming without letup. If we only had the munitions and heavy weapons that the American has he would have gone to the devil a long time ago, but, as it is, there is only a silent holding out to the last man.

Our people are overtired. When Ami really attacks again he has got to break through. I can't believe this land can be held any longer. Many of our boys just run away and we can't find them and we have to hold out with a small group, but we are going to fight.

Then two days later came the final entry:

Last night was pretty bad. We hardly got any sleep, and in the morning the artillery is worse than ever. I can hardly stand it, and the planes are here again. Once more the quiet before the storm. Then suddenly tanks and then hordes of Amis are breaking out of the forest. Murderous fire meets him, but he doesn't even take cover any more. We shoot until the barrels sizzle, and finally he is stopped again.

We are glad to think that the worst is past when suddenly he breaks through on our left. Hand grenades are bursting, but we cannot hold them any longer. There are only five of us. We have got to go back. Already we can see brown figures through the trees. As they get to within 70 paces I turn around and walk away very calmly with my hands in my pockets. They are not even shooting at me, perhaps on account of the red cross on my back.

On the road to Grosshau we take up a new position. We can hear tanks come closer, but Ami won't follow through his gains anyway. He's too cowardly for that.

Perhaps this German who called the Infantry cowardly and then surrendered to it will never hear the story of one 4th Division soldier in Huertgen. He stepped on a mine and it blew off his foot. It was one of those wounds in which the arteries and veins are forced upward so they are in a manner sealed, and bleeding is not so profuse as it otherwise would be.

The man lay there, but he wasn't able to bandage his own wounds. The medics tried to reach him but were fired upon. One was hit, and the trees around the man were white with scars of the machinegun bullets that kept the medics away. Finally—after 70 hours—they managed to reach him.

He was still conscious, and for the medics it was a blessing that he was conscious; and for the man himself it was a blessing. For during the darkness the Germans had moved up to the wounded man. They took his field jacket from him, and his cigarettes. They booby-trapped him by setting a charge under his back so that whoever lifted him would die. So the wounded man, knowing this, lay quietly on the charge and told the men who came to help him what the Germans had done. They cut the wires of the booby trap and carried him away.

The green monument of Huertgen is a bitter thing.

Market Garden

After the Breakout of Saint-Lô, the German disaster at the Falaise Gap, and Patton's "end run" with the 7th Armored Army through France, the Allied armies had suddenly won the Battle of France. Inevitably, time for consolidation of these gains had to be taken, but this allowed the Germans equal time to consolidate their losses.

Chester Wilmot says, "Within three weeks of the fall of Paris and the overwhelming defeat of the German armies in the Battle of France, the Wehrmacht had almost recovered its balance; at all events, it was no longer on the run. The Germans were again holding a coherent line—admittedly thin and taut and with meagre reserves behind it—but a line nevertheless. And, because of their successful defense and demolition of the Channel ports and the approaches to Antwerp, they were denying to Eisenhower the supplies with which to maintain the full momentum of his advance. He, in turn, had unwittingly aided their recovery by his reluctance to concentrate the bulk of his logistic resources behind a single thrust at the Ruhr. Even when he had at last determined upon this course, he had not been able to give his northern armies the priority they required.

"When D-Day came for Operation Market Garden, although Eisenhower now had 52 divisions under his command, his sole chance of retaining the initiative, of recreating conditions of mobile warfare and of dealing a decisive blow at the Wehrmacht in the West that autumn rested with the three airborne divisions waiting at their airfields in England, and with the three divisions of XXX British Corps standing at the Dutch frontier. With them, though they could not know it, lay the last, slender chance of ending the German war in 1944." *

Market Garden would be the biggest airdrop of troops ever made—three airborne divisions at once. Field Marshal Montgomery was to be

*The Struggle for Europe, by Chester Wilmot, published by Harper & Bros., p. 497.

580

given the chance to be first across the Rhine. His plan was to drop the 1st British Airborne division on the north bank of the lower Rhine, to seize the bridge-crossing at Arnhem. Bridges at Nijmegen and Grave would be assaulted by the 82nd Airborne (U.S.) and the 101st Airborne (U.S.) would secure the road from Grave to Eindhoven. Then the XXX British Corps would fight their way up the road to Eindhoven and on to Arnhem along a "carpet of airborne troops, hoping to find the bridges over the three major water obstacles already safely in their hands." *

Heavy risks were being taken: surprise was essential—the weather *had* to be good for a successful drop, and for later drops since there were not enough planes and gliders to make the operation all at once.

Unfortunately, surprise was the first element to be lost.

THE ROAD TO ARNHEM

by Chester Wilmot

Sunday, September 17, was fine but overcast. There was little wind and the clouds were high, ideal weather for an airborne drop. By noon more than 1000 troop-carriers and nearly 500 gliders were heading for Holland, for the greatest airborne operation ever undertaken. This aerial armada carried the best part of three divisions which were to be dropped along the line Eindhoven-Nijmegen-Arnhem with the task of capturing the road bridges over the Maas, the Waal and the Neder Rijn and over five other waterways, thus clearing a corridor for the armoured and motorised columns that were to drive north from the Meuse-Escaut Canal to the Zuider Zee. With this one sabre-stroke Montgomery intended to cut Holland in two, outflank the Siegfried Line and establish Second Army beyond the Rhine on the northern threshold of the Ruhr. If all were to go well, the armour would reach the

* *Tide of Victory*, by Winston Churchill, p. 196.

Zuider Zee on the fourth or fifth day, but the hazards were great—especially for the airborne forces.

Because they were to form a corridor fifty miles long, the three divisions had to be landed in depth:

The 101st American (Major-General Maxwell Taylor) between Veghel and Zon, north of Eindhoven;

the 82nd American (Major-General James Gavin) between the Maas and the Waal, south of Nijmegen;

the 1st British (Major-General R. E. Urquhart) beyond the Neder Rijn, west of Arnhem.

The 1st and 82nd Divisions were to operate under command of H.Q. I British Airborne Corps (Lieut.-General F. A. M. Browning), which was also to land south of Nijmegen. A fourth division, 52nd Lowland, was available to be brought in by Dakota as soon as an airfield had been captured.

No such deep penetration, no such mass landing in daylight had ever been attempted. Holland was thick with flak. The Luftwaffe had ample bases within easy range, and its jet-aircraft had recently made their debut. The whole force might be crippled before it even landed. Blown bridges might check the relieving armour, or the slender corridor might be cut behind it, leaving the forward troops stranded. It was a gamble. The dividend could be high but the margin would be narrow.

The greatest danger was the weather, for there were not sufficient transport aircraft to carry the full strength of all three divisions in one "lift." With some 500 aircraft (tugs and troop-carriers) available for each division, it was decided that on the first day both the 82nd and the 101st should land their three parachute regiments,* and that 1st Airborne should bring in one parachute brigade and the bulk of its air-landing brigade. When provision had been made for these, and for essential service troops, there was little room for either field or anti-tank artillery.

*An American parachute regiment was roughly the equivalent in strength of a British parachute brigade.

On D plus 1 and D plus 2 the Americans were to receive their gliderborne artillery and infantry, while two more parachute brigades (one British and one Polish) and the rest of the 1st Airborne Division were to be landed near Arnhem. It was vital, therefore, that there should be fair weather for at least two days so that the airborne divisions could be re-supplied and brought up to full strength.

This was a matter of particular concern to the British division for there was a fundamental weakness in its plan. The outstanding lesson of the Normandy operations was that airborne landings should be made on or hard by the objective, especially when that is a bridge. This had been amply proved by Gale, and the opinion of experienced Allied commanders, such as Gavin, was that "it is in general better to take landing losses and land on the objective than to have to fight after landing in order to reach the objective." *

In making the Arnhem plan this lesson was not observed, because the expert advice which Urquhart received was that heavy losses would be suffered if he attempted to make his initial landings south of the river close to the Arnhem bridge. The flak, it was said, would be intense, and the fenland here too soft for the landing of gliders. It was difficult for Urquhart to overrule this expert opinion, since he had no previous experience of airborne operations. Moreover, he had inherited a division which had suffered heavily in Sicily because its landings had been scattered and strongly opposed. Since then, the doctrine had grown up within the division that it was more important to land accurately and safely than to land close to the objective. Urquhart seems to have been influenced by this doctrine, for he accepted the view that the only feasible dropping and landing areas were north of the river, *six to eight miles west of the Arnhem road bridge which was his principal objective.*

The risk of frustration, inherent in landing so far away, was the greater because the whole division could not arrive in one "lift." Had this been possible, Urquhart could

* James M. Gavin, *Airborne Warfare*, p. 81.

have planned to move against the bridge with his force concentrated and then to seize a dropping-zone for re-supply south of the river. But, because his force was to arrive in three instalments, he decided that he must deploy the air-landing brigade outside Arnhem to protect the DZ-LZ area at least until the second "lift" came in on D plus 1. This meant that during the first critical afternoon he would be able to send to the Arnhem bridge only his lightly-armed parachute battalions and his reconnaissance squadron, and that another twenty-four hours must elapse before the main strength of the division would be available to reinforce the paratroops in the town. Thus the plan appeared to sacrifice the advantage of surprise and to expose Urquhart's divided force to the danger of destruction in detail. Consequently, the success of his operations seemed to rest, even more than did those of the American divisions, on continued fine weather and a slow enemy reaction.

There was a similar, though not so serious, weakness in the plan of the 82nd Division, but in this case it was unavoidable. Gavin had four major objectives: the bridges at Grave, at Nijmegen and over the Maas-Waal Canal, and the Groesbeek Ridge which runs along the German frontier dominating the area between the Maas and the Waal. These objectives were so widely separated that Gavin could not expect to secure them all with the forces which would be available to him in the first twenty-four hours. He decided, therefore, to concentrate his initial landings around Grave and Groesbeek, for Browning, the Corps Commander, had ordered him "not to attempt the seizure of the Nijmegen bridge until all other missions had been accomplished." This was sound, for that bridge would be of little use if Gavin failed to secure the bridges leading to it or the high ground that was essential to its defence.

Next to the weather, the greatest danger was that the relieving forces would not be able to advance rapidly enough to reinforce the airborne troops before they were counter-attacked by German units more heavily armed than themselves. Second Army now had three corps along the Meuse-Escaut Canal, but VIII Corps on the right was not yet ready to attack and XII Corps on the left was facing a belt of difficult, marshy country.* Moreover, there were sufficient supplies forward to maintain a deep penetration only by XXX Corps.

The relief of the airborne forces depended, therefore, on Horrocks's three divisions and especially on Guards Armoured. From its bridgehead on the Meuse-Escaut Canal, however, there was only one clear route for the armour and there was every possibility that its advance would be checked, if not stopped, at one of the many water obstacles which lay athwart the road. In case some bridges should be blown, Horrocks had made elaborate preparations to bring forward columns of bridging material, DUKWs and assault-boats, but the task of moving these heavy columns and the necessary infantry and artillery along one road was indeed formidable. Since the Corps plan required the movement through the tenuous "airborne corridor" of some 20,000 vehicles, the success of the whole operation might well turn on the maintenance of the flow of transport by efficient traffic control and good driving.

For Browning, then, the vital questions were: Would the weather hold until his airborne reinforcements arrived? Would XXX Corps get through the corridor faster than the Germans could move against it?

*Once the airborne forces had landed, the Order of Battle of Second Army was to be:

VIII CORPS	XXX CORPS	XII CORPS	I AIRBORNE CORPS
11th Armd. Div.	Gds. Armd. Div.	7th Armd. Div.	1st Br. Airborne Div.
3rd Inf. Div.	43rd Inf. Div.	15th Inf. Div.	82nd U.S. Airborne Div.
	50th Inf. Div.	53rd Inf. Div.	52nd Lowland Div. (Air-portable)
	8th Armd. Bde.	4th Armd. Bde.	
	101st U.S. Airborne Div.		

These dangers were fully appreciated by Montgomery, but he hoped that the very violence and magnitude of the assault would leave the Germans so shaken and confused that they would not react with sufficient speed or strength. Second Army Intelligence estimated that the forces immediately opposing XXX Corps amounted to six infantry battalions supported by twenty tanks and twenty-five guns, including a dozen 88s. The crust was expected to be hard but brittle, and behind it, so far as Second Army knew, there were only meagre reserves. Dutch Resistance sources reported that there were a half a dozen low-grade battalions in the Nijmegen area and that some battered Panzer units from France were refitting north of Arnhem. It was suspected by British Intelligence that these might be the survivors of the 9th and 10th SS Panzer Divisions, which had not been identified by contact since the start of the month.* Even if this were so, it appeared to be unlikely that the two divisions together would amount to more than one motor brigade and one armoured brigade. Nevertheless, it was certain that the Germans would strike back with all the forces they could muster, for Southern Holland had to be held if they were to maintain their communications with the forces blocking the approaches to Antwerp and with the launching sites in The Hague, from which V2s were already being fired on London.

The Allied air fleet flew into Holland protected by 1240 fighters. The way was prepared for it by more than 1000 bombers which struck at enemy anti-aircraft batteries along the route and around the dropping-zone. There was little sign of the Luftwaffe, except for fifteen FW-190s encountered over Wesel. Since the previous evening Bomber Com-

*On September 15 the following message was received in London by radio from the Dutch Resistance: "SS Div. Hohenstrufl [sic] along Ijssel, sub-units observed between Arnhem and Zutphen and along Zutphen-Apeldoorn road. . . . Along Ijssel work on field fortifications in progress." This report, however, did not get through to the airborne forces in time to affect the plan.

mand and the Eighth Air Force had attacked the fighter bases from which the Germans could have intervened, but this was not the principal reason for the Luftwaffe's absence. The Allied air offensive against the synthetic oil refineries had been renewed during the past week, and the bulk of the German fighter force was concentrated in Central and Southern Germany. That afternoon not one British troop-carrying aircraft or glider was lost by enemy action, and the casualties suffered by the Americans (35 transports and 13 gliders) were almost entirely due to flak. Altogether, 4600 aircraft of all kinds took part in the airborne operation on this day alone, and of these only 73 were shot down.* Both the Luftwaffe and the ground forces were taken by surprise.

If there was any German commander who should have foreseen this airborne assault, it was Student, whose First Parachute Army was holding the line of the Meuse-Escaut Canal. In his daily report to Model on the 16th, however, he had given no indication that he expected an airborne landing. He had merely said that "increased motor transport activity and confirmed armoured preparations strengthen the appreciation . . . that a heavy attack must be expected very shortly." On the 17th Student's H.Q. was in a cottage at Vught, only eight miles west of one of the American dropping-zones. "About noon," he says, "I was disturbed at my desk by a roaring in the air of such mounting intensity that I left my study and went on to the balcony.

*The forces involved were the following:

COMBAT AIRCRAFT			TRANSPORT AIRCRAFT		
	U.S.	BRITISH		TROOP-CARRIERS	GLIDERS
Bombers	891	222	1st British	155	358
Fighters	869	371	82nd U.S.	482	50
Fighter-Bombers	212	—	101st U.S.	436	70
			Corps H.Q.	—	13

(These figures do not include the aircraft of 2nd T.A.F. which, in support of the breakout by XXX Corps, flew 550 sorties.)

Wherever I looked I saw aircraft; troop-carriers and large aircraft towing gliders. An immense stream passed low over the house. I was greatly impressed but during these minutes I did not think of the danger of the situation." *
He was moved more by envy than fear and, as he watched, he said to his Chief of Staff: "Oh, how I wish that I had ever had such powerful means at my disposal!" The wheel had gone full circle since Student himself had planned and led the airborne assault on Rotterdam four years earlier.

Student was not the only German commander who had a "ringside seat" for the airborne landing. Model was even closer, for his Tactical H.Q. was at Oosterbeek on the western edge of Arnhem. As the British parachutists floated down above and around him, Model did not wait to watch. He drove post-haste into Arnhem and there, finding that the local garrison commander had been killed in an air raid, he took command himself, quickly restored order and called in reinforcements from the 9th SS Panzer Division which, as the Dutch had reported, was stationed north of Arnhem.

Thus it was that by a double twist of fortune the two Germans primarily responsible for the defence of Holland found themselves so placed that they could act at once to counter the advantage the Allies had won by gaining surprise. Nor was this all. The German reserves were slender, but Model and Student soon knew exactly where to use them. Early that afternoon an American glider was shot down close to Vught, and, says Student, "a few hours later the orders for the complete airborne operation were on my desk." **

*Interrogation (Liddell Hart). The SS Commander in Holland, Rauter, reports that when he suggested to Model the possibility of an airborne landing the Field-Marshal replied: "Montgomery is a very cautious general, not inclined to plunge into mad adventures." (Netherlands War Ministry Interrogation.)

**It was this series of mischances, not the betrayal of the plan, that accounted for the swift German reaction. In a series of

588

By half-past one that afternoon the sky over Arnhem, Nijmegen and Veghel was filled with the throb of engines which drowned the soft sigh of gliders swooping in to land. In half a dozen towns and villages eager, grateful people rushed out to greet the airborne troops with flowers, and with food they could ill spare. But in most places the celebrations were cut short by the onset of battle and people fled from gay streets to anxious cellars.

West of Arnhem the paratroops and gliders of the 1st British Airborne Division landed accurately and with little interference from the enemy. Although none of Urquhart's 358 gliders were shot down, 38 failed to arrive. In nearly every case the reason was that the tow-rope broke—a common cause of mishaps in airborne operations—but it was particularly unfortunate that in the missing gliders were most of the armoured jeeps of the Reconnaissance Squadron which was to have rushed the road and rail bridges and seized them by *coup de main.* This was a bad start, but, while the 1st Air-Landing Brigade (Brigadier P. H. W. Hicks) organised the defence of the dropping-zones, the 1st Parachute Brigade (Brigadier G. W. Lathbury) assembled quickly and within an hour of landing was en route for Arnhem.

The drive for the bridges was led by Lt.-Col. J. D. Frost with the 2nd Parachute Battalion which moved smartly

articles in the London *Sunday Dispatch* in April and May 1950, however, Colonel O. Pinto (the wartime head of Dutch counter-espionage at SHAEF) alleged that the Germans were forewarned by a Dutchman, Christian Lindemans, who had been a Resistance Leader until he was suborned by the Abwehr in March 1944. It is true that Lindemans, after returning from Brussels on September 15th, warned the Chief of the Abwehr in Holland (Giskes) that the British were about to attack and would land airborne troops at Eindhoven on the 17th. Giskes has declared, however, that Lindemans "did not mention Arnhem . . . obviously because the objective of the planned air-ground offensive along the road that followed the north bank of the Neder Rijn. Frost sent C Company to seize the railway bridge, but just as his troops got there it was blown, seeming, says one eyewitness, "to curl back on us." The other two companies pressed on, but at Den Brink, less than two miles from the road bridge, they encountered such strong opposition that Frost had to detach B Company to deal with it.

While these operations were in progress, the road bridge lay unguarded. During the afternoon its garrison, some twenty-five men of First War vintage, had fled, and at 7:30 p.m. a Dutch policeman* found the defences deserted. From his post at the northern end of the bridge he looked anxiously westward for the first sign of the paratroops, but, even as they appeared in the September dusk, a party of SS troops drove up from the direction of Nijmegen and secured the southern end. Shortly after eight o'clock Frost —with A Company, his H.Q. and some sappers—took possession of the buildings around the northern approaches, but when he sent a platoon to storm the German positions on the south side, it was thwarted by fire from flak guns and an armoured car. Before long Frost was joined by most of B Company and by part of Brigade H.Q., but, having only 500 men and one anti-tank gun, he could do no more than hold his ground and wait for reinforcements. That night the great steel span was No-Man's-Land.

Meanwhile, the rest of the 1st Parachute Brigade, follow-

was not known to him." Nor did the Germans profit by such information as Lindemans provided, for Student has admitted that he was "completely surprised." The presence of 9th and 10th SS Panzer Divisions in the Arnhem-Nijmegen-Deventer area was the result of orders issued on September 8th, a week before Lindemans reported to Giskes.

*Constable van Kuijk. To him and other members of the Arnhem police force, and to Charles Labouchère of the Dutch Resistance, I am indebted for information about the condition and reaction of the Germans in Arnhem during the battle.

ing on Frost's northern flank, had become heavily engaged within two miles of the DZ. SS Training Battalion Kraft (425 strong) which had arrived in the Oosterbeek-Wolf-heze area only the day before, held up the advance of both the 1st and 3rd Parachute Battalions, and gave time for a battlegroup of 9th SS, dispatched by Model, to take up blocking positions north of Oosterbeek, and between that suburb and Arnhem. Since this battlegroup contained half a dozen tanks and some armoured cars, the paratroops could not drive it off. One company managed to slip through to the bridge after dark, but the rest of the brigade made little progress.

During the night Urquhart and Lathbury were stranded at the H.Q. of the 3rd Battalion, and so did not realise that the overall situation was already becoming precarious. The Germans, thanks to Model's personal intervention, had responded more quickly and more strongly than could reasonably have been anticipated. Because of this, the 500 paratroops at the bridge were now isolated. Five miles to the west the other two parachute battalions, fighting separate battles, could not develop a concerted thrust. They were only a mile apart but, owing to a wireless failure, they had no communication with each other. Farther west, the air-landing brigade was widely dispersed in defence of the DZ-LZ area. Here Hicks had his own three battalions (less two companies which were coming with the second "lift") and a battalion of the Glider Pilot Regiment which was to prove in the course of the battle the value of the British policy of training glider crews to fight as infantry. If this brigade could have been committed that night it might have broken through to the bridge before the Germans could establish their blocking force, but Urquhart's plan required Hicks to stay where he was, awaiting the reinforcements that were due to arrive at ten o'clock next morning.

While the British were thus heavily involved at Arnhem, the Americans in the Nijmegen-Eindhoven stretch of the "corridor," finding less opposition, enjoyed more success. They met few Germans near the dropping-zones and most of these fled in panic. By dropping astride the Maas bridge

591

at Grave, one battalion of the 82nd gained this vital objective within an hour of landing. Before dark Gavin's troops had secured the route into Nijmegen by capturing one of the bridges over the Maas-Waal Canal and establishing a cordon across the neck of the rivers along the Groesbeek ridge. Having secured his "air-head," Gavin sent the only battalion he could spare into Nijmegen to test out the defences of the massive bridge that spans the Waal. Four hundred yards from the southern end, however, the paratroops were checked, for the German garrison had already formed a tight perimeter to protect the bridge.

South of the Maas, the 101st Division had a rough passage through the flak defences around Eindhoven but, once on the ground, the Americans had a comparatively clear run. In Veghel they took all four bridges intact, but their southernmost objective, the bridge over the Wilhelmina Canal at Zon, was blown in their faces. Nevertheless, one parachute regiment scrambled across the canal during the night and by dawn was approaching Eindhoven, where it was due to link up with the armour advancing from the south.

At 1330 hours on the afternoon of the 17th, Horrocks was standing on a slag-heap beside the Meuse-Escaut Canal a few yards from "Joe's Bridge." He had just received word that the airborne drop was going "according to plan," and had therefore given orders for the ground attack to begin at 1435 hours. For some time his powerful field-glasses had been sweeping the northern skies but now they were trained along the straight white concrete road that led to Eindhoven. On this one road the success of his whole plan depended. Down this road the entire Corps had to move. Along this road the Guards Armoured Division had to break out.

Five hundred yards north of the Dutch border the Germans had set up a barricade across the road, but Horrocks calculated that because the road was concrete there would be no anti-tank mines embedded in its surface. He planned, therefore, to breach the German defences by the simple ruse of sending an armoured column straight down the road to blast and batter the barricade away and burst into Holland on a one-tank front. Behind the leading squadron were to come two more, carrying infantry on the backs of their tanks and in the wake of this spearhead the rest of the Guards were to follow in close order.

There was no other way north, nor was there any scope for armoured manœuvre, since the ground on either side was soft and swampy. The tanks would have to stay on the road and this would take them through a series of cypress plantations which provided natural cover for anti-tank guns and bazookas. There was no time to send infantry to clear these plantations. They would have to be neutralised by concentrations of fire from artillery and aircraft, concentrations so close and intense that the defenders on either side of the road would be driven from their weapons while the tanks went through. Such was the plan.

Ten minutes before H-Hour the guns of XXX Corps began putting down a rolling barrage one mile wide and five miles deep along the Eindhoven road. From the air a constant stream of Typhoons reinforced the barrage, skimming down to the tops of the trees before firing their rockets and machine-guns. Eight Typhoons from 83 Group arrived every five minutes and as each aircraft made several "strikes" it appeared to the onlooker that the stream was continuous. After the first half-hour a "cab-rank" of eight Typhoons was on call overhead all the time.

As the tanks of the Irish Guards rolled forward up the road, the Typhoon pilots were directed to their targets by radio from an armoured half-track, moving with the column. The white road, standing out against the dark pines, was easily identified, and all the tanks carried fluorescent orange screens which were plainly visible from the air and were soon to be hailed by the Dutch people as banners of liberation. The Typhoons were so efficiently directed that they were able to strike at targets within 200 yards of the tanks.

The Germans were so subdued by this onslaught that the leading squadron of Irish Guards, having shot its way through the barricade, was able to drive on beyond the first belt of woods without mishap. Nevertheless, the enemy

593

(parachutists on one side of the road and SS troops on the other)* recovered quickly and, when the first of the squadrons carrying infantry tried to follow, it came under heavy fire, especially from bazookas. Eight of its tanks were quickly "brewed up," but the infantry jumped clear and began scouring the woods on either flank. After some difficult and confused skirmishing, several "bazooka-parties" were flushed, an anti-tank gun was knocked out and its crew captured. Having no means of sending their prisoners back, the Guards ordered them to climb aboard the surviving tanks, an order which so dismayed the Germans that they promptly revealed the whereabouts of the rest of their battery. This information was relayed at once to the Typhoons and the medium artillery. With their aid the remaining opposition was gradually overcome and by dusk the Irish Guards had reached the day's objective, Valkenswaard, five miles south of Eindhoven.

Horrocks's plan had worked with a remarkable economy of force. One armoured battalion and one infantry battalion, supported by 400 guns and 100 Typhoons, had opened the road for a whole corps. By the afternoon of September 18 (D plus 1) the Guards and the 101st had joined forces in Eindhoven and the way was clear for the armour to drive on through the corridor to Nijmegen, as soon as the bridge at Zon had been rebuilt, a task which would take the sappers no more than twelve hours.

In Rastenburg at midnight on the 17th–18th Hitler conferred with his staff. Although they did not know of the captured orders, they accurately appreciated the scope and objective of the airborne invasion and were clearly taken aback by its imaginative daring. The successful defensive operations of the past ten days had led Hitler to believe that

---

*The Germans had concentrated five battalions to defend the road: two from the 6th Para. Regiment, one from 9th SS, one from 10th SS, and Penal Battalion No. 6—a unit in which convicts were given the opportunity of regaining their civil rights. Captured documents revealed that these units were organised into an *ad hoc* formation, "Division Walther."

the Western Allies had been halted, and that for the moment he could safely concentrate on repairing the breach in his Eastern Front caused by the collapse of Rumania. He was now faced with a situation which, he admitted, was "much more serious than that in the East," but it is apparent from the record* of this conference that there was not a single field division he could send at once to Holland. Jodl reported that the 59th Division, which had just been withdrawn across the Scheldt Estuary, was moving against the corridor from the west, and that the 107th Panzer Brigade, which was travelling by train from East Prussia to Aachen, had been re-routed to Venlo and would attack from the east. "Emergency units" were being formed throughout Holland and Western Germany; two scratch divisions were already in the Reichswald-Venlo area southeast of Nijmegen; and in the course of a few days the Home Army would be able to provide two depot divisions, though these would be made up of low-grade troops.

The only fresh resources which Hitler could throw into the battle immediately were those of the Luftwaffe. On the 17th his jet-propelled fighter-bombers (Me 262s) had been unable to intervene because their airfields near Rheine had been severely bombed. Hitler was now informed, however, that these bases were being rapidly repaired, and that two fighter *Geschwader* had already been transferred from Berlin to western Germany and would be fit for action over Holland on the day that had just begun, September 18.

That morning the aerial convoys which left England were much more vulnerable than those which had flown in the day before, for this second "lift" was made up almost entirely of tugs and gliders—slow, unwieldy combinations incapable of protecting themselves by violent evasive action. Nevertheless, their fighter screen was so vigilant and strong that of the 1203 gliders which took off from England only 13 were shot down. It was the weather, not the Luftwaffe, that prevented the timely arrival of these reinforcements.

In England thick fog, lying heavy on the airfields, had delayed the departure of the gliders and transports. In

*Führer Conferences, Fragment 42, September 17, 1944.

Holland it was an anxious morning for the airborne troops on the ground. The Germans counter-attacked from the Reichswald and overran the landing-zones of the 82nd Division just before the gliders were due to arrive. There was no opportunity of warning or re-directing the pilots, and Gavin was unaware that his reinforcements had left England two hours late. Expecting the gliders to appear overhead any minute, the Americans counter-attacked in desperate fury and drove the Germans back with half an hour to spare. Even so, the gliders landed under fire and it took all the men Gavin could muster to hold the enemy off. The late arrival of the gliderborne troops saved them from heavy casualties, but it destroyed any chance there had been of capturing the Nijmegen bridge that day.

At Arnhem the delay, and its consequences, were yet more serious. Grounded even longer than the Americans had been, the British troop-carriers and gliders did not arrive until three o'clock, five hours late. By this time the two parachute battalions, which had been checked near Oosterbeek the night before, had forced an entry into Arnhem, but had been cut to pieces in a series of bitter actions around the Elizabeth Hospital, and their combined strength had been reduced to less than 250. They had neither the troops nor the ammunition to break through to the bridge, where Frost with no more than 600 men was still maintaining a gallant but precarious foothold at the northern end.

That morning his troops had effectively blocked the bridge by knocking out six armoured half-tracks which tried to rush through from the south. This road-block was covered by British fire from buildings beside the northern approach to the bridge, but late in the afternoon the Germans counter-attacked with infantry and tanks, and the paratroops had to yield ground when four of the houses they were holding were set alight. By the mere process of burning down the buildings, the Germans were bound to overpower the defenders before long unless substantial reinforcements could get through to them from Nijmegen or from the rest of their own division.

596

On the evening of this day (Monday, September 18) the situation north of the Neder Rijn was extremely confused. In Arnhem itself the 1st Parachute Brigade, apart from Frost's battalion, was fast disintegrating. Early that morning Lathbury, the Brigade commander, and Urquhart had tried to reach the troops in the town, but had been cut off and compelled to take cover until the late afternoon. Then, as they sought to make their way back to Oosterbeek, Lathbury was wounded. Urquhart and another officer left him in the care of Dutch civilians, but were themselves forced to hide in the loft of a house. Even after dark, they could not escape, for there were Germans all around and an S.P. gun was stationed in the street outside.

In Urquhart's absence, Hicks (of the air-landing brigade) took command of the division, but he had no contact, even by radio, with Urquhart, Lathbury, Frost or any elements of 1st Parachute Brigade. This was partly due to the use of sets which would not work efficiently in a built-up area, and partly to the fact that a powerful British station was operating on the same frequency that had been allocated to the divisional command net. The frequency had to be changed, but the units isolated in Arnhem could not be advised, nor could they be heard on the old frequency. More serious still was the breakdown of communications with the outside world. Hicks urgently needed air support to deal with German tanks, but he could not call for it, as planned. The wireless link to the R.A.F. was not working, and he could not establish contact either with Airborne Base in England or with Browning's Corps H.Q. only 15 miles away.

For information about events in the town Hicks had to rely on reports from members of the Dutch Resistance who had seized the local telephone exchange. These reports cannot have revealed the full gravity of the situation in Arnhem, for Hicks continued to give prior consideration to the security of the "air-head." Into Arnhem he sent only two of his seven battalions, and he directed the newly-arrived 4th Parachute Brigade (Brigadier J. W. Hackett) to drive the Germans from the high ground north of Oosterbeek and thus strengthen the divisional perimeter. This attack proved

597

to be a costly diversion of effort. The Germans were strongly entrenched in the woods and two parachute battalions lost half their strength in one day's fighting.

The battalions which headed for the bridge suffered even more heavily. It took them thirteen hours to cover three miles and, although they reached the Elizabeth Hospital and the survivors of 1st Parachute Brigade, they could advance no farther. Nor could any reinforcements get through to them. On the following day (Tuesday the 19th) this beleaguered force attacked and attacked in the hope of forcing a passage to the bridge, but German tanks and S.P. guns were covering every approach. When their anti-tank ammunition was exhausted, the airborne troops were driven back street by street through Oosterbeek to Hartenstein, where Urquhart, again in command, was forming a tight perimeter. There he hoped to stand his ground and conserve his strength until the arrival of XXX Corps.

The possibility of 1st Airborne being reinforced, or even re-supplied, by air was now remote, for it was not holding a large enough dropping area and the Germans had greatly increased their flak and fighter defences. That afternoon bad weather, and the appearance of more than five hundred enemy fighters, disrupted the reinforcement plan. Because of thick fog in the Midlands, the Polish Parachute Brigade and the glider infantry regiment of the 82nd Division were not able to leave their airfields. Some 655 troop-carriers and 431 gliders did take off from other bases, but only 60 per cent reached their destinations, and of those that failed to get through 112 gliders and 40 transports were lost. Worst of all, 390 tons of ammunition and food, dropped by parachute for 1st Airborne, fell almost entirely into enemy hands. The prearranged Supply Dropping Point was not located within the original landing area and the division had not been able to capture it. Urquhart had sent a signal suggesting a new dropping area but this had not been received in England.

The non-arrival of the Polish Brigade removed the last chance of any airborne forces coming to the rescue of the paratroops at the bridge in Arnhem. Since the previous morning, when a troop of anti-tank guns had broken through to him, Frost had been completely cut off. Nevertheless, he was still preventing the Germans from using the Arnhem bridge as a route for sending reinforcements to Nijmegen. But now, on the Tuesday evening, his situation was becoming desperate. His men were holding only a dozen houses and a school, and these were being heavily mortared and shelled. The cellars were filled with wounded. The surrounding houses were ablaze. The anti-tank ammunition was almost spent, and the 400 men still fit to fight could no longer drive off the tanks which were systematically demolishing their positions. And yet they fought on, withdrawing only when the buildings they held were set afire; still hoping that help might come from Oosterbeek, and not knowing that this hope was gone, for they had been out of radio communication since the Sunday evening.

On the morning of Wednesday, September 20, they regained contact with Divisional H.Q. through the Arnhem exchange, which was still being operated by Dutch patriots. Only then did Frost learn that there was no hope of rescue or relief unless he could hold out until the ground forces reached him from Nijmegen. There that day a combined attack was to be made upon the Waal bridge by the 82nd and the Guards who had strict instructions that the road to Arnhem must be opened at all costs.

On the morning of Tuesday, the 19th, the Grenadier Guards Group, the spearhead of their division, had driven rapidly through the corridor from Zon to the woods south of Nijmegen. There, however, they had found the Americans so hard pressed by attacks from the Reichswald that no move could be made against the Nijmegen bridges until mid-afternoon. Even then, Gavin could spare only one parachute battalion to operate with the Guards, for, as already mentioned, his glider infantry regiment had not been able to leave England. Since the road and rail bridges were both intact, a column was directed against each, but neither column could penetrate the defences which the Germans had had ample time to prepare.

All the approaches to the road bridge ran through some

gardens, called Huner Park, which the Dutch had fortified before the war and had held for three days in 1940. The Germans in turn had strengthened the detences of the park, especially those of an old mediæval fort and a large wooded knoll, the Valkhof. At the southern edge of the Huner Park the Anglo-American attack was halted. Tanks which tried to rush the bridge were knocked out. Guardsmen and parachutists who tried to infiltrate through the defences were cut off. That night, as Allied troops waited within reach of this great prize, they expected to see it blown to destruction. They did not know that Model himself had given orders that the bridge was not to be blown. "Model," says Student, had "prohibited the demolition of the bridge in the belief that it could be successfully defended."

During the night of the 19th–20th, while a battlegroup of 10th SS was being ferried across the Neder Rijn to stiffen the Nijmegen garrison, Horrocks and Browning made a new plan, designed to give them full possession of the Nijmegen road bridge by simultaneous attacks from north and south. Next day an American parachute regiment (the 504th) was to cross the Waal a mile downstream and seize the northern end of the bridge in concert with an attack on the southern defences by the Grenadier Guards and a battalion of parachutists. First, however, the town of Nijmegen had to be cleared of Germans so that the assault troops could gain access to the south bank of the Waal.

This mopping-up took all the Wednesday morning and it was nearly three o'clock before the 504th were in position to launch their storm-boats into the fast-running river. The combined effect of the current and the severe enemy fire was such that only half the boats carrying the first wave reached the north bank. Undaunted, some 200 men scrambled or swam ashore and established a slender foothold which was gradually reinforced and expanded as the afternoon wore on. This bold assault in clear daylight across a defended river, 400 yards wide, was a most brilliant and courageous feat of arms and was duly rewarded. By 6:30 the Americans had routed the opposition and were advancing towards the road bridge. En route, they secured the northern end of the railway bridge and there they raised the American flag.*

When this signal of success was seen by watchers on the southern bank, the Guards pressed home their attack. Here, in an afternoon of heavy fighting, while an American battalion was clearing the eastern half of Huner Park, the Grenadiers had driven the Germans from the Valkhof and had taken the fort by storm. The capture of these two strongholds opened the way to the bridge. At dusk, shortly before seven o'clock, five British tanks drove through the park, paused to engage some 88s shooting from the far bank, and then raced on with guns alive. Two tanks were hit by bazookas fired from the girders, but two others continued across the 600-yard length of bridge, through the road-block at the northern end and beyond it to link up with the Americans who were just approaching from the west. The Nijmegen bridge was in Allied hands undamaged, and a straight red road ran north to Arnhem.

There by now the staunch defenders of the road bridge had been cut down from 600 to 140 and Frost himself had been wounded. His men were still fighting from half a dozen houses around the northern pylons, but they were no longer holding the school from which for nearly three days they had maintained their road-block, preventing the southward movement of armour and artillery. That afternoon, under point-blank fire from several tanks, the schoolhouse had collapsed in flames and its garrison had been driven into the open streets. Thus it was that three hours before the first British tank crossed the Nijmegen bridge, heading north, the first German tank crossed the Arnhem bridge, heading south.

During the night the Germans made good use of the bridge which had been denied them so long, and on the morning of Thursday, the 21st, R.A.F. reconnaissance reported that twenty tanks were moving south from Arn-

*When Dempsey saw Gavin after this exploit he said: "I am proud to meet the commander of the greatest division in the world to-day." That opinion was endorsed by many another British officer who saw the 82nd in action.

hem and that the Germans appeared to be establishing fresh defences between the Neder Rijn and the Waal astride the Arnhem-Nijmegen road. Nevertheless, Horrocks still hoped to secure a bridgehead over the Neder Rijn, link up with 1st Airborne and drive on to the Zuider Zee in fulfilment of the original plan. Owing to the breakdown of Urquhart's radio communications, however, Horrocks did not know how grave the situation really was.

At nine o'clock that morning, one of Horrocks's artillery units, the 64th Medium Regiment, had established radio contact with the airborne division and had obtained the first direct news from Arnhem since XXX Corps began its attack. Through this channel Urquhart, unaware that Frost's force had at last been overrun, reported:

> Enemy attacking main bridge in strength. Situation critical for slender force [there]. Enemy also attacking divisional position East from HEELSUM vicinity and West from ARNHEM. Situation serious but am forming close perimeter around HARTENSTEIN with remainder of division. Relief essential both areas earliest possible. Still retain control ferry-crossing HEVEADORP.

From this signal Horrocks naturally concluded that Urquhart had some troops at the bridge in Arnhem and had a foothold west of the town large enough to be exploited, if quickly reinforced. He had already ordered the Guards Armoured Division to strike north "as early as possible and at maximum speed" along the main Arnhem road in the hope of breaking through to the bridge before the enemy could organise a new defence line. He now gave orders that, if the direct route were blocked, the Guards should work round west of the main road and head for the Heveadorp ferry. Arrangements had been made for dropping the Polish Parachute Brigade that afternoon near Driel to secure the southern end of the ferry, and it seemed that the Guards and the Poles together should be able to secure a base from which infantry could cross the river into Urquhart's perimeter. Then, with both banks in Allied hands, a bridge could be built at the ferry-site.

602

The plan was clear but the resources to carry it out were not immediately available. North of the Maas, Horrocks had only two divisions, the Guards and 82nd Airborne. Bad weather had so far prevented the arrival of Gavin's glider infantry regiment, and the rest of the 82nd, with the Coldstream Group in support, was fully engaged in defending the area between the Maas and the Waal, where the Germans were making frequent counter-attacks from the Reichswald flank.* In the Nijmegen bridgehead Horrocks had one parachute regiment and two groups of Guards, but the latter could not resume the offensive until they were relieved by infantry of the 43rd Division which was only just crossing the Maas.

On the one road by which XXX Corps and the American airborne divisions had to be reinforced and maintained traffic was moving slowly. For most of the 45 miles between the Meuse-Escaut Canal and the River Maas the roadway was narrow, and it passed through Eindhoven and half a dozen villages and over two rebuilt bridges. Because this single road was extremely vulnerable to air attack and artillery fire, the columns were ordered to move with vehicles well spaced and, accordingly, it had not been thought that they would be able to average more than ten miles in the hour. This might have been adequate if a steady flow could have been kept up, but an unexpected brake was imposed at the very start of the corridor.

On the first evening two three-tonners, following the armour, had been destroyed by mines which the Germans had laid in the grass verges immediately beside their road-block. In passing through this, the two trucks had gone off the concrete on to the grass and had been blown up. Next morning the wreckage of these vehicles was seen by all drivers moving north and, lest the warning should be dis-

*Gavin was also handicapped by shortage of artillery ammunition, for the four U.S. truck companies sent up from France to maintain the American airborne divisions did not reach the Meuse-Escaut Canal until the 20th. It was then found that they were loaded with the wrong type of 105 mm ammunition, and that some trucks had come up empty!

regarded, some overconscientious sapper had set up a notice: DON'T LET THIS HAPPEN TO YOU. KEEP ON THE ROAD. VERGES NOT CLEARED OF MINES.

By this time, in fact, all the mines at the road-block had been lifted, and it was most unlikely that the Germans would have been able to mine the verges of the road ahead since this had been their own supply line until the previous afternoon. Necessary or not, the warning was there, and British drivers, ever cautious, took due note of it. Over the next five miles to Valkenswaard the concrete road was only just wide enough for two vehicles. There were ample grass verges, but whenever convoys were halted to let more urgent columns through, the drivers clung to the concrete, creating a succession of traffic blocks which took hours to clear. The stretch of road between the frontier and Valkenswaard became a bottleneck which governed and constricted the northward flow of convoys.* Another bottleneck soon developed in Eindhoven which was heavily attacked by the Luftwaffe on the evening of the 19th. Here the Germans bombed an ammunition column of the Guards Armoured Division and for the next twenty-four hours the main streets of the town were blocked with wreckage.

The movement of traffic was further delayed by German activity on the flanks of the corridor, for the other two corps of Second Army, compelled to advance across an almost trackless wasteland of heath and swamp, made slow progress. By September 21 they had drawn level with Eindhoven but here they were checked. For the next thirty miles to Grave the corridor was little wider than the road itself, and bottlenecks, such as the Zon bridge and the tortuous streets of St. Oedenrode, were frequently shelled. On the 19th and 20th the Germans attacked this sector of the road from both sides. These attacks were driven off, but the passage of the road continued to be hazardous. The

*On the afternoon of the 18th, returning to file a dispatch, I found a traffic jam, two vehicles wide, almost the whole way from the Valkenswaard bridge to the Meuse-Escaut Canal. I was able to move south only by driving along the verge of the road.

604

advance had been made on such a narrow front that the line of communication was almost the front line; indeed, it had a front on either side. The result was that it took three days to transport the 43rd Division from the Albert Canal to the Maas, a distance of 60 miles, which the troops might have covered almost as quickly on foot.

It was, therefore, the afternoon of the 21st before the Irish Guards were able to attack from the Nijmegen bridgehead, and then they were halted almost at once by the anti-tank screen which the enemy had set up south of Elst. The terrain between the Waal and the Neder Rijn was reclaimed land, laced with innumerable small dykes and drainage channels which made cross-country movement impossible. The Guards had to advance along a road which was raised well above the surrounding polder and was flanked by deep ditches which the armour could not negotiate. On the road the tanks were "sitting shots" for the guns the Germans had sited in orchards and farmyards on either side. A direct attack with infantry and an outflanking movement by the Welsh Guards were equally unsuccessful, primarily because there was so little supporting fire. Owing to the shortage of ammunition, only one battery of artillery was available, and the Guards could not enlist the aid of the Typhoons as they had done so successfully on the first day. The aircraft were on call—in fact, they were overhead—but they could not be directed against the anti-tank guns, because the radio sets in the R.A.F. "contact car" failed to work. This was a grave misfortune. Without the help of the Typhoons there was no chance of the tanks breaking through that afternoon to Arnhem.

While the Guards were halted in front of Elst, the Polish Parachute Brigade was dropped between Elst and Driel in the face of heavy opposition from flak and fighters. But, by the time the Poles reached the south bank of the Neder Rijn, the Heveadorp ferry had been sunk and the northern end of the ferry-sight was in German hands. Urquhart's troops had been driven from it only two hours earlier.

On the previous day when Urquhart ordered his scattered and weakened battalions to withdraw inside the Hartenstein perimeter, some units, finding themselves cut off, had to fight their way in and lost heavily in the process. This was particularly the case with the 10th and 156th Parachute Battalions which had been trying to clear the woods north of Oosterbeek. When they reached the perimeter their combined strength was 135 men, fewer than ten per cent of those who had landed. Moreover, the Germans followed up so strongly that the 3500 survivors of the division were compressed into an area 1000 yards wide and 2000 yards deep. This area was brought under heavy and continuous fire from three sides and was repeatedly attacked by infantry and armour. Thus, although some of the supplies dropped on the 21st fell inside the perimeter, it was almost impossible for the troops to collect them.

The only help that XXX Corps could give the airborne troops on this day came from the guns of the 64th Medium Regiment. Having established radio contact, the regiment was able to bring down considerable and accurate fire on German positions around the Hartenstein perimeter. This relieved the pressure, but that evening, with stocks of food and water almost exhausted and ammunition running low, Urquhart reported: "No knowledge elements of division in ARNHEM for twenty-four hours. Balance of division in very tight perimeter . . . our casualties heavy. Resources stretched to utmost. Relief within twenty-four hours vital."

Early on the morning of the 22nd Horrocks signalled, "43 Div. ordered to take all risks to effect relief today and are directed on ferry. It situation warrants you should withdraw to or cross ferry." Urquhart replied, "We shall be glad to see you."

Horrocks now abandoned the idea of breaking through to the Zuider Zee, but he still retained the hope that he might secure an adequate bridgehead beyond the Neder Rijn for subsequent exploitation when the corridor had been widened and fresh forces had been brought forward. The plan for Friday, the 22nd, therefore, was that the 43rd Division (Major-General G. I. Thomas) should attack from the Nijmegen bridgehead at dawn with two brigades:

one striking along the main road through Elst to Arnhem, and another, on its left, following a side road through Oosterhout to the Heveadorp ferry. As both these brigades had reached Nijmegen on the 21st, Horrocks assumed that, in execution of these orders, Thomas would move his troops across the Waal during the night so that they would be deployed to attack in strength at first light. This, how-ever, was not done and the opportunity of surprising the enemy under cover of the early morning mist was lost. Taking advantage of that mist, armoured cars of the House-hold Cavalry drove through Oosterhout soon after seven o'clock and made contact with the Poles before Thomas's infantry had even begun their attack.

The mist had cleared when, at 8:30 a.m. on the 22nd, the 7th Somersets advanced towards Oosterhout supported by a squadron of tanks, a troop of 17-pounders, mortar and machine-gun platoons, a battery of self-propelled 25-pounders and a field regiment. An hour later, however, on reaching the outskirts of Oosterhout, the leading platoon was "held up by fire from a tank and some infantry"—to quote the battalion's own history.* The operation then proceeded according to the book, for Thomas had not told the C.O. "to take all risks." The platoon that had been halted was extricated under cover of smoke. Another com-pany with a troop of tanks endeavoured to work round the village but was "held up by heavy mortar fire." These manœuvres occupied most of the morning.

In mid-afternoon, when a battalion attack was made, "resistance was not heavy and was quickly overcome. . . . By 1700 hours the village was clear." This was not surpris-ing. The attack was supported by more than a hundred guns, and the garrison can hardly have been formidable, for Oosterhout yielded only "139 prisoners, one quarter-master's store completely equipped, one Mark III tank, one 88 mm gun and five small A.A. guns." In the entire day's fighting, when the fate of the 1st Airborne Division

*The Story of the Seventh Battalion, the Somerset Light Infantry, by Captain J. L. J. Meredith, p. 73.

607

and the saving of the whole operaton were at stake, the Somerset's casualties amounted to "nineteen wounded." *

In fairness to the battalion, however, it must be said that they did no more than they had been trained to do. By nature Thomas was cautious and methodical and his troops followed his example. He was extremely thorough in the organisation of his attacks—so thorough that his battalions, like most of the infantry in Second Army, had come to believe that they could not advance without overwhelming fire support.** There was considerable truth in the criticism the Germans had made in Normandy that British infantry sought "to occupy ground rather than to fight over it." The consequences of that policy were never more apparent than on this day at Oosterhout.

Near Driel that morning the Household Cavalry had picked up two officers sent back by Urquhart and had re-layed the following message from him: "We are short of ammunition, men, food and medical supplies. DUKWs are essential, two or three would be sufficient. If supplies do not arrive tonight it may be too late." To this signal Horrocks replied, "Everything possible will be done to get the essentials through." Consequently, when he discovered that neither of Thomas's brigades had made any real progress, and that Elst was strongly held, he ordered him to concentrate on opening the road through Oosterhout. The moment the village was clear, Thomas was to dispatch to Heveadorp a strong mobile column carrying supplies for 1st Airborne. At 6 p.m. the column, made up of two infantry companies riding on tanks, carriers and DUKWs, drove through Oosterhout and went on to join the Poles in Driel. Moving nose to tail, the vehicles covered the ten miles in an hour, but darkness had fallen before they

* *The Story of the Seventh Battalion, the Somerset Light Infantry,* by Captain J. L. J. Meridith, p. 75.

** That evening, when I saw General Horrocks, he was inclined to excuse the 43rd's slowness, for he did not know how little opposition there had really been at Oosterhout. Thomas's chief of staff (Lt.-Col. David Meynell), however, said to me, "I rather think it is our fault. We have been slow."

608

reached the river. It was then found that the banks were so steep and soft that the much-needed DUKWs could not be launched, and it was too late and too dark to reconnoitre firmer crossing places. No assault-boats were available and, although the troops toiled all night with improvised rafts, they were able to ferry across only fifty men of the Polish Brigade and a few small loads of food and ammunition.

It was now clear that a bridgehead could be established west of Arnhem only by a large-scale assault across the Neder Rijn, but the necessary troops and craft could not be brought forward immediately. Early that afternoon German tanks and infantry had cut the corridor between Veghel and Uden, thus isolating all forces north of the Maas. In consequence Horrocks was compelled to send the 32nd Guards Brigade back to reopen the road, a task which they, and American parachutists attacking from the south, were not able to accomplish until the following afternoon. This diversion of half the Guards Armoured Division to clear the corridor weakened the attack towards Arnhem. The direct road from Nijmegen was still blocked by the Germans in Elst and the minor route by which Thomas's troops had reached the Neder Rijn was under fire from Elst and was, in any case, unsuitable for heavy traffic.

On the evening of September 23, after "aerial re-supply" had again been thwarted by bad weather and enemy intervention, Urquhart signalled: "Morale still adequate but continued heavy mortaring and shelling is having obvious effects. We shall hold out but . . . hope for a brighter twenty-four hours ahead." That night, however, no major crossing of the Neder Rijn could be attempted, for 1st Airborne was so desperately in need of ammunition that the relieving forces had to concentrate on the ferrying of supplies. Between dusk and dawn only 250 Poles were able to cross the river and of these barely 150 reached the Hartenstein perimeter.

On Sunday the 24th—for the first time in the eight days since the start of MARKET GARDEN—the R.A.F. was able to provide strong air support for Urquhart's troops. Throughout the afternoon Typhoons struck at German positions around the perimeter and at enemy reinforcements moving towards it. This was the prelude to the assault-crossing, planned for that night, by Polish paratroops and the 4th Dorset. Inside the perimeter the writer of 1st Airborne's war diary noted, "Never was darkness more eagerly awaited." But darkness brought only disappointment. The attack was to have been launched at 10:30 p.m. but when the time came there were no assault boats available for the Poles and only four for the Dorsets. This was a direct consequence of the cutting of the road. After midnight, with these boats and five others that came up later, some 250 men crossed the river, a platoon at a time; but the swiftness of the current and the blackness of the night caused such disorganisation that the landings were widely spread and, before the Dorsets could find the airborne perimeter, the Germans closed in around them.

As dawn was breaking on the ninth day, Urquhart received a letter from Thomas advising him that Second Army had been obliged to abandon the attempt to establish a bridgehead and that 1st Airborne would have to be withdrawn. Urquhart replied that, if this was the plan, his troops must be withdrawn that night.

On the afternoon of the previous day (September 24) Dempsey and Horrocks, meeting at St. Oedenrode, had decided that on the night of the 25–26th, they would make a final attempt to gain a bridgehead north of the Neder Rijn. Their ability to do this, however, depended on the road remaining open for the northward movement of ammunition, assault boats and bridging equipment. Horrocks left St. Oedenrode at 4:30 p.m., but, even as he was driving through Veghel a few minutes later, the Germans came in from the west behind him and cut the corridor again: this time in such strength that it was to remain closed for forty-eight hours. This counter-stroke, combined with information from air reconnaissance that German infantry were digging in on the north bank of the Neder Rijn and that panzer reinforcements were moving towards the only sector of the river where a crossing could be made, forced upon Horrocks and Dempsey the reluctant decision to withdraw the 1st Airborne Division.

Within the shrunken perimeter Urquhart now had only

2500 men. For them, for the past five days, it had been, in the words of the division's own report, "a question of withstanding continuous attacks, mortaring and shelling. The force was dwindling steadily in numbers and strength . . . and was becoming increasingly short of ammunition. Much patching by small parties and frequent minor adjustments of the perimeter were necessary but, except for the deliberate closing-in of the northern face of the perimeter, little or no ground was lost." That, in itself, is a measure of the steadfast endurance and abiding courage of Urquhart's men, for the enemy pressure against the perimeter had been relentless and sustained ever since the paratroops at the bridge had been overwhelmed. From the 22nd onwards, the survivors of the division were heavily outnumbered and heavily out-gunned, but they maintained such a resolute defence, even under attack by tanks and assault guns, that, by the afternoon of the 25th, the Germans were content to contain them.

During this afternoon the airborne troops prepared to make their withdrawal and, at Divisional H.Q. in the Hartenstein Hotel, a signals officer, Lieut. J. Hardy, set free the last of the carrier-pigeons they had brought from England. One of these pigeons reached the H.Q. of VIII British Corps in Belgium, carrying this message:

1. Have to release birds owing to shortage of food and water.

2. About eight tanks lying about in sub-unit areas, very untidy but not otherwise causing us any trouble.

3. Now using as many German weapons as we have British. MGs most effective when aiming towards Germany.

4. Dutch people grand but Dutch tobacco rather stringy.

5. Great beard growing competition on in our unit, but no time to check up on the winner.

They left that night in heavy rain and high wind. A barrage from the guns of XXX Corps screened their departure and kept the enemy quieter than usual. Through woods and gardens, streets and houses which had been their battleground for so many days, they slipped away silently in small parties, each man clinging to the hand or the jacket of the man ahead. At the river's edge boats were waiting for them, manned by British and Canadian sappers. All night the ferrying continued under spasmodic fire from mortars and artillery, but the Germans made no direct attempt to prevent the withdrawal, for they did not realise what was happening. The heavy shelling from the south bank, and a gallant diversion by the Dorsets from the narrow foothold they had gained downstream, kept the Germans standing to in anticipation of another assault. Throughout the night the perimeter appeared to be manned, for wounded who could not be moved lay beside weapons and wireless sets and maintained the usual pattern of radio traffic and defensive fire. At daybreak on September 26 the evacuation had to stop, for German machine-guns began sweeping the river. By then 2163 men of the 1st Airborne Division and the Glider Pilot Regiment (together with 160 Poles and 75 Dorsets), had reached the safety of the south bank. Of the ten thousand who had landed north of the Neder Rijn only these few were rescued, and, as near as can be told, 1130 airborne troops remained at Arnhem for ever. Three hundred wounded inside the perimeter, and another two hundred men of the 4th Dorset, were taken prisoner, bringing the total of those captured in and around Arnhem to more than 6000, of whom nearly half were wounded before they fell into enemy hands.* Several hundred more remained at large, succoured and befriended by the Dutch. These were mostly men who had been cut off in the confused fighting of the past ten days or who, like Lathbury and Hackett, escaped from hospitals which the Germans captured. The majority eventually found their way back across the river, but another seven months were to elapse before British troops again set foot in Arnhem.

*The Germans, in a signal sent out by OKW on September 27 and recorded in the diary of the Naval War Staff, claimed that "6,450 prisoners were taken," and gave their own losses as "3,300 men," killed or wounded.

612

Before the Bulge

During October, 1944, there were no large scale assaults by the Allies, and Hitler was able to strengthen his front. He believed that he still might inflict enough damage upon the British and Americans to bring about a stalemate and force them to negotiate peace. Immediately after Arnhem, Hitler and Jodl drew up a plan for an offensive through the Ardennes, designed to break through all the way to the Channel coast. Hitler's generals argued for a much smaller offensive, but he would not listen. The complete plans for the Ardennes attack were given to Von Rundstedt, labeled "Not to Be Altered." And as so often in the past, Hitler had accomplished the impossible—he had scraped up more reserves than his commanders or the Allies believed possible at the time; and his faith in the ability of his troops to hold their positions through the fall was sustained. If the Ardennes attack fell short of the coast, at least valuable supplies would be captured, particularly the oil dumps stocked at Liege. The German General Staff knew that such a grandiose offensive could do little more than expend and exhaust the build-up Hitler had achieved. But the Fuehrer had been right often enough, and still had enough personal magnetism to bend the generals to his will.

In the Allied Lines, no hint of what was to come disturbed the troops, who engaged in routine patrols. As the following wartime *Life* Magazine report shows, "routine" was hardly the word for it.

The italicized opening section and the footnotes are from Capt. Laurence Critchell's *Four Stars of Hell*.

613

THE INCREDIBLE PATROL

by Cpl. Russ Engel

The officer in charge of regimental intelligence was a youthful-looking, well-proportioned first lieutenant named Hugo Sims. Sims was married and came from Orangeburg, South Carolina, where he had been studying law before the war. He had a soft, slow, deliberate voice and a rather superior air, an air that sometimes annoyed other officers of the same grade. Nobody denied that Sims was competent, but everyone doubted whether he was as good as he thought he was.

Sims was worried. Since the lines had quieted down, his battalion patrols were doing poorly. A sense of injustice was evidently strong among the soldiers selected for the task: they felt they were risking their lives to no good purpose while their comrades slept safely in foxholes behind the line. So strong was this sense of injustice that some patrols went only as far as the German shore, rested for an hour or two in some place hidden from sight of our lines and then returned with a negative report.

Sims was in the dark concerning the nature of the German forces opposing the regiment on the other side of the river [Rhine]. For all he knew, the enemy was building up strength for an attack in force. If it came unexpectedly, the blame was his.

Turning these thoughts over in his mind one night, he conceived the idea of leading a classroom patrol into the enemy territory across the river: not an ordinary patrol—he expected ordinary patrols from the battalions. This should be a patrol that would shame the rest of the regiment. Studying one of the maps of the area, he thought of going inland five or six miles to the main Utrecht-Arnhem highway. There he could set up an observation post, stay hidden

614

for twenty-four hours, report the traffic, take a few prisoners and return with them the following night.

He put the request in writing to Colonel Ewell. It came back with five letters scrawled across it: "O.K.—J.J.E."

Like a great many Southerners of old families, Sims had great self-assurance and a strong sense of what he thought the world ought to be. Given permission for the first time in his military career to devise an ambitious project entirely without supervision, he made preparations for what would be the perfect patrol.

From a group of aerial photographs he selected a house on the Arnhem-Utrecht highway, about six miles within the enemy lines. Plotting the coordinates of this house on the map, he could predetermine the azimuth line of march from the river.

The next step was to arrange for the British heavy guns to fire a single shell at regular intervals of time at a fixed and known point in the area. The explosions of these shells would give him a further check on the accuracy of his line of march. Finally, to deceive the enemy, he arranged for his own mortars to fire a flare half-hourly into the enemy lines. Flares were the usual indication that no patrols were out from lines firing them.

From S-4 he drew a 300 radio. From the regimental intelligence team and the prisoner of war interrogation group he got five volunteers: Private First Class Frederick J. Becker, Private Roland J. Wilbur, Private First Class Robert O. Nicholai, Corporal William R. Canfield and Master Sergeant Peter Frank. Frank spoke fluent German.

As such things usually happen, the rumor of this impossible patrol reached the soldiers of the regiment almost at once. Those who knew Sims, and especially those officers whose patrols had failed, grinned happily to themselves and settled down to watch the fun.—L. C.

The night of the patrol was very dark.

"All of us were a little nervous in the last few hours," testified Private First Class Frederick J. Becker of Atlantic, Ohio.[1] "We all had blacked-out our faces and we began to

---

[1] This interview, written by Corporal Russ Engel of the 101st

615

look as if we were really going on this deal instead of planning it. I was stuck with one of the musette bags with half the radio in it. One of the other boys was to carry the other half, and I was a little griped because I was stuck with the heaviest part. But the other boys had their jobs, too. They had demolition blocks for blowing the railroad we planned to cross on the return trip.

"Instead of the steel helmets we had been wearing for the last month or two, we wore our soft overseas hats. Each of us had our pockets full of extra ammunition plus grenades and honed knives. We were really going prepared. In addition to our regular weapons we all carried .45 pistols. Wilbur was the only one of us taking an M-1 rifle, the rest of us chose the Tommy gun for more firepower. We tried to talk him out of the M-1, but we knew it would be nice to have him along with it. Wilbur has the reputation of being pretty accurate with that gun and is famous for never shooting at a man unless he can aim dead center for the head. He doesn't miss.

"After a dress rehearsal in front of headquarters, where Lieutenant Sims checked over our equipment, we decided we were set. Now it was only a matter of waiting for darkness. We sat around for a while and then went in for some hot chow. The cooks seemed to know what was up, and the boys in the mess line gave us a few pats on the back. Lots of our buddies came up and wished us well and said they were sorry they couldn't go along. They really were, too. We all tried to act as if it meant nothing at all. After we washed our mess kits one of the cooks came up and gave each of us three K-ration chocolate bars and said when we came back he'd have a swell hot meal waiting. It was getting dark now and we all sat around the S-2 office getting fidgety."

Here Pvt. Roland J. Wilbur, the M-1 rifle expert, took

Airborne Division public relations office, and copyrighted by Time Inc., 1945, appeared in *Life* for January 15, 1945, entitled "The Incredible Patrol." It is reprinted here by courtesy of the publishers. The interview, as given to Corporal Engel, included all members of the patrol except Lieutenant Sims.—L.C.

616

over. He comes from Lansing, Michigan, where he used to work for Nash-Kelvinator. Now he almost looked like a soldier in one of their magazine ads, sitting there with a grim look on his face, cleaning the M-1 as he spoke.

"The S-2 office wasn't too far from the dike on the Neder Rijn. We took off about 7:39. We rechecked all our stuff and piled into two jeeps. In a few minutes we were up near the area where we planned to cross. We stopped and got out of the jeeps and began to wonder if the clothes we had on were enough to keep us warm. It was overcast and cold and it had begun to rain. We were wet before we had really gotten started. A couple of hundred yards away we ran into the group who had the boats ready to take us across.

"We were awfully careful about reaching the dike because a lot depended on those first few minutes. We knew that a couple of other patrols had been knocked off before they had gotten to the water. Our main hope was that the Jerries weren't on the alert because we were going over a little earlier than the other patrols. We started to go down towards the bank when a whisper from Lieutenant Sims halted us in our tracks. He thought he had heard a sound from the other side. After a couple of minutes of shaky waiting we decided to take a chance. Edging down to the bank, we came to the two rubber assault boats. Lieutenant Sims and two of the boys carefully slid into one and the rest of us crouched low at the bank and waited with our guns ready in case Jerry should open fire as they crossed. It seemed to take them hours to get across and we could hear every dip of the paddles in the water. We were certain they would be heard and the whole deal would be off, but they weren't. They made the opposite side and crouched low to wait for us.

"Finally we landed. Arrangements were made with the men with the boats so we could signal them by flashlight when we came back. They wondered if we had any idea when it would be and we told them that we hoped it wouldn't be until the next night. We hunched down and told the boatmen to be quiet going back. We could just barely see them as they hit the opposite shore."

Pfc. Robert O. Nicholai, a former member of the Merchant Marine who comes from Midlothian, Illinois, now broke into the story. He was given the Bronze Star for his part in the Normandy campaign and is the cocky member of the group.

"All of us started up the bank to the top of the dike, Lieutenant Sims in the lead. Nothing ahead looked like a Kraut, but there was something that we hadn't expected. A little way ahead there was a big pond directly across the route we had planned to take. We decided that it would be better to go around and change our route a little.

"We skirted the edge of the water but found we still had to do some wading in the dark. By the time we passed the pond our feet were slogging wet. Lieutenant Sims seemed to have on a pair of boots about ten sizes too large and they squished with every step he took. Someone said, 'Dammit, pick up your feet.' [2]

"Suddenly the first of our mortar flares lit up the sky and we were all flat on the ground. We cautiously looked around the countryside but there wasn't a Jerry in sight. It was now 8 p.m. and the flares were working just as we had planned. As soon as the flare died out we got up again. About 200 yards ahead we saw a light and a few shadows moving. We held a confab and decided that because we didn't want to take prisoners too early we would alter our course again. We bypassed the light and circled around to the right. Then we heard the unmistakable sound of Germans digging in for the night. It was the sound of folding shovels digging into the earth and the clunking noise they made as they were tapped on the ground to loosen the mud. We now turned left again and as we did someone stumbled into the brush in the darkness. Immediately we stood still as statues

[2] This entire account minimizes Lieutenant Sims. In point of fact, the patrol would never have taken place without his initiative. It would never have succeeded without his inventiveness, and most of the decisions mentioned in the narrative were his own. From the introductory remarks in the *Life* story, here omitted, it seems evident that none of the patrol members understood what part Sims had played.—L. C.

618

and waited. Then we heard the zip of a German flare going up. We hit the ground and froze as more of the flares lit up the countryside. To either side of us we could hear Germans moving around. Now and then one of them shouted to ask what the flares were for. They had heard something and had whole batches of flares ready to shoot off. Each time a flare burned out we crept forward between the two enemy groups. In a half hour, when our own flare next went up, we had covered less than 300 yards.

"Then we crossed a road and found ourselves within twenty yards of a lighted tent. I was all for going in and taking whoever was there a prisoner. I thought it might be a Jerry officer and a good bag but once again we decided that it was best to skirt the area. We went one way and then the other through the fields. Every time we heard activity we edged in the other direction."

Corporal William R. Canfield of Selman, Oklahoma, now interrupted the story. "I was a little to one side of the group and suddenly I heard someone blowing his nose. I moved over to the left and saw a group of Jerries stopped for a minute on the road. I asked Lieutenant Sims if I might capture them and take them along but he said not now. I was sure feeling cocky.

"A little later I heard Becker make a noise and as I glanced at him he began to pull himself out of a slit trench he had slipped into. I walked over to him and saw a big, fat Jerry snoring away in the hole. For a moment we thought he might waken and looked down ready to pounce on him if he made a noise. When he remained asleep we went on and joined the rest up ahead. Now we were in a wooded area and we had to be careful of every step. At a clearing in the woods we came to a small road and not ten yards away we saw a couple of Jerries walking down the road with something on their shoulders. Nicholai sneaked along the road and looked more closely. He came back and reported that they were carrying a mattress. A little farther down the road we saw them walk into a house with their mattress. We waited but they didn't come out so we figured they must have turned in for the night.

"Farther on we crossed the road and stumbled right into

619

an ammunition dump. Sergeant [3] Frank, the interpreter, went over to check the writing on the boxes. He found they were shells for a heavy 150-mm. infantry gun which Lieutenant Sims marked down in a little book he was carrying. He also marked the position of the ammo dump and the location of the mattress house. Just as we were starting to make a more thorough inspection around the ammo dump we heard the unmistakable sound of a German Schmeisser gun bolt being snapped back. In a second there came another. We stood rooted to the spot, afraid to breathe. The things seemed to come from just across the road. There wasn't much else for us to do but go sneaking back through the area of the sleeping men."

Sergeant Frank now pointed out that he hadn't been too scared when the bolt snapped back. He had a story all ready for the situation. Every time they came to a new emergency he would review in his mind a story that might work the patrol out of it. This time he was ready to raise hell with the Jerries for making so much noise with their machine-gun bolts. Frank continued:

"Now we cut straight across the fields for about two miles. Nicholai was getting hungry and he simply reached down and grabbed a handful of carrots from a vegetable patch and began to eat them. Soon we had enough of the fields and decided that we were deep enough in the enemy territory to brazen it out on the road. When we came to a good paved road we walked right down the middle of it. Just ahead we heard the clank and rumble of a Jerry horse-drawn vehicle. We crawled into the ditch along the road and waited for it to pass. In a couple of minutes we were on the road again.

"Farther on we checked our compass course and started off to the right. We hadn't gone more than twenty yards when I saw Becker throw his hands in the air. [4] Right in front of us was a huge German gun emplacement. The gun and pits for the ammunition were there but there didn't

[3] Later lieutenant.—L. C.

[4] This was the infantryman's hand signal for contact with the enemy.—L. C.

620

seem to be any Jerries. About a hundred yards farther on we came to a strange collection of silhouettes. We couldn't be sure what they were and kept on going until we made them out. It was a Jerry motor pool with all types of vehicles parked for the night. We were all for taking one of the cars but Lieutenant Sims again turned thumbs down. He pulled out his map and noted the exact location. Soon we were on the edge of the town of Wolfheeze and decided that it would be best to work around it. As it later turned out, this was a good thing. The place was lousy with SS troops.

"We skirted the town pretty closely and could even smell the smoke from stinking German cigarettes. We now crossed the railroad which we knew marked the two-thirds point on our trip. We were some distance behind the enemy lines and had the feeling we would be able to bluff our way out of almost any situation that might arise. The last three miles of rushing through the fields was pretty hard. The tall grass slowed us down but it also sheltered us from observation. Nicholai was in the lead, eating carrots again. When he heard the rush of a car going by he whispered to Sims that this must be the road we had crossed so much country to reach. Within a few hundred yards we came out on the road." [5]

Nicholai broke in again: "We all waited a few minutes at the side of the road while Lieutenant Sims brought out a map and checked our location. We were right behind a house that marked the exact spot where we had planned to hit the road. This was only luck [6] but it made us feel as if everything was going according to plan. Lieutenant Sims, looking over the house and the area, decided we might as well occupy the house for cover. We sneaked up carefully, listening for the slightest sound. Becker and Canfield now went through a window and a minute or so later came back to whisper that all was clear inside. But after a conference we decided that this was not so good after all. If Jerry were to see any activity around a house which he knew to

[5] The Arnhem-Utrecht highway.—L. C.
[6] A mild understatement.—L. C.

be empty he would become suspicious. Becker and Canfield climbed back out and we headed down on the road again. In front Sergeant Frank was carrying on a monolog with Becker in German. This was funny because Becker didn't understand a word of it. We all fell into the spirit of it, feeling we could fool any Germans who came along. Soon one of the boys was singing *Lili Marlene* and we all joined in.

"After about a mile of walking along the road without meeting a single German we came to a couple of houses. One of them had a Red Cross marking on the front. It was a small cross and the place hardly looked as if it were a hospital. At any rate it looked like the better of the two houses. As Sergeant Frank and myself edged close we could hear what sounded like snoring inside. We walked to the back door and found it open. In the front room of the house we found two Germans sleeping on piles of straw. They wore big shiny boots and I was sure they were officers. Sergeant Frank said they were cavalrymen. Leaving Frank on guard I went back outside and reported to Lieutenant Sims. He said we would take the men prisoner and stay at this house. I told Frank the plan and he began to shake the Germans. One of them finally began to rub his eyes. He stared at us and Frank kept telling him over and over that he was a prisoner. They just couldn't believe it."

After the dazed Germans had been thoroughly awakened they were questioned by Sergeant Frank. He got all the information he could from them and relayed it to Lieutenant Sims. Sims was now up in the attic setting up the radio with another man. In about ten minutes the men heard him saying into the radio, "This is Sims, Sims, Sims. We have two prisoners. We have two prisoners." They knew the radio was working and everyone felt swell. Soon Sims was sending information about the things he had noted along the way.

After questioning the prisoners Sergeant Frank told them to go back to sleep but they just sat up and stared. Frank asked them if they expected any more soldiers in the area. They said that another man was supposed to pick them up at about 5:30 in the morning.

622

After the radio had been set up everything was quiet until daybreak. The men took turns watching the road while the others tried to get a little sleep. At about 7 a.m., Nicholai reported the arrival of a young civilian at the front door. The civilian proved to be a boy of about sixteen in knee pants. He was both surprised and pleased to be taken captive by the "Tommies." The men took some time to explain to him that they were not Tommies but airborne GIs. When this had been taken care of, Sergeant Frank was allowed to go ahead with his questioning. The boy explained that the house belonged to some friends of his and he had just come over for some preserves. He knew the people had been evacuated and said they might not be back for some time.

The boy went on to say that his older brother, who was a member of the local underground, would also be along shortly. Almost immediately the brother was brought in by Nicholai. He was a slick-haired, effeminate young man and the patrol had doubts about him. He spoke a little English and produced papers to prove that he was a member of the Dutch underground. He began to tell the men about the various enemy installations in the area. He gave them artillery positions and unit numbers and all this was immediately relayed back over the radio.

In the following hour six more civilians were guests of the patrol. They all seemed to know that there was no one home and all wanted something from the house. They were told they would have to stay until after the patrol had left. The civilians were happy to see the men, but they didn't like the idea of having to stay. One of the captives, a very pretty Duch girl accompanied by what appeared to be her boy-friend, wouldn't take no for an answer. The men said she was not averse to using all of her charms to get out, either, but they were firm.

At noon the traffic on the road began to increase. Convoys of big trucks appeared to be heading from the Utrecht area toward Arnhem. The men observed all kinds of vehicles and guns. Presently an unsuspecting Jerry entered the courtyard for a drink of water. Opening the front door a little, one of the men pointed his Tommy gun at the German and commanded him to come in. The German came

623

in laughing, apparently not quite convinced that the whole thing wasn't a joke. He turned out to be a mail orderly who had lost his way after taking mail to a near-by town. He seemed to be an intellectual type and was very philosophical about being captured.

Shortly afterwards the idea of food occurred to everyone in the house. The men in the patrol got out their K-ration chocolate and the civilians began to dig into the little bags they all carried. It began to look as if the civilians had been going on a picnic. They brought out bread and cheese and shared it with the Americans. An hour or so later the German who was supposed to meet the first two prisoners at 5:30 finally showed up with two horses and a cart. The men let him enter the courtyard and water the horses. Then they called out to him, "Put up your hands, you are a prisoner." He didn't seem to understand and it was necessary to repeat the order. Then he answered calmly, "I must feed my horses." Finally he raised one hand and came toward the house, muttering that it just couldn't be true. Now the civilians helped in the questioning, because the Germans were not too sure about the names of towns where their units were stationed.

Once the men watching from the windows were tempted to whistle at a passing car. It was driven by a pretty German WAC. The men said that the only thing that restrained them was the fact that their lives depended on it. Because everything had gone so smoothly the men were feeling pretty cocky. They wanted to capture a truck, a couple of staff cars with German WACs and drive back to Renkum.

Two more Germans entered the courtyard and were immediately taken prisoner. They were very sore, mainly because they had come along the road just to goldbrick away a little time. By this time a big fire had been built up in the front room where the prisoners were kept. The prisoners kept the fire going and the men argued to see who would stand guard in the warm room.

As darkness approached the men began to assemble their equipment. Becker was left on guard in the house with the prisoners and civilians while Lieutenant Sims and the others went out to look for a truck. The German mail

orderly, who seemed the happiest to be captured, was chosen to help them. He agreed that as soon as Sergeant Frank told him, he would help stop the truck by shouting, *"Halt Kamerad!"* As they waited the German said to Frank, "I am happy because the war is over for us." Frank replied that it would all depend on the next few hours and that he would be able to say with more certainty the next day.

Becker reported that when the lieutenant and the others left the house the remaining prisoners looked a little scared. Finally one man came and asked Becker in pantomime if they would be shot. Becker told them that such things aren't done in the American Army. All of the Germans in the house wore the Iron Cross and had seen service against the Russians.

While the men were waiting along the road a whole German company passed on bicycles. As each German rode by he would shout, *"Guten Abend"* to the men along the road and they shouted back the same. One man stopped and asked Sergeant Frank if this were the right road to the next town. Rather than become engaged in conversation, Frank told him he didn't know.

Getting impatient after an hour and a half, the men decided they would stop the next truck that came along, no matter what kind it was. In the meantime a motorcyclist stopped by the road and went into the courtyard of the house. Nicholai rushed across the road and grabbed him. It developed that he was checking up on the absence of the other men. When Nicholai brought him across the road he saw the mail orderly and rushed up to shake his hand. They were old friends and had served together for years.

A few minutes later the men heard a truck coming down the road and told the two Germans to step out and shout, *"Halt Kamerad!"* When the truck came, all the men shouted at once and the truck stopped. It turned out to be a big five-tonner carrying 15 SS men. Nicholai jumped on the back and herded the Germans off, taking their weapons as they got down. They were all very surprised. At first the driver refused to leave his seat, but after a number of strong threats, namely shooting, he finally got off. He was a tall man and very cocky. When asked to put up his hands

625

he said, "Who says so?" When he was told that he was a prisoner of war he looked astonished and said that it was impossible. As he spoke he put one hand up and with the other drew a pistol, but only to hide it in his pocket. Sergeant Frank took it away.

The driver was told to get back in the truck and pull it off the road. He seemed reluctant and Frank had to hold a gun against his ear while he started the motor. He seemed unable to keep the motor from stalling every few seconds and when he moved into the courtyard he had trouble turning. It was obvious that he was stalling for time. He kept looking at Frank and saying in German, "This can't happen to me." He told Frank he was on his way to meet the captain of his battalion. When he was told he was to drive the truck and the men to the Neder Rijn he said there wasn't enough gas. He was told that if that were true then he would be shot, so he said there was enough gas for twenty miles.

Now Becker and the prisoners in the house came out and piled into the truck with the SS men. The Americans spaced themselves around inside the truck so they could keep guard. Lieutenant Sims and Sergeant Frank sat in front with the driver. When they were on the road the truck stalled again. As the driver tried to start the motor an amphibious jeep pulled up and a tall SS officer began to bawl him out for blocking the road. Canfield was off the truck in an instant and had brought the officer inside. As it turned out, this was the captain the truck driver had been going to meet.

Again the sergeant concentrated on getting the driver to start the truck. He worked hard at stalling the motor and had to be threatened before he would drive at all. Finally he got the truck under way and they set out on the return route they had mapped out before the patrol. Every now and then the driver would get temperamental, folding his arms and saying, *"Hab' ich eine Wut!"* ("Am I mad!"). After a prod or two with the gun muzzle he would go back to safer driving. Farther along the road toward Arnhem he was told to turn off to the right. Shortly the truck came to a muddy place in the woods and bogged down hub-deep.

No amount of trying by the SS driver was able to move it. It was now 10 p.m. and the patrol decided they might as well try to make it back on foot.

Now the men regretted having so many prisoners. As they piled down from the truck the SS captain bolted to the side of the road in the darkness. In a flash he was in the woods. Nicholai shouted for him to stop and ran after. In a moment the others heard two shots and Nicholai's only two words of German, *"Hände hoch, you son of a bitch!"* followed by a great crashing in the underbrush. Becker also ran into the woods to see if he might help. Following the noise he found Nicholai and the captain. Nicholai was still shouting, *"Hände hoch"* and with every shout he would kick the captain in the seat of the pants. When they came back to the truck the captain was cowed and willing to go quietly.

Lining the Germans up in two columns, Sergeant Frank now gave them a little lecture. He said they could just as easily be shot as taken back and that all six Americans were risking their lives to get them back safely. He told them that if anyone tried to escape or made an unnecessary noise he would be shot immediately. Starting out again with the SS captain and Sergeant Frank in front, the column made its way along the road toward the river. As they walked the SS captain told Frank that it was useless to try to cross the Rijn with the prisoners. He said the Americans might as well turn over their guns because they would surely be caught by the Germans.

The captain also asked if he might have a cigarette. He was told he couldn't have one now, but that later he would have more and better cigarettes than there were in all of Germany. The captain said the Germans had nothing against the Americans and he couldn't see personally why the Germans and Americans didn't get together to fight the Russians and Japanese. We are both white races, he said. Sergeant Frank answered that the Russians were also white. Yes, replied the captain, but they are inferior. Finally the captain asked if it were not possible for them to rest a while, or at least to slow down. He was told that he had the misfortune to be a captive of American paratroopers, who just didn't walk any slower. Now as they walked along they constantly heard German voices.

Arriving at the railroad crossing the patrol decided finally that they didn't dare blow up the tracks with the two and a half minute fuse they carried. Reluctantly they crossed the tracks and ditched their demolition charges in bushes by the road. Along this last stretch of the road they passed countless houses with Germans inside.

When they came to the town of Renkum the patrol marched boldly down the center of the main street with a great clicking of German hobnailed shoes. It was obvious from the sound alone that they could be nothing but a group of marching Germans. They went through the town without incident and headed straight for the near-by dike. Everyone was feeling wonderfully light-headed. Arriving at the dike, they had marched right down to the water when they saw a squad of Germans at a river outpost. As they came close Sergeant Frank called out to them in German that there was nothing to worry about. When they stopped two of the men rushed over and told the Jerries to put up their hands. The column moved on, cleaning out two more posts along the river. The six-man patrol now had a total of 32 prisoners.

On the dike Lieutenant Sims gave the prearranged flashlight signal to the other side. Soon the answer came—three blinks. The SS captain,[7] his truck driver and one of the patrol were the first to get to the other side. Part of the patrol stayed behind to cover the crossing while the rest of the prisoners were ferried over. Finally the last three men touched the Allied side of the Rijn. The incredible patrol was over. Shortly afterwards the soldiers were awarded Silver Stars. Lieutenant Sims, who received the Distinguished Service Cross, had dinner with General Taylor and was promoted to captain. The story of the patrol went the rounds of the European Theater, and the battalion intelligence officers of the 501st Parachute Infantry tightened their belts and sighed.

[7] Who remarked: "I congratulate you. I didn't believe it was possible."—L. C.

In the Ardennes

The Germans were still building up for the attack in the Ardennes; the Allies were still weak on precisely that front. En route to a meeting with Montgomery in the first week of December, 1944, Eisenhower had passed through the Ardennes area, and made note of the thin support behind the main American lines. There were four divisions stretched along a front of twenty-five miles. As Gen. Bradley states in A Soldier's Story, Eisenhower discussed this with him but Bradley was torn by commitments to Patton in the Saar, and those to the 9th U.S. Army, soon to assault north of Aachen at the Roer River. There had been intelligence reports, in mid-December, indicating a shift of some German divisions from the north into the Ardennes area (Hitler had assembled twenty-eight divisions in the Ardennes with new supplies, tanks and assault guns; the Allied High Command had no inkling of anything this size). However, Bradley took a calculated risk that the Americans would be able to mount an attack of their own before the Germans had an opportunity to discover and exploit his weakness in the Ardennes. He was not to get away with it.

On December 16th, the Germans began an artillery barrage of over 2,000 guns; the infantry moved up close behind it, five Panzer divisions following on their heels. The Germans, without proper air reconnaissance or aerial bombardment support from the Luftwaffe, needed bad weather to launch the attack. The morning of the 16th was foggy and misty, and the American High Command, also deprived of air reconnaissance because of the weather, didn't immediately realize this was a major attack, even though division after division was being thrown at the American lines, penetrating in five different sectors. Bradley admits that he thought it a spoiling attack at first. His staff had simply not believed the Germans could assemble strong enough forces for such an assault. And part of the lack of immediate response at Bradley's headquarters can be charged to poor communications. The Germans had dressed some of their troops in captured American uniforms, to infiltrate the Allied lines to the rear and stir up confusion, with special attention to communications. The air forces were to be grounded right up to December 25th because of the weather, and the Germans could supply and reinforce their attacking divisions without interference. Gen. T. H. Middleton's VIII Corps, facing the Ardennes at the time of the breakthrough, had three infantry divisions—the 106th, sent to the front lines only four days before the German attack, the 4th and 28th Divisions, which had been badly hurt in the Huertgen Forest, and the 9th Armored Division. The Americans, even though cut off and surrounded, fought back courageously and tenaciously in islands of resistance. But by December 18th the Germans had achieved a major breakthrough, their troops and Panzer columns fanning out toward the Meuse River. But the Americans still maintained two salients in the area under attack. From the north, the St. Vith salient was a solid arm thrusting out at the Germans, manned by the 7th Armored Division under Gen. Hasbrouck. To the south was Bastogne, sitting astride several important roads, over which the German armor would have to move if they were to drive on to the west. Gen. Middleton issued orders to hold Bastogne, calling on the nearest reserves, including the 101st Airborne Division.

Many men of the 101st Airborne were on leave in Paris, and with both division commanders home in the U.S., the artillery commander, Brig. Gen. Anthony J. McAuliffe took over. The night of the 17th, via a huge truck convoy, the division set out for Bastogne.

Capt. Laurence Critchell, author of Four Stars of Hell, and the following account of the fight at Bastogne, says, "The truck convoy ride to the Ardennes was unforgettable. The division had usually gone into battle by air drop, but now jampacked in approximately 380 trucks it rolled along through a countryside pockmarked with excavations of World War I. The convoy traveled with lights on, a deliberate risk to gain time and speed. Up and down the shaven hills of northern France went the convoy, and wherever the road made a sharp turn, the vehicles could be seen for miles ahead and miles behind." The commanders, McAuliffe and his Cols. Ewell and Kinnard, had arrived in Bastogne ahead of most of the units and had been making reconnaissance to prepare for the expected Panzer divisions. When the division got to Bastogne, they met straggling groups of soldiers in retreat.

BASTOGNE

by Capt. Laurence Critchell

It was foggy and damp at six o'clock in the morning. The 1st Battalion had been selected to lead off on the push out the Longvilly road. The coatless men moved through the streets of Bastogne, sloshing in mud and dirty water. Between their double lines, on the road itself, heavy armor still was moving eastward, away from the oncoming enemy. It was a ludicrous sight to see a few of the airborne troops wave at the retreating armor—fire power much stronger than any of them could have. One paratrooper, still without a weapon, picked up a stick and, for the benefit of the demoralized columns, shook it in the direction of the enemy. Here and there unhelmeted men were wearing wool caps or were bareheaded. Few wore overcoats. But they pushed forward out of the town with a sense of confidence, and in a little while they were in the silent, foggy countryside.

Following the 1st Battalion as it moved out of Bastogne was B Battery of the 81st Anti-Aircraft with eight 57-mm. guns. Behind that unit in turn—considerably behind it, as a matter of fact—were the 2nd and 3rd Battalions of the 501st. The latter was getting itself badly tangled in the snarl of traffic within the town, and since Ewell was not yet certain of how and where he would employ those battalions, he contented himself with the advance of the 1st Battalion and its supporting unit along the Longvilly road. On one occasion the men turned off by mistake towards Marvie, due east. But Ewell was able to set them right, and by 0730 in the morning, with the light just breaking, the situation looked fair enough.

In that region the Bastogne-Longvilly highway ran along

a valley dominated on each side by gently sloping hills. Those hills were partially covered with sparse vegetation, but the overgrowth offered little concealment. On this morning, however, the fog was dense. It was so thick that the left flank guards of the 1st Battalion by-passed two platoons of enemy infantrymen dug in on a hill in the vicinity of Bizory; though slight sounds carried distinctly on the damp air, neither the Germans nor the Americans became aware of each other's presence. Unsuspecting, the 1st Battalion marched straight towards the main body of the enemy.

The Germans, of course, were equally unsuspecting. Until that moment they had forced back the stubborn 28th Division, and the less stubborn, badly fragmented 9th Armored Division, without meeting heavily organized resistance. This had given the ordinary German soldiers new confidence; their morale was higher on the morning of December 19th than it had been since the invasion of the Normandy coast. In documents and letters later taken from German prisoners or from German dead, the enemy soldiers were writing home, "At last the war has become fun again." [1] They described the slaughter of armored and infantry divisions along the way as "a glorious blood bath" and prophesied to their families in the clean little towns of Germany that the European struggle would soon be at an end. Once again, evidently, it was *Deutschland über Alles*.

The first encounter with the deployed 1st Battalion of the 501st Parachute Infantry in the early hours of December 19th must have been a shock to them.

Contact was made at what seemed to be an enemy road block near the village of Neffe. The division reconnaissance platoon, which had somehow gone astray at the beginning of the advance, was on the point of overtaking the lead scouts of the battalion when, from the fog directly ahead, there was the unmistakable fast rattle of a German machine gun.

Almost to a man, the battalion went flat. With the first

---

[1] From a document taken by a 501st prisoner of war interrogation team.

sounds of fire the two German platoons which had been by-passed in the fog discovered their enemy in front and behind them. The confusion was so great that the German guns were quickly disposed of. However, the machine gun that had opened up at the crossroads and given the first alarm of the Bastogne siege, evidently outposted a lead element of considerable weight.

The valley road at that point did not pass through the center of the valley, but ran close to the rising ground on the left flank. Thus it was only on the right, where the valley sloped away to a small stream, that it was possible to deploy the men adequately. In keeping with McAuliffe's words, Ewell drily told the commander of the 1st Battalion, Lieutenant Colonel (then Major) Bottomly to "develop the situation." He himself found a stone house in a pocket of the hillside and established a temporary command post. Within a short time Bottomly reported to Ewell by radio that he was opposed by approximately two platoons of infantry and two Mark IV tanks. Ewell, to whom the report was put in the form of a question, told him to go ahead and fight his own fight.

The Mark IV tanks were firing, from a defiladed position near Neffe, straight down the highway. Consequently, the 57-mm. guns of the anti-aircraft company could not be brought to bear on them. And by ten o'clock in the morning, with no advance having been made on either side, the situation became a deadlock. Little more could be done just then; in Bastogne the 2nd and 3rd battalions still were struggling to get through the choked traffic of the VIII Corps, fleeing to the rear.

Off on the left flank of Ewell's position was a group of large farm houses in a broad valley. The valley ran down towards Neffe, but before it reached that village (held, Ewell judged, by the enemy) the ground rose up again to conceal the two villages from sight of each other. It occurred to Ewell that if the 2nd Battalion were to seize the town of Bizory, which lay in that direction, his men would be well situated to move onto the high ground adjacent.

Lieutenant Colonel Homan was in command of the 2nd Battalion. Implementing Colonel Ewell's orders as soon as

633

he got free of Bastogne, he seized Bizory with no opposition and only a little fire from the direction of the deadlock at Neffe. During this time the 3rd Battalion, still in Bastogne, was trying to get out of town by an auxiliary side route. Ewell ordered the commander, Lieutenant Colonel Griswold, to strike for Mont, farther to the right of the forward positions then held by Bottomly and Homan. Ewell eventually intended to use Griswold's battalion in a flanking attack on Neffe, but he kept these intentions to himself. What chiefly concerned him was getting the battalion out of town.

Bastogne at that hour still was crowded with drifting and staring men. So great was the shock they had received that many of them were inarticulate. They trickled through the German lines in two and threes, making no attempt to organize themselves, refusing to be organized by anyone else. When they asked the paratroopers what they were doing, and the paratroopers replied, "Fighting Germans," they only stared. To them, at least temporarily, the war seemed lost.

Not all were like that, however. Some of the haggard, beaten men accepted a K ration, ate it silently, and then asked for a rifle. They were ready to go back and fight. Some of the armor was in good shape, and the morale of the armored men who elected to remain at Bastogne and fight it out was high. Among them, seven tanks and three tank destroyer crews organized themselves into a combat team and voluntarily attached themselves to the 2nd Battalion, while another platoon of armored infantry stuck it out with the regiment until the siege was lifted.

By noon of the 19th the situation was clearer. The 1st Battalion was halted at Neffe, fighting what Ewell thought was only a difficult road block. The 2nd Battalion had seized Bizory and was deployed on favorable high ground. The 3rd Battalion had reached Mont, but because the ground between there and Neffe was flat, and the enemy fire heavy, the soldiers had been unable to carry out the second phase of the order and sweep down on the road block at Neffe. By these three operations, however, a line had been stretched along commanding ground outside of Bastogne to the northeast. This was the critical and—as events later proved—decisive deployment.

Ewell decided to move his 2nd Battalion to Magaret, which would still further improve their position. He sent Colonel Homan with one company of men to secure the approaches to that town by seizing a small patch of woods on a long ridge above it. Homan did so, but was presently engaged along his entire front.

Company I had been separated from the 3rd Battalion and was making a reconnaissance of wooded areas to the front. It was ordered into the town of Wardin to investigate the reported existence there of an armored road block. The ill-fated company encountered the enemy in the town, but at 1500 radioed that its men were doing all right. When a company of volunteer tank destroyers arrived at Ewell's command post, however, he sent them to the 3rd Battalion to help out in case the group at Wardin needed support.

It was then 1600. Ewell had formed three battalions approximately abreast and in contact with the enemy all along his front. For the first time since the German break-through, the enemy was meeting a line of troops which refused to give ground.

At dark Ewell ordered the battalions to break contact and form to defend a general line along the high ground to the west of Bizory-Neffe and roughly parallel to this line to the southward. Taking his plan back to the red stone buildings where division headquarters had been established, he got McAuliffe's approval. On the way he assured himself, for the first time since daybreak, that Bastogne had not been seized.

Walking along the main street of the town, he met a sergeant of Company I.

"Have you heard about Company I?" asked the sergeant. "It's been wiped out."

Ewell, hurrying back to his radio, didn't believe it.

The town of Wardin lay on the extreme right flank of the Bizory-Neffe-Wardin line, which Ewell had formed on the commanding terrain northeast of Bastogne. Wardin was a small place of a dozen-odd houses, set at a little distance from one of the main roads entering Bastogne. Captain Wallace had taken his men of Company I into the village as part of the general reconnaissance ordered by Homan in compliance with Ewell's instructions. What ensued there was tragic.

When Wallace and his men entered the town, they encountered only a few Germans. Without much difficulty, they drove those men from the dreary Belgian houses and took possession. Wardin had strategic value and, though it was closer to the enemy than Bizory and Neffe, Wallace believed he could hold his place.

He and his men had been in the town only a short while, however, when a force of German armor appeared unexpectedly on the outskirts. As the tanks—they were Tiger Royals—spread out to prevent Wallace's force from escaping, the tank gunners opened fire point-blank. Under cover of this fire, a whole battalion of German infantrymen, who had all the ardor of their late successes, closed in to the streets. Wallace hastily withdrew part of his force to fight at the flanks of his command post and to keep one avenue of retreat open. The remainder of the Americans held out in the concealment of the houses.

The din was soon terrific—the fast rocketing *"whisht-bang!"* of heavy-caliber shells at close range, the clattering of fallen rock, the explosions of bazooka shells, the rattle of small arms and the queer vibrating *"brrrrrrrp!"* of German automatic pistols. Bazooka gunners deliberately squatted in the open where they were plainly visible to the Germans and fired point-blank on the tanks. Soldiers in the houses held their positions until shells burst through the rooms and demolished the lower floors. Other soldiers snatched up the bazookas of men who had died.

House by house, fighting in a blaze of fire, the Americans retreated. The smoke of explosions from the tank guns clouded vision from one side of the street to the other. The Germans were systematically demolishing every house. Everywhere was the ammoniac stink of cordite; in the rubble of the demolished buildings hands, heads, legs protruded. Those paratroopers who still were alive fought their way towards Wallace and the command post. One

636

youngster, running out into the center of the street, deliberately knelt in a furious rattle of small-arms fire and discharged a bazooka shell squarely into the lead tank. The tank was halted and, though the boy was dead an instant later, the rest of the oncoming armor was momentarily canalized.

Wallace, giving the infantryman's equivalent of "abandon ship," ordered the remainder of the men to split up— to get back to Bastogne singly or in pairs—any way they could.

On the street before the command post the men threw up a hasty tank obstacle. As the armor and the swarms of German infantrymen approached this final point, Wallace directed all the fire power at his disposal to cover the withdrawal of the men who were left. One by one, as the small-arms and heavy-caliber fire grew heavier, they passed through the barricade, Wallace urging them on. Then the officer ordered the men at the barricade, too, to fall back. A few of them refused. The final survivors of the trap of Wardin saw, as they looked back, the figure of their captain, still at the barricade, still fighting—the last they were ever to see of him.

All that afternoon and night the survivors trickled into Bastogne. At the regimental command post, a great room which had once been a school study hall was set aside for them, where they cleaned their weapons on the children's desks. They were very silent. A few of them sat against the wall, under a statue of the Crucifixion, with their heads in their hands.

Wallace, like many of his men, left a wife and child behind him. Of approximately 200 of his soldiers who had gone into Wardin eighty-three survived.

Undertones of tragedy marked the evening of the first day at Bastogne. As the light dimmed in the sky, the streets of town became deserted. The inhabitants disappeared into their cellars. In the great dark rooms of the regimental command post the only illumination came from the flicker of the squad cookers as the survivors of Company I heated their K rations. Nothing had been heard of a truck column bringing ammunition and other supplies to the town. Father Sampson was missing. And there were rumors that our division hospital, set up to the rear of Bastogne, had been captured.

The 501st Command Post was plainly visible from the enemy lines. With the exception of the church across the street, it was the most prominent building in Bastogne. Downstairs on the main floor were a dining hall, an immense cloister with Doric columns, a skylight, and an adjacent chapel. The chapel was used for a temporary aid station, while the cloister was designated for use by the company and regimental kitchens (if the equipment got through). The dining room, which occupied a wing of its own, was left to the Franciscan nuns, who were taking care of twenty or thirty very young, very curious children. It was interesting to note that, when the German artillery began to fall on Bastogne, those children disappeared underground with the nuns and did not reappear until three weeks later.

Upstairs in the seminary were dozens of connecting rooms, each of them piously decorated. Above the second floor were dormitories for the former pupils, while on the fourth floor was a vast chamber which had been occupied before the Ardennes break-through by VIII Corps military police. The haste with which the M.P.s had abandoned their quarters was evident in the discarded material strewn about the floors: paper-bound books, magazines, pin-ups, galoshes, webbing, blankets, even uniforms. The few of us who explored this room felt a little satisfaction in the debacle of the withdrawal—mute testimony of that upheaval of life which had come to a rear echelon when it had suddenly become a forward area.

By morning of the next day, December 20th, the temperature had dropped below freezing. There was little wind before dawn, and the unmoving blanket of clouds limited visibility in the darkness. The 501st men were in the same positions they had taken up at nightfall and not much had been done to extend the flanks. Though other units had

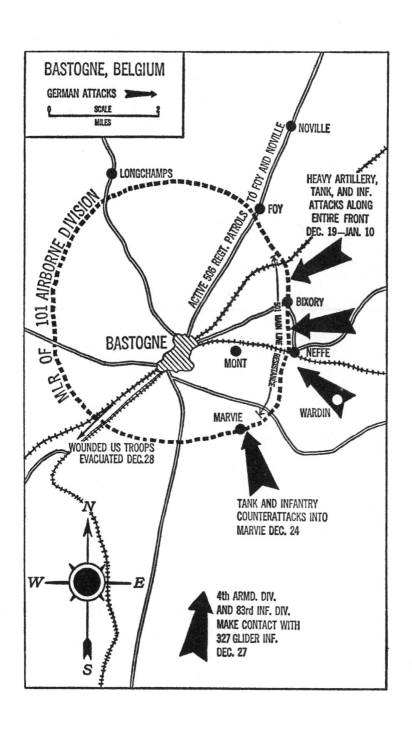

BASTOGNE, BELGIUM

GERMAN ATTACKS

SCALE

0   2

MILES

NOVILLE

LONGCHAMPS

HEAVY ARTILLERY,
TANK, AND INF.
ATTACKS ALONG
ENTIRE FRONT
DEC. 19—JAN. 10

ACTIVE 506 REGT. PATROLS TO FOY AND NOVILLE

FOY

MLR OF 101 AIRBORNE DIVISION

BIXORY

101 MAIN LINE RESISTANCE

BASTOGNE

MONT

NEFFE

WARDIN

MARVIE

WOUNDED US TROOPS
EVACUATED DEC. 28

TANK AND INFANTRY
COUNTERATTACKS INTO
MARVIE DEC. 24

N

W   E

S

4th ARMD. DIV.
AND 83rd INF. DIV.
MAKE CONTACT WITH
327 GLIDER INF.
DEC. 27

been brought up to either side, the 501st still was squarely in the line of the German advance.

One of the first moves made by McAuliffe, as an artillery commander, was to dispose his airborne artillery and tank guns in such a manner as to bring coordinated fire from all of the pieces on any one point of the line which he intended to "develop," or which was attacked by the enemy. Subsequently, when Bastogne was encircled, he was able to deliver the same concentration of fire on any point of the 360° defense. On the morning of the 20th, however, his main concern was the sector occupied by Ewell's regiment. And the honors of the day were about evenly divided between Ewell's men and McAuliffe's artillery.

The night had been reasonably quiet. From the Americans captured at Wardin the Germans had identified the division opposing them, and they evidently spent the hours of darkness massing their forces for a major drive. The much criticized G-2 of the Allied armies at the time of the Ardennes break-through was not the only one to be surprised in those days; documents later captured from the German staff revealed the enemy's astonishment of finding the 101st Airborne Division (which their intelligence had reported to be at Mourmelon, France) directly in the path of their advance at a key focal point of communications, a hundred miles from where they were supposed to be.

The first troubles on the 20th began at 0530, before there was light in the wintry sky.

East of Bizory, where Homan's 2nd Battalion men were deployed, was a rise of high ground. Between that high ground and the American front line was a clear field of fire, extending more than 3,000 yards. On that expanse, the only cover for an attacking enemy was the natural defilades where the farmland rose and fell. Homan's position was ideal for defense—so ideal, as a matter of fact, that, when an observation-post spotter who had field glasses reported that six enemy tanks were starting across the fields, accompanied by what he estimated to be a battalion of German infantrymen, the event took place at such a distance that

640

the Americans, though alerted, could only sit by their guns and wait.

A scratch force of American tank destroyers had attached itself to Homan's battalion during the night. At word of the impending attack, the crews disposed their vehicles north of the village of Bizory on either side of a small road that was a key approach to the American lines. Meanwhile, Homan had notified Ewell about the approaching enemy; Ewell had notified Kinnard, and Kinnard, through McAuliffe, the artillery. One by one the guns within Bastogne were brought to bear on a predetermined coordinate—where, when the signal came to fire, their shells would drop in a screen across the oncoming Germans.

The expanse of ground in front of Homan was so great that the Germans advanced for a whole hour before they were close to the coordinate for the artillery barrage. During part of this time the men of the 2nd Battalion could keep them in sight, and, the nearer they approached, the brighter grew the morning. When the American machine gunners suddenly opened fire, the tank destroyers fired simultaneously, and, within an instant or two, in a curtain of artillery bursts, the German lines were struck squarely by hundreds of shells from McAuliffe's guns.

From full silence to the blaze of fire took only a few moments. The Germans still were at such a distance from Homan's men that the automatic weapons' fire had little visible effect. But so intense was the coordinated artillery fire from within Bastogne that the paratroopers, who had a grandstand view of the entire episode, witnessed the Germans begin to falter. Here and there, among the mushrooming clouds of artillery smoke, the tiny black figures stumbled and fell. Behind them one of the heavy tanks turned back towards its own lines—then rolled and halted. Two of the tanks were destroyed, and a third disabled.

The tiny figures of the Germans began to run. More and more of them fell. For twenty minutes the rolling barrage continued to pursue them. When it lifted, the only Germans who remained on the open fields were the scores of still bodies.

The shock of that first repulse must have been a severe one to the German troops. Until that morning they had met other pockets of stubborn resistance—the 7th Armored Division, whose soldiers had made a gallant stand at St. Vith, and the elements of the 28th Division already mentioned. But when the Germans, filled with confidence, attacked Bastogne on the morning of the 20th, they were repulsed not only with heavy casualties, but also by a group of organized soldiers who obviously intended to deny—to twenty-five enemy divisions—a critical road-net in the heart of the salient.

Towards midmorning of the 20th it started to snow. The German forces, under cover of thick woods to the northeast, began to shell Bastogne, devoting particular attention to the huge building by the church steeple.

This was the building which we had selected for a regimental command post. It was the largest command post any regiment could have had. It was five stories high and perhaps a quarter of a mile in circumference. The walls were about three feet thick. This was thick enough to withstand shellfire, but unfortunately, the operations offices had been selected in the very first hours, before anyone knew the direction of the enemy. When the lines were consolidated outside Bastogne, it was found that the Germans could— with good luck in their marksmanship—put artillery through the windows.

The snow came down steadily, gently. Soon it blanketed the bodies of the dead Germans at Neffe and those beyond Homan's positions outside of Bizory. The paratroopers were seeing the last bare earth they were to see for two months. Meanwhile, the shelling of Bastogne continued. The Germans regrouped for a concerted attack in force, and the fateful day was quiet.

The 1st Battalion, which had fired the first shots of the Bastogne siege, had been unable to seize Neffe beyond the turn of the valley road. Company B had successfully taken a house on the side of the critical Neffe road, and, from the windows of that house, the soldiers were able to command all the approaches to the battalion front. Machine guns were set up in there, while the infantrymen of the other companies dug foxholes and, where they could, lined the interiors with straw.

In Homan's area at Bizory, where the first enemy attack in force had been repulsed, there was no change. But at Griswold's 3rd Battalion, which had taken up positions at Mont, the 1st Platoon of Company B of the 705th Tank Destroyer Battalion had attached itself during the night. This was a valuable reinforcement. Griswold posted one of the vehicles at a bend in the Neffe road, where it commanded the stretch leading to that enemy-occupied town, and where it also commanded a draw leading off to the south. Another destroyer was placed to complement the fire of the first, while the second section of the platoon, from concealed positions, guarded the approach directly across the valley.

Everywhere there was silence. The skies were leaden; the snow came down steadily, almost audibly. No planes were in the air anywhere. At division headquarters, McAuliffe, in contact with General Middleton by radio, happened to remark that Bastogne would probably be surrounded.

The soldiers blew on their stiffening fingers and waited.

At seven o'clock a few shells fell in Bizory and Mont. These were followed by a few more and, shortly, by a great number. Finally, a heavy barrage dropped on all the critical points along the defensive line. So intense was the artillery fire from the German positions that within a few minutes every telephone wire connecting the battalions to regimental headquarters was severed.

When the firing slackened off, the German forces struck simultaneously in a two-pronged offensive against the 1st and 3rd battalions.

Bottomly, at the 1st Battalion, radioed Ewell that the enemy troops were charging straight down the highway. They came with the shouts and high morale of men convinced they were going through. Not even in Normandy had the paratroopers encountered such high morale. Bottomly re-

643

ported to Ewell that it was too dark to see much, but that he could hear tanks coming along with the troops.

It was a bad hour for the regimental staff at Bastogne. On orders from someone, the records were packed, the equipment readied, the men dressed for retreat. If the two flanks collapsed . . .

The snow had ceased. The night was bitter cold.

There were eleven battalions of guns at McAuliffe's disposal within Bastogne. All eleven battalions dropped a "dam of fire" across the Neffe road, approximately 200 yards ahead of the town. It was the most effective American defensive fire during the siege. Three German tanks—two Panthers and a Tiger Royal—were struck almost at once; they had drawn up beyond the last houses in the village when they were hit, and there they stayed.

The short delay before the artillery barrage, however, had enabled a considerable number of German infantrymen to approach so close to the American lines that the greater number of shells fell behind them. Those men charged wildly towards the Americans, firing and shouting. Company B, posted in and around the house, on commanding ground at the side of the road, took the shock without yielding an inch of ground. The automatic weapons in the windows controlled the approaches so effectively that not a single German soldier got within bayonet distance of the American lines. Everywhere in the darkness the enemy troops stiffened and fell and died, and their blood spotted the snow. Weeks afterward they were still there, grotesque and stiff, the foremost bodies 300 yards in advance of the wrecked German armor.

The action in this area continued with intensity for some time. The soldiers were fighting in that bitter fume of smoke and sweat and cold where each man seemed hopelessly alone. There was no consciousness of cold or snow or wet clothes or hunger. When men are fighting each other, and the issue remains in doubt, there are only the simplest and most basic elements of human experience.

Meanwhile, the men of the 3rd Battalion were struggling to hold back a simultaneous enemy attack from a different quarter. It was evident that the Germans had aban-

644

doned their attempt to enter Bastogne across the wide field of fire opening down from Homan's positions, where they had failed that morning. The dual attack by dark left Homan's forces alone and evidently had the object of bending the two flanks of the 501st until those flanks collapsed and Homan was trapped in the middle.

The Germans attacking Griswold's forces also had supporting armor. But the enemy tank commander must have observed the tank destroyers behind the American lines, for his armor did not leave the concealment of a little wood just west of a château at Neffe. From that position the tanks could put down a base of fire for their advancing and—as events shortly proved—suicidal infantrymen.

The open and comparatively smooth slope which separated Mont and Neffe afforded a field of fire for Griswold's battalion almost as extensive as that which fronted the 2nd Battalion under Colonel Homan. In addition to this wide field of fire, the slope was crisscrossed with man-made obstacles—a checkerboard of barbed-wire fences erected by the Belgians to make feeder pens for cattle. The fences were in rows about thirty yards apart. Each fence was five or six strands high. Because of the manner of their construction, is was almost impossible to crawl underneath the fences: a man approaching Griswold's forces at Mont had to halt at each obstacle and climb through.

Whether the German commanders knew of the existence of these obstacles and decided to risk the attack anyway, or whether the leading enemy soldiers just stumbled onto them by accident in the darkness, will probably not be known. But the attack, once launched, had to be carried on. The German infantrymen ran forward with the same enthusiasm, the same wild yells and eagerness which had characterized all their offensive actions since the break-through. When they reached the fences, they simply climbed through. But it broke them.

As fast as they reached the obstacles, Griswold's machine gunners swept them down. The Germans were in great strength, and the forces behind, pressing upon the forces ahead, made a massacre inevitable. Bodies of the dead piled up around the wire fences, and the attackers who followed, climbing over those bodies, became bodies themselves a few steps beyond. The volume of tracer fire from Griswold's gunners was spectacularly intense; prisoners questioned later said that its visible effect, as much as the holocaust around the fences, was to them the terrifying element of the night attack.

What Griswold's men were facing was a whole German regiment—the 901st *Panzergrenadiers,* better soldiers than the *Volksgrenadiers* who had attacked Homan to. no effect in the early morning. These Germans rushed towards the 3rd Battalion of the 501st with such high spirit that, despite the wire fences and the field of fire, Griswold was forced to regroup part of his battalion to reinforce his left flank. By the time he accomplished this, the action had become intense and the German casualties terrible. The total destruction of one side or the other was so imminent that the American tank-destroyer men, having no targets for their guns, fired the .50-caliber weapons from their vehicles, jumped out, and joined the infantrymen on the line.

By the time the German fire began to slacken off, the insane double attack of divisional strength 'had lasted four hours. It was close to midnight. Enemy dead were piled up in such numbers around the wire fences that even the German withdrawal was difficult. Around Neffe, where the other attack had taken place, the situation was much the same, and, though the casualties on the American side had been very heavy, the *Panzergrenadiers* had been decimated. Ewell's eye for ground had given the paratroopers an advantage they were never afterwards to lose.

As he remarked later: "I think that, as of that night, the 901st had 'had it.' They no longer had enough men to be an effective offensive force. They had been pretty well chewed up before they got to us, and we completed the job."

At the regimental command post, the staff unpacked to stay.

As everyone knows, the newspapers in the United States did not announce that the 101st Airborne Division had been

646

cut off and surrounded by the enemy until a day or two before the relief of the besieged city. Oddly enough, most of us at Bastogne were almost as slow in getting the news.

Newspaper maps of front lines in a war usually show a salient in clear black, like a pool of spilled ink. The impression is that within that pool the land is thick with soldiers, that every square inch of terrestrial space has its allotted guardian. Nothing of the sort is true, of course. The breakthrough of the German tanks in Holland and their advance on Veghel through the heart of the enemy country were more typical than unique. Where the vehicles crossed the highway, and where they approached Veghel—both being guarded areas—they were engaged. But the remainder of their movements was through virtually deserted countryside, like the land on the road from Addeville to La Barquette.

Something of the sort was just as true at Bastogne. The first evidence of enemy forces to the rear of Bastogne came when a reconnaissance patrol engaged a small force of Germans on the road leading back to the hospital. In a few hours the enemy forces had moved elsewhere; but, as time passed, engagements on the roads to the rear became more frequent. McAuliffe at division headquarters knew that Bastogne would be ringed by the enemy, but at the respective regimental headquarters, and especially on the battalion lines, only rumors of the engagements to the rear reached the men. On the night of the 20th and the morning of the 21st the whole situation was in doubt. Yet the front lines of the German drive had already gone beyond Bastogne.

Von Rundstedt was aiming for Liége, where the largest supply dumps behind the Allied lines were situated. His plan was to seize those dumps and thus equip his army for the drive on Antwerp. Once Antwerp had been reached, the Allied forces would be split in half.

Nothing of this was known, however, on the morning of the 21st in Bastogne. After the Germans had fallen back, all was still and cold. The gentle descent of the snowflakes by the old church on the main street gave Bastogne the picturesque air of an old-fashioned Christmas card. By morning the snow had made the whole town clean and white—dangerously white for patrols; so Captain Phillips, with Lieutenant Frank as interpreter, ransacked the houses of Bastogne for bed sheets to use as camouflage.

That day—for the first and last time of the war—the operations offices of regimental headquarters moved underground.

A narrow corridor about ten feet below the surface of the earth, reached by a flight of stone steps, admitted to a series of cement-walled chambers underneath the convent command post. Each room was about ten by fifteen feet. When desks and chairs were put in, there was not much room to move around. The regimental commander, his executive officer, the adjutant, the intelligence officer, the operations officer, and their enlisted staffs were all crowded together into the connecting rooms. With the exception of the apartment in a private house across the street, occupied by the prisoner of war interrogation team, and with the further exception of a few aid stations, those underground chambers were the only warm rooms in Bastogne during the siege. They were not only warm, they were also safe. And consequently very crowded.

One of the last convoys to go through to Bastogne from outside brought the regimental kitchens. For lack of space in the forward positions the mobile stoves were set up— with nothing to cook—along the sides of the glass-ceiled cloister upstairs and beneath a huge statue.

The wounded who came from the lines were put temporarily in the cold chapel adjacent to the cloister. Major Carrel, the regimental surgeon, was ill, but Captain W. J. Waldmann of Bakersfield, California, a man with a high forehead and a grave manner, took his place. Operations and transfusions were performed by the yellow light of two gas lamps. The wounded men, wrapped in the few blankets on hand, were laid on the freezing floor of the chapel. As new casualties were brought from the lines, aisles were made between the litter cases. Soon the floor was covered with wounded men, who lay where they could see the crazy shadows dancing on the plasma tubes and the gas bottles for the lamps.

Presently, the enlisted men of the staff realized that no

wounded were being evacuated. And that was how the word of the encirclement finally spread.

Four German divisions and elements of three others faced the 101st Airborne Division when Bastogne was finally surrounded. Each of our men was outnumbered four to one. No one felt heroic about this, and no one made any speeches about it, written or otherwise. The troops were never called upon—as democratic statesmen are so fond of doing, especially after lunch—to give no inch of their embattled ground. Nor were they ever told that what they were doing was important, significant, or destined by any combination of circumstances to go down in military history. It was even doubtful that General McAuliffe's mimeographed Christmas message to the troops reached every foxhole.

But as soon as the word spread among the troops, both in town and on the lines, that the roads out of Bastogne had been cut off and the division surrounded, a curious, very subtle change took place in the atmosphere. It was difficult to understand. Perhaps it was this:

A certain good-natured rivalry had existed from the beginning among the various units of the division—the 501st, the 502nd, the 506th, the 327th Glider Infantry, the airborne artillery, and the others. In England, in Normandy, in Holland, in France the good-natured conviction of each unit that its own soldiers were the best had persisted. However, the various units as a whole considered themselves head and shoulders above the other divisions in the E.T.O.

So when Bastogne was surrounded, and the circle of the defense was manned, not by strangers, but by the "old gang"—the "Hell Raisers" of Newbury and Lambourne and Chilton Foliat and Littlecote and Greenham Common and Carentan and Eindhoven and Nijmegan—and we knew that the rear was protected and the flanks secured by what we considered the only kind of soldiers worth fighting with, the atmosphere in Bastogne became much as it would have been if someone had erected a sign on the highest point of town—*HOME STATION—SCREAMING EAGLES*.

No matter where the Germans attacked around the circle,

the men of the other units could say to themselves: "The Five-O-Deuce is getting it right now," or "Poor Sink. He's having a bad night." They could trust the 502nd or the 506th or any of the others. Those were not regiments a self-respecting 501st man would want to join, naturally (on account of Sink or Michaelis or too much "chicken," or any one of a dozen reasons), but they were a damned sight better regiments than any others in the E.T.O.

The stray units and fragments of units which had stayed to fight with us were not accepted just as additional fire power. By their free decision to remain and fight they were raised to the level of the airborne troops; were given, so to speak, honorary membership in the division. There were no strangers in Bastogne during the siege. Only after the siege had been lifted, and sad-faced, weary infantrymen of the relieving units filed by the hundreds through the ruined streets, did our men, and those who had fought with us, realize what had come to us for a little while and gone, and would never come again.

The day of the 21st was quiet for our regiment. The Germans had decided to abandon the attempt to gain Bastogne through the positions chosen by Colonel Ewell around Bizory, Mont, and Neffe, and were spreading around the town.

McAuliffe, worried by the dwindling supply of ammunition, and still in contact with higher headquarters by radio, asked for air resupply as soon as the weather cleared. He was promised it—*if* the weather cleared. But with the leaden skies over the town, as they had been closed over all of Europe almost without break since early November, there seemed little hope.

Captain Waldmann, working in the chapel hospital, knew that his supply of plasma would last only another day or two. Even by then, in spite of everything that he, Captain Axelrod, Captain Jacobs, and the other medical officers could do, some of the wounded had died. Outside in the courtyard, piled in the trailer of a jeep, were dead soldiers from the line, their bare legs, yellow in color, sticking out from under a frozen canvas cover. Everywhere, things

650

were half-completed or not done at all. As the German shelling grew heavier and heavier, and the third night fell, the American artillerymen within the town counted their ammunition. On the lines the inadequately clothed men fought back strong, continual, probing attacks and counted their own ammunition. The situation at Bastogne that night and the morning of the 22nd was at its lowest ebb.

Around 11:30 in the morning of a dirty gray day—the 22nd—four tiny German figures waded up through the snow on the road from Remoifosse to the American lines. The soldiers of the artillery unit who had dug themselves into fortified positions along that sector drew a bead on the target. But they held their fire. The Germans were carrying a large white flag.

Word passed down through the front lines like an electric shock: the Germans wanted to surrender!

The road from Remoifosse happened to lead to Colonel Harper's medical station. There, to the astounded medics, the German group—a major, a captain, and two enlisted men—reported themselves in crude English and demanded to be taken to the commander of troops in Bastogne. Both officers were arrogant, and it annoyed them to be blindfolded. So Colonel Harper left them at his command post.

On the line many soldiers crawled out of their foxholes, stretched upright in full sight of the Germans across the way, and, for the first time since their arrival, took time to shave. Men of the other sectors were more cautious, but Colonel Harper's men knew they were safe as long as the German emissaries were inside Bastogne. So they relaxed and ate their K rations with legs dangling over the edges of foxholes.

Division headquarters had been set up above and below ground in a series of red-brick storehouses, not unlike garages, where the VIII Corps had had its own headquarters. German artillery shells had been falling on the brick houses at least once an hour. But during the presence of the German intermediaries the morning was still.

Colonel Harper and Major Jones took the surrender message to General McAuliffe. The note read as follows:

"The fortune of war is changing. This time the USA forces in and near Bastogne have been encircled by strong German armored units. More German armored units have crossed the river Ourthe near Ourtheville, have taken Marche and reached St. Hubert by passing through Hompres-Libret-Tillet. Libramont is in German hands.

"There is only one possibility to save the encircled USA troops from total annihilation: that is the honorable surrender of the encircled town. In order to think it over, a term of two hours will be granted beginning with the presentation of this note.

"If this proposal should be rejected, one German artillery corps and six heavy AA Battalions are ready to annihilate the USA troops in and near Bastogne. The order for firing will be given immediately after this two hours' term.

"All the serious civilian losses caused by this artillery fire would not correspond with the well-known American humanity."

And now let Colonel Marshall tell what happened:

McAuliffe asked someone what the paper contained and was told that it requested a surrender.

The General laughed and said, "Aw, nuts!" It really seemed funny to him at the time. He figured he was giving the Germans "one hell of a beating" and that all of his men knew it. The demand was all out of line with the existing situation.

But McAuliffe realized that some kind of reply had to be made and he sat down to think it over. Pencil in hand, he sat there pondering a few minutes and then he remarked, "Well, I don't know what to tell them." He asked the staff what they thought, and Colonel Kinnard, his G-3, replied, "That first remark of yours would be hard to beat."

General McAuliffe didn't understand immediately what Kinnard was referring to. Kinnard reminded him, "You said 'Nuts!' " That drew applause all around. All members of the staff agreed with much enthusiasm and because of their approval McAuliffe decided to send that message back to the Germans.

652

Then he called Colonel Harper in and asked him how he would reply to the message. Harper thought for a minute but before he could compose anything, General Mc-Auliffe gave him the paper on which he had written his one-word reply and asked, "Will you see that it's delivered?"

"I will deliver it myself," answered Harper. "It will be a lot of fun." McAuliffe told him not to go into the German lines.

Colonel Harper returned to the command post of Company F. The two Germans were standing in the wood blindfolded and under guard. Harper said, "I have the American commander's reply."

The German captain asked, "Is it written or verbal?"

"It is written," said Harper. And then he said to the German major, "I will stick it in your hand."

The German captain translated the message. The major then asked: "Is the reply negative or affirmative? If it is the latter I will negotiate further."

All of this time the Germans were acting in an upstage and patronizing manner. Colonel Harper was beginning to lose his temper. He said, "The reply is decidedly not affirmative." Then he added, "If you continue this foolish attack your losses will be tremendous." The major nodded his head.

Harper put the two officers in the jeep and took them back to the main road where the German privates were waiting with the white flag.

He then removed the blindfold and said to them, speaking through the German captain: "If you don't understand what 'nuts' means, in plain English it is the same as 'Go to Hell.' And I will tell you something else—if you continue to attack, we will kill every goddam German that tries to break into this city."

The German major and captain saluted very stiffly. The captain said, "We will kill many Americans. This is war."

"On your way, bud," said Colonel Harper.[2]

The small party of the enemy, carrying their white flag,

[2] From *Bastogne—The First Eight Days,* by Colonel S. L. A. Marshall.

disappeared down the snowy road in the direction of their own lines. The USA troops climbed back into their foxholes.

And the threatened artillery barrage failed to materialize.

Shortage of ammunition, especially for the artillery, was McAuliffe's chief concern. That day the 463rd Field Artillery Battalion had only 200 rounds of ammunition.

McAuliffe passed the word to ration the firing to ten rounds per gun per day. He clarified his order for one artillery commander just before an enemy attack: "If you see 400 Germans in a 100-yard area, and they have their heads up, you can fire artillery on them—but not more than two rounds."

There was food—two boxes of K rations a day per man —but not for long. And the snow was blanketing the lines deeper. Already trench foot had set in.

Not enough maps, not enough ammunition, not enough clothing, not enough plasma, not enough food . . . What *was* there enough of?

Well, there was enough spirit.

And the next morning, after a night of heavy fighting in other sectors, the miracle happened. It was a simple miracle. Yet for a continent where months of winter had already grayed the skies day after day without change and would gray them again solidly for months and months afterwards, leaving only that one small patch of good weather in the dead center of a crisis, it *was* a miracle.

For the skies cleared and the sun came out.

And up from England by the hundreds roared the C-47 supply planes and the fighters—throttles open—destination: Bastogne.

"The fortunes of war are changing. . . ." It was a double-edged phrase.

The sun had not been up an hour before our first American fighter planes appeared. They were cheered by the frozen paratroopers at Mont and Bizory and Neffe and all along the lines—small silver planes which came swiftly from very high up and in a few moments were roaring in

654

circles around the town, a thousand feet above the fox-holes. Men who had gone to sleep in covered positions underground were awakened by the familiar thunderous buffeting of air pressure cause by exploding bombs. Within Bastogne the few windows still unshattered shook and rattled and subsided and then shook again.

Those men who had a good view of the German lines—like Major Pelham, who occupied an observation post in a private farmhouse clearly visible to both sides—could watch the planes dive on some object behind the German positions, then pull up in a fine curve a few hundred feet off the ground, leaving behind, where the bomb struck, a perfectly-formed balloon of orange flame and black smoke which expanded soundlessly, brilliantly, and with spectacular beauty over the dazzling, snow-white hills. Moments later the sound would come.

The noise continued all day. Between the concussions of the exploding bombs we could hear the occasional *"whiff-fisssssss!"* of rockets from the Typhoons—a sound that brought to mind, all in a piece, the golden lines at Eerde and along the Neder Rijn. Close liaison was maintained by radio with the air support around Bastogne, and one infantryman, who reported five German tanks bearing down on his position, had six P-47s darting upon the tanks within a few minutes.

Close to the red-brick buildings which housed division headquarters was a gentle slope of hillside clear of shrubbery or trees. It was concealed from the lines by a higher rise of land beyond. This bare slope, dazzling white with snow in the sun, was selected as the drop zone for the C-47 supply ships. Division S-4, Colonel Kohls, placed Captain Matheson of the 506th and Major Butler of the 501st in charge of the bundle recovery, and notified each regiment to send five jeeps with trailers. Distribution of the parachuted supplies would be made directly from the field.

No hour had been given McAuliffe for the expected arrival of the C-47s. So from the break of dawn on a freezing crystal morning, December 23rd, Butler, Matheson, and the supply officers of the other units, each with a jeep of his own, stamped their feet, blew on their fingers—and

655

waited. The rumor of an air resupply had reached the men on the lines, and, with the Germans virtually immobilized by the daylight bombing, they were having a quiet, cheerful morning. In straw-filled foxholes, dugout command posts, and farmhouses the American soldiers waited.

The first C-47s to reach Bastogne dropped parachutists. They were pathfinders out of England—men who had been called from classes at school several days before, and who had been waiting all this time for clear weather. They landed safely, set up radar sets—refinements of those which had been used in Normandy—and guided the resupply ships to the drop zone.

At 11:50 the planes roared in—241 of them.

What ought to be said is difficult to say. A tribute is an awkward thing. Even the men who felt like waving their arms and yelling did nothing at all except stare up in silence at the roaring planes. Bastogne vibrated with the thunder of American engines. These were the pilots, many of them, who had flown the division to the invasion of Normandy half a year before. They were the men who had been criticized or scorned by the parachutists for taking evasive action under fire—and who had then flown them to Eindhoven and Zon and Eerde and Veghel without mistake.

And now here they were again, the other half of the airborne equation, our young fellow countrymen, the youngest of all soldiers, sweeping in with their olive planes through the clear, blue December sky of Belgium, and low over the snow-covered hills, to resupply—in a town the world was watching—the same old gang.

Crowds of Belgian townspeople emerged from their catacombs under the houses to stare. It was difficult for us not to feel a sentimental pride of country. The equipment parachutes, blossoming over the white field where Butler and the other men waited to receive them, were green and blue and yellow and red—ammunition, plasma, food, gasoline, clothing. . . .

The planes made a circle of the besieged town and then turned away to the north, flying at an altitude of about a thousand feet. Flak had become heavy, but not a single plane took evasive action. The controls of one ship were shot away just as it swept, empty of its parachuted supplies, over the German lines. Its pilot had been gaining altitude. As the bullets struck it, a little wisp of brown smoke gusted out in a faint streak from its tail. Slowly the plane curled upon one wing and nosed down into a vertical dive. The airborne troops who watched, and who had ridden so often in the familiar C-47 cabin, could imagine the scene inside: the two American youngsters struggling with the controls, the cockpit windows showing nothing but up-rushing earth, the instinctive start backwards towards the cabin, and then . . .

A balloon of smoke and fire went up from the earth where the plane fell.

The drop zone was only a mile square. Yet 95 per cent of the 1,446 parachuted bundles were recovered. One hundred and forty-four tons of fresh supplies had come to Bastogne.

So speedily did the supply crews make distribution and load the bundles into jeeps (without stopping to detach the parachutes) that the artillery units were firing the new ammunition before all the bundles on the field had been recovered.

When the second aerial resupply was made, the ammunition shortage was no longer a problem. Gasoline had the lowest priority; since the division was not going anywhere, only 445 gallons were delivered. But food supplies, which had the second highest priority, remained far below the margin for safety, even after the deliveries had been made; the 26,406 K rations that had been dropped were, though impressive in figure, enough to feed the division personnel for only a little more than a day.

McAuliffe authorized foraging.

Troops like to forage, and nobody is better at it than the American soldier. An abandoned corps warehouse yielded 450 pounds of coffee, 600 pounds of sugar, and an equally large amount of Ovaltine. Most of those items were delivered to the aid stations for the use of the wounded. In an abandoned corps bakery, flour, lard, and salt were uncovered, while from a Belgian warehouse came margarine, jam and additional supplies of flour. Also found in the latter storehouse were 2,000 burlap bags. These were sent out to the front lines for the soldiers to use as padding for their feet.

The farms at the outskirts of town yielded potatoes, poultry and cattle, the staples most needed for the men. Because discipline and selflessness were at the highest during the siege, the soldiers who commandeered such items took them back to the kitchens at the regimental command post, instead of roasting or cooking them makeshift on the spot. As a result, the butchered farm animals were skinned and cleaned properly, and the meat was divided evenly among each of the battalion kitchens. It was not uncommon, in those uncommon days, to see the skinned, bloody carcass of a whole cow or a gigantic hog being hosed down by the cooks on the stone floor of the cloister at the regimental C.P., under a blue and gold statue of the Virgin Mary.

Oddly enough, the cooks themselves worked under intermittent shellfire. The glass ceiling of the cloister was also the roof of the building, and shells from the German guns to the northeast sometimes burst among the stone cornices. The KPs were kept busy sweeping away the broken glass. It is a statement of fact that no place in Bastogne could be termed a rear area. After the first German bombing, the town was sometimes more dangerous than the lines.

The fighting that took place on the 23rd and 24th, in different sectors of the all-around defense, was intense. The lines of the 501st Parachute Infantry underwent continual probing attacks by the Germans, especially each nightfall, but after the first two days the Germans had clearly abandoned the costly effort to enter Bastogne over the wide fields of fire which opened from the regimental positions. Division headquarters had no such respite, however, and for every six-hour period in Bastogne there were one or more attempts by the enemy to break through in force. Those who lived within the town seldom guessed how many men were dying in the suburbs to keep the streets empty of all but Americans.

McAuliffe had conceived the expedient of drawing a small reserve from each of the organizations on the line. These reserves were formed into a task force, with armor and tank destroyers, and were used as a mobile support, capable of moving to any sector of the line seriously threatened by an enemy attack. Ewell, copying the plan, created Task Force X, under Captain Frank McKaig and Lieutenant Ernest Fisher, to support his own battalions. For some reason, the Germans never attacked simultaneously on all sectors of the perimeter defense, so the mobile task forces were an effective device.

Approximately 2,000 civilian inhabitants of Bastogne remained in the town during the siege. They lived underground in mass shelters, one beneath a convent in the center of the town, another beneath the regimental command post. A few lived under their own houses. Those who lived in the great cellars of the two convents dwelt in conditions of indescribable filth. Old men, too crippled to move, sat in chairs at the side and stared into the darkness; young children crawled about the cement floors; men and women lay together on rough blankets or piles of burlap. At the regimental command post, this condition became such a threat to the health of the soldiers that at length certain male civilians were assigned the task of policing their own shelters and, under shellfire, of emptying the refuse outside.

An interesting, though rather ugly sidelight of life in Bastogne during the siege was the impossibility of digging slit trenches or making other arrangements for field sanitation. A large privy was dug in the courtyard outside the regimental command post, but because that area was under constant shellfire, few of the men would use it. In the beginning they utilized a large indoor latrine obviously built for school children. However, the plumbing froze after the first day; so in time the place was boarded up. From then on, at all hours of the day and night, soldiers could be found searching for unused toilets through the smaller rooms upstairs in the seminary.

The days and nights were bitter cold. Ewell authorized his men to wear whatever would keep them warm. That no loss of discipline occurred during the resultant individualism was a tribute to the discipline already ingrained in the troops. A few hours after the word had gone around, many soldiers appeared in civilian sweaters, crude blouses of parachute silk, and Belgian winter caps. One officer wore a Canadian combat jacket which he had saved from Holland. An enlisted man appeared at the command post in an army blanket, with holes cut for his arms and a rope binding it about his waist. He was the personification of the Sad Sack, but no one seeing the stubble of beard on his chin, the lines of weariness around his eyes, the tight, humorless slit of his mouth and the dirty hands cracked from exposure, gripping the one clean thing in his possession—his rifle—could have smiled.

The parachutes recovered from the equipment bundles were used to cover the wounded men. The command post personnel donated their blankets to the men on the line. Every civilian sheet and blanket in town had already been collected and put to use. Also every bottle of liquor.

On the afternoon of December 23rd, word came to Bastogne that Patton's armor was fighting its way to the besieged town. If luck held, Patton—with the division commander, General Taylor, in the vanguard—would reach Bastogne by Christmas Day.

Early in the evening of December 23rd, just after the winter darkness had fallen and a brilliant three-quarter moon lighted the snow-bound little town with a blue glare, Chaplain Engels, Lieutenant Peter Frank, Sergeant Schwartz and Sergeant Harvey were having a premature Christmas dinner in the second-floor apartment of the prisoner-of-war team, across the street from the regimental command post.

The chaplain had just come in from the lines, where the night was almost as quiet as it was in town. In the blacked-out, rickety apartment there were light and warmth. Lieutenant Frank, a Viennese by birth and an American by choice, had a flair for entertainment. He had set the supper table with linen, silver, wine glasses, plates, and candles—all (except the seminary candles) borrowed from the aban-

660

doned supplies of the house. Three bottles of looted wine were open on the sideboard; a stock of good Belgian cigars had been set out, and in the frying pan on the stove was steak, a gift from Chaplain Engels.

In half an hour the party had become merry and mellow. It is traditional with soldiers to feel more and more immortal as the wine is drained, and, the more immortal they feel, the more they toast each other's imminent death: this must be the root of that brooding melancholy which characterizes so many drinking songs. The officers and men toasted one another's distant wives and sweethearts, departed friends, and one another's lives and imminent deaths; they all toasted, in the old, old manner, confusion to their enemies.

"Gentlemen," announced Lieutenant Frank, "the Queen."

Everyone rose.

"Stalin," proposed Sergeant Schwartz.

"General Ike."

Glasses clinked.

"Benes . . ."

"McAuliffe . . ."

"Lady Macbeth . . ."

When the dinner was over and cigars had been handed around, the group, with Lieutenant Frank at the piano, sang Christmas carols.

They were midway through *Silent Night* when a buffeting of air pressure shook the floors and rattled the windows.

"Somebody's getting bombed," said Frank, pausing.

"Go on, Lootenant," said Harvey, " 'sh probably Berlin."

But a moment later a soldier put his head in the door. "German planes," he announced. "They're bombing the town."

There was a little silence. Then Frank said: "The hell with it. I'm staying here."

"Of course," said the chaplain, lighting a cigar.

But the next bomb exploded with such violence that one of the windows burst inward. The floors wobbled and shook. Plaster fell. Rushing to the door, the chaplain shouted the time-honored battle-cry of the infantry school—"FOLLOW ME!"—and fell head-over-heels downstairs.

The first bombs were dropped uptown in the vicinity of

661

a railroad overpass near division headquarters. An aid station was hit, killing most of the men and, with them, a Belgian girl who had volunteered to work as a nurse. Other bombs then struck the houses on the square below division headquarters, bracketing the group of shelters where the Belgian citizens had taken refuge and demolishing a memorial statue to the Belgian dead of World War I. One bomb had struck only fifty feet from the command post.

Another bomb tore through two floors of the command post itself and lodged—unexploded—in the ceiling of a potato cellar.

The force of aerial-bomb explosions defies description. Soldiers in Bastogne that night could tell by the rattle of anti-aircraft fire whenever the planes were coming to dive down. The small-arms fire always grew heavier as the plane reached the bomb-release point of its dive: this crescendo of noise had the same effect on the nervous system as a crescendo of drums. When the plane had swept by, the firing ceased, and then everyone knew that the bomb was on its way. Conversation ceased. Sometimes we could hear the high, whistling flutter of the descending projectile, and then death was very close.

Fires burned later in the town that night. Out on the lines, one or two of the battalion command posts had had near misses, but no one had been injured. Desolation gripped the upper regions of the town, however, and when the fires burned themselves out, only the charred skeleton of buildings remained around the main square. Bastogne, which had been untouched when the troops moved in, wore that ghastly air of desolation which had come to so many European towns in the war. In the still night a man walking past the ruins could smell the sickly-sweet odor of the untended dead.

This was Christmas, 1944.

Into the Reich

The day after Christmas, the first men from the 4th Armored Division drove into the lines of Bastogne; now it would be only a matter of hours before full reinforcements and supplies were rolling in. However, the 101st Airborne was not relieved; they were needed in Bastogne, now part of the front lines, and there they would stay until January 19th.

And now the bad weather, which had grounded the air forces during the whole breakthrough, lifted on December 25th; from then on the Allied air forces flew round-the-clock missions, smashing at the supply convoys and troop columns moving up. Weather continued good long enough for the Allies to force the Germans to keep pulling back their supply lines, to keep moving their rail assembly centers farther and farther back to escape bombing and strafing.

The Germans had gotten to within four miles of the Meuse River, but by the end of January the Allies had pushed them back to their original line of departure.

The Ardennes campaign was the last desperate convulsion of the Wehrmacht in the west; while the campaign delayed the end of the war, it cost the Germans tremendous losses in manpower and supplies. It also brought about a real crack in the shaky façade of the Allied Field Command. When the Germans drove their salient into the 1st Army, elements were split off to the north in Montgomery's sector; Hodges, commanding these elements, had little communication with Bradley. In the early stages of the breakthrough, Eisenhower decided the northern elements of the 1st and 9th Armies might be better attached to the command of Montgomery. This infuriated Bradley, and he told Eisenhower he would refuse to accept such an order, preferring to resign his command.

Bradley, incidentally, contends the tide had already been turned against the Germans before Montgomery committed British troops to action. Wilmot defends Montgomery—he was on his staff during the European campaign—by describing his strategy as waiting for the Germans to exhaust themselves in their drive. He assumed they were trying to reach Liége, he knew he was ranged in position to prevent its cap-

663

ture; Montgomery wasn't devoted to the American theory of constant offense as the best defense. Montgomery frequently delayed attack until he was sure he had the advantage.

With the Germans back to their original starting line by the end of January, SHAEF devised the following strategy: in the north, Montgomery was to strike across the Rhine and head for the Ruhr, the 1st Canadian Army attacking through the Reichswald Forest, and the 9th U.S. Army crossing the Roer River to join up with the Canadians. The 1st and 3rd U.S. Armies were also to strike for the Rhine in the south, but were not to cross over until Montgomery could also cross. Farther south, part of the 3rd Army and the American 7th Army were to hammer at the approaches to the Siegfried Line in an effort to break into the Saar, and push on as far as possible with an eye to an eventual envelopment of the Ruhr from the south. Predictably enough, conflict developed between Bradley and Montgomery once more. The Americans now had more divisions committed to the fighting than the British, and while Bradley and Patton accepted the strategy of Montgomery's striking from the north, they resented having to hold their own striking power until Montgomery had moved across the Rhine. In addition, the 9th Army was to remain under the command of Montgomery for this operation, and Eisenhower suggested that several divisions of the 1st Army might also be transferred to Montgomery, if his drive was successful.

Bradley and Patton agreed that if any more divisions went up to Montgomery, they'd never get them back, and so they decided to conduct an "aggressive defense." Montgomery's attack on Germany's Rhineland began on February 8th, when the 1st Canadian Army attacked the Reichswald. The Siegfried Line had been prepared as a major defense along the borders of Germany, but its line of fortifications didn't reach to the Reichswald, although the Germans had had time to prepare and utilize the forest's natural defenses. As in the Huertgen Forest, the Reichswald was the scene of bitter fighting. The Germans were able to throw in strong reinforcements here because they had let out the dams to raise the level of the Roer River, which would keep the American 9th Army from crossing the Roer to join the Canadians for two weeks.

The following selection from Lance-Cpl. R. M. Wingfield's *The Only Way Out* records his personal experience in the Queen's Royal Regiment of the 7th Armored Division, which fought its way through the Reichswald. Perhaps no other selection makes so vivid the dilemma of the infantryman—"*the only way out of the infantry is on a stretcher, or six feet under.*"

664

"HIDE AND SEEK" IN THE REICHSWALD

by Lance-Cpl. R. M. Wingfield

We waited on our start-line just inside the Reichswald. For the last few days we had had a very quiet time,
the pleasant glades of the woods affording welcome peace
and rest, apart from a few stray bullets from keen Canadian
rabbit-hunters on our left.

Knowing Jerry as we did and the heavy casualties suffered by the Canadians, we realized that this quiet was
suspicious. We were on edge, all dressed up for battle and
nowhere to go. Two hours after we left, Jerry blew our part
of the Reichswald to hell.

We breakfasted on "Armoured Pig" and "Armoured
Dog." Pausing only to spit the "Yellow Peril" Vitamin C
pills on to the growing pile round the corner from the cookhouse, we moved off.

The first German village we came to slowed down the advance. There were no snipers or mines, but an enemy village, the first we'd seen, was strange. Mostly from sheer
curiosity, we examined and searched each house in the local
Josef Goebbelsstrasse. Outside the village a farm was on fire
and a poor old lady was trying, single-handed, to round up
the panicky animals, the tears rolling down her old cheeks.
Fraternization ban or no, our lads couldn't bear to see the
old and weak in trouble. We trundled all the animals into a
barn and slung some hay in with them. As we marched off
down the road a quavering cry followed us.

"Danke! Danke!"

Now we moved into an entrenched knoll at the top of a
road gradient to await further orders to advance. In an end-

This selection is condensed from the author's *The Only Way
Out.*

less stream on the road passed section after section of Canadians of the Princess Patricia's Light Infantry. We could see them marching slowly and steadily down the road to Goch. This road stretched straight in front, a finger pointing into the heart of the German defences. Jerry tried to blast that road off the map. A dusty cloud flashed and puffed among the marching blobs. A section which had passed us jauntily ten minutes before vanished. The other blobs moved on steadily, passed into the drifting smoke and reappeared on the other side, never faltering. Another puff of smoke, this time much nearer, dirty yellow High-Explosive at its heart, appeared on the road in the middle of a section. The section fell apart like skittles. The survivors got to their feet. They moved on.

Now it was our turn to run the gauntlet. Once we hit the road we spaced out automatically. We reached the crater of the first shell. The hedge was spattered with strips of flesh and uniform. A white enamel mug danced pathetically on a windy branch.

Now we advanced cautiously through the town of Udem. The streets were choked with rubble and splintered timber. Our tanks slowly ground their way up and over the debris of homes, spraying before them with Besa. Snipers in the rubble bounced bullets off the tanks and some ricocheted near us. We left the cover of the tanks and took our chance in the open, dodging from cover to cover in the rubble. The tanks thrashed up clouds of dust and their steel bodies ploughed through a smoky, choking fog. Sniper fire turned from the fruitless task of trying to pierce the tanks half-hidden in the dust, and sought out the units following us. The old, chilling cry of "Stretcher-bearer!" echoed along what had been streets.

One sniper was spotted in the circular window of a church. A tank spat Besa fire at the wall. Puffs of dust spouted, moving steadily, inexorably up the building, inch by inch, flaming, leaping, leaden death. The sniper crouching in the circle was blasted to his feet, danced a jig on the bullets and slowly tilted and fell headlong, sprawling across the rubble.

He was soon avenged. A *"Panzerfaust,"* the German in-

666

fantry anti-tank weapon like a flying gas-lamp, wobbled through the air and smashed into the back of the turret. Brown smoke gushed up from the turret and down the gun barrel, which drooped down lifeless. From the smoke the tank-commander spilled out of the turret. He was alone. We climbed up and dragged him from the smouldering steel. He wasn't injured, just dazed. We climbed up once more to rescue the others, but were stopped by a feeble cry from the commander.

"The rest have had it."

Tongues of flame came from the hatch. We backed away quickly and hit the ground as the tank "brewed up" with a muffled roar. Soon it was a mass of flame, rocked by the ammunition exploding inside the white-hot hull. A bursting shell blew the front away and we could see, silhouetted in the spitting flame, the driver sitting at his post, the hair on the back of the hands slowly burning.

"Let's get out!"

We did.

That night we dug in round the tanks against a glowing back-cloth of burning tanks and homes. We patrolled to flush any snipers. None of our troops was in the town, so we shot at anything that moved.

We waited. The tanks stood silent. Dawn came. The sun climbed. The morning was warm with a slight breeze—a nice day to die. The day's work was to advance still further to the Hochwald Forest. From Maas to Rhine the Germans had dug a huge anti-tank ditch. We had to capture and breach it.

Our tanks started up and we climbed aboard. This put us six feet off the ground, but we had to give the Jerry snipers a sporting chance after their splendid but vain efforts to penetrate the tanks. We stood there, shuffling and stamping our feet impatiently. No one spoke.

Finally we moved off to the open fields, swerved off the road into the country and on again. Immediately a Spandau burst bounced off the tanks. So did we. I heard the crack overhead and listened for the thump which always echoed from the gun itself. Got it! That clump of bushes! I told one of my riflemen to put five rounds of tracer into it. The other

667

two section-commanders did the same. The criss-cross rounds signalled the target to our three tanks. They heeled as they turned and hosed the scrub with their three Besas. The bushes jerked and shook beneath the leaden flail. The machine-gun stopped.

We crept on, keeping to the hedges. To our right a farmhouse went on fire. From the blazing building spilled German Infantry, hands clasped behind their necks. One man came out by himself, a S.S. man, a leaping, hammering Schmeisser at his hip. He ran for a hayrick. Besa tracer stitched the air behind him. The earth at his heels boiled with dust. Now the Besa hit him and threw him into the haystack, which immediately "brewed up." The Besa cut off. Two German and two British Infantrymen rushed to save him. The heat was too great.

I got to my feet and my section followed me. We skirted the potato clamp cautiously. By now the smoke had drifted away. The fins of the smoke bomb stuck up from the ground. Standing on its head against the clamp was a German corpse. There was no trace of anyone else, just half a steel helmet lying by the two scorched divots of the bomb and grenade. We passed hurriedly. Ahead, up a slight gradient four hundred yards in front of us, was the anti-tank ditch.

There was someone in there.

We lay down to regroup. All was ready. There was only one thing left to do. No one wanted to give the order. I gulped and, turning to my section, shouted, "Fix bayonets!" That seemed to bring us all to life. I heard the nasty snick of the bayonets locking home. I pulled out the "Safety" of my Sten and stood up. Men to right and left stood up.

No one moved. We all stared at the ditch ahead. This was a bayonet charge. We had practised it before, stupid men in training trying to raise an empty scream while prodding a sandbag. This was no practice. It was the dread problem of "Him or Me," that problem which had never arisen yet and which we assumed would never arise. These men in the ditch were not going to give up easily. Oh God, let it be *him!*

I fingered my Sten, looked to right and left and set off at

a rapid walk. I glanced at my mate "Smoky" on my right. He licked his lips, grinned a dead grin and closed me to bring me under the protection of his bayonet. I should have to spray with my Sten and hope for the best.

The alignment was all to hell. I was leading an arrowhead. We broke into a trot, a run, a mad charge, screaming, yelling. One hundred yards away the lip of the ditch was lined with waving bits of white paper.

"So you're trying to pack up now, you bastards! It's too bloody late!" we roared and swept on. I sprayed a burst at the paper. It went down. Fifty yards . . . forty yards . . . thirty . . . twenty . . . and, with a wild yell, I was over and in.

The trench was ten feet deep. I hit the bottom with a crash and saw grey-green figures. I squeezed the trigger. Oh, God! A jam! Before I could shake out the cartridge a voice said:

"What the fornication do you lot think you're doing?"

We had charged our own "B" Company with an assortment of Germans varying from very dead to petrified with fright.

The next ten minutes, with the bubble of fear pricked, were spent in mutual recriminations, curses and remarks on the Higher Authority's ancestry. There might have been serious casualties, casualties which would have been unnecessary. Some stupid bastard had blundered. It was a bloody miracle we won the war when nobody knew where the hell anybody else was half the time.

In the middle of the curses and attempts to regroup, Jerry Defensive Fire came down. We hit the ground, "B," "D" and the German prisoners in a hopeless jumble. The gunnery was, fortunately, of a low standard as no shells came in among us. One straggler on the edge of the ditch was hit in the shoulder as he dived into the trench, rolling to the bottom in a shower of earth and stones. We bandaged him as neatly as we could. He didn't seem too bad, so we said how much we envied him, wrapped him in his gas-cape to prevent shock and gave him a cigarette. From the smile on his face we gathered that "Jack" was certainly All Right.

The barrage stopped.

That seemed to be the lot for the time being. We consolidated. I helped to booby-trap the trench with trip-flares and the inevitable tin cans. Two men took the only casualty to the Regimental Aid Post. We watched him go with envious eyes. The C.S.M. came round with the mail. The letters and parcels thumped unheeded on the ground. We were too busy doing the essential job—digging in. Slowly the trenches were dug out. The earth piled up on each side. The swinging shoulders and spades sank below the surface. Soon the trenches were dug and their parapets beaten flat. We replaced the turf as camouflage. The Bren was in the centre so that it could fire each side to protect the rest of the section and platoon. Grenades and clips of ammunition stood ready on the parapets. One at a time the men of the section went up and left their Bren mags with the gun. I stood my Sten magazines on the lips of the trench, open ends upwards, bullets pointing away. With one movement I could load and fire. I set to work with the cumbersome magazine filler to replace the burst I had given the German soil. There was only one round left in. I must have blazed off twenty-six rounds in my fright and fury!

The first shell came over as we settled down after the usual "stand-to." Everything happened at once. The shell's slathering scream came quickly, then the explosion, followed by the fluttering scythe of shrapnel. 88! My platoon was dug in well. Quickly I went the round of my section positions to see if they had enough food and cigarettes to last the night if the shelling persisted.

"Right, it seems to me as if Jerry's pulling out, but—take no chances! If and when the stonk stops, up with your weapons and all-round defence! That's when they start counter-attacks!"

I completed my round and dropped back into my trench. Smoky sat at the other end, his knees drawn up to his chin. His face would have made an interesting subject for a painter of the "Chiaroscuro" School. Each rising and falling circle of red from his cigarette showed a youthful face leaning on the dark wood of the rifle, a face streaked with dirt and sweat. The eyes were tired but calm, reflecting the quick

"Laugh and to Hell" resilience of the young. There was no trace of the introspective, brooding stare of the older members of the platoon. Maybe the Army *did* know what it was doing in ensuring a majority of youngsters in combat Battalions.

"Think they're pulling out, Corp?"

"Maybe! This stonk seems the usual racket, but if the barrage starts creeping that means trouble!"

Suddenly there flashed through my mind the warning in the sound-track of a "School of Infantry" film—"*Never* use an enemy's slit-trench and *never* dig near a prominent feature—Jerry's probably got it 'zeroed' for mortars!"

God! What a bloody fool I was! The slit-trenches of my section were all sited—by me—within fifteen yards of the anti-tank ditch! My own was within six feet! This was a hell of a time to remember! Too late to worry now. I had done the best I could think of at the time. The anti-tank ditch was well booby-trapped and it was unlikely that Jerry would start anything with the barrage still going strong.

The barrage slackened.

"O.K. Watch it!" I was pleased to see the speed with which those lads were up. These veterans of nineteen were no mugs. The barrage intensified.

A quavering voice from somewhere up on the earth began to sob, "Forty-two . . . Forty-three . . . Forty-four" with a shell-burst punctuating each number.

I shouted: "Stop that! The man in the trench with him—talk to him, tickle him, kick him, clock him—anything!—but stop him counting! He'll go bomb-happy!"

The noise stopped abruptly.

"How did you manage him?"

"Winded him! He's O.K. now."

"Right! Watch him!"

The shelling, with its monotonous beat, drugged us to silence. I sat, five feet down in the earth, staring—at nothing. The Sten, standing upright between my knees, shook with each concussion. I gripped it for something solid to cling to. A shell burst within a few feet and I looked up. In the bright flash I saw a small blade of grass on the edge of the trench, nodding gently in the steel breeze. I watched it, fascinated. "You're too small to be hit!" At that moment there was a thud and glow as a white-hot piece of shrapnel plunked into the wall of the trench and glared at me. I looked up. The grass was gone. Oh God! I turned on my side and tried to get my head lower. Many was the time that I'd wished the head and its brain Telephone Exchange were in the middle of the body to dodge high-flying bullets and shrapnel. Still, it would probably have been mangled by a mine, so what was the use of worrying.

My brain suddenly clicked back to the grass. The poor little piece of grass which points to *me* has gone. They'll never find my grave. *Grave!* I must snap out of it! Be *calm*, be *logical! Think! Think!* You're snug in the bullet-proof earth. You're safe in a trench four foot six down, two feet across and six feet long—just the dimensions of a grave! Shut up, you bloody fool! Think! *Think!* These are shells, not mortars! Their trajectory is almost horizontal, not vertical! They can't get you. Remember the bloke in "B"? He got a mortar bomb in with him. The bomb burst upwards and outwards. He was all right, I tell you, *all right!*

I settled down again. The shelling continued. I had a mad desire to get out and walk about in the night air. The shells wouldn't hurt me if I turned sideways. I imagined that I would be able to dodge the shrapnel as I tried to dodge raindrops as a child. Wouldn't it be better to nip up top and get "the chop" quickly and cleanly instead of having to face hell day after day! week after week—if you lasted a week? Don't be a fool, shrapnel's jagged. It would hurt like hell!

We slowly stood up. Our heads mounted into the dawn. It was a dreadful spectacle which met our eyes. The platoon area, no bigger than an average soccer pitch, was pitted with craters, interwoven, crumbling. Someone counted them. Over three hundred. I waited for the heads to rise from the earth.

No one was hurt.

It was a miracle.

We moved like automata back from the ditch and down the slope. We dug in to avoid any more shells and to silhouette the ditch and any attackers. The trenches were finally dug. We breakfasted. I don't remember what we had. No one else did either. I can remember drinking tea, but I don't know where it came from. That tea was the first thing we recognized in life. We were still awfully vague and dazed. We shaved. The wind, whipping the smooth cheeks, stung us to life. The shave wiped out the night's ordeal.

Throughout the day we waited. A runner came.

"Section-commanders to 'O' Group!"

"The Monmouths have bumped it again. They always do. The survivors are hanging on by their eyebrows. Some Companies are down to a dozen. They are approximately two miles to the west of us. We are passing through them at dusk. The plan is this. First, four flail tanks of 79th Armoured will clear the mines. We shall travel on tanks behind them, 'D' Company leading the Battalion, 18 Platoon leading the Company. Two hundred yards from the ditch, the flails will turn left and right and demine the approaches. The Infantry will get off the tanks and fan out into the fields. They will then advance to the ditch, which they will hold till the Engineers' Fascine tanks fill it in—then, back on to the tanks and keep going! The Yanks aren't very far away and Jerry is being heavily squeezed. Defensive Fire is expected to be heavy. (Much later we discovered that Jerry had 1,054 guns in the area.) Everyone to be as quiet as possible. Check ammo and food. Pull out of your present positions one hour before dusk and report here to Company H.Q. You will be taken by guides to the 15th/19th Hussars, who, as usual, will be our playmates. Off you go!"

We dispersed to pass on the information.

The comments in my section were very sarcastic.

" 'All ranks to be as quiet as possible'—with twenty-four bloody great roaring Cromwells, not counting those flail tanks with their bashing chains!"

"Usual muck-up! Why the hell can't we go over the part of the ditch we've captured here and take the bastards from the rear?"

"Steady on, mate, that'd be too easy. We might win the war, and that'd never do!"

"Think of it. A night attack with tanks. Those bastards are blind enough in daylight!"

"Cor! It'll be murder!" How right he was!

The hour of waiting was dreadful. We tried to occupy our time. We tried not to think. We all had premonition of trouble—big trouble. Our weapons were ready. We retested them. There was nothing to do. We talked. We smoked. The minutes ticked away. There was nothing to do. We looked to the west. We could see nothing. We could hear nothing.

A whistle blew from Company H.Q. Here we go! We put on our packs. The dry click of the metal buckles was the only sound. We moved back slowly, suddenly frightened of the ditch when we were to leave it. Any minute Germans might straddle the skyline.

"Don't worry, mates, we've got it covered," said a voice from behind. An evil-looking Vickers pointed from the scrub.

The light faded. Our feet moved automatically, left, right, left, right, winding through the wood. Our enemy was the weight of the pack, the stifling closeness of the pine forest, the unknown danger we had coming to us.

We came into a clearing. Stopped and silent lay the Cromwells, the crews sitting by the turrets, their boots tapping uneasily on the tracks. We moved past the sinister booms of the flails, their chains dangling lifeless, down the boom arm to the squat, steel boxes and on to the first Cromwell.

"O.K. Rex! Your section on that one!" God! We're the first in! We gingerly climbed aboard and settled with our backs to the warm exhaust-chute. The clatter of boots climbing on to the tracks and so to the armoured hulls faded down the line as the rest of the Battalion embarked.

We waited.

We waited a whole ruddy hour. By this time our bladders, distended by the tea and fear, were screaming to be let out. I asked for permission to dismount. No! We sprayed the surrounding area. We were easy.

We waited.

A faint squealing came from the interior of the tank. The Wireless Op. slowly got to his feet and climbed reluctantly into the turret.

"Move in five minutes!" The voice came hollow from the turret.

The rest of the crew came to life and climbed inside.

"Start up!"

A whine, a thunderous cough, and the tank trembled as the Merlin engine fought its way to full power.

From up front there came a deep roar and a clashing of whipping chains as the flails ground forward. We jerked back. We were off.

The night roared and snarled with the engines. Dust came back in choking clouds. We swayed and rolled on the pulverized track. My section moved up to the turret and held on to its solid, comforting coldness. . . . The tank-commander put his head out.

"Happy?" A chorus of groans greeted him.

"Rather you than me, mates!"

Yet we felt much safer than the tank crew behind their armour. An Infantryman may be more vulnerable, but he's a darned sight more mobile.

The tank column slowed and stopped.

"How's it going, mates?" asked a voice from below. We peered over the side of the hull. Two pale faces seemed to be resting on the ground. We shouted down from our height.

"You the Monmouths?"

"Yes."

"Had a good time?"

"Bloody awful, mates. We've been stonked and machine-gunned to hell. I think we're the only two left from our platoon. Didn't think we'd last out till you got here. I've never been so glad to see the dark. It's been very quiet for the last hour. You know what sort of quietness I mean. Best of luck, mates. You'll need it!"

We lurched on and stopped again.

The night was blasted by a sudden purple flash. The flails vanished in a roaring cataract of flame. I don't know to this day why they blew up. We had heard no shells.

I found myself with my section in a field twenty yards away. I don't remember getting off the tank. Our tank, stung to fury, blazed away with Besa tracer. The glowing beads sprayed at the trees, struck and whirled off, moved slowly left and right, up and down, blasting the whole of

675

the front of the wood. We lay there with our weapons ready and pointing at the trees which leaped and dropped in the glare of the blazing flails. From our right a lazy burst of tracer sailed, a hundred feet up, over our heads. My Bren-gunner rose to his knees and hammered back.

Simultaneous with the last round of the Bren burst, I felt a searing pain start at my left hip, flash across and numb my right thigh. There was a shout to my left and the dull burst of a "36" grenade.

Then I knew.

"Christ! I've been hit!" I panicked. I'd been hit internally, so I should be bleeding from the mouth. I coughed into my hand. It was dry. Thank God! I felt better.

It was puzzling. I'd been hit all right, but apart from the first burning slash it wasn't too bad. I felt perfectly O.K. I was disappointed. No mortal agony, no frenzied writhing and no shattering pain churning my body.

A thump by my side and Smoky was there.

"Where've you been hit, Corp?"

"In the guts."

"Can you move?"

"I don't know. I'll try."

I tried to move my legs but my thighs and legs wouldn't respond. Oh, God! I'm paralyzed!

Smoky sat up, and once more I heard that chilling sound echoing, picked up and relayed into the distance:

"Stretcher-bearers!" Only this time it was for me.

I hoped that I would soon be out of it, and appealed to passing shadows to send the Medics when they could. All the figures were moving forward. All of them showed a morbid interest in where I'd been hit. To my shame, I found myself answering very proudly. I was the great hero. I'd been hit. They all told me how lucky I was. I suddenly realized that there would be no more battle for me. I felt fine.

Now I tried to move, with Smoky helping me. Each time I levered myself up, a pain shot through my guts. I still had no right thigh. I tried to remain calm and take stock of my position. I couldn't move. I was prone on the ground, so I should be safe from any more damage. Then I suddenly realized that I'd been hit when lying on the ground. Next

676

time anyone said, "When in doubt, fall flat," I'd have something to say to them!

The greatest danger from wounds was shock. "Keep the patient warm," the book said. I rolled on to my back and unclasped my belt. A surge of warmth flooded through my abdomen and thighs. My right leg came back to me. I thought that it was only a temporary cramp which had attacked me and I tried to stand. The pain started at my abdomen and welled up over my body to my head and armpits. I felt sick. I lay down again, took my gas-cape off my belt, put it on and re-buckled the belt. The pain abated. So, in some way, my belt was acting as a partial tourniquet. I still didn't know what had hit me or where it came from. I had seen nothing.

A curious silence had fallen since I had been hit. It was broken by a sound from my left—a bubbly, heavy breathing which got hoarsely stronger and stronger—and stopped. Someone else had gone. A figure crawled across.

"Fred's had it! Hit through the lungs. What hit you, Corp?"

"I don't know."

"Maybe it was the machine-gun over by us. Just before Fred stopped his he'd slung in a grenade. It cut short a burst—but that burst got him."

A curious mutter arose from the ground and swelled to a shout—a pleading, cursing hubbub.

"They're leaving us! Come back, you cowardly bastards!"

The tanks were withdrawing. With them went our hopes, our prayers. The tanks moved slowly back, hosing the woods. Tracer faded and cut out. The last spinning burst ebbed and died and the tanks were gone. Their motors turned to a distant hum.

All around voices came from the darkness, discussing, despairing. Slowly, painfully, I crawled over to a dark mound on my right to draw comfort from a fellow sufferer. Smoky came with me.

"Pretty bloody, isn't it, mate?" No answer.

"I said, 'Pretty bloody, isn't it, mate?' "

Smoky touched the figure and recoiled. I didn't see his face. I wish I had. The man was staring straight ahead, his rifle gripped in his hands. He still said nothing. I moved round to his front and peered at his face. The pale forehead was stitched with four neat black holes.

"Get me out, Smoky, for God's sake!" I moved, half-crawling, half-carried by Smoky. I shivered and was sick.

Mere figures moved through us, another Company going forward. Suddenly tracer began to spray the area, probing towards the shadowy men. Some of them dived flat. One was late. The tracer vanished into the cardboard carton of P.I.A.T. bombs on his back. A split second of silence followed, then the most appalling crash and blossom of flame. I tucked my head to the ground, and round the edges of the steel helmet I felt the hot blast of the explosion hit my shoulders. Each of these six bombs could blow a hole in a tank. A body hit the ground heavily.

"Christ!" it said.

A miracle had happened. The man was only bruised by his long fall. There wasn't even a scorch on his battle-dress! Another man with him swore that he'd seen a blob sailing up in the air, turning over and over.

The man stumbled on.

A scuffing of boots sounded in the grass and a figure knelt by me—one of the Medics from Battalion H.Q. We recognized each other.

"Where have you got it?"

I tried to tell him with as much accuracy as possible. By the light of a blue shaded lamp he wrote my name, number, Company and where I thought I'd been hit.

"Do you want any morphia?"

"No, thanks. It doesn't hurt."

"Right! I'll take this back to the M.O. so that he knows what wounds to prepare for. We'll be back for you in half an hour."

"What's the time?"

"About nine o'clock." I'd been there for two hours already.

I turned to Smoky.

"Looks as though you can get moving. I'll be O.K. now! Thanks, mate, for staying with me."

"That's O.K., mate. You'd have done the same for me."

678

I would. "I'll try to see you again before they move you any further back." He moved away and his shadowy figure advanced to be lost in the wood.

I felt thirsty and tried to get at my water-bottle, but it was just too far away. The stretcher-bearer came back, looked at me, and without saying a word, took my Sten, dismantled it and threw the pieces away.

God! He thought I might commit suicide. Still, I suppose some people in their despair might do it. I had too much to live for. I also hadn't the guts.

"Don't drink," he said and walked away.

I didn't try to drink. I wondered whether it would be safe to suck a boiled sweet. Better not. It would be suicide to light a cigarette. Throughout the time since I had been wounded I had been mentally alert and I decided to try an experiment.

Many times I had heard that, in moments of danger, psychic messages could be sent to near ones. I concentrated very hard and tried to tell my mother that I had been hit. She heard me. There is no explanation.

There is also no explanation for the dreadful dream I had in Ypres.

I woke up one morning at two o'clock screaming. My mate asked me what was wrong. I dreamed that we had attacked a house. The Sergeant kicked the door open, threw in a grenade, and slammed the door. The grenade burst. The Sergeant kicked the door open again and dived flat. A machine-gun opened up and seven bullets hit me in the throat. I woke up screaming.

Two months later we attacked a house—*the house*. I was quite powerless to act. I was going to die and I couldn't do a thing about it. The Sergeant kicked the door open, threw in a grenade and slammed the door. The grenade burst. The Sergeant kicked the door open again and dived flat. So did I. The man behind me was hit seven times in the throat. The Sergeant killed the gunner.

In front I heard a sharp whistle, rapidly approaching, and over it went! The shell burst half a mile behind. I had been afraid of that. Defensive Fire, cunningly directed, was plunging into our supply route and rear areas. The stretcher-bearers wouldn't get through that lot. A universal groan from the other wounded told me that others had thought of that too. Patience! Patience!

The barrage moved slowly from the rear area. It was moving backwards and we were in the way. Now the shells burst among us, threaded their way back again and settled to a steady beat one hundred yards behind me. Our escape route to the rear was gone. We could only go forward.

The shelling stopped and figures appeared on the edge of the wood, coming towards us.

Counter-attack!

We could only play dead and pray. The men moved carefully between us.

"*Tot!*" said a voice.

Several things happened at once. At that moment a Vickers cut loose from behind. The tracers flared three feet overhead, stopped and went on again—but the beat of the gun hadn't stopped. One of the men's boots was right by my head when the burst started. A horrid sound, midway between a cough and a belch, and a body fell heavily across my legs, quivered, thrashed and lay still. His Schmeisser toppled across my shoulders, clouting me over the ear.

The Vickers stopped. There was a sound of running, weaving, dodging feet as the counter-attack melted back to the wood. A green Very light spun up the sky, poised, and fell. The shell storm burst with renewed fury. The counter-attack had failed. Jerry was pulling out. It was a question of waiting.

I wriggled clear of my burden. The night wore on.

Another danger came. Our own counter-barrage sparkled and crashed amid the woods. In its bright glow we saw branches chopped down and whirled away.

Then it happened. Our barrage corrected itself at the anti-tank ditch and slowly walked back—and back—*and back!* Thirty yards ahead a wounded man cried out. There was a cut-off scream as the body changed to a smoking crater. A steel helmet bowled off into the darkness.

God! Please, God! No more! *No more!* Save my miserable skin! I tried to deceive God that I was pleading for my family's sake. *He* knew better. So did I. The next shell

680

bloomed ten yards ahead of me. Its scorching heat hit my shoulders and slammed me two yards backwards. A tiny piece of shrapnel spanged off my helmet. So these helmets were some use!

The shells plunged right amongst us. Their concussion threw me this way and that, forward and backward. The earth heaved. It shook. I seemed to bounce like a ball. I turned a complete somersault and landed on my knees with a crash. I buried my face in the ground. I closed my eyes. I daren't look any more. My helmet grated in the soil, dug itself a channel and was still. With my hands I gripped the turf, determined to stay down, to pull myself into the sheltering earth. Shells screamed and whooped, blew aloft. Earth pattered down. The groans stopped.

The warmth of the shells passed in front of me, moving further and further away. I looked up. Twenty . . . twenty-five . . . thirty yards away, on to the ditch and into the wood.

Tearfully I poured out my thanks to God in an agony of relief. I stretched my fingers. I flexed my limbs. They worked. I shook the earth from my gas-cape. The dry crackle of its waterproofing was the first new sound I was aware of. Our barrage was now fifty yards in front and the German shells were fifty yards to the rear. We were stuck in the middle. I wriggled to look round at the German corpse. He wasn't there. In the next shell-flash I saw him, draped like a rag doll, hanging on a hedge fifty yards away.

Muffled voices came from the field as the wounded checked to see how many were still alive. Someone said, in a quiet, calm, matter-of-fact way:

"There *were* forty, to my knowledge."

Someone else lit a cigarette. Those who could move crawled towards it for companionship. The black shapes slithered towards the red pin-point. I couldn't move.

A shell fell right in the middle of the group. I turned my head. I couldn't bear to look. When the roar died away, I did look. There was nothing. I stared at the wood and was sick. Two feet in front of my face a cigarette glowed.

The barrage seemed less violent. The noise changed to a steady rumble. Tracer jetted into the wood. Thank God!

The tanks were back! Ragged cheers broke out all over the area. There they were, the great steel bastards, moving relentlessly on, an endless train snarling into the heart of the forest.

The barrage stopped.

I heard the sound of boots scuffing on the grass.

"Here we are, mate! The sheriff's bleedin' posse always gets through!"

The stretcher-bearers had arrived.

"Room for one on top! Have the exact fare ready. Regimental Aid Post and all stops to Blighty. Fez pliz."

My face cracked into what I hoped was a grin. Strong arms lifted me on to the stretcher. Pain shot through me.

"Put me on my stomach, for God's sake!"

Slowly, gently, they turned me over. The pain vanished. I felt comfortable, secure. As we swung off across the field someone shook my hand warmly. I turned my head. It was Smoky.

"Glad to see you're out of it, Corp. Can I have the tin of soup you've got clasped to your manly bosom?"

I laughed and pulled the can from my blouse.

"So long, Corp. You're better off where you're going. You might like to know the rest of the section's O.K. Look after yourself, mate!" Smoky shook my hand again and left.

We picked our way carefully through the craters and down the track. We met no one. Ahead and to the right was a dimly lit door. My stretcher was put down on trestles. The hard wood bit into my shins and chest.

"O.K.," said the M.O., "turn him over!"

The pain must have put me out. I can remember someone asking for my field-dressing. I tapped my right thigh, and felt something move on there. When I came round, I could see the M.O.'s face, streaked with grime and sweat. There was a strong hospital smell. I felt cold at my stomach. I lifted myself on my elbow and stared at my stomach. No wonder I was cold. They'd cut all my battle-dress and underwear away from the knee to the chest. My field-dressing was round my right thigh. From the left hip across my loins

682

was just a white field of gauze and bandage, slightly stained red.

The M.O.'s face appeared above me.

"What do you want doing with this lot?" He showed me a tin full of cigarette ends. I looked, puzzled.

"This collection was in your map pocket. There's a hundred and eighty of 'em."

I remembered. The nine hours' stonk last night.

"Chuck 'em away, please." A sudden thought occurred to me.

"What's the time, sir?"

"Three o'clock in the morning. You were picked up an hour ago."

I had been out there for seven hours.

The M.O. spoke again.

"Right, lad! You seem to be alert enough to learn what's happened. You've been hit by at least two tracers. They went in at your left hip and out at the right thigh. The hole was too big for one bullet, but they did you a good turn. The tracer powder cauterized the wound as it went through, so it's a clean hole. It's not my job to excavate, so I'm sending you to a Casualty Clearing Station. You mustn't drink till they know the internal damage. All your personal possessions are in this bag. Here you are. This will be a long job, son, but you'll be all right. Yes, Sergeant, give him a cigarette. Good-bye, son. Good luck!"

The cigarette tasted good.

Outside, I was lifted on to a Bren-carrier. The Padre sat there. I was scared.

"Don't worry, boy! I'm not with you in case you die on the way! I'm just coming down to the C.C.S. to see the rest of our boys. You're our last customer!"

The Bren-carrier throbbed, swivelled and turned on to the road. Its well-sprung movement carried me on a moving feather-bed.

The night was quite warm for February. A faint breeze blew.

So I left the Battalion.

I *was* "out."

Over the Rhine

Montgomery's armies were trying to break through to the Rhine in the north; at the same time columns from the American 1st Army drove to the Rhine, only to find that the Germans had blown its bridges. By March 7th, a dozen bridges across the Rhine had been destroyed

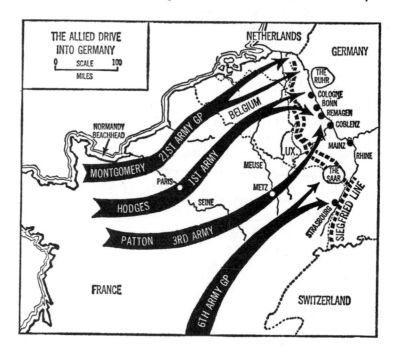

THE ALLIED DRIVE
INTO GERMANY

0   SCALE   100
MILES

NETHERLANDS

GERMANY

THE RUHR

COLOGNE
BONN
REMAGEN
COBLENZ

NORMANDY BEACHHEAD

BELGIUM

21ST ARMY GP

MAINZ

RHINE

LUX.

MEUSE

THE SAAR

MONTGOMERY

1ST ARMY

PARIS

METZ

HODGES

SEINE

STRASBOURG

SIEGFRIED LINE

PATTON   3RD ARMY

FRANCE

6TH ARMY GP

SWITZERLAND

by the Germans. However, on the same day, the 9th U. S. Armored Division of the 1st Army, rolling into the hills above Remagen, was astonished to find the Ludendorff Railway Bridge still standing. The story of its daring capture follows, carefully prepared and researched by Capt. Hechler, one of the historians attached to the 9th Armored.

684

THE CAPTURE OF REMAGEN BRIDGE

by Capt. Ken Hechler

Late in the forenoon of March 7, a gray, drizzly day, a little group of American soldiers on the Birresdorf road near the abandoned R.A.D. camp above Remagen were talking excitedly. The Ludendorff Bridge was over a mile away, and Karl Timmermann and his men did not dream that it would still be standing when they reached it.

Timmermann and his second platoon leader, Lieutenant Burrows, were peering through field glasses at the distant bridge.

"Jim, look at those damn Krauts going over the bridge," said Timmermann.

"Hey, look at the cows and horses, too," Burrows said. "With all those people trying to cross over, that bridge would make a good target."

Burrows glanced around quickly for his mortar squad. "Amick," he yelled, "you and Mercadante set up and prepare to fire on that bridge." There was a hasty scuffling with the heavy base plates and stovepipe tubes as the men adjusted their mortars.

"Tim, I'm not so sure about this," Burrows said to his company commander. "Do you think our mortars will do the trick?"

"It sure tempts me."

"Let's plaster 'em, Lieutenant," one of the mortarmen called out.

"Well, we've got some heavy stuff back of us, and there's no sense in sticking a pin in their tail just to see 'em jump.

This selection is condensed from the author's *The Bridge at Remagen.*

Let's do it this way: get hold of Colonel Engeman and he can bring up his tanks and call for some artillery."

A runner took off to alert the task force commander about the big bonanza that Timmermann had found.

A few minutes later, Engeman roared up, followed by Major Murray Deevers, the commander of the 27th Armored Infantry Battalion, and Deevers' Operations Officer, Major Don Russell. They watched the procession of German troops, vehicles, and animals far below, making their ant-like way across.

"Let's lower the boom," Engeman decreed. A radio message flew out, and presently somebody shoved a reply into his hand.

"Damn. They won't fire the artillery. Claim there are friendly troops in the vicinity. How can I get it through their thick— Oh, what's the use! Murray, we've got to take that town, and it looks like the doughs ought to go down first and clean it out. I'll bring up my tanks to cover you. Let me know how you want to plan your attack on the town."

The minutes ticked by. The stream of traffic across the bridge slowed down. There was frustrating delay on top of the hill, as the debate proceeded on how to seize this tiger by the tail without inciting him to bite. Deevers spoke to the commanders of A and C companies, Lieutenants Timmermann and William E. McMaster: "Tim and Mac, you make a reconnaissance down into town and give me a report on how to go in there."

Timmermann and McMaster made their way a little over five hundred yards down the hill along a footpath into Remagen. They met no enemy fire, but they saw a lot of activity near the bridge and on the opposite side of the river. Timmermann paused a moment at the bottom, on the road entering Remagen, and contemplated a battered old sign: "Citizens and Friends: Preserve our parks." It had obviously been intended to restrain the out-of-town tourists from scattering papers. He laughed humorlessly and started climbing back.

On the road to Remagen lived Josef Büntgen and his wife. They were unwilling eyewitnesses, along with several

German soldiers quartered in the home, of the entry of the American troops into Remagen. Herr Büntgen was a very patriotic local official, heading the construction office in the town government. The soldiers and the Büntgen family watched the American troops at the top of the hill pausing to take stock and figure out the next move. They saw Timmermann and McMaster descend the hill to reconnoiter. They saw the terrifying tanks poised for combat. They could see American soldiers start to fix their bayonets at the top of the hill. A German sergeant took a moment to say goodbye to Mrs. Büntgen. He waved his *panzerfaust* and shouted: "I'm going out and knock off one of those tanks."

She tearfully argued with him: "Do that, and they will level all our houses and destroy the town."

"Lady, there's no better place to stop them than at the Rhine. Heil Hitler!"

(Later, the Büntgens saw the sergeant's body in a ditch, an unnamed and forgotten German hero who had tried to create his own Thermopylae.)

Timmermann and McMaster returned from their reconnaissance, and Timmermann got the nod from Deevers for the all-important task of breaking into Remagen. Lieutenant Jack Liedike's B Company followed, its mission to clear the southeastern part of town while protecting the right flank of the advance. Lieutenant McMaster's C Company was assigned to clear the northwestern part and protect the left flank.

Timmermann held a quick conference with his platoon leaders to issue the attack order, and singled out Lieutenant Burrows to point the assault with his second platoon. It was about one o'clock in the afternoon. He told Burrows to take the main road and work his platoon through the center of Remagen, hugging the buildings because of snipers. Sergeant DeLisio was to fan out along the river road on the left flank, crouching low along the river because the Germans could observe clearly from the east bank. Sergeant Chinchar's platoon was to capture the railroad station and move through town on the right flank of A Company before heading for the bridge.

Once Timmermann's men had started for Remagen, a

687

further series of developments put new life and speed into the attack. Major Ben Cothran, General Hoge's operations officer, had charge of moving the command post for the combat command on the morning of March 7. Because the main effort of the 9th Armored Division was to capture bridges over the Ahr, Hoge had stayed with the south column of his combat command and turned over to Cothran the job of moving his CP from Stadt Mechenheim to Birresdorf, three miles west of Remagen. Cothran, an adventurous officer, had been a newspaper editor in Nashville, and had a nose for news as it developed. After seeing the combat command's bag and baggage to Birresdorf, Cothran hopped into his jeep to find out how close to the Rhine Colonel Engeman's task force had come. He got the same tingling sensation in his spine as everyone else when he emerged from the woods and saw the Rhine and the intact bridge below. He looked just long enough to see the German vehicles streaming across and several locomotives on the other side of the river getting up steam.

"Don't you think we ought to bring some artillery down on all that?" asked Colonel Engeman.

"My God, I've got to get the Old Man," yelled Cothran, scarcely aware of the question.

He radioed to General Hoge, who tore across the countryside to the scene, arriving shortly after one o'clock. Things began to happen fast. The general stormed at the delay in taking Remagen. He told everybody in sight to take the town immediately. Speed, speed, and more speed, he raged, was the key to the whole operation. Colonel Engeman, who had been trying to size up the situation and make careful plans, was spurred into action and issued a series of decisive orders to his subordinates. Directly or indirectly, every man on the top of the hill felt the wrath of the general who demanded and got results.

Satisfied that his calculated display of anger had speeded up the operation and saved many precious minutes, General Hoge began to think about the bridge that, incredibly, still stood before his eyes. "You know," he said in rather subdued tones to Colonel Engeman, "it would be nice to get that bridge too while we're at it."

688

He quietly studied the procession of troops and vehicles crossing the river, and weighed the risks involved in trying to rush the bridge. An aide tapped his arm.

"Want me to drive back and tell General Leonard?"

Hoge continued to stare through his field glasses, and the aide waited apprehensively.

"We might lose a battalion," replied General Hoge, irrelevantly.

The aide shifted his weight to the other foot and tried again: "Do you see anything special?"

"Engeman, Deevers, Russell, get those men moving into town!" General Hoge barked, taking the field glasses from his eyes.

"Already on their way," the three replied, almost in unison.

It was true—Timmermann had already led his men down the hill and into Remagen. But the renewed interest up above speeded the attack noticeably.

Burrows' platoon had its biggest scuffle in the main square near the City Hall, where an automatic weapon momentarily slowed down the advance. As Burrows started to maneuver his men to flank the German gun, two of Lieutenant Grimball's tanks rumbled up and fired several 90-millimeter rounds into the square. The machine gun shut up suddenly. Grimball's tanks then intermingled with Burrows' second platoon of infantry and they pushed toward the bridge.

Timmermann's old platoon, the first, did not have too much trouble. Sergeant Chinchar proved an excellent interpreter of the frenzied remarks of Polish and Russian displaced persons and prisoners who were anxious to reward their liberators by indicating where the German soldiers were hiding.

The third platoon, headed by DeLisio, moved out rapidly under the aggressive leadership of the little sergeant.

"C'mon, you guys, just another town," DeLisio cried, waving his arm and giving a hitch to his M-1. His men fixed bayonets as they moved down the hill in single file past the stately St. Apollinaris Church. Bates, Foster, Plude, Kreps, Rusakevich, Pol, Rundbaken, Acosta, White, Kenny

689

—these were some of the men whom DeLisio led down to the river bank. They crept carefully along, squeezing close against the walls of buildings and keeping their submachine guns and M-1's cocked for trouble. From behind lace curtains, the apprehensive citizens watched. Some shivered. Some laughed and said: "Why do the Americans hug the buildings and move so slowly? There are no German soldiers left to fight!" If Company Commander Timmermann had overheard these remarks, he would have complimented his men for conducting themselves like the combat veterans that they were—sticking to the book, taking no chances.

DeLisio came to a road block which the Remagen *Volkssturm* had set up and then neglected to close. He posted four men at the road block and set up a machine gun 100 yards farther inside the town. It was a perfect trap, in which they caught a number of German soldiers trying to slip through town to get across the Rhine. All were taken prisoner.

Shortly after the road block had been set up, an excited American soldier dashed up to DeLisio and yelled:

"Joe, Sergeant Foster wants you on the double! He's got a German general."

DeLisio ambled down the street behind the messenger, and soon observed a very strange sight. Foster had the muzzle of his M-1 pressed against the stomach of a gaudily attired German, with elaborately braided blouse and trousers and enough "scrambled eggs" for several admirals on his hat.

"Here's yer general, Joe," Foster announced. "Now we'll find out the straight dope about that bridge."

"Lower your gun, Foster. Lemme see him," DeLisio began. He asked the prisoner a couple of questions in halting German, and then turned to the hangers-on from his platoon who had gathered to kibitz.

"General, my tail! You know what this guy is? He's the chief station agent for the railroad! Now scatter out, you guys, and let's check these houses."

The men took off, some sheepish, some laughing, and resumed the job of locating and silencing sniper fire. At several points civilians ran out and stopped American soldiers to point out cellars where German soldiers were hiding. Thoroughly demoralized, the Germans invariably surrendered without a shot; many of them realized the futility of resistance and some had even sent civilians to bring in the American soldiers. Still, it was not an easy job to clean out the town. Sniper fire rattled from unseen locations, some 20-millimeter German fire was landing in the town, and each quiet street carried the threat of a death trap at every corner.

Shortly after two o'clock, Timmermann's men had cleaned out enough of Remagen to turn their rifle fire directly on the bridge. Before they actually reached the bridge, the men saw a volcano of rocks and dirt erupt into the air—Captain Friesenhahn had exploded the preliminary demolition which gouged a crater thirty feet wide in the approach to the bridge.

Gradually, DeLisio, Burrows and Chinchar worked their platoons up to the bridge approach where they were joined by the tanks which had helped to clear out the town.

"Look at that hole," grumbled Grimball. "It's not enough that they want to blow the bridge, they won't even let us get near it."

Timmermann came up for a brief confab with his platoon leaders.

"Well, what're we goin' to do?" Burrows asked.

Across the river, they could see the German troops making frantic preparations to blow the bridge. Timmermann glanced along the bridge and clearly saw the wires and the telltale charges, ready to go off. Turning to his platoon leaders, he said:

"They'll probably blow it any minute now. Watch this— it ought to be good." He put his field glasses to his eyes and scanned the far bank. "They look like they want to get us out on the bridge before they blow it."

"Screw that noise," DeLisio said simply.

By three o'clock most of the infantrymen of A Company and the supporting tanks had taken up positions near the bridge. Myron ("Pluto") Plude, one of DeLisio's machine gunners, set up his gun and started throwing a few tracers across. The regular *thwump* of the tank cannon echoed against the Erpeler Ley across the river. Looking back at the top of the hill from which he had first seen the bridge, Timmermann could observe more tanks belching smoke as they threw their shells across the Rhine. Everybody was tense, waiting for the Germans to deliver the inevitable *coup de grâce* to the shaky bridge.

Alex Drabik, the shy, gangling butcher boy from Holland, Ohio, ambled up to the bridge and made one of his rare utterances to his company commander. "Lieutenant Timmermann, looks like we're gonna get some sleep tonight."

"Yeh, Alex," Timmermann answered. "We'll get some hot meals, too, and shack up here for a couple of days."

The same thought had been in General Hodges' mind when he told General Millikin that after joining up with Patton everybody could take a rest for a while.

Just south of Remagen, at Sinzig on the Ahr River, an incident occurred which had a profound effect on the tankers and infantrymen in Remagen. About the time that Timmermann's men were approaching the bridge in Remagen, a task force under Lieutenant Colonel William R. Prince, making the main effort of the 9th Armored Division, was meeting considerably tougher opposition in its attempt to seize the bridge over the Ahr. Prince's task force succeeded nevertheless in rushing the bridge before the Germans could blow it up. This notable feat was accomplished almost two hours before Timmermann led his men through Remagen to the bridge.

Colonel Prince's task force captured about 400 prisoners among the rabid defenders of Sinzig. His men also rounded up some *Volkssturmers* and civilians who were making menacing gestures. A couple of the civilians indicated that they had information "of great importance" which they would like to transmit to the American authorities. Lieutenant Fred de Rango, intelligence officer of the 52nd Armored Infantry Battalion, interrogated the civilians. Impressed with the attention paid to them, the civilians tried to enhance their own importance by giving a good story. They could not have made a better choice in their selection of subject matter: they told de Rango that the German command planned to blow up the Remagen Bridge at four o'clock on the dot.

De Rango received this information about half past two, and he naturally considered it to be of the greatest importance. Acting swiftly, he sent a priority radio message to Combat Command B headquarters, alerting them of this new intelligence. The message had an authoritative ring, and the combat command forthwith relayed it to Task Force Engeman. De Rango, feeling there was not a minute to lose and fearing that his radio message might have to pass through too many channels, also dispatched a special messenger to carry the news to Colonel Engeman. Soon the messages started to ricochet around Remagen as everyone hurried to inform everyone else.

The German troops at the bridge later swore their plan to blow the bridge had no set time schedule but hinged on the appearance of American forces. Furthermore, it seems scarcely plausible that civilians in a neighboring town would have detailed information on a secret military plan of this nature. Authentic or not, the news spurred the American commanders and troops to quicker action in order to cross the bridge before it was blown.

It was 3:15 when General Hoge received the message that the bridge was to be blown at 4:00. He immediately stormed down to give the word to Colonel Engeman. The scrappy Minnesotan already had the news, but General Hoge wanted action. "Put some white phosphorus and smoke around the bridge so the Krauts can't see what we're doing, cover your advance with tanks and machine guns, then bring up your engineers and pull out those wires on the bridge because we're going to take that bridge," General Hoge roared.

General Hoge champed nervously as the minutes ticked by. He directed Majors Deevers and Russell, the commander and operations officer of the 27th Armored Infantry Battalion, to get down to the bridge and order their men across. He turned again to Colonel Engeman: "I want you to get to that bridge as soon as possible."

Engeman bristled: "I'm doing every damn thing possible to get to the bridge."

General Hoge glowered. Without waiting for another word, Engeman started down the road in his jeep to Remagen. On the way he cut open his 508-radio and called Grimball: "Get to that bridge."

Grimball's rich South Carolina accent clearly pierced the static: "Suh, I am *at* the bridge."

Engeman told him to cover the bridge with fire and keep the Germans off it. He then sent a messenger to summon Lieutenant Hugh Mott, a platoon leader in Company B, 9th Armored Engineer Battalion. The pair met in the rear of one of the big resort hotels about two hundred yards from the bridge.

These were Engeman's orders: "Mott, General Hoge wants you to get out onto that bridge and see if it's mined or loaded with TNT, and whether it'll hold tanks. I'll give you fire support from my tanks and you'll have infantry scouts out there too." It was a tough assignment.

Lieutenant Mott, a tall, dark and cool-headed twenty-four-year-old from Nashville, swiftly got hold of the two most reliable men in his platoon—Eugene Dorland, a big Kansas stone mason, and John Reynolds, a little North Carolina textile worker. On their way up to the bridge, they saw the crater blown at the bridge approach, and when the smoke had cleared they jumped into the crater for protection. They also saw Majors Deevers and Russell talking with Karl Timmermann, and pointing at the bridge. Mott waved his two men forward with him.

Deevers and Russell had made their way independently to the bridge, and both of them made contact with Timmermann to give the tall Nebraskan the order to take his men across.

"Do you think you can get your company across that bridge?" the battalion commander asked.

"Well, we can try it, sir," Timmermann answered.

"Go ahead," Deevers snapped.

Timmermann took a split-second look at the bridge, the gaping crater at the approach, and the little knots of German soldiers making frantic preparations on the far bank.

694

"What if the bridge blows up in my face?" Timmermann asked quickly.

Deevers avoided Timmermann's steady gaze. He turned and walked away without a word. Timmermann knew then that this was a suicide mission. But he did not hesitate.

"All right," he barked to his platoon leaders, "we're going across."

Just as Timmermann was giving the order to cross the bridge, General Hoge back at the top of the hill was faced with a soul-searching decision. Hoge was jolted by a message from 9th Armored Division headquarters, ordering him to push south with all possible speed, objective unlimited, to link up with the 4th Armored Division of General Patton's army. The message gave him serious pause as he surveyed the bridge with his field glasses. In the light of this latest message, to concentrate on crossing the bridge instead of moving south would be a deliberate violation of orders from higher headquarters. Success might excuse such a violation; failure might mean a court martial and disgrace. Hoge could see that the Germans were preparing to blow the bridge. Suppose they blew it up while Timmermann's men were on it? Or, even worse, suppose they blew it after sucking across a large number of troops and vehicles?

General Hoge weighed his decision cold-bloodedly. He figured that he would lose no more than a battalion if the Germans blew up the bridge and cut off the first men who crossed. And if that happened there was still a chance that the men would be captured alive. Hoge also figured that he would lose no more than a platoon if the Germans chose to blow the bridge while Timmermann's men were on their way across. He made up his mind to go through with the crossing.

Back in West Point, Karl Timmermann's wife had given birth to a daughter who was now eight days old. General Hoge's command decision could not consider Timmermann's wife and baby girl, nor Drabik's eighty-year-old father in Holland, Ohio, nor Burrows' mother and father in Jersey City. Nor would Hoge, or Deevers, or anyone else in the world try to answer Timmermann's simple question: "What if the bridge blows up in my face?"

On the surface, Karl Timmermann tried to treat his mission as if it were a big lark. This was part of his art of leadership. While giving orders to his three platoon leaders, he casually passed out some candy he had "liberated" in Remagen. "Here, try one of these Kraut rock candies, and don't break your teeth," he said with a flip to Forrest Miner, an assistant squad leader at the edge of the group.

"Now we're going to cross this bridge before—"

A deafening rumble and roar swallowed up the rest of Timmermann's sentence. The German Sergeant Faust had set off the emergency demolition two-thirds of the way across the bridge. Able Company watched in awe as the huge structure lifted up, and steel, timbers, dust and thick black smoke mixed in the air. Many of the G.I.'s threw themselves to the ground or buried their faces in their hands.

Everybody waited for Timmermann's reaction.

"Thank God, now we won't have to cross that damned thing," Mike Chinchar said fervently, trying to reassure himself.

Johnny Ayres fingered the two grenades hooked onto the rings of his pack suspenders, and nodded his head: "We wouldn't have had a chance."

But Timmermann, who had been trying to make out what was left of the bridge through the thick haze, yelled:

"Look—she's still standing!"

Most of the smoke and dust had cleared away, and the men followed their commander's gaze. The sight of the bridge still spanning the Rhine brought no cheers from the men. It was like an unwelcome specter. The suicide mission was on again.

A thousand feet away, the German soldiers were working frantically around the far end of the bridge. They looked as if they were going to make another attempt to blow the bridge.

"Maybe they're just teasing us to get us out there and then blow us all to kingdom come," Sabia said. "I tell ya it's a trap."

Timmermann's casual air had disappeared. He had thrown away his candy and the grin was gone from his face as he strode up to the bridge. He saw at one glance that although some big holes had been blown in the flooring of the bridge, the catwalks were clear for infantrymen. The Germans were still in a frenzy of activity on the other side and on the bridge itself.

He quickly circled his arm in the air to call his platoon leaders together. Other men clustered around, eager and apprehensive. "O.K., Jim, Mike and Joe, we'll cross the bridge—order of march, first platoon, third platoon and then second platoon."

There was a moment of silence.

Timmermann turned to Burrows, cupped his hand, and said in a low tone: "Jim, I want your platoon to bring up the rear so we have an officer in charge of the last platoon across." Then, in a louder tone which everybody could hear: "And when you get over, Jim, take your platoon up that high hill on the other side. You know, the old Fort Benning stuff: take the high ground and hold it?"

There was no sudden rush to cross the bridge. To the tired, dirty, unshaven men it looked like sudden death. Stomachs were queasy, not only from some wine discovered in Remagen, but from fear.

Timmermann moved tentatively up to the bridge, and started to wave his arm overhead in the traditional "Follow me" gesture. A chattering of machine guns from the towers made him duck. Jack Berry ran up to one of the General Pershing tanks, located Lieutenant Jack Grimball, and pointed at the towers.

Grimball did not hesitate. His Pershing let loose a blast.

Mike Chinchar, leader of the platoon ordered to spearhead the crossing, was knocked off his feet by the concussion. So was Dean Craig. Chinchar and Craig had their faces buried in the mud by the blast. Sabia was lifted off his feet, and shook his head dazedly. Berry laughed uncontrollably as the trio staggered around, spitting out mud and trying to regain their equilibrium.

The tank shell opened a big crack in the tower, and the German machine-gun fire let up.

"Dammit, what's holdin' up the show? Now git goin'!" Timmermann yelled.

Big Tony Samele, who had been in the lead while the first platoon was cleaning out Remagen, turned to his platoon leader, Mike Chinchar: "C'mon, Mike, we'll just walk it across."

At this point, the battalion commander, Major Murray Deevers, called out: "I'll see you on the other side and we'll all have a chicken dinner."

"Chicken dinner, my foot. I'm all chicken right now," one of the men in the first platoon shot back.

Major Deevers flushed. "Move on across," he yelled, sharply.

"I tell ya, I'm not goin' out there and get blown up," the G.I. answered. "No sir, major, you can court-martial and shoot me, but I ain't going out there on that bridge."

While Deevers was arguing, Lieutenant Timmermann was using more direct methods: "Git goin', you guys, git goin'." He moved onto the bridge himself.

Chinchar shouted at Art Massie: "You leapfrog me up as far as that hole that's blown out." Massie had a quick and natural reaction: "I don't wanna but I will."

As they started out onto the bridge, suddenly the man who had been arguing with Major Deevers turned away from Deevers and joined the group from the first platoon which was moving across.

Timmermann's men had just started out onto the bridge when Lieutenant Mott and Sergeants Dorland and Reynolds of the engineers ran out to join them and started cutting wires connected to the demolition charges. The engineers were a doubly welcome sight, because the infantrymen had not expected them. When the big German emergency charge had gone off on the bridge Mott had decided that the main job of his engineers would be to locate and cut the wires to the other demolition charges. The three men joined Timmermann and his lead scouts just as they were starting across the bridge, and there was no time to coordinate any plans as the whole group surged forward.

The right side of the bridge was torn up by the German blasts, and so Chinchar's platoon started down the left catwalk. Here the men had some protection because most of the German rifle and machine-gun fire was coming from

698

the stone tower on the far right end of the bridge. The fire had quieted down after Grimball's tank blast, but it started up again as the first infantrymen picked their way across.

When Chinchar's men were about a third of the way over, they came to a halt as the machine-gun fire intensified. The American tanks were still firing, but the German return fire from both the towers and the tunnel was growing stronger. Nobody dared move ahead.

From a half-submerged barge about two hundred yards upstream, the lead troops were getting more fire. It was not heavy and constant, but two snipers on the barge were beginning to zero in. There were no American tanks on the bridge, and so Timmermann ran back to yell to one of the German Sherman tanks at the bridge approach:

"How about putting something on that barge?"

The tank found the range and blasted the barge with its 75-millimeter gun until a white flag began to flutter.

"That's one thing they never taught us at Fort Knox," said a member of the tank crew later in reviewing his naval exploit.

Even with the barge menace removed, Timmermann faced a crisis. He ran forward to find that his old first platoon was frozen. The tank support was not silencing the opposition. The Germans were still running around on the far side of the river as though they were going to blow the bridge with the American troops on it. Timmermann waved for Sergeant DeLisio, leader of the third platoon.

"Joe, get your platoon up there and get these men off their tail," he yelled above the clatter of tank and machine-gun fire.

The little Bronx sergeant with the twitching mustache started weaving and bobbing across the bridge. One of the motionless figures hugging the flooring of the bridge grumbled as he passed:

"There goes a guy with more guts than sense."

If DeLisio heard him he gave no sign. Soon the rest of his platoon was starting over, and in a minute a few men from Burrows' second platoon had started also.

The reinforcements fired at the tunnel and the towers, and soon the enemy fire began to lessen.

Forrest Miner came up behind one of the men on the bridge and yelled:

"What's holding you guys up?"

"Don't you hear that machine-gun fire?"

"Fer cryin' out loud," Miner lied, "that's our own machine-gun fire coming from behind us."

The man looked incredulous and then hobbled to his feet with a blank and resigned expression on his face.

Above all the noise came Timmermann's constant: "Git goin', git goin'." The company commander was everywhere, spurring, encouraging, and leading his men.

DeLisio worked his way up to the first man on the bridge, a third of the way across, and shouted: "What's the trouble?"

"Trouble? Chrissakes can't you see all that sniper fire?"

"Why worry about a coupla snipers?" DeLisio laughed. "If this bridge blows up we've got a whole battalion on it. Let's get off. C'mon, guys."

DeLisio, of course, was exaggerating—there wasn't a whole battalion on the bridge, only part of A Company; but the psychology worked.

He helped uncork the attack. Other men with "more guts than sense" started to get up and weave and bob behind him.

Sabia started to run, but the bridge turned into an endless treadmill. His leaden feet got heavier and heavier, and he felt as if he had been running for hours and getting nowhere.

Ayres, his grenades and canteen bobbing up and down, suddenly wished he had not consumed so much wine in Remagen, and he vomited on the bridge. Through a blown-out hole in the bridge flooring he saw the swift current below.

"If I fall," he asked himself, "will this pack drag me under?"

Across the river, a German train steamed into view, chugging south.

Colonel Engeman, back in Remagen with his tanks, spotted the train and joyfully exclaimed: "Hallelujah! I've always wanted to fire a tank at a locomotive." Four or five tanks opened up. The firebox of the engine exploded. Ger-

700

man troops started pouring out of the train, and set up positions to fire at their tormentors on the bridge and in Remagen.

DeLisio waved back for his support squad, led by Joe Petrencsik and Alex Drabik. Then he edged forward. Heavy fire started to come down on the bridge—20-millimeter shells from German anti-aircraft guns. Petrencsik with a sudden hunch yelled: "Duck!" DeLisio crouched, and something swooshed over his head and took a piece out of one of the stone towers.

In the middle of the bridge, Mott, Dorland and Reynolds found four packages of TNT, weighing 20 to 30 pounds each, tied to I-beams underneath the decking of the bridge. They climbed down and worked their wire-cutters hot until the charges splashed into the Rhine. Above them they heard the heavy tramp of the infantrymen and the hoarse cry of Timmermann which everybody had now taken up: "Git goin'."

Back on the bridge, Dorland started to hack away at a heavy cable.

"Why don't you shoot it in two with your carbine?" Jack Berry asked.

Dorland put the muzzle up against the cable, and blasted it apart.

By this time DeLisio had traveled two-thirds of the way across the bridge. The little sergeant had a theory that if you advanced fast enough you wouldn't get hit, so instead of hugging the bridge when the Germans fired on him from the towers, he simply ran on until he got behind the towers on the German side of the bridge. DeLisio chortled to himself at his good luck, until he looked back and saw that the German fire from the towers was still pinning down the men who were supposed to be following him.

Somebody yelled: "Who's gonna clean out that tower?"

DeLisio took the question as a challenge, and ran back to the tower where most of the fire was coming from.

He pushed aside a few bales of hay blocking the door to the tower. Just as he started into the door, a stray bullet went into the stone wall and ricocheted off. Sabia came up and yelled: "You're hit, Joe."

"You're crazy, Sabia. I don't feel nothin' at all."

Sabia insisted: "I saw that bullet, I tell ya I seen it go right through ya."

DeLisio ran his hands quickly around his field jacket, and finding no blood he brushed Sabia away and went on up into the tower.

Chinchar, Samele, and Massie then went up into the left tower. Everybody else moved forward. Many of them recalled what Nelson Wegener, DeLisio's old platoon sergeant, used to say after nearly every battle: "Guinea, you're one of the luckiest men alive. I dunno how you do it, but you always seem to get out of the toughest scrapes."

DeLisio started running up the circular staircase. There were three floors in the tower, and he couldn't take anything for granted. He heard machine-gun fire above him, and then it suddenly stopped. Had the Germans heard him coming, and was he heading into a trap?

He slapped open a steel door with the heel of his hand and burst in on three German soldiers. They were bending over a machine gun, as though it were jammed. There was an agonizing second as the three men jerked their heads around. DeLisio pumped out a couple of shots with his carbine, firing from the hip.

"*Hände hoch!*" he yelled.

The three Germans wheeled around with their hands in the air. DeLisio motioned them to one side with his carbine, and seizing the gun they had been using he hurled it out of the window. Men starting across the bridge saw the gun plummet from the tower and began to move with more confidence.

In his pidgin German and his sign language, DeLisio tried to find out if there were any more soldiers left in the tower. His captives assured him that there weren't. But DeLisio was skeptical and he motioned for them to precede him up the stairs.

On the top floor of the tower, DeLisio pushed the three Germans into a room, where he found a German lieutenant and his orderly. The lieutenant dived for the corner of the room, but DeLisio stopped him with a couple of shots. He took away the lieutenant's Walther pistol. Then he marched

702

all five prisoners down the stairs and told them to proceed unescorted over the bridge to Remagen. They were the first in a long parade of German prisoners taken near the bridge.

Over in the left tower, Chinchar, Samele and Massie also tossed a German machine gun out the window and captured one cowering soldier. The flushing of the towers cost all of those involved the honor of being the first across the Rhine.

Alex Drabik, one of DeLisio's assistant squad leaders, had not seen him go into the tower and started looking for his platoon leader. He asked several people on the bridge, but nobody seemed to know. He made up his mind that there was only one thing to do.

"Let's go!" he shouted. "DeLisio must be over there on the other side all alone."

Drabik took off for the east bank, weaving and wobbling. Just before he got across the bridge he jounced so much that he lost his helmet. He did not stop to pick it up but kept running at top speed until he became the first soldier to cross the Rhine.

At Drabik's heels came the Minnesota plasterer named Marvin Jensen, repeating: "Holy crap, do you think we'll make it, do you think we'll make it?"

Drabik was the first man over, followed closely by Jensen, Samele, DeLisio, Chinchar, Massie, Sabia, a Missourian named Martin Reed and a North Carolinian named Joseph Peoples. A few seconds later Karl Timmermann, the first officer over, set foot on the German side of the Rhine.

Once over the bridge Drabik wheeled to the left, still looking for DeLisio, and raced about two hundred yards up the river road. The rest of his squad followed close behind, and he hastily set up a skirmish line in a series of bomb craters to ward off a possible German counterthrust.

The bridge itself was still a big question mark for the Americans. Every man that crossed it wondered if the Germans had yet played their final card. Were they saving up a more devastating stroke that would at any moment topple the entire structure into the Rhine? The three engineers, Mott, Dorland and Reynolds, methodically searched for the master switch that controlled the German demolitions. Near

703

the eastern end of the bridge, Dorland finally located the box that housed the switch, went to work on the heavy wires leading from it, and blasted them apart with a few rounds from his carbine. A few minutes later, the three engineers came upon a large unexploded 500 to 600 pound charge with its fuse cap blown. Mott and his men examined it closely and found it correctly wired and prepared for detonation. Cutting all attached wires, they made it harmless.

At the Remagen end of the bridge, Colonel Engeman, Captain Soumas, and Lieutenant Miller drove their men hard to clear the way for tanks and vehicles. While Mott and his two sergeants were ripping out demolition wires and determining whether the bridge could hold traffic, other engineers checked the approaches for mines and pondered the problem of filling up the tremendous crater at the bridge approach. Miller finally called up Sergeant Swayne, whose tank was equipped with a blade to operate like a bulldozer, and Swayne began pushing dirt and debris into the big hole.

On the east bank DeLisio, who had stepped off the bridge shortly after Drabik, had already been sent by Timmermann on another trouble-shooting assignment. With four of his best men, the little sergeant crept forward to investigate the menacing railroad tunnel at the end of the bridge. None of the Americans knew how strong a force the Germans had hidden in the blackness of the tunnel. All they knew was that it gave the enemy excellent cover and concealment and that from it the occupants had ideal observation over the entire length of the bridge.

The five men moved forward cautiously, hugging the ground as shots rang out of the dark. When they reached the entrance, DeLisio fired two shots into the tunnel, and several German engineers quickly ran out, hands high above their heads, as if they had been eagerly awaiting this chance to give themselves up. Misled by the easy capture of this handful of the enemy, DeLisio failed to realize that there was a much stronger force deep in the tunnel. Moving his prisoners back, he reported to Timmermann that the tunnel looked clear and then joined Drabik along the river road.

Inside the tunnel, a German major and captain had received word shortly before four o'clock that the Americans had crossed the bridge. The news spread immediately through the milling throng of soldiers and civilians, and it became almost impossible to maintain even a semblance of order. Tank shells were bursting inside the tunnel, rifle fire was ricocheting off the walls, and three railroad tank cars were dripping gasoline that formed pools of potential destruction at the feet of the miserable tunnel occupants. Panic-stricken civilians were clawing at the soldiers to stop resistance. Except for the few prudent engineers near the entrance who had made the most of their opportunity to surrender to DeLisio's patrol, few of the terrified Germans were aware even that five Americans had come and gone.

By a little after four o'clock Timmermann had only about 120 men on the east bank. As an experienced infantryman he had recognized immediately from the other side of the river that the Erpeler Ley, the highest point in the immediate area, had to be taken fast. Summoning Lieutenant Burrows, he ordered him to take the second platoon up the precipitous slope. The heights of the Erpeler Ley, as well as the tunneled depths, had become crucial.

Burrows later said: "Taking Remagen and crossing the bridge were a breeze compared with climbing that hill." The lower slope was very steep, and the face of the cliff was covered with loose rock. Footing was slippery, and several men were severely injured when they fell. About halfway to the summit the Americans began receiving 20-millimeter fire. The trees were leafless, and there was little underbrush in which to hide. Silhouetted against the face of the black cliff, the climbing men were easy targets for the German anti-aircraft gunners. The Erpeler Ley quickly became known as Flak Hill.

At first the fire seemed to come from the west bank. Colonel Engeman sent one of his light tank platoons, under Lieutenant Demetri Paris, to clean out the pocket; but the anti-aircraft fire continued with such intensity that Burrows' men soon became convinced that it was coming from the northern part of the bridgehead. Some of them crawled around the nose of the bluff to the right to get out of the

705

line of fire. Others slid or rolled to the base of the cliff.

Burrows' casualties mounted. His platoon sergeant, Bill Shultz, was severely wounded in the leg by a 20-millimeter shellburst. Ralph Munch and Frankie Marek took refuge in a small crater-like depression, and Munch had just moved to another spot when a mortar shell burst close to Marek and sent a piece of shrapnel through him below his lungs. Those men who finally managed to reach the top saw only a few small sheds across a field about a hundred yards away and a handful of German soldiers wandering around unconcernedly. Jim Cardinale, one of the American machine gunners, called excitedly, "Come on, lemme paste those guys but good."

"Shut up or we'll shoot you by God," one of the other men threatened in low but urgent tones. "We'll shoot you and push you off the cliff—you want to give our position away?"

Cardinale calmed down, and the Americans atop the cliff began a period of cautious and worried waiting. They could see numerous German infantrymen and vehicles in neighboring towns. At the base of the hill and along the side the firing got heavier. The enemy seemed to be moving in for a counterattack.

The advance guard of the Remagen crossing was in a precarious position. With no weapons more powerful than light machine guns, Timmermann called for his anti-tank platoon under Lieutenant Dave Gardner to come to the east bank, instructing them to bring as many of their .50-caliber machine guns as they could and employ them on ground mounts covering the roads into the bridgehead. Gardner's men also brought over four rocket launchers and set them up in pairs with the machine guns.

Timmermann then appealed for more men, more weapons and more support. The battalion commander, Major Deevers, sent over Lieutenant Bill McMaster's C Company, followed by Lieutenant Jack Liedike's B Company about half-past four. Their arrival eased the situation, but the battalion was still woefully weak and too strung out to present a very firm defense against a counterattack. Had German tanks struck at the flimsy American force between four and

706

five o'clock, the Remagen bridgehead would certainly have been wiped out.

This possibility troubled Timmermann a great deal as he took stock of his thin line of men. It also troubled the men, and weighed heavily on the minds of the B and C Company reinforcements that came across the bridge. Everybody was either asking about the arrival of American tanks or fearing the arrival of German tanks. The sound of German vehicles came from neighboring villages. Patrols on the edge of the bridgehead confirmed the suspicion that German forces were moving up for a counterattack.

On the Remagen bank Lieutenant Mott and armored engineers were doing everything possible to make the bridge serviceable for tank traffic. Makeshift repairs were made in the shattered planking, but it soon became clear that the bridge would not hold tanks before dark.

The officers and men on the east bank chafed at the delay. They knew that infantry alone would never be able to hang on to their slim toehold. Runners started back across the bridge with urgent requests for help. Not long before dusk, the sight of these runners caused a flurry of uneasy excitement. The backfire of German vehicles in the distance started more rumors that Tiger tanks were moving toward the bridge. Along thousands of yards of thinly held front the troops were so widely scattered that many of them lost contact. Small groups drifted back across the bridge. In the space of an hour parts of the three companies on the east bank slipped back to Remagen in confusion and disorganization.

But the majority of the 27th Armored Infantry Battalion held on. Among those who remained were many who looked about for fellow Americans without seeing any; and the story later spread that only a few men had held the east bank of the Rhine on the night of March 7. Actually, the reinforcement of the bridgehead was resumed at dusk, and from then on throughout the night an almost steady stream of men crossed the bridge to bolster the defenses on the east bank.

The Enemy at Bay

It would be at least two weeks before the 1st Army could get permission to drive farther into the Rhineland from the Remagen bridgehead. But meanwhile Patton had got a division of his 3rd Army across the Rhine before Montgomery had. Even so, SHAEF was still holding out for Montgomery to launch the main drive at the Ruhr from the north. Now all that remained of the German forces west of the Rhine was in the Saar, and here Gen. Jacob Devers had Gen. Patch's 7th Army poised to drive through the defenses. Eisenhower wanted to clear the whole line west of the Rhine so there would be no bridgehead for a German counteroffensive. Bradley persuaded Eisenhower to let Patton strike across the Moselle River and wheel southward behind the Saar defenses, isolating the Germans in their Siegfried Line. The 1st and 3rd Armies were to conduct an encirclement of the Ruhr, while Devers pounded away frontally at the Siegfried Line.

The 7th Army began to cut into the tough Siegfried Line defenses, and met with desperate fighting. One of the assault regiments was the 274th, and one of its colonels, Wallace Cheves, has prepared one of the few histories, either regimental or divisional, that report the fighting from the perspective of the infantryman. The following chapter is a condensed version of the last bitter days of the fighting.

SMASHING THE SIEGFRIED LINE

by Lt. Col. Wallace Cheves

By March 2nd, the entire 274th Infantry regiment was looking down onto the vast plain which harbored the French border cities of Forbach, Stiring-Wendel and Neue-

Glashutte. In foxholes extending from Spichern Heights to Kreutzberg Ridge, nearly everyone of us had a grandstand view of the German fortifications inside the towns. The 276th had already taken most of Forbach after bitter house to house fighting. Stiring-Wendel and the cluster of small villages around it formed the last major barrier before the Siegfried Line and the Saar Basin.

The valley looked like a picture of peace and contentment, but to us who had to fight for it, it looked like the front yard of hell. The Germans had sowed a murderous crop of mines in the fields around the towns, and their field guns had every avenue of approach zeroed in. The 274th had one of the toughest jobs before it. We weren't just taking another town, we were cracking the strongest net of fortifications ever constructed by the human race. Our job was to breach the famed wall and establish a corridor through which our armies could race to the heart of Germany.

German artillery pounded the ridges with great ferocity. In addition, the infamous rocket gun, the "Screaming Meemie" or "Ole Rusty Barrel," was brought into action. It proved to be one of the most effective weapons the Krauts possessed.

"We could hear it fired in the distance," recalls Pfc. Harry Bealor. "It made a grating noise like the bark of a seal, or like someone scratching his fingernails across a piece of tin. Then for several seconds, everything would be quiet until it hit. The explosion sounded as though someone struck a match in the Krupp Works. You'd think the whole damn mountain had exploded. I've seen guys picked right up off the ground and thrown several feet through the air by the concussion."

By the afternoon of March 2nd, rumor that a full scale push was close circulated through the foxholes. TD's came up from the rear and poked their heavy guns out of the trees toward Stiring-Wendel.

"That's no good," swore Pfc. Ralph Schaefer as one of the iron monsters rolled up near his dugout. "Those bastards draw fire."

As if to prove he was telling the truth, a short time later

709

the hills were jarred by rockets and 88's. Every time the TD's moved, a half dozen more rounds would come in.

That evening company commanders and platoon leaders were called to battalion CP's to get attack orders for the morning. One paragraph in the attack order explained everything. It read:

"Attack H-hour from present positions. Overrun Stiring-Wendel, detaching units to clear the enemy from the city. Special attention to hostile positions covering the Forbach-Stiring-Wendel road. Continue the advance and seize that part of the Division Objective in Regimental Zone of Action. Organize and defend final objective. Mop up enemy within Regimental Zone by-passed during the advance. Relieve armored force blocking NE approaches to Stiring-Wendel. Maintain contact with 276th Infantry. Not less than one company will remain on Kreutzberg Ridge."

Colonel Conley chose Col. Boyd's second and Col. Landstrom's third battalions to make the main assault. Each had a company of French troops to mop up after it and take care of prisoners. The First Battalion was to remain on Spichern Heights and co-ordinate a defense there with the 275th Infantry. The big question then was which companies would catch the hell and which would be in reserve. In the Second Battalion, Fox and George were selected to make the advance with Easy in reserve, and in the 3rd Battalion, Item and King would assault, with Love in reserve.

It's hard to sleep the night before a big push. Most of us stayed awake all night trying to get our equipment ready, or just lay out under the stars thinking. Others gathered around in small groups and told stories far into the night. Still others, like Pfc. Bobby Hawthorne, threw a raincoat over the entrance of his foxhole to keep out the candlelight and read the New Testament.

In the early morning hours of March 3rd, while the moon was high, bathing the battlefield in a strange, ethereal light, we were quietly awakened by messengers from the CP. The empty dread that "this was it" arose in every man's mind. We crawled out of our blankets, slipped into our packs and waited. Sgt. Robertson of Item Company drew the first assignment. He was to go down to the little village of Sophia on the left flank and protect the main assault force against counterattack from that direction.

Back on the ridges, preparations for the attack were in full swing. It was a bright, clear spring morning, but the gaiety, the joy of being alive on such a morning was noticeably absent. In the trees above, birds were singing and darting back and forth among the branches. Some of us who took a few seconds off to watch the sun climb over the hills across the valley wondered if we would ever see the sun rise again.

By 0800 we were swarming through the woods heading for the line of departure. Companies F, G, I and K lined up to spearhead the drive. Tanks were to furnish support as soon as the roads into the town were cleared. Air missions were available upon one hour notice. Just a short time before H-hour, several squadrons of P-47's bombed and strafed the Metz Highway which was the main German supply route.

Promptly at 0817 after a ten minute artillery barrage, all units jumped off on schedule. All companies moved out abreast, keeping close contact, swinging slightly to the right and going down the hill. The 3rd Battalion went down on the left with Capt. Keith's Item Co. and Lt. Crowson's King Co. assaulting, Love in reserve. Col. Landstrom directed the entire battalion drive from a CP on top of Kreutzberg Ridge where the whole breadth of the battlefield could be observed.

Shortly after the drive got underway, King ran against a pillbox and a heavy minefield and was stopped cold. Item and Fox Companies, on either flank, were also forced to stop until the obstacles had been knocked out, to prevent a dangerous gap from forming. "King" fought hard to smash through, but death waited at the end of every step. Thousands of murderous shu-mines dotted the ground concealed under a few inches of dirt. One ill-placed step and a man's legs were blown horribly from his body.

"The machine gunners were out in front supporting the leading third platoon," said S/Sgt. Forrest Boughton. "We were trying to work forward to positions where we could button up the pillbox. Lt. Rytting was up forward on reconnaissance crawling around through the mines as calmly as though he were walking through a potato field back home in Idaho. War was a game to 'Riddle' as we called him. To him the only way to win it was to get in the thick of it and play hard. Physically, he was as big and tough as the West he came out of. When he came overseas he was the first one in the company to be battlefield commissioned. The bar didn't mean anything to him. He would have been leading if he were only wearing a Pfc.'s stripe. That's what he was doing when he went after the pillbox. He went up so close that he got down on his hands and knees and started crawling. He hadn't gone very far when the ground seemed to blow up from under him. We saw his leg go flying through the air and his whole body leap up and then roll on the ground. The pain and the shock almost paralyzed him. He never lost consciousness, though. He just lay quietly on the ground and waited for stretcher bearers to pick him up."

Fortunately both T-4 Kinsley, the platoon aid man, and a litter squad under Pfc. Dunning were close by.

"Going up to get Lt. Rytting was a dangerous job," said Dunning. "He was lying right in the middle of the mines. The guy who went after him stood a good chance of having the same thing happen to him. Kinsley took the chance though. He picked his way along, living a thousand years with every step he took. It's hell going through mines. It takes every gut a guy's got to move his feet.

"Kinsley reached Rytting's side safely and gave him a morphine injection to stop the pain, and then bandaged the stump of his leg as best he could. About that time we heard another explosion not far away and a cry for medic, and Kinsley started over to help. He only went a couple of feet when he himself stepped on a mine."

Kinsley tried to get up and walk on the stump of his leg but fell helplessly to the ground. Dunning heard him cry out and started up with his litter squad to get him. When they reached the spot, Kinsley was sitting on the ground trying to tie a tourniquet around his leg. One of the litter bearers tried to give him a shot of morphine but he couldn't push the needle through the skin.

"Kinsley grabbed the syringe out of my hands," said Pfc.

712

Tepper. " 'Give me that thing,' he said. 'I'll give it to my-self.' Dunning and I fixed up the tourniquet and before we could help him, Kinsley climbed onto the stretcher himself. The pain must have been pretty bad. All the while we were carrying him back he kept saying, 'My leg is gone. I saw it fly through the air. I'll never be able to walk or finish college again.' We brought him and Lt. Rytting to the aid station together. Rytting was pretty far gone. He didn't want to leave the rest of his men. When they gathered around his litter to wish him luck he just said, 'You guys take it easy.' Then we carried him away."

In the meantime the pillboxes and mine field had brought the entire attack to a standstill. The halt was just what the Germans were waiting for. From OP's in town and the hills across the valley they had a perfect picture of us standing in the open near the base of the hill. Artillery, mortars, rockets . . . everything that the Kraut possessed was thrown at us. The earth was ripped and torn and the whole area pockmarked with shell holes. The trees were sheared down to shattered trunks. All along the line we clawed into the ground trying to escape the flying shell fragments. A thick, black, dry, suffocating curtain of smoke hung over the whole area. Every few seconds another shell would explode with a murderous red flash and send death-dealing shrapnel shrieking among the prostrate troops. It looked for a while as though the attack would end before it began. It seemed impossible that men could come out of the barrage alive. Yet, the battalion held its ground. There was no sign of a break, or a panic. Everybody just gritted his teeth and held on. "King" continued to hammer at the pillbox. Item started down the hill on the extreme left flank with the second platoon in the lead. Lt. Wilson, the company executive officer, declined to remain with the rear CP when the push started and joined Lt. Beck at the head of the column. The leading platoon was armed with three bazookas, several rifle grenades, a flame thrower and, in addition, each man carried a white phosphorous grenade.

The first barrage came in fast and caught the men off guard. Both Wilson and Beck kept the company moving, pushing down through the trees with scouts out. Enemy fire

713

became more intense. A pattern of mortar shells exploded all around the platoon and the men dove into the ground. Recognizing the danger, Wilson immediately got the men to their feet.

"Beck, this is costing us lives," he said. "We'd better keep moving." So we drove on. We hadn't gone far when another concentration of mortars fell around us . . . this time with deadly effect. Lt. Beck, walking near the head of the column, was hit by a piece of shrapnel which punctured the phosphorous grenade he carried in his belt. A sheet of dazzling white flame enveloped and nearly consumed his body. In the same barrage, Pfcs. Paris, Harlen, Adams, Sanvas and Jessop were hit. Lt. Wilson led the rest of the platoon across an open fire break, through a net of barbed wire and into the trees on the other side. By this time the full force of the barrage was falling in back of us. Wilson's decision to keep moving had saved many lives.

Lt. Eblem's Fox and Lt. Cassidy's George Companies, moving down on the right flank of King, also came to a halt after they pulled abreast of the general line of attack. There, they too felt the force of the artillery barrage. All efforts were bent upon getting King through the mine field and net of pillboxes. Finally, about 1030, Col. Landstrom decided to bypass both pillbox and mine field, leaving them for Love Company, which was in reserve, to neutralize. Lt. Crowson then swung King wide to the left, leaving a large gap in the lines which was to be closed as soon as the mines were cleared.

A killing concentration of fire continued to pour in on King as it moved out from the foot of the hill. T/5 Jimmie Owen, medic for the first platoon, found himself with a double job after Kinsley had been evacuated. The whole forest rang with cries of the wounded and shouts of "Medic!"

"I emptied my medical pouches that day," said Owen. "I tried to take care of the worst cases first but there were so many I hardly knew which ones needed help the most. As soon as possible I got a line of walking wounded started back up the hill to the aid station. It was almost impossible to evacuate the serious cases. The casualty collecting point

714

was in the edge of a woods clear at the top of the ridge. About two trips up that hill with a litter was all a guy could stand."

As the casualties began to mount, additional litter teams from our 370th Collecting Company were rushed to the 3rd Battalion aid station. By 0900 in the morning the wounded were streaming in. Most of them were numb from shock. The courage displayed by the men who had been hit was remarkable.

"No matter how bad they were hit they wanted us to look out for their buddies first," said Pfc. Monroe Gable. "I met M/Sgt. Lewis Ripley coming back from the front with a crude bandage wrapped around a hole as big as an egg in his elbow. His face was an ashen gray and he could hardly walk, but he refused to let me give him first aid or a shot of morphine. He told me to help the other boys first."

After King Company passed on, one squad of Love, supported by a tank, was dispatched to take care of the troublesome pillbox.

"While we kept the bunker buttoned up with rifle and machine gun fire, the tanks threw a couple of 75-mm armor piercing shells into the embrasure. After a while we heard the Krauts hollering inside and saw them stick a white flag out the door. We thought there were only a couple in there but it seemed like half of the Wehrmacht came streaming out with their hands up in the air. By the time it was all over we counted twenty-five scared Krauts."

The whole line of attack once again started to move forward, this time opposed by every bit of power the Germans could muster against it.

"We slipped and slid and dove for holes wherever we could find them," said Sgt. McNeely of Item Co. "Every time the rounds came in some one else would scream for medics. Lt. Wemple was hit in the ribs and Sgt. Hoot in the legs and stomach. Pfc. Ryan ran over to them and administered first aid but Hoot died on his way to the aid station. Everyone clawed the ground and waited in mortal dread that the next round would be for him. I saw Sgt. Harm picked up and thrown down again by an exploding 88 that dug holes all around him and then went sailing off into the air to rip off the branches of a tree that fell down on top of him. In the midst of the din I heard Lt. Wilson shout for us to move on again. Mortar and artillery rounds were coming in as fast as they could be shot out of guns. We wondered how long they could keep it up . . . and how long we could stand it. As we got in closer we could hear rifles beginning to fire. I knew we must be in closer now. Long bursts from our light machine guns and BAR's cracked nearby—followed by answering bursts from enemy Burp guns. There were a lot of pillboxes in front of us to be blown and a squad of engineers was following close behind us loaded down with high explosives. If one of their shape charges were ever hit it would have cleaned out an area of about 100 yards."

George Company had come all the way from billets in Etzlingen to take part in the attack. We moved up into the ridges and took up positions just to the right of Fox. Most of the men were fresh after a short rest in French homes and in spite of the seriousness of the situation, went into the attack with a cocky cheerfulness. Pfc. William Bloom was nicknamed "The Walking Pineapple" by the other members of his platoon. In addition to three fragmentation grenades tied onto his belt, he carried a white phosphorous grenade, a thermite grenade, and a Kraut flare pistol with 16 flares of different colors. Lt. Cassidy led off with the second platoon and followed a small trench along the crest of the ridges just before peeling off down the hill.

"We could hear King's boys running into a lot of trouble below us, and we were forced to hold up awhile," said Sgt. Robert Kirk. "King's casualties were streaming back, both on litters and on foot. The sight of them was enough to take the heart right out of a guy. Kraut artillery was falling as far back as we were and some of their boys were being hit again. We moved down along the trenches, sweating out heavy enemy mortars. Some of our own 4.2's were located just behind us and the Krauts were raking the area with counter-battery. Most of it was falling on us instead of on the mortars. After a while we were ordered to move up to a large cave which Lt. Cassidy was using as temporary Company CP. We started to dig in but the ground was so rocky it was almost impossible. About that time Pfc. Tice came up with orders to start moving again."

"It was then that the Krauts saw me," continued Tice. "I knew it was coming as soon as I heard the croak of a Screaming Meemie off in the distance. Everybody else heard it too, and just stopped in his tracks and wondered if it was coming our way. Then it hit. The first rounds struck a trench where the second squad was waiting and wounded Pfcs. Neagle, Malcolm and Daniels. The whole squad was nearly buried in the eruption of earth. Several rifles were smashed to pieces, Sgt. Dunbar was stunned by the shock but refused to be evacuated and helped reorganize the squad. We never lost our respect for the 'rusty barrel' after that. It was a killer."

After that first blast the Krauts let up on the fire somewhat, probably figuring that most of the target had been obliterated. Lt. Cassidy took advantage of the lull to make a reconnaissance down the hill with Lt. Sims and Pfc. Tice. About 150 yards ahead they found a heavily armed pillbox. The company then moved out with the third platoon on the left and the second platoon on the right. The advance was extremely dangerous because the Germans had excellent observation while our own visibility was blocked by a dense growth of trees. Enemy mortars again picked us up as we moved down the hill. Burst blanketed the whole area, falling with fatal suddenness upon the advancing platoons. Several men were seriously wounded. The rest darted from cover to cover never knowing who was going to be the next one wounded.

The third squad of the third platoon went forward to act as point. Suddenly, the scouts pushed out over the nose of the hill and were silhouetted against the sky. The Germans were waiting for them. Almost immediately a withering blast of machine-gun fire from a row of camouflaged bunkers in a wooded ravine below poured into them. Pvts. Flynn and Fixler were hit instantly. Pfc. John Hudak, acting as squad leader, came up to get his men out of trouble and in doing so was caught in a blast of automatic fire and killed. The rest of the squad hit the dirt and waited. After several minutes our artillery observer came up and directed

717

a concentration of 105's on the bunkers and succeeded in forcing them to button up. We rushed in on the heels of the barrage and swarmed around the bunkers. Within a short time the occupants of several of them were flushed out with hand grenades. Several prisoners were taken . . . others stubbornly refused to come out and were blown up inside the pillbox. By this time the company had reached the edge of the woods and halted there until Lt. Cassidy could contact Col. Boyd and receive further orders.

On the extreme right flank Charlie Co. was pushing down the hill toward the small town of Golden Brahn through scattered resistance. During the early part of the attack German observers failed to see us sweeping down toward the village and the company was able to approach its objective undetected and thereby escaping the tremendous artillery barrage which was being poured into the other assaulting units. Soon after that, however, Sgt. Swinehart, who was near the point of the advance, seemed to jump into the air. A shattering explosion followed and a large cloud of dirt and mud flew into the air. The terrifying cry of "Mines" rang through the forest.

"We froze in our tracks," recalls Sgt. Hazelwood. "We didn't know how far we had gone into them and no one knew whether or not his next step would blow him into eternity. We then started moving to the left to get on a small road which we were pretty sure was clear. Every man walked with his heart in his mouth. Pretty soon we stopped again as an other explosion went off nearby. We saw Pfc. Leach, the medic, take off running through the mine field and knew someone else had been hit. Later we found it was Pvt. Kinney. We kept on going, feeling out every step until we finally reached the road."

We then moved down the left side of the road along a high stone wall which afforded some protection from mortar and artillery shells. Each man followed in the footsteps of the man in front of him. Pfc. Fulkerson, first scout of one of the squads, wandered slightly out of line and lost his foot in the explosion of a mine. We continued to move on until we reached the first outlying houses of the town. No hostile fire was met and at first it was believed that the Ger-

718

mans had pulled out and left the village to its fate. Hazelwood's squad cleared the first house without opposition. Sgt. Walker's squad worked around through a tank ditch to take the second house when our own artillery, late in coming in, began to fall dangerously close. Several members of the squad, who had advanced on the houses, were blown back into the ditch by the concussion. Word was immediately hollered back to "Lift that goddamn artillery."

Walker then went into the second house and fired his rifle down the cellar stairs into the darkness. His shots were answered by a scream and cry of pain. Several men were stationed around the outside of the house to block all and any chances of escape, and Walker, Martin, and Lloyd started down to blow the Krauts out. German artillery now began falling with deadly accuracy throughout the area. The windows of the house were blown out and shrapnel tore through the walls. Pvts. Swirepa, Shake and Reilly, standing outside in the yard, were wounded. All casualties were brought inside where they waited until late afternoon before they could be evacuated. The heavy artillery fire made it impossible to get them out during the day.

Germans could be heard moving around down in the basement. Pfc. Hays crept around the outside of the house keeping close to the walls until he came to a basement window with a stove pipe protruding from it. Hays glanced at the pipe and drew a grenade. Sgt. Yeryar saw him from across the street and shouted, "Hays, put that damn grenade away, I'm going to get a bazooka."

"I can't," replied Hays, "I lost the pin."

"All right, then, throw it."

Hays rolled the grenade down the stove pipe and ducked around the corner. In a few seconds, soot, pipes, stove and Krauts blew for half a block. Thirteen Germans, including one infantry Lieutenant, all black as the characters in a minstrel show, came up out of the cellar and surrendered. From them, Walker learned that there were no more enemy troops in the block. In rapid succession the next three houses were occupied. Strong points were established at the end of the street and the company waited there for reorganization and instructions for its next move.

In the meantime, Item and King companies were continuing to run the gauntlet of fire. Casualties were severe. Practically every non-com in King Company's third platoon had been hit. Conflicting orders and lack of leadership added to the chaos. Twice the company tried to pull out of position and assault and twice it was forced back. Item was driving through a woods thick with small fir trees and lofty pines.

"The only way we had a semblance of control was by constant yelling," said Sgt. McNeely. "The undergrowth was so thick we could hardly get through it. Sometimes we'd get caught in the bushes and have to back up and find a new way through. We found a few small caves that looked like they might be hiding places for Krauts so we dropped grenades in and moved on. Before long we drew near to the place where we knew a line of pillboxes was located. We got down on our stomachs and started to crawl toward them. Pretty soon we ran into a thick net of barbed wire. Apparently the Krauts were waiting for us to stop here like ducks in a shooting gallery because they had several machine guns all set up and as soon as we hit the wire they opened up. Lt. Wilson told us to hold our ground and to spread out so we could set up a base of fire. We got a bead on the Kraut guns and as soon as they opened up we let them have it. Everyone got pretty excited and started to yell—'Pour it on 'em. Give 'em hell! Let's show 'em there are some Yanks up here!' The Krauts must have thought that an army of 'banshees' was after them for soon all of the machine guns were silenced. I don't know if we killed them or not, but if they weren't dead, they were too scared to fire."

All this time Lt. Wilson was bringing up more men to build a stronger firing line. However, because of the jungle maze of barbed wire, which was undoubtedly thickly mined, he decided not to attack at this particular spot. There was no glamour, no dash about it when Lt. Wilson gave an order. He spoke with a quiet voice which encouraged rather than demanded.

"All right, boys," he would say. "Let's go around to the right now. Everybody up, come on, let's go."

We pulled back away from the wire and followed Wilson around toward the right flank.

"We went through the woods to the right until Wilson was satisfied that we had gone far enough," said Pfc. Corrigan. "Then he said, 'Okay, out of the woods and into the clearing, boys, just keep walking until fired upon.'"

We formed another skirmish line and headed toward the edge of the woods. As soon as we got into the clearing, machine guns opened up on us and everyone hit the ground. The only one left on his feet was Wilson. He just said, "That's all right, men, we'll just keep going. We'll cross this in short rushes. Come on now, let's go!"

One by one the men leaped up and dashed across the open ground in short bounds. Wilson remained on his feet among them, urging them on. "That's it," he would say when a man made a good rush. "About ten steps and hit the dirt!" Then he saw another that didn't quite satisfy him. "You there, soldier. That wasn't a rush . . . that was just a flop. Let's see you get up and give a good rush."

"It was one of the most amazing things I've ever seen," continued Corrigan. "He was standing up just like he was umpiring a training problem back in the states. I don't know how he escaped being killed. He was moving erect right in the middle of the enemy fire just as though bullets couldn't hurt him."

A huge tank trap was running down the middle of the clearing parallel to the railroad tracks.

"All right," said Wilson. "Let's see who's going to be the first man to hit that tank ditch!"

Driven by the sight of cover and protection from the deadly machine gun bullets, everyone raced low across the open ground and dove into the ditch. It was a huge excavation about twelve feet deep and ten feet wide. Wilson was one of the last to come sailing in from above. He soon saw, however, that unless we moved on, the attack would bog down there. Before he had time to take a breathing spell he was urging the men on again.

"Let's pull ourselves out of here," he said. "Up, now. Come on, let's get together and crawl out."

We slipped and slid and clawed and scratched at the

721

muddy embankment . . . pulling ourselves up and falling helplessly back. The greatest concentration of small arms fire against us seemed to be coming from the cellar window of one of the houses on the outskirts of town. As the men emerged from the trap they poured a heavy volume of rifle fire into the position. We crossed the railroad tracks with guns blazing.

"When we got close to the house the Krauts poked a white flag out the window," continued Corrigan. "When the guys saw it they only got sore. Everyone was for moving in and cleaning them out, but Wilson wouldn't let them. He told me to holler over that if the Krauts wanted to surrender they must come out with their hands over their heads and they wouldn't be hurt. I yelled at them across the street and soon after the first one came running over. He was a corporal and was sweating and trembling like he figured we were going to murder him right there in the street. I asked him where the rest of them were, and he said they were too afraid to come out of the house. I gave him one more chance to get them out in a hell of a hurry or else. Everyone was getting impatient and wanted to go over and blow them out with grenades, but Wilson wanted to take them alive if possible. Finally the corporal succeeded in getting them out. They were three of the most frightened men I've ever seen."

As soon as the Germans surrendered, Wilson went into the house to insure that it was all clear. Machine gun bullets were still ripping through the walls and knocking plaster all over the floor. At a signal from Wilson, Corrigan came running across the street and entered the house from a window on the side.

"We are being fired upon from the next room," said Wilson. "I want you to holler in there and tell them to come out and give themselves up."

Corrigan shouted but received no answer. Corrigan and Doyle then forced open the door and found the room empty. Then they realized that the fire was coming from one of the pillboxes they had bypassed outside. As the two men were standing there, Sgt. McNeely came running over from across the street to enter the house. As he was climbing through the window two shots rang out from outside and hit him in the head. He dropped to the floor, his feet still on the sill. Then he started gasping and coughing and

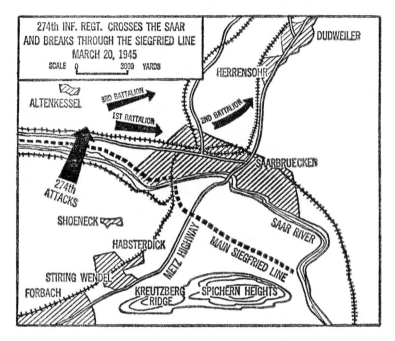

274th INF. REGT. CROSSES THE SAAR AND BREAKS THROUGH THE SIEGFRIED LINE MARCH 20, 1945 SCALE 0 3000 YARDS

DUDWEILER
HERRENSOHR
ALTENKESSEL
3RD BATTALION
1ST BATTALION
2ND BATTALION
SAARBRUECKEN
274th ATTACKS
SHOENECK
HABSTERDICK
METZ HIGHWAY
MAIN SIEGFRIED LINE
SAAR RIVER
STIRING WENDEL
FORBACH
KREUTZBERG RIDGE
SPICHERN HEIGHTS

rolled back his half open eyes. Blood was coming from his nose and mouth. Corrigan and Doyle dragged him away from the sill.

"Don't worry, Sergeant," said Wilson. "We'll fix you up."

The three men took care of him as best they could until medical help arrived. In the meantime Wilson and Corrigan went down into the basement of the house to see if any more snipers were concealed there.

"I asked Wilson if I should toss a couple of grenades down before us," said Corrigan. "He said not to, though, because he didn't want to mess it up. So he went down first and walked right into the basement. If there had been anyone down there he would have made a perfect target. Luckily the place was deserted. When we made certain that everything was all clear we went upstairs. Just as we did

723

so, one of the engineers who had accompanied us was shot in the hips and back as he was coming through the window. Of the twelve engineers who started out with us at the top of the hill, only three got down to the bottom . . . and now one of them was wounded."

The sniper in the pillbox apparently was using some sort of a machine gun pistol because his shots always came in twos. He had the window of the house zeroed in perfectly and was picking off every man who tried to get in or out. Finally Wilson took two men, Brancieri and Donovan, and went up to the second floor to see if they couldn't knock the sniper out. Upstairs Wilson walked over to the window to see if he could find the sniper when he saw several of his men outside who were starting to dig in near the railroad tracks. He leaned near the window and shouted for them to come over to the house in five minute intervals when suddenly he jerked and stepped back pale-faced from the window.

"My God, I'm hit!" he cried.

Before anyone could realize what had happened he was standing in the middle of the room with his feet spread wide apart trying to brace himself. "That's all right, I'm . . ." he tried to reassure them. Then he must have felt himself starting to fade.

"Slap my face! Slap my face!" He knew he was going but couldn't make himself accept the fact.

Brancieri struck him across the cheeks but his life had already drained from him. He fell to the floor and doubled up his legs and kicked a heavy oak table across the room. That was all. He was dead.

"When I went upstairs it was all over," recalls Corrigan. "I opened his shirt and found two small bullet holes just above his heart. There was not a trace of blood on the outside. He must have bled internally. I realized sooner or later he would have been killed but now that it happened none of us could quite believe it. I took the codes and overlays out of his pockets and looked at his AGO card. He was only 21 and as he lay there he didn't look anywhere near that. His hair was cropped close and he had no beard at all. He was just a kid, yet he proved himself to be the driving factor of the whole company. He was everything that could be expected of an officer and soldier. When he died, the spirit of the company died with him."

The rest of us set up a defense within the house and tried to establish contact with the units on the flanks. Wire and communications men from the Third Battalion headquarters valiantly tried to keep in touch with the attacking forces but their lines were pounded to shreds by the artillery. Cpl. Donald Frye tried to get down to us but was hit severely by shell fragments. Frye came all the way back to the top of the hill smiling as though nothing had happened.

No one believed he was hit until they saw the gaping holes in his shoulder and arms. Later on, Cpl. Norman Spencer and Stanley Daniels were hit while out on the lines. Spencer lost both feet at the ankles and Daniels had a large hole torn in his chest.

During Lt. Wilson's dash to the town, King Company was still fighting its way out of one of the most devastating artillery barrages it had ever undergone. The constant shrieking and hammering of the shells together with the sight of comrades being torn to pieces beside them had worn the men to the breaking point. No one was certain as to his objectives, but each knew that he could not last much longer where he was. Finally Lt. Edward Crowson took matters into his own hands, organized the remnants of his company and led them in a wild avenging charge into Stiring-Wendel. In a rage of madness the men swept over the open ground, across the railroad tracks and plunged into the first houses on the outskirts of town. Pfc. Charles Kocemba was one of the first to reach the buildings, followed closely by the slightly corpulent, but very aggressive Sgt. Dallas Waite. Waite peeled off and led an assault on the second row of houses while Kocemba followed the explosion of Pfc. Comer's grenade through a window. Not far behind came Lt. Crowson with a smoking rifle and a blazing cigar clamped between his teeth.

Crowson set up a CP in the house and then pushed on into the front rooms to observe up the street. There he was spotted by a Kraut sniper and received a painful bullet wound in the leg. Crowson merely took an extra long drag on his cigar and continued to direct the attack up the street. Tec. 5 Jim Owen, the medic, tried to get him to stop long enough so that he could dress the wound, but by the time he got a first aid bandage around it, Crowson was off again. Together with his Executive Officer, Lt. James De-Lorme, who was also from North Carolina, the two drove the assault forward with the greatest amount of vigor the South has displayed since the Battle of Bull Run.

The platoons and squads separated and began to work their way up the streets toward the Metz Highway clearing the houses as they went.

"The Krauts had all taken off for the cellars," said Pfc. Warriner. "I heard a noise in the basement of the first house I entered so I yelled down in French for any civilians to come out. All I got for an answer was a low guttural, *'Geben Sie mir meine Pistole,'* followed by a shot. I tossed a grenade down the steps and when the thing went off a shower of canned fruits, smoked meats, and a couple of pickled Krauts came flying up. We moved on to the next house where a very pretty French girl threw her arms around me, gave me a big kiss and hailed me as her liberator. She told me that there were five Germans in the next house and said for me to go there and *'treiz les sales boches'* (shoot the filthy Germans). I got Sgt. Shahan and Sgt. Coleman to help me and we went over to the house and flushed them out of the basement with grenades and M-1s."

As soon as it had gained its initial objective, King company consolidated in the protection of the houses and took stock of its strength before continuing the attack. In the whole company only approximately sixty-two men were left. Its dead and wounded had been left behind to be picked up by the medics. Litter bearers worked back and forth through the mine fields all day long. The Medical Corps, as always, was performing its utmost and was taking more than its share of the casualties. In the afternoon Pfc. Carl Rylke was taking a litter team down the hill when he stepped on a mine and his left foot was blown off. The concussion threw him into the air and when he fell he struck another mine with his elbow and received serious wounds all over his body. Several German PW's were nearby and three of them were ordered to go to Rylke's assistance. All three of them, however, stepped on mines as they tried to get to Rylke. Again more prisoners were sent out to bring in the wounded men. This time they were successful and Rylke was brought in to the aid station unconscious and near dead. Several attempts were made to revive him by giving him blood plasma but each was unsuccessful and he died a half hour later. Lt. Zeling Cooper was hit while leading King's second platoon into the town and was lying out on the open ground unable to move.

"He laughed and joked with me all the while I worked on him," said Pfc. Monroe Gable. "It seemed like he was getting a big kick out of the whole damned thing. The Germans kept throwing more artillery all over the area where the wounded were. Cooper was already hurt bad and while he was lying there he was hit again. In spite of that he kept telling jokes and trying to keep up the spirits of the rest of the wounded. I knew we couldn't get them out of there for a long time. It was a pitiful sight. They were lying in the mud pleading for help and we had to pass on. Some of them had to lie there all night long before they could be evacuated."

During the night of March 3rd, Col. Conley reviewed the day's action. Our losses had been heavy, but we had succeeded in pushing a stubborn enemy back, the same 559th Division which only a few days before had been the aggressor. In forcing their retreat, we had come through extensive mine fields and barbed wire entanglements. Numerous trenches and concrete pillboxes had been overrun and captured by our assault down the hill. Another belt of the Siegfried Line had been breached, and our leading companies occupied houses along the outskirts of the town of Stiring-Wendel.

As the morning of the 4th dawned, leading companies once more drove forward through the town . . . this time supported by heavy tanks. Every building that was thought to contain German troops was pulverized by the heavy guns on the armored vehicles. The regimental anti-tank guns moved up and helped neutralize remaining pillboxes and fortifications. One of the gun crews found an old French

727

lady and two young granddaughters living in a house they used as a billet. Although shells, rockets and mortars were raining down in that vicinity, she refused to leave, placing all her trust in the Lord, as she explained it. Several shells fell within six feet of the house and blew all the windows out but none of them were hurt and no shells hit the house itself. Right in the middle of the battlefield the woman did the men's washing and heated their rations . . . so completely did she ignore the horrors of war.

The assault companies jumped off around 0630 and proceeded rapidly through the town. Most of the German resistance faded before the onslaught of the tanks. Enemy artillery, directed from excellent OP's on the heights surrounding the northwest side of town, continued to rain down on the attackers, however, causing numerous casualties. While clearing the town many instances were seen of civilians, including women and children, firing on the American soldiers. Pfc. Bennett caught and killed one young boy sniping at a GI. This was a border town and German sympathies ran high. Some of the men found both French and German flags hidden in the homes they entered . . . one or the other to be displayed depending upon who was in control of the town. Some of our men claimed they had observed houses flying the Nazi Swastika from up on the hill . . . but when they entered the town they saw the tri-color of the French hanging from the same pole.

All companies made steady progress through the town finding scattered points of German resistance. Lt. Cox's Easy Company moved into town and took over a sector of houses from Fox and George. French troops followed the Americans into the town and were taking over and occupying the houses after they had been cleared. Easy cleared houses all day without suffering one casualty. "That's the way I like to fight this damned war," remarked Pfc. Haley. Mortar and artillery fire kept them jumping in and out of houses all through the day, however, and often the men tore out walls to pass from one house to another to avoid going out in the shrapnel littered street.

By the end of the second day we had crossed the Metz Highway, and most of the town was in American hands.

728

Only the large and heavily defended Simon Mine still held out. Companies and platoons selected quarters and set up OP's from which they could observe to the front and both flanks. The Germans continued to pound the positions with artillery and rocket fire but casualties were slight. Snipers continued to fire from different quarters of the town long after it had been cleared and taken. Vehicles could only reach the positions at night after racing down a 1,500 yard stretch of highway under direct enemy fire.

That night Lt. Peterson, 3rd Bn. S-4, was leading a group of jeeps up with chow for the third battalion but after searching vainly through a vast network of streets he was unable to find any of the companies he was looking for. Finally he saw what he believed to be a guard standing in the shadow of the doorway of one of the houses.

"Where's the K Company CP?" he asked.

The guard stepped out of the doorway and came over to the side of the jeep like he hadn't quite understood.

"Vas ist das?"

For a fraction of a second Peterson stared petrified. Then there was a resounding roar and a clashing of gears as he threw the jeep in reverse and went sailing down the streets backwards.

Wire sections were having a difficult time maintaining communication with the attacking units. Artillery kept tearing up telephone lines at regular intervals. Losses in the 3rd Bn. section were especially heavy.

The Simon Mine was now the big obstacle upon which the regimental attack was centered. For several days it had been shelled and bombed but still the trapped Germans inside of it showed no signs of surrender. Time and again attempts had been made to take it by storm but each assault was driven back. A huge steel wall surrounded the place topped by a net of barbed wire. Tanks attempted to blow holes in the walls but were driven off by enemy anti-tank fire. It was estimated that approximately three to four hundred civilians were being held prisoner deep down in the shafts. A large Red Cross flag hung from one of the entrances but any attempt to enter there was met with a hail of machine gun fire.

729

On the afternoon of the 5th a huge column of men was seen streaming toward the American line from the direction of the German lines. At first it was thought that a large scale German counterattack was being launched.

"They were straggling for miles all up and down the Metz Highway," said T/Sgt. James Wilson. "They seemed to wobble over the road like they were drunk. Some of them would fall to the ground and then drag themselves up again with a great effort. Then we found out that they were Russians who had escaped from a large prison camp on the edge of town. Most of them were in a pitiful condition. They had not had anything to eat for days and were so weak and emaciated they could hardly stand up. When the Germans saw them getting away they turned machine guns on them and killed a lot of them. Others wandered into the mine fields along the road and were blown to eternity. Still they kept coming towards us. Those who were too weak to walk just fell along the side of the hill and lay still. The rest of them came plodding on. They were so hungry they would scrape the empty cans our K rations were in, even when they were infested with ants and flies."

"We got the German prisoners to help them back," continued Pfc. Hershey. "It was nothing to see half a dozen of them sprawled on the road half dead from hunger and exhaustion. We gave them all the rations we could spare but they didn't half go around. We put some of them in trucks and sent them back to the rear where they set up special camps for them."

On the morning of the Sixth, Lt. Doane's Love Co. was ordered to attack the Simon Mine on the battalion left front. King was to furnish fire support from Neue-Glashutte and Item would be in reserve.

"We pushed through the woods up to the outside of the factory," remembers Pfc. Robinson, "and captured 12 prisoners and two machine guns there, but were then driven back by heavy machine gun fire from pillboxes hidden in the trees and from fire from the Mine itself. Every time we withdrew to let the artillery pound the factory, the Krauts would go down into the underground passages of the place and wait until the shelling was over. Then they would come up in time to catch us as we started to assault."

"It was impossible to attack the building from the side," continues Sgt. Gray. "We had to hit it head on because there was a deep sludge area around the sides. Tanks tried to come up but were knocked back by Kraut anti-tank guns. By taking it in rushes we got to within 50 yards of the outside wall. Then the Krauts turned everything they had on us. The whole company was pinned down."

Sgt. Cathey spotted one of the machine gun positions and tried to bring fire on it. He called Pfc. Bissenger to come up with a bazooka, but before Bissenger could get into position to fire, a sniper shot him through the chest and he died about fifteen minutes later.

We continued to press the attack but stubborn resistance made it impossible to get beyond the iron fence. Pfc. Wagner was shot through the head and killed and Pfc. Zoebelein lost a foot when he stepped on a mine.

"When he saw it was impossible to go any further, Sgt. Cathey went back to bring up a tank," said Sgt. William Smith, "Cathey rode on top of it up toward the wall right out in plain sight. When the tank got up to the wall Cathey jumped over and started going after a German machine gun nest. The tank fired four rounds with its 75-mm cannon and then the Germans hit it with a bazooka round. Not much damage was done but fragments from the shell flew off and hit Cathey. The tank then took off in reverse as fast as it could go and left Cathey lying there wounded inside the factory wall. When the Krauts saw him alone they started firing at him with machine guns and hit him again in the arms and legs."

It was almost certain suicide to attempt to rescue him. German guns fired at anything that moved inside the wall. Outside, the whole company was pinned down by fire. Nevertheless, Pfc. Lawrence and two others risked certain death and went up through the curtain of fire and dragged Cathey back to a ditch inside the wall out of the line of fire.

About two hours later Sgt. Kohn sent a litter squad to bring out the wounded man. Three times the squad attempted to get to him but three times it was driven back by hostile mortar, rocket and tank fire. The next time Kohn started out alone.

"I climbed over the wall only to drop in a tangle of barbed wire on the other side," said Kohn afterward. "I tore my clothes to pieces but finally pulled myself free and got over to where Cathey was lying. I told him to lock his arms around my neck and I would drag him away.

" 'I can't,' he replied. 'Both of them are broken.'

"Then I ripped his shirt up the back and tied it around my neck and started dragging him toward the wall. Mortar shells were dropping all around and a German tank had come to within fifty yards of us. Cathey was suffering pretty bad from the pain and I had to tell him to quiet down or he would attract the Kraut's attention to us. When I got him to the wall both of us got caught in the barbed wire. I pulled and jerked on his clothes until they were nearly torn off him but finally tore free. Then I lifted him to the wall and dropped him to litter bearers on the other side. The wire tore my Red Cross brassard off my arm and I picked it up and held it between my teeth. Going over the wall, though, I started to cuss and lost it."

The litter bearers from the 370th Medical Bn. took care of the rest of the evacuation by waving a Red Cross flag to see if it would be fired upon. When nothing happened a litter team was led across the field and brought Cathey back to the aid station.

The whole time we were in Stiring-Wendel the Krauts continuously hammered the area with artillery. Thousands of rounds pounded this small town daily and our own 882nd Field Artillery expended itself trying to neutralize the enemy artillery pieces with counter-battery fire. We had heard that the Germans would not fire if we kept our liaison cub planes up in the air to spot them, so our "cubs" practically lived in the skies. This did no good either and we finally resigned ourselves to fate and decided that the German artillery was just another part of the Seigfried Line, guns imbedded in concrete with only the muzzles projecting. We had also heard that the Germans were short on ammunition, but during this period they were outshooting us 5 to 1—and we were throwing every round of ammunition we could get our hands on.

Capt. Keith's Item Company led the 3rd Battalion march towards Schonecken, to be followed later by King and Love Companies. Keith moved his men out early in ·the morning and kept going all day. No contact was made with the enemy, however; so late in the day, Keith decided to hold up and then resume the pursuit in the morning. The company pulled into an old barn and settled down in the mouldy hay and cow dung to get a few hours' rest before driving on in the morning. Shortly afterwards, though, word arrived that the chase would continue without stopping.

"We hardly got our eyes shut when we were shaken out of the sack to start on again," said Sgt. Bailey. "This time our objective was Schonecken. The way out from the barn was a zigzag course around mine fields and finally out to the road again. Lt. Westbrook went out in front to find the best route for the company to follow. He took one squad and had just about made it into the town when the squad ran into some barbed wire. They stopped there because everybody suspected they would run into something out of the ordinary ahead. It was still pitch dark so Westbrook got down on his hands and knees and crawled under the wire and started feeling around with his hands. Pretty soon he touched a boxlike object.

" 'Mines,' he said."

After waiting for a short time to figure out what to do next, they decided they had to find a route through for the rest of the company. So they continued crawling forward, feeling the ground as they went. Every time someone would come to a mine, he would feel around it, remove the detonator and then dispose of the explosive charge and the box. They were small yellow "shu" mines designed to blow off the foot or leg of anyone who stepped on them. It was a ticklish business crawling through a mine field at night deactivating mines as you went. Foot by foot, mine by mine, they finally made it. They continued on into the town and found that the Germans had deserted it. Then Westbrook said he would need a good man to go back and

733

guide the rest of the company up. He asked Bob Doyle if he would be willing to go back.

"Why, hell yes," answered Doyle, his voice disguising the natural fear any man would have had to pick his way through a mine field at night. Bravery wasn't lack of fear, but the control and overpowering of fear.

Walsh volunteered to go back with Doyle, and the two of them set off through the mines. When they got to the field they made a guess as to where Westbrook had crossed, and started the blind groping and feeling. It was necessary to mark a path so the rest of the company could find it, so they left trails of tooth powder on either side of them. Before they got across, the tooth powder gave out, despite their careful efforts to conserve it. They crossed the rest of the way and found the company still in the barn where they had left several hours before.

Capt. Keith thought that the tooth powder trail would not be enough to get the men safely through the field so he asked Doyle if he could mark a clearer lane. Finally, Yarus, the Commo. Sgt. brought out a roll of toilet paper. Doyle went back to mark out the field while Walsh stayed behind to guide the company through. He picked out his earlier powder trail and marked off the rest of the path with toilet paper. Walsh soon brought the rest of the company down and the entire unit crossed the field despite the darkness without casualties. Then we proceeded into Schonecken.

The company stopped for about an hour in the middle of town, but since we met no resistance, we were ordered to keep going.

"King" then passed through Schonecken and continued down the road heading for the Saar River. Morning dawned with a bright warm sun creeping above the horizon. The streets were crowded with civilians shouting *"Vive l'Amérique"* and *"Bravo,"* but most of the men paid little attention to them for most of them had said the same thing to the Krauts when they marched through the town a few years before. Streets were littered with propaganda leaflets. Some of them warned that the terrible Siegfried Line was just ahead and the men defending it were bold and brave

734

and that no Yank would cross it and live. Most of the men tossed them aside and vowed they would hang their washing on the vaunted Line.

The 274th had surmounted another hurdle in its struggle to crash through the Siegfried barriers and was now across the border facing the last line of pillboxes. On the left in the 3rd Bn. sector, the Saar River afforded a natural barrier between us and the last line of defense. On the right in the 1st Bn. sector, a formidable thick layer of protruding concrete dragon teeth ran continuously across the front. Ours was a tough assignment, and much of the success of the Seventh Army depended upon our ability to complete the cracking of this wall and thereby opening the strategic Metz Highway N 3 over which the Army could travel to the heart of Germany.

The plan was again for the 70th Division to make the main effort, with the 63rd Division on the right prepared to exploit our successes. The 274th was to continue spearheading the Trailblazer drive. The 276th Infantry had kept abreast of us but the 275th had remained in defensive positions on the right ever since the capture of Spicheren.

Both Army and Corps Headquarters were pressing hard so General Barnett ordered Col. Conley to attack without delay. We were not prepared for a river crossing; therefore Col. Conley chose Major Cantrell's 1st Bn. to attack on the right through the dragons' teeth.

Neither were we prepared for a land assault on the Seigfried Line. Self-propelled guns were not available and our supporting tanks had not been able to negotiate a route forward to our foremost positions.

Baker Company was selected to spearhead the attack. The ground ahead was covered with cleverly concealed pillboxes and long rows of dragons' teeth. There didn't seem to be much hope for Capt. Mitchell's men. It was flesh and bones against concrete and steel . . . truly a modern mechanized war.

"We were told that each pillbox was manned by about 17 men," said Lt. Chappel of B Co. "Most of them were supposed to be transfers from the Luftwaffe. It made no difference whether they knew anything about infantry tac-

735

tics or not. All they had to do was sit inside the thick concrete bunkers and pull the trigger of a machine gun. It was sure suicide to cross the flat fields swept by perfect enemy fire, but orders were orders and we were going to try it. Our artillery turned loose an all-out barrage to help knock out the enemy bunkers, but they did no good. Even our '8' shells failed to dent the fortifications. I don't think they even shook up the occupants, and we might as well have saved our ammunition."

"My platoon jumped off first," said S/Sgt. Rysso. "I had two squads forward and one back. As soon as we started to move the Krauts threw over a lot of artillery and mortars, but most of it fell in back of us. Pfc. Condict was the first man over the knob of the hill in front of the Line. When he came back, he was sweating and his face was pale. 'It's going to be rough,' was all he said. We kept going until the two leading squads were at the top of the hill. We could all see the dragons' teeth, pillboxes, dugouts, and trenches from there. The hill was completely bare and we stood out in plain sight like sore thumbs. The Krauts couldn't help but see us. They waited until we were out on the flat ground in front and then cut loose.

"Nicokoris, a lead scout, hit the ground and then got up to run to some barbed wire, where he hit the dirt the second time. He didn't get up again. Penland ran up to help Nicokoris and tried to find out where the worst fire was coming from. He got as far as a small mound of earth when the Krauts turned on him. Dunn came up beside Penland behind the mound. Every time they tried to move, the Krauts started cutting off the top of the mound with machine gun fire. The Germans could see every move they made. Before long the mound was riddled and the men thought the bullets would soon be coming through it.

"The rest of the squad flattened on the ground squeezing into every little depression that could be found. The Krauts mistook several piles of manure for men and blasted hell out of them. We were completely pinned down. We called back for artillery on the pillboxes. It came over but just bounced harmlessly off the sides. We were told over the

736

radio that tanks would soon be coming up. Five came, but one's gun jammed and it turned around and went back. When the Krauts saw the tanks, they opened up with all the 88's and machine gun fire they had."

Nicokoris stirred a little out on the ground when things got worse. He had been hit in the chest the first time. Then he tried to pull himself back toward the mound where Penland was, but was hit again in the arm. When the tanks came up, he was wounded a third time by 88 fragments.

"I saw Frazier get it while he was running to get behind one of the tanks," continued Sgt. Penland. "An 88 burst nearby and got three of them. Palmer fell to the ground and tried to get up but the Germans opened up on him again. We later found him dead, riddled with machine gun bullets. Rakowsky was hit and knocked to the ground, but he got up and joined the rest of the boys behind the tank. Those who weren't wounded got behind two of the tanks and started firing at the pillboxes. After about 15 minutes the tanks decided to withdraw because they claimed the ground was too soft and they couldn't get across the drag-ons' teeth anyway. When they pulled back the infantrymen were left exposed to the murderous fire out in the open, so we took to the cover of a line of trees behind the hill."

"Once we had reached temporary safety I started to reor-ganize the men we had left," continues Sgt. Rysso. "Dunn made two attempts to go out into the field to get the wounded but was driven back by machine gun fire. Then Newton, the medic, went out, accompanied by Penland, Dunn, Boering, and Mann. Strange to say they drew no fire even though they were plainly visible to the Germans. They found Palmer dead, Casto with a broken leg, and Jannick unconscious with a hole in his head. He was still wearing a packboard with four bazooka rounds in it. Cuervo and Condict were also lying on the ground badly wounded. Newton did what he could for the men. He gave them all a shot of morphine and then waited for litter bearers to come up."

The platoon then withdrew farther back to a row of trenches, leaving Penland and Newton to take care of the

737

wounded. Just about that time, two short rounds of American artillery came over and appeared to fall right in the middle of the wounded lying on the hill top.

Penland immediately yelled at Rysso who was not far away, "Tell those bastards to lift that artillery! It's falling among our own men!"

Rysso was already shouting the same thing into the radio.

Just then three wounded men were seen coming out of a low row of shrubs near where the shells were falling, helping each other back. It was later learned that they were Andrews and Helaszek, supporting Darling between them. Suddenly another round came over and made a direct hit on them. The story of the tragedy can best be told by Penland:

"Two artillery shells whistled across the top of the hole Newton and I were in and exploded only a short distance away. I could see that they landed right among our wounded still lying in the field. Out of the corner of my eye, coming from the left, I saw two men supporting a third coming toward the shell crater. I glanced about and recognized Andrews on the right, supporting Darling who had been wounded in the right thigh. I did not have time to tell who the third man was, but was later told it was Helaszek. I just got out the first word of warning 'Get down!' when a large caliber shell screamed over very low and hit directly on the three men. I saw a tremendous flash of fire and a fearful cloud of black smoke. Pieces of men's bodies came flying through the air. The concussion blew off my helmet and threw me to the bottom of the crater which was filled with mud and water. One man's horribly torn body flew over my head and hit in the water beside me. Newton was standing beside me nearest the shell and was blown down into the water. I grabbed him to keep him from sinking under. He was covered with blood from the men who had been hit by the shell. I asked him if he was hit. He said he didn't know and crawled over to help another man who was pushing himself toward the water with only his legs. This was probably Helaszek who later was found dead in the hole.

"I looked around and saw just a man's chest and hands
738

sticking out of the water. I grabbed to pull him out, thinking that possibly he might still be alive and was drowning. When I got him out, though, I saw he was mangled and dead so let him slip back into the water. While Newton was working on the wounded, I went back to the platoon and assembled it. I could only account for ten men. Litter bearers eventually came up but were driven back immediately by fire from the Germans. They waited until after dark and then picked up all the wounded they could find."

In the morning Lt. Chappel went out to the shell crater to identify the bodies. He was able to pick out Helaszek by his dog tags and Darling by a letter. Throughout the day American artillery shelled the sector with 155's and 8-inchers.

The next day, March 16th, TD's and tanks moved up into the woods where they could bring direct fire on the Siegfried fortifications. Captain Murphy, Bn. S-3, reconnoitered forward positions to determine whether TD's could knock out the pillboxes in co-ordination with the infantry assault. Later it was decided to use 8-inch guns. For several minutes the huge guns rained hell on the fortifications. Direct hits were scored on several of the pillboxes. Often the powerful shells were seen to glance off the concrete structures and go sailing off into the air or explode harmlessly leaving nothing but a dent in the side.

During the night "B" and "C" Companies sent patrols out to inspect the damage. Both received small arms and machine gun fire. They reported several direct hits on the bunkers directly to the front.

That night a reconnaissance party went down to the woods in the 3rd Bn. area to observe enemy fortifications on the other side of the river. It was discovered that the primary firing lanes of the bunkers were facing up and downstream. Farther to the rear, however, were more installations from which cross fire could be maintained over the river. These showed signs of activity and the apertures were blackened to indicate use.

From interrogation of prisoners it was learned that six enemy troops manned each bunker armed with a heavy MG and 6,000 rounds of ammunition. Each fortification contained enough food to last the crews two weeks. It was also learned that our artillery had had little effect on the structures and they were operating as strongly as before.

During this time our 3rd Bn. was holding down a long line abreast of the Saar River. A tall, 150-foot water tower was used by Colonel Landstrom as an OP and by artillery observers to bring fire on targets across the Saar. A large gap formed on the right while the 1st Bn. was trying to break through the Siegfried defenses. The Battalion's mission was to patrol the river for crossing sites and locate the occupied pillboxes. It soon became apparent that all pillboxes were occupied and there was one every one hundred yards.

All the power the 70th Division could mass was brought up along the lower bank and turned upon the impressive fortifications on the opposite side. Against us was the most powerful section of the most elaborate system of fortifications ever built in the history of the world. Pillboxes blocked the way miles in depth. No one tried to think of what could happen while we floundered around in the water right in front of these electrically controlled guns on the other side.

Patrols moved at night between adjacent units. An "Item" Patrol was going down the main drag in pitch blackness when someone heard voices a short distance away. The patrol hit the ground and listened, feeling sure that the Germans had come across during the night and were digging in on the American bank. The men crept closer until they could see the dark figures digging in a heavy field gun. One of the patrol members exclaimed, "The bastards even brought artillery across!"

Then one of the voices was heard to say, "Aw, Sonubabitch! Bringing a man out in the middle of the night." . . . They were Americans, a TD outfit emplacing their guns.

By the night of March 18th, armored spearheads from the Third Army had punctured to within 60 miles of Saarbrucken and were menacing the German right flank. It was believed that the enemy might withdraw during the night under the threat of being surrounded and cut off.

The original plan had been for the 276th Infantry to

make the initial assault crossing and all anti-tank guns in the area had been placed under that regiment's control to support the operation; however, plans were being changed now and it looked as though the 274th would spearhead again.

Col. Landstrom asked for permission to fire on the pill-boxes across the way with these anti-tank guns. Permission was delayed until 1720 in the afternoon because clearance had to be obtained from the 276th. Finally it came, and Major Greenhalgh relayed the message over the phone, giving the OK to fire:

"All right, out there, shoot everything you've got. Start whenever you want to and don't stop till it gets so dark you can't see."

That was all the anti-tank and TD gunners were waiting for, along with the cannon company gunners. The whole southern bank of the river opened up with a furious bar-rage. Some of the guns went at the pillboxes while others lambasted factories and possible OP's farther back. This was the first time our guns ever had good direct fire targets. Plaster and concrete flew all over the other side of the river. After a half hour's pounding one of the gunners saw a white flag waving from the steeple of a church which the Germans appeared to be using as an OP. The gunners just dropped the next round below the flag and by slightly raising each succeeding round, raised the banner right up into the sky. As soon as the barrage lifted, however, the ever present machine guns still returned fire from the pill-boxes.

During the night the 289th Engineer Bn. brought up 38 boats to carry the 3rd Bn. over the river. Regimental S-3 told Col. Landstrom he would have 2,000 rounds of artil-lery to back him up on call. At 2010, Col. Conley con-tacted Col. Landstrom on the phone and said:

"The Commanding General expects us to cross tonight. You are to select the time for crossing. If you need any assistance, it is ready on call. If you are successful, the 2nd Bn. will follow you."

Higher headquarters still believed the enemy had re-treated. We disagreed, and on the night of March the 19th they were still blazing away. Col. Landstrom summed up his ideas on the subject as follows:

"If we start across, we will complete it. I am not in favor of patrols. Prefer to go all out. The time for crossing will be sometime between midnight and daybreak. We are still receiving fire from enemy 50 and 88-mm guns. This points to same resistance as before."

The night of March 19th was quiet and peaceful. The warming winds of spring swept up from the south and sent patterns of ripples twinkling in the starlight on the river. In foxholes along the shore the men looked up at the sky and waited.

The Last of It

The 274th Regiment jumped off at dawn, March 20th. The crossing had been feared, but the 3rd Army's roll-up of the defenses behind the Saar River made the German positions untenable; they withdrew bare hours before the 274th and the rest of the 7th Armored Division managed the crossing. With few losses, they continued into Saarbrücken.

The Americans kept breaking through the Rhine defenses, establishing more bridgeheads; by the end of March Hitler could see the end in sight. But he refused to give up. The Fuehrer commanded the German people to carry out a scorched earth policy. There was no hope for them at this point anyway, he announced, so the Allied victory must be made as costly as possible. Hitler had led his people to disaster; he was now determined to lead them to destruction. Many, still mesmerized, followed him, but the German field commanders secretly worked to undermine this order.

By April 18th, the Americans had scored a crushing victory, the 1st and 9th Armies completing the envelopment and capture in the Ruhr of more than 300,000 German troops, together with the armament factories that fed the German war machine. This was a greater loss than the Germans suffered at Stalingrad.

The Americans now streaked across central Germany, reaching the Elbe River and holding a line there. They were to wait for the Russians to close in from the east, by previous agreement. In northern Germany, Montgomery had moved north from the Lower Elbe, sealing off the coastal ports. On April 30th, the Russians were fighting their way through the rubble of Berlin. Hitler had already shouted that the German people were unworthy of him, and on the 30th he abandoned them, via suicide—to the intense relief of the German generals. They had followed Hitler's last-ditch orders long after all reasonable hope of resistance was gone. Now they could make peace. They had to.

Early on May 7th an armistice was signed at Rheims between Germany and the Allies; the terms were unconditional surrender, and delivery to the Allies of all the German forces on all fronts.

The military war in Europe was over. Its destruction to life and property staggers the imagination.

The Battle of the Atlantic cost the Allies more than 20,000,000 tons of merchant shipping, in retaliation for which 781 German submarines and their crews were sent to the bottom.

Army casualties in Europe were over 700,000. The infantry, representing only 20% of the U. S. overseas forces, absorbed 70% of the casualties.

The U. S. itself extended lend-lease aid to Allied countries, including Russia, in the amount of almost fifty billion dollars.

Such statistics are chosen at random. Perhaps they mean little to the reader, perhaps even less to the fighting man. What of him? Would his many sacrifices be forgotten, washed over by the cold war?

Eric Sevareid said, in one of his broadcasts to the nation:

War happens inside a man. It happens to one man alone. It never can be communicated. That is the tragedy—and perhaps the blessing. A thousand ghastly wounds are really only one. A million martyred lives leave an empty place at only one family table. That is why, at bottom, people can let wars happen, and that is why nations survive them and carry on. If, by the miracles of art and genius, in later years two or three among them can open their hearts and the right words come, then perhaps we shall all know a little of what it was like.

Aftermath

War is an exciting tonic to many men. Combat itself seems to release an exhilaration which can surely be felt in some of the narratives in this volume—in the daring raids, airdrops, and even in the destruction of the *Scharnhorst* in the frigid Arctic waters.

Yet in the aftermath of war the "taste of courage" that drives men in battle loses a certain essence, and is exchanged for a mood of melancholy. This restores a necessary balance and objectivity with which men may then reexperience the trauma of combat.

This awareness of "the passage over" is beautifully evoked in the next selection by Captain Laurence Critchell.

THE DISTANT DRUM WAS STILL*

by Capt. Laurence Critchell

From the small mountain stream at the bottom of the valley it is a climb to the main level of the town. Where the air is quiet there is a fragrance of wild flowers, and up to the very last turn of the road the climber can hear the slip and chuckle of the stream below. Set under the bushes along the way is a very old shrine to Mary and the Christ Child. Moss has grown over the wood.

At the top of the hill the road forks. One way leads past a four-story hotel of white stone and glass. If you are

*From *Four Stars of Hell.*

745

thirsty after the climb you can stop there for a stein of beer or a glass of cold *Liebfraumilch*. The drinks are served on a terrace, under beach umbrellas, where, in the evening, there are piano and violin concertos by starlight, and one can watch the moon rise over the snowy peak of the Vatzmann, twenty miles across the valley.

Follow the road to the right. It dips, like a slack rope, by a small park. There are scores of children. Like the young women, they are almost all blond. The girls are tanned a rich gold-brown which makes you think of wheat fields in the summertime. They wear flowered skirts and loose blouses, and if you look at them directly they will meet your eye.

There are art shops on the main street of town. Where there are no art shops, the walls themselves are painted. Above the archways on the square by the old palace is a fresco of Christ on the Cross, and around Him the heroic figures of the common people: laborers, farmers and soldiers. There is a little memorial to the war dead in the cool, sweet-smelling hallway of the church—a Christian cross supporting a helmet—and beneath it banks of wild flowers.

The houses are tinted pastel. Balconies lean over the narrow, crowded streets. Everywhere there is the clatter of life: of carts bringing families from the country, of bicycle riders, of sandals slip-slopping on the cobblestones. There is a tailor shop; there is a barber shop; there is a camera store; in another park there is a small motion-picture theater.

The hill road leads out of town, past the cemetery and the Catholic church, and overlooks the valley. Below is the other half of the town. It stands by the junction of two mountain streams. The railroad line from the north comes to an end at this point, but you can follow with your eyes where the tracks run out along the valley, adjoining the slate-colored river. The high snow mountains are all around. The clouds which make showers in the valley only make the snows deeper on those peaks. In the morning the mountains are violet and in the evening they are rose; by starlight they are as cool and remote as the firmament itself.

746

One of the streams that meet in the village is fed from a blue lake, about two miles away. Around the lake the snow mountains drop down in sheer stone cliffs, as they do at the *fjords* of Norway. There are boats for hire. There is also an electric launch which slips noiselessly out to the extreme end of the waterway, while the old boatman, who wears short pants and a hunting vest, blows a tin horn to demonstrate the echoes, and runs his vessel close to the waterfalls. At the far end of the lake there is a spit of land, and on it a small church dedicated to Saint Bartholomew, where the silence by the altar is so deep that one can hear the waterfalls a mile away.

This is where they thought he would be hiding.

This is Berchtesgaden.

For two months after the close of hostilities in Europe our regiment, with the 101st Airborne Division, occupied the area of Berchtesgaden, where we lived in the rich Bavarian living quarters of former SS troops. Towards the end we went to Linzen, in Austria, where we were on the border of Russian-occupied territory. In the latter part of August all the men of the division who were eligible to go home were assigned to the regiment, and, with Colonel Ballard still in command, entrained from Germany to Bar-le-Duc, France, a lonesome yellow town by a milk-white canal. Eventually, we were moved south to Marseilles and on August 8, 1945, we sailed for the United States.

The job was done.

Twice before in this story I have had to admit inability to convey a state of mind. The first of such references was during the long gloomy winter before the invasion of Normandy. The second was the state of mind, or, more strictly speaking, the state of being, of the soldier under fire. The first I attempted to suggest; the second I could only remark. But there was yet a third, of which I have made no mention at all. It was our state of mind when the firing ceased in Europe.

We had hated the war much more deeply than we had expected. Between the days of high spirits at Camp Toccoa

747

to the sunny, quiet, mid-summer warmth of Berchtesgaden there had been, for almost all of us, experiences of horror endurable only if the heart steeled itself against kindliness, against hope, against life itself. There had been moments of bitterness so dark that, to survive, we could do nothing except go on. We had had to shut our minds against all that justified our presence here on earth and exist as the outer shells of human kind, devoid of pride, devoid of love, devoid even of faith and hope. Of modern war, nothing can be said in mitigation.

With the end of the fighting we expected these emotions to subside. And in a sense they did. But they were succeeded for a brief period by a feeling we had never known before.

Let me see if I can put it down:

During the first weeks after the end of the fighting I flew by C-47 from Salzberg to Paris. My plane was piloted by two young Americans whose names I did not ask. They were in their early twenties. Their navigation was casual— it is termed pilotage in the Air Forces—and anyone watching over their shoulders could tell that Europe had become as familiar to them, in terms of bomb-pitted fields and terra-cotta ruins, as the pleasant farmlands, the clean villages and the long white roads of home. The copilot, with a map across his knees, followed the course with his forefinger and only glanced down now and then at the silver Rhine, the shell craters slowly filling with green water, the silent, deserted gun batteries of the enemy.

It was not peace. It was only silence. And in that silence there was something strange. . . .

In Paris the great flags of the United Nations hung, unfurled, beneath the Arc de Triomphe, over the light of the Unknown—and, it sometimes seemed, eternal—Soldier. Overhead roared B-24s and B-17s, their pilots taking the ground crews on tours of the destruction in the Ruhr valley. And while I watched, one pilot, flying low over the Champs Elysées, coming straight as an arrow from the Place de la Concorde, dipped his wings in thunderous salute as he passed the arch.

748

But the Frenchmen on the streets below did not look up.

The crowds of men and women along the great boulevards walked slowly, silently, as though dazed and going in a dream. The American soldiers talked in subdued voices or did not talk at all. Everywhere there was a strange oppression. And in the occasional skips and hops of the little children, who had not yet recovered from the great excitement of the day of victory, and who still carried tricolors in their hands—in the sight of this childish joy there was something unmistakably obscene.

There it was. . . . That was it.

For this strange state of mind which fell upon us for a little while after the guns had been silenced was a vague sense of obscenity. It was the faint, lingering aftertaste of having achieved something monstrous. We had unleashed powers beyond our comprehension. Entire countries lay in waste beneath our hands—and, in the doing of it, our hands were forever stained. It was of no avail to tell ourselves that what we had done was what we had had to do, the only thing we could have done. It was enough to know that we had done it. We had turned the evil of our enemies back upon them a hundredfold, and, in so doing, something of our own integrity had been shattered, had been irrevocably lost.

We who had fought this war could feel no pride. Victors and vanquished, all were one. We were one with the crowds moving silently along the boulevards of Paris; the old women hunting through the still ruins of Cologne; the bodies piled like yellow cordwood at Dachau; the dreadful vacant eyes of the beaten German soldiers; the white graves and the black crosses and the haunting melancholy of our hearts. All, all, were one, all were the ghastly horror of what we had known, of what we had helped to do. . . .

Face it when you close this book.

We did.